GENETICS
ETHICS, LAW AND POLICY

Fifth Edition

■ ■ ■

Maxwell J. Mehlman
Distinguished University Professor
Arthur E. Petersilge Professor of Law
Case Western Reserve University

Mark A. Rothstein
Herbert F. Boehl Chair of Law and Medicine
University of Louisville

Sonia M. Suter
Jonathan Kahan Family Research Professor of Law
The George Washington University

WEST
ACADEMIC
PUBLISHING

© West, a Thomson business, 2002, 2006
© 2010 Thomson Reuters
© 2015 LEG, Inc. d/b/a West Academic
© 2020 LEG, Inc. d/b/a West Academic
    444 Cedar Street, Suite 700
    St. Paul, MN 55101
    1-877-888-1330

West, West Academic Publishing, and West Academic are trademarks of West Publishing Corporation, used under license.

Printed in the United States of America

ISBN: 978-1-64242-769-1

For Rory, Gabe, Julia, Lisa, Rachel,
Molly, Ariana, Kelsey, and Mateo

PREFACE TO THE FIFTH EDITION

This book designed for use by not only law students but students in health sciences, public health, sociology, public policy, bioethics, and other disciplines. In law schools, the book can serve an additional function. Courses using Genetics: Ethics, Law and Policy can act as a capstone to the law school education, providing a context for students to apply the knowledge they learned in tort, constitutional, health care, criminal, insurance, employment, and intellectual property law.

The fifth edition covers most of the topics contained in previous editions, but is thoroughly updated and considerably shorter. We deleted or moved to notes some material on family law, research ethics, education, cloning, and behavioral genetics. The purpose is to make the material more accessible to students and instructors, as well as to reduce the cost of the book. Additionally, since the book is aimed at students in non-law disciplines as well as law students, it is hoped that students in those disciplines find the revised format more familiar. Finally, the book includes some text boxes to highlight key points.

Note that we use the term "genetics" to refer both to the entire field generally and to single-gene, Mendelian scientific approaches. We use the term "genomics" to refer specifically to next-generation science such as whole genome sequencing.

We are grateful to our many talented colleagues from law, social sciences, molecular biology, clinical genetics, philosophy, bioethics, economics, genetic counseling, and public health whose ideas and interactions with us have helped shape this book.

With this edition, Lori Andrews is no longer an active co-author, but the book continues to benefit enormously from her previous work. Professor Sonia Suter, Jonathan Kahan Family Research Professor of Law at GW Law, joins as a new co-author.

MAXWELL MEHLMAN
MARK ROTHSTEIN
SONIA SUTER

ACKNOWLEDGMENTS

Allen, Anita L., Genetic Privacy: Emerging Concepts and Values, in Genetic Secrets: Protecting Privacy and Confidentiality in the Genetic Era, 31, 33–34 (Mark A. Rothstein, ed. 1997). Copyright © 1997 by Yale University. Reprinted by permission.

American Academy of Pediatrics, Newborn Screening: A Blueprint for the Future; A Call for a National Agenda on State Newborn Screening Programs, Report of the Task Force on Newborn Screening excerpted from Birth to the Medical Home; Pediatrics, volume 106: 389–390 (2000), used with permission of the American Academy of Pediatrics. Copyright © August 2000 American Academy of Pediatrics.

American Society for Reproductive Medicine, Minimum Genetic Testing for Gamete and Embryo Donors, 99 Fertility and Sterility, 2013, No. 1. Reprinted by permission from the American Society for Reproductive Medicine (Fertility and Sterility, 2013, Vol. 99, 45).

American Society of Human Genetics, Points to Consider: Ethical, Legal, and Psychosocial Implications of Genetic Testing in Children and Adolescents, in American Journal of Human Genetics, volume 97, 6–10 (2015). Copyright © 2015 by the American Society of Human Genetics. All rights reserved. Reprinted with permission of Elsevier Inc.

American Society of Human Genetics, Statement on Informed Consent for Genetic Research, American Journal of Human Genetics 1996; volume 59, 471–473. Copyright © 1996, the American Society of Human Genetics. Reprinted with permission of the University of Chicago Press.

Andrews, Lori B. et al., Assessing Genetic Risks: Implications for Health and Social Policy, 40–41 (1994). Copyright © 1994. Reprinted with the permission of National Academy Press, Washington, D.C.

Andrews, Lori B., Future Perfect: Confronting Decisions About Genetics, 56–62 (2001). Copyright © 2001, Lori B. Andrews. Columbia University Press. Reprinted with the permission of the publisher.

Andrews, Lori B., Predicting and Punishing Antisocial Acts: How the Criminal Justice System Might Use Behavioral Genetics, in Behavioral Genetics: The Clash of Culture and Biology, 120–122 (Ronald A. Carson and Mark A. Rothstein eds., 1999). Copyright © 1999 Johns Hopkins University Press. Reprinted with the permission of Johns Hopkins University Press.

Andrews, Lori B., Prenatal Screening and the Culture of Motherhood, 47 Hastings L.J. 967, 970–971, 994–1000 (April 1996). Copyright © 1996, the University of California, Hastings College of the Law. Reprinted from 47 Hastings Law Journal (1996), with permission.

Andrews, Lori B., The Clone Age: Adventures in the New World of Reproductive Technology, 142–144 (2001). Copyright © 1999 by Lori B. Andrews. Reprinted by arrangement with Henry Holt & Company, LLC.

Andrews, Lori and Dorothy Nelkin, Body Bazaar: The Market For Human Tissue in the Biotechnology Age, 60–62, 102–103 (2001). Copyright © 2001, Random House Inc. Reprinted with permission of Random House.

Berg, P. et al., Letter: Potential Biohazards of Recombinant DNA Molecules, Science, volume 185, 303 (1974). Reprinted with permission.

Bowser, Rene, Race as a Proxy for Drug Response: The Dangers and Challenges of Ethnic Drugs, 53 DePaul Law Review 1111 (2004). Reprinted with permission.

Brothers, Kyle B. & Mark A. Rothstein, Ethical, Legal, and Social Implications of Incorporating Personalized Medicine into Healthcare, 12 Personalized Med. 43 (2015). Copyright © Future Medicine, Ltd. Reprinted by permission.

Buchanan, Allen, Dan W. Brock, Norman Daniels, and Dan Wikler (eds.), From Chance to Choice: Genetics and Justice, 27–28 (2000). Reprinted with the permission of Cambridge University Press. Copyright © 2000 Cambridge University Press.

Center for Genetics and Society, Genetically Modified Humans? Seven Reasons to Say "No", May 7, 2015. Reprinted by permission.

Churchill, L.R. et al., Genetic Research as Therapy: Implication of 'Gene Therapy' for Informed Consent, 26 Journal of Law, Medicine, & Ethics 38 (Spring 1998). Copyright © 1998, Reprinted with the permission of the American Society of Law, Medicine & Ethics. All rights reserved.

Collins, Francis S., Shattuck Lecture—Medical and Societal Consequence of the Human Genome Project, New England Journal of Medicine, volume 341, 31–33 (1999). Copyright © 1999 Massachusetts Medical Society. Reprinted with permission. All rights reserved.

Duster, Troy, Behavioral Genetics and Explanations of the Link Between Crime, Violence, and Race, in Wrestling with Behavioral Genetics: Science, Ethics, and Public Conversations, 154–156 (Erik Parens, Audrey R. Chapman, and Nancy Press eds.) (2006). Copyright © 2006 Johns Hopkins University Press. Reprinted with permission of Johns Hopkins University Press.

Faden, Ruth R., Neil A. Holtzman, Judith A. Chwalow, Parental Rights, Child Welfare, and Public Health: The Case of PKU Screening, American Journal of Public Health, volume 72, 1396, 1397–1398 (1982).

Reprinted with permission of the American Public Health Association. Copyright © 1982, the American Public Health Association.

Farrell, Ruth M., Women and Prenatal Genetic Testing in the 21st Centruy, 23 Health Matrix 1, 4–6 (2011). Reprinted with permission.

Fost, Norman, Genetic Diagnosis & Treatment Ethical Considerations, American Journal of Disease of Children, volume/edition 147, 1190 (1993). Copyright © 1993 American Medical Association. Reproduced with permission of American Medical Association in the format Textbook via Copyright Clearance Center.

Foster, et al. Excerpts from Foster et al., A Model Agreement for Genetic Research in Socially Identifiable Populations, American Journal of Human Genetics, volume 63, 696–702 (1998). Copyright © 1998. Reprinted with the permission of the University of Chicago Press.

Garraway, Levi A., Genomics Driven Oncology: Framework for an Emerging Paradigm, 31 J. Clinical Oncology 1806, 1806–1813 (2013). Copyright © 2013 American Society of Clinical Oncology. Reprinted by permission.

Goldstein, Norm, Owner of 'Genius' Sperm Bank Pleased by Results, The New York Times, December 11, 1984, A17. Reprinted with permission of the Associated Press. Copyright © 1984 the Associated Press.

Goulding, Rebecca et al., Alternative Intellectual Property for Genomics and the Activity of Technology Transfer Offices: Emerging Directions in Research, B.U. J. Sci. & Tech. L. 194, 202–05 (2010). Reprinted with permission.

Gyngell, Christopher, Hilaru Bowman-Smart, and Julian Savulescu, Moral Reasons to Edit the Human Genome: Picking Up from the Nuffield Report. J. Med. Ethics, January 24, 2019, open access.

Hall, Mark A., Legal Rules and Industry Norms: The Impact of Laws Restricting Health Insurers' Use of Genetic Information 40 Jurimetrics 93, 94–99, 122 (1999). Copyright © 1999 American Bar Association; Mark A. Hall. Reprinted by permission.

Harris, Cailin, Statutory Prohibitions on Wrongful Birth Claims & Their Dangerous Effects on Parents, 34 Boston College J. L. & Soc. Just. 365 (2014). Reprinted with permission.

Harsanyi, Zsolt and Richard Hutton, Genetic Prophecy: Beyond the Double Helix, 187–188 (1981). Copyright © 1981. Reprinted with permission of the authors.

Imwinkelried, Edward and D. H. Kaye, DNA Typing: Emerging or Neglected Issues, 76 Wash. L. Rev. 413, 416–440 (2001). Copyright © 2001 Washington Law Review Association. Reprinted with permission of the authors.

Kettering, Kalena R., Note, "Is Down Always Out?": The Right of Icelandic Parents to Use Preimplantation Genetic Diagnosis to Select for a Disability, 51 Geo. Wash. Int'l L. Rev. ___ (forthcoming 2020). Reprinted with permission.

Krimsky, Sheldon, The Profit of Scientific Discovery and Its Normative Implications, 75 Chicago-Kent L. Rev. 15, 21–22, 28–37 (1999). Copyright © 1999, IIT Chicago-Kent College of Law. Reprinted with permission of Chicago-Kent Law Review.

Lacy, James V. et al., Technology Transfer Laws Governing Federally Funded Research and Development, 19 Pepp. L. Rev. 1, 9–11, 13–14 (1991). Copyright © 1991. Reprinted with the permission of the Pepperdine Law Review.

Lander, E.S. Scientific Commentary: The Scientific Foundations and Medical and Social Prospects of the Human Genome, 26 Journal of Law, Medicine & Ethics 184, 184–185 (1998). Copyright © 1998, Reprinted with the permission of the American Society of Law, Medicine & Ethics. All rights reserved.

Lewin, Tamar, Boom in Genetic Testing Raises Questions on Sharing Results, The New York Times, July 21, 2000, A1. Reprinted with permission from The New York Times Agency. Copyright © 2000, The New York Times Agency.

Lombardo, Paul A., Three Generations, No Imbeciles: New Light on Buck v. Bell, in the New York University Law Review, volume 60, 30, 50–61 (1985). Reprinted with permission from the New York University Law Review.

Lowden, J. Alexander, Genetic Risks and Mortality Rates, in Genetics and Life Insurance: Medical Underwriting and Social Policy, 95–98 (Mark A. Rothstein ed. 2004). Copyright © 2004, MIT Press. Reprinted with permission.

Lynch, Holly Fernandez, et al., Implementing Regulatory Broad Consent Under the Revised Common Rule: Clarifying Key Points and the Need for Evidence, 47 J. L., Med. and Ethics 213 (2019), Reprinted by permission.

Malinowski, Michael J., Dealing with the Realities of Race and Ethnicity: A Bioethics-Centered Argument in Favor of Race-Based Genetics Research, 45 Hous. L. Rev. 1415, 1433–1436 (2009). Reprinted by permission of the Houston Law Review.

Marchant, Gary E., Genetic Susceptibility and Biomarkers in Toxic Injury Litigation, 41 Jurimetrics 67, 87 (2000). Copyright © 2000 by American Bar Association, Gary E. Marchant. Reprinted by permission.

Marchant, Gary E., Toxicogenomics and Environmental Regulation, in Genomics and Environmental Regulation: Science, Ethics, and Law, 11–14 (Richard R. Sharp, Gary E. Marchant, and Jamie A. Grodsky eds. 2008). Copyright © Johns Hopkins University Press. Reprinted with permission of Johns Hopkins University Press.

Marshall, Eliot, Tapping Iceland's DNA. Excerpted with permission from Science, volume 278, 566 (1997). Copyright © 1997, American Association for the Advancement of Science.

Matthews, Anne L., Genetic Counseling, in the Encyclopedia of Ethical, Legal & Policy Issues in Biotechnology, volume 1, 349–350 (T.H. Murray and M.J. Mehlman, eds., 2000). Reprinted with permission of John Wiley & Sons, Inc. Copyright © 2000.

McGuire, Amy L., Rebecca Fisher, Paul Cuseman, Kathy Hudson, Mark A. Rothstein, Deven McGraw, Stephen Matterson, John Glasser, and Douglas Henley, Confidentiality, Privacy, and Security Considerations for the Storage of Genetic and Genomic Test Information in Electronic Health Records: Points to Consider, 10 Genetics in Med., 495, 495–499 (2009). Reprinted by permission.

Mehlman, Maxwell J., Modern Eugenics and the Law, in A Century of Eugenics in America: From the "Indiana Experiment" to the Human Genome Era, Paul A. Lombardo, Ed. (Indiana University Press, Forthcoming 2010). Used with permission.

Mercer, Stephen & Jessica Gabel, Shadow Dwellers: The Underregulated World of State and Local DNA Databases, 69 N.Y.U. Ann Surv. Am L. 639, 653–46 (2014). Reprinted with permission.

Morse, Stephen J., Genetics and Criminal Responsibility, 15 Trends in Cognitive Sciences 378, 379 (2011). Copyright © 2011 Elsevier. Reprinted by permission.

Murphy, Erin, Law and Policy Oversight of Familial Searches in Recreational Genealogy Databases, 292 Forensics Sc. Int'l e5, e5–e8 (2018). Copyright © 2018 Elsevier. All rights reserved. Reprinted with Permission.

National Research Council, Applications of Toxicogenomic Technologies to Predictive Toxicology and Risk Assessment, 173, 186–189 (2007). Reprinted with permission by the National Academy of Sciences, Courtesy of the National Academies Press, Washington, DC.

National Research Council, The Evaluation of Forensic DNA Evidence, 171–173 (1996). Copyright © 1996, National Academy Press. Reprinted with permission of the National Academy of Sciences.

Obasogie, Osagie K., Playing the Gene Card? A Report on Race and Human Biotechnology (Center for Genetics and Society 2009). Used with permission.

Rothstein, Mark A., Predictive Genetic Testing for Alzheimer's Disease in Long-Term Care Insurance, 35 Ga. L. Rev. 707, 716–731 (2001). Copyright © 2001 Georgia Law Review Association, Inc.; Mark A. Rothstein. Reprinted by permission.

Rothstein, Mark A., Preventing the Discovery of Plaintiff Genetic Profiles by Defendants Seeking to Limit Damages in Personal Injury Litigation, 71 Ind. L.J. 877, 878–891 (1996). Copyright © 1996 by the Trustees of Indiana University; Mark A. Rothstein. Reprinted by permission.

Rothstein, Mark A., Time to End the Use of Genetic Test Results in Life Insurance Underwriting, 46 J.L. Med. & Ethics 794, 795–797 (2018).

Rothstein, Mark A. and Mary R. Anderlik, What is Genetic Discrimination and When and How Can it Be Prevented? 3 Genetics in Med. 354, 354–355 (2001). Reprinted by permission.

Rothstein, Mark A., Yu Cai, and Gary E. Marchant, Ethical Implications of Epigenetics Research, 10 Nature Reviews Genetics 224 (2009). Copyright © 2009 Nature Publishing Group. Reprinted by permission.

Rothstein, Mark A. and Phyllis Griffin Epps, Ethical and Legal Implications of Pharmacogenomics, 2 Nature Reviews Genetics 228–230 (2001). Copyright © 2001, Macmillan Magazines, Ltd.

Rothstein, Mark A. and Yann Joly, Genetic Information and Insurance Underwriting: Contemporary Issues and Approaches in the Global Economy in Handbook of Genetics and Society, 130–132 (Paul Atkinson, Peter Glasner, & Margaret Lock, eds., 2009). Copyright © 2009. Reprinted with author permission.

Rothstein, Mark A. and Meghan K. Talbott, Compelled Disclosures of Health Records: Updated Estimates, 45 J.L.Med. & Ethics 149, 153–154 (2017).

Rothstein, Mark A. and Stacey A. Tovino, California Takes the Lead on Data Privacy, 49 Hastings Center Report No. 5, 4–5 (2019).

Sandel, Michael, The Case Against Perfection: What's Wrong with Designer Children, Bionic Athletes, and Genetic Engineering, Atlantic Monthly (April 2004). Reprinted with permission.

Sherkow, Jacob S. & Jorge Contreras, Intellectual Property, Surrogate Licensing, and Precision Medicine, 7 Intell. Prop. Theory 1, 4–6 (2018). Reprinted with permission.

Stolberg, S., The Biotech Death of Jesse Gelsinger, The New York Times Sunday Magazine, November 28, 1999, 137. Reprinted with permission, The New York Times Agency. Copyright © 1999, The New York Times Agency.

Suter, Sonia M., All in the Family: Privacy and DNA Familial Searching, 23 Harv. J.L & Tech. 309, 311, 318–20 (2010). Reprinted with permission.

Suter, Sonia M., Did You Give the Government Your Baby's DNA? Rethinking Consent in Newborn Screening, 15 J.L. Sci. & Tech. 729, 734–48, 754-56 (2014). Reprinted with permission.

Suter, Sonia M., Genomic Medicine—New Norms Regarding Genetic Information, 15 Houston J. Health L. & Pol'y 83, 89–93 (2013). Reprinted with permission.

Suter, Sonia M., The Tyranny of Choice: Reproductive Selection in the Future, 5 J.L. Biosci. 262, 264–65, 267–68 (2018). Copyright © 2018, Oxford University Press. Reprinted with permission.

Trefethen, Amanda, The Emerging Tort of Wrongful Adoption, 11 J. Contemp. Legal Issues 620, 620–624 (2000). Copyright © 2000, Journal of Contemporary Legal Issues. Reprinted with the permission of the Journal of Contemporary Legal Issues.

Vogelstein, Bert, et al., Cancer Genome Landscapes, 339 Science 1546 (2013). Copyright © 2013 American Association for the Advancement of Science. Reprinted with permission.

Willing, Richard, DNA and Daddy, USA Today, July 29, 1999, 1A. Copyright © 1999, USA Today. Reprinted with permission.

Wolf, Susan M. and Jeffrey P. Kahn, Genetic Testing and the Future of Disability Insurance: Ethics, Law, and Policy, 25 J.L. Med. & Ethics (Supp. 2) 6, 11, 13 (2007).

Wright Clayton, Ellen, Screening and Treatment of Newborns, 29 Houston Law Review, 85, 103–134 (1992). Reprinted with permission from the Houston Law Review, Copyright © 1992.

Zick, Cathleen D. et al., Genetic Testing, Adverse Selection, and the Demand for Life Insurance, 93 Am. J. Med. Genetics 29, 29–32, 35–38 (2000). Copyright © 2000 by Wiley-Liss, Inc. Reprinted by permission of Wiley-Liss, Inc., a subsidiary of John Wiley & Sons, Inc.

Zick, Cathleen D. et al., Genetic Testing for Alzheimer's Disease and Its Impact on Insurance Purchasing Behavior, 24 Health Affairs 483, 484–488 (2005). Copyright © 2005, by Project HOPE—The People-to-People Foundation, Inc. Reprinted by permission.

PHOTO ACKNOWLEDGMENTS

Leja, Darryl Henrietta Lacks (HeLa) Timeline. National Human Genome Research Institute, www.genome.gov.

Rosalind Franklin's Original DNA Radiograph. Photo. Reprinted with permission of King's College London.

Photograph of Carrie Buck and Mother. Arthur Estabrook Papers, M.E. Grenander Department of Special Collections & Archives, University at Albany, SUNY.

Photograph of John Moore. Reprinted with permission.

Photograph of Watson and Crick, Photo Researchers, Inc., 307 Fifth Avenue, 3rd Floor, New York, NY 10016. With permission.

Photograph of White House announcement of completion of the Human Genome Project with the permission of the Associated Press.

President Obama signing the Patient Protection and Affordable Care Act on March 23, 2010. Photo credit: Pete Souza. Photo was altered to black and white. Reprinted under CC by 2.0, http://creativecommons.org/licenses/by/2.0/.

SUMMARY OF CONTENTS

PART V. NON-MEDICAL USES OF GENETICS

PART VI. PRIVACY AND CONFIDENTIALITY

PART VII. INSURANCE

PART VIII. EMPLOYMENT DISCRIMINATION

TABLE OF CONTENTS

PART II. GENETIC SCREENING AND TESTING
IN MEDICINE AND RESEARCH

PART III. GENE THERAPY

PART V. NON-MEDICAL USES OF GENETICS

TABLE OF CASES

The principal cases are in bold type.

GENETICS
ETHICS, LAW AND POLICY

Fifth Edition

PART I

HISTORICAL AND SCIENTIFIC OVERVIEW

■ ■ ■

This part gives a brief overview of the history of human genetic science. Chapter 1 begins by describing basic discoveries, including the role of genes in the inheritance of human traits, the first efforts to manipulate DNA directly, and the growing understand of the nature and function of DNA. The chapter then describes the growing use of genetic science in clinical medicine and crime-fighting, "direct-to-consumer" genetic testing, and advances in editing human DNA, including "germ line" changes that are passed on to an individual's children. For more information on the science of human genetics, see https://learn.genetics.utah.edu/content/basics/; https://www.genome.gov/About-Genomics/Introduction-to-Genomics.

Chapter 2 discusses eugenics, the beliefs and practices that seek to improve the quality of human genes by preventing some people from reproducing and encouraging others.

Chapter 3 discusses the question of whether there is a genetic basis for differentiating human races, and the implications of the answer.

Finally, Chapter 4 presents a number of emerging developments in genetics.

CHAPTER 1

HISTORY OF GENETIC SCIENCE

■ ■ ■

ERIC S. LANDER, SCIENTIFIC COMMENTARY: THE
SCIENTIFIC FOUNDATIONS AND MEDICAL AND SOCIAL
PROSPECTS OF THE HUMAN GENOME PROJECT
26 J.L. Med. & Ethics 184, 184–185 (1998).

* * *

Genetics is a remarkable discipline, because it offers a generic approach that enables scientists to pursue any disease-related question, from inflammatory bowel disease to schizophrenia. How is this possible? The foundations of this story, as almost everything in genetics, go back to the fundamental insight of Gregor Mendel in 1865.

> **Take Note:** In this casebook, "genetics" refers both to the entire field of genetics-related science and to the science that focuses on genes—the stretches of the DNA molecule that contain instructions for making proteins, which form the structural components of cells and tissue and the enzymes that control biochemical reactions. "Genomics" refers specifically to aspects of the entire DNA molecule, both genes and the stretches of DNA between the genes.

Mendel noted that hereditary traits in the pea plant could be explained by the action of certain invisible but predictable "factors" (the word gene was coined only at the beginning of the twentieth century). Mendel noted that each individual inherited two copies of each factor—one from each parent. And, each individual passed on one copy to its offspring. For example, when a pure-breeding green plant is mated with a pure-breeding yellow plant, the offspring will inherit one color gene from the green parent and one from the yellow parent. Finally, when the resulting plant is crossed with itself, the genes reassort: offspring of different types reemerge in the next generation.

Mendel's extraordinarily important and simple concept—that discrete factors control inheritance—was not regarded as earthshaking in its time, probably because it was so abstract. Mendel did not know the identity of the factors. He simply inferred their existence to explain the results of his pea experiments. About thirty-five years passed before cell biologists studying the division of cells noticed strange structures that appear red when cells underwent division. When cells underwent meiosis to make gametes (sperm or eggs), the structures lined up in pairs, and one copy of each pair would be transmitted. When two gametes fused to give rise to an offspring, each parent thus contributed one copy of each such structure.

This strange choreography—pairs splitting, sending one to the offspring, and then rejoining—behaved just as Mendel's abstract factors had behaved. The cell biologists did not know what these objects were, but, because they stained them with certain dyes, they named them chromosomes—a Latinate term meaning colored things. These chromosomes seemed likely to hold the secret of inheritance.

Soon after this discovery, scientists set out to understand how chromosomes controlled inheritance. By about 1911, a student at Columbia University named Alfred Sturtevant made a key observation: by following the inheritance patterns of genes, it was possible to infer whether genes were nearby one another on a chromosome. Nearby genes would tend to be transmitted together, whereas distant genes would tend to be separated by recombination events (that is, exchanges of genetic material). In other words, one could measure the location of genes on chromosomes by how frequently they were transmitted together. Sturtevant began building genetic maps, showing the locations of genes that controlled various traits in the fruit fly, such as body color and eye color. He was teasing apart the secrets of inheritance patterns that controlled traits, without knowing anything about the actual DNA that encoded them.

The idea that one could trace inheritance in this fashion was applied widely to flies, corn, and many other organisms. Moreover, it soon became clear that, in principle, the same basic ideas applied to the human being. However, one could not set up human matings to study inheritance, as in the fly or in corn. Also, one did not have simple, single-gene traits with which to trace inheritance patterns (with a few exceptions, such as a blood group). Thus, for most of this century, our understanding of human genetics was largely theoretical, not operational. Seventy years of scientific progress were required before human geneticists could do what Sturtevant was doing in 1911. The DNA revolution offered the key.

[Eds.—By the 1950s, many scientists around the world were attempting to discover the structure of DNA. Rosalind Franklin, a chemist and X-ray crystallographer at King's College, London, took an X-ray diffraction image of DNA. That image led to the discovery of the double-helix structure of DNA.

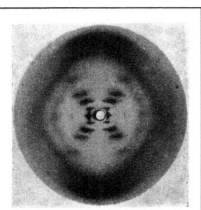

Rosalind Franklin's original DNA radiograph. *Photo Credit: King's College, London.*

After viewing Franklin's image, James Watson and Francis Crick performed their seminal work to understand the structure of DNA and how its double-helical properties enabled it to encode information, to divide apart, and to pass the information on to daughter cells.] * * * Work conducted in the 1960s showed how DNA actually encodes information in the language of the genetic code, which specifies the instructions for making proteins. Finally, the tools of recombinant DNA, developed during the 1970s, allowed molecular biologists to copy (or clone) and read the sequence of individual pieces of DNA. After all of that work—from 1910 to 1980—it was finally possible to apply Sturtevant's techniques of genetic mapping to humans. To trace inheritance, one could not use curly wings and white eyes as with *Drosophila*. However, one could use simply the spelling differences in DNA.

The discoverers of the structure of DNA, James Watson at left and Francis Crick, seen with their model of part of a DNA molecule in 1953.
A Barrington Brown/Science Source.

I.   ALTERING DNA

An important breakthrough in genetics was the ability to manipulate DNA. Previously, this could only be accomplished by selective breeding, making dogs more docile, for example, by only letting the most docile ones have puppies, and by hybridization, splicing plants together to produce new or better specimens. But these are indirect techniques; could genes be altered directly?

In 1972, Paul Berg, a Stanford biochemist who in 1980 would win half of the Nobel Prize in Chemistry, took DNA from Escherichia coli, a common type of bacteria that lives in the human digestive tract, and inserted it into the DNA of SV40, a virus found in monkey kidneys. Berg's laboratory thus created a new type of living organism, one that shared DNA from the bacterium and the virus. Because the method resembled "recombination," part of the reproductive process in humans and other animals in which DNA molecules from the parents are combined and transmitted to their offspring after first being chopped up and reassembled into new molecules, the technique that Berg's laboratory pioneered was called "recombinant DNA." Obviously, there is enormous potential in being able to create a new life-form that combines the attributes and abilities of other organisms. Why not create a bacterium that can completely digest and degrade oil spills, for example, by combining DNA from four different naturally occurring bacteria, each of which has the digestive equipment to only do part of the job? A microbiologist working for General Electric named Ananda Chakrabarty applied for a patent for just such a recombinant bacterium.

Recombinant DNA can provide direct benefits for human health. A few years after Chakrabarty created his oil-eating bacterium, a fledgling company called Genentech programmed E. coli with human DNA so the bacterium could manufacture a human protein. One year later, Genentech announced that its researchers, working with the City of Hope National Medical Center in Duarte, California, had spliced a human gene into E. coli that made it produce human insulin. Since then, the FDA and the European Medicines Agency have approved more than 150 drugs manufactured with recombinant DNA technology.

However, there could be complications. When Paul Berg created his new DNA molecule, he combined DNA from E. coli and SV40, a virus found in monkey kidneys. It turns out that the Salk polio vaccine that was developed during the 1950s was produced by culturing polio virus in a culture made from monkey kidneys, and SV40 had been detected in samples of the vaccine. This made the vaccine researchers curious about the properties of SV40, and in 1961, they discovered that it caused cancer in hamsters. This meant that there was a chance that it could cause cancer in humans as well, and the government took the threat to humans so seriously that it screened the entire polio vaccine stock to weed out any vaccine that had been contaminated with SV40. Berg was undoubtedly aware of this, but he nevertheless decided to work with SV40 because it was easy to use. By happenstance, one of his colleagues, a cancer researcher named Robert Pollack, got wind of Berg's experiment and became alarmed; Berg was about to combine this cancer-causing virus with a bacterium that flourished in the human gut. Could the resulting virus-containing bacterium find its way into the human digestive system? Would Berg's students or lab workers become infected? Could this spread throughout the population, like outbreaks of food-borne E. coli? Would there be any way to stop it?

When Pollack confronted Berg with his fears, Berg stopped his experiments and warned colleagues of the dangers of recombinant DNA at the next annual Gordon Research Conference on Nucleic Acids. Along with nine other scientists, among them four Nobel laureates, Berg then published a letter in the journal *Science* calling for a voluntary, worldwide moratorium on further recombinant DNA experiments "until the potential hazards of such recombinant DNA molecules have been better evaluated or until adequate methods are developed for preventing their spread."

PAUL BERG ET AL., LETTER

185 Science 303 (1974).

POTENTIAL BIOHAZARDS OF RECOMBINANT DNA MOLECULES

Recent advances in techniques for the isolation and rejoining of segments of DNA now permit construction of biologically active recombinant DNA molecules in vitro. For example, DNA restriction endonucleases, which generate DNA fragments containing cohesive ends especially suitable for rejoining, have been used to create new types of biologically functional bacterial plasmids carrying antibiotic resistance markers and to link *Xenopus laevis* ribosomal DNA to DNA from a bacterial plasmid. This latter recombinant plasmid has been shown to replicate stably in *Escherichia coli* where it synthesizes RNA that is complementary to X. laevis ribosomal DNA. Similarly, segments of *Drosophila* chromosomal DNA have been incorporated into both plasmid and bacteriaphage DNA's to yield hybrid molecules that can infect and replicate in *E. coli*.

Several groups of scientists are now planning to use this technology to create recombinant DNAs from a variety of other viral, animal, and bacterial sources. Although such experiments are likely to facilitate the solution of important theoretical and practical biological problems, they would also result in the creation of novel types of infectious DNA elements whose biological properties cannot be completely predicted in advance.

There is serious concern that some of these artificial recombinant DNA molecules could prove biologically hazardous. One potential hazard in current experiments derives from the need to use a bacterium like *E. coli* to clone the recombinant DNA molecules and to amplify their number. Strains of *E. coli* commonly reside in the human intestinal tract, and they are capable of exchanging genetic information with other types of bacteria, some of which are pathogenic to man. Thus, new DNA elements introduced into *E. coli*. might possibly become widely disseminated among human, bacterial, plant, or animal populations with unpredictable effects.

Concern for these emerging capabilities was raised by scientists attending the 1973 Gordon Research Conference on Nucleic Acids, who requested that the National Academy of Sciences give consideration to these matters. The undersigned members of a committee, acting on behalf of and with the endorsement of the Assembly of Life Sciences of the

National Research Council on this matter, propose the following recommendations.

First, and most important, that until the potential hazards of such recombinant DNA molecules have been better evaluated or until adequate methods are developed for preventing their spread, scientists throughout the world join with the members of this committee in voluntarily deferring the following types of experiments.

Type I: Construction of new, autonomously replicating bacterial plasmids that might result in the introduction of genetic determinants for antibiotic resistance or bacterial toxin formation into bacterial strains that do not at present carry such determinants; or construction of new bacterial plasmids containing combinations of resistance to clinically useful antibiotics unless plasmids containing such combinations of antibiotic resistance determinants already exist in nature.

Type II: Linkage of all or segments of the DNA's from oncogenic or other animal viruses to autonomously replicating DNA elements such as bacterial plasmids or other viral DNA's. Such recombinant DNA molecules might be more easily disseminated to bacterial populations in humans and other species, and thus possibly increase the incidence of cancer or other diseases.

Second, plans to link fragments of animal DNA's to bacterial plasmid DNA or bacteriophage DNA should be carefully weighed in light of the fact that many types of animal cell DNA's contain sequences common to RNA tumor viruses. Since joining of any foreign DNA to a DNA replication system creates new recombinant DNA molecules whose biological properties cannot be predicted with certainty, such experiments should not be undertaken lightly.

Third, the director of the National Institutes of Health is requested to give immediate consideration to establishing an advisory committee charged with (i) overseeing an experimental program to evaluate the potential biological and ecological hazards of the above types of recombinant DNA molecules; (ii) developing procedures which will minimize the spread of such molecules within human and other populations; and (iii) devising guidelines to be followed by investigators working with potentially hazardous recombinant DNA molecules.

Fourth, an international meeting of involved scientists from all over the world should be convened early in the coming year to review scientific progress in this area and to further discuss appropriate ways to deal with the potential biohazards of recombinant DNA molecules.

The above recommendations are made with the realization (i) that our concern is based on judgments of potential rather than demonstrated risk since there are few available experimental data on the hazards of such

DNA molecules and (ii) that adherence to our major recommendations will entail postponement or possibly abandonment of certain types of scientifically worthwhile experiments. Moreover, we are aware of many theoretical and practical difficulties involved in evaluating the human hazards of such recombinant DNA molecules. Nonetheless, our concern for the possible unfortunate consequences of indiscriminate application of these techniques motivates us to urge all scientists working in this area to join us in agreeing not to initiate experiments of types I and II above until attempts have been made to evaluate the hazards and some resolution of the outstanding questions has been achieved.

Paul Berg, *Chairman,* David Baltimore, Herbert W. Boyer, Stanley N. Cohen, Ronald W. Davis, David S. Hogness, Daniel Nathans, Richard Roblin, James D. Watson, Sherman Weissman, Norton D. Zinder, Committee on Recombinant DNA Molecules, Assembly of Life Sciences, National Research Council, National Academy of Sciences

NOTES AND QUESTIONS

Researchers around the world heeded Berg's letter, and so far as is known, recombinant DNA experiments did not resume for over a year until the NIH established safety guidelines to govern the experiments.

A voluntary moratorium is a form of self-regulation, an alternative to external restraints, such as legal prohibitions. What are its strengths and weaknesses as a regulatory approach? For an early discussion of these issues, see Barry Furrow, Governing Science: Public Risks and Private Remedies, 131 U. Pa. L. Rev. 1403 (1983).

> **Food for Thought:** A fundamental dispute in legal and economic policy is whether we need government regulation or whether individuals and enterprises can regulate themselves. What are the goals of regulation? Can scientists adequately police themselves? See Maxwell J. Mehlman, Transhumanist Dreams and Dystopian Nightmares 41–49 (2012).

Following publication of the Berg letter, another conference was held at the Asilomar Conference Center in California. The meeting was attended by 150 scientists, 4 lawyers, and 16 journalists. The focus was on how experiments in recombining DNA could be conducted safely. As one attendee observed:

> The recombinant DNA issue was defined as a technical problem to be solved by technical means. Larger ethical issues regarding the purposes and the long-term goals of the research were excluded, despite the rich discussion that had occurred among geneticists and other biologists in the 1960s about where to draw the line when it became possible to do genetic engineering. * * * Instead of these longer-term issues, the focus at Asilomar in 1975 was on safety of newly-developed technical tools for genetic engineering, on the means not the ends.

Charles Weiner, Recombinant DNA Policy: Asilomar Conference, in 2 Encyclopedia of Ethical, Legal and Policy Issues in Biotechnology 909, 910–911 (Thomas H. Murray & Maxwell J. Mehlman eds. 2000). For a description of the conference by one of the lawyers who attended, see Roger B. Dworkin, Science, Society, and the Expert Town Meeting: Some Comments on Asilomar, 51 S. Cal. L. Rev. 1471 (1978).

Shortly before the Asilomar Conference, the director of NIH had established an advisory committee called the Recombinant DNA Advisory Committee, the "RAC." The RAC originally had 12 members, all scientists. It met for the first time immediately after the conference, and began to draft safety guidelines for recombinant DNA research based on the conference proceedings. The guidelines, published at 41 Fed. Reg. 27902 (1976), required all large-scale NIH-funded recombinant experiments to be approved by the RAC.

In 1978, the RAC was expanded to 25 members, one-third of whom were "public" members, including lawyers and bioethicists, and the RAC issued revised guidelines (42 Fed. Reg. 49596) which, recognizing that recombinant DNA experiments were less risky than originally had been thought, relaxed some of the restrictions on recombinant DNA research. For a history of the early RAC, see Sheldon Krimsky, Genetic Alchemy: The Social History of the Recombinant DNA Controversy (1982).

II. THE HUMAN GENOME PROJECT

NATIONAL HUMAN GENOME RESEARCH INSTITUTE, NIH, UNDERSTANDING OUR GENETIC INHERITANCE: THE U.S. HUMAN GENOME PROJECT THE FIRST FIVE YEARS: FISCAL YEARS 1991–1995
(1990).

The Human Genome Initiative is a worldwide research effort that has the goal of analyzing the structure of human DNA and determining the location of all human genes. In parallel with this effort, the DNA of a set of model organisms will be studied to provide the comparative information necessary for understanding the functioning of the human genome. The information generated by the human genome project is expected to be the source book for biomedical science in the 21st century. It will have a profound impact on and expedite progress in a variety of biological fields, including those such as developmental biology and neurobiology, where scientists are just beginning to understand the underlying molecular mechanisms. The analysis and interpretation of the information will occupy scientists for many years to come. Thus, the maximal benefit of the human genome project will only be achieved if it is surrounded by research efforts that are focused on understanding and taking advantage of the human genetic information.

REMARKS BY THE PRESIDENT, PRIME MINISTER TONY
BLAIR OF ENGLAND, DR. FRANCIS COLLINS, DIRECTOR
OF THE NATIONAL HUMAN GENOME RESEARCH
INSTITUTE, & DR. CRAIG VENTER, PRESIDENT AND
CHIEF OFFICER, CELERA GENOMICS CORPORATION, ON
THE COMPLETION OF THE FIRST SURVEY OF THE
ENTIRE HUMAN GENOME PROJECT

June 26, 2000.

THE EAST ROOM

The President [William Clinton]: Good morning.

* * *

Nearly two centuries ago, in this room, on this floor, Thomas Jefferson and a trusted aide spread out a magnificent map—a map Jefferson had long prayed he would get to see in his lifetime. The aide was Meriwether Lewis and the map was the product of his courageous expedition across the American frontier, all the way to the Pacific. It was a map that defined the contours and forever expanded the frontiers of our continent and our imagination.

Today, the world is joining us here in the East Room to behold a map of even greater significance. We are here to celebrate the completion of the first survey of the entire human genome. Without a doubt, this is the most important, most wondrous map ever produced by humankind.

The moment we are here to witness was brought about through brilliant and painstaking work of scientists all over the world, including many men and women here today. It was not even 50 years ago that a young Englishman named Crick and a brash even younger American named Watson, first discovered the elegant structure of our genetic code. Dr. Watson, the way you announced your discovery in the journal "Nature," was one of the great understatements of all time. "This structure has novel features, which are of considerable biological interest."

How far we have come since that day. In the intervening years, we have pooled the combined wisdom of biology, chemistry, physics, engineering, mathematics and computer science; tapped the great strengths and insights of the public and private sectors. More than 1,000 researchers across six nations have revealed nearly all three billion letters of our miraculous genetic code. I congratulate all of you on this stunning and humbling achievement.

Today's announcement represents more than just an epic-making triumph of science and reason. After all, when Galileo discovered he could use the tools of mathematics and mechanics to understand the motion of celestial bodies, he felt, in the words of one eminent researcher, "that he had learned the language in which God created the universe."

Today, we are learning the language in which God created life. We are gaining ever more awe for the complexity, the beauty, the wonder of God's most divine and sacred gift. With this profound new knowledge, humankind is on the verge of gaining immense, new power to heal. Genome science will have a real impact on all our lives—and even more, on the lives of our children. It will revolutionize the diagnosis, prevention and treatment of most, if not all, human diseases.

In coming years, doctors increasingly will be able to cure diseases like Alzheimer's, Parkinson's, diabetes and cancer by attacking their genetic roots. Just to offer one example, patients with some forms of leukemia and breast cancer already are being treated in clinical trials with sophisticated new drugs that precisely target the faulty genes and cancer cells, with little or no risk to healthy cells. In fact, it is now conceivable that our children's children will know the term cancer only as a constellation of stars.

But today's historic achievement is only a starting point. There is much hard work yet to be done. That is why I'm so pleased to announce that from this moment forward, the robust and healthy competition that has led us to this day and that always is essential to the progress of science, will be coupled with enhanced public-private cooperation.

Public and private research teams are committed to publishing their genomic data simultaneously later this year, for the benefit of researchers in every corner of the globe. And after publication, both sets of teams will join together for an historic sequence analysis conference. Together, they will examine what scientific insights have been gleaned from both efforts, and how we can most judiciously proceed toward the next majestic horizons.

What are those next horizons? Well, first, we will complete a virtually error-free final draft of the human genome before the 50th anniversary of the discovery of the double helix, less than three years from now. Second, through sustained and vigorous support for public and private research, we must sort through this trove of genomic data to identify every human gene. We must discover the function of these genes and their protein products, and then we must rapidly convert that knowledge into treatments that can lengthen and enrich lives.

I want to emphasize that biotechnology companies are absolutely essential in this endeavor. For it is they who will bring to the market the life-enhancing applications of the information from the human genome. And for that reason, this administration is committed to helping them to make the kind of long-term investments that will change the face of medicine forever.

The third horizon that lies before us is one that science cannot approach alone. It is the horizon that represents the ethical, moral and spiritual dimension of the power we now possess. We must not shrink from exploring that far frontier of science. But as we consider how to use new discovery, we must also not retreat from our oldest and most cherished human values. We must ensure that new genome science and its benefits will be directed toward making life better for all citizens of the world, never just a privileged few.

As we unlock the secrets of the human genome, we must work simultaneously to ensure that new discoveries never pry open the doors of privacy. And we must guarantee that genetic information cannot be used to stigmatize or discriminate against any individual or group.

Increasing knowledge of the human genome must never change the basic belief on which our ethics, our government, our society are founded. All of us are created equal, entitled to equal treatment under the law. After all, I believe one of the great truths to emerge from this triumphant expedition inside the human genome is that in genetic terms, all human beings, regardless of race, are more than 99.9 percent the same.

What that means is that modern science has confirmed what we first learned from ancient fates. The most important fact of life on this Earth is our common humanity. My greatest wish on this day for the ages is that this incandescent truth will always guide our actions as we continue to march forth in this, the greatest age of discovery ever known.

White House announcement of completion of the Human Genome Project, Craig Venter left, Francis Collins right. AP Photo/Ron Edmonds

NOTES AND QUESTIONS

1. The term "Human Genome Project" (HGP) technically refers to the publicly-sponsored effort to map and sequence the human genome. The HGP originally expected to complete its sequencing of the human genome by 2005, at a cost of approximately $3 billion. In the U.S., funding was provided by Congress to the National Institutes of Health (NIH) and, to a much smaller extent, the Department of Energy (which had an interest in genetics as a result of its concern about the effects of atomic radiation). The NIH in turn channeled the funds to a consortium of nine research establishments, with most of the funds going to Washington University at St. Louis, Baylor College of Medicine, and the Whitehead Institute in Cambridge, Massachusetts. At the NIH, the HGP initially was overseen by an "Office of Human Genome Research," created in 1988, and headed by James Watson. In 1990, the "office" was transformed into a free-standing "center," and in 1997, the center finally achieved the status of a full-fledged "institute." In the U.K., the Wellcome Trust sponsored research at the Sanger Center. Additional public efforts were made in other countries under a loose affiliation called HUGO (for "Human Genome Organization").

Compared to publicly-funded efforts, only a small amount of mapping and sequencing initially took place in the private sector. This changed in 1998 with the formation of a company called Celera Genomics. Celera grew out of the development of faster sequencing machines. With $200 million in funding from Perkin-Elmer Corporation, an old-line medical equipment manufacturer, and with a scientist named Craig Venter as its president, Celera set out from scratch to complete its own sequence map by 2001 by running 200 of the machines around the clock.

The sequencing technique Celera used, called a "shotgun" approach, differed from the HGP approach. The HGP identified specific regions of DNA and proceeded to sequence them. Celera sequenced chunks of DNA without knowing where they were located, and then relied on computers to identify overlapping sequences at the ends of the chunks to piece them together.

At first the two programs regarded each other with antagonism. This was due in part to the high historical and scientific stakes and to the impact of success and failure on personal reputations, but also to a fundamental difference in regard to the intended use of results. As a public-funded project, the HGP was committed to making its sequencing immediately available to the public for free, while Celera, a private, for-profit company, intended to extract commercial value from its research efforts. (For more discussion about the intellectual property aspects of the HGP, see Part IV.) Francis Collins, the director of the National Human Genome Research Institute (NHGRI) at NIH, responded to Celera's challenge by vowing to speed up the HGP and complete a "rough draft" of the human genome by 2000 and a final version by 2003, rather than by the original date of 2005. When Venter scoffed that the HGP would not meet this timetable, some HGP scientists raised concerns about whether Celera could reassemble its fragments into an accurate map of the entire genome. Both sides seemed vindicated when the HGP began cranking out large portions of sequences in keeping with its new schedule, and Celera published an accurate sequence of the genome of the fruit fly, *Drosophila*. The race heated up.

Ultimately, Ari Patrinos, the head of the Human Genome Project at the Department of Energy, invited Collins and Venter to his home for pizza and beer and, after several more meetings, the two rivals agreed to cooperate in issuing a joint statement with President Clinton at the White House announcing the completion of their sequencing efforts, excerpts of which appear above. The HGP subsequently published its sequence map in the journal *Nature* while Celera published its map in *Science*.

Ironically, at the time of the June 26, 2000, announcement, neither sequencing effort was complete. The HGP had only finished a "working draft," with 97 percent of the human genome sequenced and only 85 percent placed in the proper order. Venter stated that Celera had sequenced 99 percent of the genome, but that its supercomputers (which comprised the largest private supercomputing capacity in the world) were still piecing the fragments together.

On April 14, 2003, the International Human Genome Sequencing Consortium announced that it had really finished the sequencing of the human genome. But even then, the sequencing was not quite complete. It was not until May 2006 that researchers announced that they had completed the sequencing of the last chromosome, chromosome 1.

2. Whose genome was sequenced? The NHGRI report said that the DNA came from a number of sources. But most of the DNA sequenced by the public consortium came from one man, although there were segments from eleven other people from different backgrounds. Celera sequenced DNA from three females and two males. The males were Caucasians; there was one African-American woman, one Hispanic woman, and one woman of Asian descent. Craig Venter has said that he was one of the two males.

> **Food for Thought:** Most of the research on human genetics has been conducted with subjects of European descent. This raises questions about how much of the knowledge gained applies to individuals from other backgrounds. For example, genetic tests that purport to be able to detect disease-related genetic variants may be based on findings from populations of European descent that do not apply or apply as accurately to individuals from other backgrounds. What are the medical and policy consequences?

3. The cost of DNA sequencing has continued to decline. The Human Genome Project originally estimated a cost of $1 per nucleotide base pair. (Given the estimated three billion base pairs in the entire human genome, this cost was the basis for the original estimate that the project would cost $3 billion.) By 2005, the cost had dropped to less than 1/10th of a cent. Currently it costs about $1,000 to sequence an entire human genome.

4. Certain stretches of DNA contain instructions for making proteins. Proteins form the structural components of cells and tissue and the enzymes

that control biochemical reactions, including the functioning of the genes themselves. The stretches of DNA containing protein instructions are called *genes,* and genes are said to *code for* specific proteins. Until recently, geneticists believed that a single human gene coded for a single protein. Since there are about 100,000 proteins, this meant that there should be about 100,000 human genes. It now appears that there are only around 20,000 to 25,000 human genes. This means the some genes can code for more than one protein, depending on how the amino acids are arranged and how the protein is shaped or folded. This has several implications. First, it shows that we still have a lot to learn about human genetics. Second, the greater complexity of a human, compared to other organisms such as the small flowering plant *Arabidopsis thaliana,* with about the same number of genes, is not due to the difference in the number of genes. Third, the more complex relationship between genes and proteins is likely to complicate the task of linking genes to specific diseases or traits and of finding effective treatments.

Initially, the non-gene stretches of DNA were referred to as "junk DNA" on the assumption that they had no important function. In 2003, the National Human Genome Research Institute at NIH established a research program called the Encyclopedia of DNA Elements (ENCODE) to identify all the functional elements of the human genome, not just the genes themselves. In 2007, researchers announced that a pilot project that had examined 1 percent of the genome had found that, while the protein-coding components of genes account for only about 2 percent of human DNA, 93 percent of the DNA is functionally active, in that it is transcribed into RNA. The non-protein-coding gene elements include genes that do not code for proteins, regulatory elements that control the transcription process, and elements that maintain the structure of chromosomes and mediate their replication. These non-protein coding regions of DNA are indeed important, for they contain instructions for turning genes on and off, and non-coding portions of human DNA have been associated with risks for prostate, breast, and colon cancer, and heart attacks.

In addition, the ENCODE results showed that genes were not strings of nucleotides like beads along the DNA molecule, as had long been assumed, but instead, that many genes overlap one another and share stretches of DNA. In short, the ways in which DNA functions are far more complex than previously thought.

Meanwhile, other researchers embarked on a new mega-project: creating a haplotype map of the human genome.

NATIONAL HUMAN GENOME RESEARCH INSTITUTE, INTERNATIONAL HAPMAP PROJECT OVERVIEW
Sept. 2005.

The DNA sequence of any two people is 99.9 percent identical. The variations, however, may greatly affect an individual's disease risk. Sites in the DNA sequence where individuals differ at a single DNA base are called single nucleotide polymorphisms (SNPs). Sets of nearby SNPs on the same chromosome are inherited in blocks. This pattern of SNPs on a block is a haplotype. Blocks may contain a large number of SNPs, but a few SNPs are enough to uniquely identify the haplotypes in a block. The HapMap is a map of these haplotype blocks and the specific SNPs that identify the haplotypes are called tag SNPs.

The HapMap should be valuable by reducing the number of SNPs required to examine the entire genome for association with a phenotype from the 10 million SNPs that exist to roughly 500,000 tag SNPs. This will make genome scan approaches to finding regions with genes that affect diseases much more efficient and comprehensive, since effort will not be wasted typing more SNPs than necessary and all regions of the genome can be included.

In addition to its use in studying genetic associations with disease, the HapMap should be a powerful resource for studying the genetic factors contributing to variation in response to environmental factors, in susceptibility to infection, and in the effectiveness of and adverse responses to drugs and vaccines. All such studies will be based on the expectation that there will be higher frequencies of the contributing genetic components in a group of people with a disease or particular response to a drug, vaccine, pathogen, or environmental factor than in a group of similar people without the disease or response. Using just the tag SNPs, researchers should be able to find chromosome regions that have different haplotype distributions in the two groups of people, those with a disease or response and those without. Each region would then be studied in more detail to discover which variants in which genes in the region contribute to the disease or response, leading to more effective interventions. This should also allow the development of tests to predict which drugs or vaccines would be most effective in individuals with particular genotypes for genes affecting drug metabolism.

NOTES AND QUESTIONS

1. The haplotype mapping project, called the International HapMap Project, or simply, HapMap, began as a three-year program in 2002 with pledges of $100 million from six nations (Canada, China, Japan, Nigeria, the United Kingdom and the United States). By February 2005, the project had reached its initial goal of mapping one million SNPs. Currently over 10 million SNPs have been identified.

2. HapMap began analyzing blood samples from donors from five populations: Han Chinese in Beijing, Japanese in Tokyo, Yoruba in Ibadan, Nigeria, and Utah residents with ancestry from northern and western Europe. No medical or personal identifying information was obtained from the 270 donors. However, the samples are identified by the population from which they were collected. What ethical, legal, and social issues does this raise?

3.   In 2002, Craig Venter resigned as head of Celera and started a foundation called The J. Craig Venter Institute.

4.   Studies that take advantage of new high-speed sequencing technologies (discussed in Chapter 4) have accelerated the search for SNPs associated with disease. These studies, referred to as whole genome or genome-wide association studies (GWAS), search for SNPs by comparing the entire genome of large numbers of individuals with particular diseases to the genomes of control groups without the diseases.

5.   Another post-Human Genome Project research program is the 1000 Genomes Project, an international research consortium formed to sequence the genomes of approximately 1,200 people from around the world to provide medically useful information on human genetic variation. The project was funded by the Wellcome Trust Sanger Institute in England, the Beijing Genomics Institute Shenzhen in China, and the National Human Genome Research Institute at the National Institutes of Health. The results of the project were made public in January 2009.

6.   In 2007, the NIH initiated the Human Microbiome Project. The goal of this project is to use DNA sequencing to obtain a better understanding of the microbial communities that inhabit the human digestive system. These microorganisms are essential for human metabolism, and their cells outnumber human cells by a factor of ten to one.

7.   See Chapter 4 for discussion of additional developments in genetics since the Human Genome Project.

CHAPTER 2

EUGENICS

■ ■ ■

No phenomenon has done more to shape the ethical, legal, and policy attitudes toward human genetics than the philosophy of eugenics and the actions that it inspired.

This chapter begins with an explanation of the term "eugenics" and a historical description of the movement that bears its name. The chapter then explores the reaction of American law, and discusses the ways in which eugenic thinking continues to be reflected in public attitudes and policy.

ALLEN BUCHANAN ET AL., FROM CHANCE TO CHOICE: GENETICS AND JUSTICE
27–28 (2000).

The current revolution in molecular biology is not the first but the second large-scale attempt to modify the pattern of human heredity for the better. The eugenics movement of 1870–1950 came first. These large-scale social movements, originating in England but ultimately involving public advocates and membership organizations from Brazil to Russia, located the source of social problems in the genes of individuals and sought to alter the pattern by which these genes would be transmitted to future generations. In the United States, the movement received substantial funding from the great family fortunes, including Carnegie and the Rockefellers, and it was endorsed, with varying degrees of enthusiasm, by most scientists working in the field of human genetics. Indeed, eugenics was the motivation for much of the early scientific research in this field.

Nevertheless, the history of eugenics is not a proud one. It is largely remembered for its shoddy science, the blatant race and class biases of many of its leading advocates, and its cruel program of segregation and, later, sterilization of hundreds of thousands of vulnerable people who were judged to have substandard genes. Even worse, eugenics, in the form of "racial hygiene," formed part of the core of Nazi doctrine. Hitler endorses it in *Mein Kampf,* and once in power expanded both eugenic research and, borrowing from U.S. models, a program of sterilization that became the first step toward the murder of handicapped "Aryans" and ultimately millions of victims of the Holocaust.

PHILIP R. REILLY, EUGENICS, ETHICS, STERILIZATION LAWS, IN 1 ENCYCLOPEDIA OF ETHICAL, LEGAL, AND POLICY ISSUES IN BIOTECHNOLOGY

204, 204–208 (Thomas H. Murray & Maxwell J. Mehlman eds. 2000).

ORIGINS AND RISE OF THE EUGENICS MOVEMENT

Although speculations about the perfectibility of humankind date at least as far back as the flowering of philosophy among the ancient Greek city states, the first serious social policy proposal to improve the gene pool of our species that was tied to scientific claims arose in England in the second half of the nineteenth century. Francis Galton, a Victorian polymath who was probably influenced by the revolutionary impact of *The Origin of Species* published in 1859 by his cousin, Charles Darwin, began investigating the inheritance of talent among eminent English families about 1864. He coined the term eugenics (from the Greek, fusing words for good and birth) in 1883 in *Inquiries into Human Faculty and its Development.* Public interest in the notion that success and failure in life might be closely tied to the germ plasm that one inherited grew rapidly, especially in England and the United States, and the new word enjoyed a certain vogue. * * *

In the United States eugenic policies, which flowered in the early twentieth century, germinated in the climate of progressive reform that took root in the last quarter of the nineteenth century. From 1850 to 1880, the states had built many prisons, hospitals, insane asylums, and colonies for the mentally retarded. Initial enthusiasm faded as funding problems arose and conditions declined. Richard Dugdale, a well-to-do Englishman who made New York City home, was an ardent social reformer and one of many who sought to improve such facilities. It was while inspecting prisons in upstate New York that he discovered a large family many of whose members seemed to be inhabiting one state facility or another. His book, *The Jukes,* based on an exhaustive study of the family, detailed the cost to taxpayers of their incarceration and support. He also championed two ideas that would become core beliefs among many Americans within a decade: that feeblemindedness, epilepsy, drunkenness, criminality, and insanity had strong hereditary influences, and that affected individuals tended to produce larger than average numbers of offspring.

Interest in eugenics was widespread in the United States just as biologists rediscovered the laws of inheritance that Gregor Mendel had postulated in 1865, but which had been reported in an obscure local scientific journal and been little noticed. Charles Davenport, a talented young biology professor, played an instrumental role in propagating "mendelism" in the United States. He was quick to apply the theory to problems of human heredity and about 1905 he secured a large gift from Mrs. E.H. Harriman (the wife of the railroad magnate) to develop and sustain a eugenics research facility at Cold Spring Harbor on Long Island, an entity which operated independently of the Station for Experimental Evolution that he had founded there a couple of years earlier. One of his most important decisions was to recruit a midwestern high school teacher named Harry Hamilton Laughlin to direct the Eugenics Record Office. In so doing, Davenport, a highly respected biologist who would become a member of the National Academy of Sciences, tied human genetics to eugenics and provided eugenics with a cloak of scientific legitimacy that it wore for more than three decades.

* * * Between 1910 and 1920 eugenicists working in association with the Eugenics Record Office and sometimes assisted by Laughlin's field-workers published a number of lengthy monographs with colorful names, such as *The Hill Folk: Report of a Rural Community of Hereditary Defectives*. These monographs reinforced the eugenic ideas propounded in *The Jukes* and the equally famous *The Kallikaks* (1912), written by Henry Herbert Goddard, a prominent psychologist who worked at the Vineland Training School in New Jersey and who imported IQ testing from France about 1905.

* * *

During the 1920s Laughlin also spent an immense amount of time drafting and lobbying for the enactment of laws to permit state officials to sterilize institutionalized retarded persons without their consent. He helped propagate the second wave of such laws that swept through America in the 1920s, and he provided an important deposition in the lower court proceedings that led to *Buck v. Bell*, in which the United States Supreme Court ultimately upheld the constitutionality of a law he helped to craft. This opinion removed lingering doubts in many state legislatures and made possible the enactment of about a dozen new laws (discussed below) in the ensuing five years.

* * *

FIRST STERILIZATION LAWS

The nation's first sterilization bill was introduced in the Michigan legislature in 1897, but did not come to floor vote. In 1905 the Pennsylvania House of Representatives became the first legislative body to pass a bill proposing involuntary sterilization of certain institutionalized persons, but the governor vetoed it. On April 9, 1907, Indiana governor J. Frank Hanly, a month after a sizable majority of both houses had voted favorably, signed the nation's first eugenic sterilization law. The statute authorized the compulsory sterilization of "confirmed criminals, idiots, imbeciles and rapists" residing in a state institution if, after appropriate review, a panel of one physician and two surgeons concluded that it was "inadvisable" that the individual procreate and that there was "no probability of improvement." * * *

In 1909 the legislatures in California, Connecticut, Oregon, and Washington passed similar laws. Despite overwhelming support in the legislature, the governor of Oregon vetoed the bill sent to him; the other three governors promptly signed their bills into law. In the ensuing four years (1910–1913), ten states (Iowa, New Jersey, Nevada, New York, North Dakota, Michigan, Kansas, Wisconsin, Vermont, and Nebraska) passed sterilization laws. In general, there was little opposition and most votes were lopsided. Only in the state where the vote was close (96–82 in the House), Vermont, did a governor cast a veto.

* * *

By 1913 involuntary sterilization programs were active in 14 states. There were significant differences in their scope and pace, partly because in a number of the states opponents of eugenics attacked the constitutionality of the enabling laws. In every instance (Indiana, Iowa, Michigan, Nevada, New Jersey, New York, and Washington) in which the constitutionality was put at issue, the courts invalidated the laws, usually on the grounds that they violated the requirements of the Due Process Clause of the Fourteenth Amendment. Laws that targeted prisoners were held to violate the Eighth Amendment prohibiting cruel and unusual punishments. In Oregon the sterilization law, which also was challenged on constitutional grounds, was repealed by public referendum only months after the governor signed it. [The grounds for reversal were, in one state, that the law violated the prohibition against cruel and unusual punishment; and in other states, that these laws violated equal protection because they only applied to institutionalized persons, or that they violated due process by not providing adequate procedural safeguards.—Eds.] * * *

RESURGENCE OF STERILIZATION LAWS

Eugenic Thinking in the 1920s

During the 1920s the eugenics movement, which prior to the World War had begun to decline, grew and prospered. * * * Especially in the midwest, interest in positive eugenics (the search for methods to have genetically superior children) captured the imagination. County fairs sponsored "fitter family" contests in which people, not unlike the prize hogs or cattle they showed, competed for blue ribbons based on their pedigree, physical examinations, and their children's report cards.

At the Eugenics Record Office, Laughlin, stung by the constitutional defeats suffered by the involuntary sterilization laws between 1913 and 1918, produced a massive tome on the societal benefits of eugenic sterilization. He carefully analyzed the laws that the courts had found flawed, and then drafted and circulated a model sterilization law that he hoped would satisfy the constitutional concerns. In the early 1920s his work was widely used by legislators who wanted to sponsor such bills. His polemics on sterilization found their way to Nazi Germany where Laughlin was held in such high regard that he was awarded an honorary degree by the University of Heidelberg in 1934.

Beginning in 1923 there was a major resurgence of sterilization laws. After five years of legislative inactivity, new laws were enacted in Delaware, Michigan, Montana, and Oregon. Virginia adopted a law in 1924, and governors signed seven of the nine bills that were passed in 1925. By January 1926 eugenic sterilization laws were on the books of 17 states and small bands of pro-sterilization lobbyists were urging many others to follow suit. In some states directors of state institutions permitted involuntary eugenical sterilizations to occur despite the absence of enabling laws.

In mid-1925 the Michigan Supreme Court upheld the constitutionality of the new law which it held was "justified by the findings of Biological Science," and was a "proper and reasonable exercise of the police power of the state." This greatly encouraged other legislatures, but many still wondered how such laws would fare before the United States Supreme Court. In a bold move, pro-sterilization forces in Virginia decided to find out. The resulting decision, *Buck v. Bell*, was the single most important event in the history of the sterilization laws in the United States.

BUCK V. BELL
274 U.S. 200 (1927).

MR. JUSTICE HOLMES delivered the opinion of the Court.

This is a writ of error to review a judgment of the Supreme Court of Appeals of the state of Virginia, affirming a judgment of the Circuit Court of Amherst County, by which the defendant in error, the superintendent of the State Colony for Epileptics and Feeble Minded, was ordered to perform the operation of salpingectomy upon Carrie Buck, the plaintiff in error, for the purpose of making her sterile. The case comes here upon the contention that the statute authorizing the judgment is void under the Fourteenth Amendment as

Carrie Buck and her mother.

denying to the plaintiff in error due process of law and the equal protection of the laws.

Carrie Buck is a feeble minded white woman who was committed to the State Colony above mentioned in due form. She is the daughter of a feeble minded mother in the same institution, and the mother of an illegitimate feeble minded child. She was eighteen years old at the time of the trial of her case in the Circuit Court, in the latter part of 1924. An Act of Virginia, approved March 20, 1924, recites that the health of the patient and the welfare of society may be promoted in certain cases by the sterilization of mental defectives, under careful safeguard, etc.; that the sterilization may be effected in males by vasectomy and in females by salpingectomy, without serious pain or substantial danger to life; that the Commonwealth is supporting in various institutions many defective persons who if now discharged would become a menace but if incapable of procreating might be discharged with safety and become self-supporting with benefit to themselves and to society; and that experience has shown that heredity plays an important part in the transmission of insanity, imbecility, etc. The statute then enacts that whenever the superintendent of certain institutions including the above named State Colony shall be of opinion that it is for the best interests of the patients and of society that an inmate under his care should be sexually sterilized, he may have the operation performed upon any patient afflicted with hereditary forms of insanity, imbecility, etc., on complying with the very careful provisions by which the act protects the patients from possible abuse.

The superintendent first presents a petition to the special board of directors of his hospital or colony, stating the facts and the grounds for his opinion, verified by affidavit. Notice of the petition and of the time and place of the hearing in the institution is to be served upon the inmate, and also upon his guardian, and if there is no guardian the superintendent is to apply to the Circuit Court of the County to appoint one. If the inmate is a minor notice also is to be given to his parents if any with a copy of the petition. The board is to see to it that the inmate may attend the hearings if desired by him or his guardian. The evidence is all to be reduced to writing, and after the board has made its order for or against the operation, the superintendent, or the inmate, or his guardian, may appeal to the Circuit Court of the County. The Circuit Court may consider the record of the board and the evidence before it and such other admissible evidence as may be offered, and may affirm, revise, or reverse the order of the board and enter such order as it deems just. Finally any party may apply to the Supreme Court of Appeals, which, if it grants the appeal, is to hear the case upon the record of the trial in the Circuit Court and may enter such order as it thinks the Circuit Court should have entered. There can be no doubt that so far as procedure is concerned the rights of the patient are most carefully considered, and as every step in this case was taken in scrupulous compliance with the statute and after months of observation, there is no doubt that in that respect the plaintiff in error has had due process of law.

The attack is not upon the procedure but upon the substantive law. It seems to be contended that in no circumstances could such an order be justified. It certainly is contended that the order cannot be justified upon the existing grounds. The judgment finds the facts that have been recited and that Carrie Buck "is the probable potential parent of socially inadequate offspring, likewise afflicted, that she may be sexually sterilized without detriment to her general health and that her welfare and that of society will be promoted by her sterilization," and thereupon makes the order. In view of the general declarations of the legislature and the specific findings of the Court, obviously we cannot say as matter of law that the grounds do not exist, and if they exist they justify the result. We have seen more than once that the public welfare may call upon the best citizens for their lives. It would be strange if it could not call upon those who already sap the strength of the State for these lesser sacrifices, often not felt to be such by those concerned, in order to prevent our being swamped with incompetence. It is better for all the world, if instead of waiting to execute degenerate offspring for crime, or to let them starve for their imbecility, society can prevent those who are manifestly unfit from continuing their kind. The principle that sustains compulsory vaccination is broad enough to cover cutting the Fallopian tubes. Jacobson v. Massachusetts, 197 U.S. 11. Three generations of imbeciles are enough.

But, it is said, however it might be if this reasoning were applied generally, it fails when it is confined to the small number who are in the institutions named and is not applied to the multitudes outside. It is the usual last resort of constitutional arguments to point out shortcomings of this sort. But the answer is that the law does all that is needed when it does all that it can, indicates a policy, applies it to all within the lines, and seeks to bring within the lines all similarly situated so far and so fast as its means allow. Of course so far as the operations enable those who otherwise must be kept confined to be returned to the world, and thus open the asylum to others, the equality aimed at will be more nearly reached.

Judgment affirmed.

MR. JUSTICE BUTLER dissents.

PAUL A. LOMBARDO, THREE GENERATIONS, NO IMBECILES: NEW LIGHT ON BUCK V. BELL
60 N.Y.U.L. Rev. 30, 50–62 (1985).

The trial of Buck v. Bell took place November 18, 1924. Strode [counsel for the superintendent of the state institution] presented eight witnesses from the area near Carrie's home in an attempt to prove her "social inadequacy." Additionally, Strode introduced a lengthy deposition from a eugenical expert from New York and had another eugenicist testify at the trial, both of whom informed the court about Carrie's feeblemindedness in light of eugenical theory. He also put two Virginia physicians on the stand to bolster the case in favor of the sterilization law.

In contrast, Whitehead [counsel for Buck] called no witnesses to dispute the specific allegations against Carrie or to cast doubt on the "scientific" theories about which Strode's four "experts" had testified. Moreover, Whitehead's cross-examination of the witnesses for the State was so weak that it was often unclear which side he was representing. * * * A cursory review of the trial transcript readily supports this view; a more thorough analysis of the case Whitehead could have presented suggests a deliberate decision not to defend Carrie.

Among the allegations Whitehead chose not to dispute were several assertions about Carrie's background. For example, famed eugenicist Harry Laughlin never examined Carrie, but drew firm "scientific conclusions" from very sketchy information supplied by Priddy [id.][superintendent of the state institution], compelling one commentator to label Laughlin's analysis as "near-psychic." Laughlin's deposition relied on Priddy's "facts" as proof not only of Carrie's alleged feeblemindedness, but also of her generally undesirable character. She had, said Priddy, a "record during life of immorality, prostitution, and untruthfulness; [had] never been self-sustaining; [and] has had one illegitimate child * * * supposed to be mental defective." Her mother, Emma Buck, "was maritally unworthy; having been divorced from her husband on account of infidelity * * * [and] has had one illegitimate child and probably two others inclusive of Carrie Buck * * *." With regard to the Buck family generally, he concluded, "[t]hese people belong to the shiftless, ignorant, and worthless class of anti-social whites of the South * * * [about whom] it is impossible to get intelligent and satisfactory data * * *."

Most of these comments, left unchallenged by Whitehead, were not only of questionable relevance, but untrue. Had Whitehead chosen to investigate Carrie's background he easily could have collected evidence to refute most of Priddy's charges. For example, on the question of her illegitimacy, he could have found that her parents, Frank and Emma Buck, were married in 1896. The available records indicate that when Carrie was born in 1906, her parents were still married. A common law presumption effective in Virginia at that time would have established Carrie's legitimacy. Was Carrie feebleminded? This was the purported justification for her commitment to the Colony, yet the majority of witnesses called by Strode had no firsthand knowledge of Carrie. Seven of the eleven witnesses either had never met Carrie or refused to offer any conclusion about her mental condition. Several of Carrie's own teachers could have attested, with supporting documentation, that Carrie was not mentally deficient. School records indicate that Carrie was a normal child: In the five years that she attended school, she was promoted to the sixth grade. In fact, the year before she left school, her teacher entered the comment "very good—deportment and lessons" and recommended her for promotion. That teacher and her records would have contradicted the testimony of the single witness who claimed that Carrie was "anti-social" because she had written notes to boys in school.

Was Carrie immoral? Apart from how ridiculous this charge sounds today, broadly defined character traits such as immorality were at issue in the trial. Priddy linked Carrie's supposed predisposition to "anti-social" behavior to the same characteristics he had observed in her mother and the "generally accepted theory of the laws of heredity." Whitehead easily could have questioned the charge of "immorality" by calling witnesses of his own. Carrie had attended church and church school and had been a member of two church choirs in her hometown. Such testimony would have, at the least, posed doubts about the accuracy of the investigation into her character.

The eugenical basis of the Virginia sterilization law required that Carrie's inadequacies be hereditary—that she be the "probable potential parent of socially inadequate offspring." To show this hereditary link, Strode elicited testimony that Carrie's mother, Emma, was a feebleminded patient at the Colony, that Carrie had exhibited "peculiarities" since childhood, that supposed members of Carrie's family were "peculiar," and that Carrie's child was slow. Strode's evidence was weak, yet Whitehead's cross-examination, when it took place at all, failed to attack the evidence.

Why, given the weakness of Strode's evidence, was Carrie chosen as the perfect candidate for sterilization? The answer to this question clarifies the unstated purpose of the sterilization policy: she had delivered a child, but was unmarried. Poor, and born of a disgraced mother herself, Carrie was likely to be the parent of more of the "shiftless, ignorant and worthless class of anti-social whites" from which she came. The single fact of her unwed motherhood was Priddy's proof of her deficiency.

However, strong evidence existed to mitigate Carrie's responsibility for her bastard child. The circumstances of her commitment and the contradictions in the testimony of her foster parents would have alerted any conscientious attorney to probe further. As Carrie's commitment papers show, the foster parents [the Dobbses] with whom she lived for fourteen years were very anxious to have her put away.

* * *

What the trial did not reveal was that, despite all the discussion of her immoral behavior, Carrie was pregnant because she had been raped.

Mrs. Dobbs was away "on account of some illness," in the summer of 1923. During her absence Carrie was raped by Mrs. Dobbs's nephew.

Commitment to the Colony would hide Carrie's shame; more importantly for Mr. and Mrs. Dobbs, it would save the family reputation.

* * *

Whitehead neither called the Dobbses as witnesses nor challenged Priddy by introducing readily available data on Carrie's parents, her church attendance, or her school record—data Priddy (and presumably Whitehead) had considered "impossible to get." Whitehead failed as Carrie's attorney not because he was incompetent, underpaid, or merely ineffectual. He failed because he intended to fail.

Whitehead had long been associated with Strode and Priddy. He helped Strode with his election campaign and helped him obtain an Army commission. As a member of the Colony Board, Whitehead authorized Priddy's sterilization requests. A building named in Whitehead's honor was opened at the Colony just two months before Carrie's arrival. Strode, in turn, recommended Whitehead for a government position only six days before Carrie Buck's trial. Proof that Whitehead intended to lose Carrie Buck's case does not, however, rely primarily on the evidence of these close, personal associations. Whitehead's role and intent are amply documented in the minutes of the Colony Board.

* * *

In 1930 Doctor Bell reported that after her sterilization, Carrie Buck "was immediately returned to society and made good." That evaluation was only partially true. Although she was paroled as a domestic helper to a family in Bland, Virginia, she remained under the control of the Colony. Her discharge, like that of all sterilized Colony women, was conditioned on an annual visit to Doctor Bell for a physical examination. Had there been any complaints of ill behavior, she could have been returned to the Colony at once.

After Carrie left the Colony, she married and became a member of the Methodist Church in Bland where she sang in the choir as she had as a teenager in Charlottesville. After twenty-four years of marriage, her husband died and she traveled to Front Royal, Virginia, where she met and later married Charles Detamore. He took work in farms and orchards and Carrie assisted a local family in caring for an elderly relative.

In 1970, with Carrie suffering from ill health, the couple returned to Carrie's hometown. They moved into a single-room cinder block shed with no plumbing, which the owner allowed them to inhabit rent-free. They lived there ten years in abject poverty, until in 1980 Carrie was hospitalized for exposure and malnutrition. After she recovered partially, she and her husband were taken to a state-operated nursing home outside Waynesboro, Virginia. She died there on January 28, 1983, at the age of seventy-six. Her body was returned to Charlottesville, where she was buried only a few steps from the graves of her daughter, Vivian, and her foster parents, Mr. and Mrs. Dobbs.

Throughout Carrie's adult life she regularly displayed intelligence and kindness that belied the "feeblemindedness" and "immorality" that were used as an excuse to sterilize her. She was an avid reader, and even in her last weeks was able to converse lucidly, recalling events from her childhood. Branded by Holmes as a second generation imbecile, Carrie provided no support for his glib epithet throughout her life.

Carrie's daughter Vivian, like her mother, was wrongly accused. On the basis of a nurse's comment that she was "not quite normal," Vivian Buck was used to prove her mother's hereditary "defects." Although she lived barely eight years, she too disproved Holmes's epigram. In her two years of schooling, she performed quite well, at one point earning a spot on the school "Honor Roll."

Of the three generations, the least is known about Emma Buck. She died at the Colony, leaving few records of her life. She was, at worst, the "moron" that Priddy claimed; no one but Holmes charged her with imbecility. Her true shortcomings probably stemmed from poverty and perhaps promiscuity.

NOTES AND QUESTIONS

1.   The decision in *Buck* was generally considered to be a progressive result. Brandeis, Stone, and Taft joined in Holmes' majority opinion. Only Justice Butler, the Court's only Catholic, dissented (without opinion). (Many Catholics at the time were troubled by eugenics, which some people thought should authorize non-treatment of "defective" newborns.) The outcome in *Buck* was embraced by such progressives of the time as Clarence Darrow, Helen Keller, and Margaret Sanger, who founded Planned Parenthood.

2.   Note the elaborate procedural protections provided for in the statute pursuant to which Carrie Buck was sterilized. Are there any additional protections that might have been provided? Given the scope of the existing protections, how can the outcome in her case be explained? Does this suggest anything about the usefulness of procedural protections to prevent abuses?

3.   Is Justice Holmes correct in analogizing sterilization to "call[ing] upon the best citizens for their lives" to promote "the public welfare"? When is the government permitted to require someone to die for the public welfare? Could the state kill someone to prevent the spread of an infectious disease?

4.   A recurrent theme in this book is the degree to which the government should be permitted to control human reproductive behavior. What does the *Buck* case suggest are the limits on the power of the state to restrict reproduction? Are there any circumstances in which the state would be justified in sterilizing people against their will? Does the answer turn on whether only certain types of individuals, such as those considered "defective,"

are being singled out? In the mid-1970s, one Indian state adopted a policy of sterilizing women after their third child. See Note, India's Compulsory Sterilization Laws: The Human Rights of Family Planning, 8 Cal. W. Int'l L. J. 342 (1978). Is population control a sufficiently important social purpose to justify forced sterilization?

5.   Justice Holmes stated that "[t]he principle that sustains compulsory vaccination is broad enough to cover cutting the Fallopian tubes," and cited Jacobson v. Massachusetts, 197 U.S. 11 (1905). That case upheld a Massachusetts requirement of smallpox vaccinations against a challenge that they infringed personal liberty. In his opinion, Justice Harlan observed:

> According to settled principles the police power of a State must be held to embrace, at least, such reasonable regulations established directly by legislative enactment as will protect the public health and the public safety.

* * *

> [I]n every well-ordered society charged with the duty of conserving the safety of its members the rights of the individual in respect of his liberty may at times, under the pressure of great dangers, be subjected to such restraint, to be enforced by reasonable regulations, as the safety of the general public may demand.

* * *

> [T]he means prescribed by the State to that end [must have a] real and substantial relation to the protection of the public health and safety.

197 U.S. at 25, 29, 31. Does the statute at issue in *Buck* meet these standards?

6.   Beyond compulsory vaccination, "[g]overnment engages in a broad range of restrictions of the person to reduce the spread of infection—civil confinement (isolation, quarantine, and compulsory hospitalization), mandatory treatment, and criminal penalties for knowing or willful exposure to disease." Lawrence O. Gostin, Public Health Law: Power, Duty, Restraint 203 (2000). To what extent does a genetic disease resemble a communicable disease? Is a genetic disease sufficiently "communicable" that the government is entitled to invoke its public health authority to prevent the disease from being "spread"? If so, what public health measures would be appropriate? For example, could the government, under its power to protect the public health, require someone to undergo genetic testing to determine if a fetus was affected with a genetic abnormality or disorder? Would the answer depend on whether or not the condition was treatable?

7.   Following *Buck*, a total of 28 states had enacted compulsory sterilization laws by 1931. In California, the number of reported sterilizations rose from 322 in 1925 to 2,362 over the course of 1928 and 1929. Nationally, approximately 3,000 operations were reported annually prior to the Second World War. More occurred that were not reported. For more complete

information, see Phillip R. Reilly, Eugenics, Ethics, Sterilization Laws, in 1 Encyclopedia of Ethical, Legal, and Policy Issues in Biotechnology 204 (Thomas H. Murray & Maxwell J. Mehlman eds. 2000).

8.   Eugenics theories also were seized upon by the descendants of early, Northern European immigrants to preserve their political power in the face of later waves of immigration. As Celeste Condit writes in her book, The Meanings of the Gene (1999), at 35:

> The turn of the century was an anxious era for the relatively well-to-do Americans whose ancestors had come from Europe and who had dominated the continent for 200 years. Massive migration from rural areas to cities was occurring. From 1800 to 1920 the population in the United States shifted from overwhelmingly rural (75 percent) to majority urban (51 percent). This migration was creating and amplifying what we now know to be the standard problems of urban poverty in industrializing areas. However, the scope and scale of these problems were probably both new and shocking to the members of the society. While absolute numbers of those involved in crime and poverty might not have increased, the proximity to crime, poverty, prostitution, and other social ills that accompanies life in a city environment was nonetheless capable of creating distress. The shock was exacerbated by the immigration of a variety of different ethnic groups with a vast array of languages, cultural values, and cultural practices different from those preferred by the people derived from Northern European ancestry and culture. As Diane Paul has noted, a third of the population in 1920 consisted of immigrants and their children, and the proportions were higher in cities. The descendants of the Northern Europeans who had gained dominance by displacing the native population 200 years earlier were now faced with losing that dominance in turn.

9.   World War II marked a watershed in the eugenics movement because of the association between eugenics and the Nazis. As described by Buchanan et al.:

> Eugenics was central to the entire Nazi enterprise, joined with romantic nativist and racist myths of the purebred Nordic. The emphasis on "blood" called for a purifying of the nation's gene pool so that Germans could regain the nobility and greatness of their genetically pure forebears.
>
> As Robert Proctor and other historians have shown, the subsequent programs of sterilization, euthanasia of the unfit (a program that took the lives of tens of thousands of "Aryans," mostly young children), and eventually the Holocaust itself were part of the unfolding of this central idea. The sterilization and "euthanasia" programs, which did not initially target Jews and other minorities, were an exercise in negative eugenics designed to improve the native German stock from its degenerated condition. Legislation barring

sexual relations between Jews and "Aryans," and ultimately the Holocaust were intended to prevent further adulteration of the "pure" German nation with inferior genes. Jews and others who contributed "evil" genes were the disease afflicting the German nation, which Hitler, the physician, would cure.

Allen Buchanan et al., From Chance to Choice: Genetics and Justice 37 (2000).

The Nazi sterilization program, although much larger in scope, employed many of the same legal mechanisms as the Americans:

A comprehensive German eugenic sterilization law was enacted on July 14, 1933. Pursuant to it, the nation set up a network of Hereditary Health Courts empowered to sterilize persons about whom, in "the experience of medical science, it may be expected with great probability that their offspring may suffer severe physical damage." At first persons with any one of nine conditions were targeted: inborn feeblemindedness, schizophrenia, manicdepressive [sic] insanity, hereditary epilepsy, Huntington's chorea, hereditary blindness, hereditary deafness, severe hereditary physical deformity, and severe habitual drunkenness. Each special court had three members: a district judge, a local public health official, and a physician deemed to be expert in making the evaluations of the individuals thought to be at risk.

The scale of the eugenic sterilization program in Nazi Germany dwarfed those in all other nations, including the United States. In 1934 more than 200 courts received 84,500 petitions to sterilize. These were sometimes filed by doctors or local public health officials, but often they were filed by one family member about another. In one of the more extreme examples of patriotism, substantial numbers of deaf persons volunteered to be sterilized as a show of support for the "fatherland." Of the 64,499 petitions that were heard, the courts decided for sterilization in 56,244 for a eugenic conviction rate of 87 percent. By 1935 more than 150,000 sterilizations had been approved, many based on judicial proceedings that must have taken under an hour.

Over the ensuing years the scope of the law was broadened. For example, in 1934 it was amended to apply to non-Germans living in Germany. During the 1940s people were often sterilized on the weakest of pretenses, such as being half-Jewish. In 1951, the Central Association of Sterilized People in West Germany estimated that the Nazi programs had sterilized 3,500,000 persons, although it is not possible to document the claim.

Philip R. Reilly, Eugenics, Ethics, Sterilization Laws, in 1 Encyclopedia of Ethical, Legal, and Policy Issues in Biotechnology 210 (Thomas H. Murray & Maxwell J. Mehlman eds. 2000).

10. The American eugenics movement was a major influence on the Nazis. Hitler was in jail and working on *Mein Kampf* in 1924 when he read about the Virginia sterilization statute, and a sterilization provision was the first law the Reichstag enacted after he gained power. Hitler's intent originally was to use sterilization to eliminate inferior populations, but once the war started and he needed hospital beds for wounded soldiers, he decided to empty the mental wards by killing the patients. This policy then grew to encompass the extermination of other undesirables, including Jews and Gypsies.

11. The German sterilization law was based on a "prototypical Model Sterilization Law" drafted by Harry Laughlin, the director of the Eugenics Record Office at Cold Spring Harbor, Long Island. As noted in the Reilly excerpt, Laughlin was held in such high regard by the Nazis that he received an honorary degree from the University of Heidelberg in 1934.

12. Although eugenics-based sterilization in the United States declined markedly after World War II, it did not disappear altogether. As Reilly reports, between 1948 and 1955, approximately 186 women were sterilized in North Carolina. In 1958, Georgia, North Carolina and Virginia reported 574 sterilizations, 76 percent of the national total. At one South Carolina facility for the incurably mentally ill, 104 inmates, 102 of whom were black, were sterilized between 1949 and 1960. From 1970 to 1974, 23 sterilizations were performed in North Carolina state institutions, although most often at the request of relatives concerned that an inmate would become pregnant against her will.

13. For more historical information about the eugenics movement in America, see Paul A. Lombardo, Three Generations, No Imbeciles: Eugenics, the Supreme Court, and Buck v. Bell (2008); Paul A. Lombardo, 'The American Breed': Nazi Eugenics and the Origins of the Pioneer Fund, 65 Albany L. Rev. 743–830 (2002), Paul A. Lombardo, Taking Eugenics Seriously: Three Generations of ??? are Enough?, 30 Fla. St. U. L. Rev. 191–218 (Winter 2003), and Michael J. Malinowski, Choosing the Genetic Makeup of Children: Our Eugenics Past-Present, and Future?. 36 Conn. L. Rev. 125–224 (2003).

14. In 1977, a federal court invalidated regulations issued by the Department of Health Education and Welfare [now Health and Human Services] that authorized the sterilization of adults, minors, and mental incompetents by federally-funded family planning programs on the ground that the sterilizations were not voluntary. Relf v. Weinberger, 372 F.Supp. 1196 (D.D.C. 1974), vacated as moot, 565 F.2d 722 (D.C. Cir. 1977). Judge Gerhard Gesell noted that "minors and other incompetents have been sterilized with federal funds and that an indefinite number of poor people have been improperly coerced into accepting a sterilization operation under the threat that various federally supported welfare benefits would be withdrawn unless they submitted to irreversible sterilization. Patients receiving Medicaid assistance at childbirth are evidently the most frequent targets of this pressure, as the experiences of plaintiffs Waters and Walker illustrate. Mrs. Waters was actually refused medical assistance by her attending physician

unless she submitted to a tubal ligation after the birth. Other examples were documented." The court ruled that the sterilizations were not authorized by applicable federal laws. The court's opinion observed that "since these conclusions are based on statutory rather than constitutional grounds, the Court need not reach the question of whether involuntary sterilization could be funded by Congress." The case ultimately was vacated after the Department of Health and Human Services adopted regulations conforming to the district court's order. Relf v. Weinberger, 565 F.2d 722 (D.C. Cir.1977).

15. The minors sterilized with federal funds that Judge Gesell referred to in *Relf* included Mary Alice and Minnie Lee Relf, black children aged 12 and 14 respectively, who were sterilized without their knowledge or consent by authorities in Montgomery, Alabama. An older sister, Katie, 17, avoided surgery only by physically resisting. The children's mother, who was unable to read, had placed an "X" on the consent document without knowing what it said. She assumed, she explained later, that she was merely authorizing continued use of Depo-Provera injections, which the girls had been receiving as an experimental contraceptive. For more details on the Relfs and similar cases, see Donna Franklin, Beyond the Tuskegee Apology, Washington Post, May 29, 1997, at A23. How do the protections mandated by the court in *Relf* prevent this from happening again?

As the administration of Depo-Provera to the Relf children suggests, compulsory contraception is a eugenic alternative to compulsory sterilization. After the FDA approved Norplant, a surgically-implanted, long-lasting contraceptive, legislators in a number of states proposed linking Norplant use to eligibility for welfare benefits. Although no such requirement has been adopted, Norplant has been covered under all state Medicaid programs.

16. The United States and Germany are not the only countries to have engaged in eugenics-based sterilizations. Between 1935 and 1976, approximately 60,000 people, mostly women, were sterilized in Sweden. They were typically poor, had learning disabilities, or were non-Nordic, and were labeled as genetically or racially "inferior." One of the major justifications for this sterilization program was that it would reduce the cost of the Swedish welfare state by reducing the number of people who would have to be supported. One woman is reported to have been sterilized because she could not master her confirmation studies well enough to satisfy her priest. Another was judged to be mentally slow as a child because she could not read the blackboard; it later turned out that she merely needed glasses. For a fuller account of the Swedish program, see Dan Balz, Sweden Sterilized Thousands of "Useless" Citizens for Decades, Washington Post, Aug. 29, 1997, at A1. In 1999, the Swedish government agreed to pay $20,780 to each surviving person who had been sterilized.

17. In 1994, the Chinese national legislature passed a law entitled "Law of the People's Republic of China on Maternal and Infant Health Care." The statute requires every couple to undergo a premarital medical examination, and where this shows "genetic disease of a serious nature which is considered

to be inappropriate for child bearing from a medical point of view, the two may be married only if both sides agree to take long term contraceptive precautions or to take ligation operation for sterility." Moreover, termination of pregnancy must be advised when a fetus has a "defect of a serious nature" or a "genetic disease of a serious nature." "Relevant mental diseases" include schizophrenia and manic depressive psychosis. The Chinese legislation is described in an editorial by Martin Bobrow, head of the genetics department at Cambridge University, Redrafted Chinese Law Remains Eugenic, 32 J. Med. Genetics 409 (1995).

A related use of compulsory sterilization is to punish the commission of a crime. The Supreme Court had occasion to consider the constitutionality of such an approach in the following case.

SKINNER V. OKLAHOMA

316 U.S. 535 (1942).

MR. JUSTICE DOUGLAS delivered the opinion of the Court.

This case touches a sensitive and important area of human rights. Oklahoma deprives certain individuals of a right which is basic to the perpetuation of a race—the right to have offspring. Oklahoma has decreed the enforcement of its law against petitioner, overruling his claim that it violated the Fourteenth Amendment. Because that decision raised grave and substantial constitutional questions, we granted the petition for certiorari.

The statute involved is Oklahoma's Habitual Criminal Sterilization Act. Okla. Stat. Ann. Tit. 57, §§ 171, et seq.; L. 1935, pp. 94 et seq. That Act defines an "habitual criminal" as a person who, having been convicted two or more times for crimes "amounting to felonies involving moral turpitude," either in an Oklahoma court or in a court of any other State, is thereafter convicted of such a felony in Oklahoma and is sentenced to a term of imprisonment in an Oklahoma penal institution. Machinery is provided for the institution by the Attorney General of a proceeding against such a person in the Oklahoma courts for a judgment that such person shall be rendered sexually sterile. §§ 176, 177. Notice, an opportunity to be heard, and the right to a jury trial are provided. §§ 177–181. The issues triable in such a proceeding are narrow and confined. If the court or jury finds that the defendant is an "habitual criminal" and that he "may be rendered sexually sterile without detriment to his or her general health," then the court "shall render judgment to the effect that said defendant be rendered sexually sterile" (§ 182) by the operation of vasectomy in case of a male, and of salpingectomy in case of a female. § 174. Only one other provision of the Act is material here, and that is § 195, which provides that "offenses arising out of the violation of the prohibitory laws, revenue acts, embezzlement, or political offenses, shall not come or be considered within the terms of this Act."

Petitioner was convicted in 1926 of the crime of stealing chickens, and was sentenced to the Oklahoma State Reformatory. In 1929 he was convicted of the crime of robbery with firearms, and was sentenced to the reformatory. In 1934 he was convicted again of robbery with firearms, and was sentenced to the penitentiary. He was confined there in 1935 when the Act was passed. In 1936 the Attorney General instituted proceedings against him. Petitioner in his answer challenged the Act as unconstitutional by reason of the Fourteenth Amendment. A jury trial was had. The court instructed the jury that the crimes of which petitioner had been convicted were felonies involving moral turpitude, and that the only question for the jury was whether the operation of vasectomy could be performed on petitioner without detriment to his general health. The jury found that it could be. A judgment directing that the operation of vasectomy be performed on petitioner was affirmed by the Supreme Court of Oklahoma by a five to four decision.

Several objections to the constitutionality of the Act have been pressed upon us. It is urged that the Act cannot be sustained as an exercise of the police power, in view of the state of scientific authorities respecting inheritability of criminal traits. It is argued that due process is lacking because, under this Act, unlike the Act upheld in Buck v. Bell, 274 U.S. 200, the defendant is given no opportunity to be heard on the issue as to whether he is the probable potential parent of socially undesirable offspring. It is also suggested that the Act is penal in character and that the sterilization provided for is cruel and unusual punishment and violative of the Fourteenth Amendment. We pass those points without intimating an opinion on them, for there is a feature of the Act which clearly condemns it. That is, its failure to meet the requirements of the equal protection clause of the Fourteenth Amendment. We do not stop to point out all of the inequalities in this Act. A few examples will suffice. In Oklahoma, grand larceny is a felony. Okla. Stats. Ann. Tit. 21, §§ 1705, 5. Larceny is grand larceny when the property taken exceeds $20 in value. Id. § 1704. Embezzlement is punishable "in the manner prescribed for feloniously stealing property of the value of that embezzled." Id. § 1462. Hence, he who embezzles property worth more than $20 is guilty of a felony. A clerk who appropriates over $20 from his employer's till (id. § 1456) and a stranger who steals the same amount are thus both guilty of felonies. If the latter repeats his act and is convicted three times, he may be sterilized. But the clerk is not subject to the pains and penalties of the Act no matter how large his embezzlements nor how frequent his convictions. A person who enters a chicken coop and steals chickens commits a felony (id. § 1719); and he may be sterilized if he is thrice convicted. If, however, he is a bailee of the property and fraudulently appropriates it, he is an embezzler. Id.§ 1455. Hence, no matter how habitual his proclivities for embezzlement are and no matter how often his conviction, he may not be sterilized. Thus, the nature of the two crimes is intrinsically the same and they are punishable in the same manner. Furthermore, the line between them follows close distinctions— distinctions comparable to those highly technical ones which shaped the common law as to "trespass" or "taking." There may be larceny by fraud rather than embezzlement even where the owner of the personal property delivers it to the defendant, if the latter has at that time "a fraudulent intention to make use of the possession as a means of converting such property to his own use, and does so convert it." If the fraudulent intent occurs later and the defendant converts the property, he is guilty of embezzlement. Whether a particular act is larceny by fraud or embezzlement thus turns not on the intrinsic quality of the act but on when the felonious intent arose—a question for the jury under appropriate instructions.

It was stated in Buck v. Bell, that the claim that state legislation violates the equal protection clause of the Fourteenth Amendment is "the usual last resort of constitutional arguments." Under our constitutional system the States in determining the reach and scope of particular legislation need not provide "abstract symmetry." They may mark and set apart the classes and types of problems according to the needs and as dictated or suggested by experience. It was in that connection that Mr. Justice Holmes, speaking for the Court in Bain Peanut Co. v. Pinson, 282 U.S. 499, 501, stated, "We must remember that the machinery of government would not work if it were not allowed a little play in its joints." Only recently we reaffirmed the view that the equal protection clause does not prevent the legislature from recognizing "degrees of evil" by our ruling in Tigner v. Texas, 310 U.S. 141, 147, that "the Constitution does not require things which are different in fact or opinion to be treated in law as though they were the same." Thus, if we had here only a question as to a State's classification of crimes, such as embezzlement or larceny, no substantial federal question would be raised. For a State is not constrained in the exercise of its police power to ignore experience which marks a class of offenders or a family of offenses for special treatment. Nor is it prevented by the equal protection clause from confining "its restrictions to those classes of cases where the need is deemed to be clearest." As stated in Buck v. Bell, " . . . the law does all that is needed when it does all that it can, indicates a policy, applies it to all within the lines, and seeks to bring within the lines all similarly situated so far and so fast as its means allow."

But the instant legislation runs afoul of the equal protection clause, though we give Oklahoma that large deference which the rule of the foregoing cases requires. We are dealing here with legislation which involves one of the basic civil rights of man. Marriage and procreation are fundamental to the very existence and survival of the race. The power to sterilize, if exercised, may have subtle, far-reaching and devastating effects. In evil or reckless hands it can cause races or types which are inimical to the dominant group to wither and disappear. There is no redemption for the individual whom the law touches. Any experiment which the State conducts is to his irreparable injury. He is forever deprived of a basic liberty. We mention these matters not to reexamine the scope of the police power of the States. We advert to them merely in emphasis of our view that strict scrutiny of the classification which a State makes in a sterilization law is essential, lest unwittingly, or otherwise, invidious discriminations are made against groups or types of individuals in violation of the constitutional guaranty of just and equal laws. The guaranty of "equal protection of the laws is a pledge of the protection of equal laws." When the law lays an unequal hand on those who have committed intrinsically the same quality of offense and sterilizes one and not the other, it has made as invidious a discrimination as if it had selected a particular race or nationality for oppressive treatment. Sterilization of those who have thrice committed grand larceny, with immunity for those who are embezzlers, is a clear, pointed, unmistakable discrimination. Oklahoma makes no attempt to say that he who commits larceny by trespass or trick or fraud has biologically inheritable traits which he who commits embezzlement lacks. Oklahoma's line between larceny by fraud and embezzlement is determined, as we have noted, "with reference to the time when the fraudulent intent to convert the property to the taker's own use" arises. We have not the slightest basis for inferring that that line has any significance in eugenics, nor that the inheritability of criminal traits follows the neat legal distinctions which the law has marked between those two offenses. In terms of fines and imprisonment, the crimes of larceny and embezzlement rate the same under the Oklahoma code. Only when it comes to sterilization are the pains and penalties of the law different. The equal protection clause would indeed be a formula of empty words if such conspicuously artificial lines could be drawn. In Buck v. Bell, the Virginia statute was upheld though it applied only to feeble-minded persons in institutions of the State. But it was pointed out that "so far as the operations enable those who otherwise must be kept confined to be returned to the world, and thus open the asylum to others, the equality aimed at will be more nearly reached." Here there is no such saving feature. Embezzlers are forever free. Those who steal or take in other ways are not. If such a classification were permitted, the technical common law concept of a "trespass" based on distinctions which are "very largely dependent upon history for explanation" could readily become a rule of human genetics.

* * *

Reversed.

MR. CHIEF JUSTICE STONE, concurring:

I concur in the result, but I am not persuaded that we are aided in reaching it by recourse to the equal protection clause. If Oklahoma may resort generally to the sterilization of criminals on the assumption that their propensities are transmissible to future generations by inheritance, I seriously doubt that the equal protection clause requires it to apply the measure to all criminals in the first instance, or to none.

Moreover, if we must presume that the legislature knows—what science has been unable to ascertain—that the criminal tendencies of any class of habitual offenders are transmissible regardless of the varying mental characteristics of its individuals, I should suppose that we must likewise presume that the legislature, in its wisdom, knows that the criminal tendencies of some classes of offenders are more likely to be transmitted than those of others. And so I think the real question we have to consider is not one of equal protection, but whether the wholesale condemnation of a class to such an invasion of personal liberty, without opportunity to any individual to show that his is not the type of case which would justify resort to it, satisfies the demands of due process.

There are limits to the extent to which the presumption of constitutionality can be pressed, especially where the liberty of the person is concerned and there the presumption is resorted to only to dispense with a procedure which the ordinary dictates of prudence would seem to demand for the protection of the individual from arbitrary action. Although petitioner here was given a hearing to ascertain whether sterilization would be detrimental to his health, he was given none to discover whether his criminal tendencies are of an inheritable type. Undoubtedly a state may, after appropriate inquiry, constitutionally interfere with the personal liberty of the individual to prevent the transmission by inheritance of his socially injurious tendencies. Buck v. Bell, 274 U.S. 200. But until now we have not been called upon to say that it may do so without giving him a hearing and opportunity to challenge the existence as to him of the only facts which could justify so drastic a measure.

Science has found and the law has recognized that there are certain types of mental deficiency associated with delinquency which are inheritable. But the State does not contend—nor can there be any pretense—that either common knowledge or experience, or scientific investigation, has given assurance that the criminal tendencies of any class of habitual offenders are universally or even generally inheritable. In such circumstances, inquiry whether such is the fact in the case of any particular individual cannot rightly be dispensed with. Whether the procedure by which a statute carries its mandate into execution satisfies due process is a matter of judicial cognizance. A law which condemns, without hearing, all the individuals of a class to so harsh a measure as the present because some or even many merit condemnation, is lacking in the first principles of due process. And so, while the state may protect itself from the demonstrably inheritable tendencies of the individual which are injurious to society, the most elementary notions of due process would seem to require it to take appropriate steps to safeguard the liberty of the individual by affording him, before he is condemned to an irreparable injury in his person, some opportunity to show that he is without such inheritable tendencies. The state is called on to sacrifice no permissible end when it is required to reach its objective by a reasonable and just procedure adequate to safeguard rights of the individual which concededly the Constitution protects.

MR. JUSTICE JACKSON concurring:

I join the CHIEF JUSTICE in holding that the hearings provided are too limited in the context of the present Act to afford due process of law. I also agree with the opinion of MR. JUSTICE DOUGLAS that the scheme of classification set forth in the Act denies equal protection of the law. I disagree with the opinion of each in so far as it rejects or minimizes the grounds taken by the other.

Perhaps to employ a broad and loose scheme of classification would be permissible if accompanied by the individual hearings indicated by the CHIEF JUSTICE. On the other hand, narrow classification with reference to the end to be accomplished by the Act might justify limiting individual hearings to the issue whether the individual belonged to a class so defined. Since this Act does not present these questions, I reserve judgment on them.

I also think the present plan to sterilize the individual in pursuit of a eugenic plan to eliminate from the race characteristics that are only vaguely identified and which in our present state of knowledge are uncertain as to transmissibility presents other constitutional questions of gravity. This Court has sustained such an experiment with respect to an imbecile, a person with definite and observable characteristics, where the condition had persisted through three generations and afforded grounds for the belief that it was transmissible and would continue to manifest itself in generations to come. Buck v. Bell, 274 U.S. 200.

There are limits to the extent to which a legislatively represented majority may conduct biological experiments at the expense of the dignity and personality and natural powers of a minority—even those who have been guilty of what the majority define as crimes. But this Act falls down before reaching this problem, which I mention only to avoid the implication that such a question may not exist because not discussed. On it I would also reserve judgment.

NOTES AND QUESTIONS

1.   Under *Skinner,* what sorts of sterilization laws, if any, would survive constitutional challenge? What other governmental interventions involving genetics and the regulation of human reproduction would the decision in *Skinner* support? What interventions would be prohibited?

2.   Compare *Skinner* with Buck v. Bell. Does *Skinner* overrule *Buck*? What language in *Skinner* supports the answer?

3.   Was the Oklahoma statute at issue in *Skinner* drafted to use sterilization as a punishment and deterrent for crimes or a eugenic strategy for reducing crimes in future generations?

4.   Which constitutional theory, equal protection or due process, do you think provides the most appropriate basis for striking down the statute?

5.   Why were thieves but not embezzlers were covered by the statute?

6.   Although *Skinner* is often cited as a great anti-eugenics decision, note how the Douglas and Stone opinions incorporate eugenic language and rationale.

7.   Justice Jackson's concurrence, in which he questioned the legitimacy of "biological experiments," is ironic. After World War II, Justice Jackson was appointed chief prosecutor for the Nuremberg trials.

8.   In contrast to *Skinner,* where state law authorized sterilization as a punishment for committing a crime, sterilization and other restrictions on reproduction may also be employed to deter the commission of future crimes. For example, in 1996 California enacted a law authorizing voluntary chemical or surgical castration for the first offense of child molesting and mandating castration as a condition of parole for repeat offenders. Cal. Penal Code § 645. Georgia, Florida, and Montana have adopted similar statutes. Chemical castration involves the use of Depo-Provera, a synthetic progesterone that decreases testosterone, causing a reduction in sex drive and an improved ability to control sexual fantasizing. For more on chemical castration, see Avital Stadler, Comment, California Injects New Life Into an Old Idea: Taking a Shot at Recidivism, Chemical Castration, and the Constitution, 46 Emory L. J. 1285 (1997). One judge conditioned parole for a convicted child abuser on surgical implantation of the contraceptive Norplant. The defendant challenged the requirement, but the case was dismissed as moot after other parole violations occurred.

9.   Are there other current examples of eugenics programs in the United States? What about government maternal and prenatal health care programs? What about the use of the courts to collect wrongful birth damages from health care professionals whose negligent failure to provide appropriate genetic counseling or testing results in the birth of a child with genetic diseases or abnormalities?

TAYLOR V. KURAPATI

600 N.W.2d 670 (Mich. App. 1999).

WHITBECK, J.

Plaintiffs Brandy and Brian Taylor, individually, and Brandy Taylor as next friend and mother of Shelby Taylor, a minor, appeal as of right the trial court's order granting summary disposition in favor of defendants Surender Kurapati, M.D., and Annapolis Hospital with respect to their wrongful birth and negligent infliction of emotional distress claims.

* * *

The Taylors filed their complaint in August 1996. The Taylors alleged that Brandy Taylor had a doctor-patient relationship with Kurapati, a specialist in radiology, and Annapolis. On April 19, 1994, Brandy Taylor gave birth to the couple's daughter, Shelby Taylor. Throughout her pregnancy, Brandy Taylor had been treated by Dr. Leela Suruli. Suruli had ordered that a routine ultrasound be performed in Brandy Taylor's second trimester. The ultrasound was conducted on December 4, 1993, and interpreted by Kurapati, an agent of Annapolis. Kurapati concluded that the pregnancy was seventeen weeks along, plus or minus two weeks, and that there were no visible abnormalities with the fetus. A second ultrasound was conducted on March 16, 1994, and interpreted by another physician, Dr. M.B. Cash. Cash indicated that the baby's femurs could not be adequately identified and believed that a high resolution ultrasound could be helpful for further investigation. Suruli told Brandy Taylor that the baby had short femur bones and would merely be shorter than average. Brandy Taylor decided not to have another ultrasound. Shelby Taylor was born on April 19, 1994, with "gross anatomical deformities including missing right shoulder, fusion of left elbow, missing digits on left hand, missing femur on left leg and short femur on right." A study at the University of Michigan Hospital suggested that Shelby Taylor had femur-fibula-ulna syndrome.

In their complaint, the Taylors alleged that the standard of care in performing the initial ultrasound had been breached by Kurapati when he failed to locate all four limbs at the time of the ultrasound. The Taylors alleged that the ultrasound should have shown Shelby Taylor's disabilities and that the failure to reveal the disabilities deprived the Taylors of their right to make a reproductive decision regarding the pregnancy. In addition to their claim of medical malpractice, the Taylors also alleged that, because of defendants' negligence, they suffered emotional distress at witnessing the birth of their child.

* * *

This review of the elements of tort liability points up the extraordinary nature of the trial court's holding that the plaintiffs were entitled to no recovery as a matter of law. We have here a negligent, wrongful act by the defendant, which act directly and proximately caused injury to the plaintiffs. What we must decide is whether there is justification here for a departure from generally applicable, well-established principles of law:

* * *

At its intellectual core, the wrongful birth tort this Court created in Eisbrenner relies on the benefits rule this Court adopted in Troppi. To say the very least, continued reliance on this rule has some far-reaching, and profoundly disturbing, consequences. This rule invites the jury in wrongful birth cases to weigh the costs to the parents of a disabled child of bearing and raising that child against the benefits to the parents of the life of that child. This rule thus asks the jury to quantify the unquantifiable with respect to the benefits side of the equation. Further, to posit a specific question: how does a jury measure the benefits to the parents of the whole life of the disabled child, when the potential of that child is unknown at the time of suit? How, for example, would a hypothetical Grecian jury, operating under Michigan jurisprudence, measure the benefits to the parents of the whole life of Homer, the blind singer of songs who created the Iliad and the Odyssey? Absent the ability to foretell the future and to quantify the value of the spoken and then the written word, how, exactly, would the jury do that?

Further, the use of the benefits rule in wrongful birth cases can slide ever so quickly into applied eugenics. The very phrase "wrongful birth" suggests that the birth of the disabled child was wrong and should have been prevented. If one accepts the premise that the birth of one "defective" child should have been prevented, then it is but a short step to accepting the premise that the births of classes of "defective" children should be similarly prevented, not just for the benefit of the parents but also for the benefit of society as a whole through the protection of the "public welfare." This is the operating principle of eugenics. James E. Bowman provides a dark, single sentence description of eugenics: "Eugenics espouses the reproduction of the 'fit' over the 'unfit' (positive eugenics) and discourages the birth of the 'unfit' (negative eugenics)." Paul A. Lombardo more broadly, and more charitably, defines eugenics as the idea that the human race can be gradually improved and social ills simultaneously eliminated through a program of selective procreation and describes its most enthusiastic American advocates:

> Francis Galton, Karl Pearson, and others who called themselves eugenicists believed in improving the human condition through the use of science. They understood their field as the marriage of the biological sciences, including medical genetics, with the then new discipline of biostatistics. The most passionate of American eugenicists, such as Charles Davenport

and Harry Laughlin, wished to develop a taxonomy of human traits and to categorize individuals as "healthy" or "unhealthy," and "normal" or "abnormal," within their classification scheme. Working under the presumption that most, if not all, human traits are transmitted genetically, the eugenicists encouraged educated, resourceful, and self-sufficient citizens to mate and produce "wellborn" eugenic children. In contrast, the dysgenic were discouraged from reproducing. Harry Laughlin called dysgenic groups "socially inadequate" and defined them to include: the feebleminded, the insane, the criminalistic, the epileptic, the inebriated or the drug addicted, the diseased—regardless of etiology, the blind, the deaf, the deformed, and dependents (an extraordinarily expansive term that embraced orphans, "ne'er-do-wells," tramps, the homeless and paupers.)

To our eyes, this concept appears simultaneously cruel and laughable, but we should remember that the concept, and the values, of eugenics had a profound effect on American society. We should also recall that the courts were not above the use of this type of rhetoric. One of the most respected jurists in American history, Justice Oliver Wendell Holmes, wrote the decision in Buck v. Bell.

* * *

Finally, we should not forget the influence that the Third Reich's experiments with sterilization had on the American eugenics movement. As Lombardo notes, Dr. Joseph DeJarnette, who testified as an expert witness in the Buck trial, made the following comments about those experiments:

> No person unable to support himself on account of his inherited mental condition has a right to be born. . . . In Germany the sterilization law embraces chronic alcoholics, certain hereditary physical diseases, the hereditarily blind and deaf, the criminally insane, feebleminded and epileptic. By December 31, 1934 Germany had sterilized 56,224 [persons].

Lombardo notes that Dr. DeJarnette continued to express his admiration for Hitler's campaign in the good doctor's last official comment regarding sterilization in 1938:

> Germany in six years has sterilized about 80,000 of her unfit while the United States with approximately twice the population has sterilized about 27,869 to January 1, 1938, in the past 20 years. The death rates in Virginia from sterilization is [sic] negligible— not over one in a thousand. . . . The fact that there are 12,000,000 defectives in the United States should arouse our best endeavors to push this procedure to the maximum.

To our ears, at the close of the twentieth century, this talk of the "unfit" and of "defectives" has a decidedly jarring ring; we are, after all, above such lethal nonsense. But are we? We know now that we all have at least five recessive genes but, according to Bowman, when scientists map the human genome, they will unveil many more potentially harmful genes in each of us. Bowman states that "psychoses, hypertension, diabetes, early-and late-appearing cancers, degenerative disorders, susceptibility genes for communicable diseases, genes for various mental deficiencies, aging genes, and other variations and disorders will be ascertained." Will we then see the tort of wrongful birth extended to physicians who neglect or misinterpret genetic evidence and thereby fail to extend the option of a eugenic abortion to the unsuspecting parents of a genetically "unfit" and "defective" child? Our current acceptance of the wrongful birth tort would require the answer to this question in Michigan to be: yes. We further note that it is but another short half step from the concept of preventing the birth of an "unfit" or "defective" child to proposing, for the benefit of the child's overburdened parents and of the society as a whole, that the existence of the child should not be allowed to continue. Again, this sounds preposterous, but is it? As described by Bowman:

> Daniel Callahan, the former President and Founder of the Hastings Center, the preeminent center for bioethics in the United States, has proposed age-based rationing of health care for elderly persons to alleviate escalating health care costs. Pain relief would be in order, but not life-saving measures, including nutrition. In short, aged individuals past their late seventies or early eighties should go quietly into the night in order that the generation to follow would have access to health care—in their early years.

If the elderly have a duty to die—indeed, to be starved to death—then why not the disabled child? After all, if that child never should have been born, then that child has no real right to go on living, thereby imposing the costs of the child's continued existence on the parents and society. This, we conclude, is the logical end of the slippery slope inherent in the application of the benefits rule through the wrongful birth tort.

CONCLUSION

We conclude that this intermediate appellate court should not continue to recognize the wrongful birth tort without the slightest hint of approval from the Michigan Supreme Court or our Legislature.

NOTES

1. See the discussion of wrongful birth actions in Chapter 8.

2. The *Buck* case dealt primarily with what is called "negative eugenics"—the use of state power to prevent the birth of "undesirable"

offspring. Another form of eugenics is "positive eugenics," which encourages the birth of children with "desirable" traits.

The father of modern eugenics, Francis Galton, influenced by the views of Malthus, was appalled by his observation that "inferior" people were reproducing at great rates while the best and the brightest had small families. Positive eugenics captured the popular imagination during the 1920s, when state fairs hosted "Fitter Families Exhibits" and "Perfect Baby Competitions"; livestock was judged in one barn, human lineage in another. Students on field trips who obtained a good eugenics evaluation might win a "Goodly Heritage" medal. The American Eugenics Society also sponsored awards for church sermons extolling marriages of "the best" with "the best."

An extreme example of positive eugenics was the Nazi's "Lebensborn" program, where public health officials selected Aryan women to breed with SS soldiers and raised the resulting children in special foster families. At the same time, in a program promoted by the Army Air Corps in the United States, the Pioneer Fund, created by a group of wealthy conservatives, offered military pilots and crews who had three children $4,000 (about $45,000 today) to help educate a fourth. (For a description of what happened to the twelve children who were born under the program, see Douglas A. Blackmon, A Breed Apart: A Long-Ago Effort to Better the Species Yields Ordinary Folks, The Wall Street Journal, Aug. 17, 1999, at A1.)

Are there any examples of positive eugenics programs in the United States today? Consider the following:

ASSOCIATED PRESS, OWNER OF "GENIUS" SPERM BANK PLEASED BY RESULTS

The New York Times, Dec. 11, 1984, at A17.

Robert Graham still gets some negative reaction to his sperm bank, but his list of genius donors is slowly growing and 15 children have been born to women chosen as recipients.

Mr. Graham vigorously denied that he was trying to create a super race through his Repository for Germinal Choice, popularly known as the Nobel Prize sperm bank, but he says he envisions a better society populated by smarter children born to parents who meet his standards for health and emotional stability.

"We are, I would think, selective," Mr. Graham said in a recent interview at his downtown office. "But we're not racist. We'll accept excellence in any race. What we're really trying to do is optimize the conditions for having children."

Most of the women who receive the semen, which is kept in a frozen state, are in their mid-to late 30's. Many have tried unsuccessfully for years to bear children with their husbands. Occasionally, the recipient's husband has a hereditary problem that he does not want to pass on.

* * *

Secrecy shrouds most of the names involved with the repository, started in 1979. Only William B. Shockley, who shared a Nobel Prize for the invention of the transistor and who says blacks as a group are intellectually inferior to whites for genetic reasons, has made his donations public.

Nine other men, all possessing an I.Q. of at least 140, are regular donors, Mr. Graham said.

Women who inquire about insemination through the repository are given a booklet showing the characteristics of the donors, who are not identified by name.

Sperm is given to the women free except for a $50 application fee, $10 a month for liquid nitrogen for storage and shipping costs. The women are required to be married and to prove it.

* * *

Mr. Graham, 78 years old, does not pay any fee to the repository's donors, but sends someone to pick up their donations.

"These are men who would never be on call to a doctor," Mr. Graham said. "And they don't do this because they need the money."

But running the nonprofit repository and paying its four employees costs Mr. Graham several hundred thousand dollars annually. He said money was no problem because he made a fortune by inventing shatterproof eyeglasses.

HE NOW SEEKS ATHLETES

Since the repository's founding, Mr. Graham has been primarily interested in attracting men whose area of excellence is sciences or the arts. Since the 1984 Olympics in Los Angeles, he also has been looking for donors who are outstanding athletes and have high intelligence.

"We have an interview with a gold medal winner in a week or two," Mr. Graham said. "Our present donors are all geniuses. Now we're also emphasizing outstanding bodies."

* * *

MAXWELL J. MEHLMAN, MODERN EUGENICS AND THE LAW, IN A CENTURY OF EUGENICS: FROM THE INDIANA EXPERIMENT TO THE HUMAN GENOME ERA
(2010).

* * *

Commentators often distinguish between "state-sponsored" and "private" reproductive decisions, suggesting that only the former can be considered to be eugenics. [Troy] Duster states, for example: "[I]t is imperative to distinguish between state-sanctioned eugenics programs on the one hand, and private, individualized, *personal* decisions that are socially patterned on the other." But the exercise of state power, and the dividing line between state-sponsored and private decision-making, are less clear-cut than Duster implies. At one extreme, the state can prohibit a eugenic practice. In Skinner v. Oklahoma, for example, the Supreme Court held that it was unconstitutional for a state to require certain habitual criminals to be sterilized but not others. * * *

At the other extreme, the state may compel a eugenic practice, such as Indiana did when it enacted [the nation's first] involuntary sterilization law [in 1907]. Between these two extremes, however, there are a number of gradations. For example, the government can provide financial inducements for eugenic practices, such as tax breaks and welfare penalties for having desirable or undesirable children, or damages awarded by the judicial system to families whose physicians failed to prevent the birth of children with disabilities. Even when the government merely refrains from limiting or prohibiting eugenic practices, it might be said to be sanctioning them implicitly. Duster might regard reproductive decisions by parents as "personal," but the government arguably collaborates when it turns a blind eye.

In short, when the law influences reproductive decision-making in such a way as to encourage or discourage the birth of specifically types of desirable or undesirable individuals, this is at least suggestive of a eugenics objective. The more overt this objective, or the greater the impact of the law on individual reproductive decisions, the more frankly eugenic the law can be considered. This is not meant to imply that forced sterilization is on a par with government inaction in the face of private behavior. Yet * * * society has employed indirect as well as direct means to control reproductive behavior in order to achieve eugenic goals. The memory of the victims of the Indiana law and its successors would be dishonored if we examined the current state of affairs using too narrow a view of this history.

A.   LEGALLY TOLERATED PRACTICES.

A number of practices typically are thought of as private because they result from private rather than public decision-making. But the fact that the law permits them to take place indicates a measure of public acquiescence, if not approval.

This category includes attempts to achieve what might be considered positive neoeugenic objectives. One example is selective breeding to produce a "better" genetic lineage. This has long taken place with animals, but it also takes place in humans. The most notorious recent case is the Chinese basketball player Yao Ming, whose parents were mated by the Chinese government because of their height and athletic prowess and who was forced to play basketball at an early age. Private forms of selective breeding are rampant in the United States, including mating within certain social circles, such as "coming out" at debutant balls, arranged marriages and semi-arranged marriages in which the couple is brought together by the parents, and most recently, computerized dating services in which participants select one another according to desirable traits. One such service, eHarmony.com, provides information about 29 personal characteristics, including appearance, intellect, industriousness, ambition, family background, education, and character. Those who avail themselves of these dating services can compress investigations that used to take a number of "dates" into the click of a button.

Some of the most glaring selective breeding practices are associated with gamete donation. The Genetics & IVF Institute, for example, provides the following information about egg donors: adult photos, childhood photos, audio interviews, blood type, ethnic background of donor's mother and father, height, weight, whether pregnancies have been achieved, body build, eye color, hair color and texture, years of education and major areas of study, occupation, Scholastic Aptitude Test (SAT) scores and grade point averages, special interests, family medical history, essays by donors, and personality typing based on the Keirsey test, which uses a Jungian approach to classify temperaments into 12 categories, such as "rational and reserved" or "artisan and introspective." The California Cryobank, Inc. provides purchasers of donor sperm with a 26-page donor profile. A company called Fertility Alternatives pays a premium to "exceptional" egg donors. To qualify, the donor must have graduated from a major university, or be currently attending one, preferably Ivy League; have a GPA of 3.0 +; SAT scores of 1350+ or ACT scores of 30+; and have a documented high IQ.

The degree to which the law accommodates these assisted reproductive practices is striking. Although health care is one of the most heavily regulated industries in the country, the only federal law specifically governing in vitro fertilization (IVF) services is the Fertility Clinic Success Rate and Certification Act of 1992, which merely requires infertility clinics to report success rates in a standardized fashion. State regulation is minimal. The criticisms leveled at the recent IVF-assisted birth of octuplets to an unmarried, unemployed woman illustrate this regulatory lacuna.

Conceivably, state law might encourage selective breeding by permitting parents to sue infertility clinics for negligence in failing properly to screen gamete donors. The leading case is Harnicher v. University of Utah Medical Center. [See Chapter 8]

* * *

While the parents in the *Harnicher* case used selective breeding in the hopes of achieving a positive neoeugenic goal, the law also countenances a number of practices that might be deemed negative neoeugenics. One obvious example is fetal testing followed by aborting the fetus for reasons that do not relate to the mother's health. Another is preimplantation genetic diagnosis (PGD) of fertilized embryos in the course of IVF, where only those embryos with the best genetic endowment are implanted in the uterus and allowed to gestate. The law leaves IVF services essentially unregulated. A third technique is community-based genetic testing for matchmaking purposes, such as screening programs for Tay-Sachs and other recessive genetic diseases prevalent in Jews of Ashkenazi descent. The pioneer program is Chevra Dor Yeshurim ("Association of the Upright Generation"), which screens Orthodox Jewish adolescents in New York and does not allow a matchmaker to arrange a marriage between two individuals who both carry a recessive mutation.

Finally, there are private family planning initiatives. One is Project Prevention (formerly "CRACK"). This was started in California in 1997 by a woman who wanted to punish the drug-addicted mother who had given birth to 4 children she had adopted. When she failed to persuade the state legislature to criminalize drug-addicted mothers, she created CRACK, which gives drug addicts $200 if they undergo sterilization or use long-term birth control. In 2003, the organization claimed to have 23 chapters nationwide and had paid 907 persons, including 361 who had tubal ligations. African Americans and Hispanics accounted for 401 of the participants. At present, there is no state or federal law that would interfere with this project.

B.   LEGALLY FACILITATED PRACTICES.

In some instances, the law goes farther than turning a blind eye; it actually aids the practice of neoeugenics. One example is the ability of parents to bring so-called "wrongful birth" actions. [See Chapter 8]

* * *

Another method by which the government involves itself in what might be considered neoeugenics is providing public funding for family-planning programs aimed at preventing the birth of children to poor mothers. According to the Alan Guttmacher Institute, the government in 2001 spent $1.26 billion on reversible contraceptive services and $95 million on sterilization services. These funds are distributed through several programs: Medicaid, Title X, Title V (Maternal Child Block Grants), Social Services Block Grants, and TANF (Temporary Assistance for Needy Families). These programs would not be particularly neoeugenic if they provided family-planning assistance to all socio-economic groups, but virtually all of these funds are earmarked for the poor. * * *

Organizations that provide these federally-funded family planning services are typically non-profits, and therefore another way that the government facilitates their activities in by giving them a subsidy in the form of exempting them from federal and state taxes. * * *

Another government tax policy that might be considered neoeugenic is federal child tax credits. Until statutory limits are reached, the more children the taxpaying family has, the larger the number of credits that it can claim. The policy might be regarded as eugenic in that, since only families with enough income to pay taxes benefit from the credit, the policy creates an incentive for better-off families to have more children.

Contrast child tax credits with so-called family caps under state welfare programs. Unlike child tax credits that encourage taxpaying families to produce more offspring, family caps apply to families on welfare, discouraging them from becoming larger by halting increases in welfare benefits once there are more than a certain number of children. Currently 24 states have some version of this policy. Dorothy Roberts observes that "[l]ike birth control programs and reproductive punishments, contemporary welfare policies share features of eugenic thinking. * * * Of course, the current welfare family caps are not premised on notions of recipients' genetic inferiority. But, like eugenic programs of the past, they are seen as a way of ridding America of the burden poor people pose."

In Dandridge v. Williams, the Supreme Court upheld family caps in the face of constitutional challenge. The Court ruled that the state of Maryland did not violate the Equal Protection Clause of the Fourteenth Amendment because it had a reasonable basis for the policy, namely, "the state's legitimate interest in encouraging employment and in avoiding discrimination between welfare families and the families of the working poor." Interestingly, the state itself had articulated an additional goal—"providing incentives for family planning"—on which, without comment, the Court apparently declined to rely.

C.   LEGALLY MANDATED PRACTICES.

So far we have considered government toleration or subsidization of practices that can be considered neoeugenic. Additionally, there are some practices that the government currently mandates by law. All of them are in aid of negative eugenics objectives in that they discourage reproduction by undesirable segments of the population. One example is sterilization and other restrictions on reproduction employed ostensibly to deter the commission of future crimes. For example, California in 1996 enacted a law authorizing voluntary chemical or surgical castration for the first offense of child molesting and mandating castration as a condition of parole for repeat offenders. * * * Although the intent of these laws arguably is to prevent child molestation, they are eugenic in that they decrease the likelihood that child molesters will reproduce.

The criminal justice system deters reproduction not only by sex offenders but by all incarcerated criminals. In a broader sense, then, the entire criminal system is a negative neoeugenic program. Only five states (California, Mississippi, New Mexico, New York, and Washington) permit prisoners to have conjugal visits with their spouses, despite some evidence that such visits reduce the incidence of prison rape.

In the early 20th century, eugenic goals fueled restrictive immigration laws. Similar objectives arguably are associated with current efforts to limit immigration, including the plan to construct a fence along the border with Mexico. * * *

* * *

The state-mandated initiative that most overtly raises eugenics concerns, however, is newborn screening for nontreatable disorders. [See Chapter 10] * * *

The development of faster and cheaper technologies such as tandem mass spectrometry and microchip arrays enable programs to screen for far greater numbers of disorders, including many for which no readily effective treatments presently exist. Screening for these nontreatable disorders can be beneficial, in that it could spare families years of uncertainty once symptoms emerged; alert them to be on the watch for new discoveries that could provide their children with treatment; provide children with adjunctive if not curative interventions; and facilitate participation of the children in research on their disorders. Yet some public health advocates offer an additional rationale for screening for nontreatable disorders: that it can serve as a valuable tool in family planning. One recent article explains, for example: "Arguments for considering broader benefits from the early diagnosis that only newborn screening can provide include . . . knowledge on which to base reproductive decision-making years before a disease would be diagnosed for the affected child. . . ."

Moreover, as noted above, newborn screening is mandatory. * * *

* * * Newborn screening for treatable disorders is laudable. Screening for nontreatable disorders, however, is another matter. The screening is mandated by the state, and is imposed on parents over their objection. Nontreatable disorders would be included in part in order to discourage parents from giving birth to additional children with those disorders. This will prevent these children from inheriting genes that will make them a burden on society. Viewed in this manner, the resemblance between this program and classic eugenic practices, especially on this, the centennial of the first eugenic law, is, at least, disconcerting.

NOTES AND QUESTIONS

1.   To what extent should the programs and practices described by Mehlman count as eugenics?

2.   In what ways do they rekindle or avoid the concerns raised by the efforts of the eugenics movement in the 20th century?

3. In 1994, Charles Murray and Richard Herrnstein authored a book entitled *The Bell Curve* in which they argued that genetic differences were associated with social and racial inequality. For scientific critiques of the book, see Intelligence, Genes, and Success: Scientists Respond to the Bell Curve (Bernie Devlin, Stephen E. Fineberg, Daniel P. Resnicj, and Kathryn Roeder eds. Springer Science+Business Media 1997). Former New York Times science reporter Nicholas Wade made arguments similar to Murray and Herrnstein in a 2014 book entitled *A Troublesome Inheritance: Genes, Race and Human History*. Wade's book also was heavily criticized. A review in The New York Times Sunday Book Review, for example, described it as "a deeply flawed, deceptive and dangerous book." David Dobbs, Sunday Book Review: The Fault in Our DNA "A Troublesome Inheritance" and "Inheritance," July 10, 2014, www.nytimes.com/2014/07/13/books/review/a-troublesome-inheritance-and-inheritance.html?_r=0.

4. President Trump's disparaging descriptions of immigrants from Mexico and elsewhere evoke the eugenic views that supported earlier anti-immigration measures. See Abigail Abrams, Trump's New Plan Would Require Immigrants to Pass a Test. Here's What Happened When the U.S. Tried That Before, Time, May 20, 2019 (https://time.com/5591277/trump-immigration-test-history/).

CHAPTER 3

GENETICS AND RACE

■ ■ ■

I. GENETIC BASIS FOR RACE

OSAGIE K. OBASOGIE, PLAYING THE GENE CARD? A REPORT ON RACE AND HUMAN BIOTECHNOLOGY
Center for Genetics and Society 2009, www.thegenecard.org.

What does it mean to say that race is not biologically significant? Researchers in the social and life sciences have argued that race is not a meaningful biological category, that it is a "social construction" rather than a scientific fact.

But what does this mean? These phrases are typically used to convey the ideas that

- the importance placed on the outward physical distinctions that societies traditionally use to draw racial boundaries vary substantially over time and place,

- these physical distinctions do not reflect any inherent meanings, abilities, or disabilities, and

- racial differences in social and health outcomes do not correlate meaningfully with underlying biological or genetic mechanisms.

In short, as University of California, Berkeley Law Professor Ian Haney Lopez argues, the constructionist view "rejects the most widely accepted understanding of race . . . [which holds that] there exist natural, physical, divisions among humans that are hereditary, reflected in morphology, and roughly captured by terms like Black, White, and Asian."

There are certainly biological components to race and health outcomes, though often only because of the way certain groups are treated in relation to how they are perceived. A key example of this phenomenon was demonstrated by Johns Hopkins epidemiologist Michael Klag, who found that rates of hypertension among Black Americans correspond to skin complexion; those with darker skin have higher rates. Klag showed that this is not simply a genetic or biological phenomenon, but rather a health outcome linked to skin tone discrimination and the higher degree of stress experienced by dark-skinned Blacks. While the effect was biological, the cause was largely social.

Of course, genes (along with other biological and environmental factors) shape human variation and outward physical appearance, and many of these characteristics are heritable. Evolutionary dynamics have conferred some different phenotypic traits and genetic signatures to geographically separated groups that may loosely resemble social categories of race. Thus, as Francis Collins notes, the ability to identify genetic variations that provide "reasonably accurate" yet "blurry" estimates of portions of an individual's ancestry suggest that "it is not strictly true that race or ethnicity has no biological connection."

But it is important to put even loose correlations between race and genes or genetic predispositions in an appropriate context. An early and enduring finding in human genetic studies is that there is typically more genetic variation within socially defined racial groups than between them. Another consistent finding is that for any observable "racial" trait, there are no corresponding genetic boundaries between population groups. They are discordant—that is, the collection of observable physical cues that society often uses to create the idea of discrete racial groups are not mirrored by corresponding genetic boundaries. Instead, biologists find graded variations in the percentages of groups with each characteristic.

In other words, the sharp delineations that society makes with regards to racial categories are not meaningfully reflected in our genes. That is why scientists such as Yale geneticist Kenneth Kidd conclude that "there's no such thing as race in *Homo sapiens*. . . . There's no place [in our genes] where you can draw a line and say there's a major difference on one side of the line from what's on the other side." To say that race is a social construction is to emphasize that in most cases, racial categories based upon phenotype (physical appearance) ultimately provide a poor way to proxy individual genotype, or genetic variations that may be exclusive to certain populations.

MICHAEL J. MALINOWSKI, DEALING WITH THE REALITIES OF RACE AND ETHNICITY: A BIOETHICS-CENTERED ARGUMENT IN FAVOR OF RACE-BASED GENETICS RESEARCH
45 Hous. L. Rev. 1415, 1433–1436 (2009).

Those in the scientific and medical communities opposed to research based on race and ethnicity emphasize that these groupings are inconsistent with the scientific reality of human genetics. They draw from the ample body of literature by Professors Cavalli-Sforza, Lewontin, and their contemporaries, and also reference recent findings that bolster the argument that race and ethnicity are more social constructs than genetic realities. Opponents assert that a preferred methodology for population genetics is research centered on diseases or at least specific and more reliable genetic particulars. They argue this approach will help avoid wasting resources, forcing outcomes, and chancing the affirmation of racial and ethnic groupings and social stereotypes. According to bioethicist and Ph.D. scientist Mildred Cho, the race and ethnicity categories are unworkable: "Because social perceptions of the meaning of race and ethnicity are extremely fluid, basing research findings on these categories or applying scientific findings based on perceived race or ethnicity is fraught with problems. Thus, attempts to better define [the racial and ethnic] structure [of drug response] will be futile."

Sociologist Troy Duster and many other opponents raise concerns about biologic determinism, meaning that genetic protocols crafted around race and ethnicity will become self-fulfilling prophecies. They emphasize the genetic commonality in any group due to the youth of the human species and its overwhelming genetic sameness. Professor Duster also addresses the broader social implications of underscoring lines traditionally drawn around groups based upon race and ethnicity through genetics research protocols that suggest their validity. He warns that singling out these groups further affirms prejudices and increases their vulnerability to discrimination, exploitation, and health inequality. According to Professor Duster, the scientific community has shifted from "genetic sameness" as the mantra for mapping the human genome to a mantra of "genetic differentiation" through ongoing efforts to make medical sense out of the genome map, including population genetics, pharmacogenomics, and identification of SNPs.

A number of law academics have entered the debate and argued against the perpetuation of race in the biomedical context with cautions about the weighty social and legal implications involved. In fact, there is a discernible majority opinion among law academics that race-based genomics research is undesirable on multiple levels and perhaps even illegal. The literature includes articles by Professors Erik Lillquist and Charles Sullivan, Professor Sharona Hoffman, Professor Jonathan Kahn, and a University of Minnesota symposium chaired by Professor Wolf, which includes an article by Professor Dorothy Roberts.

Proposals have been made to distinguish basic, clinical, epidemiological, and other forms of research, and to introduce legal restraints on the use of race and ethnicity in a manner tailored to each research specialty. The general consensus among law opponents is that the use of race and ethnicity in biomedical research always warrants caution and legal restraints, but there is a continuum: use of race in clinical research is least acceptable; use in epidemiological research, such as research on the correlation between race and health disparities, is most acceptable; and other types of research place between the two. Also, the general consensus is that the use of race in research and medicine runs contrary to U.S. law and policy that broadly proscribes it. Lillquist & Sullivan conclude that the use of race in research and medicine should be severely circumscribed, if not prohibited almost entirely. Their proposed standard for using race in medical treatment is extremely restrictive. They would require a scientific basis to establish not simply that the use of race is helpful in diagnosis and treatment, but that it is the best known method at the time. Professor Hoffman declares that " 'race-based' medicine is an inappropriate and perilous approach" and proposes regulatory reforms to heavily restrain, if not entirely eliminate, both race-based research and medicine. She proposes "attributes-based" identification as a race-neutral alternative.

Collectively, legal academics generally approach race-based research from the standpoint of U.S. jurisprudence and public policy against discrimination and associated social and ethical concerns. Their analysis of potential legal constraints on race-centered research begins with restrictions on intentional disparate treatment based on race by government entities under the Equal Protection Clause of the Fourteenth Amendment and the Due Process Clause of the Fifth Amendment. They emphasize that government use of racial classifications triggers strict scrutiny, but recognize that government actions, including programs thoughtfully crafted to promote affirmative action, survive such scrutiny where there is a compelling government interest and the use of race is narrowly tailored to promote that interest. They generally concede that, under established jurisprudence, government sponsorship of responsible race-based genetics research is likely to survive such challenges, though the present Court recently questioned Seattle and Louisville school diversity policies and subjected them to further inquiry.

II. SICKLE CELL SCREENING

LORI ANDREWS ET AL., ASSESSING GENETIC RISKS: IMPLICATIONS FOR HEALTH AND SOCIAL POLICY
40–41 (1994).

A serious set of errors was made in the establishment of sickle cell screening programs in the African-American community in the early 1970s. Some of these screening programs were established without adequate consultation and education of the affected communities. A test then in common use failed to distinguish individuals with the disease from those who were only carriers. No treatment was available or on the horizon. The only benefit of early detection for infants with the disease was to ensure that children would receive medical care promptly when they became sick, yet improved access to medical care was not usually part of the programs. Nor was prenatal diagnosis available at that time; the only way parents could avoid having affected children was not to have children at all or to avoid mating with another carrier.

Since 8 percent of African Americans are carriers of the sickle cell trait, many carriers were detected in screening programs. However, knowledge of having the trait was appropriate only for reproductive purposes since there is a 1 in 4 risk of having an infant with sickle cell anemia if both parents carry the trait. However, confusion about the significance of carrying the common sickle cell trait (about 1 in 12 African Americans) and the rare sickle cell anemia (with a frequency of about 1 in 600) often led to stigmatization and discrimination.

In the early 1970s, seven states passed mandatory laws requiring sickle cell screening, while ten others had voluntary laws. Some laws called for newborn screening. Others erroneously regarded sickle cell anemia as an infectious disease and called for screening before a child could enter school. Others required it as a condition of obtaining a marriage license. In at least one state law, as well as in the National Sickle Cell Anemia Control act of 1972, it was evident that legislators had confused the frequency of the trait (about 1 in 12 African Americans) with the frequency of the disease of about 1 in 600. The national act required programs supported with federal funds to be voluntary, not mandatory. Nevertheless, even in the late 1970s, some screening in at least one state was done without informed consent.

The experiences in the sickle cell screening programs of the early 1970s reinforce the need for education before screening and for counseling after screening. Enthusiasm turned to suspicion as many African-Americans concluded that the intent was to eradicate the sickle cell gene by preventing carriers from reproducing—thereby reducing the birth rate in the black community. These genetic testing programs were perceived by some as genocidal in intent.

Considerable time, effort, and money have been required to overcome these early mistakes. To promote research and develop high-quality programs of screening and counseling, the National Heart, Lung, and Blood Institute provided funding in the 1970s under the national act to establish 10 centers for sickle cell disease research and 25 clinics to carry out education, screening, and counseling in high-risk populations. Under these auspices, protocols for more effective education, screening, and counseling were developed and the criteria for appropriate management of sickle cell anemia were developed. Early studies by the Centers for Disease Control (CDC) found that the laboratories providing tests often made technical errors and were sometimes doing primary screening with a test that did not distinguish sickle cell trait from the disease. Federal support through the CDC proficiency testing and assistance program helped laboratories to improve the quality of testing. Similarly, federal support for community-based sickle cell programs included education of providers and consumers, improving the understanding of both groups. It was not until 1978 that sickle cell anemia could be diagnosed in amniotic fluid cells obtained by amniocentesis. Prior to that time, diagnosis was possible on fetal blood, although obtaining it carried much greater risks to the fetus than amniocentesis. And not until 1986, as the result of a collaborative nationwide randomized control trial, was it established that penicillin prophylaxis reduced infant and childhood mortality from sickle cell anemia, thereby providing a therapeutic rationale for screening newborns for sickle cell anemia. Although 42 states now screen newborns for sickle cell disease, not all infants with the disease receive treatment.

NOTES AND QUESTIONS

1.   In her book *Killing the Black Body*, Dorothy Roberts explains that "what began as a strategy to improve the health of Blacks soon turned into an instrument of medical abuse. Because screening programs often provided no counseling, there was rampant confusion between carriers of the trait and those who had the disease. Many people who had only sickle-cell trait were mistakenly convinced that their health was in jeopardy. Even the preamble of the federal law stated erroneously that 2 million Americans had sickle-cell *disease* rather than the *trait*." Dorothy Roberts, Killing the Black Body: Race, Reproduction, and the Meaning of Liberty 257–258 (1997). Roberts notes that 14 states required sickle-cell screening in order for Blacks to attend public school and obtain a marriage license; Blacks were denied admission to the Air Force Academy; most of the commercial airlines fired or grounded Black pilots; and Blacks had problems obtaining insurance. Roberts also describes efforts to prevent Blacks from having children. Carriers for the trait were often counseled to avoid reproducing, and in 1971 members of the Department of Obstetrics and Gynecology at Tennessee College of Medicine published an article recommending sterilization for women with the disease.

2.   For additional background on the sickle cell screening program, see Keith Wailoo, Dying in the City of the Blues: Sickle Cell Anemia and the Politics of Race and Health 165–196 (2001).

III. RACE-BASED DRUGS

FOOD AND DRUG ADMINISTRATION, FDA APPROVES BiDIL HEART FAILURE DRUG FOR BLACK PATIENTS
June 23, 2005.

The Food and Drug Administration (FDA) approved BiDil (bye-DILL), a drug for the treatment of heart failure in self-identified black patients, representing a step toward the promise of personalized medicine.

Heart failure is a condition in which the heart is weakened and does not pump enough blood. It can be caused by a variety of damage to the heart, including heart attacks, high blood pressure, and infections.

The approval of BiDil was based in part on the results of the African-American Heart Failure Trial (A-HeFT). The study, which involved 1,050 self-identified black patients with severe heart failure who had already been treated with the best available therapy, was conducted because two previous trials in the general population of severe heart failure patients found no benefit, but suggested a benefit of BiDil in black patients. Patients on BiDil experienced a 43% reduction in death and a 39% decrease in hospitalization for heart failure compared to placebo, and a decrease of their symptoms of heart failure.

"Today's approval of a drug to treat severe heart failure in self-identified black population is a striking example of how a treatment can benefit some patients even if it does not help all patients," said Dr. Robert Temple, FDA Associate Director of Medical Policy. "The information presented to the FDA clearly showed that blacks suffering from heart failure will now have an additional safe and effective option for treating their condition. In the future, we hope to discover characteristics that identify people of any race who might be helped by Bidil."

BiDil is a combination of two older drugs, neither approved for heart failure—hydralazine and isosorbide dinitrate.

As an anti-hypertensive agent, hydralazine relaxes the arteries, and decreases the work of the heart. The anti-anginal agent, isosorbide dinitrate, relaxes the veins as well as the arteries. Isosorbide seems to work by releasing nitric oxide at the blood vessel wall, but its effect usually wears off after half a day. Hydralazine may prevent this loss of effect. But how the two drugs work together is not fully known.

RENE BOWSER, RACE AS A PROXY FOR DRUG RESPONSE: THE DANGERS AND CHALLENGES OF ETHNIC DRUGS
53 DePaul L. Rev. 1111 (2004).

* * *

IV.　RACIAL REPACKAGING—THE STORY OF BIDIL

Even though race has not been shown to be a strong proxy for drug metabolism, a drug called BiDil is poised to become the first drug ever approved by the FDA to treat heart failure in African Americans, and only in African Americans. BiDil is a combination of two vasodilators, hydralazine and isosorbide dinitratre (H/I). Vasodilators dilate blood vessels and ease the strain put on the heart in pumping blood. BiDil is thought to have an added benefit of improving levels of nitric oxide in the blood, which is also thought to be of great benefit to individuals suffering from heart failure.

BiDil is an underused drug that has been around for decades; it certainly did not begin as an ethnic drug. This brief review of BiDil's origins demonstrates the centrality of commerce and the exploitation of racial categories in the repackaging of BiDil as a wonder drug for African Americans.

It all begins with the first Vasodilator Heart Failure Trial (V-HeFT I). In this medical trial, which lasted from 1980 to 1985, cardiologists found that the H/I (BiDil) combination appeared to have a beneficial impact in reducing mortality from heart disease. The V-Heft I trial was soon followed by another trial, V-HeFT II, which lasted from 1986 to 1991. This trial compared the efficacy of the H/I (BiDil drugs) against the drug enalapril, an angiotensin-converting enzyme (ACE) inhibitor. The second trial found that enalapril had a more beneficial effect on mortality than the H/I combination. The results of the second trial established ACE inhibitors as the front-line therapy for heart failure. ACE inhibitors have not totally replaced H/I, however, because between 20% and 30% of congestive heart failure patients do not respond well to them. That is roughly 1.5 million patients annually (including members of all racial groups), and current guidelines still recommend the H/I combination for these patients.

The V-HeFT investigators presented the H/I (BiDil drugs) as generally efficacious in the population at large, without regard to race. In 1987, Dr. Jay Cohn, one of the principal investigators in the V-HeFT studies applied for and received a patent on the H/I drugs. In the patent description, Cohn made no mention of race, asserting that H/I substantially and significantly reduces the incidence of mortality in congestive heart patients. Clearly, he believed the BiDil drugs would be used to treat all people suffering from heart failure.

The H/I drugs are generic drugs. Cohn and others combined them into a single pill for easy administration. By 1994, tests were conducted to make sure that the pill form was just as effective as the administration of the drugs separately. They were. Cohn and Medco, which had acquired the intellectual property rights from Cohn, were now ready to approach the FDA for the approval of BiDil for use in the general population.

In 1996, Medco submitted a new drug application (NDA) to the FDA. Jay Cohn optimistically asserted at the time that the BiDil formulation represented a very convenient dosage that, once approved by the FDA, would lead to an increased usage of this therapy in the general population. An industry report estimated a potential market of up to sixty million dollars in annual sales for BiDil.

In an unanticipated move, however, the FDA voted nine to three against approving BiDil, even though extensive findings in peer reviewed journals supported Cohn's claim that the H/I combination substantially and significantly reduced the incidence of mortality in congestive heart failure patients. The agency concluded that while the drug had clinical significance, it failed to meet the biostatistical criteria of probability and efficacy sufficient for the FDA to grant a NDA. In particular, the FDA noted that data from the V-Heft studies contained too many variables specified as endpoints for them to interpret the data with biostatical certainty. The next day, Medco's stock dropped by 25%.

To salvage the drug, the BiDil promoters repackaged it along racial lines. Jay Cohn went back one more time to the V-HeFT data, this time to analyze the differential effects of BiDil and enalapril by race. In 1999, Cohn and others published a paper asserting that the H/I combinations worked better in blacks than ACE inhibitors. Specially, they concluded:

> The H-I combination appears to be particularly effective in prolonging survival in black patients and is as effective as enalapril in this subgroup. In contrast, enalapril shows its more favorable effect in the white population . . . the consistency of observations of a racial difference in response in V-HeFT I and V-HeFT II . . . lend credence to the suggestion that therapy for heart failure might appropriately be racially tailored.

That same year Daniel Dries coauthored a study in the prestigious New England Journal of Medicine suggesting that racial differences exist in the natural progression of congestive heart failure. The implicit conclusion is that heart disease is a different disease in blacks and whites and, therefore, it must be treated with different therapies. This theory of biological difference is consistent with Jay Cohn's claim that the black/white disparity in death rates from heart failure is partly attributable to "a pathophysiology found in black patients that may involve Nitric Oxide (NO) insufficiency arising from either reduced NO production, enhanced NO inactivation or both."

In 1999, NitroMed Inc., a Boston area biotech firm specializing in the development and commercialization of nitric oxide enhanced medicines, acquired the intellectual property rights to BiDil. NitroMed announced its plans to amend the NDA to seek approval for the use of BiDil to treat and prevent mortality associated with heart failure in African-American patients. After a meeting in Washington, the FDA approved the use of BiDil as a drug to treat heart failure in African Americans, pending the successful results of a confirmatory trial. That trial, A-HeFT, the African American Heart Failure Trial, is currently underway.

The FDA's tentative approval represents a significant expansion of the potential BiDil market. NitroMed currently estimates that approximately 750,000 African Americans suffer from heart disease. The implication is that all African Americans suffering from heart disease should be taking

BiDil (because it is a different disease), not just those who cannot tolerate or do not respond well to ACE inhibitors. Without doubt, the huge commercial implications of the first ethnic niche market allowed NitroMed to raise over $31.4 million from several private venture capital firms to support the confirmatory trials. Recently, pharmaceutical giant Merck & Co., Inc. formed a multi-year research collaboration with NitroMed, even though BiDil is the company's most advanced product to date.

V.   A NEW THERAPY OR A NEW MARKET FOR AN UNDERUSED DRUG?

BiDil started as a drug for use in the general population but has emerged as a drug for use only in African Americans. A fundamental question is whether significant scientific evidence demonstrates that all African Americans with heart problems should take this drug, or are NitroMed's claims merely a scheme to expand and exploit a potentially lucrative market. As discussed below, substantial evidence raises serious questions about the underpinnings of NitroMed's claims.

First, the study authored by Peter Carson along with Jay Cohn, claiming that blacks respond better to H/I than to ACE inhibitors, retrospectively analyzed data from V-HeFT I and II. It was not prospectively designed to study racial differences in response to treatment, rather, an existing and rather old data set was reanalyzed. There are well documented statistical problems involving randomization and stratification by race in such retrospective studies.

Second, black participants had higher levels of comordid [sic] factors such as diabetes and hypertension. Essentially, the white and black populations were not the same. Few doctors would use monotherapy (a single drug) for cardiovascular disease in patients with concomitant diabetes and hypertension. Therefore, this study may simply confirm what we already know: use of a single ACE inhibitor at a standard dose is not effective for patients who also have diabetes and hypertension, but is effective for patients without these conditions.

Third, the study purports to consider relevant nongenetic environmental influences on the development and progression of heart failure, and includes two such factors—education and "financial distress (yes vs. no) during the past twelve months." While education and experience of financial distress are relevant factors to consider in examining nongenetic environmental influences, the implicit understanding is that they are exhaustive of all such relevant factors.

Vast medical and public health literature shows that a host of deleterious conditions accompany black status in the United States, including differential exposures to environmental toxins, discrimination, residential segregation, and differential political power, both in terms of individual level of control and the allocation of resources. Indeed, a

Harvard study shows that the stress of experiencing racism raises blood pressure. It is now well established that physiological processes respond to psychosocial stress. Therefore, the unmeasured variation in environmental exposures could account for the differential response in hospitalization and survival, not differences in drug metabolism.

Fourth, as fortune would have it, one of the strongest critiques has come from one of the coauthors of the original study, Dr. Daniel Dries. In 2002, Dries took issue with the earlier New England Journal of Medicine piece arguing that the ACE inhibitor, enalapril, worked equally well in blacks and whites:

> Despite recent concerns that angiotensin-converting enzyme (ACE) inhibitors may be less efficacious in black patients with [heart failure], the present study demonstrates that enalapril significantly reduced the risk of development of [heart failure] in both blacks and whites * * *. The consistency of results in black and white subjects strengthens the argument that ACE inhibitor-therapy should continue to be used in black patients with [heart failure].

These findings are consistent with the recent African American Study of Kidney Disease and Hypertension that demonstrated a benefit of ACE inhibitor therapy in patients with renal disease.

Finally, NitroMed has relied heavily on the claim that African Americans have twice the risk of dying from heart failure than whites. If this is true, then it is highly plausible that the difference is due to genetic rather than environmental factors. This two-to-one disparity has been floating around uncontested in the scientific literature for decades. Dr. Jonathan Kahn of the University of Minnesota has demonstrated conclusively that the NitroMed claim about the scope of black and white differences is simply untrue. Dr. Kahn traced the citation sources back nearly two decades, and found that the difference between blacks and whites is actually 1.2 to 1. While there is a difference, it is far less than the two-to-one ratio that would warrant special trials for blacks. Thus, "substantial scaffolding of the BiDil clinical trials is based upon incorrect statistical data on racial disparities."

NOTES AND QUESTIONS

1. For a general discussion of pharmacogenomics, the use of genomic information in pharmaceutical research, development, and marketing, see Chapter 14.

2. BiDil initially received widespread support from African-American leaders, including the Congressional Black Caucus, the NAACP, and the Association of Black Cardiologists:

The Association of Black Cardiologists, Inc. (ABC), co-sponsor of the landmark African-American Heart Failure Trial (A-HeFT), is pleased that the U.S. Food and Drug Administration (FDA) approved BiDil® (isosorbide dinitrate/hydralazine hydrochloride) for the treatment of heart failure in black patients on [sic] yesterday. A-HeFT was the first clinical trial conducted in an all black heart failure population. BiDil is an orally-administered medicine shown in A-HeFT to improve survival, reduce the rate of first hospitalization for heart failure and improve patient-reported functional status, as an adjunct to current standard heart failure therapy in self-identified black patients.

"The approval of BiDil is a major step toward eliminating existing cardiovascular-related health disparities affecting African Americans, a population that is disproportionately burdened by heart failure," said B. Waine Kong, Ph.D., J.D., chief executive officer of the Association of Black Cardiologists, Inc. "The ABC is proud to have played an integral role in the African American Heart Failure Trial and we look forward to continued progress in cardiovascular health for African Americans."

Press Release, Association of Black Cardiologists, FDA Approval of BiDil® Brings New Hope to Black Heart Failure Patients (June 24, 2005).

In an article in the Cambridge Quarterly of Healthcare Ethics, Joon-Ho Yu, Sara Goering and Stephanie Fullerton provide an interesting explanation for the support for BiDil among many leaders in the African-American community:

> BiDil's approval has been widely critiqued in academic circles on numerous grounds. Nevertheless, many advocates for African American health concerns have argued that BiDil is an important step toward reducing disparities in healthcare by creating medical therapies that are responsive to African American needs. Many of these advocates also publicly rejected the notion that BiDil is a race-specific drug, arguing that social race is a poor surrogate for the biological differences that underlie BiDil's efficacy. Thus, competing commitments to reducing health disparities while rejecting a biologically deterministic view of race have placed African American community leaders and health advocates in a state of conflict, both among themselves and with academic scholars of race, with respect to the desirability of BiDil.
>
> In this paper, we offer a sympathetic reading of this response to BiDil by some African American community leaders and aim to show how many of the academic critiques have failed to adequately account for the competing commitments of community stakeholders. We argue that justice involves not only the fair distribution of benefits but also an element of recognition, such that socially marginalized groups have the opportunity to be heard and to participate in

decisionmaking. In the case of BiDil, we believe that African American community leaders capitalized on an opportunity to bring attention to African American health issues, even as they risked complicity with an inaccurate portrayal of race as biological. Using Nancy Fraser's bivalent theory of justice (involving both recognition and redistribution), we argue that community leaders can be viewed as strategically affirming the use of race in hopes of ultimately transforming the process of drug development and garnering more careful attention to the problem of health disparities. Given the context of health disparities and statements made by community advocates that explicitly link BiDil to remedying such disparities, we believe this strategy is best understood not simply as a calculated risk assumed for the sake of some consequentialist benefit but rather as a means of asserting a demand for justice.

Joon-Ho Yu, Sara Goering & Stephanie M. Fullerton, Race-Based Medicine and Justice as Recognition: Exploring the Phenomenon of BiDil, 18 Cambridge Q. of Healthcare Ethics 57, 57–58 (2009).

3.   BiDil has proved to be a commercial failure. There are two main reasons. First, BiDil was, arguably, a breakthrough of convenience. The standard dosing is two pills, three times a day, for a total of six pills per day. Taking the generic versions of hydralazine and isosorbide dinitrate (nitroglycerin) requires four pills, four times a day, for a total of 16 pills per day. But, there is a heavy price for this convenience. BiDil costs about $4,000 per year, or about four to seven times more than the generic equivalents. Many health insurance companies have refused to cover BiDil on their formularies. Second, many African-American patients, upon learning that BiDil was approved only for self-identified African Americans, told their physicians that they would rather have the drug prescribed for white patients. Clearly, genetics, drugs, and race remain very complicated issues. For a comprehensive discussion, see Jonathan Kahn, Race in a Bottle (2014).

IV.   THE ELSI PROGRAM

The experience with eugenics in the early twentieth century, as well as other controversial programs such as the sickle cell screening effort, created concern about the potential abuses of the scientific advances made possible by the Human Genome Project. The response was to establish a special program within the Human Genome Project, called the Ethical, Legal and Social Implications or ELSI program, to focus on the project's ethical, legal, and social implications. The ELSI program was conceived by the first director of the Human Genome Project at the National Institutes of Health (NIH), James Watson, who, along with Francis Crick, had discovered the structure of the DNA molecule.

Watson himself gives the following account of the origin of the ELSI program:

In putting ethics so soon into the genome agenda, I was responding to my own personal fear that all too soon critics of the Genome Project would point out that I was a representative of the Cold Spring Harbor Laboratory that once housed the controversial Eugenics Record Office. My not forming a genome ethics program quickly might be falsely used as evidence that I was a closet eugenicist, having as my real long-term purpose the unambiguous identification of genes that lead to social and occupational stratification as well as genes justifying racial discrimination. So I saw the need to be proactive in making ELSI's major purpose clear from its start—to devise better ways to combat the social injustice that has at its roots bad draws of the genetic dice.

James Watson, A Passion for DNA: Genes, Genomes & Society 202 (2000).

Watson insisted that between 3 and 5 percent of the federal budget for the Human Genome Project be devoted to ELSI-sponsored studies by researchers outside of the government. Administration of the ELSI program was shared by the NIH, which created an ELSI Branch within what became the National Center for Human Genome Research, and the Department of Energy, which was interested in the Human Genome Project as a result of its effort to measure the biological effects of atomic radiation. For a history of the Department of Energy's involvement in the inception of the Human Genome Project, see Robert M. Cook-Deegan, The Gene Wars: Science, Politics, and the Human Genome (1994).

The ELSI program was unprecedented as an attempt to shape US science policy, and it has had its share of critics. As reported by Eric Juengst, the first chief of the ELSI Branch at NIH, one senior NIH official complained: "I still don't understand why you want to spend all this money subsidizing the vacuous pronouncements of self-styled 'ethicists'!" Watson replied that, for better or worse, "the cat was out of the bag." The official retorted: "But why inflate the cat? Why put the cat on TV?" Juengst adds:

> Pro-genomicists, like the NIH official quoted above, saw it as at best a waste of (increasingly scarce) NIH research dollars, and at worst an overblown hand-waving that could backfire badly on the scientific community if it actually succeeded in getting the public's attention. Anti-genomicists suspected that the program was, at best, a clever attempt to create a screen of ethical smoke behind which the [Human Genome Project's] juggernaut could build up speed, and, at worst, an attempt to buy off the very critics who might otherwise make trouble for the scientists.

Eric Juengst, Self-Critical Federal Science? The Ethics Experiment Within the U.S. Human Genome Project, 13 Social Philosophy & Policy 63, 66–67 (1996). Another criticism, voiced by George Annas and Sherman Elias, was that the one policy issue that received no attention from ELSI was whether the Human Genome Project should proceed in the first place. From its inception in 1990 to 2019, the ELSI program at NIH has sponsored more than 575 projects at a total cost of $433 million.

Food for Thought: It is exceedingly rare for scientific research programs to fund research on the ethical, legal, social, and policy implications of their activities. Efforts to create such research opportunities can trigger resistance from scientific researchers funded by these programs who worry that their funding will suffer. How should society compare the benefit from progress in scientific research and the value of research on the societal implications of the research?

CHAPTER 4

NEW DEVELOPMENTS

■ ■ ■

Beginning in the late 1990s, researchers began to employ faster and less expensive techniques to sequence human DNA called "next-generation" or "high-throughput" methods. As researchers learn more about the relationship between genetic factors and disease, efforts are being made to integrate that knowledge into the practice of medicine, a process known as "clinical translation." Clinical translation is hampered, however, by lingering uncertainty about the clinical significance of many genetic variations, the lack of genetic expertise on the part of many physicians and other health professionals, and the small number of genetic counsellors and others with clinical genetic proficiency.

I. PRECISION MEDICINE

The growing interest in incorporating genetics into clinical practice has led to efforts to sequence the DNA of large numbers of individuals and, by accessing their medical records, correlate the results with their health status. With enough participants, researchers can make new correlations between genetic variations and how individuals manifest illness and respond to treatments. These insights in turn can lead to more individualized care and, it is hoped, better outcomes.

The effort to make medical care more individualized was initially called "personalized medicine," but was changed to "precision medicine." As the National Research Council of the National Academies of Sciences explains, "there was concern that the word 'personalized' could be misinterpreted to imply that treatments and preventions are being developed uniquely for each individual; in precision medicine, the focus is on identifying which approaches will be effective for which patients based on genetic, environmental, and lifestyle factors." (https://ghr.nlm.nih.gov/primer/precisionmedicine/precisionvspersonalized). In other words, "personalized medicine" promised too much. See Eric Juengst, Michelle L. McGowan, Jennifer R. Fishman, and Richard A. Settersten Jr. From "Personalized" to "Precision" Medicine: The Ethical and Social Implications of Rhetorical Reform in Genomic Medicine, 46 Hastings Ctr. Rep. 21–33 (2015).

In 2015, President Obama announced the launch of the Precision Medicine Initiative, and a year later, NIH started the All of Us Research

Program, with the goal of obtaining DNA samples and data from electronic medical records for a million diverse individuals, including patients at academic medicine centers, the VA, and community health centers, as well as other volunteers. See https://allofus.nih.gov/. The program is an example of a research approach known as "citizen science." Other examples include volunteers who monitor pollution, identify and count birds, and in health care, play video games to learn more about retinal neurons and share information about their autoimmune disorders and the microorganisms in their gut. All of Us also involves the research use of large amounts of data and data sources, often referred to as "Big Data." See Mark A. Rothstein, Ethical Issues in Big Data Health Research, 43 J. L., Med. & Ethics 425–429 (2015).

The focus on precision medicine and the All of Us program intensifies a number of ongoing ethical and legal debates about large-scale genetic research projects. Once researchers have access to DNA samples and associated medical records, they can conduct innumerable investigations searching for clinically-relevant correlations. Do subjects have to give their informed consent to each specific research use of their information, or can they give some form of general consent for a variety of future studies? If, when using the samples and records in the future, researchers discover clinically-significant information about a participant's health, do they have a duty to try to notify the participant? To notify family members of the participant for whom the information also is clinically significant? Can participants withdraw from the program, and if so, can they insist that their DNA samples be destroyed? See Chapter 5 for additional discussion of these issues.

Precision medicine and similar initiatives require the collection, storage, and sequencing of large numbers of DNA samples in what are called "biobanks." As discussed more fully in Chapter 5, biobanking raises a number of concerns about protecting the interests of the individuals from whom DNA is collected.

One application of precision medicine research is the field of pharmacogenomics. As discussed more fully in Chapter 14, pharmacogenomics is the study of how genetic factors affect a patient's response to drugs. Increasingly, the Food and Drug Administration is requiring drug manufacturers to include information about genetic influences on drug response in their drug product labelling, and in some cases, to recommend that physicians run genetic tests on patients before prescribing them a drug. Another example of precision medicine research involves sequencing the DNA of patients' cancer tumors to more accurately design their chemotherapy treatments.

II. MORE EFFICIENT AND LESS COSTLY GENE EDITING TECHNIQUES

Modifying or "editing" genes is a promising approach for the prevention and treatment of human disease. Treatment using edited genes is discussed more fully in Part III. Early efforts to edit genes involved using programmable enzymes called nucleases, but engineering nucleases was difficult and time-consuming, and they were not very useful in treating conditions caused by multiple genomic variations. Beginning in 2012, scientists developed a new technique called CRISPR/Cas9, which is much easier and less expensive to use, and which can target multiple genes simultaneously. This has raised hopes of accelerated progress in using gene editing to combat disease. For more information on CRISPR/Cas9, see https://ghr.nlm.nih.gov/primer/genomicresearch/genomeediting.

III. HUMAN GERMLINE GENE EDITING

Gene editing can affect "somatic" cells, which are cells other than egg and sperm cells, and are not passed from one generation to the next. However, gene editing instead can target "germline" cells, that is, egg or sperm cells, or the genes of an early-stage embryo, in which case the modifications could be passed to descendants. In 2015, Chinese scientists used CRISPR/Cas9 to edit early-stage human embryos. The embryos had a defect (an extra set of chromosomes as the result of being fertilized by two sperm instead of one), and therefore could not have resulted in a live birth. See Jocelyn Kaiser and Dennis Normile, Chinese Paper on Embryo Engineering Splits Scientific Community, April 24, 2015 (https://www.sciencemag.org/news/2015/04/chinese-paper-embryo-engineering-splits-scientific-community). In 2018, an outcry greeted an announcement by a different Chinese scientist that he had successfully edited the genes of twin girls to confer resistance to HIV. Gina Kolata, Sui-Lee Wee, and Pam Belluck, Chinese Scientist Claims to Use Crispr to Make First Genetically Edited Babies, N. Y. Times, Nov. 26, 2018 (https://www.nytimes.com/2018/11/26/health/gene-editing-babies-china.html#). Germline gene editing is discussed further in Part III.

IV. DIRECT-TO-CONSUMER GENETIC TESTING

Beginning in the early 2000s, companies began selling DNA tests directly to consumers to help them research their ancestry. Customers submit a saliva sample and receive the test results online. It is estimated that U.S. genetic ancestry testing companies possess DNA from more than 26 million people. Antonio Regalado, More Than 26 Million People Have Taken an At-Home Ancestry Test, MIT Technology Review, Feb. 11, 2019 (https://www.technologyreview.com/s/612880/more-than-26-million-people-have-taken-an-at-home-ancestry-test/). For a description of genetic

ancestry testing, see https://ghr.nlm.nih.gov/primer/dtcgenetictesting/
ancestrytesting.

In 2007, a company called 23andMe began selling tests directly to
consumers for 107 conditions and traits, including BRCA cancer mutations,
Crohn's disease, cystic fibrosis, hemochromatosis, prostate cancer,
Parkinson's disease, and type 1 and 2 diabetes, as well as non-disease traits
as "avoidance of errors," "breastfeeding and IQ," "measures of intelligence,"
and "memory." Other companies followed. In 2013, the FDA issued warning
letters to these "direct-to-consumer" testing companies stating that they
were selling unapproved tests, and the companies halted health-related
testing. Then, in 2015, the FDA reviewed data submitted by 23andMe
under a new review approach and authorized it to sell a test to identify
carriers of a rare, autosomal-recessive blood disorder called Bloom
syndrome. In 2017, the FDA approved ten more DTC direct-to-consumer
health-related tests, followed, in March, 2018, by three breast cancer tests.

As discussed in Chapter 5, direct-to-consumer genetic testing raises a
number of concerns, including whether the tests actually measure what
they purport to, how well customers can understand the test results, how
well the testing companies protect customer privacy, and whether the
companies can sell or otherwise transfer the test results to others for
research or commercial purposes.

V. DNA FOR FORENSIC IDENTIFICATION

Law enforcement officials have used DNA to solve crimes since the
mid-1980s. More recently, they have used the results of geneology testing
to identify suspects in unsolved past crimes. Heather Murphy, Sooner or
Later Your Cousin's DNA Is Going to Solve a Murder, N. Y. Times, April
25, 2019 (https://www.nytimes.com/2019/04/25/us/golden-state-killer-dna.
html). As discussed in Chapter 20, this has raised concerns about the need
for more transparency about government access to test results and greater
privacy protections for direct-to-consumer genetic testing consumers.

VI. DO-IT-YOURSELF GENE EDITING

The development of cheaper, easier, and more accurate gene editing
techniques has expanded the ability to conduct gene editing experiments
outside of traditional corporate, academic, and government research
institutions. Experiments are taking place in basements and garages, and
in community laboratories, where people share materials and equipment.
One company sells CRISPR/Cas9 bacterial gene editing kits online. See
http://www.the-odin.com/diy-crispr-kit/. With one exception, there is little
regulation of these non-traditional forms of genetic experimentation; the
main oversight is by the FBI, which is concerned about bioterrorism. The
exception is a 2019 California law that prohibits the sale of CRISPR gene

editing kits without a notice that the kit is not for "self-administration." (Cal. Senate Bill 180, July 30, 2019). See Antonio Regalado, Don't change your DNA at home, says America's first CRISPR law, MIT Technology review, Aug. 9. 2019, https://www.technologyreview.com/s/614100/dont-change-your-dna-at-home-says-americas-first-crispr-law/. Questions have been raised about whether additional oversight is needed as gene editing techniques improve. See Patricia Zettler, Christi Guerrini, and Jacob Sherkow, Regulating Genetic Biohacking: Emphasize Community Engagement, Not Perfect Compliance, 365 Science 34–36 (2019).

VII. EPIGENETICS

The excitement over the increasing understanding of genetics has led to concerns that the role of genes may be overstated. The eugenics movement discussed in Chapter 2 is in part a reflection of such an overstatement. But how do genes and the environment interact? To what extent are humans and other organisms the product of their genes, and to what extent are they the product of environmental factors? Consideration of this question is known as the debate over "nature versus nurture."

Clearly genes are not solely responsible for how we appear or act. To take an obvious example, children may inherit genes for being tall and physically robust, but if they are not well-nourished and well-cared-for, they may well be short and frail when they grow up. For that matter, maternal exposure to certain harmful substances can affect offspring, without the effects necessarily being programmed in the children's genes. On the other hand, genetic science seemed to discredit the notion that changes produced by environmental factors could be passed on to descendants, a view most often associated with the 18th-century French naturalist Jean Baptiste Lamarck.

A growing field called epigenetics has caused a reappraisal of the effect of the environment on the functions of genes. It turns out that environmental conditions can cause certain chemical compounds to attach to DNA without changing the structure of the genes themselves. Instead, these compounds affect the functioning of the genes, such as activating or inactivating them. When cells make copies of their DNA as they divide, they also can copy these chemical compounds, passing them from one cell to the next. More surprisingly, they can be passed down from one generation to the next. For a description of epigenetics, see NIH National Human Genome Research Institute, https://www.genome.gov/about-genomics/fact-sheets/Epigenomics-Fact-Sheet.

Consider the implications of this discovery for social policy.

PART II

GENETIC SCREENING AND TESTING IN MEDICINE AND RESEARCH

■ ■ ■

There is considerable debate over the effects that new discoveries in human genetics will have on the practice of medicine. In an address to the Massachusetts Medical Society in May 1999, Francis S. Collins, then the director of the National Human Genome Research Institute at NIH, described how the isolation of disease genes will provide "the best hope for understanding human disease at its most fundamental level." Francis S. Collins, Shattuck Lecture—Medical and Societal Consequences of the Human Genome Project, 341 New Eng. J. Med. 28, 30 (1999). "Even before a gene's role in disease is fully understood," he went on, "diagnostic applications can be useful in preventing or minimizing the development of health consequences." He noted that "successes in reducing disease through treatment have been achieved for the hereditary disorders hemochromatosis, phenylketonuria, and familial hypercholesterolemia, among others. Risk reduction through early detection and lifestyle changes may be possible in the case of disorders associated with predisposing mutations, such as some cancers. As therapies build on knowledge gained about the molecular basis of disease, increasing numbers of illnesses that are now refractory to treatment may yield to molecular medicine in the future."

Collins also described the manner in which genetic knowledge will facilitate what is called "personalized genomic medicine":

> Identifying human genetic variations will eventually allow clinicians to subclassify diseases and adapt therapies to the individual patient. There may be large differences in the effectiveness of medicines from one person to the next. Toxic reactions can also occur and in many instances are likely to be a consequence of genetically encoded host factors. That basic observation has spawned the burgeoning new field of pharmacogenomics, which attempts to use information about genetic variation to predict responses to drug therapies.

* * *

Not only will genetic tests predict responsiveness to drugs on the market today, but also genetic approaches to disease prevention and treatment will include an expanding array of gene products for use in developing tomorrow's drug therapies. Since the Food and Drug Administration's approval of recombinant human insulin in 1982, over 50 additional gene-based drugs have become available for clinical use. These include drugs for the treatment of cancer, heart attack, stroke, and diabetes, as well as many vaccines.

Not all therapeutic advances for gene discovery will be genes or gene products. In other instances, molecular insights into a disorder, derived from gene discovery, will suggest a new treatment.

Id. at 33.

Francis Collins was just as optimistic six years later, when, in an article he wrote with Alan F. Guttmacher, he stressed the continued reduction in the cost of genetic sequencing as hastening the introduction of genomic medicine into clinical practice.

Not everyone agrees with these optimistic predictions about the imminence or significance of new genetic insights for the practice of medicine. In an essay entitled "Will Genetics Revolutionize Medicine?" for example, Neil Holtzman and Theresa Marteau assert that the development of treatments will lag behind the identification of genes that cause inherited disorders, and that only a small proportion of the population suffers from such disorders. Holtzman and Marteau caution against concentrating on genetics rather than the contributions that changes in social structure, lifestyle, and environment can make in improving the public health. For their views, see 343 New Eng. J. Med. 141 (2000). Limited successes in genetic medicine seem to bear out the pessimists' views: "Ten years after President Bill Clinton announced that the first draft of the human genome was complete, medicine has yet to see any large part of the promised benefits. For biologists, the genome has yielded one insightful surprise after another. But for some time, the primary goal of the $3 billion Human Genome Project—to ferret out the genetic roots of common diseases like cancer and Alzheimer's and then generate treatments—remained largely elusive. Indeed, after 10 years of effort, geneticists found themselves almost back to square one in knowing where to look for the roots of common disease." Nicholas Wade, A Decade Later, Genetic Map Yields Few New Cures, The New York Times, June 13, 2010, at A1.

Nevertheless, as costs of sequencing decline, genomic analysis is affecting clinical care. It is used to guide the treatment of cancer, offer improved prenatal screening tests, and is providing "early triumphs with rare inherited diseases." Just four years after the pessimistic declaration in the New York Times, an article in the Washington Post predicted that "medicine will, within a few years, start advancing at the same pace as the Internet and software" leading to "a revolution in health care." Vivek Wadhwa, The Triumph of Genomic Medicine is Just Beginning, Wash. Post, Mar. 13, 2014, https://www.washingtonpost.com/news/innovations/wp/2014/03/13/the-triumph-of-genomic-medicine-is-just-beginning/.

This part examines the various ways in which genetic advances are used in the medical context, whether to identify susceptibility to disease, to influence treatment decisions, or to make reproductive decisions. Although genetic testing can be for non-clinical purposes, such as forensics, (discussed in Part V, Chapters 18–21), this Part focuses on genetic testing and screening in medicine and research.

Chapter 5 sets the stage by describing the development of genetic technologies that are used in both clinical care and research. It then examines the use of biobanks so central to genetics and genomics research, as well as the relevant regulations of human subjects research. In addition, it explores the regulation of genetic testing and laboratories, as well as the growing field of direct-to-consumer genetic testing.

Chapters 6 to 10 explore genetic testing in various medical contexts. Chapter 6 begins with a description of genetic counseling, which is offered with most types of genetic testing in clinical settings. The main focus of this chapter is on genetic testing to identify susceptibility to disease and the associated ethical and liability issues that may arise with such testing. Chapter 7 explores issues associated with genomic analysis and identification of incidental findings, cancer genomics, and genetic testing of children.

Chapter 8 turns to reproductive genetic testing and screening during pregnancy or before implantation of embryos created through in vitro fertilization. In addition to describing the various technologies for such testing, it discusses the unique wrongful birth and life claims that are sometimes brought when health care providers are allegedly negligent in this context. It also addresses issues associated with carrier testing, which can inform reproductive decisions. Chapter 9 then considers the ethical and legal concerns when reproductive genetic testing is used to make reproductive decisions based on non-medical traits in the fetus or embryo, to select for future children *with* disabilities, or to select for future children based on whether they could be donors for sick children. Finally, Chapter 10 discusses genetic analysis through newborn screening programs administered through state public health programs, including the appropriate scope of such screening, parental consent, and the use of newborn samples for research.

CHAPTER 5

GENETICS RESEARCH AND THE REGULATION OF GENETIC TESTING AND MARKETING

■ ■ ■

I. GENETIC TESTING TECHNOLOGY

Information about an individual's genetic endowment can come from a variety of sources, such as family history, physical appearance, and physical examination (including laboratory tests for levels of cholesterol, blood glucose, and other chemicals that may vary, to some degree, as a result of genes). This chapter focuses on one specific type of laboratory testing: DNA analysis.

Until fairly recently, knowledge about an individual's genetic inheritance was based on indirect information, such as observations of the symptoms of genetic disease, detection of gene products (e.g., elevated chloride levels in the sweat of persons with cystic fibrosis), or descriptions of symptoms in other family members. In addition, cell nuclei can be collected and cultured and a visual image (karyotype) obtained of the chromosomes. This permits the detection of chromosomal abnormalities such as trisomy 21 or Down syndrome, caused by an extra copy of chromosome 21. Originally, the chromosomes were visually inspected under a microscope. More recently, a technique called FISH (for "Fluorescence In Situ Hybridization") employs fluorescence to "paint" the chromosomes.

A more direct type of information about genes can be obtained by linkage analysis. This technique is used when the exact location and sequence of the disease gene (or genes) is not yet known. Linkage analysis relies on the identification of "markers," which are stretches of DNA believed to be near to or containing disease genes—and on an analysis of DNA from family members. (The analysis of DNA from family members is necessary because markers differ among families.)

In the mid-1980s a young scientist, Kary Mullis, developed a method called polymerase chain reaction or PCR. This technique is used to copy, or amplify, small fragments of DNA within a test tube. For DNA testing, a sample of DNA is mixed with three types of chemicals: a primer, which attaches to the DNA and begins the duplication process; an enzyme that makes copies of the DNA; and the nucleotides that are necessary to form the duplicates. This mixture is put in a machine that increases and reduces the temperature every few minutes, doubling the "target" sequence with each cycle. This results in hundreds of millions of copies in a matter of hours. When the final mixture is run through an electrophoretic gel, the amplified stretch of DNA can be seen visually as a band at a known position on the gel. This technique can be used to copy a specific stretch of the DNA that contains the target mutation. If the target mutation is present, it will be amplified and appear on the gel.

PCR is fast and inexpensive. However, it has some limitations, such as the fact that it does not provide information about the entire sequence of the gene, so that if certain mutations are not known or are not tested for, they can be missed.

The third and most sophisticated technique is called DNA sequencing. In the most common type of sequencing, developed by Fred Sanger, a stretch of DNA is amplified and single strands of it are produced. Again, a primer chemical and enzymes are added which make copies of the DNA, but this time the mixture contains special nucleotides that stop the copying at specific points depending on where they are incorporated into the copied sequence. This produces fragments of different lengths. The reaction is repeated four times, for each of the four nucleotides, and the result is run through an electrophoretic gel which reveals the location of the different nucleotides on the original stretch of DNA. The resulting sequence of bases is then analyzed to reveal mutations. This technique yields the most detailed information compared to the others, but is more expensive and time consuming and requires large quantities of DNA.

While Sanger sequencing is still considered the gold-standard to sequence a person's DNA, it is costly and time-inefficient. Since the mid-2000s, next-generation sequencing (NGS) has offered a cheaper and faster method to analyze both short and long DNA sequences. NGS amplifies a section of DNA clonally and then, like Sanger sequencing, tags the DNA. However, NGS allows for multiple analyses to run in parallel instead of sequentially, like that of Sanger sequencing. The improvement in speed and cost has increased the use of NGS for whole genome analysis. In addition, NGS allows for short and long DNA strand analysis for research and diagnostic purposes.

Most recently, DNA chips have been developed that speed the analysis by several orders of magnitude. These consist of a small glass plate encased in plastic which is manufactured using a process similar to the one used to make computer microchips. The surface of the glass plate, or chip, contains a number of synthetic, single-stranded DNA sequences corresponding to stretches of bases in a "normal" gene. A sample of the individual's DNA, together with a sample of "normal" DNA, are separated into single strands, cut into more manageable sizes, and labeled with different fluorescent dyes—for example, green for the individual's and red for the normal sample. Both samples are then inserted into the chip. There, they bind with any sequences on the chip that have a complementary set of bases. Both a normal sequence from the individual and the corresponding sequence from the normal sample will bind to the complementary sequence on the chip, creating a position on the chip that is red and green. If the individual's sample has a mutation in that sequence, however, only the normal sample will bind to the chip, leaving a position that is red. The result is then analyzed to reveal which mutations, if any, are present in the patient's DNA. The advantage of chips over conventional methods is that they require smaller DNA samples, and can run tests in parallel to detect large numbers of mutations.

For more information about advances in genetic testing, see Sara Goodwin, et al., Coming of Age: Ten Years of Next-Generation Sequencing Technologies, 17 Nature Rev. Genetics 333 (2016); Sara Katsanis & Nicholas Katsanis, Molecular Genetic Testing and the Future of Clinical Genomics, 14 Nature Rev. Genetics 415 (2013).

II. BIOBANKS AND GENETIC RESEARCH

NATIONAL BIOETHICS ADVISORY COMMISSION (NBAC), RESEARCH INVOLVING HUMAN BIOLOGICAL MATERIALS: ETHICAL ISSUES AND POLICY GUIDANCE
1–14 (1999).

Biomedical researchers have long studied human biological materials—such as cells collected in research projects, biopsy specimens obtained for diagnostic purposes, and organs and tissues removed during surgery—to increase knowledge about human diseases and to develop better means of preventing, diagnosing, and treating these diseases. Today, new technologies and advances in biology provide even more effective tools for using such resources to improve medicine's diagnostic and therapeutic potential. Yet, the very power of these new technologies raises a number of important ethical issues.

Is it appropriate to use stored biological materials in ways that originally were not contemplated either by the people from whom the materials came or by those who collected the materials? Does such use harm anyone's interest? Does it matter whether the material is identified, or identifiable, as to its source, or is linked, or linkable, to other medical or personal data regarding the source?

* * *

Although protection of human subjects in research is of primary concern in the U.S. biomedical research system, research that uses biological materials—materials that often are distanced in time and space from the persons from whom they were obtained—raises unique challenges regarding the appropriate protection of research subjects.

* * *

Policies and guidelines governing human subjects research should permit investigators—under certain circumstances and with the informed, voluntary consent of sample sources—to have access to identifying information sufficient to enable them to gather necessary data regarding the subjects. Provided that adequate protections exist (which usually, but not always, include informed consent), such information gathering could include ongoing collection of medical records data and even requests for individuals to undergo tests to provide additional research information. In some cases, it even will be acceptable for investigators to convey information about research results to the persons whose samples have been studied. Where identifying information exists, however, a well-developed system of protections must be implemented to ensure that risks are minimized and that the interests of sample sources are protected.

* * *

How well does the existing Federal Policy for the Protection of Human Subjects (the so-called Common Rule, codified at 45 C.F.R. Part 46) meet these objectives? Specifically, does it provide clear direction to research sponsors, investigators, IRBs, and others regarding the conduct of research using human biological materials in an ethical manner? NBAC finds that it does not adequately do so. In some cases, present regulatory language provides ambiguous guidance for research using human biological materials. For example, confusion about the intended meaning of terms such as "human subject," "publicly available," and "minimal risk" has stymied investigators and IRB members. Beyond these ambiguities, certain parts of current regulations are inadequate to ensure the ethical use of human biological materials in research and require some modification.

HEATHER L. HARRELL AND MARK A. ROTHSTEIN, BIOBANKING RESEARCH AND PRIVACY LAWS IN THE UNITED STATES

44 J. L. Med. & Ethics 106, 106–114 (2016).

* * *

II.   Biobanking Framework

"Biobanks are repositories that assemble, store, and manage collections of human specimens and related data."2 Biobanks may be either specialty (e.g., cancer) or more general banks and may or may not have associated data, although most do. Databases may contain genetic sequencing information, as well as medical, demographic, family history, environmental, and other data. As used in this article, the term "data" refers to any or all of these types of information.

Technological advances have allowed for the creation and storage of more health and personal data. By combining samples and data from numerous sources researchers are better able to elucidate subtle connections between genetics and health, identify ways in which genetic variants contribute to illness, and obtain powerful research results through large sample sizes. The biobank and database framework in the United States reflects the fact that many biobanks and databases participate in consortia or collaborations. The umbrella organizations in these consortia may function as biobanks themselves (e.g., Genetic Alliance Registry and Biobank) or may provide policies and guidelines that facilitate partnerships for their member banks (e.g., International Cancer Genome Consortium (ICGC) and Global Alliance for Genomics and Health (GA4GH)). Even biobanks without a relationship with other biobanks or databases may have policies for specimen and data sharing.

A.   *Structure and Contents*

In 2012, there were more than 630 biobanks in the US, and most had an affiliation with other health care or research institutions. In 2015, President Obama announced the creation of a new biobank of data and samples from more than one million Americans under the Precision Medicine Initiative directed by the NIH. The federal government is also building a database and biobank of one million veterans established by the Department of Veterans Affairs.

Few biobanks are stand-alone entities. In one study, 88% of responding biobanks indicated they were part of larger organizations and 16% said they were part of a network, consortium, or other group of biobanks that engage in collaborative research. For instance, the Children's Hospital of Philadelphia (CHOP) Research Institute Biorepository is a member of the Children's Brain Tumor Tissue Consortium and Vanderbilt University's BioVU is part of NHGRI's eMERGE network, PAGE network, IMSGC, IIBDGC, COGENT, African American BMI GWAS Consortium, and Osteoporotic Bone Fracture Consortium of African Ancestry Populations. Most of the biobanks that are part of larger organizations are found in academic institutions and more than a quarter of biobanks are part of more than one larger organization.

Biobanks serve either academic, government, or industry researchers, with industry biobanks, unsurprisingly, serving a higher percentage of industry researchers. Similarly, academic and government biobanks tend to serve predominantly (significantly more than half) academic and government researchers. However, these classifications do not necessarily reflect bright-line policies, in part because any one biobank may have many different sources of funding. "The federal government is the largest funding source for 36% of biobanks and provided some amount of funding in the past 5 years to 57% of responding biobanks." After federal funding, financial support from a parent organization was the next largest source of funds, followed by fee for service. There are numerous organizational and financial models. For example, the Marshfield Clinic Personalized Medicine Research Project is funded by the state of Wisconsin and the Marshfield Clinic. The Cancer Human Biobank (CHB) started as a federal government organization, but plans to change into a public-private partnership.

Biobanks range greatly in the number and types of specimens stored, with serum/plasma, solid tissue, blood, and bone marrow the most common types of specimens. Most biobanks store more than one type of specimen and also have some type of associated data. Biobanks that are part of clinics or academic medical centers collect specimens predominantly, if not exclusively, from their own patient populations (e.g., CHoP, BioVU, Marshfield, Geisinger). Some biobanks collect specimens from diverse populations, such as the International HapMap Project and the Collaborative Human Tissue Network (CHTN). Others collect and share research results, such as the NCBI Database of Genotypes and Phenotypes (dbGaP).

B.   Internal Governance and Rules

Some biobanks make their internal governance more transparent to the general public than others, but approximately 80% of biobanks have internal oversight boards of some kind. Almost all responding biobanks in one study require IRB approval for researchers requesting specimen use, and 26% have a community advisory board, although these boards have different purposes, such as advising on general policies or revising protocols. For example, the Coriell Personalized Medicine Collaborative is a multi-party research study that uses genetic information along with family history, lifestyle, and environmental factors to study pharmaceutical reactions and disease risk. It has two advisory boards guiding the research project, one focused on genetic links to health conditions and one focused on pharmacogenetics. The Genetic Alliance, a health advocacy collaboration of disease-specific advocacy groups, sponsors the Genetic Alliance Registry and Biobank. It has one board composed of representatives from disease advocacy groups and experienced outside directors from a variety of disciplines, as well as its own IRB and BioTrust Ethics Team. The Genetic Alliance also has a board of directors focused on financial matters.

C.   Specimen and Data Access

Generally, specimens and data may be accessed through variations based on one of three basic access models: open access, tiered access, or controlled access. Open access allows unrestricted access to data by anyone, such as where data are placed on a public website. Controlled access is at the opposite end of the spectrum, where access is restricted to certain approved researchers and research protocols. Tiered access is conceptually in the middle and sets access restrictions based on donor consent, the nature and content of the data or specimens, or the type of research use of the specimens and data.

As noted, many of the biobanks and databases are in consortia or collaborations. One means by which a consortium or collaboration may function is having "decentralized resources deployed through a virtual network of geographically dispersed tissue centers coordinated and supported by a centralized bioinformatics and data management system networked across the country," such as the CHTN. The CHTN collects leftover clinical specimens that meet the needs of researchers submitting a request to the network; in other words, the network organizes diffuse tissue collection and distribution to requesting researchers.

Almost all biobanks require IRB approval before researchers may access specimens, and many have a panel or committee to review requests for specimens. More than half of all biobanks do not approve all researcher requests for specimens—most commonly because of a lack of scientific merit, unavailability of specimens, or donor limitations. An example of tiered access is dbGaP, which collects and distributes study results investigating phenotype/genotype associations and places group data in open access tiers; it permits individual-level data to be accessed "based on varying levels of authorization." In accessing the dbGaP, there is variation in whether IRB approval is required. However, in gaining IRB approval for data submission to dbGaP, some researchers reported that IRBs restricted release of data to dbGaP by requiring the reconsent of research participants.

The National Cancer Institute (NCI) has issued best practices for NCI-supported "biospecimen resources," which cover operational, technical, ethical, legal, and policy aspects of biospecimens. Under the policy, access levels must be approved by an institution's IRB or scientific board, and access must be limited to those whose functions necessitate access. The number of individuals who need access to data or specimens must be kept to a minimum and access must be monitored. These policies must be documented and transparent, and include auditing procedures, enforcement measures, and required training for employees.

The NIH has issued a policy on genomic data sharing that emphasizes sharing rather than restricting access to genomic data. The policy applies to all NIH-funded, large-scale human and non-human research projects that generate genomic data. The NIH funds a little over one-fourth of all research in the United States, including genomic research. Researchers applying for NIH grants are expected to explain how genetic data will be shared (usually depositing the data in an NIH repository), and peer reviewers will comment on the genomic data sharing plan, but it will not generally be factored into a grant application's overall impact score.

Although some level of data sharing is expected, privacy protections are a required part of the NIH policy. Data are stored in a two-tiered system based on data sensitivity and privacy concerns. Only if individuals give specific informed consent for open access will de-identified data about them be placed on a publicly available website. Access to controlled access genomic data generated through NIH-sponsored studies is limited to those who request access, share their plans for data use, and state their intention to abide by the NIH Genomic Data User Code of Conduct. Approval of data access is granted by the NIH Data Access Committee. For controlled-access data, access is limited to one year unless a renewal is sought. The dbGaP's data sharing policy may be perceived to contradict local IRB practices, specific consent parameters, or some countries' laws.

. . .

F.   Security

Many biobanks and databases, including many consortia, provide few details about how data and specimens are secure beyond stating that they are kept secure. Common security measures are restricted access to specimens and data, locked facilities housing specimens and data, and destruction or return of data or specimens after use. Some biobanks or consortia suggest that security measures should reflect the nature and use of the data or specimens. The NCI Biorepository and Biospecimen Research Branch, Biospecimen Research Network recommends such proportional security measures.

Other biobanks provide more specific information about security on their websites. For example, the Marshfield Clinic's Personalized Medicine Project indicates that research information is kept on a separate computer system from clinical information and that the separate system, housed in a secure location, is not connected to any external networks. Coriell states that it is audited by an independent security consulting firm. The dbGaP specifies that security is the responsibility of the recipient institution once the data have been received. The Million Veterans Program states that computer and building access will be restricted, information and specimens will be coded, sharing will be only with US academic institutions and federal agencies, and researchers will be "vetted" before data are shared.

III. Legal and Regulatory Privacy Framework

Research and privacy laws are applicable to both biobanks and researchers. The laws are often complicated and confusing, and therefore determining which laws are even applicable to biobanks can be particularly difficult. Each biobank performs a unique set of functions and has a unique set of relationships; those functions and relationships often determine which laws and policies are relevant to a certain set of circumstances. By contrast, researchers only must pass one threshold test—whether they are engaged in research.

1.   Common Rule.

The Common Rule and parallel FDA regulations are the primary human subjects protection regulations in the United States. The Common Rule gained its name because the research policy was adopted by 18 federal agencies, and is therefore "common" in federal law. The Common Rule was written by the Department of Health and Human Services (DHHS), originally the Department of Health, Education and Welfare. Because NIH is an agency of DHHS, NIH-funded research is subject to the Common Rule. Rather than adopting the Common Rule, the FDA created its own regulations addressing the same core components of research, and the FDA regulations are applicable to research performed in contemplation of submission to the FDA.

Generally, the Common Rule applies "to all research involving human subjects conducted, supported or otherwise subject to regulation by any federal department or agency which takes appropriate administrative action to make the policy applicable to such research." "Most American academic and health care institutions conducting human subjects research agree to adhere to the Common Rule for all of their research protocols regardless of the funding source for a specific study, as a condition of the institution receiving a Federalwide Assurance (FWA) from the DHHS Office for Human Research Protections (OHRP)." Thus, biobank research, if conducted through such an institution, must comply with the Common Rule regardless of funding source.

Research under the Common Rule is defined as "a systematic investigation, including research development, testing and evaluation, designed to develop or contribute to generalizable knowledge." Because research requires investigation, merely aggregating and archiving information and specimens is not considered research. In other words, a biobank may not be conducting research depending on whether it has additional functions beyond banking specimens. A researcher using specimens from a biobank, however, is engaged in research.

To be subject to the Common Rule, a biobank, database, or researcher must be involved in "human subjects research." Under the regulations, "human subject" is defined as "a living individual about whom an investigator (whether professional or student) conducting research obtains (1) data through intervention or interaction with the individual, or (2) identifiable private information." "Intervention includes both physical procedures by which data are gathered. . .and manipulations of the subject or the subject's environment that are performed for research purposes. Interaction includes communication or interpersonal contact between investigator and subject." If a biobank is involved in research, then its collection of specimens directly from the donor would mean the biobank is engaged in human subjects research.

Private information must be individually identifiable in order for obtaining the information to constitute research involving human subjects. Private information is individually identifiable when it can be linked to specific individuals by the investigator either directly or indirectly through coding systems. It is likely biobanks have identifiable private information if health data are linked to specimens, as is a common practice for biobanks. Thus, the Common Rule may apply to both biobanks (if engaged in research) and researchers under this provision.

Research involving only coded specimens, however, is not considered human subjects research if the information or specimens "were not collected specifically for the currently proposed research project through an interaction or intervention with living individuals" and either the identity of the individual(s) "cannot be readily ascertain[ed]" because of an agreement between investigators and key holder to not release the code until death, there are "IRB-approved written policies and operating procedures for a repository or data management center that prohibit the release of the key to the investigators under any circumstances, until the individuals are deceased," or some other "legal requirement prohibits the release of the key to the investigators."

Under this guidance, researchers using coded biobank materials or data are not involved in human subjects research as long as the researcher cannot access the key to the code. Biobanks may or may not be the keyholder if their specimens and data are coded. Generally, most biobanks do not have de-identified samples. Although the current applicability of the Common Rule depends on the identifiability of the data, the proposed revision of the Common Rule (discussed below) would make de-identified specimens subject to the Common Rule. Furthermore, even at the present time, overall biobank protocols are subject to IRB review, regardless of identifiability.

An exemption from the Common Rule of relevance to biobank research is for "[r]esearch involving the collection or study of existing data, documents, records, pathological specimens, or diagnostic specimens, if these sources are publicly available or if the information is recorded by the investigator in such a manner that subjects cannot be identified, directly or through identifiers linked to the subjects." Because the purpose of biobanks and databases is to compile specimens and data, this exemption more logically applies to the researcher than the biobank or database.

If a biobank, database, or researcher is subject to the Common Rule, then the research must be reviewed by an IRB, the local bodies charged with implementing the Common Rule to protect human subjects. IRBs decide whether to approve research based on an evaluation of risks and benefits, including whether the risks are minimized and reasonable in relation to anticipated benefits and the importance of the knowledge that may reasonably be expected to result. Among the risks of a particular research project, an IRB must consider whether there are adequate provisions to protect the privacy of subjects and to maintain the confidentiality of data. IRBs also review studies for compliance with informed consent and other requirements.

Informed consent must include "[a] statement describing the extent, if any, to which confidentiality of records identifying the subject will be maintained." Disclosure of privacy and confidentiality protections allows individuals to determine the sufficiency of the protections, and to decide whether to participate.

There are two instances when an IRB can waive or alter the informed consent requirement. The first instance is when the only record linking the subject and the research would be the consent document and the principal risk would be potential harm resulting from a breach of confidentiality. Such a waiver is applicable in the context of biobank research. The other instance is when the research could not practicably be carried out without the waiver or alteration, the waiver or alteration will not adversely affect the rights and welfare of the subjects, the research entails no more than minimal risk, and, as needed, the subjects will be provided with additional pertinent information after participation. Therefore, a waiver could be granted for biobank-based research if the risks are considered minimal and recontact of donors may be impossible or impracticable depending on how the specimens are de-identified or coded. Thus, even if biobank research is subject to the Common Rule, it is likely that investigators could get informed consent requirements waived and then they would only have to "adequately" protect privacy and confidentiality. If a biobank or researcher only deals with unidentifiable data and does not collect the specimens itself, the research conducted with its data and specimens is not human subjects research. Finally, research may be exempt if the investigator deals only with existing data and the subjects cannot be identified.

* * *

2. FDA Regulations

The FDA regulations generally mirror the Common Rule, thereby vesting decision-making in the hands of the local IRB. The FDA regulations are applicable when researching investigational drugs or medical devices with human subjects. "Subject means a human who participates in an investigation, either as an individual on whom or on whose specimen an investigational device is used or as a control." Thus, the FDA regulations are applicable to research on specimens, not data. Therefore, biobanks are subject to FDA regulations if they are engaged in research with their specimens, or researchers are using biobank specimens in their studies if the research studies an investigational drug or medical device. Interestingly, the FDA may be expanding its regulatory coverage over biobank research by asserting jurisdiction over sponsor-investigator genomic studies and blurring the lines between use and investigation of next generation sequencing in research.

When applicable, FDA regulations address requirements for informed consent and IRB review. Despite the importance of informed consent to privacy protection, the FDA has carved out an exception to the informed consent requirement relevant to biobank research in the exercise of its enforcement discretion. The crux of this exception is that the specimen not be individually identifiable. Consistent with the Common Rule, the FDA regulation provides: "A specimen is not individually identifiable when the identity of the subject is not known to or may not readily be ascertained by the investigator or by any other individuals associated with the investigation, including the sponsor." A specimen "will be considered to be not individually identifiable if neither the investigator(s) nor any other individuals associated with the investigation or the sponsor can link the specimen to the subject from whom the specimen was collected, either directly or indirectly through coding systems." This exception is narrower though comparable to the treatment of coded data under the Common Rule. IRBs must review "policies and procedures followed by the specimen provider to ensure that the subject cannot be identified."

3. CLIA

The Clinical Laboratory Improvement Act and Amendments (CLIA) applies to laboratories or clinical laboratories, terms defined as "a facility for the biological, microbiological, serological, chemical, immune-hematological, hematological, biophysical, cytological, pathological, or other examination of materials derived from the human body for the purpose of providing information for the diagnosis, prevention or treatment of any disease or impairment of, or the assessment of the health of, human beings." Under CLIA, it is unlawful to "solicit or accept materials derived from the human body for laboratory examination or other procedure unless there is in effect for the laboratory a certificate issued by the Secretary under this section applicable to the category of examinations or procedures which includes such examination or procedure." For all laboratories performing non-waived tests, the laboratory must ensure the confidentiality of patient information throughout all phases of the testing process that are under the laboratory's control. "The laboratory must establish and follow written policies and procedures that ensure positive identification and optimum integrity of a patient's specimen from the time of collection or receipt of the specimen through completion of testing and reporting of results."

Generally, test results must be released only to authorized persons and, if applicable, the persons responsible for using the test results and the laboratory that initially requested the test. An authorized person is an individual authorized under state law to order tests, receive test results, or both. Therefore, state laws may restrict from whom a laboratory may accept a test request and to whom test results may be provided. "Research laboratories that test human specimens but do not report patient specific results for the diagnosis, prevention or treatment of any disease or impairment of, or the assessment of the health of individual patients" are excepted from CLIA. There may be some ambiguity in interpreting this exception, mainly determining the definitions of "diagnosis," "prevention," "treatment," and "assessment of the health of individual patients." Despite the ambiguity, a majority of biobanks could fall under this exception and would not require CLIA certification.

About half the states provide that individuals may order tests directly from the laboratory and, in these states, individuals would have a right to access test results in the context of research. Furthermore, a 2013 amendment to the HIPAA Privacy Rule removed CLIA-based exceptions to individuals' right of access to protected health information. Thus, a HIPAA-covered laboratory, including a biobank, must allow access to results when the laboratory can authenticate that the test report pertains to the patient. This required return of results under HIPAA or state law may remove a biobank from the CLIA exception, thereby requiring compliance with CLIA.

DEPARTMENT OF HEALTH AND HUMAN SERVICES, PROTECTION OF HUMAN SUBJECTS, 45 CFR PART 46, SUBPART A: BASIC HHS POLICY FOR PROTECTION OF HUMAN SUBJECTS RESEARCH

§ 46.116   General requirements for informed consent.

(a) *General.* General requirements for informed consent, whether written or oral, are set forth in this paragraph and apply to consent obtained in accordance with the requirements set forth in paragraphs (b) through (d) of this section. Broad consent may be obtained in lieu of informed consent obtained in accordance with paragraphs (b) and (c) of this section only with respect to the storage, maintenance, and secondary research uses of identifiable private information and identifiable biospecimens. Waiver or alteration of consent in research involving public benefit and service programs conducted by or subject to the approval of state or local officials is described in paragraph (e) of this section. General waiver or alteration of informed consent is described in paragraph (f) of this section. Except as provided elsewhere in this policy:

(1) Before involving a human subject in research covered by this policy, an investigator shall obtain the legally effective informed consent of the subject or the subject's legally authorized representative.

(2) An investigator shall seek informed consent only under circumstances that provide the prospective subject or the legally authorized representative sufficient opportunity to discuss and consider whether or not to participate and that minimize the possibility of coercion or undue influence.

(3) The information that is given to the subject or the legally authorized representative shall be in language understandable to the subject or the legally authorized representative.

(4) The prospective subject or the legally authorized representative must be provided with the information that a reasonable person would want to have in order to make an informed decision about whether to participate, and an opportunity to discuss that information.

(5) Except for broad consent obtained in accordance with paragraph (d) of this section:

(i) Informed consent must begin with a concise and focused presentation of the key information that is most likely to assist a prospective subject or legally authorized representative in understanding the reasons why one might or might not want to participate in the research. This part of the informed consent must be organized and presented in a way that facilitates comprehension.

(ii) Informed consent as a whole must present information in sufficient detail relating to the research, and must be organized and presented in a way that does not merely provide lists of isolated facts, but rather facilitates the prospective subject's or legally authorized representative's understanding of the reasons why one might or might not want to participate.

(6) No informed consent may include any exculpatory language through which the subject or the legally authorized representative is made to waive or appear to waive any of the subject's legal rights, or releases or appears to release the investigator, the sponsor, the institution, or its agents from liability for negligence.

(b) *Basic elements of informed consent.* Except as provided in paragraph (d), (e), or (f) of this section, in seeking informed consent the following information shall be provided to each subject or the legally authorized representative:

(1) A statement that the study involves research, an explanation of the purposes of the research and the expected duration of the subject's participation, a description of the procedures to be followed, and identification of any procedures that are experimental;

(2) A description of any reasonably foreseeable risks or discomforts to the subject;

(3) A description of any benefits to the subject or to others that may reasonably be expected from the research;

(4) A disclosure of appropriate alternative procedures or courses of treatment, if any, that might be advantageous to the subject;

(5) A statement describing the extent, if any, to which confidentiality of records identifying the subject will be maintained;

(6) For research involving more than minimal risk, an explanation as to whether any compensation and an explanation as to whether any medical treatments are available if injury occurs and, if so, what they consist of, or where further information may be obtained;

(7) An explanation of whom to contact for answers to pertinent questions about the research and research subjects' rights, and whom to contact in the event of a research-related injury to the subject;

(8) A statement that participation is voluntary, refusal to participate will involve no penalty or loss of benefits to which the subject is otherwise entitled, and the subject may discontinue participation at any time without penalty or loss of benefits to which the subject is otherwise entitled; and

(9) One of the following statements about any research that involves the collection of identifiable private information or identifiable biospecimens:

(i) A statement that identifiers might be removed from the identifiable private information or identifiable biospecimens and that, after such removal, the information or biospecimens could be used for future research studies or distributed to another investigator for future research studies without additional informed consent from the subject or the legally authorized representative, if this might be a possibility; or

(ii) A statement that the subject's information or biospecimens collected as part of the research, even if identifiers are removed, will not be used or distributed for future research studies.

(c) *Additional elements of informed consent.* Except as provided in paragraph (d), (e), or (f) of this section, one or more of the following elements of information, when appropriate, shall also be provided to each subject or the legally authorized representative:

(1) A statement that the particular treatment or procedure may involve risks to the subject (or to the embryo or fetus, if the subject is or may become pregnant) that are currently unforeseeable;

(2) Anticipated circumstances under which the subject's participation may be terminated by the investigator without regard to the subject's or the legally authorized representative's consent;

(3) Any additional costs to the subject that may result from participation in the research;

(4) The consequences of a subject's decision to withdraw from the research and procedures for orderly termination of participation by the subject;

(5) A statement that significant new findings developed during the course of the research that may relate to the subject's willingness to continue participation will be provided to the subject;

(6) The approximate number of subjects involved in the study;

(7) A statement that the subject's biospecimens (even if identifiers are removed) may be used for commercial profit and whether the subject will or will not share in this commercial profit;

(8) A statement regarding whether clinically relevant research results, including individual research results, will be disclosed to subjects, and if so, under what conditions; and

(9) For research involving biospecimens, whether the research will (if known) or might include whole genome sequencing (*i.e.,* sequencing of a human germline or somatic specimen with the intent to generate the genome or exome sequence of that specimen).

(d) *Elements of broad consent for the storage, maintenance, and secondary research use of identifiable private information or identifiable biospecimens.* Broad consent for the storage, maintenance, and secondary research use of identifiable private information or identifiable biospecimens (collected for either research studies other than the proposed research or nonresearch purposes) is permitted as an alternative to the informed consent requirements in paragraphs (b) and (c) of this section. If the subject or the legally authorized representative is asked to provide broad consent, the following shall be provided to each subject or the subject's legally authorized representative:

(1) The information required in paragraphs (b)(2), (b)(3), (b)(5), and (b)(8) and, when appropriate, (c)(7) and (9) of this section;

(2) A general description of the types of research that may be conducted with the identifiable private information or identifiable biospecimens. This description must include sufficient information such that a reasonable person would expect that the broad consent would permit the types of research conducted;

(3) A description of the identifiable private information or identifiable biospecimens that might be used in research, whether sharing of identifiable private information or identifiable biospecimens might occur, and the types of institutions or researchers that might conduct research with the identifiable private information or identifiable biospecimens;

(4) A description of the period of time that the identifiable private information or identifiable biospecimens may be stored and maintained (which period of time could be indefinite), and a description of the period of time that the identifiable private information or identifiable biospecimens may be used for research purposes (which period of time could be indefinite);

(5) Unless the subject or legally authorized representative will be provided details about specific research studies, a statement that they will not be informed of the details of any specific research studies that might be conducted using the subject's identifiable private information or identifiable biospecimens, including the purposes of the research, and that they might have chosen not to consent to some of those specific research studies;

(6) Unless it is known that clinically relevant research results, including individual research results, will be disclosed to the subject in all circumstances, a statement that such results may not be disclosed to the subject; and

(7) An explanation of whom to contact for answers to questions about the subject's rights and about storage and use of the subject's identifiable private information or identifiable biospecimens, and whom to contact in the event of a research-related harm.

HOLLY FERNANDEZ LYNCH, LESLIE E. WOLF, AND MARK BARNES, IMPLEMENTING REGULATORY BROAD CONSENT UNDER THE REVISED COMMON RULE: CLARIFYING KEY POINTS AND THE NEED FOR EVIDENCE

47 J. Law, Med. & Ethics 213 (2019).

When researchers carry out their studies, the data they collect from participants may also be useful for future, distinct analyses. They might also collect biospecimens for research purposes, either specifically for a research repository or for a hypothesis-driven protocol in which some specimens may be leftover once primary research uses are complete.

Specimens collected in clinical care and left over after their clinical use also may be useful for research, and clinical data such as patient health records can offer insight into a range of research questions. There are also vast troves of data collected about us in everyday life, which may be of interest to researchers: our Google searches, AppleWatch data, credit card transactions, geotracking, and much more. Importantly, it is only when entities use federal funding to conduct research with biospecimens and data that the uses might fall within the purview of the Common Rule; that will be our focus here.

* * *

The revised Common Rule includes a new option for the conduct of secondary research with identifiable data and biospecimens: regulatory broad consent. Motivated by concerns regarding autonomy and trust in the research enterprise, regulators had initially proposed broad consent in a manner that would have rendered it the exclusive approach to secondary research with all biospecimens, regardless of identifiability. Based on public comments from both researchers and patients concerned that this approach would hinder important medical advances, however, regulators decided to largely preserve the status quo approach to secondary research with biospecimens and data. The Final Rule therefore allows such research to proceed without specific informed consent in a number of circumstances, but it also offers regulatory broad consent as a new, optional pathway for secondary research with identifiable data and biospecimens. In this article, we describe the parameters of regulatory broad consent under the new rule, explain why researchers and research institutions are unlikely to utilize it, outline recommendations for regulatory broad consent issued by the Secretary's Advisory Committee on Human Research Protections (SACHRP), and sketch an empirical research agenda for the sorts of questions about regulatory broad consent that remain to be answered as the research community embarks on Final Rule implementation.

For decades, researchers have relied on biospecimens and data leftover after collection for other purposes to make important scientific and medical advances—and the law has afforded a number of mechanisms to facilitate such "secondary" research, often without consent from the human sources from whom the specimens or data were derived. At the start of the twenty-first century, however, the previously arcane issue of aconsensual secondary research began to gain public prominence. For example, in 2004, members of the Havasupai Tribe brought a lawsuit against Arizona State University alleging that blood samples originally provided for research on diabetes had been used without their knowledge or consent for other types of genetic studies, including those exposing tribe members to stigma regarding mental illness and challenging their deeply held beliefs regarding tribal ancestry. In 2009, parents in Texas filed suit claiming research use of leftover blood spots from their newborns' mandatory public health screenings was a violation of liberty and privacy rights, as well as the right against unreasonable search and seizure; parents in other states have done the same. In both the Havsupai and blood spot litigation, resulting settlements entailed the removal of remaining specimens from research use, either through destruction or return. The debate about newborn blood spots also resulted in responsive legislation at both state and federal levels.

These examples received national news coverage, but the greatest public awakening regarding biospecimen research is probably traceable to the bestselling book, *The Immortal Life of Henrietta Lacks*, published in 2010. The book tells the story of a young African American woman, Henrietta Lacks, who received treatment for cervical cancer at Johns Hopkins in the 1950s, and died shortly thereafter. Cells collected from a biopsy of Lacks's tumor were cultured without her knowledge or permission, and additional cells may have been collected specifically for research purposes. The cells were cultivated into a self-perpetuating cell line, dubbed "HeLa," which became the most valuable cell line in history, leading to breakthroughs in cancer research and therapy, among many other scientific and clinical advances. Lacks's surviving family members, however, shared neither recognition nor profits from these advances. The story struck many reading Skloot's book as a grave injustice. Yet federal regulations governing research use of biospecimens and data do not require profit sharing and have long allowed—and still allow—secondary research to be conducted without consent so long as the researchers lack access to identifying information, as well as in a number of other circumstances.

Importantly, increasing public awareness of biospecimen research has not occurred in a vacuum. Instead, it has arisen in an era of both increasing deference to individualism and patient autonomy and recognition of concerns about the privacy of data collected on the internet, in consumer settings, and in the context of medical care. In addition to data breaches and misuse, privacy limitations have been further demonstrated by efforts in which researchers have been able to use publicly available information to re-identify individuals from datasets that appeared, on first impression, to have been de-identified by removal of typical identifiers, such as name, Social Security number, and address.

* * *

It was against this backdrop of controversial cases, broader cultural developments, and technological advances—alongside emerging empirical data on public opinion regarding consent to secondary research—that major changes were proposed to the regulations governing secondary research with bio-specimens and data, as described in detail below. Following a 2011 Advance Notice of Proposed Rulemaking, the terms set forth in the 2015 Notice of Proposed Rule Making (NPRM) "to modernize, strengthen, and make more effective the Federal Policy for the Protection of Human Subjects," i.e., to revise the "Common Rule," would have severely limited the conditions in which biospecimens could be used in federally-funded research without consent from their human sources. The proposed changes were rooted in the regulators' perception that "people want to be asked for their permission" for such research and that consent is therefore essential to trust in the research enterprise. However, that proposal was met with piercing opposition from researchers, research institutions, and patients, fearful of what the change would mean for medical progress.

The final revised Common Rule stepped back from this precipice. Promulgated on the last day of President Obama's term in January 2017, with an effective date of July 21, 2018, and a general compliance date of January 21, 2019, the Final Rule largely retains the pre-2018 status quo allowing several approaches to secondary research use of biospecimens and data without consent from their human sources. It also adds to the regulatory repertoire a new consent option intended as a compromise to facilitate research using identifiable materials: "regulatory" broad consent.

NOTES AND QUESTIONS

1. For further discussion of legal questions raised by biobanks, see the symposium issue "Regulation of Biobanks" (edited by Mark A. Rothstein and Bartha M. Knoppers), 33 J. L. Med. & Ethics 1–188 (2005).

2. At a cost of several million dollars, the National Institutes of Health collected tissue samples, including spinal fluid, from individuals afflicted with Alzheimer disease and also from healthy individuals, for use in future studies conducted by the National Institute for Mental Health (NIMH). When a researcher attempted to gain access to some of these samples for use in a new study, she was told by Dr. Pearson ("Trey") Sunderland III, the head of Geriatric Psychiatry at NIMH, that a freezer malfunction had destroyed 95% of the samples. However, Dr. Sunderland was unable to substantiate his claims and a Congressional investigation was launched to determine what happened to the samples.

The investigators discovered that Dr. Sunderland had provided over 3,000 tissue samples and associated clinical data to the pharmaceutical company Pfizer. The samples came from 538 patients over a 15-year period. Staff of H. Comm. on Energy and Commerce, 109th Cong., A Staff Report: For the Use of the Subcommittee on Oversight and Investigations in Preparation for Its Hearing, Human Tissue Samples: NIH Research Policies and Practices, June 13–14, 2006. The investigators also uncovered a previously undisclosed financial relationship between Dr. Sunderland and Pfizer. Pfizer paid Dr. Sunderland as a consultant at the same time that Pfizer was entering into official research partnerships with NIMH. As a result, Dr. Sunderland was often paid simultaneously by NIMH and Pfizer for the same work. Dr. Sunderland received hundreds of thousands of dollars from Pfizer for his consultations, but did not disclose this information or seek approval to act as a consultant for Pfizer as required by federal regulation.

Dr. Sunderland was ultimately charged with violations of a federal law that acts to prevent conflicts of interest—18 U.S.C. § 208(a)—which carried with it a potential 5-year prison sentence under 18 U.S.C. § 216(a)(2) if his actions were willful.

Dr. Sunderland was allowed to plead guilty to a misdemeanor charge with two years of probation and 400 hours of community service at a geriatric psychology service. He also agreed to pay the government $300,000.

Paul W. Lewis, one of the research participants who provided tissue samples for the Alzheimer studies, stated that he felt Dr. Sunderland received little more than "a slap on the wrist," and stated that he would attempt to retrieve his sample from the NIH. David Willman, NIH Researcher is Ordered to Forfeit Pfizer Payments, Los Angeles Times, Dec. 23, 2006, at A22. Did Dr. Sunderland do anything wrong? If so, do you think that he should have received a harsher punishment? What might be the legal basis for Paul Lewis to sue the NIH?

III. GOVERNMENT MARKETING REGULATIONS FOR TEST PRODUCTS AND LABORATORIES

Government regulation of genetic testing in the U.S. is divided into the regulation of test products by the Food and Drug Administration as medical devices under the Federal Food, Drug, and Cosmetic Act, and the regulation of the laboratories that perform the tests by the Centers for Medicare and Medicaid Services in the Department of Health and Human Services (HHS) under the Clinical Laboratory Improvement Amendments of 1988.

A. REGULATION OF TEST PRODUCTS

In regard to test products, the nature and degree of FDA regulation depends on whether the test product is a complete test kit sold commercially to a laboratory, called an in vitro diagnostic test kit; a genetic test that is developed and processed by the laboratory itself, called a "home brew" or laboratory-developed test; or a testing service provided directly to consumers, called direct-to-consumer testing.

The FDA regulates in vitro diagnostic (IVD) genetic test kits as medical devices. There are three classes of medical devices, depending on their degree of risk, with Class III being the highest risk. The FDA has classified approximately 100 IVD test kits as Class II or III medical devices, such as test kits that examine the genetic makeup of cancerous tumors to enable more targeted forms of chemotherapy. Class I device manufacturers must follow good manufacturing practices; manufacturers of Class III devices additionally must obtain pre-marketing approval from the agency;

Class II devices do not need pre-marketing approval but, in addition to meeting good manufacturing practice requirements, they must adhere to special regulatory requirements.

Most genetic tests are laboratory-developed tests rather than in-vitro diagnostic test kits or direct-to-consumer testing. Historically, the FDA has exercised extremely limited regulatory authority over laboratory-developed genetic tests, in part because until recently there were few of them, and in part due to concern that laboratory-developed tests may not qualify as "medical devices" under FDA law. The only FDA requirement has been that chemicals used in testing, called reagents, that a laboratory purchased rather than formulated itself are subject to Class I good manufacturing practice requirements. The growth in laboratory-developed testing, including genetic testing, sparked concerns about safety and efficacy, so in 2014, the agency issued two draft guidance documents proposing to phase in additional regulatory requirements over nine years. U.S. Food and Drug Administration, Draft Guidance for Industry, Food and Drug Administration Staff, and Clinical Laboratories: Framework for Regulatory Oversight of Laboratory Developed Tests (LDTs), Oct. 3, 2014 (https://www.fda.gov/downloads/MedicalDevices/DeviceRegulationandGuidance/GuidanceDocuments/UCM416685.pdf); U.S. Food and Drug Administration, Draft Guidance for Industry, Food and Drug Administration Staff, and Clinical Laboratories: FDA Notification and Medical Device Reporting for Laboratory Developed Tests (LDTs), Oct. 3, 2014. Then, in 2017, the FDA proposed a modified regulatory approach under which existing tests, but not future tests, would be exempt from new regulation. U.S. Food and Drug Administration, Discussion Paper on Laboratory Developed Tests (LDTs), Jan. 13, 2017 (https://www.fda.gov/downloads/medicaldevices/productsandmedicalprocedures/invitrodiagnostics/laboratorydevelopedtests/ucm536965.pdf).

B. REGULATION OF LABORATORIES

Whereas test products are regulated by the FDA, most laboratories that perform genetic tests used in clinical decision-making are regulated under the Clinical Laboratory Improvement Amendments of 1988 (CLIA) by the Centers for Medicare and Medicaid Services (CMS), the federal agency that oversees Medicare. CMS exempts New York and Washington from CLIA, however, and defers to strict state regulatory systems in those states. CLIA requires the laboratories to comply with good laboratory practices, conduct proficiency testing, and meet certain personnel requirements. In addition, CMS conducts routine inspections to assure that tests are valid analytically, meaning that they can accurately detect and evaluate the DNA sequences of interest. However, CLIA does not require laboratories to demonstrate clinical validity, meaning that they can show that the test actually diagnoses a genetic condition or a genetically-affected response to treatment. These gaps in CLIA oversight are one of the reasons the FDA is considering increasing regulatory oversight of LDTs, including review of clinical validity.

C. REGULATION OF DIRECT-TO-CONSUMER TESTING

Direct-to-consumer (DTC) genetic testing, including the necessary saliva collection bottles, can be purchased online and in drugstores. Consumers obtain their test results online. As described in Chapter 4, while DTC genealogy or ancestry testing was available earlier, DTC health-related genetic testing was first offered in 2007 by the company 23andMe. In 2013, the FDA issued warning letters to DTC companies stating that they were selling unapproved tests, and the companies halted health-related testing. Then, in 2015, the FDA reviewed data submitted by 23andMe and authorized it to sell a test to identify carriers of a rare, autosomal-recessive blood disorder called Bloom syndrome.

In 2017, the FDA changed its regulatory approach to DTC testing. First, it exempted DTC genetic health risk (GHR) testing from the need for premarket approval. As then-Commissioner Scott Gottlieb stated, "manufacturers of these types of tests would have to come to FDA for a one-time review to ensure that they meet the FDA's requirements, after which they may enter the market with new GHR tests without further review. The agency also established special controls for these tests in a separate de novo classification order, which outline requirements for assuring the tests' accuracy, reliability and clinical relevance and describe the type of studies and data required to demonstrate performance of certain types of genetic tests. This approach is similar to the proposed firm-based, pre-certification model that we developed for digital health technologies." Statement from FDA Commissioner Scott Gottlieb, M.D., On Implementation of Agency's Streamlined Development and Review Pathway for Consumer Tests that Evaluate Genetic Health Risks, Nov. 6, 2017, https://www.fda.gov/news-events/press-announcements/statement-fda-commissioner-scott-gottlieb-md-implementation-agencys-streamlined-development-and. The revised FDA regulations can be found at 21 CFR § 866.5950. At the same time, the agency exempted from premarket review autosomal recessive carrier screening tests—tests to determine if individuals have genetic variants that could be passed on to their children, so that a child will develop the genetic disease or condition if it inherits two copies of the variant, one from each parent. 21 CFR § 866.5940. Based on these changes, the FDA gave 23andMe approval for ten more direct-to-consumer health-related tests, followed, in March 2018, by three breast cancer tests. The agency classified these direct-to-consumer tests as Class II medical devices, and required direct-to-consumer testing companies to give consumers information about the limits of the testing, and, in particular, that it was not intended to diagnose a disease or condition, disclose anything about the consumer's current state of health, or be used to make medical decisions.

MAXWELL J. MEHLMAN, DIRECT-TO-CONSUMER GENETIC TESTING
Cyberounds® (2009).

More than a dozen companies now sell direct-to-consumer (DTC) or, as it is sometimes called, "home" genetic testing, purporting to reveal information relevant to health and lifestyle. Other companies offer only ancestry or paternity testing (e.g., www.familytreedna.com/, www.dnaancestryproject.com/, www.oxfordancestors.com, www.dna-worldwide.com/). One company, Identigene (www.dnatesting.com/), sells its paternity testing both by mail and as kits that can be purchased in drugstores. Still other companies provide nutritional guidance purportedly based on the results of genetic tests (e.g., http://www.inherenthealth.com/).

POTENTIAL BENEFITS FROM DTC GENETIC TESTING

Like patent medicines in the 19th century and modern over-the-counter drugs, DTC genetic testing offers certain advantages to consumers. It is generally cheaper than genetic testing obtained through a physician, in part because DTC testing dispenses for the most part with the services of physicians and genetic counselors. Mail-order genetic testing may be more accessible for people in rural or medically-underserved communities and those with mobility constraints. DTC testing also may provide a greater sense of privacy. Unlike genetic testing by one's physician, the fact that someone has sought or obtained DTC genetic testing, as well as the test results themselves, do not become part of the patient's medical record unless the patient shares them with his or her physician. For persons concerned about the risk of social stigma and genetic discrimination in insurance and employment, DTC genetic testing thus offers many of the same advantages as anonymous testing, which colleagues and I described as follows in 1996 in an article in the *American Journal of Human Genetics*:

> It would encourage individuals to acquire important personal information at the same time that it safeguarded the information against disclosure. Anonymous testing would promote patient autonomy by making the proband the only person who could reveal identifiable test results to third parties. It would effectively eliminate concerns over unauthorized disclosure by the test provider. By avoiding automatic or unauthorized disclosure to insurers and employers, anonymous testing would reduce the potential for discrimination. It would be up to the proband to decide whether to reveal the fact that he or she had been counseled and tested, and the test results, to insurers, employers, physicians, and family members.

Arguably, concerns about discrimination have been lessened as a result of the enactment of the federal Genetic Information Nondiscrimination Act. [Eds.—See the discussion in Chapters 26 and 32.] But people still may be concerned about the confidentiality of information from genetic tests performed by their physicians and placed in their medical records. Under the Health Insurance Portability and Accountability Act (HIPAA), medical records may be shared among an individual's clinicians and given to health insurers for claims administration purposes. Indeed, a major impetus for shifting the health care system to electronic medical records is the ease with which individual health care information in electronic form can be accessed by care givers. Individuals may blanch at the possibility that genetic information that becomes part of their medical record may be available to virtually anyone who works in a health care system where they obtain care, and they may turn to DTC companies in an effort to maintain greater control over the information.

How confidential is information from DTC genetic tests? The testing companies have privacy policies in which they state their intention not to let anyone outside the company see test information linked to a specific individual without the individual's permission, and although DTC genetic testing companies do not appear to be covered by the privacy protections of HIPAA, such as they are, some companies claim to be "HIPAA-compliant." It is unclear how easy is it for an outsider to discover the identity of the person who was tested, and how well the security systems employed by the companies work.

Ironically, despite all of the concern over genetic privacy, some DTC genetic testing companies are touting the ability of their customers to share their genetic information with others. 23andMe, for example, states: "Seeing your own genetics is just the beginning of the 23andMe experience. Our features also give you the ability to share and compare yourself to family, friends and people around the world." The company website goes on to urge people to "add some excitement at your family reunion" by "track[ing] the inheritance of specific genes in your family," having siblings "see which parts of their parents' DNA they share, and which they don't," and letting grandchildren "find out which genes they inherited from each grandparent." As a publicity stunt, 23andMe even hosted a "spit party" in Manhattan attended by such celebrities as Rupert Murdoch, film executive Harvey Weinstein, and fashion designer Diane von Furstenberg. As reported by the *New York Times*, participants spit into sample collection bottles and looked forward to using their genomes "as a basis for social networking."

CONCERNS ABOUT DTC GENETIC TESTING

Despite the possible benefits from DTC genetic testing, the practice has come in for substantial criticism. Aside from concerns about the confidentiality of identifiable information, critics complain about the validity of the tests and the difficulties of interpreting the results. 23andMe, for example, offers tests for 107 conditions and traits. * * * The company calls 28 of the tests "clinical reports," which refers to "conditions and traits for which there are genetic associations supported by multiple, large, peer-reviewed studies," and that also have "a substantial influence on a person's chances of developing the disease or having the trait." These tests include BRCA cancer mutations, Crohn's disease, cystic fibrosis, hemochromatosis, prostate cancer, Parkinson's disease, and type 1 and 2 diabetes. The company calls the remaining 79 tests "research reports," and describes them as "information from research that has not yet gained enough scientific consensus to be included in our Clinical Reports. This research is generally based on high-quality but limited scientific evidence." The company also classifies as research reports "scientifically accepted, established research that does not have a dramatic influence on a person's risk for a disease." The conditions covered by these tests include such non-disease traits as "avoidance of errors," "breastfeeding and IQ," "measures of intelligence," and "memory," as well as diseases such as asthma, brain aneurysm, lung cancer, ands ulcerative colitis. Some companies, such as Navigenics, only test for conditions which, they claim, bear directly on health.

Clearly there are different views on the validity and utility of various genetic tests. One would think that the government would play some role in assuring that only appropriate genetic tests were sold to consumers. The Food and Drug Administration (FDA) does require manufacturers of some home tests to obtain agency approval before the tests can be marketed, but this only applies to what are called "home test kits," which enable the user to obtain test results without sending a biological sample to a laboratory. (Examples of FDA-approved home test kits are tests for cholesterol, illicit drugs, fecal occult blood, glucose, hepatitis, HIV, menopause, ovulation, pregnancy, prothrombin time, and vaginal pH.) When the test sample must be sent to a laboratory for analysis, however, there may be no requirement of FDA approval for the test itself. The FDA has reviewed and approved only a handful of genetic tests, and purchasers of DTC tests are not likely to know which ones.

The Federal Trade Commission (FTC) is another government agency that is supposed to protect consumers from businesses that make false or misleading claims. In 2006, the FTC issued a warning to consumers about DTC genetic tests. In addition to explaining the limited ability of genetic testing in general to determine an individual's susceptibility to disease, the FTC advised consumers to be especially wary of claims about at-home testing. According to the commission, the FDA and the Centers for Disease Control and Prevention (CDC), which also plays a role in regulating medical tests, are not aware "of any valid studies that prove these tests give accurate results," and these agencies advise that, "because of the complexities involved in both the testing and the interpretation of the results, genetic tests should be performed in a specialized laboratory, and the results should be interpreted by a doctor or trained counselor who understands the value of genetic testing for a particular situation."

Some states also attempt to regulate DTC genetic testing. A 2007 survey by the Genetics and Public Policy Center at Johns Hopkins University reported that only 25 states and the District of Columbia allowed the marketing of DTC genetic testing; 13 states prohibit it explicitly; and the remaining 12 may prohibit it indirectly. In April 2008, the New York State Department of Health sent cease-and-desist letters to Navigenics, 23andMe, and 21 other DTC testing companies, ordering them to stop selling their tests in New York unless they obtained a permit from the state. In June 2008, the California Department of Public Health followed suit, issuing cease-and-desist orders to 13 companies. In addition to requiring the companies to obtain a state license to furnish clinical laboratory services, the state regulators warned that state law required residents to obtain genetic tests through a physician. At least one DTC genetic testing company, DNA Direct, was notified by the California Department of Public Health that it was not in compliance with state law.

One of the main concerns about DTC genetic testing is the difficulty consumers may have in interpreting the test results. The companies issue results on-line, in the form of charts and tables purporting to explain whether, compared with the general population, the individual is at increased or decreased risk for the conditions and traits for which they have been tested. Making sense of a large number of these comparisons is challenging, to say the least. The problem may be exacerbated if the results do not include information about the prevalence of the condition in the wider population. It is one thing to learn that, due to your genes, you have a 25% higher risk of suffering from a certain disease than others; it is another matter if the disease only affects only 1 out of a million people, rather than 1 out of 100. Moreover, the tests invariably reveal increased and decreased risks for different disorders. Assuming there is something individuals can do to reduce their risk, which risks should they focus on? All of them? And what preventive steps are warranted? Should someone who is told that they have a 10 percent greater risk of breast cancer obtain a prophylactic mastectomy? On the other hand, should someone told that they have a reduced risk of lung cancer start smoking?

Consumers of DTC genetic testing might have it somewhat easier if they received expert guidance in interpreting their test results. But none of the on-line testing companies requires the test results to be delivered by a physician, geneticist, or genetic counselor, although at least one company (DNA Direct), requires customers to speak with a counselor before ordering tests and gives them access to an on-line genetic specialist at no extra cost after they receive their test results. Another company, LabSafe, permits its customers to consult a staff physician by telephone at a cost of $75 for 15 minutes. Commentators also worry that company counselors who discuss testing with consumers before the tests are ordered may steer them towards making especially expensive purchases.

How do the testing companies justify the risk of confusing and misleading consumers? The answer is that they all disclaim that they are giving health advice. 23andMe, for example, states in its online consent document that "accessing your genetic information through 23andMe does not translate into a personal prediction"; that the information "should not be used to estimate your overall risk of future disease"; that its services are "not a test or kit designed to diagnose disease or medical conditions," "nor are they intended to be medical advice"; and that "you should not change your health behaviors on the basis of this information." But if customers took all these disclaimers seriously, what would be the point of spending between $300 and $1200 to obtain DTC genetic testing?

In 2006, the U.S. Government Accountability Office (GAO) issued a report on DTC sites that provided "nutragenetic" testing, that is, genetic tests that supposedly yield recommendations about nutrition and lifestyle. Like 23andMe, the four websites that were investigated all stressed that they do not provide information intended to diagnose or treat any disease or disorder. Yet all of the test results obtained by the investigators contained "predictions that a consumer may interpret as a diagnosis," including that the consumers were at risk for osteoporosis, high blood pressure, type 2 diabetes, heart disease, a reduced ability to clear toxins, brain aging, and cancer. Furthermore, the nutrition and lifestyle recommendations that supposedly were based on the results of the genetic tests were in fact based on the results of fictitious information provided by the investigators on questionnaires that were submitted as part of the testing process. To add insult to injury, two of the four sites recommended that the consumer buy expensive, "personalized" dietary supplements from them, at a cost of $1200 a year in one case and $1880 a year in the other. The investigators purchased and analyzed some of the supplements, and found that their ingredients essentially were multivitamins that could be purchased in a supermarket for about $35 a year. Far from being "personalized," moreover, each of the three fictitious consumers that the investigators created for each of the websites were told to purchase the same product, despite that the fact that the DNA samples that were sent to the companies came from two different donors, and each had a different lifestyle profile described in their questionnaires.

Some DTC genetic testing companies require consumers to agree to allow them to use test results for research purposes. As noted earlier, although the companies promise that, unless the consumer agrees otherwise, researchers will be given access only to de-identified information, consumers must take the company's word that their coding and security systems would withstand an attempt to link test results to specific individuals. In addition, consumers may be told that the company is entitled to use the research to develop commercial products and services, and that they should not expect to receive any financial benefit.

PROFESSIONAL ACCEPTANCE OF DTC GENETIC TESTING

All of these criticisms of DTC genetic testing have led some professional medical groups to declare their opposition to the practice. In 2004, the American College of Medical Genetics issued a policy statement describing DTC genetic testing as "potentially harmful" and declaring that "genetic testing should be provided to the public only through the services of an appropriately qualified health care professional." In June 2008, the House of Delegates of the American Medical Association adopted a similar policy statement that also called for the Federal Trade Commission to increase its oversight of DTC genetic testing companies.

The position of the American Society for Human Genetics, however, is more nuanced, and considers the benefits as well as the risks of DTC genetic testing:

> Potential benefits of DTC testing include increased consumer awareness of and access to testing. In the current environment, consumers are at risk of harm from DTC testing if testing is performed by laboratories that are not of high quality, if tests lack adequate analytic or clinical validity, if claims made about tests are false or misleading, and if inadequate information and counseling are provided to permit the consumer to make an informed decision about whether testing is appropriate and about what actions to take on the basis of test results.

In the same way that historic objections to patent medicines might be seen, at least in part, as an effort by physicians to avoid competition from unlicensed salespersons and commercial drug manufacturers, so too condemnations of DTC genetic testing by physicians, geneticists, and genetic counselors may strike some as self-serving attempts by medical professionals to protect their turf. This view is reinforced by studies showing that primary care physicians are not well-informed about genetics and genetic testing. If this holds true, it is unclear how much better off patients would be if they obtained genetic testing through their primary care physicians, unless the physician had specialized training in genetics.

NOTE

1.   Another issue with DTC genetic testing is that the FDA considers genetic tests ordered by physicians to be laboratory-developed tests, which the agency currently does not heavily regulate, rather than direct-to-consumer tests, even if the tests are purchased directly by consumers. Some direct-to-consumer testing companies provide online access to physicians who order the tests, but who never communicate or interact with consumers.

2.   Yet another concern is that DTC tests can be inaccurate. A 2019 study, for example, reported that, because 23andMe only tests for certain genetic variants, it missed almost 90 percent of persons who carry the BRCA breast cancer mutation. Heather Murphy, Don't Count on 23andMe to Detect Most Breast Cancer Risks, Study Warns, N.Y. Times, April 16, 2019 (https://www.nytimes.com/2019/04/16/health/23andme-brca-gene-testing.html). A 2018 study found that 40 percent of results returned by DTC companies were false positives, meaning that they indicated a genetic risk that was not present. S. Tandy-Connor, et al., False-Positive Results Released By Direct-To-Consumer Genetic Tests Highlight the Importance of Clinical Confirmation Testing for Appropriate Patient Care, 20 Genetics in Medicine 1515 (2018).

CHAPTER 6

GENETIC COUNSELING AND GENETIC TESTING FOR SUSCEPTIBILITY TO DISEASE

■ ■ ■

One type of therapeutic function for genetic testing is to facilitate a diagnosis or prognosis for a person exhibiting disease symptoms. For example, a person experiencing muscle stiffness may have a genetic disease called myotonic dystrophy, which can be pinpointed by genetic testing.

Genetic testing also can be used to predict the risk of future disease, sometimes enabling steps to be taken to prevent or mitigate the disease. One common genetic disorder which can be detected pre-symptomatically is hereditary hemochromatosis (HH), which occurs in 1 in 200 Caucasians, and which is readily treated with phlebotomy (similar to the discredited technique of "bleeding").

One of the major issues with genetic testing is its predictive accuracy. This is especially important when the test results might lead to drastic actions, such as radical preventive measures. A good example is genetic testing to detect the risk for breast cancer. In the mid-1990s, researchers identified mutations in two genes, BRCA1 and BRCA2, which were associated with an elevated risk of breast and ovarian cancer in women who have the mutations. Commercial tests for the mutations were quickly developed. Some women with a positive test result have undergone prophylactic radical mastectomies—the removal of their breasts in an attempt to eliminate the tissue at risk for cancer. The problem is that the predictive value of the genetic tests is limited. In the first place, most forms of breast cancer do not appear to be inherited: only about 5 to 10 percent of the over 250,000 women annually diagnosed with breast cancer have an inherited form of the disease. Second, these mutations are incompletely penetrant—that is, some women with the mutations will not develop breast cancer as a result. Even in families with a high risk of breast cancer, based on identified cases in the biologic line, between 10 and 15 percent of women with the BRCA 1 mutation will not develop breast cancer. The predictive value of the genetic tests increases substantially with knowledge about other factors, such as whether there is a family history of both breast and ovarian cancer, and the woman's ethnic group, since much of the initial information came from research on Ashkenazi Jews. Only rare genetic mutations, like the gene associated with Huntington disease, are fully penetrant.

Another problem raised by therapeutic genetic testing is the danger of misinterpreting a negative test result. The concern is that persons with negative test results will conclude that they will not get the disease. This could lead them to reduce their vigilance or refrain from taking preventive measures. A woman with a negative genetic test for breast cancer, for example, might reduce her frequency of mammograms. But a negative result does not mean that the person will not get the disease. As noted, most cases of breast cancer do not appear to be inherited. Even when a test for a mutation known to occur in the individual's family is negative, this only means that the individual did not inherit that particular mutation; she may have other genetic mutations for the disease that the test does not detect. Finally, the person may have had the mutation but the laboratory performing the test may have made an error in interpretation or accidentally switched samples, resulting in a "false negative" test result.

For a good overview of genetic testing, see Wylie Burke, Genetic Testing, 347 New Eng. J. Med. 1867–1875 (2002); Sara Katsanis & Nicholas Katsanis, Molecular Genetic Testing and the Future of Clinical Genomics, 14 Nature Rev. Genetics 415 (2013).

I.   GENETIC COUNSELING

> **FYI:** Various professionals can be involved in offering genetic testing and counseling. Typically they include genetic counselors and clinical geneticists. Genetic counselors have master's degrees from genetic counseling programs. A few programs offer Ph.D. training in genetics as part of genetic counseling training. Clinical geneticists are physicians who have completed a residency in medical genetics and genomics.

It is impossible to discuss genetic testing without describing the profession of genetic counseling, which is central to clinical genetics. Genetic counselors work with physicians, laboratories, and genetics researchers to deal with the "human problems associated with the occurrence, or the risk of occurrence, of a genetic disorder in the family." Ad Hoc Committee on Genetic Counseling, Genetic Counseling, 27 Am. J. Hum. Genetics 240 (1975).

Genetic counseling is essentially a communication process—about medical facts, the contribution of heredity to certain conditions, the interpretation of test results, and the options available. It also involves supportive counseling to enable patients to make decisions and to make the best possible adjustment to the presence or risk of genetic disease. Genetic counselors have master's degrees from certified programs and are certified by either the American Board of Medical Genetics or the American Board of Genetic Counseling.

Karen Heller, Genetic Counseling: DNA Testing for the Patient, 18 Baylor Univ. Med. Ctr. Proceedings 134 (2005).

Genetic counseling evolved from its infancy, when it was associated with "eugenics," to " 'informed, sympathetic counseling' for people with genetic risks who faced reproductive decisions." While initially explicitly directive or prescriptive, genetic counselors eventually "adopted a nondirective style," particularly with non-physician genetic counselors entering the profession and the recognition that "genetic information could evoke strong emotional responses and have potential long-term effects on the individual and family." Sonia M. Suter, A Brave New World of Designer Babies?, 22 Berkeley Tech. L.J. 897, 919–921 (2007).

ANNE L. MATTHEWS, GENETIC COUNSELING, IN ENCYCLOPEDIA OF ETHICAL, LEGAL, AND POLICY ISSUES IN BIOTECHNOLOGY
349–350 (Thomas H. Murray & Maxwell J. Mehlman eds. 2000).

* * *

From Sheldon Reed's first publication defining genetic counseling as "a kind of social work done for the benefit of the whole family entirely without eugenic connotations," genetic counseling has been equated with the concept of nondirectiveness. Nondirectiveness appealed to the genetics community as a way to distance itself from the eugenics movement associated with Nazi Germany. Genetic counseling embraced Carl Rogers's client-centered counseling approach. Rogers felt that counselors need to provide a warm, accepting environment free from pressure or coercion for clients to reach a successful self-acceptance and self-understanding. Nondirectiveness is understood to mean nonprescriptive. Fine defines nondirectiveness as a genetic counseling strategy that supports autonomous decision making by clients. NSGC Code of Ethics states, "Therefore, genetic counselors strive to: * * * Enable their clients to make informed independent decisions, free of coercion, by providing or illuminating the necessary facts and clarifying the alternatives and anticipated consequences." Genetic counselors therefore are facilitators and advocates of informed decision making, with the goal of having the counselee make a decision based solely on his or her own values and beliefs.

However, consensus regarding the terms directiveness and nondirectiveness is difficult to find among genetics professionals and in the literature. Kessler notes that depending on how one defines the term nondirective will determine whether or not it can be achieved. White notes that nondirectiveness is often equated with value neutrality, which may "either imply that the counseling approach as a whole does not represent any values or moral positions, or it may refer to value-free communication, representing an ideal in which concepts and facts are expressed in impartial terms." A number of authors have argued that counseling is never value-neutral. The types of information provided or not provided, the tone of voice, body language, all convey counselor values. Singer elaborates on this theme by noting that many of the decisions that patients make take place in an atmosphere of crisis and that the issues are often highly emotional. Counselors relay information that is often highly technical, while most counselees are likely to have limited knowledge of the biological and statistical issues that arise; they are a vulnerable population. Thus a counselor, who has a duty to provide all the information that clients need in order to make informed decisions, must decide what information the counselee needs and how to present the information. In this sense the genetic counselor utilizes her expertise to decide what and how much information the counselee needs to make the best possible decision for her. Brunger and Lippman would agree. They conclude that genetic counseling is not a "one-size-fits-all" endeavor; rather, it is information that is tailored to specific counselees in specific situations. For some, this would be considered a directive approach. However, authors such as Kessler or Singer would suggest that the counselor is facilitating the goal of genetic counseling by providing information upon which counselees can make autonomous, independent, and informed decisions.

One of the often quoted mechanisms for deciding whether or not a counselor is being directive is to ask whether or not counselors answer questions such as "What would you do in my situation?"

* * *

While the literature regarding nondirective counseling remains unsettled, research suggests that nondirectiveness is not the only guiding principle employed by genetic counselors. In their efforts to provide and facilitate autonomous, independent, and informed decision making by counselees, genetic counselors strive to maintain a delicate balance between a nondirective stance and enhanced counselee understanding.

NOTES AND QUESTIONS

1.   One approach Matthews describes for identifying whether counseling is directive or non-directive is whether the counselor answers the question "What would you do in my situation?" One reason people may consult health care professionals is to obtain the professional's expert opinion on what to do. How appropriate is it for professionals to refuse to provide this advice? Is there a way to provide advice in a non-directive manner? If not, is the goal of non-directiveness misguided? Can there be degrees of directiveness or non-directiveness?

> **Food for Thought:** One of the rationales for the informed consent doctrine in medicine is to recognize the importance of patient self-determination. Does nondirectiveness further this goal of self-determination for patients or does it impede it? Does the answer depend on what we mean by nondirectiveness?

2.   Although, in theory, genetic counseling is non-directive, the reality is somewhat different. See Barbara A. Bernhardt, Empirical Evidence That Genetic Counseling Is Directive: Where Do We Go From Here?, 60 Am. J. Human Genetics 17 (1997). It is also clear from consumer surveys that clients often do not want complete non-directiveness.

3.   With the rise of genetic testing, there is a growing need for genetic counselors. Unfortunately, although the field of genetic counseling has grown significantly, there is a shortage of genetic counselors involved in patient care. As of 2017, 4242 certified genetic counselors worked in the United States. Jennifer M. Hoskovec et al., Projecting the Supply and Demand for Certified Genetic Counselors: A Workforce Study, 17 J. Genetic Counseling 16 (2018). The projected growth in demand for genetic counselors between 2016 and 2026 is nearly 30 percent because of the expansion of genetic testing, including in the direct-to-consumer market (see Chapter 5). Sarah E. Richards, Can Genetic Counselors Keep Up with 23andMe?, Atlantic, May 22 2018, https://www.theatlantic.com/health/archive/2018/05/can-genetic-counselors-keep-up-with-23andme/560837/.

The goal is to have 1 genetic counselor per 100,000 people in the United States by 2020. *Id.* Data suggest, however, that individuals in 16 states would have to travel more than 50 miles to find a genetic counselor; in Wyoming, North Dakota, and Nevada, they would have to travel the farthest. Accessing genetic counseling for hereditary cardiovascular risks is especially difficult because they are fewer cardiovascular genetic counselors than cancer genetic counselors. In 35 states, for example, 57% of people would have to travel at least 50 miles to see a cardiovascular genetic counselor, and in 10 states, including Wyoming Arkansas, and New Mexico, they would have to travel more than 150 miles. Turna Ray, As Genetic Testing Access Grows, Travel Time Remains Barrier to In-Person Counseling, Genomeweb, Nov. 20, 2019, https://www.genomeweb.com/cancer/genetic-testing-access-grows-travel-time-remains-barrier-person-counseling#.Xevc4OhKg2w.

Some question whether primary care physicians can help fill these gaps given concerns about their limited knowledge of genetics. A recent study, however, found that specialists and primary care physicians were, respectively, 83.4% and 74.4% correct in interpreting genetic test results in three different scenarios. Primary care doctors were more likely to be correct if they had had experience with genetics or were educated about genetics in medical school and residency. Primary Care Professionals May Be Able to Step in to Interpret Genetic Testing Results, Nov. 25, 2019, https://www.genomeweb.com/molecular-diagnostics/primary-care-professionals-may-be-able-step-interpret-genetic-testing-results#.XevfBOhKg2w. Being able to interpret results in just three scenarios, however, does not demonstrate expertise regarding the full spectrum of genetic testing results doctors might confront, which will only expand with developments in genetics.

II. GENETIC TESTING FOR SUSCEPTIBILITY TO DISEASE

As our understanding of genetics evolves, our capacity to identify variants associated with a predisposition to conditions that develop later in life, adult- or late-onset conditions, is growing. Initially, predictive genetic testing was only available for a handful of such conditions. Huntington disease (HD), an autosomal dominant, neurodegenerative disease, was one of the first conditions for which predictive testing was offered. The disease usually develops between the ages of 30 and 50 and is characterized by involuntary movements (chorea), progressive dementia, and mood alterations, including irritability, anger, and obsessive-compulsive behavior. When the gene was identified in 1993, it became possible to do presymptomatic genetic testing for children of affected parents who had a 50% risk of inheriting the condition.

A serious concern in providing such testing was the possibility of adverse psychological consequences for those who received unfavorable results. Initial clinical experiences found "no catastrophic responses" among those at increased risk. While "all experienced some difficult episodes," like depression and anxiety soon after receiving the results, they generally appeared "to be coping fairly well." Ultimately, they tended to "become more present-centered in their awareness with a heightened perception of the here and now, but [had] increased difficulty in planning for the future." Maurice Bloch et al., Predictive Testing for Huntington Disease in Canada: The Experience of Those Receiving an Increased Risk, 42 Am. J. Med. Genetics 499, 499–507 (1992). A 2004 Dutch study found that, while the initial increased "feelings of hopelessness" in those carrying the HD mutation reduced over time, those feelings arose again for both carriers and their partners 7–10 years after receiving the adverse test results. The authors surmise that the renewed feelings of hopelessness may be related to the carrier nearing the age of disease onset. Reinier Timman et al., Adverse Effects of Predictive Testing for Huntington Disease Underestimated: Long Term Effects 7–10 Years After the Test, 23 Health Pyschol. 189, 196 (2004).

Although negative emotional responses were expected for those who received adverse results, a 1992 Canadian study also found that approximately 10 percent of those who receive favorable results from the HD predictive test experienced psychological difficulties, including "survivor guilt," stress from having made irreversible personal and financial decisions based on an expectation that they were affected, and depression once the realization sets in that many problems in their lives remain unchanged. See Marlene Huggins et al., Predictive Testing for Huntington Disease in Canada: Adverse Effects and Unexpected Results in Those Receiving a Decreased Risk, 42 Am. J. Med. Genetics 508 (1992).

Another issue that arises with predictive testing for HD is its potential impact on relatives. Children of those tested face heightened or reduced risks themselves, depending on their parents' results. Spouses not only learn about the future risks of their partners, but also the adjusted risks to their children and grandchildren. Further, if they learn their partner is a carrier of the mutation, they face a potentially altered future as their partner's primary caretaker.

To address the potential psychological risks associated with HD predictive testing, the typical protocol involves three clinical visits: 1) pre-test genetic counseling, 2) informed consent and the blood draw, and 3) a final visit to disclose the results and offer post-test counseling. In addition, test candidates usually meet with a psychotherapist to "to confirm they are appropriate candidates for receiving results with potentially dramatic emotional consequences." A neurological exam is recommended as is the presence of a "support person through the testing process." J. Scott Roberts & Wendy R. Uhlmann, Genetic Susceptibility Testing for Neurodegenerative Diseases: Ethical and Practice Issues, 110 Progress Neurobiology 89 (2013).

One of the interesting findings from a 1992 study of a Canadian Huntington testing program was how differently individuals reacted to their test results. Reactions are "usually related to entrenched personality characteristics" and are "often not fully recognized and dealt with during" the precounseling process. One candidate thought she was prepared for an increased risk, but "experienced considerable distress and prolonged difficulty coping with" her heightened risk because she actually had "a deep, powerful, and inadmissible belief that she would receive a decreased risk result." Another expected a low risk result because siblings had developed juvenile-onset Huntington disease. The precounseling therefore tries to help candidates avoid the "possible distress that may arise if they are not truly prepared for adverse results through "discussion, visual imagery, rehearsal, and other techniques . . . " Bloch et al., *supra*.

More recent investigations have found that psychological distress in response to genetic susceptibility testing "is generally mild and transient" for those who undergo testing." These findings have been replicated with respect to testing for Huntington disease as well as other diseases, including hereditary cancers and Alzheimer's disease. According to these studies, the pretest emotional state of individuals undergoing testing is a much better predictor of their subsequent distress than the test results.

Nevertheless, some believe these studies underestimate the potential psychological harm that can results from such genetic testing. These critics offer several critiques of the studies:

* * * First, several notable selection biases limit the generalizability of findings from this line of research. These

studies have typically been conducted at major academic centers in urban locations, with patient populations lacking in racial, ethnic, and socioeconomic diversity. Furthermore, psychologically vulnerable individuals are unlikely to volunteer for such studies or might be screened out based on concerns over the protection of human subjects. Second, genetic testing in these studies is generally provided in well-controlled research settings that may represent a best-case scenario for disclosure of test results. This typically means that highly trained genetic counselors are disclosing test results within standardized protocols that include intensive, in-person, pretest education and counseling. In today's rapidly changing genetic-testing landscape, these ideal conditions may not apply—particularly in the case of direct-to-consumer genetic testing, where pretest education and interaction with genetic counselors are typically absent.

A third reason for skepticism about null findings of psychological distress in response to genetic testing involves the timing of study measurements. Some studies have not administered their initial assessments of posttest responses until several weeks after disclosure of results, which may be too late to detect significant distress responses. Moreover, most studies in this area have not followed participants beyond a year after disclosure of results. These study designs would fail to capture the potential emergence of psychological distress as participants near the age where their relative developed the genetic disease in question. This phenomenon was observed in an interesting longer-term study of Huntington disease test recipients seven to ten years after receiving results, which showed increases in hopelessness and intrusive thoughts among carriers as they approached the age at which their parent experienced disease onset.

J. Scott Roberts, Assessing the Psychological Impact of Genetic Susceptibility Testing, 49 Hastings Ctr. Rep. S38, S39 (2019).

NOTES AND QUESTIONS

1.   Do the findings that there is not a great deal of psychological distress in susceptibility genetic testing suggest that the Huntington disease testing protocol should be less stringent? What about the concerns about the limitations of these studies?

2.   A 1992 report from the Canadian Huntington testing program, which follows the typical protocol, indicated that four candidates were referred for additional assessments, and testing was only postponed for one because of the risk of suicide. One candidate was found to be experiencing significant emotional distress and to be moderately depressed. However, "[a]s she did not appear to be a suicidal risk, had a stable marriage and sound social supports,

was motivated to seek additional individual psychotherapy outside the program, and was able to make an informed decision," they proceeded with predictive testing. The authors noted the significance of deciding to postpone a candidate's testing: "The stress of *undergoing testing,* receiving a result, and *adjusting to* the new risk status must be weighed against the stress and uncertainty of living at risk for HD, the blow to the candidate's self-respect by being denied testing, and the possible sense of humiliation and helplessness by having one's autonomy undermined." They also noted that "[n]o *candidate who has received an increased risk result in our program has yet made a suicide attempt or required psychiatric hospitalization.*" The candidate for whom testing was postponed ultimately resolved some of her personal issues and decided not to undergo predictive testing. The authors concluded that "only a small number of candidates will have testing postponed for psychosocial reasons." Bloch et al., *supra.*

> **Food for Thought:** There is a doctrine called the therapeutic privilege, which is a defense against claims brought by patients for physicians' failure to obtain informed consent. The exception applies when the disclosure "poses such a threat of detriment to the patient as to become unfeasible or contraindicated from a medical point of view." Canterbury v. Spence, 464 F.2d 772, 789 (D.C. Cir. 1972). Is the withholding of testing for certain patients at risk of Huntington disease a variant of, or supported by, this doctrine?

Is it appropriate to withhold testing because of concerns that patients will experience psychosocial difficulties? Is the Canadian protocol consistent with the principles of nondirectiveness that shape genetic counseling or with general principles governing informed consent to health care? To what extent, for example, is it appropriate to withhold testing because of fears that the results may emotionally upset the patient? See generally Jessica Berg et al., Informed Consent: Legal Theory and Clinical Practice 79–85 (2001).

3. While HD predictive testing offers some insight into the issues of predictive genetic testing generally, such testing is unique in two respects. First, the Huntington genetic variant is nearly fully penetrant (meaning the disease will develop with near certainty if the individual lives long enough) and second, there is currently no treatment for it. In contrast, mutations associated with many late-onset conditions, like heritable forms of breast and ovarian cancer, are not fully penetrant. In addition, medical options exist to reduce heightened risks for heritable breast and ovarian cancer and many other late-onset conditions. A worldwide study of 1,499 women, for example, found that 86% of BRCA1-positive subjects and 71% of BRCA2-positive subjects had their ovaries surgically removed by the age of 50. In the same study, 46% of both BRCA1- and BRCA2-positive subjects underwent risk-reducing mastectomy by the age of 70. Xinglei Chai et al., Use of Risk-Reducing Surgeries in a Prospective Cohort of 1,499 BRCA1 and BRCA2 Mutation Carriers, 148 Breast Cancer Res. Treat. 397 (2014).

4. In 1993, researchers announced that they had discovered a gene, APOE, that is associated with Alzheimer disease. Two years later, a working group of the American College of Medical Genetics and the American Society of Human Genetics issued a consensus statement that clinicians should not

offer predictive testing, even to members of high-risk families. See Statement on the Use of Apolipoprotein E Testing for Alzheimer Disease, 274 JAMA 1627 (1995). The group noted uncertainties about the predictive value of test results (including that 35 to 50 percent of patients with Alzheimer disease do not have the mutation), and took the position that predictive testing "may be valuable only if prevention can be affected by lifestyle changes or early drug intervention," which was not the case with Alzheimer disease. Numerous consensus statements concur in recommending against clinical use of the APOE test. See Roberts & Uhlmann, *supra*, at 90. Is this an appropriate stance? Should the decision be left up to the individuals seeking testing? What standards should be used to determine if a genetic test is predictive enough to be suitable for clinical use? Who should establish those standards?

5.   A 2005 study of the adult children of Alzheimer patients who underwent genetic testing for APOE4, associated with a higher risk of developing Alzheimer disease, found that persons whose test results were positive had no increase in anxiety or depression compared with those whose test results were negative. The study was part of a large-scale series of investigations known as REVEAL (Risk Evaluation and Education for Alzheimer's Disease). See Robert C. Green et al., The REVEAL Study: The Impact of Genetic Risk Assessment with APOE Disclosure for Alzheimer's Disease, 1 Alzheimer's & Dementia s101 (2005). Do these findings affect your views about the 1995 consensus statement regarding APOE testing described in Note 4? It is possible to be tested for APOE through direct-to-consumer genetic testing services (see Chapter 5). What are the arguments for or against offering such testing through such services given the consensus against clinical predictive APOE testing?

> **What's That?:** A monogenic disease is one caused by a single gene or single allele, whereas a polygenic disease is caused by at least two genes.
>
> **What's That?:** Penetrance refers to the likelihood that individuals with a particular genotype will express the associated trait. If a genetic disease is highly penetrant, nearly all people with the mutation will develop the condition. If a disease shows incomplete penetrance, only some individuals who have the genetic variant will develop the condition.

6. Genetic testing for asymptomatic relatives of patients with amyotrophic lateral sclerosis (ALS or Lou Gehrig disease) raises similar concerns. Although such individuals increasingly ask about genetic testing, it is not recommended in the clinical setting because the genetics of ALS is complicated. Unlike Huntington disease, which is monogenic with fairly predictable penetrance, ALS is polygenic and with uncertain penetrance and pathogenicity for the many associated mutations. See Adriano Chio et al., Genetic Counseling in ALS: Facts, Uncertainties, and Clinical Suggestions, 85 J. Neurology Neurosurgery & Psychiatry 478 (2014).

7.   One of the rationales for offering predictive testing for certain heritable conditions is not only to help individuals with life planning, but also to offer them the possibility of engaging in behaviors or medical treatments that can reduce their risk, if available. A meta-analysis of studies of patients who received DNA-based risk assessments found no positive or negative

changes with respect to risk-reducing behavior, such as smoking cessation, medication use, diet, physical activity, etc. Gareth Hollands et al., The Impact of Communicating Genetic Risks of Disease on Risk-Reducing Health Behaviour: Systemic Review with Meta-Analysis, 352 British Med. J. 1153 (2016).

In contrast, a 2008 study found that those with a heightened risk of Alzheimer disease based on genetic testing "endorsed healthy behavior changes [even] after explicitly being informed that none were proven to prevent" the disease. The authors surmised this was due to persistent information in the press claiming that "dietary measures, leisure time activities, vitamins, and medications may decrease" the risk for the disease. They noted that this contrasted with difficulty motivating behavioral change, like screening behavior after genetic testing for breast cancer, in other areas. Serena Chao et al., Health Behavior Changes After Genetic Risk Assessment for Alzheimer Disease: The REVEAL Study, 22 Alzheimer Disease & Associated Disorders 94 (2008). The study participants may have been on to something, however. A recent study found that patients with high genetic risk factors could slightly reduce their likelihood of developing dementia if they adhered to a favorable lifestyle. Iliana Lourida, Association of Lifestyle and Genetic Risk with Incidence of Dementia, 322 JAMA 430 (2019). What do these data suggest regarding the value of predictive testing?

8.   Although open communication is often encouraged for individuals who undergo genetic testing for late-onset conditions, there are risks associated with such open communication, which genetic counselors discuss with patients. These risks include vulnerability to rejection, potential emotional distress of others, and the risk of discrimination by employers, insurers, or other entities that might be interested in such information (discussed in Chapters 26–32). Bloch et al., *supra*.

Should the risk of potential discrimination by employers and insurers be part of the information that physicians or genetic counselors disclose as part of the informed consent? Is this information that would be material to a reasonable patient?

9.   Even if health professionals order genetic tests, patients' insurance plans may not pay for it, leaving the patient with the choice of foregoing the test or paying for it out-of-pocket. A 2006 report by the Department of Health and Human Services Secretary's Advisory Committee on Genetics, Health, and Society recommended that the government should promulgate a set of principles to guide coverage decision-making for genetic tests, but no such principle have been issued. See Coverage and Reimbursement of Genetic Tests and Services, Report of the Secretary's Advisory Committee on Genetics, Health, and Society, Feb. 2006, https://osp.od.nih.gov/wp-content/uploads/2013/11/CR_report.pdf. See also James D. Chambers et al., Examining Evidence in U.S. Payer Coverage Policies for Multi-Gene Panels and Sequencing Tests, 33 Int'l J. Tech. Assessment Health Care 534 (2017);

Rebecca Eisenberg & Harold Varmus, Insurance for Broad Genomic Tests in Oncology, 358 Sci. 1133 (2017).

Insurance coverage for surveillance and prophylactic surgery, if predisposition to disease is detected through genetic testing, is even more uncertain. Insurance is more likely to cover treatment than prevention, "but the medical interventions for adult onset genetic conditions occupy a hazy space between these extremes." Depending on patient's insurance policies, therefore, some "patients may be harmed by learning of genetic predispositions that they cannot prevent due to lack of insurance coverage." Anya E.R. Prince, Prevention for Those Who Can Pay: Insurance Reimbursement of Genetic-Based Prevention Interventions in the Liminal State Between Health and Disease, 2 J.L. Biosci. 365, 366–67 (2015).

What process should a medical director of a large health plan use to decide whether or not to provide coverage for a genetic test and/or prophylactic treatment? What criteria should the plan employ?

TAMAR LEWIN, BOOM IN GENETIC TESTING RAISES QUESTIONS ON SHARING RESULTS

N.Y. Times, July 21, 2000, at A1.

As genetic testing becomes increasingly common, those who choose to learn their genetic risks, and the health professionals who treat them, are facing difficult decisions about how—and whether—to share the results with family members who share their genes.

And the new genetic information is creating new kinds of rifts, when one family member finds out what another family member does not want to know, or when family members react differently to the same knowledge.

"One woman who'd had ovarian cancer was tested for the breast cancer gene mutations mostly for the sake of her two adult daughters," said Katherine Schneider, senior genetics counselor at the Dana Farber Cancer Institute in Boston. "But when she told them she had it, they were so devastated that they didn't talk with her for two years. They didn't want to know."

"I tell that story a lot. There's nothing easy about any of this. But before testing, it's important to talk not only about what the information will mean for you, but what it might mean to your sisters, your children, your cousins."

Genetic tests are now commonplace, what with prenatal tests diagnosing hundreds of syndromes, midlife tests for mutations linked to breast and ovarian cancer, and—with the human genome newly mapped—more and more familial disorders.

The scientific advances have created debate about public policy on genetic discrimination. But the private effects on family dynamics are just as complex, as patients and health professionals adjust to thinking about family not just as flesh and blood, but flesh and blood and genes.

Usually, patients are happy to share health information with family members for whom it may be important, often asking the doctor or genetic counselor for a written explanation to pass along.

But when patients want to keep the information to themselves, health professionals may encounter situations that mix social problem and soap opera, and be ethically and legally pulled into uncharted waters.

A young man in Washington State called his genetics counselor to confess a guilty conscience: Several months earlier, he told her, he had made a sperm donation. And while he knew his test results had shown that he had an inheritable syndrome that causes heart trouble and, often, early death, he did not mention it to the sperm bank. Troubled, the counselor called the sperm bank and found that there had, indeed, been successful pregnancies with the man's sperm. She offered to counsel those families but does not know whether the sperm bank even passed on the information.

In a New York family with three adult daughters, the two married daughters know that their mother, who had breast cancer as a young woman, has been tested and found to carry a gene mutation associated with a high risk of breast and ovarian cancer. The mother has forbidden them to tell their unmarried sister, who has always felt herself to be the least attractive, for fear that it might make her less marriageable. They have obeyed, but want the family doctor to make sure she has frequent mammograms and screenings.

Two sisters who know their mother had genetic testing before she died of ovarian cancer want to find out her test results. But the Pennsylvania medical center that did the testing will not release the results to the young women without the consent of their stepfather, who has a dismal relationship with them. The sisters could, of course, have had their own genetic tests, but they had hoped by learning more about their family's history to avoid the process. The center's ethics committee is now revising its consent forms to require all patients tested to specify which family members should have access to the results after their death.

* * *

Often, the decision to pass on information is a delicate one, depending not only on such factors as the relatives' closeness, ages and emotional health, but also the nature of the disease and the severity of the risk. Where there is no treatment, or the risk is small, the case for sharing painful knowledge becomes less compelling. And the need to share information may be temporary, experts say, as the era approaches when complete genetic profiles become a routine part of individual health records.

Meanwhile, the cost of testing even a single gene can run from several hundred to several thousand dollars.

Still, Josephine Wagner Costalas, a genetic counselor at Fox Chase Cancer Center in Philadelphia, has an unspoken worry whenever she counsels a patient who has tested positive for the breast cancer gene mutations.

"My worst nightmare is the scenario where I might have a patient who tests positive and doesn't tell her relatives," Ms. Costalas said, "and a few years later her sister will discover she has metastatic cancer, with a bad prognosis, and she'll find out that there was this information showing she was at risk. And maybe she'll sue me, saying I should have picked up the phone and told her, 'Your sister's positive, you should get tested.' This is all so new, and there are no clear guidelines, so I worry."

Still, Ms. Costalas does not pressure her patients to share their results. "If people aren't sure about sharing the information, I ask them to think about what it would be like if the situation were reversed," she said. "Would they want to know? But I do believe patients need to decide for themselves what they want to do."

And when several family members come in together, there are other issues. "What if they have different results?" Ms. Costalas said. "Who do you tell first? What if they have different reactions?"

* * *

Two years ago, the American Society of Human Genetics adopted a position recognizing the conflict between the health professions' duty to maintain confidentiality and the duty to warn about serious health risks. Health professionals should tell patients about potential genetic risks to their relatives, the statement said, and in some cases, they may be allowed to breach confidentiality to warn relatives at risk if the harm is ["highly likely to occur and serious and foreseeable" prevention or treatment is available, attempts to encourage the patient to disclose have failed, and the at-risk relatives are identifiable].

But there is little consensus on where to draw those lines. Generally, genetic counselors are more concerned about confidentiality and not pressuring patients, while physicians specializing in genetics are more concerned about the duty to warn, according to research by Dorothy C. Wertz, senior scientist at the Shriver Center in Waltham, Mass. As a practical matter, though, most health professionals cannot warn relatives.

"In the end it's up to the patient, because in real life, we don't have relatives' names and phone numbers," said Helen Hixon, a genetic counselor in cardiology at Cedars Sinai hospital in Los Angeles. "We do tell people pretty strongly that they should warn their relatives, that they may have a legal duty to do so."

NOTES AND QUESTIONS

1.   While the American Society of Human Genetics statement permits disclosures to relatives in narrow instances, it does not require it. The American Medical Association urges physicians to discuss the implications of genetic testing for the patient's biological relatives. Emphasizing the duty of confidentiality to patients, it states that physicians should discuss with patients "whether to invite family members to participate in the testing process." In addition, it advises physicians to tell patients when they would expect their patients to notify relatives about disease risks. AMA Council on Ethical and Judicial Affairs, The AMA Code of Medical Ethics' Opinion on Disclosure of Patients' Genetic Test Results, 14 Virtual Mentor 627 (2012).

The National Society of Genetic Counselors' Code of Ethics stresses the importance of maintaining the "privacy and security of their client's confidential information and individually identifiable health information, unless released by the client or disclosure is required by law." But it does not directly address issues related to a relative's potential medical interest in such information, and it describes no situation when a genetic counselor may disclose relevant information to at-risk biological relatives. National Society of Genetic Counselors. NSGC Code of Ethics sec. 22, pt. 7, https://www.nsgc.org/p/cm/ld/fid=12#section2.

To what extent should professional codes of ethics shape legal obligations regarding whether genetic counselors and clinical geneticists can or should share information about genetic risks to family members?

What legitimate interests do family members have in the results of an individual's genetic testing? What obligations should clinicians—primary care physicians, geneticists, genetic counselors, etc.—owe patients' family members regarding genetic information about a patient?

III. LIABILITY ISSUES

PATE V. THRELKEL
661 So.2d 278 (Fla.1995).

WELLS, J.

We have for review the following question certified to be of great public importance:

DOES A PHYSICIAN OWE A DUTY OF CARE TO THE CHILDREN OF A PATIENT TO WARN THE PATIENT OF THE GENETICALLY TRANSFERABLE NATURE OF THE CONDITION FOR WHICH THE PHYSICIAN IS TREATING THE PATIENT?

We have jurisdiction. Art. V, § 3(b)(4), Fla. Const. We answer the question in the affirmative provided the children of the patient first establish that pursuant to the prevailing standard of care set forth in section 766.102, Florida Statutes (1989), a reasonably prudent physician would give such warning to his or her patient in light of all relevant circumstances.

In March 1987, Marianne New received treatment for medullary thyroid carcinoma, a genetically transferable disease. In 1990, Heidi Pate, New's adult daughter, learned that she also had medullary thyroid carcinoma. Consequently, Pate and her husband filed a complaint against the physicians who initially treated New for the disease as well as the physicians' respective employers. Pate and her husband alleged that the physicians knew or should have known of the likelihood that New's children would have inherited the condition genetically; that the physicians were under a duty to warn New that her children should be tested for the disease; that had New been warned in 1987, she would have had her children tested at that time; and if Pate had been tested in 1987, she would have taken preventative action, and her condition, more likely than not, would have been curable. Pate claimed that as a direct and proximate cause of the physicians' negligence, she suffers from advanced medullary thyroid carcinoma and its various damaging effects.

The respondent health care providers moved to dismiss the complaint for failure to state a cause of action. Specifically, the respondents alleged that Pate did not demonstrate the existence of a professional relationship between her and respondents and thus failed to establish that respondents owed her a duty of care. The trial court granted the motion and dismissed the Pates' complaint with prejudice, finding that the plaintiffs were not patients of the respondents and that they did not fit within any exception to the requirement that there be a physician-patient relationship between the parties as a condition precedent to bringing a medical malpractice action.

The district court affirmed the trial court's dismissal. The court rejected the Pates' argument that it should, based upon past decisions recognizing a doctor's duty to inform others of a patient's contagious disease, extend a physician's duty to cover the child of a patient who suffers from an inheritable disease. The court also rejected the Pates' reliance on Schroeder v. Perkel, 432 A.2d 834 (N.J.1981), in which the parents of a four-year-old child brought suit against the child's pediatricians for failing to diagnose the child with cystic fibrosis early enough to prevent the parents from having a second diseased child. The New Jersey court in Schroeder recognized that due to the special nature of the family relationship, a physician's duty may extend beyond a patient to members of the patient's immediate family.

* * *

We conclude that to answer the certified question we must consider two questions related to duty. First, we must determine whether New's physicians had a duty to warn New of the genetically transferable nature of her disease. We find that to make this determination we must apply section 766.102, Florida Statutes (1989), which defines the legal duty owed by a health care provider in a medical malpractice case. That section provides in part:

> (1) In any action for recovery of damages based on the death or personal injury of any person in which it is alleged that such death or injury resulted from the negligence of a health care provider as defined in s. 768.50(2)(b), the claimant shall have the burden of proving by the greater weight of evidence that the alleged actions of the health care provider represented a breach of the prevailing professional standard of care for that health care provider. The prevailing professional standard of care for a given health care provider shall be that level of care, skill, and treatment which, in light of all relevant surrounding circumstances, is recognized as acceptable and appropriate by reasonably prudent similar health care providers.

§ 766.102, Fla. Stat. (1989). In applying this statute to the instant case, we conclude that a duty exists if the statutory standard of care requires a reasonably prudent health care provider to warn a patient of the genetically transferable nature of the condition for which the physician was treating the patient.

In medical malpractice cases, the standard of care is determined by a consideration of expert testimony. Because this case comes to us on appeal from an order granting the physicians' motion to dismiss, the record has yet to be developed in respect to such testimony. However, the court's dismissal requires us to assume that the factual allegations in the complaint are true. * * * Accordingly, we must accept as true the Pates' allegations that pursuant to the prevailing standard of care, the health care providers were under a duty to warn New of the importance of testing her children for medullary thyroid carcinoma. Whether these allegations are supported by the statutorily required expert medical authority will have to be determined as the action progresses. We do note, however, that the plaintiffs have pled good-faith compliance with section 766.104, Florida Statutes (1989).

The second question we must address in answering the certified question is to whom does the alleged duty to warn New of the nature of her disease run? The duty obviously runs to the patient who is in privity with the physician. * * * In other professional relationships, however, we have recognized the rights of identified third party beneficiaries to recover from a professional because that party was the intended beneficiary of the prevailing standard of care. In such cases, we have determined that an absence of privity does not necessarily foreclose liability.

* * *

Here, the alleged prevailing standard of care was obviously developed for the benefit of the patient's children as well as the patient. We conclude that when the prevailing standard of care creates a duty that is obviously for the benefit of certain identified third parties and the physician knows of the existence of those third parties, then the physician's duty runs to those third parties. Therefore, in accord with our decision in Baskerville-Donovan Engineers, we hold that privity does not bar Heidi Pate's pursuit of a medical malpractice action. Our holding is likewise in accord with McCain because under the duty alleged in this case, a patient's children fall within the zone of foreseeable risk.

Though not encompassed by the certified question, there is another issue which should be addressed in light of our holding. If there is a duty to warn, to whom must the physician convey the warning? Our holding should not be read to require the physician to warn the patient's children of the disease. In most instances the physician is prohibited from disclosing the patient's medical condition to others except with the patient's permission. See § 255.241(2), Fla. Stat. (1989). Moreover, the patient ordinarily can be expected to pass on the warning. To require the physician to seek out and warn various members of the patient's family would often be difficult or impractical and would place too heavy a burden upon the physician. Thus, we emphasize that in any circumstances in which the physician has a duty to warn of a genetically transferable disease, that duty will be satisfied by warning the patient.

Accordingly, we conclude that the trial court erred by dismissing the complaint with prejudice. Whether the Pates can recover for medical malpractice depends upon the prevailing standard of care pursuant to section 766.102. The pleadings were prematurely terminated based upon the trial court's conclusion that a lack of privity prevented the Pates from stating a cause of action. We therefore quash the decision of the district court affirming the dismissal of the complaint with prejudice and remand for further proceedings in accord with this opinion.

It is so ordered.

SAFER V. PACK

677 A.2d 1188 (N.J. Super. Ct. App. Div. 1996).

KESTIN, J.

Plaintiffs appeal from the trial court's order dismissing their complaint and denying their cross-motion for partial summary judgment as to liability only. We reverse that portion of the order dismissing the complaint and affirm the denial of plaintiffs' motion.

Donna Safer's claim arises from the patient-physician relationship in the 1950s and 1960s between her father, Robert Batkin, a resident of New Jersey, and Dr. George T. Pack, also a resident of New Jersey, who practiced medicine and surgery in New York City and treated Mr. Batkin there. It is alleged that Dr. Pack specialized in the treatment and removal of cancerous tumors and growths.

In November 1956, Mr. Batkin was admitted to the hospital with a pre-operative diagnosis of retroperitoneal cancer. A week later, Dr. Pack performed a total colectomy and an ileosigmoidectomy for multiple polyposis of the colon with malignant degeneration in one area. The discharge summary noted the finding in a pathology report of the existence of adenocarcinoma developing in an intestinal polyp, and diffuse intestinal polyposis "from one end of the colon to the other." Dr. Pack continued to treat Mr. Batkin postoperatively.

In October 1961, Mr. Batkin was again hospitalized. Dr. Pack performed an ileoabdominal perineal resection with an ileostomy. The discharge summary reported pathology findings of "ulcerative adenocarcinoma of colon Grade II with metastases to Levels II and III" and "adenomatous polyps." Dr. Pack again continued to treat Mr. Batkin postoperatively. He also developed a physician-patient relationship with Mrs. Batkin relative to the diagnosis and treatment of a vaginal ulcer.

In December 1963, Mr. Batkin was hospitalized once again at Dr. Pack's direction. The carcinoma of the colon had metastasized to the liver with secondary jaundice and probable retroperitoneal disease causing pressure on the sciatic nerve plexus. After some treatment, Mr. Batkin died on January 3, 1964, at forty-five years of age. Donna was ten years old at the time of her father's death. Her sister was seventeen.

In February 1990, Donna Safer, then thirty-six years of age and newly married, residing in Connecticut, began to experience lower abdominal pain. Examinations and tests revealed a cancerous blockage of the colon and multiple polyposis. In March, Ms. Safer underwent a total abdominal colectomy with ileorectal anastamosis. A primary carcinoma in the sigmoid colon was found to extend through the serosa of the bowel and multiple polyps were seen throughout the entire bowel. Because of the detection of additional metastatic adenocarcinoma and carcinoma, plaintiff's left ovary was also removed. Between April 1990 and mid-1991, Ms. Safer underwent chemotherapy treatment.

In September 1991, plaintiffs obtained Robert Batkin's medical records, from which they learned that he had suffered from polyposis. Their complaint was filed in March 1992, alleging a violation of duty (professional negligence) on the part of Dr. Pack in his failure to warn of the risk to Donna Safer's health.

Plaintiffs contend that multiple polyposis is a hereditary condition that, if undiscovered and untreated, invariably leads to metastatic colorectal cancer. They contend, further, that the hereditary nature of the disease was known at the time Dr. Pack was treating Mr. Batkin and that the physician was required, by medical standards then prevailing, to warn those at risk so that they might have the benefits of early examination, monitoring, detection and treatment, that would provide opportunity to avoid the most baneful consequences of the condition.

* * *

In dismissing, the trial court held that a physician had no "legal duty to warn a child of a patient of a genetic risk[.]" In the absence of any evidence whether Dr. Pack had warned Mr. Batkin to provide information concerning his disease for the benefit of his children, the motion judge "assumed that Dr. Pack did not tell Robert Batkin of the genetic disease."

The motion judge's reasoning proceeded from the following legal premise: "in order for a doctor to have a duty to warn, there must be a patient/physician relationship or circumstances requiring the protection of the public health or the community [at] large." Finding no physician-patient relationship between Dr. Pack and his patient's daughter Donna, the court then held genetically transmissible diseases to differ from contagious or infectious diseases or threats of harm in respect of the duty to warn, because "the harm is already present within the non-patient child, as opposed to being introduced, by a patient who was not warned to stay away. The patient is taking no action in which to cause the child harm."

The motion judge relied on Pate v. Threlkel, 640 So. 2d 183 (Fla.Dist.Ct.App.1994), as the only "on point" authority respecting genetically transmissible disease.

* * *

Because the issue before us arose on a motion for summary judgment, we, too, are obliged to accept plaintiffs' proffer through their medical expert that the prevailing standard of care at the time Dr. Pack treated Mr. Batkin required the physician to warn of the known genetic threat.

* * *

We see no impediment, legal or otherwise, to recognizing a physician's duty to warn those known to be at risk of avoidable harm from a genetically transmissible condition. In terms of foreseeability especially, there is no essential difference between the type of genetic threat at issue here and the menace of infection, contagion or a threat of physical harm. See generally, e.g., McIntosh v. Milano, 168 N.J. Super. 466, 483–85, 403 A.2d 500 (Law Div.1979); Tarasoff v. Regents of Univ. of Cal., 17 Cal. 3d 425, 551 P.2d 334, 344, 131 Cal. Rptr. 14 (Cal. 1976); Restatement (Second) of

Torts §§ 314, 314A (1965); T.A. Bateman, Annotation, Liability of Doctor or Other Health Practitioner to Third Party Contracting Contagious Disease from Doctor's Patient, 3 A.L.R. 5th 370 (1992). The individual or group at risk is easily identified, and substantial future harm may be averted or minimized by a timely and effective warning.

The motion judge's view of this case as one involving an unavoidable genetic condition gave too little significance to the proffered expert view that early monitoring of those at risk can effectively avert some of the more serious consequences a person with multiple polyposis might otherwise experience. We cannot conclude either, as the trial court did, that Dr. Pack breached no duty because avoidable harm to Donna was not foreseeable, i.e., "that Dr. Pack's conduct did not create a 'foreseeable zone of risk.'" Such a determination would ignore the presumed state of medical knowledge at the time.

* * *

Although an overly broad and general application of the physician's duty to warn might lead to confusion, conflict or unfairness in many types of circumstances, we are confident that the duty to warn of avertable risk from genetic causes, by definition a matter of familial concern, is sufficiently narrow to serve the interests of justice. Further, it is appropriate, for reasons already expressed by our Supreme Court, that the duty be seen as owed not only to the patient himself but that it also "extends beyond the interests of a patient to members of the immediate family of the patient who may be adversely affected by a breach of that duty."

* * *

We need not decide, in the present posture of this case, how, precisely, that duty is to be discharged, especially with respect to young children who may be at risk, except to require that reasonable steps be taken to assure that the information reaches those likely to be affected or is made available for their benefit. We are aware of no direct evidence that has been developed concerning the nature of the communications between physician and patient regarding Mr. Batkin's disease: what Dr. Pack did or did not disclose; the advice he gave to Mr. Batkin, if any, concerning genetic factors and what ought to have been done in respect of those at risk; and the conduct or expressed preferences of Mr. Batkin in response thereto. There may be enough from Mrs. Batkin's testimony and other evidence for inferences to be drawn, however.

We decline to hold as the Florida Supreme Court did in Pate v. Threlkel, supra, that, in all circumstances, the duty to warn will be satisfied by informing the patient. It may be necessary, at some stage, to resolve a conflict between the physician's broader duty to warn and his fidelity to an expressed preference of the patient that nothing be said to family members about the details of the disease. We cannot know presently, however, whether there is any likelihood that such a conflict may be shown to have existed in this matter or, if it did, what its qualities might have been. As the matter is currently constituted, it is as likely as not that no such conflict will be shown to have existed and that the only evidence on the issue will be Mrs. Batkin's testimony, including that she received no information, despite specific inquiry, that her children were at risk. We note, in addition, the possible existence of some offsetting evidence that Donna was rectally examined as a young child, suggesting that the risk to her had been disclosed.

This case implicates serious and conflicting medical, social and legal policies, many aptly identified in Sonia M. Suter, Whose Genes Are These Anyway? Familial Conflicts Over Access to Genetic Information, 91 Mich. L. Rev. 1854 (1993) and in other sources, including some referred to by the motion judge. Some such policy considerations may need to be addressed in ultimately resolving this case. For example, if evidence is produced that will permit the jury to find that Dr. Pack received instructions from his patient not to disclose details of the illness or the fact of genetic risk, the court will be required to determine whether, as a matter of law, there are or ought to be any limits on physician-patient confidentiality, especially after the patient's death where a risk of harm survives the patient, as in the case of genetic consequences. See generally Janet A. Kobrin, Confidentiality of Genetic Information, 30 UCLA L. Rev. 1283 (1983).

Issues of fact remain to be resolved, as well. What was the extent of Donna's risk, for instance? We are led to understand from the experts' reports that the risk of multiple polyposis was significant and that, upon detection, an early full colectomy, i.e., an excision of her entire colon, may well have been the treatment of choice to avoid resultant cancer—including metastasis, the loss of other organs and the rigors of chemotherapy. Full factual development may, however, cast a different light on these issues of fact and others.

Difficult damage issues portend also. Not the least of these will involve distinguishing between the costs of the medical surveillance that would have followed a timely and effective warning, and the costs of medical care attributable to any breach of duty that may be found to have occurred.

Because of the necessarily limited scope of our consideration, we have highlighted only a few of the potentially troublesome issues presented by this case. Such questions are best conceived and considered in the light of a fully developed record rather than in the abstract.

* * *

The order of the trial court dismissing the complaint is reversed. For similar reasons, the trial court's order denying plaintiffs' motion for summary judgment on liability is affirmed. The matter is remanded to the trial court for further proceedings.

NOTES AND QUESTIONS

1.   Both of the conditions about which the physicians in *Pate* and *Safer* allegedly failed to warn the plaintiffs, medullary thyroid carcinoma and familial adenomatous polyposis, are autosomal dominant disorders with nearly complete penetrance. Each child of an affected parent has a 50 percent chance of inheriting the mutation, and unless treated, has an extremely high probability of becoming ill. Does the physician's duty depend on the probability of inheriting the disorder? On its severity?

2.   What harms might be caused by disclosing genetic test results to family members at risk?

3.   If the genetic disorder is not treatable, does the health care professional still have a duty to warn third parties at risk? What benefits, if any, would disclosure provide? See Carol McCrehan Parker, Camping Trips and Family Trees: Must Tennessee Physicians Warn Their Patients' Relatives of Genetic Risks?, 65 Tenn. L. Rev. 585, 601–02 (1998).

In a recent case in England, a woman sued her physicians for failing to inform her that her father carried the Huntington mutation before she had her own child. She only learned that he had the gene after she gave birth. Her father had been convicted of manslaughter for killing his wife and was later discovered to have Huntington disease. Although physicians asked him to inform his daughter, he allegedly refused to do so for fear she would terminate her pregnancy. The woman, now in her 40s, subsequently discovered that she had inherited the gene, and therefore her daughter has a 50% risk of having inherited it as well. She alleges that she would have had an abortion had she known about her father's genetic status. The court of appeals overturned the lower court's dismissal of the case, Patient ABC v. St. George's Healthcare Trust. It is set for trial in the near future. Robin McKie, Woman Who Inherited Fatal Illness to Sue Doctors in Groundbreaking Case, Guardian, Nov. 25, 2018, https://www.theguardian.com/science/2018/nov/25/woman-inherited-fatal-illness-sue-doctors-groundbreaking-case-huntingtons;   Fergus   Walsh, Huntington's Disease: Woman Who Inherited Gene Sues NHS, BBC News, Nov. 18, 2019, https://www.bbc.com/news/health-50425039. How should this case be resolved?

4.   The classic case addressing the duty of a health care professional to warn third parties of a risk of harm created by a patient is Tarasoff vs. Regents of the University of California, 551 P.2d 334 (Cal. 1976). In that case, the Supreme Court of California held that a psychotherapist had a duty of care to a foreseeable victim of a threat of a serious danger of violence created by a patient. (The patient allegedly told the psychotherapist that he planned to kill a female acquaintance, and later did so.) The court intimated that the duty of

care might require directly warning the potential victim. In what ways do the facts alleged in *Pate* and *Safer* resemble the facts alleged in *Tarasoff*? Should the physician's duty to warn only extend to cases where the patient actively creates the harm? See Michelle R. King, Physician Duty to Warn a Patient's Offspring of Hereditary Genetic Defects: Balancing the Patient's Right to Confidentiality Against the Family Member's Right to Know—Can Or Should Tarasoff Apply?, 4 Quinnipiac Health L. J. 1 (2000).

Note: It is important to keep distinct two related questions: 1) Do health care providers owe a duty of care to the relatives of their patients, and if so when? and 2) If a duty of care is owed to the relatives, what does the duty of care require—a statement to the patient about the risks to the relatives or additional efforts by the health care provider to ensure that the risk information reaches the patient? Do the courts disagree about the first question or only about the second question?

The physician's duty to warn third parties has been extended to contagious and even non-contagious diseases. On the latter, see Bradshaw v. Daniel, 854 S.W.2d 865 (Tenn. 1993) (duty to warn husband that wife had Rocky Mountain Spotted Fever). Are genetic disorders "contagious"?

5.   Under the rule adopted by the court in *Safer*, what if the patient instructs the physician not to disclose the information to anyone? New Jersey enacted a statute in response to the *Safer* case that reads as follows:

N.J. STAT. ANN. § 10:5–47 (2013)

Conditions for disclosure of genetic information

a.   Regardless of the manner of receipt or the source of genetic information, including information received from an individual, a person may not disclose or be compelled, by subpoena or any other means, to disclose the identity of an individual upon whom a genetic test has been performed or to disclose genetic information about the individual in a manner that permits identification of the individual, unless:

(1)   Disclosure is necessary for the purposes of a criminal or death investigation or a criminal or juvenile proceeding;

(2)   Disclosure is necessary to determine paternity in accordance with the provisions of section 11 of P.L.1983, c.17 (C.9:17–48);

(3)   Disclosure is authorized by order of a court of competent jurisdiction;

(4)   Disclosure is made pursuant to the provisions of the "DNA Database and Databank Act of 1994," P.L.1994, c.136 (C.53:1–20.17 et seq.);

(5)   Disclosure is authorized by the tested individual or the tested individual's representative by signing a consent which complies with the requirements of the Department of Health and Senior Services;

(6)   Disclosure is for the purpose of furnishing genetic information relating to a decedent for medical diagnosis of blood relatives of the decedent;

(7)   Disclosure is for the purpose of identifying bodies;

(8) Disclosure is pursuant to newborn screening requirements established by State or federal law;

(9) Disclosure is authorized by federal law for the identification of persons; or

(10) Disclosure is by an insurer pursuant to the requirements of P.L.1985, c.179 (C.17:23A–1 et seq.).

b.   The provisions of this section apply to any subsequent disclosure by any person after another person has disclosed genetic information or the identity of an individual upon whom a genetic test has been performed.

Does this statute overturn *Safer?* In some states, the law immunizes health care professionals from civil or criminal liability in certain circumstances. Title 410, section 513/30 of the Illinois Compiled Statutes, part of that state's Genetic Information Privacy Act, states: "No civil or criminal sanction under this Act shall be imposed for any disclosure or nondisclosure of a test result to a spouse by a physician acting in good faith under this paragraph." Would this protect a physician who disclosed test results to a spouse without the consent of the person who was tested? Would the protection of the statute extend to disclosure to children?

6.   The Health Insurance Portability and Accountability Act (HIPAA) Privacy Rule prohibits the disclosure of individually identifiable health information without the authorization of the individual. 45 C.F.R. Parts 160, 164. One of the exceptions permits disclosures "required by law," and this includes common law as well as statutes. 45 C.F.R. § 164.512(a). Another exception permits, but does not require, disclosures "to prevent or lessen a serious and imminent threat to the health or safety of a person or the public" 45 C.F.R. § 164.512(j). The exception explicitly notes that it is consistent with *Tarasoff*-required disclosures. In theory, if a state does not have a genetic privacy statute that prohibits disclosure of genetic information without consent, the Privacy Rule would not prohibit the state from judicially recognizing a duty to warn if certain criteria were met: (1) the client's genetic information reveals a "serious and imminent threat" to the relative's health, (2) disclosure of this information would be "necessary to prevent or lessen the threat," and (3) the relative would be "reasonably able to prevent or lessen the threat." *Id.* On the other hand, the combination of widespread legislative action to protect genetic privacy, the dearth of cases clearly imposing such a duty, and the spirit—if not the letter—of the Privacy Rule, would likely deter a court from imposing such a requirement.

Are there any genetic risks that are "serious and imminent"? Imagine a genetic counselor whose client has arrhythmogenic right ventricular cardiomyopathy, a heart condition that is usually autosomal dominant and can develop later in life. The condition varies in severity but often presents no symptoms and can result in heart failure and sudden cardiac death. It is treatable if one is under the care of a cardiologist, and risks can be reduced by avoiding competitive sports. If the client, who wants to cultivate a tough image as a police officer, refuses to disclose his condition to relatives, would this exception apply? What if the genetic counselor knows his sister is a marathon runner? How does this case compare to the facts of *Safer* or *Pack*? What are the harms of disclosing and the harms of failing to disclose?

In the rare instance when a client chooses not to warn relatives, genetic counselors face an ethical dilemma. On the one hand, disclosure to relatives could help them prevent serious medical harms. The necessity of disclosure to relatives or their patients, however, may depend on the state of technology and access to genetic testing. For example, if whole genome sequencing becomes more routine, relatives with access to such technology could learn about actionable genetic risks without a genetic counselor having to breach patient confidentiality. Sometimes, however, disclosure might be the only way to avert harm.

On the other hand, clients may be trying to protect relatives. For example, a mother reportedly forbade her married daughters to tell her unmarried daughter about the mother's BRCA mutation for fear it could make the unmarried daughter "less marriageable." Breaches of confidentiality could cause various harms, such as embarrassment, impaired family relationships; stigmatization; or discrimination. Finally, they could lead to distrust of genetic counselors, deterring genetic testing, genetic counseling or participation in genetics research.

See Sonia M. Suter, Legal Challenges in Genetics, Including Duty to Warn and Genetic Discrimination, Cold Spring Harbor Persp. Med. (2019), doi: 101101/cshperspect.a036665. Suter argues that "an absolute rule forbidding disclosure to relatives or their physician raises ethical concerns." Mark Rothstein, on the other hand, argues that requiring health care providers to do anything more than encourage patients to warn relatives about genetic risks could cause harm to the interested parties. Mark Rothstein, Reconsidering the Duty to Warn Genetically At-Risk Relatives, 20 Genetics Med. 286 (2018). Whether or not there should be an ethical duty to warn, should such disclosure ever be permissible?

7.   The HIPAA Privacy Rule does not explicitly address disclosures of genetic information to family members, but the Office for Civil Rights of the Department of Health and Human Services, which enforces the rule, discusses scenarios where patients' family members want "to identify their own genetic health risks." A health care provider may share genetic information about the patient "with providers treating family members of the individual . . . , provided the individual has not requested and the health care provider has not agreed to a restriction on such disclosure." 78 Fed. Reg. 5668 (Jan. 25, 2013). If disclosure of a patient's information is ethically acceptable in certain rare scenarios, is it preferable to tell the patient's relatives directly or the relative's health care provider? What ethical considerations might be relevant?

Would a physician's disclosure of genetic risks to the provider of a patient's family member require secrecy on the part of the family members' physician? If so, is such secrecy ethical? Is it practicable?

8.   The court in *Pate* states: "Thus, we emphasize that in any circumstances in which the physician has a duty to warn of a genetically transferable disease, that duty will be satisfied by warning the patient." Is that true? Is there a situation in which warning the patient would not be sufficient to discharge the physician's duty?

9.   In Molloy v. Meier, 679 N.W.2d 711 (Minn. 2004), physicians failed to identify the Fragile X mutation in Kimberly Molloy's developmentally delayed daughter and to inform Molloy about the risk of passing on the mutation to future children. Molloy remarried and had a son with similar disabilities who was found to carry the Fragile X mutation. The court held that the physicians owed Molloy a duty of care even though she was not a patient because "a physician's duty regarding genetic testing and diagnosis extends beyond the patient to biological parents who foreseeably may be harmed by a breach of that duty." In this case, informing the patient, a child with mental impairment, would not have benefited Kimberly Molloy. As the patient's mother, however, Molloy was entitled to her minor child's medical information. Thus, unlike *Pate* and *Safer*, this case did not implicate confidentiality issues.

10.   The decision in *Safer* requires the physician to take "reasonable steps" to see that warning information reaches the person to whom the physician owes a duty to warn. What steps might be "unreasonable" and what considerations inform that judgment? The plaintiff was a child when her father was diagnosed and Dr. Pack died before she reached maturity. What effect should this have on the duty to warn?

11.   Physicians generally do not feel knowledgeable about available genetic tests. See Arch G. Mainous III et al., Academic Family Physicians' Perception of Genetic Testing and Integration into Practice: A CERA Study, 45 Fam. Med. 257 (2013). Is that relevant to questions about whether there should be a duty to warn patients of genetic risks or which providers, if any, should be held to that duty?

CHAPTER 7

GENOMIC ANALYSIS, CANCER GENOMICS, AND GENETIC TESTING OF CHILDREN AND ADOLESCENTS

■ ■ ■

I. GENOMIC ANALYSIS AND INCIDENTAL FINDINGS

SONIA M. SUTER, GENOMIC MEDICINE—NEW NORMS REGARDING GENETIC INFORMATION
15 Houston J. Health L. & Pol'y 83, 89–93 (2013).

* * *

With advances in bioinformatics and sequencing technology, the ability to sequence the whole genome or exome ("WG/ES") is becoming faster, more accurate, and cheaper. * * * Such expansive testing has not yet become a part of ordinary clinical care, although genomic analysis is being offered in certain instances based on medical indications. For example, individuals with family histories of cancer are being offered testing of panels of cancer genes. Similarly, in some instances where a complex disorder has not yet been diagnosed but a genetic variant is suspected, clinicians have used WG/ES to search for potentially responsible mutations. This kind of expansive screening is part of an effort to end the "diagnostic odysseys" for many rare disorders, sometimes with breathtaking success. * * * *

> **What's That?:** The genome is the complete set of genetic material in a cell. In humans, it made up of 3 billion base pairs. The exome represents all of the exons in the genome, that is, the parts of the genome that code for proteins. The exome represents 1–1.5% of the human genome.

[When and if] expansive genetic analysis . . . become[s] a routine part of personalized medicine in the near future as individuals undergo array-based genotyping or even WG/ES to learn about susceptibility and risks for various genetic conditions, * * * we will see an expansion of the categories of people who undergo genetic analysis from those with heightened risks of inherited disease to those with ordinary population risks of genetic disease, i.e., potentially anyone. * * *

Given that each of us has some genetic mutations, * * * genomic analysis can potentially reveal something to all of us about at least some of these variations. * * * * [One of] the most significant and perhaps most obvious change will be the sheer amount of information that array-based genotyping and especially WG/ES analysis will provide. By moving from targeted testing, which focuses on information concerning a particular gene, to genomic analysis, which produces information about different parts of the genome, the amount of information generated will be enormous. Although the goal of such expansive testing is to provide more information so that people can make important health-care and life-style decisions, * * * the explosion and complexity of information will present a number of challenges and dilemmas for the health care system related to, respectively, informed consent and the amount and kind of information that should be reported and disclosed to various categories of patients.

FYI: Most known mutations that cause disease are in exons. Therefore whole exome sequencing is an efficient way to identify most known disease-causing genetic variants. However, some genetic variants outside of exons cause genetic disorders by affecting gene activity and protein production. As a result, whole exome sequencing cannot identify the variants associated with these genetic disorders.

PRESIDENTIAL COMMISSION FOR THE STUDY OF BIOETHICAL ISSUES, ANTICIPATE AND COMMUNICATE: ETHICAL MANAGEMENT OF INCIDENTAL AND SECONDARY FINDINGS IN THE CLINICAL, RESEARCH, AND DIRECT-TO-CONSUMER CONTEXTS

(2013).

* * *

Incidental findings—traditionally defined as results that arise that are outside the original purpose for which the test or procedure was conducted—can create a range of practical, legal, and ethical challenges for recipients and practitioners. Discovering an incidental finding can be lifesaving, but it also can lead to uncertainty and distress without any corresponding improvement in health or wellbeing. For incidental findings of unknown significance, conducting additional follow-up tests or procedures can be risky and costly. Moreover, there is tremendous variation among potential recipients about whether, when, and how they would choose to have incidental findings disclosed. Information that one recipient regards as an unnecessary cause of anxiety could lead another recipient to feel empowered in making health-related decisions.

* * *

For clinicians and patients, one of the most challenging aspects of an incidental finding is determining what should be done in response. In some cases, clinical investigation of such a finding can lead to a diagnosis and beneficial, perhaps even lifesaving, treatment. In many other cases, however, further testing reveals that the incidental finding would have had no health consequences if left untreated. Pursuing an incidental finding might require conducting additional diagnostic tests or procedures that expose patients to additional risk, anxiety, or other psychological ramifications. If the finding turns out to have no medical significance, patients undertake these additional risks, including the risk of further incidental findings, without corresponding benefit.

For a variety of reasons, clinicians might be motivated to pursue diagnostic workups of incidental findings even when a clinician's professional judgment suggests that such workup is unnecessary. This motivation could stem, in part, from the prevailing notion that learning more information necessarily means providing better care. Both clinicians and patients can have difficulty accepting this uncertainty, even if certainty is unlikely to be obtained through additional testing. And ignoring an incidental finding or pursuing a "wait and see" course of action, often referred to as "watchful waiting," might be questioned if this decision results in a poor outcome. Clinicians might be motivated by patients and their families who prefer to be "better safe than sorry," without fully understanding that pursuing incidental findings often entails additional risks. Clinicians also might be motivated to err on the side of investigating incidental findings for fear of legal action, even though data on the motivations and rates of litigation do not substantiate these fears. In addition, clinicians might choose to seek secondary findings when suggested by professional guidance, such as the recent recommendations by the American College of Genetics and Genomics (ACMG) that laboratories seek and report a list of actionable genetic variants whenever clinical genomic sequencing is conducted.

* * *

Clinicians should make patients aware that incidental and secondary findings are a possible, or likely, result of the tests or procedures being conducted. Clinicians should engage in shared decision making with patients about the scope of findings that will be communicated and the steps to be taken upon discovery of incidental findings. Clinicians should respect a patient's preference not to know about incidental or secondary findings to the extent consistent with the clinician's fiduciary duty.

* * *

Professional and public health organizations should produce evidence-based standards for proposed screening programs that take into account the likelihood that incidental findings will arise. Professional organizations should provide guidance to clinicians on how to manage these incidental findings.

ACMG POLICY STATEMENT: UPDATED RECOMMENDATIONS REGARDING ANALYSIS AND REPORTING OF SECONDARY FINDINGS IN CLINICAL GENOME-SCALE SEQUENCING

17 Genetics Med. 68, 68–69 (2015).

As genome-scale sequencing is increasingly applied in clinical medicine, complex issues arise regarding the extent to which primary data should be analyzed and reported. At the present time, the most common clinical application of massively parallel sequencing lies in its use as a powerful new diagnostic tool in selected patients. When such sequencing is performed, primary data files consisting of a vast number of genomic variants are generated for each individual, with that information varying greatly with regard to relevance to the specific diagnostic question. What to do with these large numbers of "secondary" or "incidental" variants (nomenclature has varied with regard to such findings; the American College of Medical Genetics and Genomics (ACMG) has now adopted "secondary findings" as standard nomenclature, as recommended by the Presidential Commission on Bioethical Issues) has been a matter of considerable debate and discussion. Challenges include how extensively the primary data should be routinely analyzed and which of the many variants discovered should be reported to patients. These questions are especially challenging because although many of these variants are not clinically relevant or are uninterpretable, a minority may have important medical implications for the individual sequenced as well as for other family members.

In March 2013, the ACMG issued a set of recommendations regarding the use of clinical-scale sequencing. One recommendation advised laboratories performing whole-exome sequencing or whole-genome sequencing for any clinical indication to specifically analyze the sequence of 57 (later revised to 56) genes. These genes were selected based on substantial clinical evidence that pathogenic variants result in a high likelihood of severe disease that is preventable if identified before symptoms occur.

The release of this set of recommendations resulted in considerable discussion, much of it focused on whether the analysis of these 56 genes should be "mandatory" when whole-exome/whole-genome sequencing is pursued clinically, or whether patients should be able to "opt out" of such secondary analysis and reporting. This discussion was informed by a report by the Presidential Commission on Bioethical Issues regarding secondary findings and a survey administered by the ACMG to its membership in January 2014. In March 2014, the ACMG updated its recommendations, prompted in part by what appeared to be a general consensus among ACMG members and other relevant stakeholders that patients should be able to opt out of the analysis of genes unrelated to the indication for testing, and that the decision should be made during the process of informed consent before testing.

In this issue of *Genetics in Medicine*, we publish the results of this survey and articulate the current recommendations of the ACMG with regard to the analysis and return of secondary findings when clinical genome-scale analysis is pursued.

- When clinical genome-scale (e.g., whole-exome sequencing, whole-genome sequencing) sequencing is performed, written informed consent should be obtained by a qualified genetics health-care professional describing the nature of the test and addressing points such as interpretive uncertainty, privacy, possible impact on other family members, and the inevitable generation of data not immediately relevant to the clinical indication for sequencing. At the time of testing, the patient should be made aware that, regardless of the specific indication for testing, laboratories will routinely analyze the sequence of a set of genes deemed to be highly medically actionable so as to detect pathogenic variants that may predispose to a severe but preventable outcome.

- Patients should be informed during the consent process that, if desired, they may opt out of such analysis. However, they should also be made aware at that time of the ramifications of doing so.

- In accordance with the recent recommendations of the Presidential Commission for the Study of Bioethical Issues, as well as a lack of clear consensus in the ACMG membership survey administered in January 2014, the board recommends that the same policy should be adhered to in children as in adults; i.e., analysis of a set of selected genes to identify pathogenic variants associated with severe but preventable disease should be routinely performed. Parents should have the option during the consent process to opt out of such analysis.

- At this time, given the practical concerns and inherent difficulty of counseling patients about the features of each disorder and every gene on an ever-changing list, it is not feasible for patients to be offered the option of choosing a subset of medically actionable genes for analysis. Thus, the decision regarding routine analysis should apply to the entire set of genes deemed actionable by the ACMG.

The ACMG recognizes the complex nature of policies surrounding genome-scale testing and that positions will continue to evolve and change in response to new knowledge, new technologies, and ongoing input and discussion with our membership and the broader medical community. The ACMG will continue to explore these issues in the best interest of patients. A multidisciplinary working group has been formed to develop a process for updating and maintaining the list of genes to be routinely analyzed for secondary findings.

NOTES AND QUESTIONS

1.   To say, as the preceding publication states, that the original ACMG Policy Statement "resulted in considerable discussion" is a huge understatement. The original statement promulgated a list of 57 mutations that must be tested for any time that clinical gene sequencing occurred and required that the test results be reported to the clinician who ordered the sequencing, without offering the patient a choice. This provoked widespread condemnation as a violation of patients' rights. See, e.g., Lainie Friedman Ross, Mark A. Rothstein, & Ellen Wright Clayton, Mandatory Extended Searches in All Genome Sequencing: "Incidental Findings," Patient Autonomy, and Shared Decision Making, 310 JAMA 367 (2013); Robert Klitzman, Paul S. Appelbaum & Wendy Chung, Return of Secondary Genomic Findings vs. Patient Autonomy: Implications for Medical Care, 310 JAMA 369 (2013). For additional information, see Anastasia Richardson, Incidental Findings and Future Testing Methodologies: Potential Application of the ACMG 2013 Recommendations, 1 J.L. & Biosci. 378 (2014).

2.   In 2016, the ACMG issued a statement describing its new process for "accepting and evaluating nominations for updates to the secondary findings list." It also applied the process to six nominations, resulting in the addition of four genes and the removal of one, with an updated list of "59 medically actionable genes recommended for return in clinical genomic sequencing." Sarah S. Kalia, Recommendations for Reporting of Secondary Findings in Clinical Exome and Genome Sequencing, 2016 Update (ACMG SF v2.0): A Policy Statement of the American College of Medical Genetics and Genomics, 19 Genetics Med. 249 (2016).

3.   A survey of attitudes toward the return of incidental results when whole-genome sequencing is done in the clinical or research setting found four different approaches, return: 1) only results of "panels of specific genes or targeted sequencing," 2) only results that are analytically valid, clinically significant, and actionable, 3) results on "an *ad-hoc* case-by-case" basis, and 4) no results. Which approach is most defensible, ethically, and why?

Section III, *infra*, discusses concerns surrounding genetic testing for late-onset conditions in children. Would decisions about the release of incidental findings make a difference if genome sequencing was performed on an adult or a child? In the latter context, would it make a difference if there was a family history of the condition?

4.   While genetics professionals tend to believe there should be limits on the return of secondary or incidental findings, non-professionals in several

studies "concluded that the obvious solution would be to just 'ask for everything.'" They "placed value on knowledge itself regardless of whether or not it led to action ... and most welcomed 'information' regardless of its accuracy, validity, or predicted potential for harm," although "clinical actionability stood out as the benchmark against which all other characteristics were measured." These data, however, are based on responses to hypothetical situations, not actual decisions. Moreover, they do not address whether the respondents understood the number of uncertain findings that could be discovered. The study also did not explore whether respondents would choose a "handful of well-understood genomic findings or thousands of genomic findings with unknown clinical significance." Myra I. Roche & Jonathan Berg, Incidental Findings with Genomic Testing: Implications for Genetic Counseling Practice, 3 Current Genetic Med. Rep. 166, 169–70 (2015). How should we balance autonomy interests in obtaining information against the challenges of disclosing potentially vast amounts of information?

5.   Genetic counseling has long been patient-centered with respect to decision making. Is the ACMG recommendation consistent with that approach? It mentions "the practical concerns and inherent difficulty of counseling patients about the features of each disorder and every gene on an ever-changing list" or actionable variants. How can patients make informed decisions about what information to opt out of receiving, especially with too few trained genetic counselors to provide such counseling? Suter, Genomic Medicine, *supra,* at 99. How "coarsely or finely should the options" for potentially returnable variants be described? Roche & Berg, *supra,* at 168.

Further complicating the informed consent challenges is the fact that some state laws addressing informed consent for clinical genetic testing are "profoundly limited or confusing when applied to the current realities of" advances in genetic technologies like genome sequencing. For example, some statutes require disclosures of variants "known, determined, or scientifically or medically accepted or believed to be associated with disease, disorder or mutation." Given that genetic variants can be classified as "benign, likely benign, variants of uncertain significance, likely pathogenic, [or] pathogenic," it may not be clear which variants must be disclosed under the law. In other words, state informed consent requirements may not have caught up with genetic testing technologies. Kayte Spector-Bagdady et al., Analysis of State Laws on Informed Consent for Clinical Testing in the Era of Genomic Sequencing, 178C Am. J. Med. Genetics 81, 82, 86 (2018).

6.   Under the Health Insurance Portability and Accountability Act (HIPAA), individuals have the right to access genetic information in their medical records. Although, HIPAA exempted information possessed by clinical laboratories certified under the Clinical Laboratories Improvement Act (CLIA)—the type of laboratory that typically handles genetic tests for clinical (as opposed to purely research) purposes, in 2014, federal regulations under HIPAA were amended to remove the exemption for CLIA labs. Under HIPAA, therefore, patients potentially now have a right to request their genetic test results directly from the lab, bypassing the physician who ordered the test. See

79 Fed. Reg. 7289 (Feb. 6, 2014). However, the amended regulation contains the following exception: "A licensed health care professional has determined, in the exercise of professional judgment, that the access requested is reasonably likely to endanger the life or physical safety of the individual or another person." 45 C.F.R. § 164.524(a)(3)(i). In the Federal Register notice accompanying the amended regulations, the Department of Health and Human Services explained this exception as follows: "We do not believe that this rule will eliminate or interfere with the role or obligation of the treating or ordering provider to report and counsel patients on laboratory test results. The rule provides ample time to ensure providers receive sensitive test reports before the patient and to allow providers to counsel individuals on the test reports. In addition, as indicated above, we believe the rule will further encourage providers, at the time the test is ordered, to counsel patients on the potential outcomes of a test and what they may mean for the patient, given his or her medical history." The regulations give the patient the right to request a review of a lab's refusal to provide access to test results; the review is to be conducted by a "licensed health care professional who is designated by the covered entity to act as a reviewing official and who did not participate in the original decision to deny." 45 C.F.R. § 164.524(a)(4). What effect do you expect the amended regulation to have on the practice of clinical genetic testing?

Barbara Evans notes that this right of access to genomic data, which "potentially includes not just confirmed, clinically significant genomic test results but also uninterpreted variants and variants of uncertain significance," generated ongoing controversy. She acknowledges that the HIPAA access right may seem strange and ill-advised when viewed through the lens of "consumer safety regulation." She argues, however, that the better perspective is to view it "as a federal civil-rights regulation issued in response to a mandate laid down in the Genetic Information Nondiscrimination Act of 2008 (GINA)." Suggesting that the goals of consumer safety and civil rights need not be in conflict, she offers some possible solutions to reconcile the two. Barbara J. Evans, HIPAA's Individual Right of Access to Genomic Data: Reconciling Safety and Civil Rights, 102 Am. J. Hum. Genetics 5 (2018). To the extent that the two goals cannot be reconciled, which goal is more important, consumer safety or civil rights?

7.   What kind of liability do clinicians face if they fail to report incidental findings in genomic analysis? A study in 2013 found only eight U.S. cases addressing clinician liability for nondisclosure of incidental findings, and they all involved medical imaging, not genomics. The authors noted that these cases turned on the standard of care within each specialty. They conclude that, "for most clinicians, the standard of care will be defined almost entirely by the results and interpretations that are 'pushed' to them by the laboratory," although for medical geneticists who routinely "examine genomic results directly when [genome sequencing] is ordered, a separate standard of care will emerge." Ellen W. Clayton et al., Managing Incidental Genomic Findings:

Legal Obligations of Clinicians, 15 Genetic Med. 624, 627 (2013). Should disclosure obligations be different for incidental findings that reveal preventable or treatable health risks versus those that reveal reproductive risks?

A recent study found 202 genomics malpractice cases, which the authors broke down by type of alleged error. See Table 1. Although the authors found "genomic malpractice has yet to hit critical mass or become a major category of litigation," there was a "clear upward trend." In 60% of the genomics cases, plaintiffs received a payout, as compared with 22% in other medical malpractice cases. Gary E. Marchant & Rachel A. Lindor, Genomic Malpractice: An Emerging Tide or Genetic Ripple?, 73 Food & Drug L.J. 1, 15–17 (2018).

> **Food for Thought:** How might liability concerns affect what information physicians disclose? Imagine the standard of care is to disclose certain medically actionable findings unless a patient opts out. Compare the potential damages if a patient sued for disclosure of clinically actionable information she opted not to receive with the potential damages if medically actionable information was not disclosed and the patient developed a preventable medical condition. Would the differences in damages influence disclosure decisions? See Suter, Genomic Medicine, *supra*, at 117–22.

Table 1. "Genetic Malpractice Cases by Type of Error."

Error Category	# of Cases
Diagnose	57
Interpret	43
Offer	59
Return	36
Treat	8

Marchant & Lindor, Table 3, at 19.

8.   Should laboratories be liable for failing to report actionable incidental findings? In a recent case alleging wrongful death, a lab performed DNA sequencing on a young child who had begun experiencing febrile focal seizures at four months of age. Although the lab's first report correctly identified a transversion in the SCN1A gene, it "mislabeled" it as a variant of uncertain significance, rather than as a mutation associated with Dravet syndrome, a rare and catastrophic seizure disorder. A revised report later correctly identified the variant as Dravet syndrome mutation. The claim alleged that, because of the failure to identify the variant correctly initially, the child did not receive appropriate medical treatment and died. The District of South Carolina certified for procedural reasons that the laboratory could be treated as a "licensed health care provider" for purposes of the medical malpractice claim. Williams v. Quest Diagnostics, Inc., 816 S.E.2d 564 (2018). The motion to dismiss was denied in part and granted with respect to claims of a civil conspiracy. Williams v. Quest Diagnostics, Inc., 353 F. Supp. 3d 432 (D.S.C. Oct. 18, 2018).

Should the standard of care be different for laboratories as opposed to ordinary clinicians given the complexity of genomic analysis and the changing understanding of genetic variants? Some laboratories reanalyze variants annually. If that becomes more common, will that put laboratories that do not do annual reviews at legal risk? See Jennifer Couzin-Frankel, Genomics Breeds New Legal Questions, Sci., May 10, 2019, at 521.

9.   Another issue that arises with genomic analysis is whether clinicians have a duty to recontact when research reveals new relationships between a disease and a genetic variant or leads to reinterpretations of variants for which the original test was ordered. Based on existing law "a general duty to recontact patients about new genetic findings does not exist at this time, even though the unique nature of genetic data challenges medical custom." Although there is no clear duty to recontact patients at this point, the American College of Medical Genetics recently offered the following perspective:

> An ethical obligation based on the principle of beneficence requires at least attempting to re-contact the patient in circumstances that may meaningfully alter medical care. Moreover, re-contacting patients may be less of a burden due to electronic communication, electronic health record (EHR) patient portals, and direct patient access to their results from testing laboratories. It is quite possible that the legal requirements for re-contact will change as the burden of recontacting former patients is reduced and the potential resulting injury or missed opportunity for clinical benefit from failure to re-contact is better understood. It would be prudent for the provider to inform the patient prior to testing that the results have the potential to be updated and that it is important for the patient to provide up-to-date contact information.

> However, many practical issues remain in re-contacting patients. Populations are mobile, and physicians and healthcare networks may change. Navigating EHR systems to access patient information is often difficult as different EHR systems may not interface with each other and EHRs may not use current genetic nomenclature.

Karen L. David et al., Patient Re-Contact After Revision of Genomic Results: Points to Consider—A Statement of the American College of Medical Genetics (ACMG), 4 Genetics Med. 769 (2019). The ACMG also noted the additional burdens clinicians will face as new technologies detect an ever-increasing number of variants, especially in a health care system that imposes time limitations. On the other hand, asking patients to be responsible for follow up is difficult given the limits of their understanding of genetics and the medical system. Finally, "there is currently no consensus for when and how often laboratories should review the classification of a particular variant." Id. For more information on this issue, see Yvonne A. Stevens et al., Physician's Duty to Recontact and Update Genetic Advice, 14 Personalised Med. 367 (2017).

II. CANCER GENOMICS

Worldwide, cancer kills over eight million people each year. Recent developments in genomics have had a profound effect on the risk assessment, prevention, diagnosis, and treatment of a wide range of cancers. Indeed, genome sequencing of tumors is quickly becoming the standard of care in oncology. Two major initiatives are attempting to increase the scale of discovery in cancer genomics.

The Cancer Genome Atlas is a joint research program of the National Cancer Institute and the National Human Genome Research Institute at NIH. Its goal is to compile an atlas of the genomic structures of the 200 or more types of cancer. Understanding the genomic structure of the various types of cancer will aid in cancer prevention, early detection, and treatment. For further information, see cancergenome.nih.gov.

The International Cancer Genome Consortium is an international collaboration to obtain comprehensive descriptions of genomic, transcriptomic, and epigenomic changes in multiple tumor types and subtypes. For further information, see icgc.org.

The following excerpts review some of the recent advances and consider the next steps in cancer genomics.

LEVI A. GARRAWAY, GENOMICS DRIVEN ONCOLOGY: FRAMEWORK FOR AN EMERGING PARADIGM
31 J. Clinical Oncology 1806, 1806–1813 (2013).

Over the past decade, the oncology field has witnessed the advent of versatile means to test the hypothesis that comprehensive genomic information will enable rational therapeutic choices and improve outcomes for patients with cancer. The coming decade should produce the first wave of clinical studies that evaluate key tenets of genomics-driven cancer medicine. This accelerating pace of research invites consideration (albeit highly speculative) of what the world might ultimately look like on completion of the precision medicine experiment in oncology.

It should be emphasized that the genomics-driven paradigm is complementary to other frameworks currently shaping oncology therapeutic development (such as immunotherapy, targeting of the tumor microenvironment, or stem cell-based treatments). From the early observations of Sakurai and Sandberg to the present day, investigators have recognized that tumor genomic features must be evaluated as part of a larger clinical context that includes age, performance status, disease burden, cancer cell lineage, and histologic/molecular features when pondering treatment decisions. As with all medical advances, the emerging genomic framework must eventually become fully integrated within the existing spectrum of clinical knowledge leveraged by the oncologist to produce an optimal management plan.

Although knowledge of genomics may conceivably effect a profound transformation in the management of aggressive or advanced cancer, this prospect hardly represents a foregone conclusion. It is equally possible that the impact of genomics will prove more limited, particularly if clinical actionability is constrained by drug toxicity, tumor heterogeneity, or the overall complexity of tumor genomic information. Alternatively, the impact may prove substantive but not transformative; for example, genomic profiling may become relevant to some but not all cancer subtypes. Whatever the final outcome, the precision oncology hypothesis has certainly proved itself worthy of detailed interrogation during the coming years. In the words of Theodore Roosevelt, navigating the triumphs and challenges of genomics-driven cancer medicine will offer many oncologists "the chance to work hard at work worth doing."

BERT VOGELSTEIN ET AL., CANCER GENOME LANDSCAPES
339 Science 1546 (2013).

* * *

When we think about eradicating cancer, we generally think about curing advanced cases—those that cannot be cured by surgery alone because they have already metastasized. This is a curious way of thinking about this disease. When we think of cardiovascular or infectious diseases, we first consider ways to prevent them rather than drugs to cure their most advanced forms. * * *

This focus on curing advanced cancers might have been reasonable 50 years ago, when the molecular pathogenesis of cancers was mysterious and when chemotherapeutic agents against advanced cancers were showing promise. But this mindset is no longer acceptable. We now know precisely what causes cancer: a sequential series of alterations in well-defined genes that alter the function of a limited number of pathways. Moreover, we know that this process takes decades to develop and that the incurable stage, metastasis, occurs only a few years before death. In other words, of the one million people that will die from cancer this year, the vast majority will die only because their cancers were not detected in the first 90% of the cancers' lifetimes, when they were amenable to the surgeons' scalpel.

This new knowledge of cancer has reinvigorated the search for cures for advanced cancers, but has not yet permeated other fields of applied cancer research. A common and limited set of driver genes and pathways is responsible for most common forms of cancer; these genes and pathways offer distinct potential for early diagnosis. The genes themselves, the proteins encoded by these genes, and the end products of their pathways are, in principle, detectable in many ways, including analyses of relevant body fluids, such as urine for genitourinary cancers, sputum for lung cancers, and stool for gastrointestinal cancers. Equally exciting are the possibilities afforded by molecular imaging, which not only indicate the presence of a cancer but also reveal its precise location and extent. Additionally, research into the relationship between particular environmental influences (diet and lifestyle) and the genetic alterations in cancer is sparse, despite its potential for preventative measures.

The reasons that society invests so much more in research on cures for advanced cancers than on prevention or early detection are complex. Economic issues play a part: New drugs are far more lucrative for industry than new tests, and large individual costs for treating patients with advanced disease have become acceptable, even in developing countries. From a technical standpoint, the development of new and improved methods for early detection and prevention will not be easy, but there is no reason to assume that it will be more difficult than the development of new therapies aimed at treating widely metastatic disease.

Our point is not that strenuous efforts to develop new therapies for advanced cancer patients should be abandoned. These will always be required, no matter our arsenal of early detection or preventative measures. Instead, we are suggesting that "plan A" should be prevention and early detection, and "plan B" (therapy for advanced cancers) should be necessary only when plan A fails. To make plan A viable, government and philanthropic organizations must dedicate a much greater fraction of their resources to this cause, with long-term considerations in mind. We believe that cancer deaths can be reduced by more than 75% in the coming decades, but that this reduction will only come about if greater efforts are made toward early detection and prevention.

NOTE AND QUESTIONS

1.   One of the key insights of cancer genomics is that the genomic makeup of a tumor is often more important to therapy than the site of the tumor. Thus, a treatment regimen previously approved for one cancer site might be valuable to use at another site. Although such "off label" use of therapeutics is permissible, there are some questions, including the following. First, without using random controlled trials, will it be possible to prove that the new therapy works? Second, will public and private payers pay for this "unapproved" therapy?

2.   A recent study has determined that there is benefit in doing widespread hereditary cancer risk testing in people with metastatic breast cancer. The study found that this group of individuals has a "high prevalence of [pathogenic or likely pathogenic] variants that could have therapeutic implications." Such testing would not only have value for family members, but could guide certain treatment decisions, demonstrating some overlap between

germline genetic testing for predictive as well as therapeutic purposes. Kelsey Stuttgen et al., Pathogenic Germline Variants in Patients with Metastatic Breast Cancer, JAMA Oncology, August 29, 2019. doi:10.1001/jamaoncol.2019. 3116.

Despite the value of genetic testing for patients with breast and ovarian cancer, the rate of such testing is well below the levels expected under current testing guidelines. Differences in testing rates have been found based on race and socioeconomic status. The high costs may be deterring some patients from testing. See Allison W. Kurian et al., Genetic Testing and Results in a Population-Based Cohort of Breast Cancer and Ovarian Cancer Patients, 37 J. Clinical Oncology 1305 (2019).

3.   For further discussion, see Michael S. Lawrence, Discovery and Saturation Analysis of Cancer Genes Across 21 Tumor Types, 505 Nature 495 (2014); Richard Simon & Sameek Roychowdhury, Implementing Personalized Cancer Genomics in Clinical Trials, 12 Nature Reviews Drug Discovery 358 (2013).

III. GENETIC TESTING OF CHILDREN AND ADOLESCENTS

Genetic testing of minors raises special issues and has been the subject of much debate, particularly as it becomes possible to test for an increasing number of late-onset conditions. For example, when, if ever, is it appropriate to test children and adolescents, and for what conditions? Is it ever appropriate to test them without their knowledge and consent? Without the assent of their parents? What if the minor and parents disagree? Who should have access to the test results?

AMERICAN SOCIETY OF HUMAN GENETICS, POINTS TO CONSIDER: ETHICAL, LEGAL, AND PSYCHOSOCIAL IMPLICATIONS OF GENETIC TESTING IN CHILDREN AND ADOLESCENTS
97 Am. J. Human Gen. 6, 7–10 (2015).

* * *

In 1995, the ASHG and ACMG issued a joint report that offered points to consider for genetic testing in children. The clinical context of that report focused on decisions about testing for single-gene disorders in response to either a family history or within-population screening programs. The social context of that report included limited data about the psychosocial impact of such testing in children. The ASHG and ACMG recommended that clinicians and parents consider timely medical benefits related to diagnosis, prognosis, and interventions as the best justification for testing in the child. Additionally, the report recommended that the potential psychological benefits to adolescents who request such testing also be considered. The report suggested that in the absence of timely medical benefits to the child, or the expressed wishes of adolescents, testing should be deferred until adulthood, particularly for adult-onset conditions or for carrier status for reproductive decision making. However, the report acknowledged that there was limited information about the benefits and risks of genetic testing in children. The report recommended deferral of testing in the face of this uncertainty, yet it also recommended deference to parents in some circumstances. The report has been influential in encouraging caution and reflection regarding testing children but often has been over-interpreted as a stricter prohibition of predictive testing in children for adult-onset conditions than was intended.

* * *

Predictive Genetic Testing in High-Risk Families

In the 20 years since the first ASHG-ACMG pediatric testing statement, there has been a modest volume of clinical research about the impact of predictive testing in high risk families. To date, this limited research has not found evidence of significant psychosocial harms in children. Perhaps the most significant finding is that, even without testing, children and many families create narratives about a child's genetic status. That is, some families simply assume that their children are destined to have, or not have, the familial condition. Further, the baseline uncertainty about risk status can cause psychosocial distress in the absence of genetic testing. Over the last two decades, there has been a general shift toward greater parental discretion in the face of clinical uncertainty about the best interests of the child. This broad shift is not exclusive to genetics but has implications for genetic testing.

As parents consider the best course of action regarding genetic testing of their children, it remains important for parents to be aware that informed adults make a range of choices about predictive and reproductive testing, and thus many adults decline such testing. Deferring testing to adulthood allows children the opportunity to make their own decisions. This is especially important for the small subset of conditions where a minority of at-risk adults opt for genetic testing, such as for Huntington disease. Approaching parents (and children, when appropriate) with respectful but directive recommendations, along with acknowledging flexibility, might be an effective approach to forging a therapeutic alliance with families. Encouraging families to consider such decisions over a period of time might convince some families that testing will be helpful in their particular context, or it might become clear that it will be most appropriate to defer testing until adulthood. The ASHG offers the following recommendations:

- Unless there is a clinical intervention appropriate in childhood, parents should be encouraged to defer predictive

or pre-dispositional testing for adult-onset conditions until
adulthood or at least until the child is an older adolescent who
can participate in decision making in a relatively mature
manner.

- Adolescents should be encouraged to defer predictive or pre-
dispositional testing for adult-onset conditions until
adulthood because of the complexity of the potential impact
of the information at formative life stages.

- Providers should offer to explore the reasons why parents or
adolescents are interested in predictive or pre-dispositional
testing for adult-onset conditions. Providers can acknowledge
that, in some cases, testing might be a reasonable decision,
but decisions should follow thorough deliberation.

Adolescents should be provided the opportunity to discuss these issues
without the presence of their parents, although parents should be involved
in, and supportive of, any final decisions for testing. A referral to genetic
counselors and mental-health professionals is appropriate if the clinician
and family need additional support for decision making or in assessing the
psychosocial dynamics.

- Facilitating predictive or pre-dispositional testing of children
for adult-onset conditions can be justified in certain
circumstances. For example, after careful deliberations with
the family and older child, testing can be justified to alleviate
substantial psychosocial distress or to facilitate specific life-
planning decisions. The impact of predictive testing on
children and families remains uncertain and therefore can be
justified in specific cases when it is requested by families
after informed deliberations and when the testing is not
clearly inconsistent with the welfare of the child.

- Empirical research on the psychosocial impact of predictive
or predispositional testing in children is necessary for future
policy recommendations. Genetic testing of children for adult-
onset conditions in the research context can be ethically
justified because of its social importance and when risks are
minimized by appropriate counseling and support and when
appropriate parental permission and child assent are
obtained.

Genome-Scale Sequencing in Children

* * *

Genome-scale sequencing creates a tension between the need to
generate a comprehensive analysis of an individual's genome to address a
clinical challenge and the need to limit problems created by a wealth of

data, including secondary findings and findings of uncertain clinical significance. Yet, the improving coverage, accuracy, sensitivity, and cost effectiveness of genome-scale sequencing will eventually equal that of testing a single gene or performing targeted gene panels, meaning that genome-scale sequencing might become an attractive choice for interrogating a single gene or targeted set of genes. The ASHG recognizes the current debate regarding the obligation, if any, to search for selected variants with high clinical validity and clinical utility when conducting genome-scale sequencing. The ASHG makes an important distinction between using genome-scale sequencing as the method of choice for searching broadly for a diagnosis and choosing genome-scale sequencing with analysis restricted to a limited number of genes when a more targeted strategy is indicated. The recommendations below reflect ASHG's assessment that targeted tests, or selective sequence analysis, is usually preferable to less-discriminate data acquisition when the clinical challenge can be addressed through a targeted approach.

- When clinically indicated, the scope of genetic testing should be limited to single-gene analysis or targeted gene panels based on the clinical presentation of the patient.

- Targeted testing using genome-scale sequencing, but restricting analysis to a limited set of genes relevant to the clinical indication, is an acceptable alternative to a single-gene analysis or targeted gene panel in certain circumstances. When genome-scale sequencing is performed but the analysis is restricted to a limited set of targeted genes, ASHG finds it ethically acceptable for the laboratory to limit the analysis to the genes of clinical interest.

- ASHG recommends that, in the context of diagnostic testing for a child with a most likely genetic disorder, genome-scale sequencing is appropriate when prior more limited genetic testing failed to identify a causative mutation. Depending on the clinical presentation and on the quality and availability of appropriate targeted testing, comprehensive testing such as genome-scale sequencing might also be indicated in certain circumstances, even in the absence of prior, more limited genetic testing.

- At the present time, genome-scale sequencing is not indicated for screening in healthy children. Accordingly, genome-scale sequencing is not indicated for the purposes of clinical newborn screening at this time. In the research setting, genome-scale sequencing in newborns for screening purposes can be justified as part of carefully developed protocols for better understanding the potential benefits and risks of this technology in this context.

Secondary Findings

* * * The generation of a patient's genomic sequence data radically increases the probability of discovering incidental or secondary findings. For consistency, throughout this statement we use "secondary findings," defined as clinically relevant information unrelated to the condition for which the sequencing was originally ordered.

Secondary findings might have a clinical utility for a child or his or her family members. Therefore, there will be cases in which it is acceptable to return Clinical Laboratory Improvement Amendments (CLIA)-validated information derived from a child's sequence when such information has important clinical implications for the child or someone in the child's family.

Parents or guardians should have a clear understanding of when secondary findings might be generated and of the circumstances, if any, under which they can expect to be offered results. Children should be included in the informed-assent or -consent process to the extent that they are capable.

- ASHG recommends that clinicians offer to disclose secondary findings for a child to the child's parents or guardians only when the information has clear clinical utility for the child and/or his or her family members.

- In any clinical genomic endeavor that has a substantial likelihood of generating clinically relevant secondary findings, ASHG recommends that there should be a robust informed-consent process.

- If genome-scale sequencing is performed in somatic tissue, such as in tumor tissue in children with cancer, it is usually necessary to also conduct germline sequencing on the patient to adequately interpret the tumor sequence. Therefore, ASHG recommends that the same considerations in the management of secondary findings be undertaken for both somatic tissue sequencing and germline genome-scale sequencing.

Parents have wide decision-making authority, but in cases where the clinical response to a secondary finding will most likely prevent serious morbidity or mortality for the child, it can be appropriate to override a parental decision not to receive this information.

- ASHG recommends that, in general, parents should be able to decline to receive secondary findings in advance of genetic testing.

- However, when there is strong evidence that a secondary finding has urgent and serious implications for a child's health or welfare, and effective action can be taken to mitigate that threat, ASHG recommends that the clinician communicate those findings to parents or guardians regardless of the general preferences stated by the parents regarding secondary findings.

* * *

- When secondary findings are likely to be generated in the conduct of pediatric research, ASHG recommends that investigators develop and follow an IRB approved plan to manage such findings.

Questions about whether there is a duty to look for secondary findings have been actively debated. As analytic tools make searching for a limited list of high-value variants more efficient, the benefits of actively searching for such variants in the clinical context are likely to outweigh the costs and adverse consequences. However, more data, experience, and debate are necessary for defining the most ethically appropriate approach in the clinical pediatric context regarding an obligation to look for secondary findings. * * *

NOTES AND QUESTIONS

1.   Minors of the same age differ in terms of their maturity. Do the foregoing sets of recommendations take this into consideration?

Typically, age restrictions under the law, such as minimum ages for driving or voting, are irrebuttable presumptions; minors are not permitted to argue that they should qualify for the privilege despite being under-age. Should the approach for rules regarding genetic testing be different than for rules for, say, driving or voting? Why?

2.   What benefits might accrue from genetic testing of minors and adolescents? Which of these benefits do the foregoing recommendations recognize? Which harms? How do the recommendations balance benefit and harm? Is the result desirable?

One issue is the impact of genetic test information on the minor. Several studies suggest that disclosing test results to children is preferable to postponing disclosure until they are adults. For example, a 2013 study explored the reactions of adolescents who sought predictive genetic testing for adult-onset conditions. It found "remarkable consistency" in their views about predictive testing, even though the implications differ for various conditions.

For example, there are often preventive interventions for familial cancer syndromes but none for neurogenetic conditions, like Huntington disease.

Participants "conveyed feelings of disempowerment, lack of control and defeated expectations" regarding the testing process, which they found "onerous and a source of distress above and beyond simply living at risk." The adolescents reported that, before testing, "uncertainty and anxiety associated with not knowing had become a barrier to their development and participation in everyday activities." Learning their gene status, however, felt "empowering and allowed participants to get on with life and face key developmental tasks of adolescence and young adulthood such as establishing identity and making plans for the future." Cara Mand et al., "It Was the Missing Piece": Adolescent Experiences of Predictive Genetic Testing for Adult-Onset Conditions, 15 Genetics Med. 643, 646–47 (2013). Do the American Society of Human Genetics recommendations make sense given these findings? Should it matter whether the child requests the tests or not?

The participants in these studies had experience with the impact of the condition on affected family members and family dynamics. Would attitudes be different if they had not had those lived experiences?

3.   The Huntington Disease Society of America recommends against testing asymptomatic minors for Huntington disease, a nontreatable, adult-onset disease. Nevertheless, 53 percent of health professionals stated that they would perform the testing at the request of parents. In a survey of genetic testing laboratories, 22 percent reported that they performed tests for Huntington disease in children under the age of 12.

A survey of 27 guidelines and position papers finds unanimity that the "most important justification" for predictive testing of minors is medical benefit, although sometimes "the value of some preventive and therapeutic measures may be uncertain." While the concept of best interests is central to this issue, conflicts may arise between the interests of the minor and the best interest of the family. No consensus exists, however, when no preventive or therapeutic measures are available. Pascal Borry et al., Presymptomatic and Predictive Genetic Testing in Minors: A Systematic Review of Guidelines and Position Papers, 70 Clinical Genetics 374, 378–79 (2006).

Is it desirable that there be a single, uniform national policy on genetic testing of children and adolescents? Who should administer such a policy?

CHAPTER 8

REPRODUCTIVE GENETIC TESTING

■ ■ ■

For centuries, parents followed folk myths in attempts to control the characteristics of their children. In earlier generations, people believed that conceiving under certain circumstances (a full moon, wearing a particular garment or trinket, facing a certain direction, using a specific position, etc.) would influence the traits of their offspring. As physicians gained greater knowledge about inheritance, couples began to incorporate into their reproductive decisions information from family histories about the risk of passing on a particular genetic disease to their children.

In recent decades, genetic testing has entered the obstetric realm to provide more precise predictions about inheritable diseases. Couples planning to conceive can be screened to see if they are carriers of genetic diseases. During pregnancy, tests can be undertaken on the fetus. Most pregnant women in the United States now undergo some form of prenatal screening or testing, such as ultrasound, amniocentesis, chorionic villi sampling, or other tests. New technologies are available such as a blood test of the mother to analyze the health status or genetic make-up of the fetus. By testing the woman's blood for a particular gene product from the fetus (known as maternal serum alpha-fetoprotein), a physician can assess whether the child is at risk for a neural tube defect such as spina bifida or anencephaly. The physician can also analyze cell-free DNA from the fetus which is circulating in the mother's blood to determine whether there are indications of Down syndrome, other chromosomal anomalies, and potentially some single-gene disorders. Finally, individuals can do genetic analysis on embryos created through in vitro fertilization (IVF) to select embryos for implantation.

In the wake of the Human Genome Project, the range of genes that can be tested prenatally has grown exponentially. Ethical questions arise about whether fetuses should be tested for diseases that will not manifest until later in life, such as breast cancer, or for traits that do not represent diseases, such as gender. Even the question of what constitutes a disease is contested. Some deaf people argue deafness is neither a disease nor a disability, but merely a culture. Legal questions also abound about which genetic tests health care professionals should offer and the circumstances under which they may be found liable for negligence in testing.

What can people do in response to concerns that they might pass on a genetic disease to their children? A range of responses is available. Some people who are at risk of passing on a gene mutation related to a recessive genetic disorder choose not to marry a person with the same mutation. Other people choose to undergo in vitro fertilization and preimplantation screening or testing and implant only embryos that have not inherited the disease. A great many undergo prenatal screening when pregnant to determine whether they are at heightened risk for certain chromosomal disorders, like trisomy 21. Finally, some pursue prenatal diagnosis during pregnancy, if the risks are heightened because of a positive screening test, family history, carrier status, or other risk factors. They can then decide whether or not to terminate a pregnancy if the fetus is affected.

An additional option for couples at genetic risk is to use an egg, sperm, or embryo donor to provide a different genetic component of the pregnancy. As with an infertile couple's use of third-party aid in reproduction, this process raises questions about what type of genetic screening should be done on the donor. This chapter discusses the legal and ethical issues raised by the use of genetics in the context of reproduction, with a focus on testing to prevent disease. Chapter 9 will explore the use of technological advances to select future children based on non-medical traits, the propensity *for* disabilities, and their ability to serve as donors for siblings who are ill.

> **FYI:** Screening tests are distinct from diagnostic tests in general and in the prenatal context. A screening test identifies individuals at increased risk for the condition at issue, but the test results are not diagnostic. Further testing is required to determine whether the disease is present or not. Diagnostic testing, in contrast, aims to detect the presence or absence of disease.

I. PRENATAL DIAGNOSIS AND SCREENING

LORI B. ANDREWS, FUTURE PERFECT: CONFRONTING DECISIONS ABOUT GENETICS
56–62 (2001).

Family history has long been used to predict a couple's general chance of giving birth to a child with a particular disorder. Starting [in the 1960s] with the advent of prenatal diagnosis through amniocentesis, specific genetic information about a particular fetus became available to parents. Today, genetic information related to reproduction is obtainable in numerous ways. One partner may have a mutation associated with Huntington disease or breast cancer, for example, and face a decision about whether the fetus should be tested for that mutation. In other instances, the parents may not know their genetic make-up, but each (or maybe both) may be tested in advance of reproduction (or even during pregnancy) for mutations that are common in their ethnic group—such as cystic fibrosis for Caucasians, sickle cell anemia for African Americans, or Tay-Sachs for

Ashkenazi Jews. Or the fetus itself may be tested, which can reveal previously unknown genetic information about the mother, the father, or both. Parents-to-be may learn that both are carriers of a recessive disorder, that one has a mutation associated with a dominant disorder, or that the woman has passed on a mutation associated with an X-linked disorder.

The range of conditions that can be [identified] prenatally is growing exponentially each year. More than 500 different conditions can be diagnosed through chorionic villi sampling or amniocentesis. [As of 2010, there were 5000 known single-gene disorders and 1000 genetics tests for them]. The availability of these tests affects even those people who decide not to have them done. Some women say that friends and relatives have made them feel irresponsible for not having genetic testing; others have felt guilty and responsible if they had a child with a genetic disorder (either after refusing testing or after deciding to carry through the pregnancy of an affected child). Yet, as more and more prenatal genetic tests become available, parents are increasingly feeling that they are put into the position of playing God. Should they have prenatal screening for a disorder that won't affect their child until much later in life—or should they bank on a cure being developed in the child's lifetime? Should they abort a fetus whose disorder is treatable, albeit at some expense? As testing becomes available to tell whether a fetus is at a higher likelihood of suffering from breast cancer, colon cancer, heart disease, diabetes, and Alzheimer disease, should such tests be utilized? What about for alcoholism, violence, and other behavioral traits? In studies with varying degrees of scientific repute, genes have been implicated in shyness, bedwetting, attempted rape, homosexuality, manic-depressive disorder, arson, tendency to tease, traditionalism, tendency to giggle or to use hurtful words, and zest for life. Should testing for such traits be done prenatally? If so, what should be done with the resulting information?

* * *

Many couples who use genetic services in conjunction with reproduction feel that it has offered them an overall benefit by allowing them to make an informed choice about their pregnancies. In fact, couples have sued when they felt deprived of prenatal genetic information. At least one federal court [Lifchez v. Hartigan, 735 F. Supp. 1361, 1377 (N.D. Ill.1990), cert. denied, 498 U.S. 1069 (1991)] has recognized the importance of this choice by indicating that the constitutional protections of the abortion decision logically "must also include the right to submit to a procedure designed to give information about that fetus which can then lead to a decision to abort."

RUTH M. FARRELL, WOMEN AND PRENATAL GENETIC TESTING IN THE 21ST CENTURY

23 Health Matrix 1, 4–6 (2011).

* * *

* * * One category of prenatal genetic testing that has undergone important changes is the screening test. Screening tests provide information about the chance that a fetus has Down syndrome or other related chromosomal abnormalities. The advantage of screening tests is that they are performed by drawing a sample of blood from the mother without the use of more invasive procedures; thus, the pregnant woman can bypass the uncommon but real risks associated with chorionic villus sampling (CVS) and amniocentesis. When used as a triage mechanism, screening tests help to determine which women might benefit from definitive diagnostic testing, thus reducing the potential number of iatrogenic losses of chromosomally normal fetuses that could occur with generalized use of these procedures. Screening tests also have limitations. One limitation is the ability of the screen to detect all fetuses with an abnormal complement of chromosomes, so that there is a chance of a screen-negative result in the context of an affected fetus. There is also the possibility of a false positive result, in which case the screen would indicate an increased risk of a chromosomal abnormality when the fetus has, in fact, a normal complement of chromosomes. Thus, this information can only be used to inform decisions about further testing.

> **What's Aneuploidy?:** Normally, individuals have 46 (23 pairs) of chromosomes. Aneuploidy occurs when someone has more or fewer than 46 chromosomes. During meiosis—the division of germ cells that creates gametes (eggs or sperm)—the pairs of chromosomes are divided, leaving each gamete with 23 chromosomes. If nondisjunction occurs during meiosis, at least one pair of chromosomes does not divide. For example, nondisjunction of chromosome 21 results in one egg with two chromosomes 21 and the other with none. If the egg with both chromosomes 21 is fertilized with a normal sperm, the resulting embryo will have trisomy 21.

The first screening tests were developed in the late 1980s and 1990s. Initially, it was determined that the combination of three maternal serum chemicals (human chorionic gonadotropin, unconjugated estriol, and alpha-fetoprotein) conferred information about possible abnormalities caused by extra or missing chromosomes (referred to as "aneuploidy"). This test analyzing these three chemicals was known as the Triple Screen. In the years following, the Quadruple Screen was developed to increase detection rates with the addition of another maternal serum marker called inhibin A. Since that time, there has been a move towards earlier screening modalities. While the Triple and Quadruple Screens provided fetal risk information, they could not be performed until after the fifteenth week of pregnancy. Thus, choices about the pregnancy following confirmatory diagnostic testing could not be made until well into the second trimester, a time when the choice to continue or terminate the pregnancy may have very different ramifications for the woman than if the decision had been made earlier in the pregnancy. First trimester aneuploidy screening is a new screening approach consisting of assessment of maternal serum markers in conjunction with sonographic measurement of the back of the fetal neck (also known as nuchal translucency). This new tool confers similar fetal genetic risk information regarding Down syndrome as the Triple and Quadruple Screen but can be performed as early as eleven weeks into gestation. Timed one month earlier than its second trimester counterparts, this new screening modality gives patients a wider range of options over the course of their prenatal care, including immediate diagnostic procedures in the initial weeks of pregnancy.

Important advances have also taken place in another category: diagnostic testing. The procedures of CVS and amniocentesis were developed in the latter half of the twentieth century as ways to directly test fetal cells to confirm the presence or absence of a genetic condition. Both procedures involve inserting a needle into the pregnant woman's uterus to access fetal or placental cells for testing. While amniocentesis cannot be performed until the second trimester of pregnancy, CVS can be performed in the first trimester.

The procedures of CVS and amniocentesis have changed little over the decades since their development. What has changed, however, is the number of testing applications that can be performed using these procedural platforms. Initially, these diagnostic procedures were used to conduct analysis for a single genetic mutation (e.g., cystic fibrosis) or chromosomal abnormality (e.g., Down syndrome) at a time. The development of multiplex testing techniques then allowed assessment for multiple different single Mendelian mutations or fetal characteristics (e.g., gender) simultaneously. Further advances in genetic science have changed the basic paradigms of genetic conditions and shifted our perception of diseases away from the concept of their being monogenic in origin towards the idea that they often involve multiple genes in concert. As a result, there has been a move towards incorporating microarrays into prenatal care, allowing analysis to identify from tens to thousands of variants during a single testing process. Prenatal microarray testing is able to generate detailed genetic information that could not be detected using standard cytogenetic techniques.

Until recently, diagnostic information about the fetus could only be obtained through invasive procedures such as CVS and amniocentesis. Now, non-invasive prenatal genetic diagnosis is changing conventional paradigms about accessing and using fetal genetic information to guide antepartum care. Performed by drawing a blood sample from the pregnant woman, it is anticipated that non-invasive prenatal genetic diagnosis will ultimately provide the same degree of diagnostic information as more invasive procedures while bypassing the physical risks to mother and fetus. The clinical potential for non-invasive prenatal genetic diagnosis is great. Studies show that pregnant women are very interested in using this new approach to prenatal genetic testing. Preliminary studies also show that including the option of noninvasive prenatal genetic diagnosis increases women's interest in and willingness to undergo prenatal genetic testing for a number of different conditions and also alters core beliefs about genetic testing in pregnancy. Access to genetic information via a sample of maternal blood is also likely to encourage the already growing direct-to-consumer movement of genetic testing, which may further complicate legal, ethical, and social ramifications. As the development of genetic, genomic, and molecular technologies concurrently accelerates, the scope of possible in utero investigations will drastically expand.

NOTES AND QUESTIONS

1. As the Farrell article notes, most forms of fetal diagnosis are intrusive and therefore present some level of risk to the fetus and some physical risk to the pregnant woman, such as infection. The rarely used fetoscopy, which samples blood from the fetus while in utero, presents a 3 to 6 percent risk of fetal death. Amniocentesis is the most common prenatal diagnostic test. Usually performed between 15 and 20 weeks gestation, it involves the removal of amniotic fluid containing fetal cells, which can be analyzed for chromosomal anomalies or genetic disorders. The largest risk associated with amniocentesis is pregnancy loss. The risk varies according to the stage of pregnancy and is difficult to estimate because of the lack of controls and the fact that miscarriage is already a greater risk in women choosing this procedure. Estimates for spontaneous miscarriage related to amniocentesis have ranged from as low as 1 in 300 to 500 to as high as 1.0%, although a recent estimate comparing the background risks of miscarriage in women who did not undergo amniocentesis with those who did suggested the risk was 0.11%. Ranjit Akolekar, Procedure-Related Risk of Miscarriage Following Amniocentesis and Chorionic Villus Sampling: A Systematic Review and Meta-Analysis, 45 Ultrasound Obstetrics Gynecology 16 (2014).

Chorionic villus sampling (CVS), which involves sampling part of the placenta for chromosomal or genetic analysis, is typically performed in the first trimester, between ten and thirteen weeks gestation. It has been associated with a rate of pregnancy loss as high as 3.6%, but because miscarriage is most common in the first trimester, the additional risk due to CVS has been estimated to be approximately as low as 1 in 300 to 500 and as high as 1–2 %. Again, a more recent estimate comparing the risk of those who did not undergo the procedure with those who did found a procedure-related risk of 0.22%. Akolekar, *supra*. Some studies suggested that CVS presents a risk of limb deformities of about one in 3,000 cases, but that has been associated with CVS performed before nine weeks, which is why the procedure is not typically offered before ten weeks. Richard Olney et al., Chorionic Villus Sampling and Amniocentesis: Recommendations for Prenatal Counseling, 44 MMWR Recommendations & Rep. 1 (1995).

2.   Until 2007, prenatal diagnosis (amniocentesis or CVS) was offered only to women at increased risk for chromosomal anomalies or genetic disorders, especially advanced maternal age. Thirty-five was used as the age at which such testing was indicated because the risk of having a child with trisomy 21 was greater than the estimated risk of pregnancy loss from the procedure. That rationale, however, presumes all women weigh the harm of pregnancy loss as equal to the harm of failing to identify trisomy 21. In fact, women's views of these relative harms vary depending on their circumstances and personal views. Miriam Kuppermann et al., Who Should Be Offered Prenatal Diagnosis? The 35-Year Old Question, 89 Am. J. Pub. Health 160 (1999). Nevertheless, by 1990, approximately 40% of women thirty-five years or older underwent either amniocentesis or CVS. Olney, *supra*.

In 2007, the American College of Obstetricians and Gynecologists recommended that both prenatal diagnostic testing and prenatal screening tests with high detection and low false positive rates be offered to all pregnant women regardless of age. The goal was to increase the accessibility of tests that identify chromosomal abnormalities and to allow women to balance for themselves the benefit and risks of the various tests. It also emphasized the importance of informed decisions. ACOG, Committee Opinion, Screening for Fetal Chromosomal Abnormalities, 109 Obstetrics & Gynecology 217 (2007).

3.   The noninvasive prenatal test that Farrell describes above is usually offered between ten and twelve weeks. It involves analysis of cell-free fetal (and maternal) DNA in maternal serum, sometimes called noninvasive prenatal testing (NIPT). Originally used to identify the likelihood of trisomies 13, 18, and 21, as well as fetal sex, companies now market it for assessment of the risk of other chromosomal anomalies like sex chromosome aneuploidy, rare trisomies like trisomy 16 and 22, and microdeletions or microduplications of chromosomes. It has also been marketed for risk assessment of certain single gene disorders such as Huntington disease, achondroplasia, and cystic fibrosis. Although still not diagnostic, compared to previous prenatal screening tests, NIPT is much improved in identifying risks for the most common trisomies, 13, 18, and 21. The accuracy of NIPT however, varies for other conditions and in some cases can be quite low. Because it is still a screening test, physicians recommend amniocentesis or chorionic villus sampling to confirm positive results.

> **FYI:** Because analysis of cell-free DNA is a prenatal screening test, it can lead to false positives. Sometimes the false positive can indicate an adverse maternal condition, including maternal mosaicism (meaning the mother has some cells with aneuploidy), or in rare cases, maternal cancer. The risk of maternal cancer is especially great when more than one aneuploidy is identified and it is different from the fetal genotype.

4.   Although no treatments exist for most conditions that can be identified through prenatal testing, such testing is valuable to prospective parents in various ways. Not only can it inform prospective parents' decisions about whether to continue an affected pregnancy, it can also help them prepare for raising a child with a particular disability; offer reassurance about the health of the fetus; provide information about fetal sex; or, in rare cases, identify conditions that can be treated in utero. Farrell notes, however, that the field of high-risk obstetrics and fetal intervention is exploring interventions to improve fetal and neonatal outcomes, which may, for some conditions, begin to change the "calculus of prenatal testing." Farrell, *supra,* at 11–12.

5.   Informed decision making about prenatal testing depends on knowledge about the conditions that can be identified and some understanding of the benefits and risks of testing. Unfortunately, several barriers can impede informed decision making in this context. First, as more women undergo prenatal screening, many will have no family history of or membership in ethnic groups with an increased risk for identifiable genetic conditions. As a result, prospective parents may have limited knowledge about these conditions, making it difficult for them to decide whether to undergo prenatal testing/screening and what to do if results identify one of these in the fetus.

Complicating the informed consent process is the routinization of prenatal testing. Even before non-invasive prenatal testing (NIPT) was available, prenatal screening had become routine, moving out of specialists' care into general obstetric care. With this change, nondirective and comprehensive genetic counseling became more difficult and sometimes virtually nonexistent. Many factors have contributed to such routinization, including programs mandating the offer of such screening, concerns about liability for failing to identify genetic anomalies, public sentiments that "good parents" should undergo prenatal testing, and providers' biases in favor of testing. See Sonia Suter, The Routinization of Prenatal Testing, 28 Am. J. L. Med. 233 (2002).

The unprecedented role of commercial companies in the development and marketing of NIPT tests has further impeded informed consent. Unlike with other prenatal modalities, private laboratories have increasingly influenced patient expectations and even clinical practices with efforts aimed to achieve market dominance in the area of prenatal testing. Marketing campaigns, which fail to meet the standards of the American College of Medical Genetics and Genomics, have created confusion for both patients and providers about the accuracy of the tests. See Brian L. Shaffer & Mary E. Norton, Cell-Free DNA Screening for Aneuploidy and Microdeletion Syndromes, 45 Obstetrics & Gynecology Clinics N. Am. 13 (2018); Brian G. Skoto et al., Adherence of Cell-Free DNA Noninvasive Prenatal Screens to ACMG Recommendations, Genetics Med., Apr. 3, 2019, doi: 10.1038/s41436-019-0485-2.

What role can or should the law play in addressing these various limits on informed decision making with respect to prenatal testing?

6.   Some physicians undertake genetic screening tests on pregnant women without informed consent—and tell them the results of the testing only

if it indicates a problem. When questioned about this practice, physicians state that other types of unconsented-to testing are routinely done on pregnant women without their consent. Are genetic tests distinguishable from routine nongenetic pregnancy tests?

Standard, nongenetic tests—like lab tests for blood type, exposure to rubella (German measles), hepatitis B and hepatitis C infection, and urine tests to determine sugar and protein levels—are often done during pregnancy in order to be able to treat the fetus. Genetic testing, in contrast, often reveals that the fetus has a condition that is untreatable, so the "benefit" is the possibility of pregnancy termination. There is a much wider range of moral and personal opinion about the advisability of abortion as compared with treatment of fetuses or newborns. Some women may not want information about their genetic status or the fetus's genetic status because they do not intend to terminate the pregnancy. Others may not want that information because they do not want to risk genetic discrimination against themselves or their future child. Standard nongenetic tests are also generally for transitional, pregnancy-related conditions, whereas the genetic information revealed about a woman or her fetus is permanent and immutable in character.

7. Because NIPT is noninvasive, it could replace (and may already be replacing) invasive prenatal diagnostic tests like amniocentesis and CVS, which have been associated with some increased risk of miscarriages. Indeed, the use of prenatal diagnostic and screening tests is widespread, with a greater number of women desiring genetic analysis of their fetuses now that NIPT is available. A 2014 study found that most women (95–98%) would have a blood screening test to detect spinal muscular atrophy, cystic fibrosis, phenylketonuria, congenital heart defects, Down syndrome, and Fragile X syndrome in their fetus. A smaller majority of women would undergo amniocentesis to detect these conditions (ranging from 64% for phenylketonuria to 73% for spinal muscular atrophy). See Mary E. Norton et al., Women's Attitudes Regarding Prenatal Testing for a Range of Genetic Disorders of Varying Severity, 3 J. Clin. Med. 144 (2014); Lori Andrews, Future Perfect: Confronting Decisions About Genetics 62 (2001) (describing a survey that found "39 percent of people felt that every pregnant woman should have prenatal testing and 22 percent felt that a woman should be required to abort if the baby has a serious genetic defect"). What are some of the ethical and legal implications of the increased use and availability of such technology?

8. Prenatal genetic testing has raised concerns within the disability rights movement. Some raise the "expressivist objection," the notion that prenatal testing to

Food for Thought: In 1991, a talk show host criticized a pregnant anchorwoman's decision to take the 50% risk of passing on her heritable condition of ectrodactyly to her child. Ectrodactyly is a malformation of the hands and feet, which can cause the fingers and toes to fuse or be missing. The host devoted two hours to the discussion of whether it is "fair to pass along a genetically disfiguring disease." Although disability rights activists voiced strong objection to the idea that such a disability should not be tolerated, many listeners seemed to share the host's view. Have attitudes regarding disabilities changed much in the last several decades?

select against disabilities expresses disvalue of not only the fetus, but also individuals who have the disability selected against, and therefore it fosters discrimination against such individuals. In addition, it evaluates disabled individuals in terms of their disability, instead of seeing them as a whole person. See Adrienne Asch & David Wasserman, Where is the Sin in Synecdoche?, in Quality of Life and Human Difference 172 (David Wasserman et al. eds. 2005).

With the increased use of prenatal testing, especially NIPT, evidence suggests the number of children born with trisomy 21 is declining. One study found that selective termination reduced the number of children born with Down syndrome by 39% overall in nine states. The fact that people with Down syndrome now live longer than ever, however, counterbalanced the decline in births, resulting in a plateau in population levels of individuals with trisomy 21. Gert de Graaf et al., Estimation of Live Birth and Population Prevalence of Down Syndrome in Nine U.S. States, 173 Am. J. Human Genetics 2710 (2017). In addition, recent reports have suggested that, because of prenatal testing, children with trisomy 21 are disappearing in countries like Iceland. Julian Quinones & Arijeta Lajka, "What Kind of Society Do You Want to Live in?": Inside the Country Where Down Syndrome is Disappearing, CBS News, Aug. 4, 2017, https://www.cbsnews.com/news/down-syndrome-iceland.

Some critique the expressivist argument on the grounds that disabilities are like diseases and therefore trying to avoid the "disease" is not the same as rejecting individuals with the disease. Nevertheless, many in the disability rights movement argue that as prenatal testing becomes more routine and normalized, people are making decisions about pregnancy termination based on genetic disorders without an understanding of the lived experience of those with the conditions. Consequently, disability rights supporters argue that health care providers should provide patients with "experientially based," as opposed to only medical, information about conditions identified prenatally. See Felicity K. Boardman, The Expressivist Objection to Prenatal Testing: The Experiences of Families Living with Genetic Disease, 107 Soc. Sci. Med. 18 (2014).

This critique has led to legislation to ensure that prospective parents receive balanced information about the conditions identified in the fetus. In 2008, Congress passed the Prenatally and Postnatally Diagnosed Conditions Awareness Act, which requires the allocation of federal funds to "collect, synthesize, and disseminate current evidence-based information" about diagnosed conditions and to "coordinate the provision of, and access to, new and existing supportive services for patients receiving a positive diagnosis." 42 U.S.C. § 280g–8(b)(1)(A) & (B). Since 2014, more than a dozen states have enacted versions of The Down Syndrome Information Act, which requires the availability of balanced and accurate information about Down syndrome. It also requires health care providers to provide that information to parents after the diagnosis of Down syndrome in a fetus or newborn. Some of the laws prohibit providers from discussing the option of selective abortion. Mark W. Leach, The Down Syndrome Information Act: Balancing the Advances of

Prenatal Testing Through Public Policy, 54 Intellectual & Developmental Disabilities 84 (2016). Are these laws an appropriate way to address the "expressivist objection" to prenatal testing? Who should determine what information to disclose and how? Should providers be able to discuss the option of termination?

9. Some states have enacted laws banning abortions based on genetic disorders, including trisomy 21. Most such laws have been enjoined by court order. See Guttmacher Institute, Abortion Bans in Cases of Sex or Genetic Anomaly, July 1, 2019, https://www.guttmacher.org/state-policy/explore/abortion-bans-cases-sex-or-race-selection-or-genetic-anomaly. The Supreme Court recently denied the State of Indiana's petition for certiorari regarding its ban on abortions based on sex, race, or disability, which the Seventh Circuit invalidated as unconstitutional. (The Court did grant certiorari regarding provisions of the law controlling disposition of fetal remains and reversed the Seventh Circuit's decision to invalidate that portion of the law). Box v. Planned Parenthood of Indiana & Kentucky, Inc., 139 S. Ct. 1789 (2019). Justice Thomas wrote separately to defend the reason-based abortion ban as promoting "a State's compelling interest in preventing abortion from becoming a tool of modern day eugenics." *Id.* at 1783 (Thomas, J. concurring).

> **FYI:** Roe v. Wade, 410 U.S. 113 (1973), found a fundamental "right of privacy" to obtain an abortion under the Due Process Clause of the Fourteenth Amendment of the United States Constitution. Roe prohibited regulation of abortion in the first trimester, but allowed regulation of abortions to protect maternal health in the second trimester and the ban of abortions in the third trimester. Planned Parenthood v. Casey, 505 U.S. 833 (1992), affirmed the "essential holding" of Roe. It found, however, that the state's legitimate interest in the health of the mother and the life of the fetus allows it to regulate abortions previability as long as such regulations do not impose an "undue burden," i.e., do not have "the purpose or effect of placing a substantial obstacle in the path of a woman seeking an abortion of a nonviable fetus."

10. How is pregnancy termination based on genetic diseases different and/or similar to the eugenics movement described in Chapter 2? For a comparison of the similarities and differences of the eugenics movement and individual decisions to use of prenatal testing to select against disease, see Sonia M. Suter, A Brave New World of Designer Babies?, 22 Berkeley Tech. L. J. 897 (2007). How should one assess the eugenics question given that the federal government and the states invest large sums of money to support prenatal testing for conditions like trisomy 21, yet invest very little to improve the lives of individuals with Down syndrome? See Mark Leach, People with Down Syndrome Are Not Costs to be Avoided Through Prenatal Testing, Down Syndrome Prenatal Testing (Apr. 3, 2014), http://www.downsyndromeprenatal testing.com/people-with-down-syndrome-are-not-costs-to-be-avoided-through-prenatal-testing/.

II. PREIMPLANTATION GENETIC TESTING

FYI: Based on data from the Centers for Disease Control and Prevention (CDC), in 2014, approximately 4% of all IVF cycles included PGT. The CDC does not report the number of children born following PGT, but one scholar infers that the number is "around 2800 children." Judith Daar, A Clash at the Petri Dish: Transforming Embryos with Known Genetic Anomalies, 5 J.L. & Biosci. 219, 227 (2018).

Technologies designed to aid infertile couples who wish to have children can also be used by couples at risk of passing on a genetic disease to their children. In vitro fertilization is a process by which a woman's egg is fertilized with a man's sperm in a petri dish and then transferred into that woman's body or another woman's body. Before the transfer, preimplantation genetic testing can be undertaken to provide genetic information about the embryo so prospective parents can decide which embryo to implant. One form of preimplantation genetic testing (PGT) is preimplantation genetic diagnosis, where embryos are analyzed for specific genetic diseases based on family history or carrier status. The second is preimplantation genetic screening, where embryos are screened for chromosomal abnormalities in women of advanced maternal age or with a history of miscarriages.

PGT can detect roughly 400 genetic conditions that impact a child's health at birth or in childhood, including Down syndrome, Tay-Sachs, cystic fibrosis (CF), thalassemia, sickle cell anemia, Gaucher disease, and hemophilia. It can also detect other genetic disorders that pose little to no health risks (such as colorblindness) or late-onset diseases that that develop later in life (such as Huntington disease).

Once PGT is performed, prospective parents face the decision of whether to implant, discard, or freeze the embryos based on the results. In some ways, PGT is less desirable than amniocentesis or CVS. It involves the physically burdensome surgical process of egg retrieval necessary to create the embryo. In addition, like IVF, it is rarely covered by insurance. On the other hand, for individuals with a high risk of passing on a genetic condition, or infertile couples who have already undergone IVF, PGT can offer a preferable alternative to pregnancy termination to avoid giving birth to a child with a genetic condition.

NOTES AND QUESTIONS

1.   Should PGT be limited to analysis of only serious medical conditions or only those that affect individuals in childhood? What about using PGT to test for susceptibility to late-onset conditions like heritable forms of cancer? Some individuals at risk for hereditary breast and ovarian cancer are opting for prenatal diagnosis (through amniocentesis or CVS) or preimplantation genetic diagnosis (PGD) for the associated BRCA mutations. In one survey of these populations, for example, the majority of respondents believed that PGD (59%) or prenatal diagnosis (56%) should be offered to those at risk of passing

on the BRCA mutations. However, the percentage who would consider utilizing either PGD (35%) or prenatal diagnosis (30%) was substantially lower. Jessica Chan et al., Reproductive Decision-Making in Women with BRCA1/2 Mutations, 26 J. Genetic Counseling 594 (2017).

2.   A study by Kenneth Offit and colleagues analyzed some of the ethical issues raised by PGD. According to the authors, "[f]ocus group surveys and interviews have found that the U.S. public, as well as users of PGD, emphasized the importance of individual decision making regarding the use of reproductive technologies. Individuals stressed ethical as well as personal considerations, including the nature of the trait being avoided." Moreover, "[t]he emotional burden on mutation carriers, who have to cope with their high risk for cancer and make decisions regarding prevention options, is heightened by the knowledge that they might pass the mutation to their children."

The authors suggest that in deciding whether to perform a test for cancer susceptibility, a clinician should consider four questions: 1) does the disease develop at an early age of onset?, 2) if a person inherits the genetic mutation, how likely is it that he or she will develop the disease?, 3) how severe are the disease's symptoms?, and 4) what options are available for treating the disease or for risk-reducing surgery? Kenneth Offit et al., Preimplantation Genetic Diagnosis for Cancer Syndromes: A New Challenge for Preventative Medicine, 296 JAMA 2727 (2006). Is this framework effective in evaluating the use of PGD for late-onset conditions? Does it miss important considerations?

3.   Genomic Prediction, a new startup company, says that it can analyze several hundred thousand genetic variants in an embryo to create statistical estimates—called polygenic scores—to predict which embryos have the lowest risk for complex health conditions, like diabetes or cardiovascular disease. Comparing itself to "23andMe for IVF clinics," the company offers the disclaimer that its assessment is "NOT a diagnostic test." Critics argue the science is simply not good enough to "reliably predict" such risks. Antonio Regalado, The World's First Gattaca Baby Tests Are Finally Here, MIT Tech. Rev., Nov. 8, 2019, https://www.technologyreview.com/s/614690/polygenic-score-ivf-embryo-dna-tests-genomic-prediction-gattaca/. If the science were reliably predictive, would such probabilistic forecasts raise different issues from identifying disease genes that confer susceptibility to conditions like breast cancer?

4.   As a general matter, private insurance does not always cover PGD, and it rarely covers PGS. Moreover, IVF, which is a prerequisite for PGD, is usually not covered by insurance. Only 20 to 25% of private health plans cover *infertility*-related IVF, and many do not cover IVF when *fertile* couples use IVF for PGD. Does this mean access to PGD and genetic selection depends on economic means? If so, what are the implications of that reality?

III. LIABILITY FOR MALPRACTICE IN REPRODUCTIVE TESTING

CAILIN HARRIS, STATUTORY PROHIBITIONS ON WRONGFUL BIRTH CLAIMS & THEIR DANGEROUS EFFECTS ON PARENTS

34 B.C. J.L. & Soc. Just. 365, 368–372 (2014).

* * *

The wrongful birth cause of action is part of a group of pregnancy-related medical malpractice claims that have become more prevalent due to advance[s] in genetic testing, as well as the recognition of abortion rights and availability of such procedures. Wrongful birth suits are typically brought by parents who claim they would not have conceived or given birth to a child were it not for the defendant's negligence in performing genetic or prenatal testing, testing that if done correctly could have revealed the risk or presence of a health condition in the fetus.

The wrongful birth cause of action is often compared to and confused with wrongful conception (also known as wrongful pregnancy) and wrongful life causes of action. Parents bring a wrongful conception claim to seek damages for the expenses of an unwanted pregnancy and birth that occurs after a failed sterilization procedure. A wrongful life claim is brought by, or on behalf of, a child seeking compensation for the defendant's failure to properly counsel the child's parents about the child's condition. In contrast, a wrongful birth claim is brought by the parents, who claim that were it not for the defendant's negligence, they would have known about the fetus's condition, and they would have had the opportunity to decide whether or not to abort the fetus.

* * *

Wrongful birth claims can be brought based on the defendant's negligence at multiple points before or during the mother's pregnancy. When a wrongful birth claim is based on negligence before pregnancy, the cause of action may stem from a physician's alleged failure to diagnose a genetic condition or disease in an earlier child, if a later child is born with the same condition. In addition, the cause of action can also be brought based on a physician's negligence in performing or failing to perform genetic testing on the child's parents. Similarly, the cause of action may be brought based on a physician's failure to perform or properly handle a prenatal genetic or diagnostic test on the fetus. Additionally, wrongful birth claims can also be based on negligence during pregnancy when a physician fails to discover and inform parents of non-genetic fetal defects, such as a health condition in the mother that could adversely affect the health of the fetus.

In addition to duty and negligence, plaintiffs bringing wrongful birth claims must establish proximate causation. Notably, a wrongful birth claim does not allege that the defendant's negligence actually caused the child's injury. Instead, the plaintiffs allege that because of the defendant's negligence, they did not know about the fetus's impairments and, therefore, they did not have the opportunity to use that information to evaluate whether to terminate the pregnancy. Thus, parents are not suing for the child's impairment itself, but rather for the loss of their choice not to give birth to the unhealthy child. Courts typically use a subjective standard to determine causation, asking whether the particular plaintiffs were deprived of the chance to "accept or reject a parental relationship." It is not necessary for parents to prove decisively that they would have aborted an unhealthy fetus because the crux of their claim is that the defendant's negligence deprived them of the opportunity to make that choice.

Courts often struggle with how to appropriately award damages in wrongful birth cases. Although most courts are willing to compensate parents for the extraordinary medical costs associated with giving birth to and caring for an unhealthy child, some courts are hesitant to award parents damages covering the total cost of caring for their child. In most wrongful birth cases, the parents desired a child and planned to support their child, which, courts have stated, is the obligation of all parents. Thus, while the costs of raising the child that stem from the child's disability or condition may be recovered, those costs that are inherent in raising any child may not be recovered. Some courts also award parents damages for the emotional distress of giving birth to and caring for an unhealthy or disabled child.

A. WRONGFUL BIRTH

KEEL V. BANACH
624 So.2d 1022 (Ala. 1993).

SHORES, J.

The plaintiffs are Karen and Danny Keel, parents of Justin Keel, who was born on January 18, 1985, with severe multiple congenital abnormalities. Justin died in February 1991, at the age of six. The defendants are Warren Banach, M.D., who was Karen's doctor and who performed the sonographic examinations of the fetus, and his professional corporation. The Keels charged the defendants with medical malpractice in failing to discover several severe, life-threatening fetal abnormalities that, the Keels say, had they been known to them, would have caused them to terminate the pregnancy. Actions such as that filed by the Keels have come to be called actions for "wrongful birth."

* * *

The sole issue on appeal is whether this State recognizes a cause of action for wrongful birth. At the outset, we must emphasize the posture in which this case is now before this Court: The question presented for review is not whether the plaintiffs should ultimately prevail in this litigation, but whether their complaint states a claim upon which relief can be granted.

On October 22, 1984, Karen Keel had her first prenatal visit with Dr. Banach, an obstetrician practicing in Ozark, Alabama. There is conflicting testimony as to the content of the conversations between the physician and his patient pertaining to the couple's medical history. The Keels say that they relayed their concerns regarding this pregnancy because Danny had earlier fathered a stillborn infant with anencephaly, the congenital absence of brain and spinal cord, which is the most severe of spinal cord abnormalities. Spinal cord defects are known to be hereditary, and the Keels contend that they told Dr. Banach that they did not want their child to suffer such a fate.

Dr. Banach did a sonogram on October 26, 1984. He derived a biparietal diameter consistent with 19 weeks' gestation, and a femur length consistent with 22 weeks' gestation. Under "obvious anomalies" he wrote: "none seen." The Keels say that, to alleviate their fears, Dr. Banach moved the transducer around to show them what appeared to be a healthy fetus's head, body, arms, and legs. The sonogram machine produced several photographs of the sonographic images. Two were given to Karen.

Another sonogram was performed on January 4, 1985. Again Dr. Banach marked under "obvious anomalies" "none seen." During this sonogram, Dr. Banach determined that the fetus was a male. As during the first sonogram, the machine produced photographs, and all were retained in the medical records.

Justin was born on January 18, 1985, with severe multiple congenital abnormalities. He had only a two-vessel umbilical cord (as opposed to the normal three-vessel cord), a short cord, ventriculomegaly, absent right leg, imperforate anus, one testicle, one kidney, a vertebrae anomaly in the lumbar sacral region, hydrocephaly, a large fluid-filled sac extending off the right aspect of the sacrum consistent with meningocele (spina bifida). Justin underwent numerous surgeries during his life. A shunt from his brain to his heart channeled fluids, which, for the most part, prevented any brain damage due to the hydrocephaly. Blood clots from the heart, impregnating the lungs, a known but unpreventable risk of the shunt, were the direct cause of Justin's death.

According to Dr. Banach, the fact that Danny had fathered a stillborn with anencephaly was not revealed to him until after Justin was born.

The Keels sued Dr. Banach, alleging that he had failed to meet the standard of prenatal care and that, had he done so, he would have further investigated questionable sonogram findings. The plaintiffs contend that there were discrepancies in the fetus measurements that should have prompted further investigation. They contend that there were images on the sonogram that showed an oblong head with open frontal bones visible (known as a "lemon sign," frequently noted in spina bifida). They contend that the sonogram findings should have prompted an amniocentesis, which, had it been performed, would in all likelihood have diagnosed this fetus's neurotube defect.

* * *

This case involves an alleged failure by Dr. Banach to properly perform prenatal tests that would have revealed severe multiple congenital abnormalities in the fetus, which, if known to the parents, would have weighed in their decision whether to exercise their constitutional right to terminate the pregnancy.

The defendants make compelling policy arguments for rejecting the plaintiffs' cause of action. These include:

"(1) [T]he tort will be particularly subject to fraudulent claims. The cause of action is dependent entirely upon the retrospective and subjective testimony of the mother that had she known of the defects during the pregnancy, she would have aborted the child.

"(2) [T]he wrongful birth action would place a heavy burden on obstetricians/gynecologists. Appellee claims that with respect to obstetrics and gynecology the wrongful birth action will:

"a. Increase abortions;

"b. Increase abortions of healthy fetuses as a risk management action;

"c. Increase the cost of prenatal care as the result of more prenatal testing and the burden on OB/GYNs to obtain detailed informed consent; and

"d. Lead to the reduction of OB/GYNs practicing in the state.

"(3) Another concern is . . . the negative impact the cause of action may have on the child by creating an 'emotional bastard.'

"(4) Since the wrongful birth views nonexistence as being greater than life with a disability, the cause of action would have a negative impact on the disabled. The cause of action cries out that children with disabilities constitute injury to parents. This will lead to a stigmatism and high toll on the self-esteem of persons with disabilities at a time when our state and country are moving forward at great lengths to recognize the rights and privileges of the disabled as ordinary citizens."

* * *

Although the arguments of the defendants set out above are compelling, the great weight of authority to the contrary forces us to agree with the majority of the courts and the legal commentators and to hold that an action for the wrongful birth of a genetically or congenitally defective child may be maintained by the parents of such a child.

The nature of the tort of wrongful birth has nothing to do with whether a defendant caused the injury or harm to the child, but, rather, with whether the defendant's negligence was the proximate cause of the parents' being deprived of the option of avoiding a conception or, in the case of pregnancy, making an informed and meaningful decision either to terminate the pregnancy or to give birth to a potentially defective child. Like most of the other courts that have considered this cause of action, we hold that the parents of a genetically or congenitally defective child may maintain an action for its wrongful birth if the birth was the result of the negligent failure of the attending prenatal physician to discover and inform them of the existence of fetal defects.

* * *

The basic rule of tort compensation is that the plaintiff should be put in the position that he would have been in absent the defendant's negligence * * *. "It is a fundamental tenet of tort law that a negligent tortfeasor is liable for all damages that are the proximate result of his negligence."

We follow the holding of other courts that have considered this issue. "[T]he current trend with respect to damages is to allow the recovery of only the additional costs of treatment and special resources for the child, not the entire cost of rearing the child." * * * The primary element of damages that may be recovered in an action for wrongful birth is the pecuniary loss to the plaintiffs, the child's parents, resulting from the care and treatment of the child. The plaintiffs are entitled to recover for the extraordinary expenses they incur because of the child's unhealthy condition, including: (1) hospital and medical costs, (2) costs of medication, and (3) costs of education and therapy for the child.

It is generally recognized that, in a wrongful birth action, parents may recover the extraordinary costs necessary to treat the birth defect and any additional medical or educational costs attributable to the birth defect during the child's minority.

Emotional distress suffered by the parents of an unhealthy child is compensable in a wrongful birth action. A jury could conclude that the defendants, in failing to inform Mrs. Keel of the possibility of giving birth to a child with severe multiple congenital abnormalities, directly deprived her and, derivatively, her husband, of the option to accept or reject a parental relationship with the child and thus caused them to experience mental and emotional anguish upon their realization that they had given birth to a child afflicted with severe multiple congenital abnormalities.

We conclude that the following items are compensable, if proven: (1) any medical and hospital expenses incurred as a result of a physician's negligence; (2) the physical pain suffered by the wife; (3) loss of consortium; and (4) mental and emotional anguish the parents have suffered.

NOTES AND QUESTIONS

1.   What are the policy reasons for and against the recognition of wrongful birth cases?

2.   How does the traditional tort analysis of duty, breach, causation and damages apply to wrongful birth causes? Early case law dealing with wrongful birth actions rejected the notion that the failure to warn the parents of a fetus' risk of serious defect was actionable because the physician was not the proximate cause of the defect. However, liability for a missed diagnosis in other areas of medicine is common even though, in such cases, the physician did not cause the illness. Another reason that courts were reluctant to recognize the wrongful birth cause of action was that the post-conception remedy available—abortion—was illegal. This reasoning is no longer valid after Roe v. Wade, 410 U.S. 113 (1973), which upheld a woman's constitutional right to undergo an abortion during the first two trimesters of pregnancy. With the recent change in composition of the Supreme Court, many now worry that Roe v. Wade could be overturned. If *Roe* is overturned, it would make abortion illegal in many states, although other states would continue to protect abortion rights. In states where abortion became illegal again, what effect would that have on wrongful birth cases?

3.   In Azzolino v. Dingfelder, 337 S.E.2d 528 (N.C. 1985), the court refused to recognize a wrongful birth cause of action. The court was concerned, in part, about its eugenic implications (see Chapter 2). The court said:

> [S]ince the parents will decide which "defects" would have led them to abort the fetus, other questions will rapidly arise in jurisdictions recognizing wrongful birth claims when determining whether such claims will be permitted in particular cases. When will parents in those jurisdictions be allowed to decide that their child is so "defective" that given a chance they would have aborted it while still a fetus and, as a result, then be allowed to hold their physician civilly liable? When a fetus is only the carrier of a deleterious gene and not itself impaired? When the fetus is of one sex rather than the other? Should such issues be left exclusively to the parents with doctors being found liable for breaching their duty to inform parents of any

fetal conditions to which they know or should know the parents may object?

* * *

Inevitably this will place increased pressure upon physicians to take the "safe" course by recommending abortion. This is perhaps best illustrated by a story drawn from a real life situation.

A clinical instructor asks his students to advise an expectant mother on the fate of a fetus whose father has chronic syphilis. Early siblings were born with a collection of defects such as deafness, blindness, and retardation. The usual response of the students is: "Abort!" The teacher then calmly replies: "Congratulations, you have just aborted Beethoven."

4.   What types of evidence can be used to establish the standard of care in wrongful birth suits?

5.   What should be the scope of damages in wrongful birth cases? The Illinois Appellate court allowed a couple to plead damages that encompassed the care of their child born with Angelman syndrome after physicians failed to diagnose the disease in his older brother. Clark v. Children's Memorial Hospital, 907 N.E.2d 49 (Ill. App. 1st Dist. 2009), affirmed in part, reversed in part, 955 N.E.2d 1065 (2011) (clarifying that parents could not recover damages for cost of care after child had reached majority). In Basten v. United States, 848 F. Supp. 962 (M.D. Ala. 1994), liability was found for wrongful birth when physicians failed to inform a couple of the availability of prenatal testing that would help diagnose spina bifida. In addition to allowing the parents to recover millions of dollars in damages, the court allowed the healthy sister of the affected child to recover $25,000 for "loss of parental services"—the loss of care, counsel, training and education she would have received were it not necessary for her parents to devote attention to her seriously ill sibling. The court in a footnote said it was awarding those damages "reluctantly" and was doing so because the parties jointly stipulated that the sister of the affected child should recover damages for loss of parental services.

If a "healthy" child can recover damages because a sibling born with a genetic impairment takes an excessive amount of parental time, could a first-born child sue his or her parents for having several additional children, thus reducing the attention the first-born will receive?

As Harris, *supra*, notes, courts have not reached a consensus as to what damages are recoverable for wrongful birth actions. The most typical damages allowed are the extraordinary expenses associated with the condition, including medical and educational expenses, and sometimes "extraordinary" parental care. These damages are sometimes recoverable beyond the age of majority if the child remains dependent on its parents and are usually not offset by the intangible benefits of parenthood. While ordinary child-rearing costs are rarely recoverable, courts are divided as to whether parents may recover for the emotional distress of the wrongful birth. Whether such damages should be offset by the emotional benefits of parenthood is "an open question in most jurisdictions" and the only claim for loss of parental consortium was rejected. Only a few jurisdictions allow for recovery of the maternal pain and suffering of the pregnancy and childbirth or for loss of consortium damages for the marital unit. Daniel Whitney & Kenneth Rosenbaum, Recovery of Damages for Wrongful Birth, 32 J. Legal Med. 167 (2011). What are the arguments for and against such damages?

6.   In traditional tort cases, plaintiffs have a duty to mitigate damages. Should parents in wrongful birth cases be required to mitigate damages by putting their child up for adoption?

7.   Should other family members like grandparents recover for wrongful birth? A New Jersey appellate court held that a grandfather cannot bring a wrongful birth suit on his behalf to recover emotional distress damages arising from the birth of his grandson despite allegations by the grandfather that a grandparent is a "filament of family life" and that the birth of a child with Tay-Sachs disease affected the entire family. Michelman v. Erlich, 709 A.2d 281 (N.J. Super. A.D. 1998).

8.   Should wrongful birth actions only be permitted where the disorder at issue is serious? Some courts have considered the severity of the disorder as a factor in assessing the health care professional's liability for failing to provide information about genetic risks. For example, in Turpin v. Sortini, 643 P.2d 954 (Cal. 1982), a wrongful birth case, the California Supreme Court asserted, "[i]n this case, in which the plaintiff's only affliction is deafness, it seems quite unlikely that a jury would ever conclude that life with such a condition is worse than not being born at all." Using the reasoning presented in *Turpin*, a slight disadvantage such as short stature would probably not be sufficient to find liability. In Zepeda v. Zepeda, 190 N.E.2d 849, 859 (Ill. App. 1963), the court refused to allow a son born out of wedlock to sue his father for wrongful life. The court refused to recognize a cause of action because it felt it was the legislature's job to redress such a far-reaching tort. The court noted:

> Encouragement would extend to all others born into the world under conditions they might regard as adverse. One might seek damages for being born of a certain color, another because of race; one for being born with a hereditary disease, another for inheriting unfortunate family characteristics; one for being born into a large and destitute family, another because a parent has an unsavory reputation.

9.   Although the majority of states allows wrongful birth actions, the number that do not is slowly growing. Currently, at least 11 states—Arkansas, Arizona, Idaho, Kansas, Maine, Michigan, Minnesota, Missouri, Oklahoma, Pennsylvania, and South Dakota—have statutes that prohibit parents from bringing such suits against health care providers. And at least three—Georgia, Kentucky, and North Carolina—do not recognize such claims under the common law. Could such laws be challenged as a violation of the couple's reproductive liberty by eliminating an incentive for physicians to give parents-to-be information necessary to make procreative decisions? In a Utah case, a

couple challenged the constitutionality of a Utah statute that prohibited any cause of action "based on [a] claim that but for the act or omission of another, a person would not have been permitted to have been born alive but would have been aborted." Several genetic tests had been conducted, but the parents alleged that they were never accurately informed about the results of the tests or the risks of the fetus having Down syndrome. The Utah Supreme Court rejected a due process challenge to Utah's prohibition on wrongful birth lawsuits because the court found the law did not place an undue burden on a woman's ability to abort a fetus with a genetic anomaly. It also rejected an equal protection challenge to the law because it held that the class of people who choose to abort a fetus with a genetic anomaly is not a recognized class under the equal protection clause. Wood v. University of Utah Medical Center, 67 P.3d 436 (Utah 2002). Utah subsequently repealed its wrongful birth statute in 2008.

10. The Minnesota Supreme Court allowed the parents of a child born with Fragile X, a heritable form of mental impairment, to bring a medical malpractice suit against physicians, even though Minnesota statutorily bars wrongful birth and wrongful life actions when the claim is that the parents would have terminated an affected pregnancy. The parents alleged that the physicians negligently failed to identify the Fragile X mutation in their daughter, and therefore they failed to learn they were at increased risk of having another child with the condition. See Molloy v. Meier, 679 N.W.2d 711 (Minn. 2004). In this case, the couple alleged they would have chosen not to procreate (rather than abort) and therefore they could recover for wrongful conception.

Similarly, in McAllister v. Ha, 496 S.E.2d 577 (N.C. 1998), the North Carolina Supreme Court allowed parents of a child born with sickle cell disease to bring a wrongful conception case for negligently failing to advise the parents they were carriers of sickle cell disease, even though wrongful birth and life claims were statutorily barred. Nevertheless, it refused to allow the parents to recover damages for any costs associated with child-rearing (including the extraordinary costs of caring for the child due to illness). It did allow recovery of costs associated with the pregnancy and severe emotional distress.

11. After undergoing preimplantation genetic diagnosis (PGD) to avoid giving birth to a child with a particular genetic condition, should parents be able to recover for the losses associated with the child's illness if the defendants negligently failed to identify the genetic variant associated with the genetic condition? An appellate court in Massachusetts rejected what amounted to a wrongful birth claim for a child born with cystic fibrosis. After giving birth to a daughter with cystic fibrosis, the Doolans used IVF to create ten embryos. Using PGD, a commercial laboratory analyzed the embryos for the Delta F-508 mutation associated with cystic fibrosis. After deciding to implant an embryo the Doolans were told was free of the mutation, Mrs. Doolan became pregnant and gave birth to a son, Thomas, who was later diagnosed with cystic fibrosis.

The court rejected the parent's two rationales for their claim for loss of consortium against the defendants who implanted the embryo and the laboratory that analyzed it. First, it rejected the parent's reliance on a statute allowing parents to recover for loss of consortium against individuals "legally responsible for causing" the child's serious injury. The court reasoned that the "essence of [the] claim is not that the alleged negligence of the defendants caused him to be born with cystic fibrosis, but rather that the alleged negligence of the defendants denied his parents the opportunity to choose not to conceive and give birth to him." Therefore, it concluded, the defendants had not caused the child to be "born afflicted with cystic fibrosis." Doolan v. IVF America (MA) Inc., 2000 WL 33170944, at *4 (Mass. Super. 2000).

Second, the parents argued that "were it not for the alleged negligence of the defendants, they would currently be raising a boy named Thomas, [who] would not be afflicted with cystic fibrosis." This "hypothetical 'healthy Thomas Doolan,' " they reasoned, would "be more likely to be able to offer society and companionship to his parents for the duration of their lifetimes than would the actual Thomas Doolan." *Id.* at *4. The court rejected this argument for two reasons:

> First, the extent of any loss of consortium damages for a child that was never born would be far too speculative to uphold plaintiffs' cause of action. For example, the jury would have to consider the quality of the relationship plaintiffs might have had with their hypothetical son in assessing Mr. and Mrs. Doolan's loss of consortium damages. Furthermore, plaintiffs' assertion that this hypothetical Thomas Doolan would have been "healthy" discounts the possibility that he might have been afflicted with another type of birth defect or long-term illness.

Id. at 5.

Are there substantive differences between claims brought for negligence in failing to identify a genetic mutation through prenatal testing and claims brought for similar negligence in performing PGD? In other words, is there logical consistency in allowing wrongful birth claims for the first type of negligence but not the latter?

12. Most cases alleging negligence in prenatal screening deal with false negatives—situations in which parents are erroneously told that their fetus is not afflicted with a serious genetic disorder. What about false positives, though? A couple might erroneously be told their fetus has a serious genetic disease. Such a case is not a wrongful birth case because the fetus is not brought to term, but may be looked at as a wrongful abortion case. In Martinez v. Long Island Jewish Hillside Medical Center, 512 N.E.2d 538 (N.Y. 1987), the defendants negligently advised Carmen Martinez that her baby would be born with the congenital birth defect of microcephaly (small brain) or anencephaly (no brain). Based on the extraordinary circumstances, she submitted to an abortion believing that it would be justified. Because of her religious beliefs, she felt abortion was a sin, except under justifiable

circumstances such as these. When it was shown that the diagnosis was erroneous and that Ms. Martinez had aborted a healthy fetus, she was allowed to maintain a cause of action for emotional distress.

Only a handful of wrongful abortion cases have gone to court. See Ronen Perry & Yehuda Adar, Wrongful Abortion: A Wrong in Search of a Remedy, 5 Yale J. Health Pol'y, L. & Ethics 507 (2005); see also, Johnson v. United States, 810 F. Supp. 7 (D.D.C. 1993) (denying defendant's motion to dismiss a claim alleging plaintiff terminated a pregnancy after being incorrectly diagnosed with AIDS); Breyne v. Potter, 574 S.E.2d 916 (Ga. App. 2002) (allowing plaintiff to bring a claim for malpractice when plaintiff terminated a pregnancy after an inaccurate diagnosis of trisomy 21).

Why are wrongful birth claims so much more prevalent than wrongful abortion claims? The damages sought for wrongful abortion are likely to focus on emotional distress, whereas damages sought for wrongful birth would include the extraordinary expenses associated with the medical and other costs associated with the child's illness and disability. Might the differences in the types of damages one might receive be relevant?

13. Dov Fox recently published a book that explores the various kinds of reproductive negligence that can arise, including wrongful birth. It offers a framework for analyzing "reproductive wrongdoing writ large. Some of these wrongs *deprive* people of the pregnancy or parenthood they want. Others *impose* those roles on people seeking to avoid them. Others still *confound* plans not just for any child, but for one born with certain traits," including different health, sex, and other traits than the ones the parents selected. Dov Fox, Birth Rights and Wrongs: How Medical Mix-Ups Are Remaking Reproduction and the Law 6 (2019).

B. WRONGFUL LIFE

CURLENDER V. BIO-SCIENCE LABORATORIES
165 Cal. Rptr. 477 (Cal. App. 1980).

JEFFERSON, J.

The appeal presents an issue of first impression in California: What remedy, if any, is available in this state to a severely impaired child— genetically defective—born as the result of defendants' negligence in conducting certain genetic tests of the child's parents—tests which, if properly done, would have disclosed the high probability that the actual, catastrophic result would occur?

* * *

In the first cause of action against the named defendants, plaintiff Shauna alleged that on January 15, 1977, her parents, Phillis and Hyam Curlender, retained defendant laboratories to administer certain tests designed to reveal whether either of the parents were carriers of genes which would result in the conception and birth of a child with Tay-Sachs disease, medically defined as "amaurotic familial idiocy." The tests on plaintiff's parents were performed on January 21, 1977, and, it was alleged, due to defendants' negligence, "incorrect and inaccurate" information was disseminated to plaintiff's parents concerning their status as carriers.

The complaint did not allege the date of plaintiff's birth, so we do not know whether the parents relied upon the test results in conceiving plaintiff, or, as parents-to-be when the tests were made, relied upon the results in failing to avail themselves of amniocentesis and an abortion. In any event, on May 10, 1978, plaintiff's parents were informed that plaintiff had Tay-Sachs disease.

As the result of the disease, plaintiff Shauna suffers from "mental retardation, susceptibility to other diseases, convulsions, sluggishness, apathy, failure to fix objects with her eyes, inability to take an interest in her surroundings, loss of motor reactions, inability to sit up or hold her head up, loss of weight, muscle atrophy, blindness, pseudobulper palsy, inability to feed orally, decerebrate rigidity and gross physical deformity." It was alleged that Shauna's life expectancy is estimated to be four years. The complaint also contained allegations that plaintiff suffers "pain, physical and emotional distress, fear, anxiety, despair, loss of enjoyment of life, and frustration. . . ."

The complaint sought costs of plaintiff's care as damages and also damages for emotional distress and the deprivation of "72.6 years of her life." In addition, punitive damages of three million dollars were sought, on the ground that "[a]t the time that Defendants . . . [tested the parents], Defendants, and each of them, had been expressly informed by the nation's leading authority on Tay-Sachs disease that said test procedures were substantially inaccurate and would likely result is disasterous [sic] and catastrophic consequences to the patients, and Defendants knew that said procedures were improper, inadequate and with insufficient controls and that the results of such testing were likely to be inaccurate and that a false negative result would have disasterous [sic] and catastrophic consequences to the Plaintiff, all in conscious disregard of the health, safety and well-being of Plaintiff. . . ."

* * *

The term "wrongful life" has to date served as an umbrella for causes of action based upon any distinguishable factual situations; this has led to some confusion in its use. For purposes of our discussion, the term "wrongful life" will be confined to those causes of action *brought by the infant* alleging that, due to the negligence of the defendant, birth occurred; * * *.

* * *

The high court in Pennsylvania issued an exhaustive opinion in 1979 concerning the various aspects of the "wrongful-life" problem. The case was Speck v. Finegold, 408 A.2d 496 (Pa. 1979), a malpractice suit by parents and child occasioned by the birth of the child with neurofibromatosis, a seriously crippling condition already evidenced in the child's siblings. Overruling the trial court, *Speck* recognized the parents' cause of action but not that of the infant plaintiff.

We quote at length from the *Speck* court's opinion: "In the instant case, we deny Francine's [infant plaintiff's] claim to be made whole. When we examine Francine's claim, we find regardless of whether her claim is based on 'wrongful life' or otherwise, there is a failure to state a legally cognizable cause of action even though, admittedly, the defendants' actions of negligence were the proximate cause of her defective birth. Her claims to be whole have two fatal weaknesses. First, there is no precedent in appellate judicial pronouncements that holds a child has a fundamental right to be born as a whole, functional human being. Whether it is better to have never been born at all rather than to have been born with serious mental defects is a mystery more properly left to the philosophers and theologians, a mystery which would lead us into the field of metaphysics, beyond the realm of our understanding or ability to solve . . . [This] cause of action . . . demands a calculation of damages dependent on a comparison between Hobson's choice of life in an impaired state and nonexistence. This the law is incapable of doing . . . unfortunately, . . . this is not an action cognizable in law. Thus, the recognized principle, not peculiar to traditional tort law alone, that it would be a denial of justice to deny all relief where a wrong is of such a nature as to preclude certain ascertained damages, is inapposite and inapplicable here."

* * *

The circumstance that the birth and injury have come hand in hand has caused other courts to deal with the problem by barring recovery. The reality of the "wrongful-life" concept is that such a plaintiff both *exists* and *suffers*, due to the negligence of others. It is neither necessary nor just to retreat into meditation on the mysteries of life. We need not be concerned with the fact that had defendants not been negligent, the plaintiff might not have come into existence at all. The certainty of genetic impairment is no longer a mystery. In addition, a reverent appreciation of life compels recognition that plaintiff, however impaired she may be, has come into existence as a living person with certain rights.

One of the fears expressed in the decisional law is that, once it is determined that such infants have rights cognizable at law, nothing would prevent such a plaintiff from bringing suit against its own parents for allowing plaintiff to be born. In our view, the fear is groundless. The "wrongful-life" cause of action with which we are concerned is based upon negligently caused failure by someone under a duty to do so to inform the prospective parents of facts needed by them to make a conscious choice *not* to become parents. If a case arose where, despite due care by the medical profession in transmitting the necessary warnings, parents made a conscious choice to proceed with a pregnancy, with full knowledge that a seriously impaired infant would be born, that conscious choice would provide an intervening act of proximate cause to preclude liability insofar as defendants other than the parents were concerned. Under such circumstances, we see no sound public policy which should protect those parents from being answerable for the pain, suffering and misery which they have wrought upon their offspring.

* * *

The extent of recovery, however, is subject to certain limitations due to the nature of the tort involved. While ordinarily a defendant is liable for all consequences flowing from the injury, it is appropriate in the case before us to tailor the elements of recovery, taking into account particular circumstances involved.

The complaint seeks damages based upon an actuarial life expectancy of plaintiff of more than 70 years—the life expectancy if plaintiff had been born without the Tay-Sachs disease. The complaint sets forth that plaintiff's actual life expectancy, because of the disease, is only four years. We reject as untenable the claim that plaintiff is entitled to damages as if plaintiff had been born without defects and would have had a normal life expectancy. Plaintiff's right to damages must be considered on the basis of plaintiff's mental and physical condition at birth and her expected condition during the short life span (four years according to the complaint) anticipated for one with her impaired condition. In similar fashion, we reject the notion that a "wrongful-life" cause of action involves any attempted evaluation of a claimed right *not* to be born. In essence, we construe the "wrongful-life" cause of action by the defective child as the right of such child to recover damages for the pain and suffering to be endured during the limited life span available to such a child and any special pecuniary loss resulting from the impaired condition.

In California, infants are presumed to experience pain and suffering when injury has been established, even if the infant is unable to testify and describe such pain and suffering * * *.

The complaint sought costs of care as an element of special damages, an appropriate item of recovery in cases where, for one reason or another, there is no suit brought by the parents seeking recovery for this pecuniary loss. We are informed, however, that such a suit is pending by the parents of the plaintiff before us. Upon remand, consideration should be given to consolidating plaintiff's cause of action with those of the parents in the interest of efficient use of trial time and the prevention of duplication of effort, as well as the prevention of possible double recovery. Costs of plaintiff's care may only be awarded once.

Finally, we considered the matter of punitive damages. The complaint makes such a request. Our Civil Code section 3294 allows such damages "where the defendant has been guilty of oppression, fraud, or malice, express or implied"; they are given "for the sake of example and by way of punishing the defendant." We need not speculate on the means by which plaintiff plans to establish facts showing oppression, fraud or malice—as related to either the third cause of action stated in the complaint or the entitlement of plaintiff to punitive damages. Such will be the concern of judge and jury when this matter is tried. For our purposes, we find that plaintiff has adequately pleaded a cause of action for punitive damages. We see no reason in public policy or legal analysis for exempting from liability for punitive damages a defendant who is sued for committing a "wrongful-life" tort.

NOTES AND QUESTIONS

1.   What are the policy arguments for and against wrongful life actions? How do the policy arguments regarding wrongful life cases compare to those involving wrongful birth cases?

2.   Should a child be able to bring a wrongful life cause of action against his or her parents in addition to, or instead of, the negligent health care provider? In *dicta*, the *Curlender* court said:

> If a case arose where, despite due care by the medical profession in transmitting the necessary warnings, parents made a conscious choice to proceed with a pregnancy, with a full knowledge that a seriously impaired infant would be born. * * * Under such circumstances, we see no sound policy which should protect those parents from being answerable for the pain, suffering and misery which they have wrought upon their offspring.

Subsequently, the California legislature passed the following statute:

Cal. Civ. Code § 43.6

§ 43.6.   Immunity from Liability

(a)   No cause of action arises against a parent of a child based upon the claim that the child should not have been conceived or, if conceived, should not have been allowed to have been born alive.

(b)   The failure or refusal of a parent to prevent the live birth of his or her child shall not be a defense in any action against a third party, nor shall the failure or refusal be considered in awarding damages in any such action.

3.   In Doolan v. IVF American (MA) Inc., 2000 WL 33170944 (Mass. Super. 2000), described in note 11, pages 180–181, the court rejected the child's

"wrongful life" claim for being born with cystic fibrosis after the defendants were allegedly negligent in performing PGD to test for the cystic fibrosis mutation. Although the plaintiff characterized the claim as "wrongful conception," rather than "wrongful life," the court thought the "essence" of his claim was that "the alleged negligence of the defendants denied his parents the opportunity to choose not to conceive and give birth to him." *Id.* at *3–4. It reasoned that the claim raised "precisely the 'fundamental problem of logic' " of wrongful life claims in "requir[ing] a comparison of the relative monetary values of existence and nonexistence, a task that is beyond the competence of the judicial system." *Id.* at *4. Consequently, it granted the defendants' motion for summary judgment. How do the ethical and legal issues with regard to wrongful life claims in the context of PGD compare to those raised in the context of prenatal testing? In what ways are they similar and/or different?

If germline gene editing (see Chapter 13) could safely eliminate a heritable condition, should alleged negligence for failure to use gene editing be described as a wrongful life claim or a different kind of claim? Why is it or isn't it a wrongful life claim? Barbara Billauer argues for legal recognition of *"wrongful genetic manipulation"* to avoid the "toxic atmosphere surrounding the words *wrongful life*." Barbara P. Billauer, Wrongful Life in the Age of CRISPR-CAS: Using the Legal Fiction of the Conceptual Being to Redress Wrongful Gamete Manipulation, ___ Penn. State ___ (forthcoming 2020).

IV. CARRIER TESTING AND SCREENING

A. CARRIER TESTING AND SCREENING GENERALLY

When individuals have a family history of a genetic disorder and the particular familial mutation is known, they can be offered carrier testing to determine whether they and/or their partner carry the mutation. If both prospective parents are carriers, they should be counseled about the 25% risk with each pregnancy that the child will be affected with the condition, and the 75% risk that the child will be unaffected (a 50% chance that the child would be an unaffected carrier plus a 25% chance that the child would not inherit either mutation). Their options are to accept the risk; avoid reproduction and consider adoption; conceive with gamete (sperm or ovum) donations; undergo prenatal testing either to prepare for the birth of an affected child or to consider termination of an affected fetus; or undergo preimplantation genetic diagnosis (PGD).

Carrier screening, whether used in targeted or expanded form, has long been a part of preconception and prenatal care to determine whether asymptomatic individuals have genetic variants associated with certain genetic diseases. As a screening technique, however, it does not identify all individuals at risk of the screened condition. Traditionally, it was offered to individuals from specific ethnic populations—ethnicity-based screening—based on their increased risk of carrying mutations for a few serious autosomal recessive disorders. Caucasians, for example, face a heightened risk for cystic fibrosis; African Americans for sickle cell anemia; people of Ashkenazi Jewish descent for Tay-Sachs disease; and Asian, Mediterranean, and Middle Eastern populations for thalassemia.

> **FYI:** The carrier rate for Tay-Sachs disease in the Ashkenazi Jewish population is about 1 in 27, whereas it is about 1 in 250 in the general, non-Jewish population. Roughly 1 in 13 African Americans is a carrier for sickle cell anemia, whereas 1 in 333 white Americans is a carrier.

In our increasingly multi-racial society, it is becoming more difficult to predict the pretest likelihood of carrier status based on the ethnic group with which the patient identifies. As reproduction increasingly occurs across ethnicities, ancestry is becoming harder to define, and certain genetic diseases are no longer limited to specific ethnic groups. As a result, some types of carrier screening are recommended in preconception and prenatal care, irrespective of ethnicity. For example, the American College of Obstetricians and Gynecologists (ACOG) recommends the offer of carrier screening for spinal muscular atrophy, cystic fibrosis, hemoglobinopathies and thalassemias to *all* women considering pregnancy or who are currently pregnant. Nevertheless, it still recommends offering carrier screening for genetic conditions in individuals of Eastern and Central European Jewish descent or a family history of the conditions, and Fragile X premutation carrier screening to women with a family history suggestive of Fragile X. ACOG, Committee Opinion, Carrier Screening for Genetic Conditions, 129 Obstetrics & Gynecology e41 (2017).

With scientific advances, the cost of DNA analysis is declining, while the capacity to screen for a large number of conditions at one time is increasing. This capacity for expanded carrier screening has led professional groups to offer guidance to providers as to the appropriate scope of expanded carrier screening. The American College of Medical Genetics and Genomics (ACMG), for example, recommends careful consideration as to what conditions to include in expanded carrier screening, rather than "simply including as many disorders as possible." It offers several criteria for those decisions. For example, it suggests that screening should only include conditions most at-risk individuals would consider for prenatal diagnostic testing, that individuals consent to screening for any adult-onset conditions, and that there be "validated clinical association between the mutation(s) detected and the severity of the disorder." Wayne W. Grody, ACMG Position Statement on Prenatal/Preconception Expanded Carrier Screening, 15 Genetics Med. 482 (2013). ACOG recommends including disorders in screening panels that "have a carrier frequency of 1 in 100 or greater, have a well-defined phenotype, have a detrimental effect on quality of life, cause cognitive or physical impairment, require survival or medical intervention, or have an onset early in life." ACOG, Committee Opinion, Carrier Screening in the Age of Genomic Medicine, 129 Obstetrics & Gynecology 525 (2017).

Evidence suggests, however, that in practice obstetricians and gynecologists may offer more expansive carrier screening than that recommended by ACOG and the ACMG.

NOTES AND QUESTIONS

1.   After originally advocating for ethnic-based screening, ACOG now views as acceptable ethnic-specific screening, panethnic screening (screening for a panel of disorders offered to all individuals regardless of ethnicity), and expanded carrier screening (screening for a large number of conditions simultaneously). It suggests, however, that providers "establish a standard approach that is consistently offered to and discussed with each patient, ideally before pregnancy." ACOG, Committee Opinion, Carrier Screening in the Age of Genomic Medicine, 129 Obstetrics & Gynecology 525 (2017). What are the advantages and benefits of these different screening strategies? What ethical and legal concerns should shape this analysis?

2.   When carrier screening was based only on ethnicity (or family history), a minor and his parents sued a physician and a university hospital for medical malpractice in failing to test his parents for Tay-Sachs disease. The mother's ethnicity was German, English, and Canadian, while the father's was Norwegian and "some peculiar type of French." Neither was of Ashkenazi Jewish descent. Based on their reported ethnicity, the standard of care was not to offer carrier screening for Tay-Sachs. Consequently, the court granted the defendant's motion to dismiss. Munro v. Regents, 215 Cal. App. 3d 977 (Cal. App. 1990). Are the risks of liability for failing to identify conditions like Tay-Sachs greater today with the possibility of expanded and panethnic screening? What considerations would be relevant? And what are the social and ethical implications, if the threat of liability has increased?

3.   A Harvard scientist is developing a dating app called "digiD8" to help couples determine whether they "share the same recessive gene for an incredibly rare and severe genetic disease that could be passed down to future offspring." Users of the app would submit their DNA for whole genome sequencing. Is this a "dating app that only a eugenicist would love," an effort to "wipe out genetic diversity and people with disabilities," or just an extension of what genetic counselors offer clients to determine whether their future children are at risk of inheriting genetic diseases. See Meagan Flynn, A Harvard Scientist is Developing a DNA-Based Dating App to Reduce Genetic Disease. Critics Called it Eugenics, Wash. Post, Dec. 13, 2019, https://www. washingtonpost.com/nation/2019/12/13/genetics-george-church-dna-dating-app-reduce-disease-eugenics/.

B.   ASSISTED REPRODUCTIVE TECHNOLOGIES AND CARRIER SCREENING

Third parties—egg donors, sperm donors, and embryo donors—can be used to substitute for the genetic component of one or both parents. But as more actors get involved in the drama of reproduction, the law is increasingly called in to sort out rights and responsibilities. What sort of genetic screening of potential donors is appropriate? Who is liable if a donor passes on a genetic disease? Although this textbook focuses on issues associated with inheritance of genetic conditions, the use of gamete and embryo donors raises a vast array of legal and ethical issues, including how to decide who the legal parents are when a donor is involved. For more information about such issues, see Judith Daar, Reproductive Technologies and the Law (2d ed. 2013).

MINIMUM GENETIC TESTING FOR GAMETE AND EMBRYO DONORS, APPROVED BY THE BOARD OF DIRECTORS OF THE AMERICAN SOCIETY FOR REPRODUCTIVE MEDICINE

99 Fertility & Sterility 47, 62.e1 (2013).

* * *

I.   The donor

A.   Should not have any major Mendelian disorder. Mendelian disorders fall into the following categories:

a.   Autosomal dominant or X-linked disorders. Providers should be aware that some autosomal dominant or X-linked disorders can have variable expressivity (meaning that mutation carriers may not have noticeable symptoms) or have an age of onset that extends beyond the age of the donor (one example is Huntington disease).

b.   Autosomal recessive disorders. Donors who are heterozygous need not necessarily be excluded if the reproductive partner has had appropriate carrier screening. The recipient and reproductive partner (as appropriate) should be counseled about the accuracy of the carrier screening test and the residual risk to be a carrier following a negative test. Counseling regarding residual risk is complex and may be best provided by a genetic counselor.

B.   Should not have (or have had) any major malformation of complex cause (multifactorial/polygenic), such as spina bifida or cardiac malformation. A major malformation is defined as one that carries serious functional or cosmetic handicap. However, the definition of "major" is a matter of judgment.

C.   Should not have any significant familial disease with a major genetic component.

* * *

D.   Should not have a known karyotypic abnormality that may result in chromosomally unbalanced gametes. In the general population, the chance of having a chromosomal rearrangement that could be transmitted in unbalanced form to offspring is small, provided the family history is negative for risk factors. Therefore, routine karyotyping of all donors is optional.

E.   Should undergo general population and ethnicity (ancestry)-based genetic screening. Donors should give informed consent prior to carrier screening. Informed consent should include discussion of the natural history of the condition being screened, carrier frequency in the respective ethnic group, detection rate of the test, residual risk to be a carrier when testing negative, and options for persons testing positive. If a prospective donor is identified as a carrier, genetic counseling for both the donor and recipient is recommended.

The recommended list of tests may change as tests for other disorders are developed. Guidelines regarding ethnicity and population-based genetic screening are published by the American College of Obstetricians and Gynecologists (www.acog. org) and the American College of Medical Genetics (www.acmg. net). All gamete donors should be evaluated by the current tests recommended at the time of the donation.

Note: It is not appropriate to screen gamete donors for adult onset conditions (such as cancer predisposition, Huntington disease, etc.) without full consent of the gamete donor, including formal genetic counseling.

F.   Should be generally healthy and young. Advanced maternal age is associated with an increased risk for aneuploidy offspring. Advanced paternal age is associated with a moderately increased risk for new mutations in offspring, and an emerging body of evidence suggests an increased risk for complex disorders, including some congenital anomalies, schizophrenia, autism spectrum disorders, and specific forms of cancer.

II.   The donor's first-degree relatives (parents, siblings, and offspring) should be free of:

A.   Mendelian disorders as described in Section I.A.

B.   Major malformations as described in Section I.B.

C.   Significant familial disease with a major genetic component.

D.   A chromosomal abnormality, unless the donor has a normal karyotype.

E.   Mental retardation of undocumented etiology. If family history reveals a disorder for which definitive testing is available, then it is appropriate to refer the prospective donor for genetic counseling for that specific disorder. Testing without a formal genetic consultation would be inappropriate. Genetic test results may determine the appropriateness of using that donor.

NOTES AND QUESTIONS

1.   What type of genetic screening of gamete donors is appropriate? Should donors be liable if they knew (or should have known) that they risked passing on a certain genetic disease to the resulting children? Should a donor's confidentiality be protected? Should a blood sample of each donor be kept for genetic testing in the future? Should a donor be required to update the clinic on subsequently-discovered genetic diseases in his or her family so that the children can be warned?

2.   In a California case, Petitioners Diane and Ronald Johnson sued a sperm bank and physicians for negligently failing to disclose that a sperm donor had a family history of Autosomal Dominant Polycystic Kidney Disease (ADPKD). The Johnson's daughter, who was conceived with the donor's sperm through artificial insemination, was ultimately diagnosed with ADPKD. The California Court of Appeals reversed the trial court's refusal to allow plaintiffs to depose and discover information related to the anonymous sperm donor. It found no physician-patient privilege between a donor and sperm bank because sperm donors attend sperm banks solely to sell their sperm. Second, it reasoned that "a child conceived by artificial insemination may need his or her family's genetic and medical history for important medical decisions," thereby necessitating the disclosure of the donor's identity. Moreover, any contracts that preclude disclosure of a sperm donor's identity in such scenarios are "contrary to public policy and . . . unenforceable." Third, the court found that the sperm donor should not reasonably expect that his identity would never be disclosed. As a result, the Court of Appeals ordered the deposition to continue while "protecting [the donor's] identity . . . to the fullest extent possible and the identities of his family members." Johnson v. Superior Court, 95 Cal.Rptr.2d 864 (Cal. App. 2000).

Ultimately, however, the appellate court did not allow general damages or damages for lost earnings on behalf of the daughter with ADPKD because it characterized the claim as a wrongful life suit. Drawing on precedent, the court reasoned that general damages were not available because the "harmed interest of the plaintiff's physical, emotional, and psychological well-being" are impossible to weigh against her "physical existence with the capacity both to receive and give love and pleasure as well as to experience pain and suffering." Also drawing on precedent, it reasoned that because the child never had earning capacity, she could not "lose what [she] never had." Johnson v. Superior Court, 124 Cal.Rptr.2d 650 (Cal. Ct. App. 2002).

Is Johnson v. Superior Court's decision to deny a wrongful life claim consistent with the wrongful life claims discussed in section III.B above? Would the outcome have been different if the plaintiff had sought extraordinary damages associated with her condition as opposed to general damages?

Would the parents have been successful if they brought a wrongful birth claim based on the facts in Johnson v. Superior Court (see section II.B)? Should a wrongful birth claim based on alleged negligence in failing to screen a donor for genetic conditions be allowed? Is this more like a negligence claim in the context of prenatal testing or negligence in the context of PGD?

3.   Sperm banks offer the option to select donors based on a range of traits including ethnicity, favorite subject; talents; personal goals; and even resemblance to the person seeking a donor, her partner, or someone famous. Some banks have started to offer screening based on genes. For example, Gene Peeks launched a screening service in 2014, which

> screens for donors least likely to result in the birth of a child with a recessive genetic disease. Working with two sperm banks, the company used a patented algorithm that 'creates thousands of hypothetical offspring' based on the genotypes of the mothers and potential donors. By scanning 'the resulting "digital children," the program can "flag pairings with an increased risk of inheriting genetic disorders." ' The analysis 'generates a personalized catalogue of risk-reduced donors for each prospective mother, filtering out donor matches with a high probability of passing on' the more than 500 inherited recessive diseases the company targets. Noting, in 2014, that the analysis focused only on 'simple Mendelian disorders, with a one-to-one relation between genes and phenotype', the company was nevertheless optimistic about its potential to 'consider polygenic traits in the future'.

Sonia M. Suter, The Tyranny of Choice: Reproductive Selection in the Future, 5 J.L. & Biosci. 262, 292 (2018). A visit to Gene Peeks' website suggests they may not be offering this service at this time, but one could imagine sperm banks providing such services in the future as genetic testing becomes more expansive and cheaper. Should such services be offered? Why or why not?

4.   Sperm donors are often unmarried students who do not yet have children of their own. On occasion, donor insemination produces a child with a rare recessive genetic disorder when the donor did not realize he was a carrier. Should he be told that fact so that he can take it into consideration when making his own reproductive plans? What if, as is often the case, the infertility clinic has told him in advance that they will not let him know if his sperm results in a pregnancy (so that he will not track down any resulting child)? In a study of sperm banks faced with the issue of contacting donors, half tracked down the donor to warn of the genetic risk and half did not.

5.   An article in the *Journal of the American Medical Association* describes the case of a 23-year-old man in good health who donated sperm to a U.S. sperm bank almost a hundred times over a two-year period. Barry J. Maron et al., Implications of Hypertrophic Cardiomyopathy Transmitted by Sperm Donation, 302 JAMA 1681 (2009). The sperm bank followed protocols standard in the industry at the time of the donation: doctors gave the donor a comprehensive medical evaluation including a complete personal and family

medical history in addition to laboratory testing for communicable diseases. Several years later, a woman inseminated with the donor's sperm gave birth to a child diagnosed with hypertrophic cardiomyopathy (HCM)—a heart disease characterized by the thickening of the heart muscle.

What are the pros and cons of undertaking chromosomal analysis on all sperm and egg donors? Would the cost make these procedures less accessible?

Should other women who conceived children with the donor's sperm be told of the birth of the affected child? Most sperm banks do not have records of which recipients conceived. In the case reported in JAMA, however, the sperm bank notified the donor and all other recipients of his sperm that their children were at risk for HCM. Twenty-two children were born using the donor's sperm in addition to two children born to the donor's wife. Five children showed evidence of HCM including one two-and-a-half-year-old child who died waiting for a heart transplant.

6.   In Norman v. Xytex Corp., 830 S.E.2d 267 (Ga. Ct. App. 2019), a child conceived using sperm from Donor #9623 purchased from Xytex Corporation was diagnosed with Attention Deficit Hyperactivity Disorder and an inherited blood disorder. In addition, he had suicidal and homicidal ideations and had been prescribed anti-depressant and anti-psychotic medications. The parents alleged that Donor #9623 "completely fabricated" his sperm donor application when he represented that he had "an IQ of 160, multiple college degrees, a clean mental health history, and no criminal background." In fact, according to the appellants, he was diagnosed with "Schizophrenia, Narcissistic Personality Disorder, a drug induced psychotic disorder, and significant grandiose delusions" and had been repeatedly hospitalized for mental health reasons. Moreover, he allegedly did not earn a college degree until 15 years after he started selling sperm to the Xytex.

Appellants brought suit against Xytex on various grounds other than wrongful birth, including fraud, negligent representation, and strict liability. Nevertheless, the Georgia Court of Appeals reasoned that the parents'

> claims directly relate to the fact that, had they known the health, educational and criminal history of Donor #9623, they would not have purchased his sperm from the Appellees. As the Supreme Court of Georgia stated, "we are unwilling to say that life, even life with severe impairments, may ever amount to a legal injury." This is a task best addressed by the Georgia General Assembly.

Construing their claims as amounting to a wrongful birth claim, which is not cognizable in Georgia, the court affirmed the trial court's dismissal of the claims. Had this case been brought in a jurisdiction that recognizes wrongful birth, should the appellants have been able to recover for wrongful birth, assuming the facts are true?

7.   In Harnicher v. University of Utah Medical Center, 962 P.2d 67 (Utah 1998), David and Stephanie Harnicher sought treatment for infertility. Using a mix of sperm from David and a donor, they underwent IVF and had triplets.

According to the couple, they had "specifically and exclusively selected" donor #183. After the triplets were born, one of the babies became ill, requiring blood tests. The results revealed that two of the children were not the child of either David or donor #183, both of whom had "curly dark hair and brown eyes." The genetic father of the two children was instead another donor with "straight auburn hair and green eyes." The Harnichers sued the Utah Medical Center for negligent infliction of emotion distress in using sperm from a donor they claimed they did not select. They alleged that they experienced severe emotional distress because their children did "not look as much like David as different children might have and whose blood type could not be descended from his" and which therefore "thwarted the couple's intention to believe and represent that the triplets are David's biological children." The Utah Supreme Court affirmed the lower courts' decisions to grant summary judgment on behalf of the medical center because "[e]xposure to the truth of one's own situation cannot be considered an injury." Moreover, the couple failed to

> allege that the triplets are unhealthy, deformed, or deficient in any way. Nor do they claim any racial or ethnic mismatch between the triplets and their parents. In fact the couple has presented no evidence at all that the physiological characteristics of three normal healthy children, which could not have been reliably predicted in any event, present circumstances with which " 'a reasonable [person,] normally constituted, would be unable to adequately cope.' "

The dissent argued that the medical center owed the Harnichers a clear duty "to use the donor sperm selected by the Harnichers that would have permitted them to believe the children to be their full biological children." It reasoned that the breach of that duty caused a lost opportunity for the couple "to believe their children to be their full biological offspring" and resulted in damages in the form of mental distress with physical symptoms.

Is the majority or dissent correct? Dov Fox argues that remedies should be available when negligence results in the birth of a child with different health, sex, and other traits than the ones the couple selected. See Dov Fox, Birth Rights and Wrongs: How Medical Mix-Ups Are Remaking Reproduction and the Law (2019).

CHAPTER 9

USING REPRODUCTIVE GENETIC TECHNOLOGIES FOR NON-MEDICAL PURPOSES

■ ■ ■

I. SEX AND TRAIT SELECTION

LORI B. ANDREWS, THE CLONE AGE: ADVENTURES IN THE NEW WORLD OF REPRODUCTIVE TECHNOLOGY
142–144 (2001).

In many parts of the world, technology is making the admission standards for birth tougher and tougher. In India, China, Taiwan, and Bangladesh, technicians with portable ultrasound machines go from village to village scanning pregnant women who are desperate to learn whether they are carrying a boy. Many abort when they fail to see a penis on the tiny out-of-focus screen. In Bombay alone, 258 clinics offered amniocentesis for sex selection. In one study of 8,000 abortions in India, 7,999 were female fetuses, leading human rights activists to protest this clear evidence of "gyne"cide. In China, when the one-child policy was strictly enforced, families so preferred males that the sex ratio changed to 153 males for each 100 females.

At Dr. John Stephens's clinics in California, Washington and New York, Western couples too can have prenatal testing for sex selection. One Australian client actually terminated a pregnancy because she couldn't get to Stephens's clinic in time to learn the sex of the fetus. She carried the next pregnancy to term when Stephens vetted it as a boy. Although most couples want a boy, an Israeli couple went to great lengths to have a girl out of fear of losing a son in a military engagement. They aborted a fetus when they learned it was a boy. In the next pregnancy, the wife was carrying twins, a boy and a girl. She used selective reduction to abort only the boy.

Thirty-four percent of U.S. geneticists said they would perform prenatal diagnosis for a family who want a son, and another 28 percent said they would refer the couple to another doctor who would perform such testing. Dorothy Wertz, the social scientist at the Shriver Center for Mental Retardation in Waltham, Massachusetts, who conducted the study, said the percentage of practitioners willing to respond to sex selection request had increased 10 percent from 1985 to 1995. "Autonomy just runs rampant over any other ethical principle in this country," Wertz says. "And it's only going to increase."

* * *

What if a sexual imbalance occurred in the United States, as is now happening in China and India? Sociologist Amitai Etzoni speculated that since women consume more culture and men commit more crimes, sex selection would create a more frontierlike society—with less art and more violence. Since men are more likely to vote Republican, politically there would be a shift to the right.

FYI: The expected biological ratio of boys to 100 girls at birth is 105. The United States retained that ratio from 1950 to 2017. In some countries, the ratio skewed upward in the 1990s and 2000s, with peaks in some countries in the 2000s. This table shows the sex ratio of boys to 100 girls in 2000, 2006, and 2017 in countries with the most skewed ratios based on a 2019 study. See Fengqing Chao et al, Systematic Assessment of Sex Ratio at Birth for All Countries and Estimation of National Imbalances and Regional Reference Levels, 116 PNAS 9303 (2019).

Country	2000	2006	2017
Armenia	118	116	112
China	117	118	114
Azerbaijan	115	117	113
India	111	110	110
Georgia	111	111	106
Albania	110	113	108
South Korea	110	107	106
Vietnam	108	111	112

The overwhelming tilt toward boys is not as pronounced yet in the United States as it is in other countries, but social psychologist Roberta Steinbacher of Cleveland State University worries about the effect on society if couples were able to predetermine their baby's sex. Twenty-five percent of people say they would use a sex selection technique, with 81 percent of the women and 94 percent of the men desiring to ensure their first-born would be a boy. Since other research reveals firstborns are more successful in their education, income, and achievements than latterborns, Steinbacher worries that "second class citizenship of women would be institutionalized by determining that the firstborn would be a boy."

THE AMERICAN SOCIETY FOR REPRODUCTIVE MEDICINE'S POSITION ON SEX SELECTION

Sex selection can be performed preconception through the use of methods like flow cytometry to separate sperm cells based on whether they have an X or Y chromosome, and inseminating with sperm cells that will produce offspring of the desired sex. It can also be used preimplantation through preimplantation genetic diagnosis (PGD) or preimplantation genetic screening (PGS) to test embryos for sex prior to implantation. This technique may result in the discarding of embryos of the undesired gender.

Individuals can also use prenatal screening to decide postconception whether or not to continue a pregnancy based on sex.

The ASRM Ethics Committee has weighed in on the ethics of sex selection a few times. In 1999, it approved the use of PGD for sex selection in the case of sex-linked genetic diseases, like hemophilia A or Duchenne-Becker muscular dystrophy. However, it has expressed more misgivings with respect to nonmedical uses of sex selection. For example, in ethics guidelines, it concludes, "[t]he initiation of IVF with PGD solely for sex selection holds even greater risk of unwarranted gender bias, social harm and the diversion of medical resources from genuine medical need. It therefore should be discouraged." Ethics Committee of the American Society of Reproductive Medicine, Sex Selection and Preimplantation Genetic Diagnosis, 72 Fertility & Sterility 595 (1999).

> **FYI:** There is evidence that our ancestors attempted to select sex as far back as the prehistoric era and in early Chinese, Egyptian and Greek cultures. Documentation of scientific efforts to influence the sex of a pregnancy by eating certain foods, timing intercourse based on ovulation, and using vaginal douches can be found as early as the 1600s. None of these efforts seemed to be particularly effective, however.

The ASRM has taken a more permissive stance on the use of preconception sex selection than with sex selection through PGD. Although ethical concerns such as reinforcing gender discrimination, reinforcing gender stereotypes, and causing societal sex-ratio imbalances exist with preconception sex selection, it does not result in the destruction of embryos. Thus, in 2001, the ASRM stated that, "[i]f . . . methods of preconception gender selection are found to be safe and effective, physicians should be free to offer preconception gender selection in clinical settings to couples who are seeking gender variety in their offspring if the couples (1) are fully informed of the risks of failure, (2) affirm that they will fully accept children of the opposite sex if the preconception gender selection fails, (3) are counseled about having unrealistic expectations about the behavior of children of the preferred gender, and (4) are offered the opportunity to participate in research to track and assess the safety, efficacy and demographics of preconception gender selection. Ethics Committee of the American Society of Reproductive Medicine, Sex Selection and Preimplantation Genetic Diagnosis, 75 Fertility & Sterility 861, 863 (2001).

In 2015, the ASRM noted that "[s]urvey data indicate that some assisted reproductive technology (ART) clinics in the United States are offering patients access to sex selection for nonmedical reasons." To offer guidance to practitioners, it reviewed the ethical arguments for and against nonmedical uses of sex selection, although it did not reach a consensus as to its permissibility.

In favor of offering such testing are the fact that parents may have many reasons for choosing sex selection, including balancing families to experience parenting children of both sexes. Given constitutionally protected reproductive liberty interests and the "deeply private" nature of reproductive choices, "[p]olicing the underlying attitudes among individuals with preferences for the sex of a child may be judged to be beyond the scope of fertility care . . . and violate patient autonomy and privacy." In addition, preferring one sex for a particular child "need not necessarily reflect discriminatory attitudes or intent" and may not "necessarily reflect gender bias." Further, such reproductive decisions "are not inconsistent with unconditional parental love." Finally, using preconception or preimplantation means to select sex avoids abortion, but allows parents to select their offspring's sex.

On the other hand, some argue that even though "no serious risks have been identified," the unknown long-term medical risks of preimplantation genetic screening (PGS) and even sperm sorting make nonmedical uses of sex selection problematic. Some believe that sex selection through PGS "fails to show appropriate respect for embryos" and that choosing sex is not a sufficiently "strong" reason for PGS. Others worry that non-medical sex selection does not demonstrate "unconditional parental acceptance" of one's children or parental love "independent of the parents' wants and preferences." Additionally, some fear it "represents a 'slippery slope' toward selection of many other traits . . . that would be ethically problematic." Others worry it could "deny the resulting child a right to an open future" by imposing "inappropriate gender norms" and reinforcing "gender essentialism," potentially causing the child psychological harm and disrupting the parent-child relationship. When used because of bias, it could lead to "prejudice against female children." The ASRM noted that it has suggested, however, that bias "may be less evident where sex selection is used for family balancing." How free of discriminatory biases family balancing is depends on the underlying attitudes toward the different sexes.

The ASRM also addressed the broader issue of social justice by noting the importance of social context. It observed that "[c]oncerns about gender bias and social injustice are significant, at least within certain populations," like China and India where infanticide and abortion have been used to select males. In contrast, in the United States, the preference for male children over female children is less great. In a 2004 survey, for example 50% of those surveyed "wished to have a family with an equal number of boys and girls, 7% with more boys than girls, 6% with more girls than boys, 5% with only boys, 4% with only girls, and 27% had no preference." Nevertheless, the ASRM noted "the ongoing problems with the status of women in the United States" and the possibility of subgroups who choose sex selection because of discriminatory views." Finally, it addressed the need to consider "the effects on the availability of ART for more fundamental fertility care needs" when there are limited resources for ART and strong "cultural pressures for sex selection." Ethics Committee of the American Society for Reproductive Medicine, Use of Reproductive Technology for Sex Selection for Nonmedical Reasons, 103 Fertility & Sterility 1418 (2015).

NOTES AND QUESTIONS

1. Should prenatal sex selection be permitted? Would it be an unconstitutional infringement on the couple's reproductive liberty to ban it? Eight states have enacted laws banning abortions for the purpose of sex selection. Congress has also introduced similar federal legislation in recent years. Legislators argue that these laws are intended to prevent sex discrimination, but critics argue they are just one more strategy to make abortion less accessible, particularly because no laws in the United States "prohibit other sex selection methods, such as sperm sorting or preimplantation genetic diagnostics." See Guttmacher Institute, Abortion Bans in Cases of Sex or Genetic Anomaly (July 1, 2019), https://www. guttmacher.org/state-policy/explore/abortion-bans-cases-sex-or-race-selection-or-genetic-anomaly.

Some countries, such as England, ban the use of preimplantation genetic testing for sex selection for non-medical reasons. Would such a ban raise the same constitutional issues raised by bans of abortions based on sex?

If a couple seeks to have a boy and the geneticist negligently tells them they are carrying a male fetus, would they be able to sue for wrongful birth if the child turned out to be a girl? See Chapter 8, Section III.A. What damages could they recover? For example, could they recover the lifetime difference in salary, since, on average, full-time working women earn 80.7 cents on every dollar a full-time working man earns? See Sonam Sheth et al., 7 Charts that Show the Glaring Gap Between Men and Women's Salaries in the US, Business Insider, Aug. 26, 2019, https://www.businessinsider.com/gender-wage-pay-gap-charts-2017-3.

2. Are the legal and ethical concerns regarding sex selection different depending on how it is achieved: through sperm sorting prior to conception, through preimplantation genetic testing, or through amniocentesis or NIPT? Does it matter if the testing is used to select against male embryos when there is the risk of an X-linked disorder? Does it matter if it is used to select in favor of female embryos when a family already has three boys? What legal or ethical framework should guide this analysis?

How should genetic counselors, who are strongly committed to gender equality, respond to requests for sex selection given their equally strong commitment to nondirectiveness? See Chapter 6, Section I. Should they challenge or deny such requests as inconsistent with equality when the motivations are driven by discriminatory views against females? Should they remain nondirective under the theory that it protects patient autonomy and therefore helps ensure equality for women? Or should they not be held accountable for the choices that patients make with respect to reproductive testing? See Sonia M. Suter, Sex Selection, Nondirectiveness, and Equality, 3 Univ. Chi. L. Sch. Roundtable 473 (1996).

3.   Recently, there have been some hints that gay men who use gestational surrogacy (where the surrogate is implanted with an embryo created through IVF) may be using PGT to select for sex. A study of 40 gay-father families, who mostly relied on gestational surrogacy, and 55 lesbian-mother families, who relied on donor insemination, found that 60 percent of the men's children were male and 40 percent were female, whereas 50.9 percent of the women's children were male and 49.1% were female. Susan Golombok et al., Parenting and Adjustment of Children Born to Gay Fathers Through Surrogacy, 89 Child Dev. 1223 (2018). The sample size of this study is too small to provide conclusive results, but if it suggests a trend among gay men who use gestational surrogates to select for boys, does this form of sex selection raise the same issues as in other contexts? How "relevant is the concern that sex selection reinforces gender stereotyping when the parents themselves are nonconforming?" Linda Layne, Sex Selection by Gay Men Using Gestational Surrogacy: A Troubling Trend in Queer Family-Making, BioNews, July 29, 2019, https://www.bionews.org.uk/page_144104.

SONIA M. SUTER, THE TYRANNY OF CHOICE: REPRODUCTIVE SELECTION IN THE FUTURE
5 J.L. & BIOSCI. 262, 264–65, 267–68 (2018).

* * * With expanded genomic analysis, PGD could provide a wealth of information for reproductive decision making. * * * * Next-generation sequencing [NGS] and increased understanding of the links between genotype and phenotype (the observable characteristics that result from the interaction of genotype with the environment) will provide parents with dizzying amounts of probabilistic information about an enormous range of health risks and traits for each embryo. * * *

* * *

* * * Researchers are currently exploring various methods of NGS, although we should expect the nature of large-scale sequencing in the future to be different (potentially much different) from what is possible right now. Developing the sequencing technology will be easy, however, in comparison to the challenge of improving our ability to interpret the vast amount of data that NGS could generate. How well we will be able to do that in the future is not clear.

Given that genomic information varies in its significance in determining phenotype, we will need to be able to interpret the genome comprehensively so that we can establish which genetic variants are particularly meaningful and informative. Highly penetrant genetic variants (where the probability is high that the variant will lead to the associated phenotype) will be far more informative than low penetrant genetic variants. Even with lower penetrant variants, however, NGS may still be able to offer predictions about the likelihood of the phenotype's developing.

In theory, large-scale sequencing would ultimately provide comprehensive genomic information about a range of phenotypes—physical health risks, intellectual or cognitive disorders, and non-medical traits. The first two categories could be broken down based on degree of severity and age of onset ([e.g.,] do they occur in childhood or adulthood?). Non-medical traits would include things like sex, physical characteristics (height, build, hair color, eye color, etc.), temperaments (tendencies toward extroversion, introversion, anxiety, etc.), and capacities in areas such as athletics, scholastics, music, etc. Crucial information would be the probability that the genotype would actually result in the specific phenotype, whether medical or non-medical. A few genotypes would be strongly determinative of phenotype; others would only increase the odds of the phenotypes, sometimes only by insignificant amounts. The degree to which our capacity to interpret the genome improves in the coming years will strongly influence how much we will be able to predict about the health and non-medical traits of future children through [PGD].

NOTES AND QUESTIONS

1.   In a study conducted between July 2006 and February 2007, 999 patients answered a survey question: "If you were planning to have a child (or are having a child), which conditions would you want testing for?" Among the choices were blindness, deafness, cancer, heart disease, athletic ability, dwarfism, superior intelligence, mental retardation, tall stature, longevity, or shortened lifespan (death by five, twenty, forty, or fifty years). A majority of the participants indicated they would test for mental retardation, blindness, deafness, dwarfism, heart disease and cancer. Only 10% of the participants of the study would test for athletic ability and only 12.6% of the participants would test for superior intelligence. While the participants indicated that they may not personally test for enhancements, 52.2% of the participants said that there are no conditions for which genetic testing should never be offered. On the other hand, only 6.4% of participants indicated that there are conditions for which testing should never be offered. Feighanne Hathaway et al., Consumers' Desire Towards Current and Prospective Reproductive Genetic Testing, 18 J. Genetic Counseling 137 (2009).

2.   Atlas Sports Genetics offers parents a $149 test that identifies variations in their child's ACTN3 gene, which it claims is a measure of natural-born athletic ability. The company says the test can determine whether a child will be a better football player, sprinter, or distance runner. Juliet Macur, Born to Run? Little Ones Get Test for Sports Gene, N.Y. Times, Nov. 30, 2008, at A1. Scientists have found that polymorphisms in ACTN3 and another gene, ACE I/D, have some association with sports performance, but they are not strong enough to be predictive. Lisa Guth & Stephen Roth, Genetic Influence

on Athletic Performance, 25 Current Opinion Pediatrics 653 (2013). Nevertheless, genetic testing for athletics continues. Baylor University's football team, for example, is using genetic profiles to tailor training regimens for athletes. Joe Leccesi, Genetic Testing: The New Way to Identify and Train Elite Athletes, USA Today, July 25, 2017, https://usatodayhss.com/2017/genetic-testing-the-new-way-to-identify-and-train-elite-athletes. While the science behind the test is questionable, its availability raises questions as to whether parents should be allowed to use preimplantation genetic testing (PGT) to select for these traits.

> **FYI:** Genes associated with traits can be incredibly complex. For example, even though there is a genetic component to height, different genetic variants can have significantly different impacts. Scientists believe about 700 genetic variants affect height, however their effect varies considerably. Some contribute as little as a millimeter of difference, others as much as an inch.

Companies are starting to develop and offer tests for non-medical traits in embryos. Genomic Prediction (see Chapter 8, Section II), for example, offers polygenic scores—statistical analysis of genetic variants—to predict which embryos are predisposed to be "among the shortest 2% of the population" or "in the lowest 2% in intelligence." Although demand for eye-color testing in embryos has not been high, it remains to be seen how high the demand for polygenic scores for intelligence and height will be. One family with autistic children has expressed an interest in the polygenic predictions of intelligence, even though the genetic causes of autism are not likely to be identified. Antonio Regalado, The World's First Gattaca Baby Tests Are Finally Here, MIT Tech. Rev., Nov. 8, 2019, https://www.technologyreview.com/s/614690/polygenic-score-ivf-embryo-dna-tests-genomic-prediction-gattaca/.

Genomic Prediction's test could be used to select embryos predisposed to be the most intelligent or tallest. A recent study, however, suggests the predictive capacity of such testing would quite limited. Using simulations, it estimated that selecting among five embryos based on polygenic scores would result in an "average gain" of roughly 2.5 cm in height and 2.5 IQ points. If ten embryos were analyzed, the average gain would be 3 cm in height and 3 IQ points. Moreover, they showed that in 28 families, the polygenic scores of the grown children predicted the tallest child in only seven families. In five families, the child predicted to be tallest was actually shorter than average. Ehud Karavani et al., Screening Human Embryos for Polygenic Traits Has Limited Utility, 179 Cell 1424, 1426-28 (2019).

3.   Does PGT for nonmedical uses implicate "neoeugenics," that is eugenics on an individual as opposed to state level? If so, is that problematic? Are there equity concerns given the costs associated with PGT and limited insurance coverage? Would PGT allow wealthy families to select embryos for socially advantageous traits, exacerbating existing inequities if less wealthy families cannot afford the technology? See Sonia M. Suter, A Brave New World of Designer Babies?, 22 Berkeley Tech. L.J. 897 (2007). Or will the predictive ability of genetics for traits be too complex to achieve the goals of selecting for certain characteristics?

Should there be limits on the use of prenatal testing or PGT for certain kinds of information? If so, on what grounds, and what should the limits be? Should such limits be enforced through professional guidelines, insurance coverage, regulations, and/or legislation? Are there any constitutional implications of government intervention either in prohibiting prenatal tests or PGT for certain uses or in prohibiting the disclosure of certain test results?

4. Would the potential risk from PGT itself be a sufficient rationale to ban its use for non-medical reasons? Genomic imprinting disorders are a rare type of birth defect. Three types of imprinting disorders (Beckwith-Wiedemann syndrome, Angelman syndrome and hypomethylation syndrome) have been associated with IVF, which is the first step in PGT. What effect should the possibility of an increase in birth defects have on the analysis of whether to ban PGT for non-medical reasons?

> **What's That?:** Genomic imprinting is a form of epigenetics (see Chapter 4), which causes genes to be expressed based on the parent of origin. Usually both genes inherited from each parent are active or "turned on." But sometimes only one is active, which can depend on whether the gene was inherited from the mother or father. Imprinting indicates the parent of origin by marking the gene during gamete formation through a process called methylation. During methylation small molecules called methyl groups attach to part of the DNA in the gene. Errors in the imprinting process can sometimes lead to genetic disorders.

5. What about the possibility of offering testing for prospective parents to discover how their "parental DNA would likely combine"? In 2008, 23andMe received backlash for "its patent for its Family Traits Inheritance Calculator, which was designed to predict 'six variable benign traits, including "eye color" and "muscle performance," based on how parental DNA would likely combine'." The company considered using enhanced gamete donor selection, when it filed for the patent in 2008. It ultimately decided not to given "concerns that this technology amounted to 'shopping for designer donors in an effort to produce designer babies.'" Suter, *supra,* at 293.

II. SELECTING FOR DISABILITY

KALENA R. KETTERING, NOTE, "IS DOWN ALWAYS OUT?": THE RIGHT OF ICELANDIC PARENTS TO USE PREIMPLANTATION GENETIC DIAGNOSIS TO SELECT FOR A DISABILITY

51 GEO. WASH. INT'L L. REV. ___ (forthcoming 2020).

* * *

It might seem counterintuitive to imagine a parent who would intentionally select for, rather than against, a disability. Indeed, it remains one of the most controversial uses of PGD. One survey of PGD clinics in the U.S. conducted by the Genetics and Public Policy Center at Johns Hopkins University found three percent of prospective parents used PGD to intentionally select for a disability. The parents who chose "defective" genes did not see these conditions as disabilities or as "defective," but instead as a way for their children to share in the same culture and experiences as their parents. Most commonly, those who select for a disability are selecting for deafness or for achondroplasia, colloquially known as dwarfism.

This desire to share in a culture surrounding a disability is antithetical to typical societal and medical customs. While the medical community tends to view a trait such as deafness as a "condition to be cured," deaf people perceive deafness and sign language as defining characteristics of a community. Sociologists, linguists, and anthropologists now recognize the deaf population as culturally and linguistically distinct, sharing in common identities and customs. People in the Deaf community not only share a language, but common experiences. Deaf culture is full of customs including widely recognized jokes, stories, and poetry. [As a result], several studies have found that some deaf parents have a preference for deaf children.

Similarly, parents with achondroplasia want their child to belong to a distinctive community and family unit. One woman with achondroplasia conveyed to the *New York Times* that her desire to have a child with achondroplasia stems from the question "what [would life] be like for her, when her parents are different than she is?" Children of parents with disabilities also share this gravitation towards uniform disability amongst family members. One study found that 36.4% of hearing children with deaf parents at one point or another wanted to be deaf. One such child recalled, "at times I wanted to be deaf . . . I felt so comfortable being around my deaf family and friends. Being with hearing friends, I felt awkward and socially inept."

Using assistive reproductive technology to intentionally have a child with a disability is not new. In 2002, *The Washington Post* ran an article about a deaf lesbian couple who intentionally selected sperm with a gene for deafness to give birth to a deaf son. These women did not consider it a negative to bring a deaf child into the world; instead, they saw it as a way for their future son to bond with them and their culture. Similarly, a woman named Mary Ellen Little who has achondroplasia, used amniocentesis to find out whether her second daughter would also have the same trait. Additionally, there is at least one reported case of a couple with achondroplasia who corresponded with a researcher to identify the gene for achondroplasia, and assist in genetic screening and abortion of any fetus who did not possess the trait.

But strong opposition exists to allowing PGD selection on the basis of disability. Opponents of this use of PGD insist this selection creates a "harm" to the future child. Opponents claim the harm manifests itself in both the selection and the disability, creating adverse psychological and physical effects. Additionally, most physicians will not allow their patients to use PGD to select for a disability. In their mind, PGD is only about producing "healthy" babies. In addition to physician resistance, some governments' regulation of PGD make it impossible for parents to select for a disability despite their desire for cultural connectivity.

NOTES AND QUESTIONS

1.   Kettering references a study of children of deaf adults, known as "CODAs," which showed that more than a third had wished at some point that they were deaf like their parents. See Cara Mand et al., Genetic Selection for Deafness: The Views of Hearing Children of Deaf Adults, 35 J. Med. Ethics 722, 725 (2009). Should this information influence the ethics of using PGD to select for deafness in particular?

2.   Various examples exist where parents seek to have children with "disabilities." In one instance, a woman had two children with celiac disease, which made them unable to digest carbohydrates. She wanted help from a physician to conceive a third child with the disease. Because the diet for her two children was so complicated, she did not want a child who required an alternative "normal" diet.

Similarly, a couple in which both individuals had inherited the autosomal-dominant condition achondroplasia (dwarfism) had a 50% chance of having a child with this condition. They called the researcher who had cloned the gene and asked for aid in screening and aborting a fetus who would not have achondroplasia.

Ronald M. Green discusses these cases in Prenatal Autonomy and the Obligation Not to Harm One's Child Genetically, 25 J.L. Med. & Ethics 5, 13 (1997). He advocates the following standard:

> Parents are best suited to understand and shape the lives of their offspring. Their freedom of decision in this area should have presumptive priority in our moral and legal thinking. Only in extreme cases are we warranted as a society in denying them access to the professional services they need to realize their choices or in preventing them from exercising those choices. These extreme cases are characterized by the following two features: (1) the likelihood that, relative to others in the birth cohort, the child will experience significant pain, disability or limitations in life options as a result of avoidable genetic factors; and (2) the parents' reasons for bringing the child into the world in this condition do not constitute reasonable or compelling grounds for respecting their choice.

3.   Should prospective parents be allowed to use PGD to intentionally select *for* a disability, or should PGD be limited to help create "healthy" babies? Does selection for a disability create a harm to the future child, or does it depend on the disability?

If PGD is used to select for a disability, should the future child be able to sue their parents or the PGD provider for wrongful life? See Chapter 8, Section III.B. Why or why not?

4. What role should physicians play in these decisions? If laws do not regulate the selection of PGD for nonmedical uses, should physicians defer to patient's wishes? Or are they entitled to "conscientiously object" by refusing to use PGD to select for a disability? Various arguments support and counter physicians complying with such requests.

[There are] five possible bases on which a provider could acquiesce in good faith. Support for physician acquiescence is largely grounded in the preeminence of reproductive liberty, alongside the worthy goal of equal protection in the quest for biologic parenthood. This latter concern advocates equal treatment of pre- and post-implantation embryos, honoring a woman's choice to give birth, or not, to a particular would-be child. A third argument in favor of honoring patient requests for transfer looks to the growing bank of litigated cases discussing the disposition of disputed embryos in the context of divorce. While not dispositive of a clash between a patient and a provider, the body of law does shed light on the allocation of dispositional authority over preimplantation embryos. [A fourth argument concerns] the parties' inability to accurately predict the future child's well-being. Disability advocates have nicely shaped this prediction problem, which seems quite apropos for the clinical scenario at hand. Finally, an * * * argument about the benefits of existence over non-existence [can also be made]. Together, these rationales are steeped in the values of patient autonomy, reproductive equality, and the preference for birth over non-existence.

The[re are four possible] arguments for declining patient requests for transfer of genetically anomalous embryos * * *. Provider autonomy is offered as a prime, yet seriously undervalued basis on which to decline to participate in treatment the physician finds professionally or personally troublesome. Worries about discrimination or capriciousness can be minimized if refusals are applied equally on the basis of the embryo's diagnosis and prognosis. Next, two theories interchangeably support a physician's refusal to further the patient's reproductive plan. Reproductive non-maleficence and procreative beneficence invoke notions of 'do not harm' and 'fulfill a duty to do the most good' in the context of reproductive technologies. Fourth and finally, as rational actors in a litigious society, physicians may calculate their exposure to legal liability for assisting in the birth of a seriously impaired human being—assessing a greater risk for acts undertaken versus acts refused. Since a patient cannot waive the potential child's future legal claims, concerns about malpractice could motivate an ART provider's actions at the bedside.

Judith Daar, A Clash at the Petri Dish: Transferring Embryos with Known Genetic Anomalies, 5 J.L. & Biosci. 219, 226 (2018).

5.   Regulation of PGD in the United States is nonexistent; prospective parents can use PGD to select on the basis of sex, disability, or other nonmedical uses. Internationally, regulation of PGD varies greatly. Some countries impose strict limitations. All Australian states, for example, ban PGD for non-medical reasons and only allow it to prevent a genetic (sometimes limited to "serious") condition. Germany only allows PGD when prospective parents demonstrate predisposition to a serious genetic illness and receive approval from an ethics panel. Austria prohibits PGD, except in rare cases such as "potential parental death, miscarriage, or a non-treatable hereditary illness." France also limits PGD to cases where "a physician attests to a high risk of a serious hereditary genetic defect" and only allows analysis for that defect. Italy only allows prospective parents to use PGD "to foster a healthy embryo or to protect the embryo against a hereditary disease." Finally, the United Kingdom established the Human Fertilisation and Embryology Authority (HFEA), which regulates assisted reproductive technology. The UK's 2008 update of the Human Fertilisation and Embryology Act of 1990 bans both sex selection for nonmedical reasons and "the selection of embryos at risk of developing a disability." Its explanatory notes "indicate deafness is among the prohibited disabilities." Kettering, *supra*.

III. CONCEIVING A SIBLING TO BE A DONOR

When Anissa Ayala was diagnosed with chronic myelogenous leukemia, a disease usually fatal within five years, her best chance of survival was a bone marrow donation from a relative. However, neither her parents nor her brother was a close enough match. A nationwide search was unable to locate a compatible donor.

Anissa's parents decided to conceive another child to serve as a donor. Her father underwent surgery to reverse a vasectomy. Her mother was 42 years old when she conceived Marissa. Genetic testing when the fetus was six months old revealed the new daughter would be an appropriate match. When she was 14 months old, she was anesthetized, and doctors inserted long needles into her hip bone to withdraw marrow to donate to her ill older sister. Gina Kolata, More Babies Born to Be Donors of Tissue, N.Y. Times, June 4, 1991, at A1.

In the years since the Ayala case, over one hundred children have been conceived as prospective donors. Couples get pregnant, have the fetus tested prenatally to see if it is a match, and then abort and try again if the new child cannot serve as a donor. There are no figures on how many fetuses have been aborted under these circumstances. One couple who chose not to abort created three additional children, yet none was a suitable match. In another family, a baby was created to be a donor—but the infant turned out to have the same rare metabolic disease as the existing child.

In 2000, a Colorado couple, Lisa and Jack Nash, used in vitro fertilization followed by preimplantation genetic testing to conceive a child to be a tissue donor for his older sister who had a rare genetic disease, Fanconi anemia. Of 15 embryos created, only one was a genetic match. When the sibling was born, cells from his cast-off umbilical cord were transfused into his sister. Peter Gorner, A Child is Born and So Is a Genetic Dilemma, Chi. Trib., Oct. 8, 2000, at 1C. In another case, when a remarried woman learned that a child from her first marriage needed a bone marrow transplant, she used artificial insemination with sperm from her first husband to conceive a child.

NOTES AND QUESTIONS

1.   One court considered whether providers should be liable for the lost chance of creating donor siblings for a very sick child. Susan Ferrell and her daughter, Alexis Ferrell, sued Dr. Rosenbaum and Children's National Medical Center for their allegedly negligent failure to diagnose Alexis with Fanconi anemia, "a potentially fatal genetic blood disorder." The crux of their claim was that "had Alexis been diagnosed properly while under Dr. Rosenbaum's care, the Ferrells would have been informed that a matched bone marrow transplant from a sibling donor was the best treatment for their daughter's condition." However, because Alexis's condition was only diagnosed after her father, Mr. Ferrell, left the family and could no longer be found, "Alexis's only chance for a matched sibling donor ha[d] been foreclosed." As a result, the plaintiffs claimed that 'Alexis's chance to obtain the matched bone marrow transplant donor she needs for survival ha[d] been significantly reduced." The D.C. Court of Appeals found there was a "possibility . . . that, had the Ferrells known about the Fanconi Anemia and its optimum treatment with a matched donor transplant, they would have taken steps to conceive a sibling or siblings who could have provided a compatible bone marrow donor whenever the transplant was appropriate." Given that Ms. Ferrell "would have done anything possible to help Alexis," the court concluded that "had Alexis been properly diagnosed when Mr. Ferrell was in her life, and had Alexis received a transplant from a compatible sibling donor, Alexis would have had 'an appreciable chance of saving [her] life.' " Therefore, because the "defendants interfered with the plaintiff's chance to avoid the harm," plaintiffs made a prima facie showing of proximate cause, and the court overturned the defendants' motion for summary judgment. Ferrell v. Rosenbaum, 691 A.2d 641 (D.C. App. 1997). On remand, however, the jury found for the defendants.

2.   In some cases, an existing family member is a match for an ill child but does not want to go through the painful bone marrow extraction. Is it fair to create a child to be a donor and force him or her to do something that an existing sibling, cousin, or parent will not do? Where should we draw the line? Should parents conceive a second child to be a kidney donor for the first?

3.   There are also questions about access to the technologies for prenatal and preimplantation testing for tissue matching. When a child is diagnosed

with a disease that would benefit from matched tissue, should the physician have a duty to tell the parents that they could conceive a sibling for donation? Should insurers reimburse for the procedure? The cost to the Nashes of in vitro fertilization and preimplantation testing was $50,000.

4.   In 2017 alone, there were over 255,000 cycles of in vitro fertilization in the United States which were reported to the Society for Assisted Reproductive Technology. Preimplantation genetic diagnosis procedures were performed on 8,000 of the resulting embryos. See www.sartcorsonline.com/rptCSR_PublicMultYear.aspx?ClinicPKID=0. There is no way of knowing exactly how many attempts were made to create "savior siblings" (siblings conceived to be donors). According to data collected in 2006 from fertility doctors in the United States by the Genetics and Public Policy Center at Johns Hopkins University, approximately one percent of all preimplantation genetic diagnosis cycles are conducted for purposes of creating a sibling to be a donor. Beth Whitehouse, The Match: 'Savior Siblings' and One Family's Battle to Heal Their Daughter, 127 (2010).

CHAPTER 10

NEWBORN SCREENING PROGRAMS

■ ■ ■

I. THE HISTORY AND RATIONALE FOR NEWBORN SCREENING PROGRAMS

AMERICAN ACADEMY OF PEDIATRICS, REPORT OF
THE TASK FORCE ON NEWBORN SCREENING,
PUBLISHED AS A CALL FOR A NATIONAL AGENDA
ON STATE NEWBORN SCREENING PROGRAMS
106 Pediatrics 389, 389–90 (Supp.) (2000).

Newborn screening in the United States is a public health program aimed at the early identification of conditions for which early and timely interventions can lead to the elimination or reduction of associated mortality, morbidity, and disabilities. This screening takes place within the context of a newborn screening system, and involves the following components: screening, short-term follow-up, diagnosis, treatment/management, and evaluation. Inherent to each of these components is an education process.

* * *

THE HISTORY OF NEWBORN SCREENING

Newborn screening programs began in the early 1960s with the original work of Dr Robert Guthrie, who developed a screening test for phenylketonuria (PKU) and a system for collection and transportation of blood samples on filter paper. By 1962, Massachusetts launched a voluntary newborn PKU screening program that demonstrated the feasibility of mass genetic screening.

Initially, newborn screening for PKU was not a health department role or a legislated activity. Health professionals were slow to adopt the practice of screening for PKU, and the responsibility for screening was not defined (e.g., should

> **What's That?:** PKU is an autosomal recessive condition caused by a mutation in the gene that codes for an enzyme that metabolizes the amino acid, phenylalanine. If that enzyme is missing, the body will build up harmful levels of phenylalanine unless the affected individual eats a special diet that limits consumption of phenylalanine and the artificial sweetener, aspartame. Symptoms of untreated PKU include intellectual disability and other serious health problems, although the condition can range from mild to severe.

it be the responsibility of the hospital in which the infant was born, the mother's obstetrician, or the infant's pediatrician or primary care health professional). The American Academy of Pediatrics (AAP), acting as the professional association that develops policy for the care of children, raised concerns about the sensitivity and specificity of PKU screening tests, as well as the efficacy of early intervention for PKU. Out of these concerns, the need for further research about this testing was recognized, and the federal Children's Bureau (now the federal Maternal and Child Health Bureau [MCHB]) funded a collaborative study to address questions and concerns about the effectiveness of the PKU screening test.

At the same time, advocates for children remained concerned that children with undetected PKU were at high risk for mental retardation. The National Association for Retarded Citizens (now the ARC) proposed model legislation for creation of public programs to address low detection rates, and also conducted an extensive grass-roots lobbying effort to support passage of mandatory PKU screening legislation. Many state health departments supported the adoption of such legislation. The Kennedy Administration * * * was also supportive. * * * As a result of [a] multidimensional advocacy campaign, most states passed laws in the early 1960s that mandated newborn screening for PKU. Forty-three states had formal statutes by 1973. State health departments, particularly their maternal and child health (MCH) programs (funded by Title V of the Social Security Act of 1935), assumed the central role in implementation of these new laws.

* * *

As a result of the laws mandating PKU testing, and the establishment of health department newborn screening units that occurred in the 1960s and 1970s:

- Every newborn had an opportunity to be screened for PKU when laws were properly implemented; consequently, most were screened.

- Financial barriers to screening and diagnosis were removed, but families often had to pay for the special formula, special foods, and other related treatments.

- State newborn screening programs evolved, with the goal of providing safe screening tests and appropriate follow-up to every newborn.

* * *

Now, after 30 years of experience with PKU, it is clear that knowledge regarding PKU and the approach to newborn screening were rudimentary when the programs were first launched. Studies to validate the screening test, and to assess the safety and effectiveness of a special diet to prevent mental retardation, were completed after laws were implemented. However, the history of these efforts has set the context for the role of public health in newborn screening and genetics.

SONIA M. SUTER, DID YOU GIVE THE GOVERNMENT YOUR BABY'S DNA? RETHINKING CONSENT IN NEWBORN SCREENING
15 Minn. J.L. Sci. & Tech. 729, 734–45 (2014).

* * *

NBS begins with a heel prick and the collection of a few drops of blood on filter paper, or Guthrie cards. It is a preventive health measure that involves the analysis of the newborn's blood for various medical conditions, many of which are inherited, including certain inborn errors of metabolism and blood disorders. The value of conducting screening during the newborn period is both practical and clinically significant. Most infants are born in hospitals, which makes the systematic collection of samples easier at this stage of life than nearly any other. In addition, for many of the diseases screened, treatment must be started in the newborn period to prevent the development of clinical symptoms.

As its name suggests, NBS is a screening program in which an abnormal result does not necessarily identify the presence of disease. It merely indicates an increased risk that the child has the condition, necessitating confirmation through diagnostic testing.

With its inception nearly fifty years ago, NBS is the longest program of genetic screening in the history of genetics. * * *

While PKU was the primary disease screened for in the early days of NBS, the panel of NBS diseases has expanded considerably in the last few years. The initial expansion, however, was quite slow, with only a few diseases added per decade. As late as 2003, the number of diseases screened for in most states was still quite low—eight or fewer diseases. Technological advances, however, changed that. While initial NBS required a separate assay for each disorder, the development of tandem mass spectrometry (MS/MS) in the 1990s allowed for the identification of over forty conditions through a single test, contributing greatly to the expansion of NBS. After several years of much variability in screening practices, a consensus began to emerge about the need for more uniformity in NBS, especially with respect to screening panels. The American College of Medical Genetics [and Genomics] (ACMG) issued recommendations for the standardization of the selection of NBS diseases in 2005, which were endorsed by several professional groups. Now every state tests or will test for a minimum of twenty-nine conditions. Some panels include over fifty disorders.

What's That?: Tandem mass spectrometry allows laboratories to screen for metabolic disorders in newborns by separating out metabolites in the infant's blood based on their molecular weight. Metabolites are substances formed during metabolism. Errors in metabolism can lead to abnormal levels of certain metabolites.

As technologies allow us to test for more diseases more efficiently, the question of what diseases should be included in each state's NBS panel remains difficult and, as we shall see later, has some bearing on the question of whether parental consent should be required. Among the relevant criteria are, of course, scientific considerations, such as the prevalence of the condition in the population, the validity of the NBS test, and the efficacy of available treatments. But other non-scientific considerations also play a vital role. Political concerns—such as the existence of advocacy groups and cost-benefit analysis—are also hugely influential. And, of course, ethical considerations should and often do come into play. For example, because the benefits to the newborn, to the family, and to society do not necessarily overlap, decision makers must decide whose benefits should determine the selection of the screening panel.

If the goal of NBS is to benefit the newborn, the panel of diseases should be limited to those for which we have effective treatments or early intervention and whose natural history we understand well. If we also consider the benefits to the family, however, the panel of diseases might be broader because it would include diseases with no treatment that might help parents make better informed reproductive decisions about whether to undergo prenatal testing with future pregnancies. In addition, such information can avoid diagnostic odysseys, when parents search long and hard for the diagnosis of a rare condition. Finally, if we focus on the benefits to society, the panel of diseases would be even larger, including conditions about which we have limited knowledge and no effective treatments so that we can identify potential research subjects to learn more about the natural history of the disease.

For some time, the consensus has been that the benefits to the newborn should be decisive in selecting conditions for NBS since *the raison d'être* of the program is to protect infants from debilitating diseases. Despite this consensus, these criteria have not always been followed in practice. Because state health departments have substantial discretion to decide which tests to include for NBS, there is little oversight. Even the ACMG recommendations, which expressly declare that the benefit to the newborn should drive the selection of disease, include a panel of diseases, not all of which directly or indirectly benefit the newborn.

Several factors have contributed to, and will likely further contribute to, the expansion of NBS, not all of which directly benefits the newborn. Technological advances, such as [tandem mass spectrometry], have contributed to this expansion. Other technologies, like DNA microarrays, will make it possible to screen for a slew of genetic conditions. With the possibility of ever-cheaper whole genome sequencing, it is not hard to imagine a time, in the not too distant future, when NBS will be expanded to include whole genome sequencing. Indeed, the National Institutes of Health (NIH) recently funded pilot programs to "explore the promise—and ethical challenges—of sequencing every newborn's genome." This is consistent with the development of personalized medicine and the belief that it is responsible and empowering to get as much medical information as possible.

So far, most of the expansions of NBS have been beneficial, although the data about "long-term clinical outcomes" are limited. The lives of many children, who might have died years ago because their state did not screen for medium chain acyl-coenzyme A dehydrogenase deficiency (MCADD), for example, have been saved by the introduction of MCADD testing in all states. Even so, the expansion of NBS is not without costs. The more conditions we screen for, the greater the risk of the inevitable artifacts of any screening program: false negatives, false positives, and clinical and diagnostic uncertainty. False negatives may create false reassurance and slow the process of diagnosis; because pediatricians know that NBS is done for all children, they may assume that the child does not have one of the NBS diseases based on the negative NBS result.

False positives present the opposite problem. When a child is reported as being positive for one of the NBS conditions, the family can experience a great deal of anxiety and confusion. Some studies have shown that false positives can have an adverse effect on the relationship between parent and child, including parents' continued worries about the child's health even after learning that she did not have the condition after all. In addition, false positives may have a negative health impact on the child by requiring follow-up testing and treatment until it is determined that the child is unaffected; further testing and treatment both pose potential medical risks. Children who have false positive results are often mislabeled as ill even though they do not display any clinical symptoms.

The recent and rapid expansion of NBS panels may also result in the diagnosis of conditions for which there is no treatment, which may create unnecessary stress and anxiety for the family and affect the parent-child relationship. For example, parents may pursue costly treatment odysseys, hoping to find a cure even though no proven treatment exists. While such information may help parents with future reproductive decision making, this rationale moves NBS away from its stated purpose of benefitting the newborn. Moreover, it undercuts the justification for the mandatory nature of NBS * * * .

Even more complicated issues arise when laboratories make incidental findings of "abnormalities" or clinically ambiguous findings. This problem has increased with tandem mass spectrometry, which looks for a group of core conditions by identifying unusually high levels of metabolites related to these conditions. An artifact of this technology is the incidental identification of elevated levels of certain metabolites, which the laboratory was not even trying to identify, or the identification of screening values that lie outside the normal range but that do not always clearly correlate with defined disease categories. These findings can lead to a new kind of diagnostic odyssey, where children become, to use the terminology of Timmermans and Buchbinder, "patients-in-waiting," who hover "for extended periods of time under medical attention between sickness and health, or more precisely, between pathology and an undistinguished state of 'normality.' "

Several problems arise when these incidental or diagnostically uncertain findings are made and reported to parents. The child might be stigmatized as a "sick child" before symptoms develop, if they ever will. This label has been shown to have a harmful effect on the parent-child relationship and on the family as a whole. Indeed, in some cases, the child might never become clinically affected by the abnormal levels of the metabolite or the mutation. There may be a considerable time lag before physicians can determine whether high metabolites or certain mutations are clinically significant, hence the phrase "patients-in-waiting."

Timmermans and Buchbinder's ethnographic study of a genetics clinic describes the complexities and anxieties that such diagnostic uncertainties present and the ways in which entire families are affected during this period. If families learn of these findings, they might embark on treatment odysseys, investing significant money and time in search of treatments that may not exist or that are unproven. Sometimes the heightened vigilance that parents exhibit during this period is difficult to "tone down" once it becomes clear that the child is not clinically affected. NBS programs may also spend added dollars to report and follow up on conditions for which treatments may not exist. It has also presented challenges for clinicians who have to contend with the fact that expanded screening has "identified more patients than anticipated," most of whom are asymptomatic, and which requires a collective learning process and the development of new knowledge to determine who is truly affected.

If NBS ultimately includes whole genome sequencing, similar issues will arise on an even greater scale. We are unlikely to fully understand for some time the clinical implications of many mutations, let alone the complex interactions of different mutations within a particular genome and environment. In many instances, it will be difficult to determine whether a genetic variant is likely to have a significant clinical impact, or what the degree or timing of such impact would be. As a result, whole genome sequencing would likely provide a great deal of data of limited value, which could increase parental anxiety and confusion.

Although the *raison d'etre* for NBS was to promote the wellbeing of newborns, some of the expansions of NBS can only be justified by other considerations, such as allowing parents to make better informed reproductive decisions and benefiting society by allowing us to better understand the conditions. * * *

NOTES AND QUESTIONS

1.　Does it make sense for the state to be the primary provider of newborn screening? One advantage of state-run programs is that the screening is usually paid for, which avoids "the inequities inherent in the piecemeal health insurance that exists in this country." In theory, the state's presence should help ensure that all children are tested, especially where states mandate screening, although "states vary widely in the percentage of children who are tested." The state also has "more tools at its disposal with which to find children who are diagnosed with serious conditions at birth and to ensure that they receive continuity of care," although again, "the success of states in the context of finding and tracking children varies widely." Ellen W. Clayton, Screening and Treatment of Newborns, 29 Houston L. Rev. 85, 124 (1992).

2.　The justification for the state role in newborn screening is either the police power or the doctrine of *parens patriae*. Are those rationales persuasive? Consider the view of one scholar

> [I]f the affected child is the target, the state cannot justify screening as an exercise of the police power. Because genetic disorders are not "catching," the child does not pose a health risk to others. One might argue that the parents could "harm" future children by passing on the genetic disorder and that the state can appropriately intervene to prevent this injury. The problem with this argument is that the only way to protect the child from getting the genetic disorder is to prevent the child from being born. Even if one concedes that some conditions may make a child's life not worth living, the disorders for which newborn screening is currently performed do not qualify. Nor is it likely that the diseases sought in newborn screening will ever be the basis for wrongful life claims because newborn screening is most appropriate when effective treatment is available.

> The state, then, is far more likely to invoke its role as *parens patriae* as the source of its authority to conduct newborn screening. At first, the analogy between the state as parent and parents as parents seems compelling, but further analysis reveals two problems with viewing the state as "parent." First, these children have "real" parents, whether by biological or other social connections, who have far-reaching authority to make important decisions regarding their children. The state is not completely free to override the parents' choices.

Second, concern for children does not seem to be the state's primary motivation for participation in newborn screening. The fact that the state bases its decisions about which diseases to seek on cost-benefit analyses makes clear that avoiding burdens on the public fisc is a major reason for screening. Further, the cost-benefit analyses that have been done are fundamentally flawed because they are based on the invalid premise that affected children receive care. This assumption is invalid because many states neither provide treatment nor require insurers to pay for it and many families have trouble meeting the demands of dietary and other therapeutic regimens necessary to provide care for affected children.

* * *

* * * Even assuming that the states are acting within the limits of their power, it is not obvious that these programs should be in the public domain at all, particularly since similar screening efforts are undertaken as a matter of course in the context of routine medical care. No reasons suggest that the state is a particularly dispassionate or wise decision-maker in this area, for the state is subject to cost constraints that can oppose the interests of the children being screened and their families. In addition, history reveals that political advocacy by individual practitioners and special interest groups greatly influenced the development of newborn screening programs. Finally, although one can argue that the involvement of the state can lead to more uniform access, this potential has only been partially met.

Clayton, *supra,* at 127–30, 134.

3.   Over the years, several groups of experts have grappled with the question of what criteria to use in deciding which conditions to include in newborn screening. In 1975, the National Academy of Sciences issued a report setting forth a number of criteria for newborn screening tests:

1.   acceptance by healthcare professionals;

2.   previous feasibility studies;

3.   satisfactory test methodology;

4.   appropriate laboratory facilities and quality control;

5.   adequate resources for counseling, treatment, and follow-up;

6.   acceptable costs;

7.   effective education;

8.   informed consent; and

9.   adequate means of evaluation.

Another NAS report in 1994 focused on three criteria:

1.   clear indication of benefit to the newborn;

2.   a system in place to confirm the diagnosis; and

3.   available treatment and follow-up.

The Task Force on Newborn Screening of the American Academy of Pediatrics, *supra*, emphasized:

1.   screening should be of primary benefit to the infant;

2.   the test should have analytical and clinical validity and utility; and

3.   interventions to improve outcomes for the infant should be safe and effective.

What are the differences between these approaches? What values do they share?

4.   The March of Dimes, an organization focused on preventing birth defects and infant mortality, criticized the Task Force report for not calling for screening for an unlimited number of diseases: "We believe that a test (even for a rare disease)—as long as its early discovery makes a difference to the child—must be conducted for every newborn." Mike Mitka, Neonatal Screening Varies by State of Birth, 284 JAMA 2044 (2000). What kinds of "differences to the child" should count?

The National Academy of Sciences recommends against newborn screening for disorders for which no beneficial treatment is available. What if there is beneficial treatment, but it is equally effective if it is delayed until symptoms occur, rather than initiated as the result of newborn screening? Some studies suggest that this is the case with newborn screening for galactosemia, one of the standard newborn screening tests. There is also controversy over whether detecting cystic fibrosis in newborns improves patient health.

Is treatment the only benefit that might derive from screening? What about research needs? What about information to aid the child and its family in planning for the future? At least one state has screened infants for Duchenne muscular dystrophy in order to provide reproductive information for the parents. (See the discussion in Chapter 2 of newborn screening in the context of eugenics.)

5.   In an effort to achieve uniformity in NBS, a 2005 report by the American College of Medical Genetics (ACMG) commissioned by the U.S. Department of Health and Human Services identified 29 conditions as a "core panel" that should be included in every state newborn screening program. The ACMG selected the core panel of tests based on the availability of specific and sensitive test methods; the capacity to identify a condition between 24 to 48 hours after birth when it would not otherwise be clinically detected; and "demonstrated benefits of early detection, timely intervention, and efficacious treatment." It also noted that the key factor in selecting conditions was "the

potential for the affected newborn to realize a significant improvement in quality of life as a result of the screening," although it also recognized that "many others are also affected by newborn screening," including "families, public health professionals, the public, and the health care system" through cost reductions for overall health care services. Newborn Screening: Toward a Uniform Screening Panel and System, https://www.hrsa.gov/sites/default/files/hrsa/advisory-committees/heritable-disorders/newborn-uniform-screening-panel.pdf; see also Michael S. Watson et al., ACMG Newborn Screening Expert Group, 8 Genetic Med. 12 (Supp. 2006). For a list of the core and secondary disorders in the Recommended Uniform Screening Panel, see Newborn Screening Status for all Disorders, NewSTEPs, https://www.newsteps.org/resources/newborn-screening-status-all-disorders.

6.   Some are proposing the use of whole genome sequencing in newborn screening. (See Chapter 7, Section I for a discussion of genome sequencing.) As Suter mentions, pilot programs have been conducted to explore newborn genome sequencing. One research protocol offered parents who participated in newborn sequencing studies the choice to decide how much information to receive about their infants—basic information or information about conditions that could be actionable in the future. About 70% of parents wanted to receive information in all categories. These results may reflect selection bias because the parents in these studies may be particularly curious about genetic information. In some cases, parents are learning things they would not discover with typical newborn screening. One mother, for example, learned that her daughter carries a genetic variant for a heightened risk of disease as an adult, and so does she. In another study, researchers found 11% of sequenced infants had unanticipated results, and 88% were found to be heterozygous for at least one recessive allele. They also found that returning risk information about the newborns did not cause the families undue stress, change perceptions of the child's vulnerability, or disrupt the parent-child bond.

Ironically, however, genome sequencing is far less effective at picking up metabolic disorders like PKU than the standard heel prick. The genetics of such conditions may be caused by multiple variants, not all of which have been identified. Ultimately, the move toward newborn genome screening has not been incorporated into infant care as quickly as some had predicted it would, and researchers are split as to its value. Some think it's better to get information about health risks sooner rather than later. Others worry about the privacy issues and personal preferences surrounding the information that can be gleaned. In addition, genome screening and the associated follow up may not be available to everyone because it is not covered by governmental insurance for the poor. See Richard Harris, The Promises and Pitfalls of Gene Sequencing for Newborns, Morning Edition, NPR, July 8, 2019, https://www.npr.org/sections/health-shots/2019/07/08/738528989/the-promises-and-pitfalls-of-gene-sequencing-for-newborns; Monica Heger, NIH Newborn Sequencing Projects' Lessons, Next Steps Highlighted at Meeting, Jun. 26, 2019, https://

www.genomeweb.com/sequencing/nih-newborn-sequencing-projects-lessons-next-steps-highlighted-meeting#.XWx8AuhKjb0.

Should genome sequencing be offered as a supplement to newborn screening? If so, what precautionary measures should be taken to address the concerns about its use in NBS?

7. In order for NBS to be successful, children must not only be diagnosed with conditions, but also be able to access appropriate treatment. Suppose there is a treatment for the condition, but it is not readily available? Consider the following from the 2000 report of the Task Force on Newborn Screening, *supra*:

> Funding for comprehensive medical care and treatment is challenging, and treatment of some conditions identified through newborn screening is costly. Not all children have health coverage or the means to purchase needed treatment. Managed care plans and other third-party payers often do not cover items such as special formulas, special foods, neurodevelopmental assessments, and therapies. Important psychosocial services and other support services for families are also less likely to be funded through health plans. Many managed care plans restrict access to specialized services or require that in-network health professionals who lack appropriate expertise deliver care. For children with complex conditions, treatment may best be delivered by a multidisciplinary team with specialized expertise; however, development and support of such teams requires financing beyond that provided through any form of insurance. Thus, many children with the disorders identified by neonatal screening do not receive optimal care because they have inadequate insurance coverage and/or lack access to qualified health professionals. For many, the situation is exacerbated when they reach adulthood and no longer qualify for public programs such as Medicaid.

8. In 2003, a jury awarded a brain-damaged boy more than $70 million in damages in a suit claiming that the Stanford Hospital and the Palo Alto Medical Clinic where he was treated had failed to diagnose the boy's phenylketonuria (PKU) disease. The hospitals were held liable in part because the boy had been given newborn screening for PKU too soon after he was born, resulting in a false negative result. Cook v. Stanford University Medical Center et al., No. 324905, verdict returned (Cal. Super. Ct. San Francisco County, Sept. 26, 2003).

Other problems have arisen in screening programs, including collecting inadequate samples, samples failing to reach state departments of health, lab errors, and problems recording and reporting results. What challenges might arise in litigation based on such errors given that one defendant may be the State Department of Health, a government entity? What issues arise for healthy newborns who were incorrectly diagnosed with a condition?

9.   According to the Government Accountability Office, states reported that they spent over $120 million on newborn screening in state fiscal year 2001, with individual states' expenditures ranging from $87,000 to about $27 million. Seventy-four percent of these expenditures supported laboratory activities. The primary funding source for most states' newborn screening expenditures was newborn screening fees. The fees are generally paid by health care providers submitting specimens; they in turn may receive payments from Medicaid and other third-party payers, including private insurers. Other funding sources that states identified included the Maternal and Child Health Services Block Grant, direct payments from Medicaid, and other state and federal funds. Approximately four million babies are screened each year for genetic conditions. Approximately 3,000 cases of severe genetic disease are detected. In the late 1980s, the Congressional Office of Technology Assessment calculated that, for every 100,000 babies screened for PKU and congenital hypothyroidism, the nation saved $3.2 million in 1986 dollars (7.5 million in 2019 dollars), and that the net savings per detected and treated case was $93,000 in 1986 dollars (nearly $217,000 in 2019 dollars).

How should costs and benefits be assessed for newborn screening programs? Mary Ann Baily and Thomas H. Murray point out various costs of newborn screening that are often underestimated. They note that the true cost of identifying the few rare cases of children with a serious preventable condition includes the cost of screening many newborns, which is much more than the price of a single test. Each new condition added to a panel presents additional costs associated with "parental education, follow-up of all positives to a definitive diagnosis, treatment of affected children, and ongoing data collection and evaluation." When "the natural history of the condition is poorly understood and plainly effective treatments are lacking, children may receive no benefit, or may even be harmed by unnecessary interventions." There are also costs of followup and treatment that affect private insurance, for the insured, and the state and federal government, for the one third of births covered through the Medicaid program. When children test positive, families incur costs obtaining a definitive diagnosis and in "unnecessary worry and anxiety" when children are found not to have the disorder or "a clinically insignificant form of it." There are also costs "of program-related research and quality improvement."

The authors also argue that the benefits of newborn screening "must be assessed and compared to the benefits that could be achieved from other ways of using the resources." They argue that "the resources devoted to newborn screening and treatment for genetic disorders should be established in the context of determining the entire adequate level of health care and the importance of health care relative to other important social goods." Not only is the "American health care system . . . not really a system," newborn screening is even less so. Each state makes its own decisions. Moreover, there is a lack of transparency of NBS financing. Finally, there is advocacy by "health professional groups, makers of screening technologies, and consumer groups" in favor of genetic screening, but few advocates of other programs not undertaken. Mississippi, for example, "expands newborn screening at the same time that it cuts support for prenatal care for poor women" who have no advocates. Mary A. Baily & Thomas H. Murray, Ethics, Evidence, and Cost in Newborn Screening, 38 Hastings Ctr. Rep. 23, 27–28 (May/June 2008). Are there ways to better achieve a clear net benefit of newborn screening given its many costs?

II. PARENTAL CONSENT

SONIA M. SUTER, DID YOU GIVE THE GOVERNMENT YOUR BABY'S DNA? RETHINKING CONSENT IN NEWBORN SCREENING
15 Minn. J.L. Sci. & Tech. 729, 746–48 (2014).

* * *

NBS is quite unusual in being one of the few areas where the state can require medical testing of an individual or child without affirmative consent. Even so, the mandatory nature of NBS has long been well accepted with only minimal criticism. Although most states do not require affirmative parental consent for newborn screening, there is some variability with respect to what amounts to presumed consent. The majority of states allow parents to opt out, although the reasons they allow differ. Some will only allow parents to refuse for religious reasons. Many will allow parents to opt out for any reason. At one extreme, NBS is mandatory without exception. One state actually imposes criminal penalties for refusing to undergo NBS. Even in states where there is an opt-out provision, there is serious doubt as to whether parents truly have an opportunity to refuse in these jurisdictions, making the provision "opt-out" more in name than practice. Only two states [Maryland and Wyoming] require affirmative parental consent.

Not only is a requirement of consent for NBS rare, but parents are often woefully uninformed about NBS. Often states provide limited information about the nature of NBS testing or that there is an option to opt out (when there is such an option). Sometimes parents are not even informed that the child will be tested. If a child tests positive through NBS, parents often do not learn that the newborn screening results are not diagnostic and that there may be false positives or negatives. And many are not adequately educated about the nature of the condition or offered genetic counseling, even when the child tests positive.

NBS laws and practices go very much against legal and ethical norms in the United States, which recognize an individual's right to choose whether to undergo medical treatment or testing and to refuse treatment even when it can result in death. Not only is consent required for most medical interventions and treatments, generally consent must be *informed*.

There is considerable irony in the fact that parental decision making and education are so limited with NBS since it is essentially a form of genetic screening. Mandatory genetic testing is extremely unusual, in large part because a strong consensus has existed for some time that genetic screening programs should not be compulsory and should involve informed consent. After all, genetics and especially genetic counseling are among the disciplines in medicine most deeply committed to individual autonomy in medical decision making and informed decision making for genetic testing.

RUTH R. FADEN ET AL., PARENTAL RIGHTS, CHILD WELFARE, AND PUBLIC HEALTH: THE CASE OF PKU SCREENING
72 Am. J. Pub. Health 1396, 1397–98 (1982).

THE FUNCTION OF PARENTAL CONSENT

* * * Although case law links parental consent with the protection of parental self-interest and prerogatives, parental consent is generally not viewed as a mechanism for protecting the *autonomy* of parents or of parents' rights in medicine and biomedical research. Rather, parental consent is defended as a mechanism for protecting the welfare of children, on the theory that parents are their children's most conscientious advocates and have their children's best interest most accurately in focus. This analysis of the primary function of a parental consent requirement presupposes, but does not argue for, a well entrenched view in the literature of biomedical ethics, viz, that third-party consent is grounded in the principle of beneficence rather than the principle of autonomy. * * *

* * *

If the primary function of a parental consent requirement is to protect the welfare of children, how does this apply to the case of PKU screening? In this form of screening, the intervention poses minimal risk of harm to normal infants and holds promise of the remote but important benefit of preventing [intellectual disability], which threatens not only the general well-being of infants, but also their future abilities to develop as autonomous agents. Thus, there appears to be no reasonable question or issue of judgment as to what is in the best interest of infants.

Under these conditions, is a public policy that grants parents the right to consign their children to a state of irreversible [intellectual disability] morally acceptable? We think not, and it is for this reason that we question the moral justification for requiring parental consent for PKU screening. To require parental consent entails an obligation to respect parental refusal, and it is the validity of such refusals that we question. If the principle consideration is the welfare of children, their welfare is best served in this case by a program of compulsory and exceptionless screening.

CHILD WELFARE AND THE HARM PRINCIPLE

By making child welfare the overriding consideration in policy determinations about participation in child health programs, we are taking the position that in this context, any right of parents independent of their role as advocates for their children's welfare is subservient. The general outlines of this position in contemporary ethical theory can be traced historically to John Stuart Mill's *On Liberty,* where he discusses what is now popularly referred to as the harm principle. This principle states that a person's liberty may justifiably be restricted if the person's (e.g., a parent's) action or negligence poses significant risk of harm to another (e.g., the parent's child). The point of this appeal for our purposes is that parental refusal of PKU screening unjustifiably poses a risk of harm to the child.

Central to this argument for compulsory newborn screening for PKU is the absence of any reasonable question as to the welfare of children. To the extent that potential benefits to *individual* children may be present, a justification for a parental consent requirement is enhanced. Thus, from the perspective of a general policy on parental consent in public health programs, a central issue is whether risk/benefit judgments for individual children may sometimes differ from judgments about risks and benefits for children in general. If some children would be better off without the program, then parental consent may be required as a safeguard to protect the interests of those children. However, only if there is a reasonable possibility that some children would be better off should a policy permitting parental refusal be adopted.

It is important to clarify our position, which is based on the position that there is no *reasonable* question or issue of judgment as to the net beneficial character of the policy we propose. We do not mean that there can be no doubt in any parent's mind about the net benefit of the intervention. In the case of PKU, one could imagine parents opposing screening based on bizarre views about child welfare. For example, parents might believe that the screening test condemns children to eternal damnation. We would not interpret such metaphysical beliefs about damnation as providing a *reasonable* judgment as to the best interests of infants.

NORMAN FOST, GENETIC DIAGNOSIS AND TREATMENT: ETHICAL CONSIDERATIONS

147 Am. J. Diseases of Children 1190 (1993).

An important breach in the rule of informed consent occurred when newborn screening for phenylketonuria (PKU) was mandated by law in most states beginning in the 1960s. The origin of this mandate was the strong belief by advocates that the test was accurate, sensitive, and specific and that safe and effective treatment was available. Furthermore, given the rarity of the disease, there was concern that physicians left to their own devices would fail to perform the test on many infants, resulting in preventable harm. Finally, some believed that the benefits of testing and treatment were so clear and the risks of nontesting were so high that parents should not be allowed to refuse testing anyway, because to do so would constitute a form of medical neglect.

These presumptions all were later shown to be flawed. The Guthrie screening test turned out to be a remarkably nonspecific test, with a false-positive rate of between 15 and 20 to 1. As a result, many infants who, in fact, had benign forms of hyperphenylalaninemia were falsely labeled as having PKU. Confidence in the safety of the diet was also premature, resulting in brain damage and death in some infants who suffered from excessive restriction of an essential amino acid. The combination of these errors resulted in serious harm to an uncertain number of normal children.

* * * The original PKU trials were begun before contemporary standards for institutional review were established, and consent from parents, to this day, is rarely obtained. * * * Once the difficulties with PKU testing and treatment were resolved, it became common to add tests to the program, typically without institutional review or informed consent. In some cases, such as screening for hypothyroidism, there was a clearly positive outcome. In others, such as urine testing for iminoglycinuria or blood testing for CF [cystic fibrosis], the benefits were absent, as in the former case, or controversial, as in the latter. A positive outcome, of course, is not sufficient to justify bypassing the rules of experimentation; ends do not justify means.

The success of the PKU program also led to the widespread feeling that parental consent was now irrelevant because it would be unethical and possibly illegal for a parent to refuse permission for testing and treatment. It was also argued that it was inefficient to obtain consent for a simple test obtained from every newborn. These assumptions have also been shown to be flawed. Many states do allow parents to refuse testing for PKU, but they are seldom given the opportunity to do so. The notion that parents commit neglect when they expose a child to a 1:10,000 risk of serious harm is inconsistent with our general tolerance for refusal of circumcision, which is associated with comparable risks, and with decisions to allow a child to ride a bicycle or compete in gymnastics, activities with a higher risk than that of refusal of PKU testing. Finally, the claim that high standards for consent are impractical and inefficient are inconsistent with a study by Faden et al. showing that high standards for consent can result in higher compliance rates than those in states that mandate testing without consent.

These are the simple questions. The success of the PKU program is now clear if measured by the benefits and risks of preventing retardation in affected individuals. But treatments can have late effects that complicate assessment of benefits, risks, and costs. A pregnant woman who was successfully treated for PKU in childhood exposes her fetus to the most potent human teratogen, high maternal serum phenylalanine. Over 90% of such fetuses will be seriously damaged. Prevention of such damage requires strict adherence to a difficult diet throughout pregnancy, possibly from the moment of conception. It is not yet known how many children will be injured from such exposure. Because such women generally would not have borne children in the prescreening era, the net costs and benefits of screening cannot be assessed accurately. This high risk to exposed fetuses has also raised complex questions of law and ethics regarding forced treatment of women who cannot or do not consent to treatment.

NOTES AND QUESTIONS

1.　What are the arguments in favor of and against requiring parental consent for newborn screening? Which arguments do you find most persuasive? Are your views shaped by the expansion of newborn screening panels that include conditions for which the medical benefits to newborns are less clear?

In addition to the points made in the excerpt by Faden et al. in support of mandatory testing without parental consent, consider the following:

> Those who oppose the informed consent model contend that the logistical constraints of newborn-screening protocols make meaningful informed consent an unrealistic goal. The perceived limitations on time available to discuss complex screening issues prior to discharge, the logistical realities of varied birth settings, and the massive numbers of neonates to be screened can present genuine challenges to the implementation of the informed consent model. * * * In addition, some fear that it would be disruptive to established programs and might have a negative impact on both efficacy and cost-effectiveness. * * *

Elaine H. Hiller et al., Public Participation in Medical Policy-Making and the Status of Consumer Autonomy: The Example of Newborn-Screening Programs in the United States, 87 Am. J. Pub. Health 1280, 1286 (1997).

2.　A 1982 study in Maryland reported that only 27 out of approximately 50,000 mothers (0.05 percent) refused to consent to newborn screening when given the opportunity. Should data like this influence state laws regarding consent requirements (or lack thereof) for newborn screening?

3.　Maryland and Wyoming are the two states that currently seek parental informed consent for newborn screening. In Maryland, the consent is for the total screening package; parents are not asked to consent to each test. As of 2016, 45 states allow exemptions for just religious beliefs (30 states) or for religious, personal, or philosophical beliefs (15 states). Three states specifically prohibit exemptions for religious or philosophical beliefs, and four require that parents have a reasonable opportunity to object. Jaime S. King & Monica E. Smith, Whole-Genome Sequencing of Newborns? The Constitutional Boundaries of State Newborn Screening Programs, 137 Pediatrics S8 (2015).

DOUGLAS COUNTY V. ANAYA

694 N.W.2d 601 (Neb. 2005).

WRIGHT, J.

NATURE OF CASE

The Douglas County District Court ordered Josue Anaya and Mary Anaya to submit their daughter to [newborn screening] for metabolic diseases as required by Neb. Rev. Stat. § 71–519 (Cum.Supp.2002). The Anayas appeal, asserting that § 71–519 violates their rights guaranteed under the 1st and 14th Amendments to the U.S. Constitution and that the issue is moot.

* * *

FACTS

Rosa Ariel Anaya was born in the Anayas' home, without a physician present, on July 11, 2003. The birth was reported to the Department of Health and Human Services (DHHS) on July 17.

[Nebraska's newborn screening statute, § 71–519, requires all infants born in the State of Nebraska to be screened for phenylketonuria, primary hypothyroidism, biotinidase deficiency, galactosemia, hemoglobinopathies, medium-chain acyl co-a dehydrogenase (MCAD) deficiency, and such other metabolic diseases as DHHS may from time to time specify.

If no physician attends the birth, the statute requires the person registering the birth to ensure that newborn screening is conducted as required by DHHS. When Rose Anya was born, DHHS required newborn screening "to be performed within 48 hours of registration of the birth," 181 Neb. Admin. Code, ch. 2, § 008 (2002).

After a DHHS employee determined that newborn screening as required by § 71–519 had not been performed, a certified letter was sent to the Anayas explaining the statute's requirements and the screening process, which includes drawing a small amount of blood from the heel of the infant.] The Anayas declined to submit Rosa Anaya for the screening, stating that it was in direct conflict with their sincerely held religious beliefs that life is taken from the body if blood is removed from it and that a person's lifespan may be shortened if blood is drawn.

Douglas County brought an action seeking to compel the Anayas to comply with § 71–519. At a hearing on September 26, 2003, Mary Anaya testified as to the Anayas' religious beliefs.

[The district court ordered the Anayas to comply with § 71–519 by submitting Rosa Anaya for metabolic screening. It rejected their claim that the issue was moot. Although any screening would be after the timing required by the regulations, it was not too late to administer the test even if the infant was 6 months of age or older. It also held that the statute did not violate the 14th Amendment to the U.S. Constitution because the Anayas' religious beliefs did not outweigh the State's compelling interest in screening infants for preventable metabolic diseases.]

* * *

The Anayas argue that § 71–519 infringes upon their First Amendment right to freely exercise their religion and that the district court erred in concluding that the State had shown a compelling interest which justifies the infringement.

"The free exercise of religion means, first and foremost, the right to believe and profess whatever religious doctrine one desires." Employment Div., Ore. Dept. of Human Res. v. Smith, 494 U.S. 872, 877 * * * (1990). The " 'exercise of religion' " involves "not only belief and profession but the performance of (or abstention from) physical acts * * *." Smith, 494 U.S. at 877 * * *.

* * *

The Anayas argue that because they have raised a free exercise of religion claim along with a parental substantive due process claim, they have a hybrid constitutional rights claim, which requires strict scrutiny review. Under a strict scrutiny review, the law must be justified by a compelling governmental interest and must be narrowly tailored to advance that interest. See Church of Lukumi Babalu Aye, Inc. v. Hialeah, 508 U.S. 520 * * * (1993). The Anayas claim *Smith* held that strict scrutiny is required in cases in which a free exercise claim has been raised along with a claim of violation of another constitutional right.

[We reject the view that *Smith*, which upheld an Oregon law prohibiting the use of peyote during a religious ceremony, held that "a strict scrutiny review is required simply because more than one constitutional right might be implicated." The *Smith* Court stated that "the right of free exercise does not relieve an individual of the obligation to comply with a 'valid and neutral law of general applicability on the ground that the law proscribes . . . conduct that his religion prescribes . . . ' " Smith, 494 U.S. at 879, citing United States v. Lee, 455 U.S. 252 (1982) (Stevens, J., concurring in judgment). Similarly, the *Hialeah* Court stated that, "[i]n addressing the constitutional protection for free exercise of religion, our cases establish the general proposition that a law that is neutral and of general applicability need not be justified by a compelling governmental interest even if the law has the incidental effect of burdening a particular religious practice." Hialeah, 508 U.S. at 531. In addition, federal appellate courts reject the idea of strict scrutiny for hybrid rights claims. See, e.g., Swanson By and Through Swanson v. Guthrie ISD I-L, 135 F.3d 694, 700 (10th Cir.1998) (A plaintiff cannot "simply invoke the parental rights doctrine, combine it with a claimed free-exercise right, and thereby force the government to demonstrate the presence of a compelling state interest).]

We conclude that the Anayas' assertion of a hybrid rights claim does not implicate a strict scrutiny review of § 71–519. A party may not force the government to meet the strict scrutiny standard by merely asserting claims of violations of more than one constitutional right.

> **What's That?:** A strict scrutiny standard of review means that the government must demonstrate that its legislation serves a compelling governmental interest and that the law is narrowly tailored to achieve that interest.

The second constitutional rights violation asserted by the Anayas seems to suggest that § 71–519 violates their rights as parents to make decisions concerning the upbringing of their children. They rely upon Pierce v. Society of Sisters, 268 U.S. 510 * * * (1925), and Wisconsin v. Yoder, 406 U.S. 205 * * * (1972).

In *Pierce,* the Court held that a compulsory education law deprived parents of the right to select a school for their children. It held that the Oregon compulsory education statute "unreasonably interfere[d] with the liberty of parents and guardians to direct the upbringing and education of children under their control." Pierce, 268 U.S. at 534–35 * * *. The Court concluded that the challenged law served no state interest and therefore had no reasonable relation to any state purpose.

In *Yoder,* the Court held that a state could not compel Amish parents to require their children to attend formal high school and that the compulsory education law violated the 1st and 14th Amendments. The Court noted that no harm to the physical or mental health of the child was inferred but that when the health and safety of a child was involved, different considerations applied.

> To be sure, the power of the parent, even when linked to a free exercise claim, may be subject to limitation under Prince [v. Massachusetts, 321 U.S. 158 (1944),] if it appears that parental decisions will jeopardize the health or safety of the child, or have a potential for significant social burdens.

Yoder, 406 U.S. at 233–34 * * *. The Court did not conclude that strict scrutiny was required.

It is true that "the custody, care and nurture of the child reside first in the parents." Prince v. Massachusetts, 321 U.S. 158 * * * (1944). However, the Court has never held that parental rights to childrearing as guaranteed under the Due Process Clause of the 14th Amendment must be subjected to a strict scrutiny analysis.* * *. See Troxel v. Granville, 530 U.S. 57 * * * (2000). "[T]he Supreme Court has yet to decide whether the right to direct the upbringing and education of one's children is among those fundamental rights whose infringement merits heightened scrutiny." Brown v. Hot, Sexy and Safer Productions, Inc., 68 F.3d 525, 533 (1st Cir.1995). *Pierce* and *Yoder* do not support an inference that parental decisionmaking requires a strict scrutiny analysis.

The question is not whether the Anayas have set forth a hybrid rights claim but whether the law they have challenged is neutral and has general application.

This case is analogous to cases in which courts have upheld the State's right to require immunization of children. In Boone v. Boozman, 217 F.Supp.2d 938 (E.D.Ark.2002), the court upheld the constitutionality of an immunization statute, finding that the free exercise claim challenged a neutral law of general applicability. The law applied to all school children except those whose health would be endangered by immunization. Because the law was neutral, heightened scrutiny was not required even though compulsory immunization might burden a plaintiff's right to free exercise.

The court stated, "It is well established that the State may enact reasonable regulations to protect the public health and the public safety, and it cannot be questioned that compulsory immunization is a permissible exercise of the State's police power." Id. at 954. Society's interest in protecting against the spread of disease takes precedence over parental rights and the right to free exercise of religion. *Id.*

In Prince, 321 U.S. at 166–67, * * * the Court held that neither rights of religion nor rights of parenthood are beyond limitation. Acting to guard the general interest in youth's well being, the state as *parens patriae* may restrict the parent's control by requiring school attendance, regulating or prohibiting the child's labor and in many other ways. Its authority is not nullified merely because the parent grounds his claim to control the child's course of conduct on religion or conscience. Thus, he cannot claim freedom from compulsory vaccination for the child more than for himself on religious grounds. The right to practice religion freely does not include liberty to expose the community or the child to communicable disease or the latter to ill health or death * * *. [T]he state has a wide range of power for limiting parental freedom and authority in things affecting the child's welfare; and * * * this includes, to some extent, matters of conscience and religious conviction.

A law is neutral and of general applicability "if it does not aim to 'infringe upon or restrict practices because of their religious motivation,' and if it does not 'in a selective manner impose burdens only on conduct motivated by religious belief[.]' " San Jose Christian College v. Morgan Hill,

360 F.3d 1024, 1031 (9th Cir.2004), quoting Church of Lukumi Babalu Aye, Inc. v. Hialeah, 508 U.S. 520 * * * (1993). Section 71–519 is a neutral law of general applicability. It is generally applicable to all babies born in the state and does not discriminate as to which babies must be tested. Its purpose is not directed at religious practices or beliefs. Pursuant to Employment Div., Dept. of Human Res. v. Smith, 494 U.S. 872 * * * (1990), and its progeny, a neutral law of general applicability need not be supported by a compelling governmental interest even though it may have an incidental effect of burdening religion. * * *

Section 71–519 does not contain a system of particularized exemptions that allow some children to be excused from testing. See Kissinger v. Board of Trustees, 5 F.3d 177 (6th Cir.1993). The statute does not unlawfully burden the Anayas' right to freely exercise their religion, nor does it unlawfully burden their parental rights. Section 71–519 cannot be construed as directly regulating religious-based conduct. See Cornerstone Bible Church v. City of Hastings, 948 F.2d 464 (8th Cir.1991). There is no evidence that the State had an anti-religious purpose in enforcing the law. See *id.*

Whether a statute is constitutional is a question of law; accordingly, the Nebraska Supreme Court is obligated to reach a conclusion independent of the decision reached by the court below. Slansky v. Nebraska State Patrol, 268 Neb. 360, 685 N.W.2d 335 (2004). A statute is presumed to be constitutional, and all reasonable doubts will be resolved in favor of its constitutionality. *Id.*

* * *

We conclude that the effect of § 71–519 upon the constitutional claims the Anayas have asserted is properly analyzed under a rational basis review. Evidence was presented concerning the effects of the diseases that are tested for under the statute. Early diagnosis allows for prevention of death and disability in children. The State has determined that it is appropriate to test for these diseases soon after a child is born in order to address treatment options. The health and safety of the child are of particular concern, as are the potential social burdens created by children who are not identified and treated.

The State has an interest in the health and welfare of all children born in Nebraska, and the purpose of § 71–519 is to protect such health and welfare. This is a rational basis for the law, and it is constitutional.

[The discussion of mootness is omitted.]

NOTES AND QUESTIONS

1. In another case, parents and newborns alleged that Michigan's Newborn Screening Program violated their Fourteenth Amendment substantive due process and Fourth Amendment rights when blood was drawn from the newborns without the parents' consent or knowledge. The Sixth Circuit affirmed the lower court's dismissal of these claims, finding that the Michigan Department of Health and its employees were entitled to, respectively, sovereign and qualified immunity with respect to these claims. Exercising its discretion to address the children's substantive due process claims, the court concluded that children "lack a liberty interest in directing their own medical care," and therefore their substantive due process rights were not violated. While the court stated that "a program to screen children for life-threatening disease at birth may be an example of the state's proper exercise of its *parens patriae*," it refrained from deciding the question. Similarly, it did not reach the substantive issue with respect to whether the blood draw actually violated the children's Fourth Amendment rights. Kanuszewski et al. v. Michigan Dept. of Health & Human Serv., 927 F.3d 396 (6th Cir. 2019).

> **What's That?:** Sovereign immunity is a judicial doctrine that prevents the government or its political subdivisions, departments and agencies from being sued without its consent. Qualified immunity is a doctrine that, when applicable, can shield government officials from liability.

2. What should a health professional do if parents refuse to consent to screening, especially for a disease that can be treated or prevented if it is detected early enough? Consider the following definition of child abuse and neglect under the federal Child Abuse Prevention and Treatment Act (CAPTA), under which states must require health professionals to report to child protective services agencies in order to receive federal grants: "Any recent act or failure to act on the part of a parent or caretaker, which results in death, serious physical or emotional harm, sexual abuse, or exploitation, or an act or failure to act which presents an imminent risk of serious harm." 42 U.S.C. § 5106g(2). Would a parental refusal to permit newborn screening fall under these provisions?

3. Is newborn screening analogous to vaccination, as the court in *Anaya* suggests? In Jacobson v. Massachusetts, 197 U.S. 11 (1905), the Supreme Court upheld the state's right to mandate that its citizens be vaccinated against small pox. The Court found compelled vaccination was within the state's exercise of the police power as long as the means are "reasonably required for the safety of the public." *Id.* at 35. Vaccination of children protects third parties with whom the child might come into contact. Newborn screening, however, only affects the individual child, and with a 1 in 15,000 incidence of PKU, the child is unlikely to be "harmed" by the parents' refusal to test. In fact, parents consent all the time to more risky activities of their children, such as participating in football. The *Anaya* court views parents' refusal to consent to screening as creating a risk to the child. What about the fact that some of the disorders in newborn screening panels are not treatable or only offer the

benefit of identifying carrier status to aid in the parents' future reproductive choices?

4. If genome sequencing is ultimately incorporated into newborn screening, does it present additional issues regarding the constitutional authority of states to mandate such testing, given the challenges associated with genomic analysis discussed in Section I of Chapter 7, such as the discovery of information that may be inaccurate, uncertain, limited in utility, or not desired by all parents? See Jaime S. King & Monica E. Smith, Whole-Genome Sequencing of Newborns? The Constitutional Boundaries of State Newborn Screening Programs, 137 Pediatrics S8 (2015).

III. RESEARCH ON NEWBORN BLOOD SPOTS

SONIA M. SUTER, DID YOU GIVE THE GOVERNMENT YOUR BABY'S DNA? RETHINKING CONSENT IN NEWBORN SCREENING
15 Minn. J.L., Sci. & Tech. 729, 754–56 (2014).

* * *

Once the newborn blood spots are analyzed for the various [newborn screening (NBS)] conditions, residual blood remains in the form of [dried blood spots]. Increasingly, states retain these samples for future uses, although the retention time varies significantly from state to state. Some states have provisions to retain samples for only one to four weeks, some for months, some for years, some for decades, and others indefinitely. Often these samples are stored with identifying information.

[T]here are several reasons states might want to retain the samples for months or even years. * * * [T]he retention of these samples * * * is necessary for follow-up and to ensure that there will be appropriate intervention for an affected child. In addition, labs may need to perform repeat tests to make a confirmatory diagnosis or to reassure families if there is a false positive. Less directly related to NBS testing per se, but still connected to the public health aspects of NBS, is the retention of blood spots for quality assurance testing and to monitor the prevalence of various conditions in the state. NBS samples may also be helpful for post-mortem diagnosis; for example, when trying to establish whether a genetic condition was related to a child's death. Increasingly, states are interested in long-term retention of these blood spots for purposes not directly related to NBS. Some states and/or other countries retain neonate blood spots for nonmedical or non-research uses, such as identification in kidnappings or deaths. NBS samples have also been used for paternity testing and could potentially be used for the identification of criminals.

In addition, these blood spots, like most pathology samples, are a treasure trove for researchers because they are a valuable national repository of genetic material. As genetic technology develops, the blood spots are an especially rich source of research material: they are stable over time, they constitute an unbiased collection of samples since they represent the entire population, and they can potentially be linked to basic demographic information. As one author notes, "[n]ewborn screening initially began as a population health endeavor but is rapidly becoming a resource for population research." Newborn blood samples have been used in research and shared with investigators since the 1980s, sometimes with identifying information.

AMERICAN ACADEMY OF PEDIATRICS, REPORT OF THE TASK FORCE ON NEWBORN SCREENING, PUBLISHED AS A CALL FOR A NATIONAL AGENDA ON STATE NEWBORN SCREENING PROGRAMS
106 Pediatrics 389, 415 (Supp.) (2000).

* * *

ETHICAL CONCERNS RELATED TO USE OF RESIDUAL BLOOD SAMPLES

Storage and use of residual newborn screening blood samples raise a number of practical and ethical challenges. Ethical challenges include the development of guidance regarding the use of residual blood spots for purposes other than those for which they were originally obtained. The protection of privacy and confidentiality among children and families is a serious concern. In the case of newborn screening, when blood samples are collected from infants as a matter of law, there is additional reason to ensure appropriate storage and use.

At the same time, residual newborn screening samples have been used to address important public health issues. The prevalence of in utero exposure to drugs and environmental agents; the allele frequency of genes associated with significant morbidity, mortality, or disability in infancy or childhood; and the prevalence of serious maternal or intrauterine infections have been determined in various populations by anonymous use of residual blood spots. Samples linked to outcome have been used to assess the feasibility of screening for various diseases of the newborn and infant, and to determine risk factors for birth defects and developmental disabilities. To date, there have been no published reports of misuse of residual newborn screening samples in research projects; however, the potential for use and misuse is expanding.

NOTES AND QUESTIONS

1.   How does the storage and retention of these newborn blood samples compare with the practices of other DNA or tissue banks discussed in Section II of Chapter 5?

2.   What policies should govern the storage and retention of these blood samples? Although the view has long been that research on deidentified biological samples, including deidentified newborn dried blood spots, is exempt from Federal Protections for Human Research Subjects (known as the "Common Rule"), Section 12 of the Newborn Screening Saves Lives Reauthorization Act of 2014 stated that federally funded research on newborn dried blood spots constituted human subjects research. That provision, however, only applied until the Common Rule was revised. Under revisions of the Common Rule, research with nonidentified newborn dried blood spots is not considered research with human subjects. See Chapter 5, Section II, for a discussion of the revised Common Rule.

With respect to identifiable samples, The Task Force on Newborn Screening of the American Academy of Pediatrics, *supra,* states that:

> parental permission should be sought for the use of identifiable samples in research to validate tests for additional diseases, or for epidemiologic research. Identifiable samples from newborns should be used for research only if: 1) IRB approval is obtained for the proposed research, 2) consent is obtained from the child's parent(s) or guardian for the proposed research, 3) newborn samples represent the optimal source of available tissue for the research, 4) unlinked samples will not suffice, and 5) acceptable samples from consenting adults are not available.

Are these recommendations appropriate?

3.   Very few states have regulations governing future uses of the samples or requiring parents to be notified of or give consent to such uses. In a few states, there has been litigation surrounding these practices.

In 2009, parents in Texas sued to block the state from giving researchers access to newborn screening bloodspots. Pursuant to a 2011 settlement agreement, the state destroyed 5.3 million stored blood spots, and the legislature passed a law requiring the state to obtain parental permission to use residual blood spots for research purposes.

After Texas reached the settlement agreement regarding its use of bloodspots, the Texas Tribune reviewed nine years of emails and internal documents of the Department of State Health Services' newborn screening program. The communications revealed it had transferred "hundreds of infant blood spots to an Armed Forces lab to build a national and, someday, international mitochondrial DNA . . . registry." Because the case was settled before it reached the discovery phase, the plaintiffs never saw those documents. Emily Ramshaw, DNA Deception, Tex. Trib., Feb. 22, 2010, https://www.texastribune.org/2010/02/22/dshs-turned-over-hundreds-of-dna-samples-to-feds/.

In 2011, the Minnesota Supreme Court held that stored blood spots were covered by the state's Genetic Privacy Act, which required parental consent for residual uses, including research. Bearder v. State, 806 N.W.2d 766 (Minn.

2011). The state eventually destroyed all blood spots collected between the date of the court's decision and a subsequent hearing of the case on remand one year later. For a description of state laws governing retention and use of newborn screening blood spots, see Michelle Lewis et al., State Laws Regarding the Retention and Use of Residual Newborn Screening Blood Samples, 127 Pediatrics 703–712 (2011).

In Doe v. Adams, 53 N.E. 3d 483 (Ind. Ct. App. 2016), a minor child sued the Indiana State Department of Health (ISDH), alleging constitutional violations in retaining her dried blood spots from NBS without her permission. The Indiana Court of Appeals found she had no standing because she had suffered no injury. Her samples had not and would not be released to third parties without authorization for medical research under the ISDH's storage and destruction policy instituted in 2013. Moreover, the ISDH offered evidence she could request destruction of her samples at any point. Finally, her fear of misuse of her samples was merely "speculative" and insufficient to show standing. Consequently, the court affirmed the judgment in favor of ISDH.

Finally, in Kanuszewski et al. v. Michigan Dept. of Health & Human Serv., 927 F.3d 396 (6th Cir. 2019), the plaintiff parents and their children claimed Fourteenth and Fourth Amendment violations by the Michigan Department of Health, the Michigan Neonatal Bank and their employees for allegedly retaining samples, transferring samples to the Neonatal Biobank, and indefinitely storing samples for use by the state or third parties without the parents' informed consent. The Sixth Circuit held that state sovereign immunity did not bar the plaintiffs' claims for prospective relief against the "individual Defendants in their official capacities arising out of the ongoing storage of the children's blood." Although it found "the children's substantive due process rights were not violated" because "children cannot control their own medical care," it held that parents "possess a fundamental right to make decisions concerning the medical care of their children." Finding it unlikely that the defendants would be able to demonstrate a compelling interest in the retention, transfer, and storage of the blood spots, particularly because "the health of the child is no longer at stake after the samples have been tested for life-threatening diseases," the court reversed the lower court's dismissal of the Fourteenth Amendment Claim. Similarly, because "it does not seem that the health of the child justifies the state in taking any actions with respect to the blood samples after it has finished screening the samples for disease," the court reversed the lower court's dismissal of the children's Fourth Amendment claim. Was this case properly decided? How might rulings like that of *Kanuszewski* and *Bearder* affect research and public attitudes toward newborn screening and research?

PART III

GENE THERAPY

■ ■ ■

This part discusses ethical and legal issues raised by attempts to employ genetic science to prevent or treat disease, generally referred to as gene therapy. (The use of genetic screening and testing to diagnose and predict disease is discussed in Part II.)

The part begins with a brief introduction to the science of gene therapy. Chapter 11 then discusses the regulation of gene therapy research by the NIH Recombinant DNA Advisory Committee, discussed in Part I, and the Food and Drug Administration (FDA). Chapter 12 gives a brief history of gene therapy research. (Part II discusses issues raised by research to develop genetic tests.) Chapter 13 discusses germ line gene therapy, namely, therapeutic interventions that make changes in DNA that may be passed on to descendants. Chapter 14 discusses pharmacogenetics, the growing understanding of the relationship between genetic variations and the safety and efficacy of drug treatments. Chapter 15 discusses the use of genetic technologies to enhance capabilities rather than to treat or prevent disease.

The concept of gene therapy is broad and encompasses a number of different techniques that share a common approach: the alteration of DNA to combat disease. This can occur in several ways, including replacing flawed genetic material in chromosomes; adding cells with properly-functioning DNA to an organism; altering the function of existing defective genes (such as by blocking messenger RNA, which in turn produces proteins); interrupting the aberrant functioning of mutant proteins (for example, by creating other proteins that block or destroy them); or creating "gene factories" that manufacture therapeutic substances in the body. Moreover, gene therapy can be "somatic," meaning that it does not affect reproductive cells and therefore the altered DNA is not passed on to the patient's offspring, or it can be germline therapy, in which the altered DNA intentionally or unintentionally changes the genetic endowment of future generations. Finally, the same techniques of genetic modification might be aimed at altering normal, non-disease traits, in which case they would not be considered gene therapy but "genetic enhancement." For a fuller description of gene therapy techniques, see Stuart H. Orkin & Arno G. Motulsky, Report and Recommendations of the Panel to Assess the NIH Investment in Research on Gene Therapy, December 7, 1995; Theodore

Friedmann, Overcoming the Obstacles to Gene Therapy, Scientific American, June 1997, 96–101. Genetic enhancement is discussed in Chapter 15.

Gene therapy faces a number of technical hurdles. First, the DNA has to get into the patient. There are a variety of ways this might be accomplished, including the use of artificial chromosomes and "naked DNA." The most common technique in gene therapy experiments is to insert the desired DNA into an organism, such as a virus, and then insert the organism either into the patient directly, or into cells in the laboratory that are then inserted into the patient. An organism such as a virus that delivers DNA into a patient or into a cell is called a "vector." The two most common vectors are viruses and retroviruses, which contain RNA rather than DNA. It is important that the pathological or disease-causing elements of the viral vector be deleted as much as possible before the vector is used.

Once a suitable vector is chosen to deliver the DNA (or RNA), the next problem is making sure that the genetic material gets to the correct site. Some vectors may not need to be so site-specific. A treatment for hemophilia (a clotting disorder) might only need to be introduced into the circulatory system. But other treatments, such as those for cancer, might fail, or be accompanied by unacceptably serious side effects, if they cannot be delivered directly to tumors.

Even if therapeutic genes reach the appropriate site, it is necessary that they function, or are "expressed," rather than remain dormant. Every cell nucleus contains essentially a complete set of a person's DNA, but only some of the genes are "turned on"; otherwise, the genes in the nuclei of liver cells, for example, would produce not only liver enzymes but biochemicals that were supposed to be manufactured in the pancreas or the gall bladder, and so on. The therapeutic genetic material must not only function, but function correctly. It must produce the correct amount of an enzyme, for example, and not cause problems such as cell death, sterility, or uncontrolled cell division (cancer).

Finally, the gene therapy must continue to function for the amount of time necessary to achieve the desired therapeutic effect. The body discards cells after a certain amount of time; even the oldest tissues in our bodies, our bones, are completely regenerated within approximately three years. Yet the target condition may persist throughout the patient's lifetime, or for longer than the corrected genes would remain functional. One approach is to replace the therapeutic genes as they wear out or are discarded. An alternative is to insert the genetic material in such a way that it is replicated as cells divide. This is one advantage of using retroviruses, which integrate the therapeutic genetic material into the host genome, over viruses, which only have short-term effects.

For a thorough but technical description of gene therapy techniques, see Katherine A. High and Maria G. Roncarolo, Gene Therapy, 381 N. Eng. J. Med. 455, 462 (2019).

CHAPTER 11

REGULATION OF GENE THERAPY RESEARCH

■ ■ ■

Research to develop genetic tests to diagnose or predict disease is discussed in Part II. This chapter discusses research to develop gene therapies, that is, genetic modifications to prevent or treat disease.

Each year, more genetic mechanisms that underlie diseases are uncovered, new diagnostic tests to pinpoint genetic disorders are introduced into clinical practice, and experimental therapies to treat genetic diseases are developed. Since so many traits, conditions, diseases, and defects have a genetic basis, almost everyone is a potential subject of genetic research. Potential genetic research subjects range widely in age, including embryos, fetuses, newborns, children, and adults. They differ in condition—healthy, mentally disabled, physically ill. The experimental procedures and products range in the level of risk they pose to the subject. The methodology of the research varies widely as well, ranging from pedigree studies to whole genome sequencing to determine the nuances of a person's genes that correlate with disease or that increase the likelihood that a certain treatment will succeed.

Experimentation with human subjects has existed since the beginning of the science of medicine. However, it was not until the early twentieth century that ethical and legal considerations regarding such research came to the fore. The atrocities committed by Nazi physicians in experiments (some done in the name of genetics or, more properly stated, eugenics) led to the development of certain principles and guidelines that affect research on humans today. In the trials of those physicians, the court set forth standards that should be complied with both before and during research. These standards, subsequently adopted by the United Nations General Assembly, are known as the Nuremberg Code. The tenets of the code significantly influenced later state laws and federal regulations in the United States dealing with research.

The Nuremberg Code provides guidance for assuring that participation in research is voluntary and that the risks of research are minimized. The code requires that certain basic scientific research and animal research must be done before human research is undertaken, that the human research must be well-designed and undertaken only by scientifically qualified individuals, that the potential results justify the level of risk involved in the performance of the research, and that those results are not procurable by other means of study. The central tenet of the Nuremberg Code is that participation in research must be voluntary, informed, and uncoerced, and that the subject has the right to bring the experiment to an end. The code also requires the minimization of research risks through the appropriate design and conduct of the research as well as through adequate preparation and facilities. Research is forbidden if there is an *a priori* reason to believe death or disabling injury will occur (although the Nuremberg Code does allow for a potential exception if the researchers also serve as subjects) and on-going research must be stopped if there is reason to believe that its continuation will lead to the injury, disability, or death of the subject.

Subsequent societal discussion of research in the decades since the adoption of the Nuremberg Code has highlighted some additional ethical concerns. One concern is that subjects for research must be selected equitably; for example, a particular class or race of subjects should not serve as subjects for research that primarily benefits people of another class or race. With respect to potential genetics research on fetuses, there is concern that a disproportionate share of the fetal research burden might fall upon people of color. Since African-American infants have a higher morbidity and mortality rate than do Caucasian infants, it might be argued that they stand to benefit more from fetal research. However, it can conversely be argued that research on infants from minority or poor families will more likely be used to benefit wealthier white mothers and infants who have better access to new medical technologies.

There has also been a move toward requiring that research proposals be reviewed in advance by groups unrelated to the research project itself. This has led to the formation of Institutional Review Boards (IRBs), committees designed to approve, disapprove, review, and monitor biomedical research involving human subjects. The purpose of IRB review is to assure that proper steps are taken to protect the rights and welfare of human research subjects.

Federal regulations first adopted in 1975 to regulate federally-funded research focus on avoiding unnecessary physical risks to the subject, assuring informed consent and confidentiality, and assessing the merits of the proposed research in advance. Genetic research, however, raises ethical and legal concerns not necessarily addressed by the federal regulations. Much genetic research is conducted with private funds (for example, by biotechnology companies) and thus is not covered by the federal regulations protecting human subjects unless it results in a marketable product that is regulated by the Food and Drug Administration. In addition, genetics research raises risks of stigmatization not only to the individual participating in the research, but to relatives or members of the community or ethnic group that share some of the subject's genes. This has led to consideration about whether group consent, in addition to individual consent, should be required before certain types of genetic research are undertaken.

While the law has focused on protection of people from risks in their interactions with researchers, new concerns have been raised about genetic research undertaken on previously-collected tissue samples. All of us have DNA on file someplace. Since the late 1960s, virtually every newborn in the United States has undergone public health department testing for certain genetic diseases; many laboratories have saved those blood samples. Moreover, after blood tests or biopsies are undertaken in hospitals, the samples are saved and often made available for further research without the individual's knowledge or consent. A major policy question has arisen about whether the person whose blood or other tissue sample is used for genetic research should have the chance to either consent or refuse to participate in such research.

DEPARTMENT OF HEALTH AND HUMAN SERVICES, RECOMBINANT DNA RESEARCH: REQUEST FOR PUBLIC COMMENT ON "POINTS TO CONSIDER IN THE DESIGN AND SUBMISSION OF HUMAN SOMATIC-CELL GENE THERAPY PROTOCOLS"

National Institutes of Health,
50 Fed. Reg. 2940 (1985).

Experiments in which recombinant DNA * * * is introduced into cells of a human subject with the intent of stably modifying the subject's genome are covered by Section III-A-4 of the National Institutes of Health (NIH) Guidelines for Research Involving Recombinant DNA Molecules (49 FR 46266). Section III-A-4 requires such experiments to be reviewed by the NIH Recombinant DNA Advisory Committee (RAC) and approved by the NIH. RAC consideration of each proposal will follow publication of a precis of the proposal in the Federal Register, an opportunity for public comment, and review of the proposal by a working group of the RAC. RAC recommendations on each proposal will be forwarded to the NIH Director for a decision, which will then be published in the Federal Register. In accordance with Section IV-C-1-B of the NIH Guidelines, the NIH Director may approve proposals only if he finds that they present "no significant risk to health or the environment."

In general, it is expected that somatic-cell gene therapy protocols will not present a risk to the environment as the recombinant DNA is expected to be confined to the human subject. Nevertheless, item I-B-4-b of the "Points to Consider" document asks the researchers to address specifically this point.

This document is intended to provide guidance in preparing proposals for NIH consideration under Section III-A-4. Not every point mentioned in the document will necessarily require attention in every proposal. It is expected that the document will be considered for revision at least annually as experience in evaluating proposals accumulates.

A proposal will be considered by the RAC only after the protocol has been approved by the local Institutional Biosafety Committee (IBC) and by the local Institutional Review Board (IRB) in accordance with Department of Health and Human Service regulations for the protection of human subjects (45 CFR, Part 46). If a proposal involves children, special attention should be paid to Subpart D of these regulations. The IRB and IBC may, at their discretion, condition their approval on further specific deliberation by the RAC and its working group. Consideration of gene therapy proposals by the RAC may proceed simultaneously with review by any other involved federal agencies (e.g., the Food and Drug Administration) provided that the RAC is notified of the simultaneous review. The committee expects that the first proposals submitted for RAC review will contain no proprietary information on trade secrets; therefore, the review will be open to the public. The public review of these protocols will serve to educate the public not only on the technical aspects of the proposals but also on the meaning and significance of the research.

The clinical application of recombinant DNA techniques to human gene therapy raises two general kinds of questions. Part I of this document deals with the short-term risks and benefits of the proposed research to the patient and to other people as well as with issues of equity in the selection of subjects, informed consent, and privacy and confidentiality. In Part II, investigators are requested to address broader ethical and social issues pertaining to the research and its longer-term implications. These broader questions go beyond the usual purview of IRBs and reflect the kinds of public concerns discussed by a recent presidential commission in its report entitled Splicing Life: The Social and Ethical Issues of Genetic Engineering with Human Beings. Responses to the questions raised in these "Points to Consider" should be in the form of either written answers or references to specific sections of the protocol or other documentation which accompanies the proposal. In addition, Part III of the "Points to Consider" summarizes other documentation that will assist the RAC and its working group in their review of gene therapy proposals.

I. DESCRIPTION OF PROPOSAL

A. Objectives and rationale of the proposed research. State concisely the overall objectives and rationale of the proposed study. Please provide information on the following specific points:

1. Why is the disease selected for treatment by means of gene therapy a good candidate for such treatment?

2.   Describe the natural history and range of expression of the disease selected for treatment. In your view, are the usual effects of the disease predictable enough to allow for meaningful assessment of the results of gene therapy?

3.   Is the protocol designed to prevent all manifestations of the disease, to halt the progression of the disease after symptoms have begun to appear, or to reverse manifestations of the disease in seriously ill victims?

4.   What alternative therapies exist? In what groups of patients are these therapies effective? What are their relative advantages and disadvantages as compared with the proposed gene therapy?

B.   Research design, anticipated risks and benefits.

* * *

3.   Clinical procedures, including patient monitoring. Describe the treatment that will be administered to patients and the diagnostic methods that will be used to monitor the success or failure of the treatment.

a.   Will cells (e.g., bone marrow cells) be removed from patients and treated in vitro in preparation for gene therapy? If so, what kinds of cells will be removed from the patients, how many, how often, and at what intervals?

b.   Will patients be treated to eliminate or reduce the number of cells containing malfunctioning genes (e.g., through radiation or chemotherapy) prior to gene therapy?

c.   What treated cells (or vector/DNA combination) will be given to patients in the attempt to administer gene therapy? How will the treated cells be administered? What volume of cells will be used? Will there be single or multiple treatments? If so, over what period of time?

d.   What are the clinical endpoints of the study? How will patients be monitored to assess specific effects of the treatment on the disease? What is the sensitivity of the analyses? How frequently will follow-up studies be done? How long will patient follow-up continue?

e.   What are the major potential beneficial and adverse effects of treatment that you anticipate? What measures will be taken in an attempt to control or reverse these adverse effects if they occur? Compare the probability and magnitude of potential adverse effects on patients with the probability and magnitude of deleterious consequences from the disease if gene therapy is not performed.

f.   Serious adverse effects of treatment should be reported immediately to both your local IRB and the NIH Office for Protection from Research Risks (phone: 301-496-7005).

g.   Reports regarding the general progress of patients should be filed at six-month intervals with both your local IRB and the NIH Office of Recombinant DNA Activities (phone: 301-496-6051). These twice-yearly reports should continue for a sufficient period of time to allow observation of all major effects (at least three to five years).

h.   If a treated patient dies, will an autopsy be requested? If so, please indicate what special studies, if any, will be performed.

4.   Public health considerations. Describe the potential benefits and hazards of the proposed therapy to persons other than the patients being treated.

a.   What potential benefits or hazards are postulated?

b.   Is there any expectation that the recombinant DNA will spread from the patient to others or to the environment?

c.   What precautions will be taken, if any, to protect others (e.g., patients sharing a room, health-care workers, or family members) from such potential hazards?

5.   Qualifications of investigators, adequacy of laboratory and clinical facilities. Indicate the relevant training and experience of the personnel who will be involved in the preclinical studies and clinical administration of gene therapy. In addition, please describe the laboratory and clinical facilities where the proposed study will be performed.

a.   What professional personnel (medical and nonmedical) will be involved in the proposed study? What are their specific qualifications and experience with respect to the disease to be treated and with respect to the techniques employed in molecular biology? Please provide curricula vitae.

b.   At what hospital or clinic will the treatment be given? Which facilities of the hospital or clinic will be especially important for the proposed study? Will patients occupy regular hospital beds or clinical research center beds?

C.   Selection of subjects. Estimate the number of patients to be involved in the proposed study of gene therapy. Describe recruitment procedures and patient eligibility requirements. Indicate how equity consideration in the selection of subjects will be handled.

* * *

2.   How many eligible patients do you anticipate being able to identify each year?

3.   What recruitment procedures do you plan to use?

4.   What selection criteria do you plan to employ? What are the exclusion and inclusion criteria for the study?

5.   What equity issues, if any, are likely to arise in the selection of patients? How will these issues be addressed?

D.   Informed consent. Indicate how patients will be informed about the proposed study and how their consent will be solicited. If the study involves pediatric or mentally handicapped patients, describe procedures for seeking the permission of parents or guardians and, where applicable, the assent of each patient. Areas of special concern include potential adverse effects, financial costs, privacy, and the right to withdraw from further participation in the study.

1.   Will the major points covered in IA–IC of this document be disclosed to potential participants in this study and/or parents or guardians in language that is understandable to them? (Include a copy of the patient contest form as part of the documentation requested in Part II below).

2.   Will the innovative character and the theoretically-possible adverse effects of gene therapy be discussed with patients and/or parents or guardians? Will the potential adverse effects be compared with the consequences of the disease? What will be said to convey that some of these adverse effects, if they occur, could be irreversible?

3.   Will the financial costs of gene therapy and any available alternative therapies be explained to patients and/or parents or guardians?

4.   Will patients and/or parents or guardians be informed that the innovative character of gene therapy may lead to great interest by the media in the research and in treated patients? What special procedures, if any, will be followed to protect the privacy of patients and their families?

5.   Will patients and/or their parents or guardians be informed of their right to withdraw at any time from the proposed study and of the consequences of withdrawal at the various stages of the experiment? State the extent to which subjects will be specifically advised of the reversibility or irreversibility of procedures that are performed during the course of the experiment.

E.   Privacy and confidentiality. Indicate what measures will be taken to protect the privacy of gene therapy patients and their families as well as to maintain the confidentiality of research data.

1.   What provisions will be made to honor the wishes of individual patients (and the parents or guardians of pediatric or mentally handicapped patients) as to whether, when, or how the identity of patients is publicly disclosed?

2.   What provision will be made to maintain the confidentiality of research data, at least in cases where data could be linked to individual patients?

II.   SOCIAL ISSUES

The following issues are beyond the normal purview of local IRBs. However, since these issues have arisen in public debates about human gene therapy and the potential future applications of genetic techniques, the RAC and its working group request that investigators respond to questions A and B below and discuss, at their discretion, the general issues enumerated in point C.

A.   What steps will be taken to ensure that accurate information is made available to the public with respect to such public concerns as may arise from the proposed study?

B.   Do you or your funding sources intend to protect under patent or trade secret laws either the products or the procedures developed in the proposed study? If so, what steps will be taken to permit as full communication as possible among investigators and clinicians concerning research methods and results?

C.   The following issues will also be considered by the RAC and its working group in reviewing each gene therapy proposal:

1.   How strong is the evidence that the proposed somatic-cell gene therapy will not affect the reproductive cells of patients?

2.   Is the proposed somatic-cell gene therapy an extension of existing methods of health care, or does it represent a distinct departure from present treatments of disease?

3.   Is it likely that somatic-cell therapy for human genetic disease will lead to: (a) germ-line gene therapy, (b) the enhancement of human capabilities through genetic means, or (c) eugenic programs encouraged or even mandated by governments?

NOTES AND QUESTIONS

1.   Do the "Points to Consider" adequately address the ethical, legal, and social issues that might be raised by gene therapy experiments? Which issues does it mention, and which, if any, does it neglect? For a critique, see Eric

Juengst, The NIH "Points to Consider" and the Limits of Human Gene Therapy, 1 Human Gene Therapy 425 (1990).

2.   The institution where the research is conducted is required to have an Institutional Review Board (IRB) and an Institutional Biosafety Committee (IBC) to approve and oversee the research. IBCs were required by the NIH's first guidelines for recombinant DNA research (discussed in Chapter 1), 41 Fed. Reg. 27,902 (1976). According to the guidelines, institutional biohazards committees, as they were then called, are required to (1) advise the institution on policies regarding containment of recombinant DNA organisms; (2) create a reference resource; (3) develop a procedures manual; and (4) certify to NIH that they have reviewed and approved the safety of recombinant DNA experiments.

3.   The first protocol for a human experiment was received by the RAC in 1988. It was not an actual treatment experiment but a "gene marking" study in which the researcher, Steven Rosenberg, proposed to use cells (specifically, tumor-infiltrating lymphocytes) "marked" with an inserted bacterial gene to track the path of the tumor-fighting cells in cancer patients. The RAC approved the experiment, and after settlement of a lawsuit filed by the Foundation on Economic Trends, a group headed by Jeremy Rifkin, complaining of procedural irregularities in the RAC review process, the experiment took place. For a description of the suit and its aftermath, see Joseph M. Rainsbury, Biotechnology on the RAC: FDA/NIH Regulation of Human Gene Therapy, 55 Food & Drug L.J. 575, 584 (2000); Foundation on Economic Trends, Petition to Amend the National Institutes of Health Guidelines for Research Involving Recombinant DNA Molecules to Establish a Public Policy Advisory Committee, 2 Human Gene Therapy 131 (1991).

4.   In 1985, the NIH issued a revised version of its "Points to Consider." 50 Fed. Reg. 33,462. The revision contained the following new language:

> The acceptability of human somatic-cell gene therapy has been addressed in several recent documents as well as in numerous academic studies.

> * * *

> Civic, religious, scientific, and medical groups have all accepted, in principle, the appropriateness of gene therapy of somatic cells in humans for specific genetic diseases. Somatic cell gene therapy is seen as an extension of present methods of therapy that might be preferable to other technologies.

> Concurring with this judgment, the RAC and its working group are prepared to consider for approval somatic-cell therapy protocols, provided that the design of such experiments offers adequate assurance that their consequences will not go beyond their purpose, which is the same as the traditional purpose of all clinical investigations, namely, to benefit the health and well-being of the individual being treated while at the same time gathering generalizable knowledge.

The two possible undesirable consequences of somatic-cell therapy would be unintentional (1) vertical transmission of genetic changes from an individual to his or her offspring or (2) horizontal transmission of viral infection to other persons with whom the individual comes in contact. Accordingly, this document requests information that will enable the RAC and its working group to assess the likelihood that the proposed somatic-cell gene therapy will inadvertently affect reproductive cells or lead to infection of other people (e.g., treatment personnel or relatives).

In recognition of the social concern that surrounds the general discussion of human gene therapy, the working group will continue to consider the possible long-range effects of applying knowledge gained from these and related experiments. While research in molecular biology could lead to the development of techniques for germ line intervention or for the use of genetic means to enhance human capabilities rather than to correct defects in patients, the working group does not believe that these effects will follow immediately or inevitably from experiments with somatic-cell gene therapy. The working group will cooperate with other groups in assessing the possible long-term consequences of somatic-cell gene therapy and related laboratory and animal experiments in order to define appropriate human applications of this emerging technology.

Note that the RAC for the first time declared its willingness to consider protocols for human gene therapy experiments.

The Food and Drug Administration within the federal Department of Health and Human Services regulates drugs, medical devices, and a class of products called "biologics." Three weeks before the RAC issued its "Points to Consider" in 1985, the FDA issued a policy statement declaring its intention to assert regulatory authority over biotechnology products, including gene therapies, and describing the sources of its regulatory authority.

FOOD AND DRUG ADMINISTRATION, STATEMENT OF POLICY FOR REGULATING BIOTECHNOLOGY PRODUCTS
49 Fed. Reg. 50,878 (1984).

INTRODUCTION

A small but important and expanding fraction of the products the Food and Drug Administration (FDA) regulates represents the fruits of new technological achievements. These achievements are in areas as diverse as polymer chemistry, molecular biology, and micro-miniaturization. It is also noteworthy that technological advancement in a given area may give rise to very diverse product classes, some or all of which may be under FDA's regulatory jurisdiction. For example, new developments in recombinant DNA research can yield products as divergent as food additives, drugs, biologics, and medical devices.

Although there are no statutory provisions or regulations that address biotechnology directly, the laws and regulations under which the Agency operates place the burden of proof of safety as well as effectiveness of products on the manufacturer, except for traditional foods and cosmetics. The administrative review of products using biotechnology is based on the intended use of each product on a case-by-case basis.

This notice describes the regulatory policy of the FDA applicable to biotechnology in general. The manner in which regulations for biotechnology are implemented in the United States could have a direct impact on the competitiveness of U.S. producers in both domestic and world markets. Inconsistent or duplicative domestic regulation will put U.S. producers at a competitive disadvantage. In addition, certification systems which favor domestic products, if adopted by our trading partners, could create substantial nontariff barriers to trade and block market access. Therefore during the development of the U.S. regulatory procedures for biotechnology products, attention is being paid to the need for achieving consistency in national regulation and international harmonization. With respect to international harmonization the U.S. is seeking to promote scientific cooperation, mutual understanding of regulatory approaches, international agreement on a range of common technical problems such as the development of consistent test guidelines, laboratory practices and principles for assessing potential risks. In achieving national consistency and international harmonization, regulatory decisions can be made in a socially responsible manner, protecting human health and the environment, while allowing U.S. producers to remain competitive.

The Agency possesses extensive experience with the administrative and regulatory regimens described as applied to the products of biotechnological processes, new and old, and proposes no new procedures or requirements for regulated industry or individuals. Public comment is requested on scientific and regulatory policy issues raised by this notice.

The marketing of new drugs and biologics for human use, and new animal drugs, requires prior approval of an appropriate new drug application (NDA), license, or new animal drug application (NADA). For new medical devices, including diagnostic devices for human use either a premarket approval application or reclassification petition is required. If the device is determined to be equivalent to an already marketed device, a premarket notification under section 510(k) of the Federal Food, Drug, and Cosmetic Act (the act) is required. For food products, section 409 of the act requires FDA preclearance of food additives including those prepared using biotechnology. Section 706 of the act requires preclearance of color additives. The implementing regulations for food and color additive petitions and for affirming generally recognized as safe (GRAS) food substances are sufficiently comprehensive to apply to those involving new biotechnology.

Genetic manipulations of plants or animals may enter FDA's jurisdiction in other ways; for example, the introduction into a plant of a gene coding for a pesticide or growth factor may constitute adulteration of the foodstuff derived from the plant, or the use of a new microorganism found in a food such as yogurt could be considered a food additive. Such situations will be evaluated case-by-case, and with cooperation with the U.S. Department of Agriculture (USDA), where appropriate.

THE REGULATORY PROCESS

Congress has provided FDA authority under the act and the Public Health Service (PHS) Act to regulate products regardless of how they are manufactured.

GENERAL REQUIREMENTS FOR HUMAN DRUGS AND BIOLOGICS

A new drug is, in general terms, a drug not generally recognized by qualified scientific experts as safe and effective for the proposed use. New drugs may not be marketed unless they have been approved as safe and effective, and clinical investigations on human subjects by qualified experts are a prerequisite for determination of safety and effectiveness. Sponsors of investigations of new drugs or new drug uses of approved drugs file an Investigational New Drug Application (IND) to conduct clinical investigations on human subjects. The IND must contain information needed to demonstrate the safety of proceeding to test the drug in human subjects, including, for example, drug composition, manufacturing and controls data, results of animal testing, training and experience of investigators, and a plan for clinical investigation. In addition, assurance of informed consent and protection of the rights and safety of human subjects is required. FDA evaluates IND submissions and reviews ongoing clinical investigations. Significant changes in the conditions of the study, including changes in study design, drug manufacture or formulation, or proposals for additional studies, must be submitted to FDA as amendment to the IND.

FDA approval of a New Drug Application (NDA) or an abbreviated New Drug Application (ANDA) is required before the new drug can be marketed. The NDA must contain:

— Full reports of investigations, including the results of clinical investigations, that show whether or not the drug is safe and effective;

— A list of components of the drug and a statement of the drug's quantitative composition;

— A description of the methods used in, and the facilities and controls used for, the manufacturing, processing, and packaging of the drug;

— Samples of the drug and drug components as may be required; and

— Specimens of the proposed labeling.

NDA holders who intend to market an approved drug under conditions other than those approved in the NDA must submit a supplemental NDA containing clinical evidence of the drug's safety and effectiveness for the added indications. Extensive changes such as a changed formula, manufacturing process, or method of testing differing from the conditions of approval outlined in the NDA may also require additional clinical testing.

Section 351 of the PHS Act defines a "biological product" as "any virus, therapeutic serum, toxin, antitoxin, vaccine, blood, blood component or derivative, allergenic product, or analogous product * * * applicable to the prevention, treatment, or cure of diseases or injuries of man * * *." Biologics are regulated similarly to new drugs during the IND phase; approval for marketing is granted by license, which is only issued upon demonstration that both the manufacturing establishment and the product meet standards designed to ensure safety, purity, potency, and efficacy. All biologics are subject to general provisions in the regulations that assure potency, general safety, sterility, and purity. In addition, specific tests and standards are established for particular products. To obtain a license, the manufacturer must submit information demonstrating that the manufacturing facility and the product meet FDA standards, and the facility must pass a prelicensing inspection. Licensed products are subject to specific requirements for lot release by FDA.

Manufacturers of new drugs and biologics must operate in conformance with current good manufacturing practice (CGMP) regulations, which address: adequately equipped manufacturing facilities; adequately trained personnel; stringent control over the manufacturing process; and appropriate finished product examination. CGMP's are designed to protect the integrity and purity of the product. Approval of the product application is also approval of the sponsor's process techniques.

* * *

GENERAL REQUIREMENTS FOR MEDICAL DEVICES

Medical devices for human use are regulated by requirements of the act as amended by the Medical Device Amendments of 1976. In general terms, a device is defined in the act as any health care product that does not achieve any of its principal intended purposes by chemical action in or on the body or by being metabolized. Devices include diagnostic aids such as reagents, antibiotic sensitivity discs, and test kits for in vitro diagnosis of disease. Veterinary medical devices are subject to the act but are not subject to preclearance requirements.

Regulations promulgated under the Medical Device Amendments control introduction of medical devices into commerce. In May 1976 when these device amendments were enacted, expert advisory committees recommended classifications for all medical devices of the types marketed at that time. The law segregates medical devices into three classes:

Class I devices are subject to the minimum level of control; general controls include the CGMP's.

Class II devices have been declared to require performance standards to assure their safety and/or effectiveness. They must also meet the controls of class I.

Class III devices require formal FDA approval of a Premarket Approval Application (PMAA) for each make and model of the device to assure its safety and effectiveness. The controls of class I are also required.

Before a manufacturer may introduce into commerce any medical device not previously marketed, the manufacturer must formally declare that intent to FDA and proceed along one of two legal avenues. The manufacturer can file a premarket notification to FDA seeking a determination that the device is substantially equivalent to a preamendment device and proceed to market the device subject to whatever controls apply to the older versions of the device depending on its classification. This is the so-called "510(k)" process, which takes its name from a paragraph in the act.

A new device—that is, one not substantially equivalent to a preenactment device—is automatically a class III device requiring FDA approval of a PMAA unless FDA reclassifies it into class I or class II. In the premarket approval process, the manufacturer must establish that the device is safe and effective. This is typically accomplished by scientific analysis by the Agency of product performance and data from clinical trials, submitted by the manufacturer in the PMAA.

For a "significant risk device," as defined in FDA's regulations, the sponsor must submit an application to FDA for approval to conduct the investigation. This application is known as the Investigational Device Exemption (IDE). When the manufacturer believes there are sufficient data to establish the safety and effectiveness of its device, the manufacturer may file a premarket approval application, or PMAA. The law requires that FDA act on such an application within 180 days.

REGULATION OF SPECIFIC PRODUCTS

Within the framework of FDA's statutes and regulations, strategies have been developed for the evaluation of various kinds of "biotechnological" or "genetically engineered" products, as well as for other products. These strategies are product-specific rather than technology-specific. For example, review of the production of human viral vaccines routinely involves a number of considerations including the purity of the media and the serum used to grow the cell substrate, the nature of the cell substrate, and the characterization of the virus. In the case of a live viral vaccine, the final product is biologically active and is intended to replicate in the recipient. Therefore, the composition, concentration, subtype, immunogenicity, reactivity, and nonpathogenicity of the vaccine preparation are all considerations in the final review, whatever the techniques employed in "engineering" the virus.

Scientific considerations may dictate areas of generic concerns or the use of certain tests for specific situations. For example, a hepatitis B vaccine produced in yeast (via recombinant DNA techniques) would be monitored for yeast cell contaminants, while distinctly different contaminants would be of concern in a similar vaccine produced from the plasma of infected patients.

In order to provide guidance to current or prospective manufacturers of drugs and biological products, the FDA has developed a series of documents describing points that manufacturers might wish to consider in the production of interferon, monoclonal antibodies, and products of recombinant DNA technology, as well as in the use of new cell substrates. These documents, called "Points to Consider . . . ", are available from the Agency upon request.

Administrative jurisdiction within FDA's various organizational units are the same for a given product, whatever the processes employed in its production.

Nucleic acids used for human gene therapy trials will be subject to the same requirements as other biological drugs. It is possible that there will be some redundancy between the scientific reviews of these products performed by the National Institutes of Health and FDA.

* * *

SCIENTIFIC ISSUES SURROUNDING SPECIFIC PRODUCTS

There are some scientific issues raised by specific products manufactured with recombinant DNA technology. First, the molecular structure of some products is different from that of the active molecule in nature. For example, the "human growth hormone" from recombinant microorganisms has an extra amino acid, an amino-terminal methionine; hence, it is an analogue of the native hormone. Such differences may affect the drug's activity or immunogenicity and these considerations, among others, may affect the amount of clinical testing required. However, FDA possesses extensive experience with evaluation of analogues of native human polypeptides, a number of which have been approved for marketing.

Second, approval of the product application for pharmaceuticals is also approval of the sponsor's processing techniques, and FDA must determine whether the quality assurance within the manufacturing process is adequate to detect deviations that might occur, such as the occurrence of mutations in the coding sequence of the cloned gene during fermentation. Such mutations could, in theory, give rise to a subpopulation of molecules with an anomalous primary structure and altered activity. This is a potential problem inherent in the production of polypeptides in any fermentation process. One way FDA has dealt with these situations in existing IND's is to require batch-by-batch testing with appropriate techniques to ensure that the active drug substance is homogenous and has the correct identity.

SUMMARY

FDA's administrative review of products, including those that employ specialized biotechnological techniques such as recombinant DNA in their manufacture, is based on the intended use of product on a case-by-case basis. Although scientific considerations may dictate areas of generic concerns for certain techniques, e.g., the possibility of contamination with adventitious agents or oncogenes when cultured mammalian cells are the source of a drug, the use of a given biotechnological technique does not require a different administrative process. Regulation by FDA must be based on the rational and scientific evaluation of products, and not on a priori assumptions about certain processes.

NOTES AND QUESTIONS

1.   In its policy statement, the FDA states: "The Agency possesses extensive experience with the administrative and regulatory regimens described as applied to the products of biotechnological processes, new and old, and proposes no new procedures or requirements for regulated industry or individuals. * * * Nucleic acids used for human gene therapy trials will be subject to the same requirements as other biological drugs." This represents the core of the FDA's approach to biotechnology: Biotechnology products and processes, including gene therapy, are subject to the same regulatory requirements as any other product or process, no more and no less. This position is noteworthy because it heralded the agency's long-standing approach to the whole range of biotechnology products, including genetically-engineered foods, that they would not be subject to any special review for safety. This approach has unraveled to some extent. Following the death in 1999 of a subject in a gene therapy experiment, discussed in Chapter 12, the FDA also announced its intent to impose special regulatory requirements on human gene therapy experiments, discussed below.

The FDA's position in the 1984 policy statement that the agency will apply its existing regulatory requirements to gene therapy is also noteworthy because it indicates the agency's willingness to regulate practices that might be regarded as the practice of medicine rather than the marketing of a product. Historically, the FDA has been deemed to lack the authority to regulate the practice of medicine. See, e.g., Chaney v. Heckler, 718 F.2d 1174, 1179 (D.C. Cir. 1983) (noting that legislative history of the Federal Food, Drug, and Cosmetic Act reflects congressional intent to prohibit FDA from regulating the practice of medicine), rev'd on other grounds, 470 U.S. 821 (1985); David A. Kessler, The Regulation of Investigational Drugs, 320 New Eng. J. Med. 281, 285 (1989). The agency itself has traditionally accepted this view. See 37 Fed. Reg. 16,503, 16,504 (1972) (concluding that "it is clear that Congress did not intend the [FDA] to regulate or interfere with the practice of medicine"); Online Pharmacies FAQs, Jan. 28, 2000 (FDA will "continue to defer to states to regulate the practice of medicine and pharmacy"). The agency's lack of authority over the practice of medicine is what allows physicians to prescribe drugs for uses which the agency has not approved—a practice known as "off-label use"—without violating federal law. The FDA's lack of authority to regulate off-label use is discussed in Chapter 15 concerning the regulation of genetic enhancement. (The agency's lack of authority is also cited by some commentators as a reason why it does not have jurisdiction to regulate human cloning, despite its claims to the contrary. See Elizabeth C. Price, Does the FDA Have Authority to Regulate Human Cloning?, 11 Harv. J. L. & Tech. 619 (1998).)

2.   In 1985, the RAC issued a revised version of its "Points to Consider." 50 Fed. Reg. 33,462. The revision contained the following new language:

"Applicability: These 'Points to Consider' apply only to research conducted at or sponsored by an institution that receives any support for recombinant DNA research from the National Institutes of Health (NIH). This includes research performed by NIH directly."

The revision also contained a footnote stating: "The Food and Drug Administration (FDA) has jurisdiction over drug products intended for use in clinical trials of human somatic-cell gene therapy." Yet in 1987, the RAC issued a statement reiterating that gene therapy trials had to be reviewed and approved by the RAC even if they were approved by another agency.

3.   In the 1990's, the FDA intensified its efforts to regulate human gene therapy experimentation. In 1991, it issued its own "Points to Consider" document: Center for Biologics Evaluation and Research, Food and Drug Administration, Points to Consider in Human Somatic Cell Therapy and Gene Therapy (1991). In 1992, the FDA clarified that regulation of human gene therapy experiments would be coordinated by a new Division of Cellular and Gene Therapies in a new Office of Therapeutics Research and Review, housed in the agency's Center for Biologics Evaluation and Research (CBER).

4.   Toward the middle of the 1990s, gene therapy researchers and the biotechnology industry became increasingly frustrated at what many of them

viewed as a duplication of regulatory oversight by the RAC and the FDA. Efforts were made to streamline the review process and eliminate the need to submit protocols using two different formats, one for FDA and the other for the RAC. In 1995, a committee recommended to the director of the NIH, Harold Varmus, that the FDA take over the responsibility for reviewing most gene therapy protocols; the RAC would only review proposals that raised novel questions. Varmus decided to go even further. In 1996, he announced his intention to cede all regulatory authority to the FDA. His position was described in a publication in the Federal Register in July 1996 (61 Fed. Reg. 35,774) and formally set forth in a Federal Register publication in 1997 (62 Fed. Reg. 59,032, October 31, 1997). The size of the RAC was reduced to 15 members, and its functions reduced to three: (1) identifying "novel human gene transfer experiments deserving of public discussion" by the committee and transmitting its comments to the investigators, the sponsor, and the FDA; (2) identifying "novel scientific, safety, social, and ethical issues" and recommending revisions to the NIH's Points to Consider; and (3) recommending topics for "Gene Therapy Policy Conferences"—public discussions on "broad overarching policy and scientific issues related to gene therapy research." 62 Fed. Reg. 59,032. (The first Gene Therapy Policy Conference was held on September 11, 1997. The topic was the regulation of genetic enhancement.) An article in The New York Times stated that part of Varmus' motivation was his concern over the quality of the research proposals the RAC was being asked to review, and his disapproval of the way that biotechnology companies touted a favorable RAC review for business purposes. See Sheryl Gay Stolberg, The Biotech Death of Jesse Gelsinger, The New York Times Sunday Magazine, Nov. 28, 1999, at 137.

5.   As noted in its 1984 Statement of Policy, the FDA has basic regulatory authority over drugs, medical devices, and biologics (as well as foods and cosmetics). The FDA regulates drugs, devices and biologics somewhat differently, but all three regulatory schemes share common features. The manufacturer of the product, called the "sponsor," must demonstrate that the product is safe and efficacious[1] in order to be permitted to ship the product across state lines.

Under the Commerce Clause of the Constitution, federal regulatory authority is limited to interstate commerce. As in other areas, however, the

---

[1] "Efficacious" is a term of art that relates to the performance of a product in human experiments. The term "effectiveness" is reserved for the performance of a product in actual use. For a variety of reasons, a product may be efficacious, meaning that it performs satisfactorily in clinical trials, but turn out to be ineffective when marketed for widespread use. For example, the types of patients enrolled in clinical trials are usually carefully controlled to produce the maximum effects, effects that may not be seen when physicians use the product in broader patient populations. In addition, the physicians who treat the experimental subjects may be more expert at using the product than the physicians who provide the product after it is approved. The efficacy-effectiveness distinction was dramatically illustrated by the drug chymopapain, which was efficacious in clinical trials when injected into patient's spines to treat slipped lumbar discs without surgery but which proved lethal when used by less well-trained physicians following FDA approval. See Drug for Slipped Disks is Linked to 5 Deaths, 28 Serious Disorders, The Wall Street Journal, June 7, 1984, at 7.

courts have interpreted the scope of the FDA's authority over "interstate commerce" broadly. See, e.g., Baker v. United States, 932 F.2d 813 (9th Cir. 1991) (ingredients shipped in interstate commerce). In terms of gene therapies, the FDA states: "The interstate commerce nexus needed to require premarket approval under the statutory provisions governing biologics and drugs may be created in various ways in addition to shipment of the finished product by the manufacturer. For example, even if a biological drug product is manufactured entirely with materials that have not crossed State lines, transport of the product into another State by an individual patient creates the interstate commerce nexus. If a component used in the manufacture of the product moves interstate, the interstate commerce prerequisite for the prohibition against drug misbranding is also satisfied even when the finished product stays within the State." (58 Fed. Reg 53248, 53250, Oct. 14, 1993). FDA approval to ship across state lines is required for experimental products as well as for products that have received marketing approval. Before an experimental gene therapy can be given to human subjects in a clinical investigation, the sponsor must have submitted an application to the FDA describing the experiment, and the FDA must have given its approval. The process differs slightly for drugs, devices, and biologics. As described in the 1984 policy statement, sponsors of drug trials must submit an Investigational New Drug application, called an "IND." The agency then has 30 days in which to object to the study going forward, or the application is deemed approved. See 21 C.F.R. § 312.42. The same application is used for biologics. See 21 C.F.R. § 312.2. In the case of a medical device, the application is called an Investigational Device Exemption application, or "IDE." See 21 C.F.R. § 812 1(a). Once clinical trials are satisfactorily completed, the sponsor must file an application for marketing approval. For drugs, this is a New Drug Application or "NDA," described in 21 C.F.R. Part 314. Following passage of the FDA Modernization Act of 1997, 21 U.S.C. §§ 355–397, biologics manufacturers are required to obtain an approved Biologics License Application or "BLA." (Previously they had to obtain separate product and establishment licenses.)

The system for medical devices is more complicated. As described in the 1984 Statement of Policy, medical devices are divided into three classes; only Class III devices must have the equivalent of an approved NDA or BLA, called, in the case of medical devices, an approved Premarket Approval Application or "PMA." Most gene therapies that would be regarded as medical devices would be considered Class III or "significant risk devices," requiring an approved PMA.

Given the different regulatory processes for drugs, devices, and biologics, it is important for sponsors of gene therapy products to know which route to follow, that is, whether their gene therapy is a drug, device, or biologic. A device, by definition, does not achieve its effect by chemical or metabolic action in the body. See 21 U.S.C. § 321(h). Genetic test kits and the reagents used by testing laboratories therefore were medical devices, but not most gene therapies. The distinction between a drug and a biologic was more troublesome. The 1984 Statement of Policy provided little guidance. A subsequent policy statement, Center for Biologics Evaluation and Research, Points to Consider in Human Somatic Cell Therapy and Gene Therapy (1991), defined the term "gene therapy" ("a medical intervention based on modification of the genetic material of living cells"), but did not clarify whether a gene therapy was a drug or biologic. Finally, in 1993, the FDA issued a document entitled Application of Current Statutory Authorities to Human Somatic Cell Therapy Products and Gene Therapy Products (58 Fed. Reg. 53248), in which the agency explained that "synthetic products" (including "a synthetic polynucleotide sequence intended to alter a specific genetic sequence in human somatic cells after systemic administration") were drugs and required INDs and NDAs, while viral and retroviral vectors inserting natural DNA were biologics. 58 Fed. Reg. at 53251. Consequently, virtually all of the gene therapy trials to date fall into the regulatory category of biologics.

6. In April 2019, the NIH eliminated RAC review of human gene therapy protocols. As explained in the August 2018 proposal in the Federal Register (83 Fed. Reg. 41082):

NIH is proposing a series of actions to the *NIH Guidelines for Research Involving Recombinant or Synthetic Nucleic Acid Molecules (NIH Guidelines)* to streamline oversight of human gene transfer research (HGT), and to focus the *NIH Guidelines* more specifically on biosafety issues associated with research involving recombinant or synthetic nucleic acid molecules. The field of HGT has recently experienced a series of advances that have resulted in the translation of research into clinical practice, including U.S. Food and Drug Administration (FDA) approvals for licensed products. Additionally, oversight mechanisms for ensuring HGT proceeds safely have sufficiently evolved to keep pace with new discoveries in this field.

At this time, there is duplication in submitting protocols, annual reports, amendments, and serious adverse events for HGT clinical protocols to both NIH and FDA that does not exist for other areas of clinical research. Historically, this duplication was conceived as harmonized reporting, enabling FDA to provide regulatory oversight while NIH provided a forum for open dialogue and transparency. However, since these complementary functions were first envisioned, we have now seen several converging systems emerge that provide some of these functions. For instance, *ClinicalTrials.gov* has been instituted, which provides a transparent and searchable database for clinical trials. In addition, the protection of human research subjects was improved through changes that updated provisions of the Common Rule. In 2018, FDA released a suite of draft guidance documents pertaining to gene therapy that includes new guidance on manufacturing issues, long-term follow-up, and pathways for clinical development in certain areas, including hemophilia, ophthalmologic indications, and rare diseases.

While the science and oversight system have evolved, HGT protocols continue to receive special oversight that is not afforded to other areas of clinical research. This observation was also noted in a 2014 Institute of Medicine of the National Academies report, *Oversight and Review of Clinical Gene Transfer Protocols: Assessing the Role of the Recombinant DNA Advisory Committee,* in which it was recommended that NIH begin to limit RAC review to only exceptional HGT protocols that meet certain criteria and that would significantly benefit from RAC review. As very few protocols have been assessed by NIH to merit review under this new system, NIH asserts it is an opportune time to make changes to the *NIH Guidelines* to make oversight of HGT commensurate with oversight afforded to other areas of clinical research given the robust infrastructure in place to oversee this type of research.

Briefly to summarize, NIH proposes amending the *NIH Guidelines* to:

1.   Eliminate RAC review and reporting requirements to NIH for HGT protocols.

2.   Modify roles and responsibilities of investigators, institutions, IBCs, the RAC, and NIH to be consistent with these goals including:

a.   Modifying roles of IBCs in reviewing HGT to be consistent with review of other covered research, and

b.   Eliminating references to the RAC, including its roles in HGT and biosafety.

NIH suggests that the series of changes proposed in this Notice is a rational next step in the process of considering appropriate oversight of HGT. Consistent with these proposed changes to the *NIH Guidelines,* Section I-A, the Purpose of the *NIH Guidelines,* is proposed to be amended to clarify that the focus of the policy is biosafety oversight of research involving recombinant or synthetic nucleic acid molecules. NIH notes that some of the duties of Institutional Biosafety Committees (IBCs) as currently written in the *NIH Guidelines* (*e.g.,* review of informed consent documents) are duplicative with the oversight provided by FDA or Institutional Review Boards (IRBs). NIH proposes that IBCs retain responsibility to review and approve HGT protocols; however, NIH proposes that these responsibilities be modified to be similar to those responsibilities IBCs currently have for review and approval of other research subject to the *NIH Guidelines.*

With the proposed elimination of the requirements for safety reporting under Appendix M, IBC oversight should be completed immediately after the last participant is administered the final dose of product. Additionally, the role of IBC review is proposed to be amended to be consistent with FDA's current guidance regarding individual patient expanded access to investigational drugs. In this way, the role of the IBCs will be focused on providing local biosafety oversight of basic and clinical research involving recombinant or synthetic nucleic acids. In particular, NIH seeks comment on whether the expectations of IBCs, in light of these proposed changes, have been articulated clearly in the proposed revisions to the *NIH Guidelines*.

Notably, the roles and responsibilities of the RAC are proposed to be removed from the *NIH Guidelines*. NIH recognizes the value of the RAC in discussions of science, safety, and ethics. In an effort to use the RAC as a public forum to advise on issues associated with emerging biotechnologies, the RAC's charter will be modified to change the committee's focus from research solely involving recombinant or synthetic nucleic acids to emerging biotechnologies research. In light of this modification to the committee, NIH proposes eliminating references to the RAC in the *NIH Guidelines*, though NIH may continue to seek advice from the RAC on biosafety issues that fall under the purview of the *NIH Guidelines*. Similarly, NIH may choose to seek advice from internal working groups or Federal Advisory Committees on a variety of issues, when warranted.

Has the development of somatic gene therapies become so routine that this change in the role of the RAC is appropriate?

7. In 2018, the FDA issued six new draft guidance documents for developers of gene therapies. (https://www.fda.gov/vaccines-blood-biologics/biologics-guidances/cellular-gene-therapy-guidances). A 2019 article in the New England Journal of Medicine stated that this step and the elimination of RAC review of gene therapy protocols, "support the continued maturation of gene therapies as a class of therapeutics." Katherine A. High and Maria G. Roncarolo, Gene Therapy, 381 N. Eng. J. Med. 455, 462 (2019). The article states that, as of 2019, the FDA has given marketing approval to five gene therapies. 381 N. Eng. J. Med. 455, 461, Table 2.

U.S. DEPT. OF HEALTH AND HUMAN SERVICES, OFFICE OF PROTECTION FROM RESEARCH RISKS (OPRR) PROTECTING HUMAN RESEARCH SUBJECTS: INSTITUTIONAL REVIEW BOARD GUIDEBOOK

5-42 to 5-51 (1993).

HUMAN GENETIC RESEARCH

Human genetic research involves the study of inherited human traits. Much of this research is aimed at identifying DNA mutations that can help cause specific health problems. The identification of genetic mutations enables clinicians to predict the likelihood that persons will develop a given health problem in the future or pass on a health risk to their children. For many disorders, however, there will be a considerable time lag between the ability to determine the likelihood of disease and the ability to treat the disease.

Efforts to isolate DNA mutations involved in disease in order to understand the origins of the pathophysiological process are becoming increasingly common across the broad sweep of biomedical research, from cardiology to oncology to psychiatry. IRBs [Institutional Review Boards] should expect to see more of these kinds of studies in the future. * * *

* * *

Unlike the risks presented by many biomedical research protocols considered by IRBs, the primary risk involved in the first three types of genetic research [family linkage studies, identification of genes, and DNA diagnostic studies] are risks of social and psychological harm, rather than risks of physical injury. Genetic studies that generate information about subjects' personal health risks can provoke anxiety and confusion, damage familial relationships, and compromise the subjects' insurability and employment opportunities. [See Chapters 26–32 for a discussion of the legal issues raised by genetic discrimination.] For many genetic research protocols, these psychosocial risks can be significant enough to warrant careful IRB review and discussion. The fact that genetic studies are often limited to the collection of family history information and blood drawing should not, therefore, automatically classify them as "minimal risk" studies qualifying for expedited IRB review.

* * *

Subject Recruitment and Retention. The familial nature of the research cohorts involved in pedigree studies can pose challenges for ensuring that recruitment procedures are free of elements that unduly influence decisions to participate. The very nature of the research exerts pressure on family members to take part, because the more complete the pedigree, the more reliable the resulting information will be. For example, revealing who else in the family has agreed to participate may act as an undue influence on an individual's decision, as may recruiting individuals in the presence of other family members. (Both would also constitute a breach of confidentiality * * *.)

Recruitment plans, some of which are described here, can attempt to address these problems; each approach has its own strengths and weaknesses. One strategy is to use the proband as the point of contact for recruiting. [The proband is the person whose case serves as the stimulus for the study of other members of the family.] This approach insulates families from pressure by the investigator, but presents the risk that the proband may be personally interested in the research findings and exert undue pressure on relatives to enroll in the study. Furthermore, the proband may not want to act as a recruiter for fear that other family members will then know that he or she is affected by the disease. Another approach is direct recruitment by the investigator through letters or telephone calls to individuals whose identity is supplied by the proband. Direct recruitment by the investigator may, however, be seen as an invasion of privacy by family members * * *. A third approach is to recruit participants through support groups or lay organizations. Adopting this strategy requires investigator and IRB confidence that these organizations will be as scrupulous in their own efforts to protect subjects as the investigator would be. A fourth possibility is to contact individuals through their personal physicians. Prospective subjects contacted by their physician may, however, feel that their health care will be compromised if they do not agree to participate. In the end, the IRB must ensure that the recruitment plan minimizes the possibility of coercion or undue influence.

In contrast to inappropriate pressure placed on prospective participants to join the study is the possibility that a subject may agree to participate out of a misguided effort to obtain therapy. The purposes of the research and how subjects will or will not benefit by participation must be clearly explained.

* * *

Defining Risks and Benefits. Potential risks and benefits should be discussed thoroughly with prospective subjects. In genetic research, the primary risks, outside of gene therapy, are psychological and social (referred to generally as "psychosocial") rather than physical. IRBs should review genetic research with such risks in mind.

Psychological risk includes the risk of harm from learning genetic information about oneself (*e.g.*, that one is affected by a genetic disorder that has not yet manifested itself). Complicating the communication of genetic information is that often the information is limited to probabilities. Furthermore, the development of genetic data carries with it a margin of error; some information communicated to subjects will, in the end, prove to be wrong. In either event, participants are subjected to the stress of receiving such information. For example, researchers involved in developing presymptomatic tests for Huntington Disease (HD) have been concerned that the emotional impact of learning the results may lead some subjects to attempt suicide. They have therefore asked whether prospective participants should be screened for emotional stability prior to acceptance into a research protocol.

Note that these same disclosures of information can also be beneficial. One of the primary benefits of participation in genetic research is that the receipt of genetic information, however imperfect, can reduce uncertainty about whether participants will likely develop a disease that runs in their family (and possibly whether they have passed the gene along to their children). Where subjects learn that they will likely develop or pass along the disease, they might better plan for the future.

To minimize the psychological harms presented by pedigree research, IRBs should make sure that investigators will provide for adequate counseling to subjects on the meaning of the genetic information they receive. Genetic counseling is not a simple matter and must be done by persons qualified and experienced in communicating the meaning of genetic information to persons participating in genetic research or persons who seek genetic testing.

Debate about the social policy implications of genetic information is vitally important and is occurring on a national and international level, but is not literally a concern for IRBs. The IRB's concern is, first, to ensure that these risks will be disclosed to subjects, and, second, to protect subjects against unwarranted disclosures of information.

* * *

Privacy and Confidentiality Protections. Special privacy and confidentiality concerns arise in genetic family studies because of the special relationship between the participants. IRBs should keep in mind that within families, each person is an individual who deserves to have information about him-or herself kept confidential. Family members are not entitled to each other's diagnoses. Before revealing medical or personal information about individuals to other family members, investigators must obtain the consent of the individual.

Data must be stored in such a manner that does not directly identify individuals. In general, except where directly authorized by individual subjects, data may not be released to anyone other than the subject. An exception to requiring explicit authorization for the release of data may be secondary research use of the data, where the data are not especially sensitive and where confidentiality can be assured. IRBs should exercise their discretion in reviewing protocols that call for the secondary use of genetic data. Furthermore, when reviewing a consent document, IRBs should note agreements made by investigators not to release information without the express consent of subjects. Subsequent requests for access to the data are subject to agreements made in the consent process. For studies involving socially sensitive traits or conditions, investigators might also consider requesting a certificate of confidentiality.

* * *

Publication Practices. One final issue involving consent is the publication of research data. The publication of pedigrees can easily result in the identification of study participants. Where a risk of identification exists, participants must consent, in writing, to the release of personal information. Various authors have noted the problem of obtaining consent for the publication of identifying data, and have recommended that consent to the publication be obtained immediately prior to the publication, rather than as part of the consent to treatment or participation in research. It is worth noting, however, that to address this concern, IRBs must also resolve the following questions: Who determines the risk of identification, and on what grounds? Who are defined as participants (is it everyone listed in the pedigree, some of whom have been contacted by investigators, some of whom have had information about them provided by a family member)?

While IRBs must be careful to avoid inappropriate restrictions on investigators' research publications, some evaluation of publication plans is important as part of the IRB's overall interest in preserving the confidentiality of research subjects. One approach for investigators to use in evaluating their publication plans might be to work in a step-wise fashion: First, is publication of the pedigree essential? If publication of the pedigree or other identifying data (*e.g.*, case histories, photographs, or radiographs) is essential, can some identifying data be omitted without changing the scientific message? (The practice of altering data—such as changing the birth order and gender—is controversial, and no clear professional consensus yet exists as to whether this is an appropriate practice.) Finally, if the pedigree must be published, and if identifying data cannot be omitted in an appropriate manner without changing the scientific message, subjects must give their permission for publication of data that may reveal their identity.

NOTE: STATE REGULATION OF RESEARCH

The federal research regulations specifically do not preempt state or local laws or regulations that provide additional protections for human subjects. Only a handful of states, such as Virginia, have adopted comprehensive laws governing human research. See Va. Code Ann. §§ 32.1–162.16–.20. Many states, however, have adopted laws governing research on certain vulnerable populations, such as children or people with mental disabilities. See Elyn R. Saks et al., Proxy Consent to Research: The Legal Landscape, 8 Yale Journal of Health Policy, Law, and Ethics Issue 2, 37 (2013). States have also adopted restrictive laws governing research on embryos and fetuses. The state laws on research are particularly important because, unlike the federal research regulations, they apply to research no matter what the source of funding.

Starting in the mid-1990s, a new trend in state laws emerged. Some states adopted laws forbidding genetic testing without an individual's written informed consent. Yet most of those laws created exceptions that allowed researchers to undertake certain types of genetic testing without informed consent. The Massachusetts law, Mass. Stat. Ann. 111 § 70G, for example, allows investigators undertaking pharmacological or clinical research to undertake genetic testing on a person's anonymized DNA without his or her consent if the research has been approved by an IRB. Other states exempt any researcher from having to comply with the informed consent provision, without even requiring IRB approval.

LARRY R. CHURCHILL ET AL., GENETIC RESEARCH AS THERAPY: IMPLICATIONS OF "GENE THERAPY" FOR INFORMED CONSENT
26 J. L. Med. & Ethics 38 (1998).

In March 1996, the General Accounting Office (GAO) issued the report Scientific Research: Continued Vigilance Critical to Protecting Human Subjects. It stated that "an inherent conflict of interest exists when physician-researchers include their patients in research protocols. If the physicians do not clearly distinguish between research and treatment in their attempt to inform subjects, the possible benefits of a study can be overemphasized and the risks minimized." The report also acknowledged that "the line between research and treatment is not always clear to clinicians. Controversy exists regarding whether certain medical procedures should be categorized as research."

This problem currently plagues gene transfer research. A few months prior to the GAO report, an ad hoc committee appointed by National Institutes of Health (NIH) Director Harold Varmus expressed similar concerns in its assessment of NIH investment in research on gene therapy. The committee's report stated:

> Expectations of current gene therapy have been oversold. Overzealous representation of clinical gene therapy has obscured the exploratory nature of the initial studies, colored the manner in which findings are portrayed to the scientific press and public, and led to the widely held, but mistaken, perception that clinical gene therapy is already highly successful.

In mid 1996, the Recombinant DNA Advisory Committee's (RAC) five-year status report of gene therapy described the situation this way:

> It is clearly too early . . . to assess the therapeutic efficacy of gene therapy or even to predict its promise. Numerous studies have reported the ability to express recombinant DNA in vivo, but few have reported clinical efficacy. . . . The few "dramatic" successes claimed are not dissimilar to those that were reported with a variety of other therapeutic techniques for which enthusiasm ultimately dampened over time.

Yet despite this cautionary report, and despite the fact that no therapeutic benefit has been clearly demonstrated for the more than 2,100 subjects enrolled in gene transfer research worldwide, enthusiasm for gene therapy persists unabated.

* * *

At present, gene transfer research amplifies the already existing confusions between research and therapy and intensifies extant problems of informed consent.

* * *

Consider, for instance, the following excerpt from the minutes of 1991 meetings of RAC and its Human Gene Therapy Subcommittee. In the subcommittee's 1991 review of a protocol for gene therapy for familial hypercholesterolemia, not only is the research described by some discussants as treatment, but some subcommittee members also considered it "discriminatory" to "treat" adults before children were entered in the protocol. This is not an isolated example of the conflation of research and therapy. Indeed, the basis of this ambiguity is built into the ethical guidelines that RAC uses to review protocols for gene transfer research. The most recent version of RAC's "Points to Consider" document refers to research participants as "patients" in some places and "subjects" in others, and sometimes refers to clinical studies as "treatments." This oscillation in language cannot be helpful for the process of informed consent.

* * *

Yet although gene therapy is conceived as revolutionary, its administration is viewed as routine. For example, many advocates describe gene therapy as merely "a novel form of drug delivery," where this description does not refer to the practice of manufacturing traditional drugs with recombinant DNA techniques, but to gene transfer. Almost everyone agrees that germ-line intervention—affecting future generations and involving a host of unknowable consequences—presents major new ethical issues, but the accepted wisdom is that somatic cell gene transfer is simply a part of the therapeutic continuum, presenting no novel ethical dilemmas.

* * *

The revolutionary rhetoric about addressing the essence of disease in scientific research is fueled, of course, by the agendas of those with major social and economic investments in the gene therapy enterprise. Physicians and researchers working on gene transfer techniques have substantial interests in promoting this nascent field of medical science. Biotechnology companies, moreover, have an interest in turning out numerous products related to the so-called genetic revolution—for example, diagnostic tests and DNA-based medicines. The cluster of scientific, economic, and cultural hopes swirling around our genes seems to intensify and sustain the future promise of gene therapy at the same time that it frames this revolutionary concept in traditional garb—as merely the next wave of therapeutic options. The failure to discuss these factors candidly leads regulators, professionals, and the public to perpetuate confusion, misrepresentation, and disappointment in the sometimes appropriate, and occasionally misguided, pursuit of medical advancement.

* * *

CONCLUSION

Informed consent is fundamentally about language, about how doctors and patients, researchers, and subjects communicate. As a practice, informed consent is intended to foster genuinely collaborative decision making in both the research and patient care settings. But in the current milieu of therapeutic enthusiasm for research, informed consent has become a way of not talking, or more precisely, a way of not talking with sufficient candor. By failing to dispel confusion about the therapeutic intentions of gene transfer research, the consent process often perpetuates a false promise to subjects. To promote conversation, researchers must earn the trust of their subjects through communication that avoids the false appeal of a beneficence warranted only by compassionate intent and devoid of evidence of benefit. In promoting an ethically sound genetic research enterprise involving human subjects, policy-makers should craft institutional opportunities for meaningful informed consent discussions in which the nuances can be sorted out.

To achieve these goals, the minimum requirement is conceptual clarity. We argue that rectifying the language of the regulatory bodies is essential for restoring informed consent for research to its original role as a collaboration-oriented process that promotes appropriate access and yet fully informs and protects subjects from inflated promises of benefit.

Specifically, with regard to gene therapy, we suggest the following.

First, RAC, FDA, and the Office for Protection from Research Risks should delete the terms gene therapy and gene therapy research and any language that would imply that a gene therapy already exists from the informed consent process and committee deliberation. This conceptual clarity is essential in those oversight institutions that set the tone for researcher-subject discussions. The term gene transfer research more accurately conveys the experimental practice that is currently at issue.

Second, RAC should rewrite its "Points to Consider" to differentiate clearly patients from subjects and research from treatment where those references are misleading. In this regard, the recent diminution of RAC's oversight role is troubling. Over the past few years, RAC has received an abundance of criticism, including charges that it has exceeded its authority, delayed approval of protocols, and functioned in a "purely cosmetic" way. Members of RAC have seen their role differently, recognizing that they are charged with reviewing a "new form of medical experimentation." In many cases, RAC has changed the language of consent forms to delete terms like therapy and often challenged what it has perceived as overestimates of potential benefit from participation in gene transfer protocols, similar to the concerns we have discussed here. If the confusions about gene therapy are to be dispelled, we believe a more robust role for RAC is required, rather than a diminished one.

Third, all institutions [and investigators] charged with responsibility for protecting human subjects and ensuring their informed participation in research should critically rethink the ethical norms that currently shape the language of informed consent in areas like human gene transfer research. The meaning of the principle of beneficence as direct benefit to the patient-subject should be clearly distinguished from beneficence as a possible benefit to future patients. The use of beneficence to refer to motivations of compassionate intent or desperate use in research contexts is misleading, especially to patient-subjects, and should be eliminated. The appropriate place for beneficence in genetic research is almost always as a long-range, aggregate good stemming from research results, and not as an immediate benefit resulting directly from research participation. The goal of genetic research is generalizable knowledge to benefit future patients, not current subjects. This is especially relevant to the Phase I and II protocols for gene transfer now extant. Subjects are treated ethically only when a robust exercise of consent is combined with a commitment to eliminate or reduce harms. Beneficence is too often translated into false promises of therapy for subjects, and this compromises the consent process.

Fourth, consent forms should state clearly and explicitly that there is no expected benefit to the individual patient who becomes a subject in current gene transfer research. Moreover, researchers should work to minimize the unwarranted therapeutic assumptions that inevitably result when research is conducted in the physical environment and moral context of ongoing patient care. One way to achieve this would be for each protocol and informed consent document to provide a separate section entitled "Evidence of Benefit," thereby calling attention to whatever evidence for individual benefit exists and laying it open to critical scrutiny by federal oversight bodies, IRBs, investigators, and subjects.

Finally, the NIH training program in research ethics should make a significant investment in educating investigators to view informed consent as conversation, in the service of subject autonomy and professional self-scrutiny, and aimed ultimately at an improved, collaborative decision-making process in research.

NOTES AND QUESTIONS

1.   What are the differences between research and therapy? Are there differences between research subjects and patients undergoing treatment in terms of protections to prevent harm? Review the earlier discussion of the ethics of genetic research. Is the informed consent process the same in the cases

of research and therapy? If not, how do they differ? Under federal law and the terms of NIH grants, all proposals for human subjects research involving the administration of a drug, device, or biologic must be reviewed by institutional review boards (IRBs), groups of individuals at the institution conducting the study. Is there an equivalent entity or function in the case of therapy?

2.   Especially troublesome problems arise when a patient's physician is also a researcher. As George Annas states: "When physician and researcher are merged into one person, it is unlikely that patients can ever draw the distinction between these two conflicting roles because most patients simply do not believe that their physician would knowingly harm them or would knowingly use them as a means for their own ends." George J. Annas, Questing for Grails: Duplicity, Betrayal and Self-Deception in Postmodern Medical Research, 12 J. Contemp. Health L. & Pol'y 297, 311–312 (1996). Do the recommendations suggested by Churchill et al. respond to this concern?

> **Food for Thought:** Churchill suggests that the term "gene transfer research" be used instead of "gene therapy research" to avoid misleading experimental subjects about the potential benefits of an experiment. Looking back at the description of gene therapy at the beginning of this part of the casebook, does Churchill's term accurately describe the techniques in question?

3.   Is the conflation of research and therapy a particular problem in gene therapy experimentation, or a general problem with medical research? Does the article by Churchill make a persuasive argument that gene therapy research is special?

4.   Will the recommendations in the article solve the problem? If not, what other approaches might work?

CHAPTER 12

HISTORY OF GENE THERAPY

■ ■ ■

The first attempt at human gene therapy is said to have occurred in 1970, when Stanfield Rogers, a biochemist and physician, attempted to insert into three German girls a virus carrying a gene to combat an inherited liver disease. None of the girls improved.

In 1980, Martin Cline, a UCLA researcher and Chief of Hematology/Oncology at the UCLA Medical Center, attempted to insert DNA into the bone marrow of two patients, one in Italy and the other in Israel, suffering from beta thalassemia, a hereditary blood disorder. Cline submitted a protocol to the UCLA Institutional Review Board (IRB), but went ahead with the experiment before receiving IRB approval. The IRB later rejected Cline's protocol because of insufficient studies in animals. Cline's experiments were uncovered by a newspaper reporter for the L.A. Times. As a result, Cline lost his department chair and his funding from the NIH. The Cline incident raises issues of research ethics, such as the following: What is the reach of a research protocol? Should a protocol from a U.S. university extend to a professor's work abroad?

Ten years later, in 1990, the third attempt at gene therapy occurred at the NIH in Bethesda, Maryland. The patient, Ashanti DeSilva, was a four year-old suffering from SCID (severe combined immune deficiency). As a result of a genetic error inherited from both parents, patients with this disease do not manufacture the enzyme adenosine deaminase, required for proper functioning of the immune system. DeSilva led a cloistered, endangered existence, being vulnerable to severe infections. A team of physicians removed some of her white blood cells, inserted normal copies of the gene into the cells, and returned the cells into her bloodstream. After four infusions over four months, she improved. She continues to receive infusions every few months, however, because the cells with the normal gene do not continue to work indefinitely. Moreover, she continues to receive traditional drug therapy (PEGADA, a form of the missing enzyme) to supplement the effect of the gene therapy. Nevertheless, many regard DeSilva's experiment to be the first partially successful use of gene therapy.

Ten years after that, in 2000, French scientists announced that they had used gene therapy to successfully treat several infants suffering from a form of SCID (SCID-X1). Unlike in the case of DeSilva, the French researchers claimed to have inserted correctly-functioning genes in the babies' bone marrow, where they can continue to proliferate, thereby avoiding the need for repeat infusions.

Three years later, however, the French scientists announced that, although nine of the 10 babies developed normal immune systems, two of them developed T-cell leukemia, a form of cancer. The FDA placed a hold on three U.S. gene therapy trials that used the same retroviral vector, as did France and Germany. Subsequently, researchers determined that the leukemia resulted from the coincidental insertion of the retrovirus near a cancer gene that it activated. It was hoped that improved vectors could alleviate the problem. But in 2004, one of the two babies died, and in 2005, a third child in the French experiment developed leukemia.

The events in France followed years of unsuccessful efforts to use gene therapy to treat diseases such as cystic fibrosis, familial hypercholesterolemia, Gaucher's disease, and cancer. They also followed the death in October 1999, of Jesse Gelsinger.

Gelsinger, 18 years old, enrolled in an experiment at the University of Pennsylvania to develop a gene therapy for OTC (ornithine transcarbamylase) deficiency, an x-linked, dominant, single-gene liver disorder whose sufferers, numbering about one out of every 40,000 births, are unable to metabolize ammonia, which is a by-product of the breakdown of protein in the body. The disease is especially severe in newborns. Affected babies slip into a coma within 72 hours of birth and suffer severe brain damage. Half die within one month, and half of the survivors die before they reach six months of age.

Interestingly, Gelsinger himself did not inherit the disease. Instead, it resulted from a de novo genetic mutation. Furthermore, Gelsinger had what is called mosaicism—the genetic makeup of his cells was not all the same and some of his liver cells were producing the missing enzyme, enough so that he did not become comatose after birth and was able to control the illness with a combination of a non-protein diet and enzyme pills. However, by the time he reached eighteen, he was taking 35 pills a day, and was likely to have had to increase the dosage as time went on. He was eager to help find a cure—both for himself and for the more severely-affected infants.

The study Gelsinger enrolled in was not intended to treat OTC. Instead, it was what is called a "Phase I" trial. The plan was to use an adenovirus as a vector; the DNA in the nucleus of the virus would be altered by recombinant DNA techniques to carry the correct gene, and an infusion of the adenovirus vector would be inserted into the subjects' livers. The purpose of the Phase I trial was to determine if, once inserted, the corrected genes would proceed to produce the missing enzyme, and to determine the "maximum tolerated dose" of the infusion—that is, the highest dose that would produce the desired effect without serious side effects.

At first, the Penn researchers proposed to conduct the experiment on a group of severely affected newborns, since their form of the disease was the ultimate target of the therapy. But Arthur Caplan, a leading bioethicist then at Penn, objected that the parents of these infants could not give valid informed consent, since parents of dying babies were subject to too much "emotional coercion." Sheryl Gay Stolberg, The Biotech Death of Jesse Gelsinger, The New York Times Sunday Magazine, Nov. 28, 1999, at 137. Consequently, the Penn researchers decided to do the Phase I study on adults, both female carriers and persons like Gelsinger with only partial enzyme deficiencies.

The Penn research was funded by the NIH. Therefore, the researchers submitted their protocol, or plan for the design of the study, to the NIH RAC for review. The NIH reviewers were concerned about imposing the risks of the experiment on asymptomatic volunteers like Gelsinger, but Caplan's position prevailed and the NIH gave Penn the go-ahead. The researchers also submitted their protocol to the FDA, as required by federal law, and the agency approved it. Finally, the protocol was reviewed and approved by Penn's own Institutional Review Board (IRB), a group made up primarily of Penn researchers.

There were 18 subjects in all, divided into three groups, with each group getting a different dose. Gelsinger was in the highest dosage group. Everything seemed to be going fine. A story in The New York Times tells what happened next:

> The treatment began on Monday, Sept. 13. Jesse would receive the highest dose. Seventeen patients had already been treated, including one woman who had been given the same dose that Jesse would get, albeit from a different lot, and had done "quite well," Raper [the surgeon who administered the infusion] says. That morning, Jesse was taken to the interventional-radiology suite, where he was sedated and strapped to a table while a team of radiologists threaded two catheters into his groin. At 10:30 a.m., Raper drew 30 milliliters of the vector and injected it slowly. At half past noon, he was done.

> That night, Jesse was sick to his stomach and spiked a fever, 104.5 degrees. Raper was not particularly surprised: other patients had experienced the same reaction. Paul Gelsinger [the patient's father] called; he and Jesse talked briefly, exchanging I love yous. Those were the last words they ever spoke.

> Early Tuesday morning a nurse called Raper at home; Jesse seemed disoriented. When Raper got to the hospital, about 6:15 a.m., he noticed that the whites of Jesse's eyes were yellow. That

meant jaundice, not a good sign. "It was not something we had seen before," Raper says. A test confirmed that Jesse's bilirubin, a breakdown product of red blood cells, was four times the normal level. Raper called Gelsinger, and Batshaw [a physician who proposed the experiment] in Washington, who said he would get on a train and be there in two hours.

Both doctors knew that the high bilirubin meant one of two things: either Jesse's liver was failing or he was suffering a clotting disorder in which his red blood cells were breaking down faster than the liver could metabolize them. This was the same disorder the scientists had seen in the monkeys that had been given the stronger vector. The condition is life-threatening for anyone, but particularly dangerous for someone with Jesse's disease, because red blood cells liberate protein when they break down.

By midafternoon Tuesday, a little more than 24 hours after the injection, the clotting disorder had pushed Jesse into a coma. By 11:30 p.m., his ammonia level was 393 micromoles per liter of blood. Normal is 35. The doctors began dialysis.

Paul Gelsinger had booked a red-eye flight. When he arrived in the surgical intensive care unit at 8 Wednesday morning, Raper and Batshaw told him that dialysis had brought Jesse's ammonia level down to 72 but that other complications were developing. He was hyperventilating, which would increase the level of ammonia in his brain. They wanted to paralyze his muscles and induce a deeper coma, so that a ventilator could breathe for him. Gelsinger gave consent. Then he put on scrubs, gloves and a mask and went in to see his son.

By Wednesday afternoon, Jesse seemed to be stabilizing. Batshaw went back to Washington. Paul felt comfortable enough to meet his brother for dinner. But later that night Jesse worsened again. His lungs grew stiff; the doctors were giving him 100 percent oxygen, but not enough of it was getting to his bloodstream. They consulted a liver-transplant team and learned that Jesse was not a good candidate. Raper was beside himself. He consulted with Batshaw and Wilson, and they decided to take an extraordinary step, a procedure known as ECMO, for extracorporeal membrane oxygenation, essentially an external lung that filters the blood, removing carbon dioxide and adding oxygen. It had been tried on only 1,000 people before, Raper says. Only half had survived.

"If we could just buy his lungs a day or two," Raper said later, they thought "maybe he would go ahead and heal up."

The next day, Thursday, Sept. 16, Hurricane Floyd slammed into the East Coast. Mickie Gelsinger [the patient's stepmother] flew in from Tucson just before the airport closed. (Pattie Gelsinger, Jesse's mother, was being treated in a psychiatric facility and was unable to leave.) Batshaw spent the day trapped outside Baltimore on an Amtrak train. He ran down his cell phone calling Raper; when it went dead, he persuaded another passenger to lend him his. The ECMO, Raper reported, appeared to be working. But then another problem cropped up: Jesse's kidneys stopped making urine. "He was sliding into multiple-organ-system failure," Raper says.

That night, at his hotel, Paul Gelsinger couldn't sleep. He left his wife a note and walked the half mile to the Penn medical center to see Jesse. The boy was bloated beyond recognition; even his ears were swollen shut. Gelsinger noticed blood in Jesse's urine, an indication, he knew, that the kidneys were shutting down. How can anybody, he thought, survive this?

On the morning of Friday the 17th, a test showed that Jesse was brain dead. Paul Gelsinger didn't need to be told: "I knew it already." He called for a chaplain to hold a bedside service, with prayers for the removal of life support.

The room was crowded with equipment and people: 7 of Paul's 15 siblings came in, plus an array of doctors and nurses. Raper and Batshaw, shellshocked and exhausted, stood in the back. The chaplain anointed Jesse's forehead with oil, then read the Lord's Prayer. The doctors fought back tears. When the intensive-care specialist flipped two toggle switches, one to turn off the ventilator and the other to turn off the ECMO machine, Raper stepped forward. He checked the heart-rate monitor, watched the line go flat and noted the time: 2:30 p.m. He put his stethoscope to Jesse's chest, more out of habit than necessity, and pronounced the death official. "Goodbye, Jesse," he said. "We'll figure this out."

Sheryl Gay Stolberg, The Biotech Death of Jesse Gelsinger, The New York Times Sunday Magazine, Nov. 28, 1999, at 137.

Gelsinger was believed to be the first patient to die in the course of a gene therapy experiment. In the aftermath of Gelsinger's death, it was discovered that there had been a number of adverse events associated with gene therapy experiments that had never been made public. Many of them had been reported to the FDA, as required by FDA regulations. See 21 C.F.R. § 312.32 (requiring IND safety reports within 15 days of any serious or unexpected adverse events, and immediate notification of fatal or life-threatening adverse events). In accordance with long-standing FDA policy, however, these reports were considered trade secrets and not disclosed to the public. Even the fact that a sponsor had filed an IND (or IDE) was kept secret.

NIH also required that it be notified of serious adverse events occurring in gene therapy studies that it funded or that were conducted at an institution that received NIH funding. In contrast to the FDA, however, the NIH made these reports public. Sponsors therefore were reluctant to make the reports. After Gelsinger's death, the NIH received reports of 691 serious adverse events; only 39 had been reported when they occurred, as required by the NIH rules.

The lack of public awareness of safety problems with gene therapy trials not only impaired the ability of researchers to inform subjects of potential risks in obtaining informed consent; it hampered the researcher's ability to design and conduct safe studies. In reviewing gene therapy research INDs, the FDA was not always able to consider the full implications of the adverse event reports it received for other investigations, and researchers would only hear about these events if their occurrence was "leaked" by their colleagues, for example, at science conferences or in private conversations.

Gelsinger's death and the resulting disclosures of the lack of awareness of adverse events prompted several government reactions. In March 2000, the Department of Health and Human Services announced a new Gene Therapy Trial Monitoring Plan whereby the FDA would more closely review the procedures employed by a sponsor to monitor gene therapy trials, and established a program of Gene Transfer Safety Symposia which would bring researchers together 4 times a year to review safety results from gene therapy experiments. See Food and Drug Administration, New Initiatives to Protect Participants in Gene Therapy Trials, March 7, 2000. The Secretary of Health and Human Services proposed to ask Congress for new authority to levy $250,000 fines against investigators who violated human subjects protection rules, and $1 million fines against their institutions.

Finally, the FDA published proposed regulations which would have provided for the public disclosure of IND safety reports for two types of experiments: gene therapy and xenotransplantation (the transplantation into humans of non-human organs or tissue). The proposal can be found at 66 Fed. Reg. 4688 (2001). This marked the first time that the FDA proposed to adopt formal regulations specifically dealing with gene therapy; all previous FDA pronouncements had been in the form of policy statements. If adopted, the regulations would have marked a significant change in the agency's attitude toward gene therapy and biotechnology more generally. As noted earlier, until now, the FDA has taken the position that biotechnology products should be subject to the same regulatory requirements as any other products. The proposed regulations, by pertaining only to gene therapy and xenotransplantation would signal that the agency had abandoned this viewpoint. This might lead to a broader shift in the government's regulatory policy toward biotechnology, with repercussions for areas such as genetically engineered foods and plants. However, the FDA withdrew the proposal in 2016. 81 Fed. Reg. 79,400, Nov. 14, 2016.

In March 2004, the NIH and FDA announced the creation of a new web data base, the Genetic Modification Clinical Research Information System (GeMCRIS). Information reported to the NIH about adverse events that occur in gene therapy trials is posted on the data base and available to researchers and to the public.

Two months after Gelsinger's death, the FDA inspected the research operation at Penn and, after finding a number of deficiencies, suspended all gene therapy experiments. The deficiencies included problems with the informed consent process in the OTC trial. The FDA also determined that Gelsinger was not a proper subject for enrollment into the study, since his liver was not functioning well-enough at the time he received the adenovirus infusion.

One of the most troubling revelations involved the significant financial conflicts of interest of the lead researchers who owned stock in a biotech company trying to monetize the gene therapy. The experiment in which Jesse Gelsinger died was part of a large-scale gene therapy research program at the University of Pennsylvania's Institute of Gene Therapy, headed by James M. Wilson. At the time, the institute had 250 employees and an annual budget of $25 million, and was considered the largest academic gene therapy research program in the country. Wilson was also the founder and a stockholder, along with the university, in a company called Genovo. Genovo did not fund the Gelsinger study, but it did provide twenty percent of the institute's budget, and had the exclusive right to commercialize any institute discoveries. According to the university's general counsel, the relationship between Wilson, Genovo, and Penn was so complicated that the university set up two committees to oversee it. When Genova was sold in 2000 to a company called Targeted Genetics Corp., Wilson was due to receive stock worth $13.5 million.

In May 2000, the FDA criticized researchers at the St. Elizabeth's Medical Center in Boston for failing to report a death in an experiment designed to determine if patients with blocked blood vessels of the heart could be improved by injecting them with genes that produce a substance that promotes revascularization. It turned out that the patient was not appropriate for the study because he had a lung tumor and was a heavy smoker, raising the concern that the inserted genes would promote tumor growth. The chief researcher was a founder of and major stockholder in the company sponsoring the experiment.

A great deal of attention has been given to the problems created by researchers' financial stake in the outcome of their experiments. See Catherine D. DeAngelis, Conflict of Interest and the Public Trust, 284

JAMA 2237 (2000); David Korn, Commentary: Conflicts of Interest in Biomedical Research, 284 JAMA 2234 (2000); Bernard Lo et al., Conflict-of-Interest Policies for Investigators in Clinical Trials, 343 New Eng. J. Med. 1616 (2000); S. Van McCrary et al., A National Survey of Policies on Disclosure of Conflicts of Interest in Biomedical Research, 343 New Eng. J. Med. 1621 (2000).

In 2005, the Justice Department settled a lawsuit against the Gelsinger researchers that had accused them of making false statements to the FDA, including misrepresentations that would have resulted in the FDA shutting down the experiment. Under the terms of the settlement, the University of Pennsylvania agreed to pay $517,000 in fines and the Children's National Medical Center (where Batshaw worked) $514,622. This was twice the amount of NIH funding for the experiment. The agreement also barred Wilson until 2010 from conducting clinical research under FDA jurisdiction, and imposed a 3-year ban on clinical research by Raper and Batshaw.

After several months during which he defended the researchers at Penn, Gelsinger's father filed a lawsuit for wrongful death. Arthur Caplan was initially named as a defendant, in what is regarded as the first suit against a biomedical ethicist for advice in connection with the design of a clinical trial. Caplan was subsequently dismissed as a defendant, however, and the suit eventually settled for an undisclosed amount.

For a poignant account of these events written by the father of Jesse Gelsinger, see Paul L. Gelsinger, Uninformed Consent: The Case of Jesse Gelsinger, Law and Ethics in Biomedical Research: Regulations, Conflict of Interest, and Liability (Trudo Lemmens & Duff R. Waring eds. 2006).

CHAPTER 13

GERMLINE THERAPY

■ ■ ■

"Germline therapy" is a therapeutic genetic intervention that, intentionally or not, affects the genetic material of reproductive cells. As a result, the modifications can alter the genetic endowment of the person's offspring, and their progeny in turn.

The distinction between somatic cell and germline therapy is not always clear. Somatic cell treatments that enabled people to have children, whether by repairing their reproductive systems or simply by saving their lives while they were still capable of reproducing, would affect the genes of offspring by making the lives of the offspring possible. Similarly, abortions performed because of fetal health problems or health-based decisions about which embryos to implant following IVF might be considered germline therapy because they affect the genes of a person's children, precluding the aborted fetuses or discarded embryos from passing on their genes via reproduction. But these interventions all involve naturally inherited genes; therapeutic abortions and embryo selection for implantation merely select among offspring on the basis of their natural genetic endowment. Most commentators reserve the term "germline therapy" for interventions that actually change the genes of surviving offspring.

Some commentators also distinguish somatic and germline therapy in terms of the target of the intervention. The goal of somatic cell therapy, they say, is to treat the person who is the subject of the procedure, while the goal of germline therapy is to treat that person's children. This distinction is blurred as well, however. As discussed below, one therapeutic approach might be to insert genes into an early stage embryo or fetus with the intent of correcting an abnormality or preventing a disease. If the insertion is made at an early-enough stage of development, the altered genes will be incorporated not only into the somatic cells of a surviving individual but into that person's reproductive cells.

Germline therapy refers to genetic manipulation of germ cells or "gametes": the egg and the sperm. In practice, it also refers to genetic alteration of the fertilized egg and genetic alteration of the cells of an early embryo (or embryonic stem (ES) cells), because these alterations will be incorporated in all the cells of the resultant child, including his or her germ cells. Therefore, the altered gene will pass down the generations.

In its 1985 Revised Points to Consider, the FDA stated that it would not approve any protocols for germline therapy:

> A distinction should be drawn between making genetic changes in somatic cells and in germ line cells. The purpose of somatic cell gene therapy is to treat an individual patient, e.g., by inserting a properly functioning gene into a patient's bone marrow cells in vitro and then reintroducing the cells into the patient's body. In germ line alterations, a specific attempt is made to introduce genetic changes into the germ (reproductive) cells of an individual, with the aim of changing the set of genes passed on to the individual's offspring. The RAC and its working group will not at present entertain proposals for germ line alterations but will consider for approval protocols involving somatic-cell gene therapy.

50 Fed Reg. 33,462, 33,464 (1985). In 1996, the U.S. Congress approved a federal budget with the Dickey-Wicker amendment, which forbids federal funds from being used for research that creates, destroys, or harms human embryos. (Balanced Budget Downpayment Act of 1996, Public L. 104–99 (1996)). In 2015, NIH reaffirmed its policy that it "will not fund any use of gene-editing technologies in human embryos." National Institutes of Health, The NIH Director, Statement on NIH funding of research using gene-editing technologies in human embryos (2015); www.nih.gov/about/director/04292015_statement_gene_editing_technologies.htm. In 2016, Congress included language prohibiting the NIH or FDA's use of funds "in research in which a human embryo is intentionally created or modified to include a heritable genetic modification." Consolidated Appropriations Act, 2016, Public Law 114–113 (2015).

One technique to treat a form of infertility has raised objections because of its resemblance to germline gene therapy. The technique, ooplasmic transfer, treats a type of female infertility in which embryos do not properly grow and develop in the womb because of deficiencies, often related to age, in the portion of the egg, called the cytoplasm, that surrounds the nucleus. To correct the deficiencies, doctors remove the nucleus and insert it into an egg from another woman that has had its nucleus removed, leaving only the other woman's healthier cytoplasm. Using standard IVF techniques, the egg then is fertilized in the laboratory and implanted. Researchers using this approach reported the first successful birth in 1997.

Although most of a person's genetic material is found in the cell nucleus, a very small amount is contained in organelles or structures in the cytoplasm called mitochondria, which produce energy. Therefore, when an infertile woman's nucleus is implanted in the cytoplasm from another woman's donor egg, the resulting egg contains not only the mother's nuclear genetic material, but the donor's mitochondrial DNA, and as the fertilized egg divides, this mitochondrial DNA will be incorporated in the cells of the resulting child, including its reproductive cells, and passed on to its children. In short, a germline modification has been introduced, as confirmed by researchers in New Jersey who examined the resulting mitochondrial DNA in two children born as the result of ooplasmic transfer.

Given the RAC's de facto ban on germline alterations as reflected in its 1985 revised Points to Consider, how could any of these ooplasmic transfers have been lawfully conducted in the United States? In an editorial in Science, Eric Juengst and Erik Parens gave the following answer:

> First, their intervention did not use recombinant DNA (rDNA). When RAC's guidelines, which apply only to interventions using rDNA, were articulated in the late 1980's, no one was thinking about transplanting ooplasm to treat a form of infertility. Insofar as the ooplasmic transfer technique does not involve rDNA, it falls outside of RAC's purview. However, as a recent American Association for the Advancement of Science (AAAS) report suggested, RAC's purview is unduly restricted to a consideration of techniques that now are more than two decades old. The AAAS working group (of which we were a part) argued that if new techniques raise the same ethical concerns as those raised by "traditional" germline gene transfer techniques, then either RAC's purview should be expanded to encompass them, or a new, RAC-like body should be created to oversee them. The working group argued that even though some inheritable genetic modifications (IGMs) might not involve rDNA, might not alter single genes, and might not alter nuclear DNA (nDNA), they should be subject to the same public scrutiny if they raise the same ethical questions as the traditional germline interventions. Examples of IGMs in the report included the introduction of artificial chromosomes, the use of oligonucleotides to repair genes in situ—and the transfer of mtDNA [mitochondrial DNA].

> Second, federal funds did not support this ooplasmic transfer experiment. RAC guidelines are binding only on those who receive federal funds. If, however, their protocol had aimed at achieving traditional germline interventions, they probably would have felt compelled to approach RAC, as do other privately funded researchers whose work raises novel issues. Given their recognition that they were engaged in "germline modification," it is unfortunate—though perfectly legitimate—that they did not bring their protocol before RAC.

Third, gene transfer was an inadvertent effect of their intervention. Since the creation of the RAC guidelines, however, researchers have had to demonstrate that the chances of inadvertent germline gene transfer are miniscule. When an in utero gene transfer pre-protocol was recently put before RAC, the idea was rejected largely because the chances of inadvertent germline effects were too great. If the ooplasmic transplantation protocol had been within RAC's official purview, it probably would not have received RAC's blessing. We will never know.

Erik Parens & Eric Juengst, Inadvertently Crossing the Germ Line, 292 Science 397 (2001). Note that at least some attempts at ooplasmic transfer were being made before the RAC's authority to review gene transfer protocols was ceded to the FDA.

In June 2001, the FDA sent a letter to six fertility clinics warning them that ooplasmic transfer was a clinical experiment for which an approved Investigational New Drug application was required.

In March and early April, 2015, separate groups of scientists published commentaries calling for voluntary moratoria on human germ line engineering. Edward Lanphier et al., Don't Edit the Human Germ Line, 519 Nature 410–411 (2015); David Baltimore et al., A Prudent Path forward for Genomic Engineering and Germline Gene Modification, 348 Science 36–38 (2015). The commentaries were inspired by the recent development of highly-effective techniques for editing DNA, including CRISPR-Cas9, zinc fingers, and TALENS.

Then, on April 18, 2015, a paper was published online in an open-access journal by a group of Chinese researchers reporting that they had attempted to correct a mutation that causes serious blood diseases in human embryos. P. Liang, et al., CRISPR/Cas9-mediated gene editing in human tripronuclear zygotes, 6 Protein Cell 363–372 (2015). The embryos had an abnormality that prevented them from being viable. The news led to world-wide calls for a prohibition on germline gene editing, although a committee of the National Academies of Sciences, Engineering, and Medicine was more equivocal:

> Given both the technical and societal concerns, the committee concludes there is a need for caution in any move toward germline editing, but that caution does not mean prohibition. It recommends that germline editing research trials might be permitted, but only after much more research to meet appropriate risk/benefit standards for authorizing clinical trials. Even then, germline editing should only be permitted for compelling reasons and under strict oversight. In the United States, authorities are currently unable to consider proposals for this research due to an ongoing prohibition on use of federal funds by FDA to review

"research in which a human embryo is intentionally created or modified to include a heritable genetic modification." The committee defined a set of criteria under which heritable germline editing could be permitted if U.S. restrictions are allowed to expire, or if countries without legal prohibitions were to proceed with this line of research.

The criteria includes:

- absence of reasonable alternatives;

- restriction to preventing a serious disease or condition;

- restriction to editing genes that have been convincingly demonstrated to cause or strongly predispose to that disease or condition;

- restriction to converting such genes to versions that are prevalent in the population and are known to be associated with ordinary health with little or no evidence of adverse effects;

- availability of credible pre-clinical and/or clinical data on risks and potential health benefits the procedures;

- during the trial, ongoing, rigorous oversight of the effects of the procedure on the health and safety of the research participants;

- comprehensive plans for long-term multigenerational follow-up that still respect personal autonomy;

- maximum transparency consistent with patient privacy;

- continued reassessment of both health and societal benefits and risks, with broad, ongoing participation and input from the public; and

- reliable oversight mechanisms to prevent extension to uses other than preventing a serious disease or condition.

National Academies of Sciences and National Academy of Medicine, Human Genome Editing: Science, Ethics, and Governance, Highlights (https://www.nap.edu/resource/24623/Human-Genome-Editing-highlights. pdf). An interesting question that the report did not address is who should decide whether a condition or disease is serious enough to justify germline gene editing and whether there are reasonable alternatives. Government officials? IRBs? Physicians and geneticists? Parents?

On November 26, 2018, another Chinese researcher named He Jiankui claimed to have altered the genomes of twin baby girls to make them resistant to HIV. The announcement prompted an international outcry. In March, 2019, the World Health Organization called for a global registry of all human gene editing experiments and stated that germline gene editing at that time was "irresponsible." An investigation by Chinese officials found that He had violated Chinese regulations, he was fired from his academic position, and he disappeared from public view under apparent house arrest. He also was accused of failing to properly obtain the parents' informed consent. See Preetika Rana, How a Chinese Scientist Broke the Rules to Create the First Gene-Edited Babies, Wall St. J., May 10, 2019 (https://www.wsj.com/articles/how-a-chinese-scientist-broke-the-rules-to-create-the-first-gene-edited-babies-11557506697). For a list of statements by organizational and expert bodies on germline gene editing, see Christopher Gyngell, Hilaru Bowman-Smart, and Julian Savulescu, Moral Reasons to Edit the Human Genome: Picking Up from the Nuffied Report, J. Med. Ethics, Published Online First: 24 January 2019. doi: 10.1136/medethics-2018-105084, p. 2.

In July 2018, the British Nuffield Council on Bioethics released a report on germline gene editing, which can be found at 2018 http://nuffield bioethics.org/project/genome-editing-human-reproduction. The following excerpt is from a response to that report:

CHRISTOPHER GYNGELL, HILARU BOWMAN-SMART, AND JULIAN SAVULESCU, MORAL REASONS TO EDIT THE HUMAN GENOME: PICKING UP FROM THE NUFFIELD REPORT

J. Med. Ethics, Published Online First: 24 January 2019.
doi: 10.1136/medethics-2018-105084.

. . .

[T]he central conclusion of the Nuffield report on HGE was that there are no categorical limits on its use, provided applications are consistent with its guiding principles and preceded with broad public debate. We believe much stronger conclusions regarding the ethics of HGE can be drawn.

Technologies like HGE cannot be good or bad absolutely. We can speak of whether a particular *application* of a technology is good or bad, or whether their availability has good or bad effects on society—but technologies themselves are not the type of object to which the property of 'good' or 'bad' attaches.

The most basic ethical questions regarding HGE is therefore whether particular applications of it are good, bad, permissible, desirable, etc. In this section, we will examine some possible applications of HGE and show that rather than being merely morally permissible, some applications will be moral imperatives.

Single gene disorders

A mark of success of medical genetics has been the diagnosis of the disease phenylketonuria (PKU) at birth. This is an inherited metabolic disorder in which levels of the enzyme phenylalanine hydroxylase are lowered. This means individuals cannot metabolise the amino acid phenylalanine. In 1962, a test was devised that allowed PKU to be diagnosed through a blood test. The 'heel prick test' is now routinely given to infants as part of newborn screening. Those children who are identified as suffering from PKU are put on a low phenylalanine diet or else they will develop severe intellectual disability. This diet means no bread, pasta, soybeans, egg whites, meat, legumes, nuts, watercress and fish. Such an environmental intervention is demanding. There is always a risk that foods containing phenylalanine will be consumed by mistake. The ubiquitous sweetener, aspartame, can cause a crisis.

Imagine an artificial enzyme was developed to replace phenylalanine. If this was administered regularly it would allow sufferers of PKU to consume a normal diet. Such a cure would be hailed as a breakthrough. There would be a moral imperative to provide this cure, just as there is an imperative to provide blood transfusion for severe bleeding, and antibiotics for infection.

Now imagine that instead of getting a pharmaceutical company to manufacture the enzyme, we could get the body to manufacture it. By altering the DNA of someone with PKU, we could get a patient's own cells to produce the missing enzyme, phenylalanine hydroxylase. There are many advantages to not relying on pharmaceutical companies. Production inside the body allows for a more targeted response and more accurate dosages. Furthermore, it removes all chance that a patient would be unable to access the treatment, such as when the company has supply chain problems.

Just as there would be a moral imperative to provide a replacement enzyme therapy for PKU, there would be an imperative to make safe genome edits which prevent PKU. If it becomes possible for carriers of the PKU mutation to prevent PKU in their future children through HGE, they will have an obligation to use this technology, in the same way they would have an obligation to use an enzyme replacement therapy.

Preimplantation genetic testing and HGE

The Nuffield report notes that in all but 'extremely rare' (p.44) cases, monogenic diseases like PKU can already be prevented through IVF in combination with preimplantation genetic testing (PGT), with the proviso that 'it might not be reasonable to expect sufficient viable embryos with the characteristics sought to be available' (p. 46). Let us try to put some numbers around the cases in which HGE would provide benefits over PGT in preventing single gene disorders due to a lack of viable embryos. In 2013 (the last year for which data are available), 18% of IVF cycles conducted in the UK produced only one viable embryo. So, for every 100 couples who go through IVF with the intention of using PGT to avoid disease, approximately 18 will produce a single viable embryo. In 2016 (the last year for which there is data), there were roughly 700 cycles of PGT for genetic disease in the UK. So, every year in the UK, around 126 IVF cycles are conducted for PGT and only produce one viable embryo. In these cases, it will not be possible to use genetic selection to avoid diseases. As people choose to attempt to conceive children later and later in life, in part for educational and career reasons, there will be a greater and greater scarcity of embryos.

The most common scenario in which couples use PGT is when they are both are carriers for recessive conditions. In these cases, there is a 25% chance that an embryo will carry both copies of the disease-predisposing mutation. This would imply that there are 31 cases in the UK per year in which HGE could avoid genetic disease in an embryo which PGT cannot. However, this is likely a conservative estimate. When parents are homozygous for dominant conditions like Huntington's disease, or cases where there are multiple undesirable independently sorting variants, the number of affected embryos will be closer to 50%. One IVF company is on record as estimate that 48% of embryos which undergo PGT are affected by a genetic condition, although this will vary clinic to clinic.

Extrapolating from the above numbers would imply that, worldwide, there are several hundred cases a year where HGE would be the only option to produce unaffected offspring.

While several hundred cases a year can be considered rare, it is not negligible. If a public health measure could reduce the incidence of serious disease by several hundred a year, then we would have strong reasons to implement it. It would not merely be 'morally permissible' to take such a measure, but something that we actively ought to do. Of course, in situations of limited resources we have reasons to prefer interventions that maximise benefit, but this does not negate the moral reasons we have to benefit the few.

In sum, the application of HGE to prevent of single gene disorders is a good application of technology, and something we have moral reasons to pursue. If it were possible to use HGE to prevent single gene disorders, there would be a moral imperative to use it for this purpose. Of course, given this application alone may not benefit a large number of people, it may not justify using limited health resources developing HGE which could be spent on more effective health measures. But HGE also has potential to prevent far more common causes of disease, as we will explain in the next section.

Polygenic diseases

Most diseases are not the result of just a few genetic changes. They are the result of many, sometimes hundreds, of genes combining together with environmental effects. Such polygenic diseases are among the world's biggest killers. Cardiovascular disease is emerging as the biggest cause of death in the low-income and middle-income world. Together deaths from chronic diseases in those under 70 years are responsible for approximately 30% of all deaths worldwide. In addition to causing pain and death to individuals, chronic diseases place a huge burden on national health systems, consuming resources that could be used elsewhere. One study found that the healthcare cost associated with treating cardiovascular disease totalled €104 billion annually, for countries within the European Union.

We know that there are genetic contributions to chronic diseases. Genome-wide association studies have identified at least 44 genes involved in diabetes; 35 genes involved in coronary artery disease and over 300 genes involved in common cancers.

It is possible to differentiate between individuals based on their genetic risk of developing chronic diseases. Using next-generation sequencing technologies (like whole genome or whole exome sequencing), polymorphisms occurring across many genes can be tallied and weighted giving an individual a 'polygenic risk score' that reflects their genetic predispositions to develop particular diseases and traits. Individuals can then be stratified into different risk categories (such as high risk, medium risk and low risk) based on their polygenic risk score.

As genome editing technologies can target many genes at one time, it may become possible to use them to alter an individual's polygenic risk score at the embryonic stage, and shift individuals from a high-risk category to a low-risk category.

Alternatively, it will be possible for individuals who know they have a high polygenic risk to particular diseases to use HGE to alter their gametes to ensure they do not pass this high risk on to their children.

For example, by editing around 27 mutations associated with coronary heart disease, it would be possible to reduce an individual's lifetime risk by 42%; by editing 12 genetic variants one's lifetime risk of bladder cancer could be reduced by almost 75%.

This application cannot be achieved through current methods of genetic selection. Say a couple want to use PGT to select for 15 different genes in an embryo, to reduce their likelihood of cardiovascular disease. Then they would need to create thousands of embryos to make it sufficiently likely that one will have the right combination at all 15 loci.

The chance of the couple having such an embryo would be <1% with traditional IVF and PGD.

Given the massive disease burden caused by chronic diseases, we have strong moral reasons to develop technologies that reduce their incidence— whether these operate through genetic or environmental mechanisms. Imagine scientists develop a new technology which potentially could be incorporated into exhaust filters, and would drastically reduce the amount of air pollution cars emit. In cities where cars are fitted with the exhaust filter, the incidence of respiratory disease would be decreased by 40%.

There are clearly strong moral reasons to develop this technology and pursue its applications. Developing the exhaust filter is not merely something it would be permissible to do, but something that there is an imperative to do. The very same reasons apply to the development of HGE.

One might respond that the clear difference between this case and HGE, is that HGE makes heritable changes and will thus affect future generations. However, air pollution is a known epigenetic modifier, that is, it makes changes to gene expression which can be inherited by future generations. Hence, reducing air pollution could also affect future generations. Of course, we need to consider what the long-term effects of any changes will be. But if the likely effect of a genetic change in one generation is to reduce risk of disease in future generations, this seems only to strengthen the case in favour of those changes.

If HGE could make genetic changes which reduce risks of polygenic disease in current and future generations, there would be an imperative to use it. Obviously, this application is a long way away from being plausible, possibly decades. One major difficulty is that we do not understand polygenic scores well enough to accurately predict the effects of large-scale changes. Still, we have moral reasons to develop HGE with the intention of using them for this purpose. First, it will reduce rates of premature death and disability due to chronic disease. Second, the use of HGE to make the highest risk individuals the same as the lowest risk individuals will be equality-promoting. Third, using HGE to lower the incidence of chronic disease will also promote justice. As stated above, health systems spend billions in resources to treat and prevent chronic disease. Using HGE in germline cells will probably be a relatively cheap way (in the proximity of US$20 000) of reducing someone's susceptibility to chronic diseases. In a world of limited resources, taking a more expensive therapy has the opportunity cost of preventing the treatment of someone else's disease. Justice requires we choose the most cost-effective option, other things being equal. If we do not invest in the most cost-effective option, we harm others who could use these resources.

Enhancement

Just as polygenic scores could in theory be used to reduce rates of complex disease, they can target complex traits like intelligence.

General intelligence—the ability to learn, reason and solve problems—is the best known predictor of education and occupational outcomes.

For decades, it has been known that around 50% of the observed variation in intelligence is due to genetic factors. A number of recent large studies have identified many polymorphisms, which help explain 20% of the heritable variation in intelligence.

As with complex disease, using the polygenic scores it is possible to stratify the population into three board groups 'high predisposition to high intelligence'; 'medium predisposition to high intelligence' and 'low predisposition to high intelligence'. It will become theoretically possible to use HGE to shift individuals from the low or medium predisposition groups, into the high predisposition group.

Enhancing based on intelligence using polygenic scores would, in the words of the Nuffield report, be a form of enhancement that uses only 'wild-type' variants (variants that already exist in the species) rather than a form of enhancing that goes beyond what currently exists in the species. In other words, it is a form of 'normal range human enhancement'. While it may be possible in the future to enhance intelligence beyond levels that are currently observed in the species—such forms of enhancement are much less feasible at present.

Imagine a prenatal nutritional programme was developed, which was predicted to increase intelligence in children born with low innate predisposition to high intelligence. This would be seen as a breakthrough. We may soon be able to achieve the same with HGE.

One of the most intuitive concerns about technologies like germline engineering is the effect on equality. It is feared that germline engineering would only be available to the rich, and that it could widen the gap between rich and poor, adding biological advantages to already existing social ones. This is an important and complex issue, faced not just by genome editing but other goods like education. Ethically, we must take steps to ensure that the benefits and costs of HGE are evenly or fairly shared. As recognised by the Nuffield Council, this is not a reason to ban the technology, or fail to develop it, but a reason to ensure it is developed responsibly.

However, it is also possible to use HGE to directly improve equality, as the intelligence example shows. Nature is a biological lottery which has no mind to fairness. Some are born gifted and talented, others with short painful lives or severe disabilities. Currently, diet, education, special services and other social interventions are used to correct natural inequality. It may be that targeting combinations of genes is an effective means of promoting equality in education. For example, there are natural variations in people's innate ability to learn how to read. This often matters little for people in higher socioeconomic groups, who can afford to spend extra time with their children teaching them how to read, or employ tutors, etc. However, for those in lower socioeconomic groups, this predisposition can leave them illiterate for life. While other measures could in theory no doubt remedy this inequity of outcomes, evening out the genetic starting point could prove the most effective way. This method would have the additional benefit of being passed to future generations. Genome editing could be used as a part of public healthcare for egalitarian reasons.

Boosting intelligence and other cognitive traits through HGE will be an 'enhancement', rather than disease prevention. As noted by the Nuffield report, this does not by itself reduce the moral reasons we have to pursue it. We have a moral imperative to use all reasonable means to produce equality in education.

Future generations and intergenerational justice

One of the key interests considered by the Nuffield Council report is that of future generations. It is crucial that the very long-term consequences of developing or failing to develop HGE be considered. Humans often exhibit a cognitive bias towards the near future and neglect then how our actions may affect the very far future. This can distort our appraisal of technologies.

The obligations we have to future generations are often described in terms of intergenerational justice. We owe future generations the same considerations that we owe our contemporaries. We should not unnecessarily deplete the ozone layer, for example, if this will greatly harm future persons at an only small benefit to ourselves.

Some worry that by engaging in HGE we risk harming future generations by negatively altering our genome. There is no doubt that some application of HGE could harm future generations (e.g., see discussion of collective action problems in Section 3); however, such applications are not the inevitable consequences of the development of HGE, and can be mitigated or avoided.

Moreover, a deep engagement with the interests of future generations will show why there is strong moral imperative to develop HGE as a matter of intergenerational justice.

Modern medicine is removing selection pressures that humans have historically been subjected to. This is increasing the rate of random mutations accumulating in the genome and poses a risk to future generations, as made clear by Michael Lynch in a 2016 article in the journal *Genetics*:

What is exceptional about humans is the recent detachment from the challenges of the natural environment and the ability to modify phenotypic traits in ways that mitigate the fitness effects of mutations, for example, precision and personalized medicine. This results in a relaxation of selection against mildly deleterious mutations, including those magnifying the mutation rate itself. The long-term consequence of such effects is an expected genetic deterioration in the baseline human condition, potentially measurable on the timescale of a few generations in westernized societies.

As we develop effective and accessible treatments for disease, we all but guarantee that the incidence of those diseases will increase in future generations. This is because mutations which arise that contribute to those diseases are no longer selected against.

For example, short sightedness (myopia) has been historically very rare because it was selected against in hunter-gatherer societies. Modern technologies such as glasses, contact lenses and Lasik eye surgery help correct such vision problems. In modern societies, those with naturally poor eyesight have the same fitness as those who have naturally good eyesight. This allows deleterious mutations to occur in the genes which influence vision and not be selected against. Rates of myopia are now over 50% in many countries, making populations increasingly reliant on technology for this basic biological function. It is likely that reduced selection against poor vision has caused some of this increase. While it is easy to correct for myopia, the same process will allow mutations to accumulate in genes which influence other biological functions.

The percentage of people who require blood pressure medication, assisted reproductive technologies and have genetic predispositions to deafness, are all increasing. While social changes play a major role in these changes (eg, poor diet and sedentary lifestyle, delayed childbearing), biological factors also play an important part. In future generations, nearly all people may be reliant on technologies for these basic functions, as well as many others.

This will be bad for individuals, who become increasingly dependent on technologies for basic functions, and need to spend much of their time and money acquiring a range of therapeutic goods. Similarly, society will become burdened with spiralling healthcare costs. Furthermore, the consequence of natural disasters will become much more severe if people are reliant on a variety of complex technologies whose supply can be disrupted.

Fortunately, there is a way for our descendants to avoid such a medicalised future. Using HGE, we could edit out disease-causing mutations as they arise in our genome. This will allow our descendants to enjoy the same level of genetic health as we enjoy today.

Of course, many diseases have a lifestyle element—we have mentioned cardiovascular disease and infertility. Many resist using biological interventions to treat lifestyle problems. For example, it seems absurd to genetically modify human beings to be able to tolerate a diet consisting solely of foods with low nutritional value.

However, as we have argued, there are biological components to many contemporary diseases that are worthy of modification. Moreover, even if such diseases were entirely lifestyle or social in origin, which intervention we ought to choose—modifying the biological, psychological, social or natural environment—depends on the costs and benefits of the particular intervention, and relevant moral values. For example, it may be possible to prevent skin cancer by avoiding exposure to the sun, or by increasing the production of melanin, or by increasing the capacity of our immune cells to attack skin cancers. Which we should choose depends on the context.

A common assumption in environmental ethics is that we have obligations to members of future generations. According to one principle of intergenerational justice, 'existing generations ought not act so as to worsen the position of future generations by depleting non-renewable resources with no compensatory action or recompense'.

It is clear that the use of modern medicine is worsening the position of members of future generation, by allowing random mutations to occur to our genome. Fortunately, there is a straightforward compensatory action—developing HGE. This is not something that is merely permissible—but a moral imperative.

Governance and public attitudes

Ultimately, it is up to the public to make decisions about the ways genome editing can be applied. This is a guiding principle of liberal democracies. As noted by the Nuffield Council (p. 162), before any changes are made to the laws governing HGE, broad and inclusive public debate is necessary.

We endorse this view, but wish to add that public debates surrounding HGE need to be supplemented by public education initiatives. Making truly informed decisions about complex scientific matters requires people to understand science. A recent study by the Pew Study showed that 86% of Americans with high scientific knowledge approved of the use of HGE to prevent diseases that would be apparent at birth. This drops to 56% of people with low knowledge of science. Such research shows how familiarity with a subject matter shapes one's view of it.

The Pew Research also shows a great divide between people who think HGE is permissible to prevent disease (72% for disease present at birth;

60% for later onset diseases) and those that think it is permissible for enhancement (18%). This is interesting because as noted by the Nuffield Council, there seems not to be essential reasons as to why the use of HGE to prevent disease is different than its use for human enhancement. What is important is that any use be consistent with promoting individual welfare, and does not negatively impact society.

Just as is the case with science, for people to make truly informed decision on *ethical* matters, ethical education is required. People should learn about concepts such as justice, freedom and well-being from an earlier age, and learn how to think critically about such topics. Only then can we truly make informed decisions about technologies like HGE.

Conclusion

Genome editing technologies are developing rapidly, and so too is our understanding of their moral implications. The consensus of various expert bodies on the ethical implications of genome editing has shifted in response to greater engagement with the underlying philosophical issues. This has been exemplified by the recent Nuffield Council report, 'genome editing and human reproduction'. Rather than drawing arbitrary lines between different possible uses of HGE, the Nuffield Council report engages with the fundamental ethical principles that should guide our appraisal of genome editing—concerns for individuals, for society as a whole and for future generations.

Nonetheless, we think deep engagement with underlying ethical issues of HGE yields much stronger conclusions than those drawn by the Nuffield Council. It will be 'morally permissible' to engage in HGE and will be morally 'required' in some instances.

The human genome was created by a blind process of mutation and selection occurring over thousands of generations. This process had no foresight for the creatures it would produce. This has resulted in vast natural inequality. The most extreme examples are single gene disorders, where some people become destined to a short life with much pain due to random quirks in their DNA. Others are born with high risks of chronic disease like heart disease and cancer. We ought to use powerful technologies like HGE to correct these inequalities and promote human flourishing. Such actions are moral imperatives.

GENETICALLY MODIFIED HUMANS? SEVEN REASONS TO SAY "NO"

Center for Genetics and Society, May 7, 2015.

1. Profound health risks to future children. Altering the genomes of our offspring—not just the first generation but all later ones as well—means irreversibly changing every cell in their bodies, forever. The risks of

such biologically extreme experimentation would be huge, from the early stages of embryonic development through the life span. Even with the latest gene-editing tools, "off-target effects" are an unsolved problem, and even if genes can be added or deleted in the right place, we can't predict what those added or deleted genes might do in the cell or the organism.

2.   Thin medical justification. Human germline modification is often presented as a way to prevent the transmission of inherited diseases. But in nearly every case, people at risk of passing on genetic diseases can have healthy and genetically related children without manipulating genes by using the embryo screening technique known as preimplantation genetic diagnosis or PGD. (Prenatal screening, adoption, and third party gametes are frequently used additional options.)

3.   Treating human beings like engineered products. Who has the right to decide the biological future of another human being? Who can ethically undertake non-consensual experimentation on someone else's body? It's one thing for parents to offer their kids opportunities like music lessons or extra coaching; it's quite another to force them into a pre-determined biological mold. We must preserve the human right to bodily integrity and an open future.

4.   Violating the common heritage of humanity. Our shared humanity is the starting point for every struggle for equality. What happens to the movements for racial, gender, sexuality, and disability justice if we lose our shared evolutionary origin? What happens if traits viewed as socially undesirable are merely problems to be solved in a system that makes "fitting the mold" a biological possibility? UNESCO's *Universal Declaration on the Human Genome and Human Rights*, unanimously passed by 77 national delegations, declares that the "human genome underlies the fundamental unity of all members of the human family, as well as the recognition of their inherent dignity and diversity."

5.   Undermining the widespread policy agreements among dozens of democratic nations. More than 40 countries and several international bodies including the Council of Europe prohibit genetic alterations that extend to future generations. In the United States, the National Institutes of Health and the Food and Drug Administration have made it clear that they will not fund or permit human germline modification to the extent of their authority. But the U.S. is the only country with a robust biomedical sector that has not established a legal prohibition on creating genetically modified humans that would be binding on privately funded scientists and fertility clinics.

6.   Eroding public trust in responsible science. Scientists working on gene therapy and regenerative medicine are rightly worried that attempts to change the genetic inheritance of our species will provoke a backlash against important scientific efforts to treat disease in people who are

suffering today. We can and should encourage beneficial applications of genetic technologies, and condemn pernicious ones.

7.   Reinforcing inequality, discrimination and conflict in the world. In the twentieth century, efforts to improve human genetic traits were known as eugenics. While twenty-first century efforts to directly modify the human germline would likely play out differently, the determination of "bad" genes that need to be replaced and "good" genes to be introduced would reflect criteria set by the economically and socially privileged. The social and commercial dynamics in which human germline modification would necessarily develop could easily exacerbate global disparities, and take structural inequality to a whole new (molecular) level.

It doesn't have to be this way. But three things must be done. First, the United States should establish an explicit prohibition on creating genetically modified humans. Second, the United States should join other countries in an international treaty that prohibits the creation of genetically modified humans. And third, civil society organizations, scientific and medical groups, and others should work to deepen public understanding of the differences between socially dangerous uses of powerful human genetic technologies and applications that can contribute to human flourishing and the common good.

NOTES AND QUESTIONS

The debate over germline gene editing raises a number of thorny questions about the relative roles of the state, clinicians, and parents in making decisions about offspring. For a discussion of the ethical, legal, and social implications, see Maxwell J. Mehlman, Transhumanist Dreams and Dystopian Nightmares: The Promise and Peril of Genetic Engineering (2012).

> **Food for Thought:** How much control do parents now exert over the futures of their offspring? From a social policy perspective, how different is it when they do so using gene editing?

If human germline experiments proceed, it is likely to be deemed necessary to monitor long-term effects on descendants. How will descendants be identified and tracked? What are the risks to them? What if they refuse to participate? See Bryan Cwik, Designing Ethical Trials of Germline Gene Editing, 377 N. Eng. J. Med. 1911–1913 (2017).

CHAPTER 14

PHARMACOGENOMICS

■ ■ ■

Pharmacogenomics refers to how an individual's DNA affects their response to drugs. The field previously was called "pharmacogenetics," and some continue to make a distinction that "pharmacogenetics" refers to how individuals differ in the way they respond to medicines due to their genes, while "pharmacogenomics" considers the effects of all components of an individual's DNA, not just the genes. As the NIH explains:

> Many drugs that are currently available are "one size fits all," but they don't work the same way for everyone. It can be difficult to predict who will benefit from a medication, who will not respond at all, and who will experience negative side effects (called adverse drug reactions). Adverse drug reactions are a significant cause of hospitalizations and deaths in the United States. With the knowledge gained from the Human Genome Project, researchers are learning how inherited differences in genes affect the body's response to medications. These genetic differences will be used to predict whether a medication will be effective for a particular person and to help prevent adverse drug reactions.

NIH National Library of Medicine, What is Pharmacogenomics? https://ghr.nlm.nih.gov/primer/genomicresearch/pharmacogenomics.

FOOD AND DRUG ADMINISTRATION, GUIDANCE FOR INDUSTRY: PHARMACOGENOMIC DATA SUBMISSIONS
(2005).

Background

The promise of pharmacogenomics lies in its potential to help identify sources of inter-individual variability in drug response (both effectiveness and toxicity); this information will make it possible to individualize therapy with the intent of maximizing effectiveness and minimizing risk. However, the field of pharmacogenomics is currently in early developmental stages, and such promise has not yet been realized. The Agency has heard that pharmaceutical sponsors have been reluctant to embark on programs of pharmacogenomic testing during FDA-regulated phases of drug development because of uncertainties in how the data will be used by FDA in the drug application review process. This guidance is intended to help clarify FDA policy in this area.

Sponsors submitting or holding INDs [Investigational New Drug applications], NDAs [New Drug Applications], or BLAs [Biologics License Applications] are subject to FDA requirements for submitting to the Agency data relevant to drug safety and effectiveness (including 21 CFR 312.22, 312.23, 312.31, 312.33, 314.50, 314.81, 601.2, and 601.12). Because these regulations were developed before the advent of widespread animal or human genetic or gene expression testing, they do not specifically address when such data must be submitted. The FDA has received numerous inquiries about what these regulations require of sponsors who are conducting such testing.

From a public policy perspective, a number of factors should be considered when interpreting how these regulations apply to the developing field of pharmacogenomics. Because the field of pharmacogenomics is rapidly evolving, in many circumstances, the experimental results may not be well enough established scientifically to be suitable for regulatory decision making. For example:

- Laboratory techniques and test procedures may not be well validated. In addition, test systems may vary so that results may not be consistent or generalizable across different platforms. A move to standardize assays is underway, and much more information should be available within the next several years.

- The scientific framework for interpreting the physiologic, toxicologic, pharmacologic, or clinical significance of certain experimental results may not yet be well understood.

- The findings from a specific study often cannot be extrapolated across species or to different study populations (e.g., various human subpopulations with different genetic backgrounds).

- The standards for transmission, processing, and storage of the large amounts of highly dimensional data generated from microarray technology have neither been well defined nor widely tested.

Despite these concerns, some pharmacogenetic tests—primarily those related to drug metabolism—have well-accepted mechanistic and clinical significance and are currently being integrated into drug development decision making and clinical practice.

It is important for FDA to have a role in the evaluation of pharmacogenomic tests, both to ensure that evolving FDA policies are based on the best science and to provide public confidence in the field. The

FDA developed this guidance to facilitate the use of pharmacogenomic tests during drug development and encourage open and public sharing of data and information on pharmacogenomic test results.

To this end, the Agency has undertaken a process for obtaining input from the scientific community and the public. On May 16 and 17, 2002, the Agency held a workshop, cosponsored by pharmaceutical industry groups, to identify key issues associated with the application of pharmacogenetics and pharmacogenomics to drug development. Subsequently, on April 8, 2003, a public presentation was made to the FDA Science Board. This presentation contained a proposal for developing guidance on the submission of information on pharmacogenomic tests and a potential algorithm for deciding whether submission of such data is voluntary or required. The Science Board endorsed moving forward with both of these proposals. In November 2003, FDA published a draft version of this guidance and received public comment on the draft guidance. The Agency also has developed internal policy related to pharmacogenomics and voluntary submissions.

The policies and processes outlined in this final guidance are intended to take the above factors into account and to assist in advancing the field in a manner that will benefit both drug development programs and the public health.

SUBMISSION POLICY

General Principles

The FDA recognizes that its pharmacogenomic data submission policies must be consistent with the relevant codified regulatory submission requirements for investigational and marketing application submitters and holders. At present, many pharmacogenomic results are not well enough established scientifically to be appropriate for regulatory decision making. This guidance interprets FDA's regulations for investigational and marketing submissions, with the goal of clarifying FDA's current thinking about when the regulations require pharmacogenomic data to be submitted and when the submission of such data would be welcome on a voluntary basis. In some cases, complete reports of pharmacogenomic studies suffice, while in others, an abbreviated report or synopsis should or must be submitted.

Because FDA regulations establish different requirements for investigational applications, unapproved marketing applications, and approved marketing applications, this guidance sets out different submission algorithms for each of these categories. The guidance also clarifies how the Agency currently intends to use such data in regulatory decision making—that is, when the data will be considered sufficiently reliable to serve as the basis for regulatory decision making; when it will be considered only supportive to a decision; and when the data will not be used in regulatory decision making.

This guidance also makes a distinction between pharmacogenomic tests that may be considered either probable or known *valid biomarkers,* which may be appropriate for regulatory decision making, and other less well-developed tests that are either observational or exploratory biomarkers that, alone, are insufficient for making regulatory decisions. Although, currently, most pharmacogenomic measurements are not considered valid biomarkers, certain markers (e.g., for drug metabolism) are well established biomarkers with clear clinical significance. Undoubtedly, the distinction between what tests are appropriate for regulatory decision making and those that are not will change over time as the science evolves. Throughout the development of these tests, as appropriate, FDA will continue to seek public comment as we evaluate whether a biomarker is a *valid biomarker* (e.g., via discussions at Advisory Committee meetings).

For the purposes of this guidance, a pharmacogenomic test result may be considered a *valid biomarker* if (1) it is measured in an analytical test system with well-established performance characteristics and (2) there is an established scientific framework or body of evidence that elucidates the physiologic, pharmacologic, toxicologic, or clinical significance of the test results. For example, the consequences for drug metabolism of genetic variation in the human enzymes CYP2D6 and thiopurine methyltransferase are well understood in the scientific community and are reflected in certain approved drug labels. The results of genetic tests that distinguish allelic variants of these enzymes are considered to be well established and, therefore, valid biomarkers.

This guidance makes an additional distinction between known valid biomarkers that have been accepted in the broad scientific community and probable valid biomarkers that appear to have predictive value for clinical outcomes, but may not yet be widely accepted or independently verified by other investigators or institutions. When a sponsor generates, or possesses, data sufficient to establish a significant association between a pharmacogenomic test result and clinical outcomes, the test result represents a probable valid biomarker. It would be expected that this biomarker would meet criteria (1) and (2) above, and its association with a meaningful outcome would have been demonstrated in more than one experiment.

The algorithms described below for investigational and marketing application holders describe when to submit to FDA data on known valid biomarkers. Data on probable valid biomarkers need not be submitted to the IND unless they are used by a sponsor to make decisions regarding specific animal safety studies or clinical trials (e.g., using biomarker data as inclusion or exclusion criteria, assessment of treatment-related prognosis, or stratifying patients by dose) or are a probable valid biomarker in human safety studies. However, we recommend that sponsors or applicants submit reports on all probable valid biomarkers to new (i.e., unapproved) NDAs or BLAs according to the algorithm in section IV.B.

Many pharmacogenomic testing programs implemented by pharmaceutical sponsors or by scientific organizations are intended to develop the knowledge base necessary to establish the validity of new genomic biomarkers. During such a period of scientific exploration, test results are not useful in making regulatory judgments pertaining to the safety or effectiveness of a drug and are not considered known or probable valid biomarkers. However, scientific development of this sort is highly desirable for advancing the understanding of relationships between genotype or gene expression and responses to drugs and, therefore, should be encouraged and facilitated. For these reasons, although submission of exploratory pharmacogenomic data is not required under the regulations, FDA is encouraging *voluntary submission* of such data, as described below.

Specific Uses of Pharmacogenomic Data in Drug Development and Labeling

As the field of pharmacogenomics advances, it is likely (and desirable) that sponsors will begin to use pharmacogenomic tests to support drug development and/or to guide therapy. Sponsors may choose to submit pharmacogenomic data that have not achieved the status of a valid biomarker to an investigational or marketing application to support scientific contentions related to dosing and dosing schedule, safety, or effectiveness. For example, a sponsor may wish to provide supportive data demonstrating that changes in drug-induced gene expression differ between species that have different toxicologic responses to a drug, thus correlating changes in certain gene expression patterns with a specific toxicity. Or, a pharmacogenomic test result might also be used to stratify patients in a clinical trial or to identify patients at higher risk for an adverse event to correlate test results with clinical outcome.

If a pharmacogenomic test shows promise for enhancing the dose selection, safety, or effectiveness of a drug, a sponsor may wish to fully integrate pharmacogenomic data into the drug development program. This integration could occur in two ways:

    1.   The pharmacogenomic data may be intended to be included in the drug labeling in an informational manner. For example, such data might be used to describe the potential for dose adjustment by drug metabolism genotype (e.g., CYP2D6*5) or to mention the possibility of a side effect of greater severity or frequency in individuals of a certain genotype or gene expression profile. In such cases, the pharmacogenomic test result would be considered a known valid biomarker. However, an FDA-approved

pharmacogenomic test may not be available or required to be available, or a commercial pharmacogenomic test may not be widely available. Given this level of complexity, at the current time, sponsors should consult the relevant FDA review division for advice on how to proceed in a specific case. However, whenever a sponsor intends to include pharmacogenomic data in the drug label, complete information on the test and results must be submitted to the Agency as described under §§ 314.50 and 601.2.

2.   The pharmacogenomic data and resulting test or tests may be intended to be included in the drug labeling to choose a dose and dose schedule, to identify patients at risk, or to identify patient responders. Inclusion of a pharmacogenomic test in the labeling would be contingent upon its performance characteristics. For example:

- Patients will be tested for drug metabolism genotype and dosed according to the test results.

- Patients will be selected as potential responders for an efficacy trial (or deselected because of a high risk) based on genotype (e.g., of either the patient or the patient's tumor) or gene expression profile.

- Patients will be excluded from a clinical trial based on genotype or gene expression profile (e.g., biomarker for risk of an adverse event).

In all of these cases, FDA recommends co-development of the drug and the pharmacogenomic tests, if they are not currently available, and submission of complete information on the test/drug combination to the Agency. The FDA plans to issue further guidance on co-development of pharmacogenomic tests and drugs.

The Office of In Vitro Diagnostics in CDRH, appropriate review divisions in CBER, and the Clinical and Clinical Pharmacology Review divisions in CBER or CDER are willing to meet jointly with sponsors to discuss both scientific and regulatory issues with regard to new pharmacogenomic tests. The CDRH has both formal (IDE) and informal (pre-IDE) processes to evaluate protocols for pharmacogenomic test development.

NOTES AND QUESTIONS

1.   Some findings from pharmacogenomics research are beginning to be commercialized and used clinically. For example, a cytochrome P450 2D6 gene test was approved by the FDA in 2004 to help identify genetic mutations that affect how patients metabolize a number of drugs. Another example is a test for a gene known as TPMT that makes some patients highly sensitive to the

chemotherapy agent used to treat acute lymphoblastic leukemia, the most common form of childhood cancer. The test reportedly can tell if a patient should get only five percent of the standard dosage to avoid serious side effects without significant loss of effectiveness. Another test can reveal if congestive heart failure will be responsive to drug therapy, or if a heart transplant will be necessary.

Warfarin (also known as Coumadin) is the most widely-used oral anticoagulant, used in patients with cardiovascular disease to prevent the formation of blood clots that can cause strokes. The dosage of the drug must be carefully calibrated for each patient to avoid catastrophic side-effects. Traditionally this was done on a risky trial-and-error basis, but pharmacogenomic research demonstrated that people with a variant of the genes CYP2C9 or VKORC1 break down the drug more slowly, which means that it stays in the body longer and causes bleeding. In 2007, the FDA announced that a new label was being prepared for Warfarin, stating under "precautions": "Certain variations in two key genes may increase the need for more frequent monitoring and the use of lower doses." Genetic tests for the two key genes cost $300–$500 and the turnaround time for test results means that initial dosing and titration of Warfarin levels must begin before the results are available. In 2009, the Centers for Medicare and Medicaid Services announced it will not pay for the genetic tests because of a lack of clinical utility. In 2010, the FDA revised the Warfarin label to lower the starting dose from 5 mg per day: "If the patients CYP2C9 and VKORC1 are not known, the initial dose of Coumadin is usually 2–5 mg per day." For an overview of pharmacogenomics, see Kelan Tantisira and Scott T. Weiss, Overview of Pharmacogenomics, UptoDate, May 14, 2019 (https://www.uptodate.com/contents/overview-of-pharmacogenomics).

2.   Not everyone is optimistic that positive developments will occur rapidly. Andrew Pollack in an article in the New York Times describes some of the problems encountered in using pharmacogenetic testing to refine the prescribing of the drugs Herceptin and tamoxifen:

> * * * The hurdles include drug makers, which can be reluctant to develop or encourage tests that may limit the use of their drugs. Insurers may not pay for tests, which can cost up to a few thousand dollars. For makers of the tests, which hope their business becomes one of health care's next big growth industries, a major obstacle is proving that their products are accurate and useful. While drugs must prove themselves in clinical trials before they can be sold, there is no generally recognized process for evaluating genetic tests, many of which can be marketed by laboratories without F.D.A. approval.
>
> Genentech, a developer of cancer drugs, petitioned the F.D.A. this month to regulate such tests. It warned of "safety risks for patients, as more treatment decisions are based in whole or in part on the claims made by such test makers."

A cautionary case is Herceptin, a Genentech breast cancer drug that is considered the archetype of personalized medicine because it works only for women whose tumors have a particular genetic characteristic. But now, 10 years after Herceptin reached the market, scientists are finding that the various tests—some approved by the F.D.A., some not—can be inaccurate.

Moreover, doctors do not always conduct the tests or follow the results. The big insurer UnitedHealthcare found in 2005 that 8 percent of the women getting the drug had tested negative for the required genetic characteristic. An additional 4 percent had not been tested at all, or their test results could not be found.

Tamoxifen, * * * illustrates the promise and current limitations of genetic testing. In 2003, more than 25 years after tamoxifen was introduced, researchers led by Dr. David A. Flockhart at Indiana University School of Medicine figured out that the body converts tamoxifen into another substance called endoxifen. It is endoxifen that actually exerts the cancer-fighting effect. The conversion is done by an enzyme in the body called CYP2D6, or 2D6 for short.

But variations in people's 2D6 genes mean the enzymes have different levels of activity. Up to 7 percent of people, depending on their ethnic group, have an inactive enzyme, Dr. Flockhart said, while another 20 to 40 percent have an only modestly active enzyme.

The implications were "scary," Dr. Flockhart said. Many women were apparently not being protected against cancer's return because they could not convert tamoxifen to endoxifen.

The economic implications could be just as scary to big pharmaceutical companies.

Tamoxifen, now a generic drug, costs as little as $500 for the typical five-year treatment. But most patients in the United States are currently treated with a newer, much more expensive class of drugs, called aromatase inhibitors, that cost about $18,000 over five years. Those drugs—made by AstraZeneca, Novartis and Pfizer—performed better than tamoxifen in clinical trials before the role of 2D6 was generally understood.

If only women with active 2D6 had been assessed, tamoxifen might have worked as well or better than the newer drugs, according to researchers at the Dana-Farber Cancer Institute in Boston.

But proving these suppositions and having them incorporated into medical practice have not been easy.

The F.D.A., in its meeting this month, said clinical trials were the ideal way to validate a test. But many test developers argue that trials would be too costly and time-consuming, so many tests are validated by reanalyzing patient data from old trials.

In the case of tamoxifen, Dr. Matthew P. Goetz of the Mayo Clinic and colleagues went back to an old trial and used stored tumor samples to test the 2D6 genes of each patient. The researchers reported in 2005 that 32 percent of the women with inactive 2D6 enzyme had relapsed or died within two years, in contrast to only 2 percent of the other women.

But while some subsequent studies have backed those conclusions, two had contradictory results. That leaves many experts hesitant to use the test, which costs about $300.

There are other complications. Dozens of variants of the 2D6 gene exist, and laboratories can differ in their interpretation of test results. And it is not always clear how to act upon the information the test provides.

* * *

Such complexities are not confined to tamoxifen testing. The labels of about 200 drugs now contain some information relating genes to drug response, said Lawrence J. Lesko, the F.D.A.'s head of clinical pharmacology. But in many cases, he said, doctors are not told specifically enough what to do with the test results, such as how much to change the dose.

Andrew Pollack, Patient's DNA May Be Signal to Tailor Drugs, The New York Times, Dec. 30, 2008, at A1.

MARK A. ROTHSTEIN & PHYLLIS GRIFFIN EPPS, ETHICAL AND LEGAL IMPLICATIONS OF PHARMACOGENOMICS
2 Nature Reviews Genetics 228 (2001).

Pharmacogenomics is changing the way that drugs are developed, approved, marketed and prescribed. The objective of pharmacogenomics is to define the pharmacological significance of genetic variation among individuals and to use this information in drug discovery, thereby decreasing the number of adverse drug responses that injure and kill thousands each year. By determining which genetic variations are likely to affect a person's ability to metabolize a drug, drug manufacturers intend to develop more predictable and effective therapeutic agents. Towards this end, pharmaceutical companies are investing huge amounts of capital in the technologies that will revolutionize both how researchers identify drug targets and the amount of time needed to move a drug through development and approval. Pharmacogenomics promises to streamline the clinical trial phase of drug development. Researchers hope to use knowledge gained from high-throughput screening and other technologies to construct clinical trial groups that are composed of people most likely to benefit from a particular drug. The ability to streamline clinical trials by genotyping will enable researchers to "rescue" drugs that could not be approved under conventional models of research trials. In other words, drugs that were previously rejected after giving unacceptable rates of adverse responses in traditionally constructed trials will yield lower adverse-response rates after testing under the new model, thereby becoming acceptable candidates for approval. Pharmacogenomics will not only produce better drugs but also yield greater efficiency in the allocation of resources in drug development.

Other changes attributable to pharmacogenomics will be less welcome. Notwithstanding the increasingly efficient research and development process, pharmacogenomic-based drugs will be expensive, because of, for example, the need to recoup the cost of investment in new technologies. The ability to develop specialized drugs that are ultimately approved for smaller populations rather than for general use will fragment the market for pharmaceuticals. Will a pharmaceutical manufacturer react to this economic reality in a way that better suits profit margins than health, and is that socially acceptable? The use of groups in clinical trials that are increasingly similar genotypically raises several important ethical issues regarding social inclusion and the adequacy of current regulatory frameworks. Because polymorphisms of pharmacological interest might vary in frequency among different population subgroups, important social issues arise in multi-ethnic countries, such as the United States. Finally, pharmacogenomics will change the standard of care for pharmaceutical companies and health professionals, including physicians and pharmacists.

This article provides an overview of some ethical and social concerns that arise with the integration of pharmacogenomics into the discovery of drugs and the practice of preventive and therapeutic medicine. Specifically, the article addresses issues associated with the design of clinical trials, the relatively higher cost of pharmaceuticals developed using pharmacogenomics, and the allocation of ethical and legal responsibility. The objective is to highlight a few of the questions and challenges that will require further attention in the near future.

A NEW MODEL OF CLINICAL TRIALS

Pharmacogenomics promises to reduce the time and money required to develop a drug. The ability to predict drug efficacy by genotyping participants during the early stages of clinical trials for a drug would enable researchers to recruit for later trials only those patients who, according to their genotype, are likely to benefit from the drug. As a result, clinical trials could become smaller, cheaper and faster to run.

The prospect of clinical trials that are composed of smaller groups with the same polymorphisms at one or more loci of interest poses some risks, however. A group that reflects the diversity of the population yields information on how a drug will behave in a greater number of people. If the clinical trial group is smaller, or is less genotypically diverse, there is a greater risk that some side effects will go undetected. So, the trials will yield a greater quantity and quality of information, but on a smaller segment of the population. Whereas the conventional model yielded information about harmful side effects in a greater proportion of the population, the concentration of individuals pre-selected for a favourable response under the newer model might not produce the same information. Compared with traditionally designed human clinical trials, genotype-specific human clinical studies might be subject to equal or greater limitations in that the relatively short duration of the study, combined with the narrower subject population and smaller size, would hinder the ability of the studies to identify rare or delayed adverse reactions or drug interactions. A drug could reach the market with less information about the side effects or risk of harm from its non-prescribed uses. An unresolved issue is whether the ethical principles of beneficence and non-maleficence (that is, not causing harm to others) would preclude the deliberate inclusion of anyone who is not likely to respond favourably to treatment. With the advent of genotype-specific clinical trials, manufacturers and regulators must be ready to carefully evaluate post-market data by strengthening the existing guidelines for phase IV, or post-approval, clinical trials.

As in other areas of genetic research that involve human subjects, the likely effect of pharmacogenomics on clinical trials raises important questions regarding informed consent, which might include considerations of privacy and confidentiality. Current ideas regarding patient autonomy and informed consent require that patients agree to enter into research on the basis of adequate information regarding the risks and consequences of participation. Genotyping that is appropriate to pharmacogenomic research might not produce information regarding susceptibility to disease or early death, but it might reveal evidence of genetic variation that could lead to individuals being classified as "difficult to treat," "less profitable to treat," or "more expensive to treat." The fear of being so classified could act as a barrier to the recruitment of research participants.

Fear of stigmatization might prove to be a significant barrier to participation in clinical trials among members of population subgroups. Genetic variations of pharmacological significance are known to occur in varying frequency in groups categorized by their ethnicity. For example, different variants of glucose-6-phosphate dehydrogenase (G6PD—an enzyme critical for NADPH (nicotinamide-adenine dinucleotide phosphate reduced) generation in mature red blood cells) are found at a high frequency in African, Mediterranean and Asiatic populations, some of which disrupt the function of the enzyme. A deficiency of G6PD can predispose individuals from these populations to haemolytic anaemia, both in individuals with loss-of-function G6PD mutations and in response to some drugs, such as the malarial drug primaquine. Isoniazid is an anti-tuberculosis drug that is inactivated by acetylation; its impaired metabolism by slow acetylation causes it to accumulate to toxic levels. Variation in the *N*-acetyl transferase 2 (*NAT2*) gene accounts for whether individuals are rapid or slow acetylators of isoniazid, as well as of other therapeutic and carcinogenic compounds. About 50% of individuals in many Caucasian populations are genotypically slow acetylators of isoniazid, but more than 80% of individuals in certain Middle Eastern populations and fewer than 20% in the Japanese population have the slow acetylator phenotype.

The significance of data that imply a role for ethnicity in research has been a source of considerable debate among the research ethics community. One issue is how to advise potential research participants about the possibility of social harms from group-based findings even where the research is conducted without using the names of participants. Another matter of considerable debate in the literature is whether it is necessary or feasible to engage in community consultation when genetic research focuses on socially or politically distinct population subgroups.

COST AS A BARRIER TO ACCESS

Pharmacogenomic drugs will be expensive, cheaper clinical trials notwithstanding. Collectively, the pharmaceutical industry is investing huge amounts of time and money in the development of new technologies that will yield drugs that are more effective than those already available. Without the opportunity to recoup their investment, drug companies will not continue their efforts. At the same time, insurance systems and consumers are struggling to absorb the rising costs of pharmaceutical products.

Pharmacogenomics is based on the idea that pharmaceutical consumers will be better served by drug therapy once they have been subdivided by genotype and matched with the most suitable drug. From the industry perspective, the subdivision of a market into smaller markets is hardly ideal. Incentives for pharmaceutical companies to invest time, effort and resources into the development of drugs to treat limited populations are few compared with the development of drugs to treat more prevalent genotypes in the context of pharmacogenomics. Most drug companies might be expected to direct their resources towards the development of drugs to treat the more prevalent genotypes.

Those groups characterized by less-profitable genotypes are at risk of becoming therapeutic "orphans". At present, pharmaceuticals for rare diseases are termed "orphan drugs." The United States and Japan have enacted legislation to stimulate research and the development of orphan drugs through market mechanisms, such as tax-based cost incentives and time-limited monopolies, with varying degrees of governmental intervention. Canada, Sweden, France, the United Kingdom and other countries rely on broader national drug policies based on more substantial governmental intervention. The European Union has entertained initiatives to stimulate legislative action on orphan drugs, and the European Agency for the Evaluation of Medicinal Products has a provision that exempts drug companies from having to pay application fees to develop a drug if it is an orphan drug. Despite allegations of overpricing of orphan drugs under the American model, nearly all efforts have been followed by a measurable increase in the number of drugs that have been developed and approved for the treatment of rare diseases. As clinical trials increasingly consist of genetically non-diverse groups, policy makers will need to consider whether to expand the concepts underlying orphan drug policies to stimulate research into and the development of drugs for populations who, by virtue of their genetic make-up, face inequities in drug development efforts.

Cost might act as a barrier to access to pharmacogenomics in that the cost of participating in clinical trials or of the resulting drug therapy might be excluded from insurance coverage. Particularly in the United States, where managed care systems attempt to contain costs by rationing medical services, public and private third-party payers have refused or been reluctant to pay for treatments that they deem "experimental" or not "medically necessary." Increasingly, these terms have more political than legal or medical significance. There is some evidence that the insurers' disinclination to cover expenses that are associated with new drug therapies can be countered by high physician or consumer demand for the new drug. If consumers must absorb rising pharmaceutical costs, pharmacogenomics will not introduce new questions so much as it will intensify existing ones about equitable access to medical care.

PROFESSIONAL STANDARDS OF CARE

As pharmacogenomic-based drugs enter into the marketplace, physicians will encounter alternatives to conventional drug therapy and prescription practices. Although the evaluation of genetic variation among patients to determine proper medication and dosage during the course of treatment is not the standard of care at present, ethical concerns, economic considerations and the threat of malpractice liability are likely to encourage physicians to begin testing for and prescribing medications designed for use by specific, smaller groups of individuals. Moral and ethical proscriptions against causing harm might require a physician to integrate pharmacogenetics into clinical practice where necessary to minimize risk to a patient. By contrast, budgetary constraints imposed by insurers could slow the acceptance of drugs developed through pharmacogenomics by limiting their use by physicians and their availability to patients. The issues raised are not unique to pharmacogenomics but do require new applications of ethical principles and legal doctrine.

In countries where the legal systems are based on common law (that is, the English tradition of law-making based on the court decisions of judges), physicians and pharmacists are subject to liability under theories of negligence, which involve the violation of a duty based on a "reasonableness" standard or a standard of reasonable care. The standard of care is defined by how a similarly qualified practitioner would act in treating a patient under the same or similar circumstances. The literature, which includes professional scholarship and guidelines published by professional societies, and clinical experience establish the standard of care. In cases based on negligence in the form of medical malpractice, the standard of care is defined through the testimony of witnesses regarding what constitutes conventional practice within the medical community.

As pharmacogenomic-based drugs increase in prevalence over the next several years, the use of genotyping or genetic testing as a diagnostic tool and the prescription of medications based on genotypic information will become the standard of care for physicians. Physicians and pharmacists might be subject to liability if they lack sufficient knowledge of genetics to adequately interpret diagnostic tests, prescribe appropriate pharmacogenomic-based drug therapy in proper dosages, consider pharmacogenomic-based drug interactions, or properly dispense pharmacogenomic-based prescriptions. With greater knowledge comes greater responsibility. Pharmacogenomics might provide greater information about the likelihood of a drug being effective or causing adverse reactions in persons possessing a particular genetic characteristic, and will certainly yield drugs that are more likely to be suitable for smaller, specific groups of individuals. By increasing the information available for consideration in drug therapy and the importance of matching the right drug to the right person, pharmacogenomics will raise the standard of care applicable to all involved in the safe prescription and distribution of pharmaceuticals.

Pharmacists are primarily charged with the dispensation of prescriptions as administered by physicians, but the scope of their responsibilities has expanded over time to include ensuring that prescriptions and patient directions are correct and appropriate. Pharmacists also have a duty to warn their customers of the potential adverse effects or other problems associated with a prescribed drug therapy. Even if a pharmacist has dispensed a prescription according to a physician's instructions, some jurisdictions have imposed liability on pharmacists for the harm that resulted from a drug that was properly dispensed in accordance with an improper or harmful prescription. As information regarding the genotype of an individual becomes increasingly important to safe prescription and dosage, pharmacists might be charged with greater knowledge of their customers' genetic information than they now require. The increased amount of genetic information in pharmacies raises privacy and confidentiality concerns, especially where pharmacists belong to large pharmacy chains or corporations with widely accessible, centralized records. For physicians and pharmacists, the issue of continuing professional education and record maintenance will become more important, not only for improving competence but also for preventing liability.

Pharmacogenomics is likely to increase the burden shared by the pharmaceutical industry to provide adequate warnings of the limitations and dangers of their products. In the United States, for example, pharmaceutical manufacturers have a duty to warn physicians about any known or knowable risks, or dangers, of the use of a manufactured drug. Many states in the US will impose strict liability on a drug company for harm caused by the failure to adequately warn against the dangerous propensities of a drug that it has manufactured. Unlike negligence theory, the rules of strict liability are not concerned with the standard of care nor the reasonableness of the manufacturer's conduct; and an aggrieved party need only prove that the manufacturer did not adequately warn of a particular risk that was knowable in the light of generally recognized and prevailing best scientific and medical knowledge available at the time of manufacture and distribution. Pharmaceutical companies must consider the potential for liability if patients are harmed because they were excluded from the subgroup for which a pharmacogenomic-based drug is deemed safe and efficacious, particularly if the exclusion leads to a failure to yield information on possible side effects or alternative therapies. Not all adverse side effects are predictable, owing to the number of genes relevant to drug responsiveness, as well as environmental factors. The question is how to allocate responsibility for taking the greatest advantage of drugs specialized to suit relatively smaller segments of the population.

In June 2000, four individuals filed a class action lawsuit against SmithKline Beecham, alleging that the manufacturer of a vaccine for Lyme disease knew that some individuals would be susceptible to arthritis on exposure to the vaccine because of their genotype, but failed to warn about this by labeling. The case is still pending. Similar cases involve malpractice actions by the patient against the prescribing physician, who in turn seeks to recover against the manufacturer for failure to provide adequate information. Put simply, pharmacogenomics will raise the legal stakes for all involved whenever a patient suffers adverse reactions from the use of a drug that might have been contraindicated based on his or her genotype.

CONCLUSION

By lessening the uncertainty associated with the selection of drug targets and the design of human clinical studies in the development of new drugs, pharmacogenomics will result in the production of safer, more effective drugs for use in therapeutic medicine. The integration of pharmacogenomic technology into the drug development process and the practice of medicine will require consideration of ethical, social and legal questions. Answers to these questions might well determine the level of social acceptance and realization of the benefits of pharmacogenomic technology.

NOTES AND QUESTIONS

1.   The prospect of drug variants for small patient populations whose genetic profile makes the variant especially safe and effective raises questions about how safety and efficacy would be determined. To meet FDA requirements, sponsors typically must conduct clinical trials in large numbers of subjects. It may be difficult to enroll enough subjects in studies of drug variants for small populations. Should the FDA relax its safety and efficacy requirements to facilitate pharmacogenetic testing? Should it proceed on a case-by-case basis for specific drugs? What factors should the agency consider in deciding what requirements to impose? Does the new FDA guidance document adequately answer these questions?

2.   The "Learned Intermediary Doctrine" makes health professionals such as physicians and pharmacists rather than the manufacturer responsible for providing safety warnings to patients, but the manufacturer can still be liable if in product labeling it does not make health professionals aware of safety information of which the manufacturer is aware (see, e.g., Schenebeck v. Sterling Drug, Inc., 423 F.2d 919, 923 (8th Cir. 1970)) or if it directs advertising to patients and omits warnings about serious side effects (see Perez v. Wyeth Laboratories, Inc., 734 A.2d 1245 (N.J. 1999)).

Would manufacturers be liable for marketing a drug if the drug harmed a subgroup of patients but was safe for others? See Margaret Gilhooley, When Drugs Are Safe for Some But Not Others: The FDA Experience and Alternatives for Products Liability, 36 Hous. L. Rev. 927 (1999). As Gilhooley notes, the newly-adopted Restatement (Third) of Torts provides that a prescription drug is defective only if it is unsafe "for any class of patients." Restatement (Third) of Torts: Products Liability § 6 (c) (1998), and a comment by the authors of the Restatement explains that "a prescription drug * * * that has usefulness to any class of patients is not defective in design even if it is harmful to other patients." (Comment b).

3.   Note that, as Rothstein and Epps point out, not only manufacturers but physicians, pharmacists, and other health professionals also may be liable if they fail to meet the applicable standard of care in regard to the use of pharmacogenetic information in treating their patients.

4.   In April 2019, the FDA issued a warning letter to Inova Genomics Laboratory for marketing pharmacogenomics tests to physicians without FDA approval.   https://www.fda.gov/news-events/press-announcements/fda-issues-

warning-letter-genomics-lab-illegally-marketing-genetic-test-claims-predict-patients. These tests were "laboratory-developed tests," which historically received little regulatory scrutiny. See the discussion of laboratory-developed tests in Chapter 5.

CHAPTER 15

GENETIC ENHANCEMENT

■ ■ ■

As the human genome is more completely deciphered and the techniques of genetic testing, gene therapy, and pharmacogenetics and pharmacogenomics are perfected, the possibility arises that these technologies might be targeted at non-therapeutic or "enhancement" objectives. As an American Association for the Advancement of Science (AAAS) Report notes, "[t]he technology for therapy and enhancement procedures is basically the same." AAAS Report, Human Inheritable Genetic Modifications at 43 (2000).

Distinguishing between "therapy" and "enhancement" can be problematic, however. One working definition of a biomedical enhancement is "an intervention that employs medical and biological technology to improve performance, appearance, or capability besides what is necessary to achieve, sustain or restore health." Eric Juengst, "The Meaning of Enhancement," in Enhancing Human Traits: Ethical and Social Implications (E. Parens ed. 1998) 29. But the concepts of health and disease can be elusive. Body shapes that were associated with health a hundred years ago, for example, are now considered obese. Moreover, there is a tendency to describe more traits as diseases and more interventions as treatments. One group of authors, for example, laments that "[e]veryday experiences like insomnia, sadness, twitchy legs, and impaired sex drive now become diagnoses: sleep disorder, depression, restless leg syndrome, and sexual dysfunction." H. Gilbert Welch, Lisa Schwartz, and Steven Woloshin, "What's Making Us Sick Is an Epidemic of Diagnoses," New York Times, 2 January 2, 2007, at F1. A similar problem arises by calling an enhancement an improvement beyond what is "natural." Vaccines confer immunity beyond what people naturally would enjoy, so are they enhancements? No, since immunization is aimed at preventing disease.

Another approach is to define an enhancement as an improvement beyond what is "normal." But what is "normal"? In some cases, it refers to the frequency with which a trait or capability occurs within a population. A person of normal height, for example, is arbitrarily defined as someone whose height lies within approximately two standard deviations of the population mean. But at other times, "normal" bears little relation to population distributions. Normal eyesight is deemed to be 20/20, but only about 35 per cent of adults have 20/20 vision without some form of correction. (The 20/20 standard of normality stems from an eye chart created by a 19th century physician; a person with 20/20 vision could read a character on the chart approximately three-eighths of an inch high from twenty feet away.)

Assuming we could agree on what is "normal," a drug that improved cognitive function in persons with below-normal cognitive ability, for example, would not be considered an enhancement. But a pharmacological agent that improved cognitive function in those individuals to such a degree that they exceeded population norms for cognitive functioning clearly would qualify as an enhancement. An intervention also might be regarded as an enhancement if it improved the cognition of someone with normal cognition to start with, even though the resulting cognitive performance remained within population norms.

In short, the distinction between enhancement and therapy is not a bright line.

Depending on how "genetic enhancement" is defined, it could be achieved by a number of different types of techniques. For example, drugs that affect non-disease traits can be made with recombinant DNA manufacturing methods. An example is recombinant DNA-manufactured human growth hormone (HGH), which is used by athletes to enhance performance. Genetic enhancement by actually inserting or deleting DNA remains a more distant prospect, since it faces the same hurdles described in Chapter 11 that beset gene therapy.

No type of biomedical enhancement generates more concern than human germline genetic enhancement, discussed in Chapter 13, whereby changes to an individual's DNA would be passed on to their offspring. See, e.g., Maxwell J. Mehlman, Transhumanist Dreams and Dystopian Nightmares: The Promise and Peril of Genetic Engineering (2012).

The debate over the ethical, legal, and social implications of genetic enhancement echoes many of the arguments surrounding the use of drugs to improve performance in sports and other competitions, such as competition for grades in education. Why should drugs that improve performance be prohibited when other techniques, such as attending better schools or having access to better coaches and equipment, be permitted? Similarly, should genetic enhancement be viewed differently than other ways of enhancing people, such as cosmetic surgery? For a discussion of enhancement generally, see Maxwell J. Mehlman, The Price of Perfection: Individualism and Society in the Era of Biomedical Enhancement (2009).

See also the discussion in Chapter 9 of the use of genetic testing in reproductive decision-making for non-disease characteristics.

MICHAEL SANDEL, THE CASE AGAINST PERFECTION: WHAT'S WRONG WITH DESIGNER CHILDREN, BIONIC ATHLETES, AND GENETIC ENGINEERING

Atlantic Monthly, Apr. 2004.

Breakthroughs in genetics present us with a promise and a predicament. The promise is that we may soon be able to treat and prevent a host of debilitating diseases. The predicament is that our newfound genetic knowledge may also enable us to manipulate our own nature—to enhance our muscles, memories, and moods; to choose the sex, height, and other genetic traits of our children; to make ourselves "better than well." When science moves faster than moral understanding, as it does today, men and women struggle to articulate their unease. In liberal societies they reach first for the language of autonomy, fairness, and individual rights. But this part of our moral vocabulary is ill equipped to address the hardest questions posed by genetic engineering. The genomic revolution has induced a kind of moral vertigo.

* * *

Though some maintain that genetic enhancement erodes human agency by overriding effort, the real problem is the explosion, not the erosion, of responsibility. As humility gives way, responsibility expands to daunting proportions. We attribute less to chance and more to choice. Parents become responsible for choosing, or failing to choose, the right traits for their children. Athletes become responsible for acquiring, or failing to acquire, the talents that will help their teams win.

One of the blessings of seeing ourselves as creatures of nature, God, or fortune is that we are not wholly responsible for the way we are. The more we become masters of our genetic endowments, the greater the burden we bear for the talents we have and the way we perform. Today when a basketball player misses a rebound, his coach can blame him for being out of position. Tomorrow the coach may blame him for being too short. Even now the use of performance-enhancing drugs in professional sports is subtly transforming the expectations players have for one another; on some teams players who take the field free from amphetamines or other stimulants are criticized for "playing naked."

The more alive we are to the chanced nature of our lot, the more reason we have to share our fate with others. Consider insurance. Since people do not know whether or when various ills will befall them, they pool their risk by buying health insurance and life insurance. As life plays itself out, the healthy wind up subsidizing the unhealthy, and those who live to a ripe old age wind up subsidizing the families of those who die before their time. Even without a sense of mutual obligation, people pool their risks and resources and share one another's fate.

But insurance markets mimic solidarity only insofar as people do not know or control their own risk factors. Suppose genetic testing advanced to the point where it could reliably predict each person's medical future and life expectancy. Those confident of good health and long life would opt out of the pool, causing other people's premiums to skyrocket. The solidarity of insurance would disappear as those with good genes fled the actuarial company of those with bad ones.

The fear that insurance companies would use genetic data to assess risks and set premiums recently led the Senate to vote to prohibit genetic discrimination in health insurance. But the bigger danger, admittedly more speculative, is that genetic enhancement, if routinely practiced, would make it harder to foster the moral sentiments that social solidarity requires.

Why, after all, do the successful owe anything to the least-advantaged members of society? The best answer to this question leans heavily on the notion of giftedness. The natural talents that enable the successful to flourish are not their own doing but, rather, their good fortune—a result of the genetic lottery. If our genetic endowments are gifts, rather than achievements for which we can claim credit, it is a mistake and a conceit to assume that we are entitled to the full measure of the bounty they reap in a market economy. We therefore have an obligation to share this bounty with those who, through no fault of their own, lack comparable gifts.

A lively sense of the contingency of our gifts—a consciousness that none of us is wholly responsible for his or her success—saves a meritocratic society from sliding into the smug assumption that the rich are rich because they are more deserving than the poor. Without this, the successful would become even more likely than they are now to view themselves as self-made and self-sufficient, and hence wholly responsible for their success. Those at the bottom of society would be viewed not as disadvantaged, and thus worthy of a measure of compensation, but as simply unfit, and thus worthy of eugenic repair. The meritocracy, less chastened by chance, would become harder, less forgiving. As perfect genetic knowledge would end the simulacrum of solidarity in insurance markets, so perfect genetic control would erode the actual solidarity that arises when men and women reflect on the contingency of their talents and fortunes.

Thirty-five years ago Robert L. Sinsheimer, a molecular biologist at the California Institute of Technology, glimpsed the shape of things to come. In an article titled "The Prospect of Designed Genetic Change" he argued that freedom of choice would vindicate the new genetics, and set it apart from the discredited eugenics of old.

> To implement the older eugenics ... would have required a massive social programme carried out over many generations.

Such a programme could not have been initiated without the consent and co-operation of major fraction of the population, and would have been continuously subject to social control. In contrast, the new eugenics could, at least in principle, be implemented on a quite individual basis, in one generation, and subject to no existing restrictions.

According to Sinsheimer, the new eugenics would be voluntary rather than coerced, and also more humane. Rather than segregating and eliminating the unfit, it would improve them. "The old eugenics would have required a continual selection for breeding of the fit, and a culling of the unfit," he wrote. "The new eugenics would permit in principle the conversion of all the unfit to the highest genetic level."

Sinsheimer's paean to genetic engineering caught the heady, Promethean self-image of the age. He wrote hopefully of rescuing "the losers in that chromosomal lottery that so firmly channels our human destinies," including not only those born with genetic defects but also "the 50,000,000 'normal' Americans with an IQ of less than 90." But he also saw that something bigger than improving on nature's "mindless, age-old throw of dice" was at stake. Implicit in technologies of genetic intervention was a more exalted place for human beings in the cosmos. "As we enlarge man's freedom, we diminish his constraints and that which he must accept as given," he wrote. Copernicus and Darwin had "demoted man from his bright glory at the focal point of the universe," but the new biology would restore his central role. In the mirror of our genetic knowledge we would see ourselves as more than a link in the chain of evolution: "We can be the agent of transition to a whole new pitch of evolution. This is a cosmic event."

There is something appealing, even intoxicating, about a vision of human freedom unfettered by the given. It may even be the case that the allure of that vision played a part in summoning the genomic age into being. It is often assumed that the powers of enhancement we now possess arose as an inadvertent by-product of biomedical progress—the genetic revolution came, so to speak, to cure disease, and stayed to tempt us with the prospect of enhancing our performance, designing our children, and perfecting our nature. That may have the story backwards. It is more plausible to view genetic engineering as the ultimate expression of our resolve to see ourselves astride the world, the masters of our nature. But that promise of mastery is flawed. It threatens to banish our appreciation of life as a gift, and to leave us with nothing to affirm or behold outside our own.

MAXWELL J. MEHLMAN, THE LAW OF ABOVE AVERAGES: LEVELING THE NEW GENETIC ENHANCEMENT PLAYING FIELD

85 Iowa L. Rev. 517, 541–544 (2000).

* * *

Is it fair for some people to have greater genetic advantages than others? This is an age-old question, forming the crux of the problem of "natural inequality" that has plagued philosophers and social theorists for centuries. If it is unfair, then presumably society should do what it can to mitigate the consequences. Yet, what forms of intervention should society take, and how feasible would they be?

* * *

Maintaining a liberal democratic form of government is an important social goal. This goal is directly threatened by wealth-based genetic enhancement: The inequality of social opportunity that results may be so great that a liberal democratic form of government becomes unsustainable, and our political system instead becomes autocratic or oligarchic. This follows from the assumption that a minimum degree of equality is necessary for the existence of a modern liberal democracy. If social inequality becomes too pronounced, liberal democratic political systems, and the capitalist economic system upon which they rest, become unstable. As one sociologist states:

> Inequality in the distribution of rewards is always a potential source of political and social instability. Because upper, relatively advantaged strata are generally fewer in number than disadvantaged lower strata, the former are faced with crucial problems of social control over the latter. One way of approaching this issue is to ask not why the disprivileged often rebel against the privileged but why they do not rebel more often than they do.

The characteristics of genetic enhancement that threaten to destabilize liberal democratic government are the features that distinguish genetic enhancement from other forms of self-improvement: its high cost, which may place it beyond the reach of all but the very wealthy; the broad and fundamental nature of the traits that it could enhance; the magnitude of its effects; their multiplicity; the resulting ability to gain advantages in multiple spheres of social activity; and the possibility—created by germ line enhancement—that these advantages would be passed on to successive generations.

These characteristics not only give rise to social inequality; more insidiously, they undermine the belief in equality of opportunity. A widespread belief in equality of opportunity is the method by which liberal democracies accommodate the reality of capitalist inequality—that everyone is not equally endowed with equally beneficial natural assets or blessed with the same luck. Sociologists point out that "whereas most Americans are willing to tolerate sizeable inequalities in the distribution of resources, they typically insist that individuals from all backgrounds should have an equal opportunity to secure these resources." John Schaar notes that the belief in equal opportunity is instrumental in maintaining the prevailing social order, stating that "no policy formula is better designed to fortify the dominant institutions, values, and ends of the American social order than the formula of equality of opportunity, for it offers *everyone* a fair and equal chance to find a place within that order."

Assuming, as discussed earlier, that the price of genetic enhancements prohibits people of ordinary means from acquiring them, genetic enhancement would create profound differences in ability that would endow the wealthy with opportunities utterly and irrevocably beyond the reach of the majority of the citizens. World history is filled with examples of societies similar to those that would result from wealth-based genetic enhancement. In medieval Europe, for example, individuals were born with a social status, and barring the infrequent case in which peasants were able to obtain education in religious institutions or became apprenticed and eventually esquired to knights, individuals remained members of the class into which they were born. Similarly, in slave-owning societies, people were born into bondage and could be freed only by escape (self-exile) or at the pleasure of their masters. The most obvious surviving example of such a society is the caste system in India. The caste system remains a constant threat to that nation's democratic institutions.

Genetic social stratification thus would undermine our current social system, but it is not certain how seriously. Perhaps society will adapt to the social artifacts of the genetic revolution and the result, while markedly different from present arrangements, will be relatively stable. The genetic underclass might cede power to their genetic superiors in return for enjoying the material benefits made possible by genetic advances. In this scenario, the underclass would accept the division between social strata, and be content with being upwardly mobile only within the confines of their own class. The genobility, in turn, would rule according to enlightened principles of noblesse oblige, taking care to permit sufficient benefits to trickle down to maintain political and social equilibrium. A democracy of sorts might even persist, with the underclass electing representatives who either belonged to the upper class or who were committed to preserving its privileges. In essence, such a system might not look very different from our own, given the extent to which we increasingly elect representatives who are considerably more privileged than their constituents.

This system, however, seems highly unstable. For one thing, the members of the genetic upper class would require great self-control to avoid over-reaching. At minimum, they would need to maintain effective means of monitoring and regulating the behavior of their peers to prevent antisocial excesses of greed. The system also would be vulnerable to demagogues who achieved power by promising to redistribute genetic endowments more evenly. Assuming that the principle of one-person/one-vote persisted, a numerically inferior genetic upper class could be out-voted by the underclass and Congress could become dominated by elected officials pledged to employ the full force of government to rectify genetic imbalances.

The genobility might respond with reprisals in an effort to preserve its privileged status. At one extreme these could range from threats to withhold the fruits of genetic medicine from non-privileged segments of society, to overt interference with the democratic process. At the other, the genetic upper class is liable to amass sufficient wealth and influence to enable it to control the media, which would in turn permit it to affect the outcome of elections in a manner quite out of proportion to its numbers. Efforts by the underclass to preserve its hegemony might prove no more successful than current efforts to reform campaign finance laws in order to dilute the power of special interests.

In the end, we might embark on an era of social chaos as the system swung in ever-widening arcs between rule by underclass demagogues and by the genetic aristocracy. Eventually, this could degenerate into mob rule and, then, anarchy. To rid itself of its status as the class of the genetically disadvantaged, the mob might even destroy the scientific foundations of the genetic revolution, perhaps by physically dismantling research centers and erasing mapping and sequencing data.

Alternatively, post-genorevolutionary society could devolve into totalitarian rule by a genetic autocracy. The genetic upper class would employ whatever repressive techniques were necessary in order to obtain power and to keep the underclass in check. Advances in genetic science might even enable the genobility to genetically manipulate the underclass in ways that make it more docile.

While it is impossible to predict with certainty what effect wealth-based genetic enhancement will have on society, what is clear is that it creates not only a moral challenge but a political threat. From a moral standpoint, those who obtain enhancement may not have done anything to deserve it. Adults may have obtained the means necessary to purchase enhancement in objectionable or morally irrelevant ways—through exploitation or the brute luck of inheritance. Moreover, it is difficult to argue that children earned their new-found advantages. Yet genetic enhancement poses more than an ethical quandary. Even if the resources necessary to purchase genetic enhancement are earned in a moral sense, wealth-based enhancement is likely to have a severe societal impact. Somatic enhancement alone could dramatically widen the gap between the haves and have-nots, and crippling class warfare would ensue. Germ line enhancement could create, quite literally, a master race. A future as bleak as this is not perhaps inevitable, but it is unquestionably within the realm of possibility. The question then becomes whether there is any practical way to prevent this.

NOTES AND QUESTIONS

1.   Is there a solution to the equality problem? See Maxwell J. Mehlman, The Law of Above Averages: Leveling the New Genetic Enhancement Playing Field, 85 Iowa L. Rev. 517, 570–574 (2000) (suggesting licensing the use of genetic enhancements for public benefit and a national lottery in which everyone was enrolled). The high cost of enhancements also would create unfairness problems when the enhanced competed with the unenhanced for scarce societal resources, whether Olympic gold medals or admission to Harvard Law School. For possible ways of leveling the playing field, see Mehlman, *supra* 576–592.

PART IV

COMMERCIALIZATION OF GENETIC RESEARCH: PROPERTY, PATENTS, AND CONFLICTS OF INTEREST

■ ■ ■

Genetic research is undertaken at universities, government laboratories, and private companies, with funding from public, corporate and philanthropic sources. But at some point, the discoveries need to be turned into tangible products, such as diagnostics and treatments. Patent law has developed in this area as an incentive to promote innovation. Part IV explores the incentives for product development and technology transfer in the genetics realm and analyzes the issues raised by the commercialization of genes and cell lines.

The framers of the U.S. Constitution realized it was important to create incentives for technological innovation. The U.S. Constitution, Art. 1, § 8, cl. 8 provides that Congress shall have the power "To promote the Progress of Science and useful Arts, by securing for limited Times to Authors and Inventors the exclusive Right to their respective Writings and Discoveries." This clause provides the foundation for federal patent law, which rewards inventors with a 20-year period of exclusivity that allows them to forbid anyone else from making, using, selling, or offering to sell their invention. The goal is to encourage novel, useful, and nonobvious inventions that might not otherwise have been created.

Scientists were searching for and finding genes long before patents were available for genes. They did so for various reasons, including to help humankind, win a Nobel Prize, achieve academic advancement, and gain professional status. When the Human Genome Project was undertaken to locate and sequence all human genes, key researchers in the field warned about the risks of granting intellectual property rights over genes. They feared that if scientists could "own" genes and reap financial rewards by having exclusive rights to any diagnostic or treatment technologies developed with the gene they found, they would be less likely to share copies of the genes or even information about those genes. And, in fact, these dangers came to pass once patents were issued on human genes.

The ascendancy of patents as a means of encouraging innovation in the life sciences became clear in courts and Congress in the early 1980s.

The Supreme Court in Diamond v. Chakrabarty, 447 U.S. 303 (1980), held that patents could issue on genetically-engineered organisms. Congress adopted a series of technology transfer laws that allowed federally-funded researchers, including those at federal laboratories and at universities, to patent and gain a commercial interest in inventions that they created with taxpayer money—something that was previously considered to be a criminal usurpation of public funds.

For nearly two decades, policy makers debated whether genes should be patented. Was a gene an "invention" or an unpatentable product of nature? Was the incentive of a patent necessary to encourage the discovery of genes or were other motivations and incentives (such as federal funding) sufficient? In 2013, the U.S. Supreme Court held that the patents on two isolated human breast cancer genes were invalid because genes were products of nature, not inventions of man. But questions remain. What uses of genomic information are sufficiently inventive applications of the laws of nature to be patentable?

As courts grapple with those questions, the policy debates about patent law continue. Does existing patent law and doctrine promote or hinder innovation? Has patent law discouraged researchers from sharing data and materials and made the fruits of biomedical research unaffordable to many? And what are the appropriate technology transfer laws to make sure that scientific discoveries are translated into health care products?

The genetic gold rush that resulted from the possibility of biotech patents also profoundly changed the relationship between patients and physicians. Some patients, such as John Moore, began to feel that they were being harvested by their doctors, who were making deals with biotech companies to sell patients' tissue, genes, cell lines, and other body parts. Courts and medical organizations began to deal with questions of the duties owed to patients when their tissue was commercialized and whether individuals have property rights in their biological material. Without the trust of people whose tissue is used, there will be no tissue available for the biotech industry's scientific endeavors. The policies created in the seemingly obscure area of patent and technology transfer law thus have life and death implications for all of us.

Chapter 16 explores patent law, technology transfer law, and the surrounding policy issues in these areas, with some brief comparisons between U.S. and foreign patent law. Chapter 17 examines case law concerning the rights of individuals whose bodies are the sources of patented genes, cell lines, and genetic information. It also explores the question of whether individuals do and should have property rights in their tissue samples and genetic information.

CHAPTER 16

THE PATENT SYSTEM

■ ■ ■

I.   REQUIREMENTS FOR A PATENT

LORI ANDREWS, THE "PROGRESS CLAUSE": AN EMPIRICAL ANALYSIS BASED ON THE CONSTITUTIONAL FOUNDATION OF PATENT LAW
15 N.C. J.L. & Tech. 537, 537–546 (2014).

When the Founding Fathers were drafting the U.S. Constitution, they thought about how best to encourage innovation in their new nation. The result was the Progress Clause of the U.S. Constitution, Article I, Section 8, Clause 8. The Progress Clause provides that Congress shall have the power "[t]o promote the Progress of Science and useful Arts, by securing for limited Times to Authors and Inventors the exclusive Right to their respective Writings and Discoveries. . . ." This clause, designed to reward the creation and sharing of new knowledge, is the constitutional basis for the intellectual property system in existence today.

* * *

Patents are not granted for all useful products or processes that result from human ingenuity. For instance, mental processes and abstract ideas are not patentable because "they are . . . basic tools of scientific and technological work." Patenting other raw materials of scientific and technological work, such as laws of nature or products of nature, similarly raises the danger of inhibiting future innovation and "foreclose[ing] more future invention than the underlying discovery could reasonably justify."

In a series of cases over the past 150 years, the Supreme Court has held that one cannot patent abstract ideas, laws of nature, products of nature, or materials isolated from products of nature if those materials behave in the same way they would in nature.

* * *

The mechanism by which Congress chose to encourage innovation was to grant an inventor a patent—a monopoly on any use of the patented invention in exchange for a disclosure in the patent application of how the invention can be made. This is thought to encourage innovation by stimulating people to invent in the first place, often by making a better, cheaper, more interesting, and more effective alternative to an existing invention. Thus, if a person patents a mousetrap made of wood, when the patent application later becomes public (a condition of the patent grant), other inventors can read about how the inventor made the mousetrap and can create variations using significantly different materials or processes.

Under the Patent Act, a patent is a limited legal monopoly given to an inventor who meets certain constitutional and statutory requirements. The invention must be novel, non-obvious, and useful.

* * *

For twenty years from the date of the filing of the patent application, a patent holder controls any use of its invention and can prevent anyone else from using, making, selling, or importing the invention. The patent holder can keep an invention away from the public altogether. The inventor can decide that he will be the only one to sell the invention and charge as much as he wants for the invention. Or the inventor can, for royalty fees, grant exclusive rights to a single licensee to use the invention or make the invention available for royalty fees in a non-exclusive fashion to all comers.

Unlike in copyright law, there is no patent law exception for fair use. Unlike patent law in other countries, there is no general statutory research exception in the United States. * * * Under American patent law, an inventor can refuse to make the invention and forbid others from making it. In contrast, under American trademark law, a person can lose the mark if he does not use it for three years. And in Europe, patent holders are required to "work" the patent and make the invention available or else their rights are constricted.

The American patent system is a three-way give-and-take among the U.S. Patent and Trademark Office ("USPTO"), the courts, and Congress. All three have active roles in assuring that the goals of the patent system are met and that the monopoly granted is not too broad. Often this means that Congress and the courts winnow back patents erroneously granted by the USPTO. Between 25% and 75% of litigated patents are found invalid during litigation, sometimes because their scope is so broad that they cover unpatentable subject matter such as abstract ideas, laws of nature, or products of nature. Sometimes the director of the USPTO has had to review and invalidate provisions of improperly granted patents—this has happened, for example, with patents on certain computer programs. In other instances, Congress has stepped in—for example, by exempting doctors from patent infringement liability if they use a patented medical or surgical procedure.

II. STATUTORY AUTHORITY

PATENT CODE
35 U.S.C. §§ 101–103.

§ 101. Inventions patentable

Whoever invents or discovers any new and useful process, machine, manufacture, or composition of matter, or any new and useful improvement thereof, may obtain a patent therefore, subject to the conditions and requirements of this title.

§ 102. Conditions for patentability; novelty

(a) Novelty; prior art.—A person shall be entitled to a patent unless—

(1) the claimed invention was patented, described in a printed publication, or in public use, on sale, or otherwise available to the public before the effective filing date of the claimed invention; or

(2) the claimed invention was described in a patent * * * or in an application for patent published or deemed published * * * in which the patent or application, as the case may be, names another inventor and was effectively filed before the effective filing date of the claimed invention.

* * *

§ 103. Conditions for patentability; non-obvious subject matter

A patent for a claimed invention may not be obtained, notwithstanding that the claimed invention is not identically disclosed as set forth in section 102, if the differences between the claimed invention and the prior art are such that the claimed invention as a whole would have been obvious before the effective filing date of the claimed invention to a person having ordinary skill in the art to which the claimed invention pertains. Patentability shall not be negated by the manner in which the invention was made.

III. POLICY ARGUMENTS RELATED TO PATENTING OF GENETIC MATERIALS

LILA FEISEE, ARE BIOTECHNOLOGY PATENTS IMPORTANT? YES!
1 PTO TODAY 9, 9–12 (2000).

Biotechnology is one of the most research intensive and innovative industries in the global economy today. While the promise of new discovery is great, this does not come without cost. It takes hundreds of millions of dollars to bring a new pharmaceutical to the marketplace. Without patent protection for biotechnological research, there would be little incentive for investors to risk their capital and many of the potential benefits of biotechnology would not come to fruition. By rewarding inventors for their discoveries for a limited time, the patent system supports innovation while, at the same time, dedicating these discoveries to the public. Thus, both the private sector and the public benefit.

Patent protection in the area of biotechnology also serves the larger economy by providing a forum that encourages both innovation and investment. It also benefits society by providing the means to reduce disease and suffering for both humans and animals. Such results promote and enhance the dignity and quality of life * * *. Biotechnology patents allow for the dissemination of potentially valuable scientific information. The availability of the information disclosed in biotechnology patents enables others in the field of science to build on earlier discoveries. Not only can other researchers use the information in a patent, but by disclosing cutting edge scientific information, the patent system avoids expensive duplication of research efforts. It is only with the patenting of biotechnology that some companies, particularly small companies, can raise capital to bring beneficial products to the market place or fund further research.

In addition, this capital provides jobs that represent an immediate public benefit independent of the technological benefits. Continuing employment opportunities represent a national resource for the future because they encourage the youth of today to become the scientists and inventors of tomorrow. Thus, the patent system not only fosters benefits to our society today, but ensures our future ability to innovate and grow.

U.S. DEPARTMENT OF ENERGY OFFICE OF SCIENCE, OFFICE OF BIOLOGICAL AND ENVIRONMENTAL RESEARCH, HUMAN GENOME PROGRAM

http://web.archive.org/web/20101003085133/
http://www.ornl.gov/sci/techresources/Human_Genome/elsi/patents.shtml.

GENETICS AND PATENTING

* * *

What are some of the potential arguments for gene patenting?

- Researchers are rewarded for their discoveries and can use monies gained from patenting to further their research.

- The investment of resources is encouraged by providing a monopoly to the inventor and prohibiting competitors from making, using, or selling the invention without a license.

- Wasteful duplication of effort is prevented.

- Research is forced into new, unexplored areas.

- Secrecy is reduced and all researchers are ensured access to the new invention.

What are some of the potential arguments against gene patenting?

- Patents of partial and uncharacterized cDNA sequences will reward those who make routine discoveries but penalize those who determine biological function or application (inappropriate reward given to easiest step in the process).

- Patents could impede the development of diagnostics and therapeutics by third parties because of the costs associated with using patented research data.

- Patent stacking (allowing a single genomic sequence to be patented in several ways such as an EST, a gene, and a SNP) may discourage product development because of high royalty costs owed to all patent owners of that sequence; these are costs that will likely be passed on to the consumer.

* * *

- Costs increase not only for paying for patent licensing but also for determining what patents apply and who has rights to downstream products.

- Patent holders are being allowed to patent a part of nature— a basic constituent of life; this allows one organism to own all or part of another organism.

- Private biotechs who own certain patents can monopolize certain gene test markets.

- Patent filings are replacing journal articles as places for public disclosure—reducing the body of knowledge in the literature.

NOTES AND QUESTIONS

1. A 2013 study found that 41% of all human genes were explicitly claimed in United States patents. Jeffrey Rosenfeld & Christopher E. Mason, Pervasive Sequence Patents Cover the Entire Human Genome, 5 Genome Med. 27 (2013). Some scholars believe, however, that this study may overestimate the share of the genome that is patented because the authors did not "specifically analyze the claims of these patents." See Shine Tu et al., 6 Genome Med. 14 (2014). A different study concluded that patents have been granted for sequences of 30% of human genes. Bhaven Sampat & Heidi Williams, How Do Patents Affect Follow-On Innovation? Evidence from Human Genome, 109 Am. Econ. Rev. 203 (2019).

2. How might a trade secret approach to genetic discoveries differ from that of a gene patenting approach? What is the likely impact of each on research? What is the likely impact of each on the development of gene therapies?

3. About one-quarter of gene patent holders did not allow any other physician or laboratory to test for "their" patented gene. The company holding the patent on a gene associated with Alzheimer disease, for example, would not let any laboratory except its own perform the test for "its" gene. Doctors and labs across the country faced a lawsuit if they tried to determine whether one of their patients has the genetic form of Alzheimer disease even though testing could easily be done by anyone who knows the gene sequence without using any product or device made by the patent holder. See Kathie Skeehan et al., Impact of Gene Patents and Licensing Practices on Access to Genetic Testing for Alzheimer's Disease, 12 Genetics Med. S71 (2010).

This exclusivity impeded research to improve diagnosis. Various mutations in the same gene can cause a particular disease. But companies that do not let anyone else test for "their" gene can make it more difficult to find mutations than if other labs were also testing the same gene. In countries where the Alzheimer gene and hemochromatosis gene were *not* patented, researchers found previously unknown mutations. These mutations could be used to diagnose people who would not otherwise be diagnosed.

4. Most drugs only work on a percentage of patients who use them. Genetic testing can help distinguish those patients for whom a drug will work from those for whom it will not. But such tests will also limit the market for drugs. A pharmaceutical company filed for a patent on a genetic test to determine the effectiveness of one of its asthma drugs. But the company said it would not develop the test—or let anyone else develop it. Geeta Anand, Big Drug Makers Try to Postpone Custom Regimens, Wall St. J., June 18, 2001, at B1. Should a company lose its patent in a case like this, where the company is not developing the invention? There is a concept in trademark law, under 15 U.S.C. § 1127, whereby the owner can lose a trademark he or she does not use for three consecutive years (since part of the requirement for trademark protection is use in commerce).

> **Food for Thought:** Would it be problematic if a patent owner sought a patent, not for financial reasons, but to prevent the creation or use of the patented invention? Some scientists have suggested creating a chimera, mixing human and chimp DNA to produce a subhuman species to do menial tasks. In 1997, biologist Stuart Newman filed a patent application on that technology. He planned to use the patent to prevent anyone from making such a creation for the 20-year period he controlled the patent. His patent was denied because the chimera "includes within its scope a human being" and people are not patentable.

IV. CASE LAW ON PATENTABLE SUBJECT MATTER

Diamond v. Chakrabarty, 447 U.S. 303 (1980), was a landmark case with respect to patent law in biotechnology. Although it did not directly address the patentability of genes, it answered an important underlying issue: is "a live, human-made micro-organism" patentable subject matter under 35 U.S.C. § 101? The patent application at issue asserted claims related to the Chakrabarty's invention of a bacterium genetically engineered to break down crude oil to help treat oil spills. This unique property does not occur in naturally occurring bacteria.

The patent claims were initially rejected on the grounds that they (1) were "products of nature, and (2) as living organisms, were not patentable subject matter under 35 U.S.C. § 101." Chakrabarty's appeal ultimately reached the United States Supreme Court, which held that the micro-organism was patentable subject matter as a "composition of matter" under 35 U.S.C. § 101. The Court noted that § 101 does not include every discovery. As it observed:

> The laws of nature, physical phenomena, and abstract ideas have been held not patentable. Thus, a new mineral discovered in the earth or a new plant found in the wild is not patentable subject matter. Likewise, Einstein could not patent his celebrated law that $E=mc^2$; nor could Newton have patented the law of gravity. Such discoveries are "manifestations of * * * nature, free to all men and reserved exclusively to none."

> [In contrast, Chakrabarty's claim was] not to a hitherto unknown natural phenomenon, but to a nonnaturally occurring manufacture or composition of matter—a product of human ingenuity "having a distinctive name, character [and] use." The point is underscored dramatically by comparison of the invention here with that in Funk [Brothers Seed Co. v. Kalo Inoculant Co., 333 U.S. 127 (1948)]. There, the patentee had discovered that there existed in nature certain species of root-nodule bacteria which did not exert a mutually inhibitive effect on each other. He used that discovery to produce a mixed culture capable of inoculating the seeds of leguminous plants. Concluding that the patentee had discovered "only some of the handiwork of nature," the Court ruled the product nonpatentable.

Because the bacterium Chakrabarty produced had "markedly different characteristics from any found in nature" and "the potential for significant utility," the Court considered his discovery to be his handiwork, not nature's. The Court observed that Congress could amend the statute to exclude patent protection for

> **FYI:** General Electric (GE), Dr. Chakrabarty's employer and the holder of the patent for the genetically modified, oil-eating bacterium, never developed the microbe for commercial use. GE believed that fighting oil spills was beyond its purview and that development of genetically modified organisms presented more political trouble than it was worth. As a result, the bacterium was not used in the infamous 1989 Exxon Valdez oil spill in Alaska. Since then, researchers have been exploring the natural, oil-eating properties of various other types of bacteria.

genetically engineered organisms or it could draft legislation to address the patentability of living organisms, but until then, it held that the invention was patentable subject matter under § 101.

ASSOCIATION FOR MOLECULAR PATHOLOGY V. MYRIAD GENETICS, INC.

569 U.S. 576 (2013).

THOMAS, J.

Respondent Myriad Genetics, Inc. (Myriad), discovered the precise location and sequence of two human genes, mutations of which can substantially increase the risks of breast and ovarian cancer. Myriad obtained a number of patents based upon its discovery. This case involves claims from three of them and requires us to resolve whether a naturally occurring segment of deoxyribonucleic acid (DNA) is patent eligible under 35 U.S.C. § 101 by virtue of its isolation from the rest of the human genome. We also address the patent eligibility of synthetically created DNA known as complementary DNA (cDNA), which contains the same protein-coding information found in a segment of natural DNA but omits portions within the DNA segment that do not code for proteins. For the reasons that follow, we hold that a naturally occurring DNA segment is a product of nature and not patent eligible merely because it has been isolated, but that cDNA is patent eligible because it is not naturally occurring. We, therefore, affirm in part and reverse in part the decision of the United States Court of Appeals for the Federal Circuit.

* * *

Scientists can * * * extract DNA from cells using well known laboratory methods. These methods allow scientists to isolate specific segments of DNA—for instance, a particular gene or part of a gene—which can then be further studied, manipulated, or used. It is also possible to create DNA synthetically through processes similarly well known in the field of genetics. One such method begins with an mRNA molecule and uses the natural bonding properties of nucleotides to create a new, synthetic DNA molecule. The result is the inverse of the mRNA's inverse image of the original DNA, with one important distinction: Because the natural creation of mRNA involves splicing that removes introns, the synthetic DNA created from mRNA also contains only the exon sequences. This synthetic DNA created in the laboratory from mRNA is known as complementary DNA (cDNA). [Ed. Note: See diagram below showing how RNA can be translated into protein or synthesized into cDNA and diagram comparing cDNA and genomic DNA.]

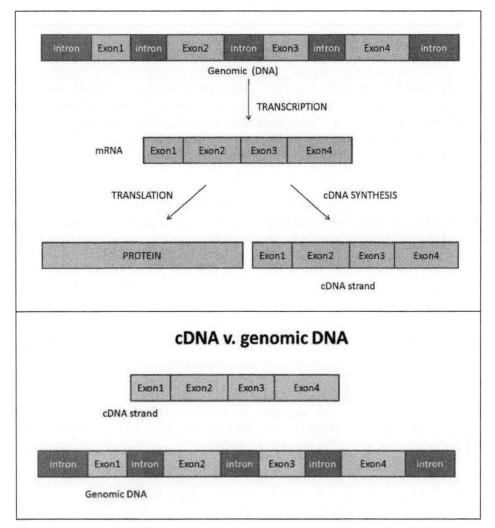

[Ed. Note: Genomic DNA contains introns between the coding portion of the genome called exons. During transcription, as shown in the top diagram, the introns are removed, and RNA molecules are created. During translation, proteins are formed based on RNA molecules. Complementary DNA or cDNA synthesis can be done in the laboratory by creating a complementary DNA (or cDNA) version of the RNA. As the second diagram shows, cDNA and genomic DNA have the same exons, but cDNA has no introns.]

Changes in the genetic sequence are called mutations. Mutations can be as small as the alteration of a single nucleotide—a change affecting only one letter in the genetic code. Such small-scale changes can produce an entirely different amino acid or can end protein production altogether. Large changes, involving the deletion, rearrangement, or duplication of hundreds or even millions of nucleotides, can result in the elimination, misplacement, or duplication of entire genes. Some mutations are harmless, but others can cause disease or increase the risk of disease. As a result, the study of genetics can lead to valuable medical breakthroughs.

* * *

Myriad discovered the precise location and sequence of what are now known as the BRCA1 and BRCA2 genes. * * * Before Myriad's discovery of the BRCA1 and BRCA2 genes, scientists knew that heredity played a role in establishing a woman's risk of developing breast and ovarian cancer, but they did not know which genes were associated with those cancers.

* * *

Once it found the location and sequence of the BRCA1 and BRCA2 genes, Myriad sought and obtained a number of patents. Nine composition claims from three of those patents are at issue in this case. Claims 1, 2, 5, and 6 from the '282 patent are representative. The first claim asserts a patent on "[a]n isolated DNA coding for a BRCA1 polypeptide," which has "the amino acid sequence set forth in SEQ ID NO:2." SEQ ID NO:2 sets forth a list of 1,863 amino acids that the typical BRCA1 gene encodes. Put differently, claim 1 asserts a patent claim on the DNA code that tells a cell to produce the string of BRCA1 amino acids listed in SEQ ID NO:2.

Claim 2 of the '282 patent operates similarly. It claims "[t]he isolated DNA of claim 1, wherein said DNA has the nucleotide sequence set forth in SEQ ID NO:1." Like SEQ ID NO:2, SEQ ID NO:1 sets forth a long list of data, in this instance the sequence of cDNA that codes for the BRCA1 amino acids listed in claim 1. Importantly, SEQ ID NO:1 lists only the cDNA exons in the BRCA1 gene, rather than a full DNA sequence containing both exons and introns. As a result, the Federal Circuit recognized that claim 2 asserts a patent on the cDNA nucleotide sequence listed in SEQ ID NO:1, which codes for the typical BRCA1 gene.

Claim 5 of the '282 patent claims a subset of the data in claim 1. In particular, it claims "[a]n isolated DNA having at least 15 nucleotides of the DNA of claim 1." The practical effect of claim 5 is to assert a patent on any series of 15 nucleotides that exist in the typical BRCA1 gene. Because the BRCA1 gene is thousands of nucleotides long, even BRCA1 genes with substantial mutations are likely to contain at least one segment of 15 nucleotides that correspond to the typical BRCA1 gene. Similarly, claim 6 of the '282 patent claims "[a]n isolated DNA having at least 15 nucleotides of the DNA of claim 2." This claim operates similarly to claim 5, except that it references the cDNA-based claim 2. The remaining claims at issue are similar, though several list common mutations rather than typical BRCA1 and BRCA2 sequences.

Myriad's patents would, if valid, give it the exclusive right to isolate an individual's BRCA1 and BRCA2 genes (or any strand of 15 or more nucleotides within the genes) by breaking the covalent bonds that connect the DNA to the rest of the individual's genome. The patents would also give Myriad the exclusive right to synthetically create BRCA cDNA. In Myriad's view, manipulating BRCA DNA in either of these fashions triggers its "right to exclude others from making" its patented composition of matter under the Patent Act.

But isolation is necessary to conduct genetic testing, and Myriad was not the only entity to offer BRCA testing after it discovered the genes. The University of Pennsylvania's Genetic Diagnostic Laboratory (GDL) and others provided genetic testing services to women. Petitioner Dr. Harry Ostrer, then a researcher at New York University School of Medicine, routinely sent his patients' DNA samples to GDL for testing. After learning of GDL's testing and Ostrer's activities, Myriad sent letters to them asserting that the genetic testing infringed Myriad's patents. App. 94–95 (Ostrer letter). In response, GDL agreed to stop testing and informed Ostrer that it would no longer accept patient samples. Myriad also filed patent infringement suits against other entities that performed BRCA testing, resulting in settlements in which the defendants agreed to cease all allegedly infringing activity. Myriad, thus, solidified its position as the only entity providing BRCA testing.

* * *

Section 101 of the Patent Act provides:

"Whoever invents or discovers any new and useful . . . composition of matter, or any new and useful improvement thereof, may obtain a patent therefor, subject to the conditions and requirements of this title." 35 U.S.C. § 101.

We have "long held that this provision contains an important implicit exception. Laws of nature, natural phenomena, and abstract ideas are not patentable." Rather, " 'they are the basic tools of scientific and technological work' " that lie beyond the domain of patent protection. As the Court has explained, without this exception, there would be considerable danger that the grant of patents would "tie up" the use of such tools and thereby "inhibit future innovation premised upon them." This would be at odds with the very point of patents, which exist to promote creation.

The rule against patents on naturally occurring things is not without limits, however, for "all inventions at some level embody, use, reflect, rest upon, or apply laws of nature, natural phenomena, or abstract ideas," and "too broad an interpretation of this exclusionary principle could eviscerate patent law." As we have recognized before, patent protection strikes a delicate balance between creating "incentives that lead to creation, invention, and discovery" and "imped[ing] the flow of information that might permit, indeed spur, invention." We must apply this well-established standard to determine whether Myriad's patents claim any "new and useful . . . composition of matter, § 101, or instead claim naturally occurring phenomena."

It is undisputed that Myriad did not create or alter any of the genetic information encoded in the BRCA1 and BRCA2 genes. The location and order of the nucleotides existed in nature before Myriad found them. Nor did Myriad create or alter the genetic structure of DNA. Instead, Myriad's principal contribution was uncovering the precise location and genetic sequence of the BRCA1 and BRCA2 genes within chromosomes 17 and 13. The question is whether this renders the genes patentable.

Myriad recognizes that our decision in [Diamond v.] Chakrabarty, 447 U.S. 303 (1980) is central to this inquiry. In *Chakrabarty,* * * * [t]he Court held that [a] modified bacterium was patentable [because] the patent claim was "not to a hitherto unknown natural phenomenon, but to a nonnaturally occurring manufacture or composition of matter—a product of human ingenuity 'having a distinctive name, character [and] use.' " * * * In this case, by contrast, Myriad did not create anything. To be sure, it found an important and useful gene, but separating that gene from its surrounding genetic material is not an act of invention.

Groundbreaking, innovative, or even brilliant discovery does not by itself satisfy the § 101 inquiry. In Funk Brothers Seed Co. v. Kalo Inoculant Co., 333 U.S. 127 (1948), this Court considered a composition patent that claimed a mixture of naturally occurring strains of bacteria that helped leguminous plants take nitrogen from the air and fix it in the soil. * * * The Court held that the composition was not patent eligible because the patent holder did not alter the bacteria in any way. His patent claim thus fell squarely within the law of nature exception. So do Myriad's. Myriad found the location of the BRCA1 and BRCA2 genes, but that discovery, by itself, does not render the BRCA genes "new . . . composition[s] of matter," § 101, that are patent eligible.

* * * Myriad's patent descriptions simply detail the "iterative process" of discovery by which Myriad narrowed the possible locations for the gene sequences that it sought. Myriad seeks to import these extensive research efforts into the § 101 patent-eligibility inquiry. But extensive effort alone is insufficient to satisfy the demands of § 101.

Nor are Myriad's claims saved by the fact that isolating DNA from the human genome severs chemical bonds and thereby creates a nonnaturally occurring molecule. * * * If the patents depended upon the creation of a unique molecule, then a would-be infringer could arguably avoid at least Myriad's patent claims on entire genes (such as claims 1 and 2 of the '282 patent) by isolating a DNA sequence that included both the BRCA1 or BRCA2 gene and one additional nucleotide pair. Such a molecule would not be chemically identical to the molecule "invented" by Myriad. But Myriad obviously would resist that outcome because its claim is concerned primarily with the information contained in the genetic *sequence,* not with the specific chemical composition of a particular molecule.

* * *

Further undercutting the PTO's practice, the United States argued in the Federal Circuit and in this Court that isolated DNA was *not* patent eligible under § 101, and that the PTO's practice was not "a sufficient reason to hold that isolated DNA is patent-eligible." These concessions weigh against deferring to the PTO's determination.

cDNA does not present the same obstacles to patentability as naturally occurring, isolated DNA segments. As already explained, creation of a cDNA sequence from mRNA results in an exons-only molecule that is not naturally occurring. Petitioners concede that cDNA differs from natural DNA in that "the non-coding regions have been removed." They nevertheless argue that cDNA is not patent eligible because "[t]he nucleotide sequence of cDNA is dictated by nature, not by the lab technician." That may be so, but the lab technician unquestionably creates something new when cDNA is made. cDNA retains the naturally occurring exons of DNA, but it is distinct from the DNA from which it was derived. As a result, cDNA is not a "product of nature" and is patent eligible under § 101, except insofar as very short series of DNA may have no intervening introns to remove when creating cDNA. In that situation, a short strand of cDNA may be indistinguishable from natural DNA.

NOTES AND QUESTIONS

1.   The United States and Canada have taken different positions on the patentability of the Harvard "oncomouse," a mouse genetically engineered to increase its susceptibility to cancer for use in cancer research. In the United States, a patent on the oncomouse was granted by the USPTO (U.S. Patent No. 4,736,866) on April 12, 1988, the validity of which has not been challenged. The patent claims also extend to all non-human mammals that have been similarly altered. In Harvard College v. Canada (Commissioner of Patents), [2002] 4 S.C.R. 45, 2002 SCC 76, the Supreme Court of Canada reasoned that "a higher life form such as the oncomouse" could not easily be "understood as either a 'manufacture' or a 'composition of matter'" under Canada's Patent Act. Reasoning that "the patentability of higher life forms is a highly contentious matter raising serious practical, ethical and environmental concerns not contemplated by the Act," it deemed the mouse unpatentable.

How might the United States Supreme Court have ruled if the oncomouse patent was challenged under 35 U.S.C. § 101 for being a non-patentable subject matter?

2.   At the time *Myriad* was decided, the prevailing view among scholars and patent attorneys was that isolated genes were patentable subject matter.

Food for Thought: In his concurrence in *Myriad*, Justice Scalia wrote: "I join the judgment of the Court, and all of its opinion except [the portions that go] into fine details of molecular biology. I am unable to affirm those details on my own knowledge or even my own belief. It suffices for me to affirm, having studied the opinions below and the expert briefs presented here, that the portion of DNA isolated from its natural state sought to be patented is identical to that portion of the DNA in its natural state; and that complementary DNA (cDNA) is a synthetic creation not normally present in nature." Is Justice Scalia being humble, or is he suggesting Justices do not have to understand those finer technical points? Is the latter view problematic?

Scholars wondered what impact Myriad would have on gene and other related patents. A 2016 empirical study found that its effect on the biotech industry has "been much less profound than some practitioners, scholars, and patent holders had anticipated." The authors found an increase in gene-related patents after *Myriad*, although they detected an overall decrease in patents for "isolated," "purified," or "natural" genes. Mateo Aboy et al., *Myriad's* Impact on Gene Patents, 34 Nature Biotech. 11 (Nov. 2016). Another empirical study published in 2018, found that, of the 6,786 patent applications that were affected by a *Myriad*-based rejection in the 5 years since that decision, 85% concerned subject matter other than genomic DNA, such as RNA, DNA arrays, and DNA-based kits. Mateo Aboy et al., Was the *Myriad* Decision a Surgical Strike on Isolated DNA Patents, or Does it Have Wider Impacts?, 36 Nature Biotech. 1146 (2018).

3. *Myriad* is not the only case that addresses the idea that "laws of nature, natural phenomena and abstract ideas," are not patentable. In Mayo Collaborative Services v. Prometheus Laboratories, Inc., 566 U.S. 66 (2012), the Supreme Court established a framework to distinguish patents that claim laws of "nature, natural phenomena, or abstract ideas" from those that claim patent-eligible *applications* of those laws. To be patent-eligible, patents directed at laws of "nature, natural phenomena, or abstract ideas" must claim methods that demonstrate an "inventive concept." In Alice Corp. Pty. Ltd. v. CLS Bank Int'l, 573 U.S. 208 (2014), the Supreme Court extended the analysis established in *Mayo* to software patents. It also clarified that effectively adding the words "apply it" to a claim directed to an abstract idea or limiting an abstract idea to a particular area of technology is insufficient to demonstrate a patent-eligible inventive concept.

Based on cases like *Myriad, Mayo,* and *Alice,* the Federal Circuit has denied patents for various diagnostic methods. For example, in Ariosa Diagnostics, Inc. v. Sequenom, Inc., 788 F.3d 1371 (Fed. Cir. 2015), it found invalid a patent for a non-invasive prenatal test that analyzed cell-free fetal DNA (cffDNA) that circulates in a pregnant woman's blood (see Chapter 8, Section I). The representative claims were directed to the detection and amplification of cffDNA. Although the patent did not claim cffDNA itself, the Federal Circuit found it applied "routine, conventional steps to a natural phenomenon, specified at a high level of generality" and therefore did not describe "an inventive concept." Concluding that the patent was "directed to an application that starts and ends with a naturally occurring phenomenon," the court ruled it was invalid.

Recently, the Federal Circuit denied an en banc rehearing of the court's earlier invalidation of Athena's patent claim for a diagnostic test for myasthenia gravis. Athena Diagnostics, Inc. v. Mayo Collaborative Servs., LLC, 927 F.3d 1333 (Fed. Cir. 2019). The eight separate opinions in the denial all called "for Supreme Court or Congressional intervention" with respect to the eligibility of diagnostic patents. Dennis Crouch, Athena Loses on Eligibility—Although 12 Federal Circuit Judges Agree that Athena's Claims Should Be Eligible, Patently-O, July 3, 2019, https://patentlyo.com/patent/2019/07/eligiblity-although-eligible.html. Athena has petitioned for certiorari, asking the Supreme Court to clarify the patent eligibility of diagnostics. Mayo, has responded, arguing that if any such clarification is needed, that is a job for Congress. Turna Ray, Mayo Tells Court Congress Should Clarify Patent Eligibility Confusion in Diagnostics, Genomeweb, Nov. 25, 2019, https://www.genomeweb.com/policy-legislation/mayo-tells-supreme-court-congress-should-clarify-patent-eligibility-confusion#.Xe1cc-hKg2w.

As of the fall of 2019, Congress was considering a proposed bill that would overturn Supreme Court decisions that create exceptions to subject matter eligibility under § 101 for "abstract ideas," "laws of nature," or "natural phenomena." The bill is motivated by concerns that these decisions create incoherent and overly stringent patent eligibility standards, which hurt biotechnology and other innovation in the US, especially when technological rivals like China face few patent restrictions. Experts disagree as to whether the proposed bill would allow patents on specific genes. Some argue the requirement for novelty precludes that, although patents for complex methods to estimate someone's risk for disease through polygenic risk scores would likely be patent eligible. Critics fear the bill would allow monopolies on discoveries vital to research and medicine. They worry that a thicket of exclusive rights in biotechnology would hinder innovations that have led to lower prices for healthcare consumers. See Chris Anderson, Whose Genes Anyway?: Congressional Action on Section 101 of U.S. Patent Law Could Reopen Path to Patenting Genes, 6 Clinical Omics 46, July 18, 2019; Kelly Servick, Controversial U.S. Bill Would Lift Supreme Court Ban on Patenting Human Genes, Sci., Jun. 4, 2019, https://www.sciencemag.org/news/2019/06/controversial-us-bill-would-lift-supreme-court-ban-patenting-human-genes.

4.   Is patent reform of the sort under consideration by Congress a wise idea? How relevant is it that European countries, pursuant to the European Biotech Directive 98/44/EC and the European Patent Convention allow patents for isolated genes and other biological samples? The European Biotech Directive states that:

> 1.   * * * [I]nventions which are new, which involve an inventive step and which are susceptible of industrial application shall be patentable even if they concern a product consisting of or containing biological material or a process by means of which biological material is produced, processed or used.

2.   Biological material which is isolated from its natural environment or produced by means of a technical process may be the subject of an invention even if it previously occurred in nature.

Although it states that "the human body, . . . and the simple discovery of its elements, including the sequence or partial sequence of a gene, cannot constitute patentable inventions," it does allow patents for elements "isolated from the human body or otherwise produced by means of a technical process, including the sequence or partial sequence of a gene, . . . even if the structure of the element is identical to that of a natural element." Some argue that the United States' prohibition against patents for isolated genes puts the United States at a competitive disadvantage, given this European directive. How relevant should that be as Congress contemplates amending patent eligibility requirements?

5.   The national patent acts of the European Union member states define research and experimental use exemptions from patent infringement. Scholars argue that with those exemptions patents promote both research and innovation. See Hans-Rainer Jaenichen & Johann Pitz, Research Exemption/Experimental Use in the European Union: Patents Do Not Block the Progress of Science, 5 Cold Spring Harbor Persp. Med. 1 (2015). Should the United States include such an exemption in the Patent Code?

6.   The European Directive also treats inventions as unpatentable if "their commercial exploitation would be contrary to *ordre public* or morality," such as the processes for cloning human beings, modifying the human germline, or genetically modifying animals that "are likely to cause them suffering without any substantial medical benefit to man or animal, and also animals resulting from such processes." Should the United States Congress prohibit patents for such processes?

7.   Much of the concern surrounding Myriad's patents was the company's use of its exclusive rights to limit the ability of others to offer BRCA genetic testing. Even with the invalidation of its patents on genomic DNA, however, Myriad retained a "key competitive advantage" in genetic testing for breast and ovarian cancer because of its expansive proprietary database that contains information "correlating gene mutation with health outcomes, family histories, and other phenotypic factors." Having built up such data when it used its patent to prevent other US labs from offering such testing, Myriad gained "a unique ability to interpret BRCA gene test results," especially with respect to variants of uncertain significance (VUS). Others are working to create publicly accessible databases. Until they catch up, Myriad can provide much more clinical information about BRCA test results than others. This asymmetry has serious clinical significance if individuals undergo invasive preventive procedures, like mastectomies, based on a VUS that could have been resolved as clinically innocuous based on Myriad's database. John M. Conley et al., Myriad After Myriad: The Proprietary Data Dilemma, 15 N.C. J.L. & Tech. 597, 599–600 (2014).

Since Myriad stopped sharing its data with public suppositories in 2004, it treated its database as a trade secret. In 2016, the American Civil Liberties

Union (ACLU) filed an official complaint with the Department of Health and Human Services Office for Civil Rights on behalf of four individuals who had undergone genetic testing with Myriad. The ACLU alleged violations of their right to access their health information under the HIPAA Privacy Rule. Although the individuals received risk assessments, Myriad refused to grant their requests for their full genetic data. Health Information Privacy Complaint, Zeughauser v. Myriad Genetics Lab., U.S. Dep't of Health & Human Servs., Office for Civil Rights (May 19, 2016), https://www.aclu.org/sites/default/files/field_document/2016.5.19_hipaa_complaint.pdf. As of 2018, HHS had made no public response and did not answer questions about the status of the case. As the public database becomes more robust, Myriad's competitive advantage will diminish and the "BRCA fight" may become moot before HHS responds to this complaint. Kat McGowan, One of America's Biggest Genetic Testing Companies Refuses to Publicly Share Date that Could Save Countless Lives, Mother Jones, June 6, 2018, https://www.motherjones.com/politics/2018/06/one-of-americas-biggest-genetic-testing-companies-refuses-to-publicly-share-data-that-could-save-countless-lives/.

V.　TECHNOLOGY TRANSFER LAWS AND COMMERCIALIZATION

JAMES V. LACY ET AL., TECHNOLOGY TRANSFER LAWS GOVERNING FEDERALLY FUNDED RESEARCH AND DEVELOPMENT
19 Pepp. L. Rev. 1, 9–11, 13–14 (1991).

* * *

Economists have long realized that innovation affects demand and is thus one of the key forces that drives capitalism. A robust economy requires investment in research and development, as technological change most often results in production shifts, which can form the cornerstone of economic development and expansion. Technological innovation, however, can only be economically meaningful when it impacts the market. Therefore, a good idea which is never commercialized simply remains only a good idea.

The absence of a federal technology transfer policy prior to 1980 resulted in an enormous investment of money in R & D, which yielded a great deal of government-owned, but unlicensed, patents. Technological, bureaucratic, legal and communications problems, as well as a lack of basic incentives, prevented the transfer of this technology to American industry.

* * *

An economic parable states: "Lease a man a garden and in time he will leave you a patch of sand. Make a man a full owner of a patch of sand and he will grow there a garden on the sand." This parable highlights one of the basic problems with federal patent policy and technology transfer prior to 1980. There was no incentive for government inventors or institutions to create commercially viable technology because there was no legal basis to gain a piece of the resulting monetary rewards. As a result, commercially viable technology was not being created, and the wealth of federal inventions that were available for licensing were not being transferred for use in the private sector.

* * *

As a result of this concern, Congress enacted a series of bipartisan initiatives in the 1980s. These initiatives were aimed at revising government patent policy, reducing legal and bureaucratic barriers, and creating incentives to improve federal technology transfer to the private sector.

* * *

In short, recipients of government contracts, grants and cooperative agreements for the performance of experimental, developmental or research work funded in whole or in part by the federal government may now elect to retain title to any subject invention made in the course of that work.

* * *

[T]he government by statute must retain certain residual rights to the invention, including a government-use license to practice the invention, the right to limit exclusive licenses into which the funding recipient may wish to enter, and so-called "march-in" rights.

The government-use license that the Bayh-Dole Act imposes on contractors and grantees must provide the federal government with, at a minimum, "a nonexclusive, nontransferable, irrevocable, paid-up license to practice or have practiced for or on behalf of the United States any subject invention throughout the world." The statute also provides that the license may provide for such additional rights in favor of the government as are determined to be necessary by the government agency entering into grant, contract or cooperative agreement.

* * *

Finally, the government retains so-called "march-in" rights to inventions made with full or partial government funding. The government is provided the right to "march-in" and retake title to inventions in those cases where: (1) "action is necessary because the contractor or assignee has not taken, or is not expected to take within a reasonable time, effective steps to achieve practical application of the subject invention;" or (2) "action is necessary to alleviate health or safety needs which are not reasonably satisfied" by the contractor or grantee; or (3) "action is necessary to meet requirements for public use specified by Federal regulations and such requirements are not reasonably satisfied" by the contractor or grantee; or (4) the contractor or grantee has granted an exclusive license in violation of the "Preference for United States Industry."

SHELDON KRIMSKY, THE PROFIT OF SCIENTIFIC DISCOVERY AND ITS NORMATIVE IMPLICATIONS
75 Chi.-Kent L. Rev. 15, 21–22, 28–37 (1999).

* * *

[S]everal pieces of legislation were enacted in 1980 to create more cooperation between industries and universities. The Stevenson-Wydler Technology Transfer Act of 1980 encouraged interaction and cooperation among government laboratories, universities, big industries and small businesses. In the same year, Congress passed the Bayh-Dole Patent and Trademark Laws Amendment, which gave intellectual property rights to research findings to institutions that had received federal grants. Discoveries and inventions from public funds could be patented and licensed, initially to small businesses, with exclusive rights of royalties given to the grantee * * *. In 1983, by executive order, President Reagan extended the Bayh-Dole Act to all industry. To close the circle of research partnerships among industry, universities and government, Congress passed the Federal Technology Transfer Act of 1986, which expanded science-industry collaboration to laboratories run by the federal government. Governmental standards for keeping an arm's length from industry were being turned on their head. Through this act, a government scientist could form a "Cooperative Research and Development Agreement" ("CRADA") with a company as a route to commercializing discoveries made in a federal laboratory. Government scientists could accept royalty income up to a given amount [$150,000], fifteen percent of the National Institutes of Health (the "NIH") share, to supplement their salaries. At the time this policy was enacted, there was virtually no public discussion about the blatant conflicts of interest that this would introduce. The CRADA required government scientists to keep company data confidential and impeded the sharing of information in government laboratories.

* * *

By the mid-1980s, genetic technology had spawned hundreds of new companies, many with academic scientists as officers, board members or consultants. Small venture capital companies colonized the faculty of prestigious universities for building their intellectual capital. Major corporations that had sector interests in drugs, therapeutics, and agriculture invested large sums into multi-year contracts with universities.

* * *

[Studies published in the early 1990s showed that] these new arrangements * * * impeded the "free, rapid, and unbiased dissemination of research results." Biotechnology faculty with industry support were four times as likely as other biotechnology faculty to report that trade secrets had resulted from their research. The vast majority of the faculty without industry support viewed the commercial relationships as undermining intellectual exchange and cooperation within departments. The surveys also revealed that faculty believed the new relationships were responsible for skewing the research agenda in biology toward applied research.

* * *

[T]wo concerns flowing from the intense commercialization of science that could not be resolved by ethical standards established within universities were conflicts of interest and scientific bias * * *. Of the 789 articles and 1105 Massachusetts authors reviewed in * * * [a] study, thirty-four percent of the papers met one or more of the criteria for possessing a financial interest. Furthermore, none of the articles revealed the authors' financial interests.

* * *

[A] study which appeared in the Journal of General Internal Medicine reported that clinical trials sponsored by pharmaceutical companies were much more likely to favor new drugs (an outcome beneficial to the sponsoring companies in this case) than studies not supported by the companies.

[Another] study [found] that * * * those authors who were supportive of the obesity drugs were significantly more likely than the authors who were neutral or critical of the drugs to have a financial agreement with a manufacturer of a calcium channel blocker (ninety-six percent, sixty percent and thirty-seven percent respectively).

* * *

Because every biomedical discovery has potential monetary value, the new culture of science will seek to protect that discovery from becoming part of the "knowledge commons." * * * Scientists, instead of sharing their discoveries in a timely fashion, are protecting them as trade secrets. This has resulted in wasteful duplication of research, not for the sake of verifying results, but rather for establishing the unpublished data needed to secure intellectual property rights over the discovery. Writing in Science, Eliot Marshall noted, "[w]hile some duplication is normal in research, experts say it is getting out of hand in microbe sequencing. Tuberculosis, like *Staph aureus* and *H. pylori* will be sequenced many times over in part because sequencers aren't sharing data, whether for business reasons or because of interlab rivalries."

* * *

Companies have taken out patents on disease causing bacteria and viruses, sometimes keeping confidential parts of the sequenced genome. This may inhibit two companies competing in the search for a cure or treatment for a disease. Why should anyone own the natural sequence of a natural microorganism? Pharmaceutical companies can now exercise property ownership over both the drug to treat a disease and the microorganism that causes it. The intense privatization of biomedical knowledge that has evolved since the 1980s threatens the entire edifice of public health medicine.

LORI ANDREWS & DOROTHY NELKIN, BODY BAZAAR: THE MARKET FOR HUMAN TISSUE IN THE BIOTECHNOLOGY AGE
60–62 (2001).

Nowhere are these fundamental changes in scientific research more evident than at the National Institutes of Health, where scientists who are paid with taxpayer dollars can patent their research and pad their salaries with royalties. Allowing publicly-funded researchers to gain commercially, however, means that government-funded laboratories are experiencing some of the same problems with secrecy and conflicts of interest as industry-funded academic laboratories.

When government scientists enter joint ventures with business, their lips must be sealed concerning their data. Cooperative research and development agreements (CRADAs) restrict free access of information in NIH labs because of the requirement that company data be kept confidential. Anthony S. Fauci, the director of the National Institute of Allergy and Infectious Diseases, is worried about the effect of "CRADA fever." For the first time in his several decades at NIH, he says, scientists are reluctant to share information.

Leslie Roberts, writing in Science, points out, "The obvious concern is that some investigators might use the resources developed with public funds for their own proprietary interest. Yet another question is how will the genome project receive impartial advice when nearly everyone has a financial stake in it?"

People increasingly feel they are paying twice for research—once to the government to fund the research, and then again to the biotech companies who sell them products developed from taxpayer-funded research. In the pharmaceutical field, patents are generally thought to be necessary in order to encourage the discovery of drugs, and to fund the testing of these drugs on animals and humans. But genetic discoveries are very different from drug development. The public pays for the research that yields discoveries of genetic associations with disease. Genetic testing can be applied to humans as soon as the gene is accurately identified, without costly clinical trials. Financial compensation is thus less warranted.

The high costs of genetic tests and treatments seems ludicrous, given that taxpayers have provided much of the funding for their discovery. The NIH paid $4.6 million toward discovery of a gene predisposing women to breast cancer.

* * * The same thing occurs with funding for drug research. * * * [For example, a] kidney cancer drug, Proleukin, benefited from $46 million in research funds. Patients nevertheless pay up to $20,000 per treatment. Taxol, a breast and ovarian cancer treatment, received a $27 million federal subsidy; the treatment cost—$5,500.

Federal subsidies could have a much different impact on drug prices. The federal research handout could come with a requirement that the drug company lower prices to the consumer.

REBECCA GOULDING ET AL., ALTERNATIVE INTELLECTUAL PROPERTY FOR GENOMICS AND THE ACTIVITY OF TECHNOLOGY TRANSFER OFFICES: EMERGING DIRECTIONS IN RESEARCH
16 B.U. J. Sci. & Tech. L. 194, 202–05 (2010).

* * *

III. Concerns About IP Practices

Large numbers of patents related to genomics research have been granted over the past several decades and [Technology Transfer Offices (TTOs)], by their own measures, license these technologies with success, generating—in some cases—significant income for their institutions. With respect to genomics research, however, there are growing statements of concern about how IP is utilized and the appropriate role of TTOs in managing innovation. These include worries about the impact of patent practices on the open practice of science and on the pursuit of research and innovation. * * *

A. Practice of Science

* * * Stated broadly, the concern for open science is that the focus on patents fostered by the growth of gene patenting, the strong emergence of a biotechnology industry and the directives offered by the Bayh-Dole Act, diminish open practices and turn universities away from public-minded research in favor of potential commercial pursuits. The implication is that genomics scientists may be less open and collaborative in the pure pursuit of knowledge as they might have been before the advent of widespread IP in this area. Some scholars have identified impacts on the types of science

and the interchange between scientific practitioners as a function of the pursuit of IP rights.

B.   Concerns about Anti-Commons and Patent Thickets

There are also concerns about the impact of IP practices on the potential for future innovation. The fear is that if the genomics research landscape is characterized by numerous patents on basic upstream research, there is, consequently, a potential for the creation of an "anti-commons" and/or patent thickets which could block further scientific development and possibly the production of healthcare products.

The "anti-commons" is a term that was first used in the biosciences context by Michael Heller and Rebecca Eisenberg to describe a situation "in which people underuse scarce resources because too many owners can block each other." A patent thicket, in turn, is commonly understood as "a dense web of overlapping intellectual property rights that a company must [get] through in order to actually commercialize [a] new technology." Both of these concepts reflect genuine concerns about the relationship between genomic research and IP and have resonated within and outside the research community.

In reality, the extent of the impact of an anti-commons in genomics is not entirely clear. As articulated in Heller and Eisenberg's seminal article, the anti-commons could result in a potential decline in scientific research as researchers are blocked from access to, or use of, key ideas. Empirical studies carried out in recent years have questioned the extent or impact of this effect. For example, Caulfield asserts that gene patents per se have not impacted how scientists pursue research, postulating instead that academic researchers are influenced more by funding opportunities and career incentives within the academic community. In a different vein, Eisenberg has suggested that researchers are largely oblivious to patents and IP. Her implication might be, therefore, that patents are considered by researchers to be largely irrelevant to academic research.

At the same time, others have pointed to the fact that, even absent direct licensing-related obstacles, the existence of numerous patents poses a challenge for scientists attempting to access and use the work of others. Taken together, this work suggests that even in the absence of a full-scale anti-commons, there are reasons to be concerned about the impact of widespread patenting practices on upstream genomics.

JACOB S. SHERKOW & JORGE L. CONTRERAS, INTELLECTUAL PROPERTY, SURROGATE LICENSING, AND PRECISION MEDICINE

7 Intell. Prop. Theory 1, 4–6 (2018).

* * *

The promises and perils of university patenting have been well-documented. On the positive side of the ledger, university patenting encourages academic scientists to study "translational" technologies—technologies with immediate or near-term practical impact. University patenting also provides academic institutions with an additional revenue stream that, ideally, can be redeployed to serve education and fund further research. On the negative side of the ledger, some argue that university patenting "force[s] US taxpayers to 'pay twice' for patented products: once when they fund the initial grant, and again when they pay supra-competitive prices for the patented product." University patents may also threaten cross-institutional collaboration; skew internal funding, advancement, and promotion decisions; and ultimately stymie follow-on research if enforced against other academic institutions. Whatever the policy considerations, since Bayh Dole, universities and other research institutions have been obtaining patents in significant numbers, particularly in the biotechnology area.

Biotechnology's marriage of academic and commercial interests has led universities and research institutions to employ a range of methods for commercializing the technologies that they patent. Some university research may be sponsored directly by industrial collaborators, which obtain preferential rights in any technology resulting from that research. Other university research may be licensed directly by the university, commonly through a technology licensing or technology transfer office, to companies granted rights to exploit the technology, usually in exchange for a royalty based on sales. But a third, and increasingly popular, mode of university technology commercialization is the creation of a new company (a "spinoff" or "spinout") specifically designed for the purpose of commercializing a particular portfolio of the university's technologies and IP. Both the university and the researchers responsible for the relevant technologies often retain an equity ownership stake in the spinout company, which then obtains a license of the relevant IP from the university.

University spinouts are not new; they have been formed to commercialize academic research for more than a century, and have grown substantially in popularity in the wake of the Bayh-Dole Act. According to the Association of University Technology Managers (AUTM), U.S. and Canadian universities formed more than 11,000 start-up companies between 1994 and 2015, contributing to economic growth, job creation, and technology dissemination. Yet, commercial product development and IP licensing are not traditionally part of universities' larger translational research efforts. Ideally then, spinouts enable universities to allocate the responsibility for technology commercialization to external professionals, freeing university researchers to perform basic research. In that vein, spinouts appear to provide an efficient vehicle for raising external capital to fund the translation of scientific discoveries in university laboratories into marketable products. Notable university spinouts over the years have included Google (Stanford University), Bose (MIT), and Myriad Genetics (University of Utah).

Many spinouts leave the university free to license IP to other companies, for other applications, as the university and its researchers see fit. But one variant of this spinout approach uses the spinout as a "surrogate" for the university's broader licensing authority. In a typical transaction of this nature, the surrogate takes an exclusive license to the university's technology, with the charge simultaneously to move the technology toward commercial development, through its own efforts but also through sublicensing the IP to others. [We term] this licensing approach "surrogate licensing": the spinout company acts as a surrogate for the university, standing in the university's shoes for purposes of commercializing and sublicensing university IP. A significant, recent example of surrogate licensing exists with respect to the IP covering CRISPR-Cas9 gene-editing technology. Separately, the University of California (UC) and the Broad Institute (a joint effort of Harvard, MIT, and Harvard-affiliated research hospitals) have exclusively licensed each of their foundational CRISPR patent estates to surrogates: UC to Caribou Biosciences and the Broad Institute to Editas Medicine.

What differentiates surrogates from ordinary spinouts is the breadth of the university's delegation of its IP. In some cases, the field of research ceded by the university to its surrogate is practically universal. * * *

In the case of CRISPR-Cas9, the field ceded to the research institutions' surrogates encompasses every conceivable application—in the case of UC's license to Caribou—or, as with Editas, every CRISPR-based human therapy directed to any of the 19,000-plus human genes. In either instance, the CRISPR-Cas9 surrogate licenses are so vast as to allow single, for-profit entities to lay claim to a broad universe of the technology's applications in treating human disease. In addition, commercial applications for CRISPR extend beyond human therapies and into the realms of diagnostics, gene screening platforms, and agricultural applications. To the extent that universities abdicate their educational and public missions to for-profit surrogate companies, surrogate licensing casts in stark relief the distinction between universities' core missions as educational institutions and research enterprises and their commercial aspirations.

NOTES AND QUESTIONS

1.   What was the purpose of the technology transfer laws?

2.   Should products such as genetic tests or gene therapies that are developed with substantial amounts of public funds be priced or marketed differently than privately developed tests and therapies?

> **Food for Thought:** How would one design a study to determine whether the technology transfer laws have been effective? What would the definition and measure of "success" be? The number of patents obtained by government employees and federally-funded researchers has increased since the laws' passage. Is that a sufficient indicator of success?

3.   When a researcher has a financial interest in the gene or drug that he or she studies, should that fact be disclosed in publications? Since the publication of the Krimsky article, the journal Nature has changed its policy and now requires disclosures of conflicts of interest. In addition, the Department of Health and Human Services requires organizations that receive Public Health Service grants to have written policies defining what financial interests must be reported to the organization. The organizations must also identify the procedures they use to review and manage those interests. 42 C.F.R. § 50.601 et seq. Intellectual property rights, "any remuneration" (other than from the research institution) greater than $5000, and equity interests in a publicly traded equity greater than $5000 are some of the financial transactions or relationships that must be reported. Organizations must post their financial conflicts of interest policies on publicly accessible websites as well as specifics about conflicts of interest they identify. The options for addressing such conflicts include terminating the financial relationship, prohibiting the researcher from conducting the study, public disclosure of the financial relationship, or appointing independent monitors for the study. See F. Lisa Murtha et al., Conflicts of Interest in Research: Assessing the Effectiveness of COI Disclosure Program, 18 J. Health Care Compliance 5 (July/August 2016). Do these policies and regulations sufficiently address the problems of conflicts of interest described in the readings above? If not, what additional regulations could be imposed?

4.   The readings above discuss how patent rights and profit motives hinder research, make it duplicative, or more expensive. And yet the rationale for patent rights is that they promote research and the sharing of ideas. Can these ideas be reconciled?

5.   Does surrogate licensing, discussed in Sherkow and Contreras, *supra*, offer a useful way to further commercial innovation? What is the downside of such forms of university spinouts? Do they focus too heavily on encouraging commercial development of basic research at the expense of basic science research or health care?

CHAPTER 17

PATIENTS: THE SOURCES OF GENES AND CELL LINES

■ ■ ■

Patent on John Moore's cells

John Moore

MOORE V. REGENTS OF THE UNIVERSITY OF CALIFORNIA
793 P.2d 479 (Cal. 1990).

PANELLI, J.

[The plaintiff, John Moore, underwent treatment for hairy-cell leukemia at the Medical Center of the University of California at Los Angeles (UCLA Medical Center). The defendants were Dr. David Golde, the attending physician; the Regents of the University of California, who own and operate the university; Shirley G. Quan, a researcher at UCLA; Genetics Institute, Inc.; and Sandoz Pharmaceuticals Corporation.]

* * *

Moore first visited UCLA Medical Center on October 5, 1976, shortly after he learned that he had hairy-cell leukemia. After hospitalizing Moore and "withdr[awing] extensive amounts of blood, bone marrow aspirate, and other bodily substances," Golde confirmed that diagnosis. At this time all defendants, including Golde, were aware that "certain blood products and blood components were of great value in a number of commercial and

> **FYI:** Hairy-cell leukemia is a rare, slow growing cancer of the blood. It causes the bone marrow to produce too many B cells, a type of lymphocyte or white blood cell that helps fight infections. This form of leukemia is named after the fact that the B cells appear hairy under a microscope. The excess B cells can cause the spleen to enlarge, which if it is ruptured or causes pain might need to be removed. Splenectomies, however, are not commonly used to treat hairy cell leukemia.

scientific efforts" and that access to a patient whose blood contained these substances would provide "competitive, commercial, and scientific advantages."

On October 8, 1976, Golde recommended that Moore's spleen be removed. Golde informed Moore "that he had reason to fear for his life, and that the proposed splenectomy operation . . . was necessary to slow down the progress of his disease." Based upon Golde's representations, Moore signed a written consent form authorizing the splenectomy.

Before the operation, Golde and Quan "formed the intent and made arrangements to obtain portions of [Moore's] spleen following its removal" and to take them to a separate research unit. Golde gave written instructions to this effect on October 18 and 19, 1976. These research activities "were not intended to have . . . any relation to [Moore's] medical . . . care." However, neither Golde nor Quan informed Moore of their plans to conduct this research or requested his permission. Surgeons at UCLA Medical Center, whom the complaint does not name as defendants, removed Moore's spleen on October 20, 1976.

Moore returned to the UCLA Medical Center several times between November 1976 and September 1983. He did so at Golde's direction and based upon representations "that such visits were necessary and required for his health and well-being, and based upon the trust inherent in and by virtue of the physician-patient relationship. . . ." On each of these visits Golde withdrew additional samples of "blood, blood serum, skin, bone marrow aspirate, and sperm." On each occasion Moore travelled to the UCLA Medical Center from his home in Seattle because he had been told that the procedures were to be performed only there and only under Golde's direction.

"In fact, [however,] throughout the period of time that [Moore] was under [Golde's] care and treatment, . . . the defendants were actively involved in a number of activities which they concealed from [Moore]. . . ." Specifically, defendants were conducting research on Moore's cells and planned to "benefit financially and competitively . . . [by exploiting the cells] and [their] exclusive access to [the cells] by virtue of [Golde's] ongoing physician-patient relationship. . . ."

Sometime before August 1979, Golde established a cell line from Moore's T-lymphocytes.[2] On January 30, 1981, the Regents applied for a

---

[2] [A T-lymphocyte is a type of white blood cells that produces lymphokines, proteins that regulate the immune system.] Some lymphokines have potential therapeutic value. [The

patent on the cell line, listing Golde and Quan as inventors. "[B]y virtue of an established policy . . ., [the] Regents, Golde, and Quan would share in any royalties or profits . . . arising out of [the] patent." The patent issued on March 20, 1984, naming Golde and Quan as the inventors of the cell line and the Regents as the assignee of the patent. (U.S. Patent No. 4,438,032 (Mar. 20, 1984).)

The Regent's patent also covers various methods for using the cell line to produce lymphokines. Moore admits in his complaint that "the true clinical potential of each of the lymphokines . . . [is] difficult to predict, [but] . . . competing commercial firms in these relevant fields have published reports in biotechnology industry periodicals predicting a potential market of approximately $3.01 Billion Dollars by the year 1990 for a whole range of [such lymphokines]. . . ."

* * *

* * * Moore attempted to state 13 causes of action[, including conversion, lack of informed consent, and breach of fiduciary duty.] Each defendant demurred to each purported cause of action. The superior court, however, expressly considered the validity of only the first cause of action, conversion [and rejected it] * * *.

[T]he Court of Appeals reversed, holding that the complaint did state a cause of action for conversion * * *.

A. BREACH OF FIDUCIARY DUTY AND LACK OF INFORMED CONSENT

Moore repeatedly alleges that Golde failed to disclose the extent of his research and economic interests in Moore's cells before obtaining consent to the medical procedures by which the cells were extracted. These allegations, in our view, state a cause of action against Golde for invading a legally protected interest of his patient. This cause of action can properly be characterized either as the breach of a fiduciary duty to disclose facts material to the patient's consent or, alternatively, as the performance of medical procedures without first having obtained the patient's informed consent.

Our analysis begins with three well-established principles. First, "a person of adult years and in sound mind has the right, in the exercise of control over his own body, to determine whether or not to submit to lawful

---

identification of genetic variants responsible for a particular lymphokine can sometimes be used to manufacture large quantities of the lymphokine using recombinant DNA.] * * *

While the genetic code for lymphokines does not vary [among individuals], it can nevertheless be quite difficult to locate the gene responsible for a particular lymphokine. * * * Moore's T-lymphocytes were [valuable] because they overproduced certain lymphokines, [making it easier to identify the corresponding genetic variant.] * * *

Cells taken directly from the body (primary cells) are not very useful for these purposes [because] they typically reproduce a few times and then die. One can * * * use cells for an extended period of time by developing them into a "cell line," a culture capable of reproducing indefinitely. [The probability of succeeding with any given cell sample, however, is generally low.] * * *

medical treatment." Second, "the patient's consent to treatment, to be effective, must be an informed consent." Third, in soliciting the patient's consent, a physician has a fiduciary duty to disclose all information material to the patient's decision.

These principles lead to the following conclusions: (1) a physician must disclose personal interests unrelated to the patient's health, whether research or economic, that may affect the physician's professional judgment; and (2) a physician's failure to disclose such interests may give rise to a cause of action for performing medical procedures without informed consent or breach of fiduciary duty.

* * *

Indeed, the law already recognizes that a reasonable patient would want to know whether a physician has an economic interest that might affect the physician's professional judgment. As the Court of Appeal has said, "[c]ertainly a sick patient deserves to be free of any reasonable suspicion that his doctor's judgment is influenced by a profit motive." The desire to protect patients from possible conflicts of interest has also motivated legislative enactments. Among these is Business and Professions Code section 654.2. Under that section, a physician may not charge a patient on behalf of, or refer a patient to, any organization in which the physician has a "significant beneficial interest, unless [the physician] first discloses in writing to the patient, that there is such an interest and advises the patient that the patient may choose any organization for the purposes of obtaining the services ordered or requested by [the physician]." Similarly, under Health and Safety Code section 24173, a physician who plans to conduct a medical experiment on a patient must, among other things, inform the patient of "[t]he name of the sponsor or funding source, if any, . . . and the organization, if any, under whose general aegis the experiment is being conducted."

* * *

[While no law prohibits physicians from doing research in the area in which they practice,] a physician who treats a patient in whom he also has a research interest has potentially conflicting loyalties. This is because medical treatment decisions are made on the basis of proportionality— weighing the benefits *to the patient* against the risks *to the patient*. * * * A physician who adds his own research interests to this balance may be tempted to order a scientifically useful procedure or test that offers marginal, or no, benefits to the patient. The possibility that an interest extraneous to the patient's health has affected the physician's judgment is something that a reasonable patient would want to know in deciding whether to consent to a proposed course of treatment. It is material to the patient's decision and, thus, a prerequisite to informed consent.

* * *

B.   CONVERSION

Moore also attempts to characterize the invasion of his rights as a conversion—a tort that protects against interference with possessory and ownership interests in personal property. He theorizes that he continued to own his cells following their removal from his body, at least for the purpose of directing their use, and that he never consented to their use in potentially lucrative medical research. Thus, to complete Moore's argument, defendants' unauthorized use of his cells constitutes a conversion. As a result of the alleged conversion, Moore claims a proprietary interest in each of the products that any of the defendants might ever create from his cells or the patented cell line.

* * *

Since Moore clearly did not expect to retain possession of his cells following their removal, to sue for their conversion he must have retained an ownership interest in them. But there are several reasons to doubt that he did retain any such interest. First, no reported judicial decision supports Moore's claim, either directly or by close analogy. Second, California statutory law drastically limits any continuing interest of a patient in excised cells. Third, the subject matters of the Regents' patent—the patented cell line and the products derived from it—cannot be Moore's property.

Neither the Court of Appeal's opinion, the parties' briefs, nor our research discloses a case holding that a person retains a sufficient interest in excised cells to support a cause of action for conversion. We do not find this surprising, since the laws governing such things as human tissues, transplantable organs, blood, fetuses, pituitary glands, corneal tissue, and dead bodies deal with human biological materials as objects sui generis, regulating their disposition to achieve policy goals rather than abandoning them to the general law of personal property. It is these specialized statutes, not the law of conversion, to which courts ordinarily should and do look for guidance on the disposition of human biological materials.

* * *

Moore, adopting the analogy originally advanced by the Court of Appeal, argues that "[i]f the courts have found a sufficient proprietary interest in one's persona, how could one not have a right in one's own genetic material, something far more profoundly the essence of one's human uniqueness than a name or a face?" However, as the defendants' patent makes clear—and the complaint, too, if read with an understanding of the scientific terms which it has borrowed from the patent—the goal and result of defendants' efforts has been to manufacture lymphokines. Lymphokines, unlike a name or a face, have the same molecular structure in every human being and the same, important functions in every human being's immune system. Moreover, the particular genetic material which is responsible for the natural production of lymphokines, and which defendants use to manufacture lymphokines in the laboratory, is also the same in every person; it is no more unique to Moore than the number of vertebrae in the spine or the chemical formula of hemoglobin.

Another privacy case offered by analogy to support Moore's claim establishes only that patients have a right to refuse medical treatment * * *. Yet one may earnestly wish to protect privacy and dignity without accepting the extremely problematic conclusion that interference with those interests amounts to a conversion of personal property. Nor is it necessary to force the round pegs of "privacy" and "dignity" into the square hole of "property" in order to protect the patient, since the fiduciary-duty and informed-consent theories protect these interests directly by requiring full disclosure.

* * *

The extension of conversion law into this area will hinder research by restricting access to the necessary raw materials. Thousands of human cell lines already exist in tissue repositories * * *. These repositories respond to tens of thousands of requests for samples annually. Since the patent office requires the holders of patents on cell lines to make samples available to anyone, many patent holders place their cell lines in repositories to avoid the administrative burden of responding to requests. [H]uman cell lines are routinely copied and distributed to other researchers for experimental purposes, usually free of charge. This exchange of scientific materials, which still is relatively free and efficient, will surely be compromised if each cell sample becomes the potential subject matter of a lawsuit.

* * *

For these reasons, we hold that the allegations of Moore's third amended complaint state a cause of action for breach of fiduciary duty or lack of informed consent, but not conversion.

* * *

BROUSSARD, J., concurring and dissenting.

* * *

With respect to the conversion cause of action, I dissent from the majority's conclusion that the facts alleged in this case do not state a cause of action for conversion * * *. [T]he pertinent inquiry is not whether a patient generally retains an ownership interest in a body part after its removal from his body, but rather whether a patient has a right to determine, before a body part is removed, the use to which the part will be put after removal. Although the majority opinion suggests that there are "reasons to doubt" that a patient retains "any" ownership interest in his organs or cells after removal, the opinion fails to identify any statutory provision or common law authority that indicates that a patient does not generally have the right, before a body part is removed, to choose among the permissible uses to which the part may be put after removal. On the contrary, the most closely related statutory scheme—the Uniform Anatomical Gift Act—is quite clear that a patient does have this right.

* * *

One of the majority's principal policy concerns is that "[t]he extension of conversion law into this area will hinder research by restricting access to the necessary raw materials"—the thousands of cell lines and tissues already in cell and tissue repositories. The majority suggests that the "exchange of scientific materials, which still is relatively free and efficient, will surely be compromised if each cell sample becomes the potential subject matter of a lawsuit."

This policy argument is flawed in a number of respects * * *. For example, if a patient donated his removed cells to a medical center, reserving the right to approve or disapprove the research projects for which the cells would be used, and if another medical center or a drug manufacturer stole the cells after removal and used them in an unauthorized manner for its own economic gain, no breach-of-fiduciary-duty cause of action would be available and a conversion action would be necessary to vindicate the patient's rights. Under the majority's holding, however, the patient would have no right to bring a conversion action, even against such a thief. As this hypothetical illustrates, even if there were compelling policy reasons to limit the potential liability of innocent researchers who use cells obtained from an existing cell bank, those policy considerations would not justify the majority's broad abrogation of *all* conversion liability for the unauthorized use of body parts.

* * *

Because potential liability under a conversion theory will exist in only the exceedingly rare instance in which a doctor knowingly concealed from the patient the value of his body part or the patient's specific directive with regard to the use of the body part was disregarded, there is no reason to think that application of settled conversion law will have any negative effect on the primary conduct of medical researchers who use tissue and cell banks.

* * *

Under established conversion law, a "subsequent innocent converter" does not forfeit the proceeds of his own creative efforts, but rather "is entitled to the benefit of any work or labor that he has expended on the [property]."

* * *

Finally, the majority's analysis of the relevant policy considerations tellingly omits a most pertinent consideration. * * * [T]he opinion speaks only of the "patient's right to make autonomous medical decisions" * * * and fails even to mention the patient's interest in obtaining the economic value, if any, that may adhere in the subsequent use of his own body parts. Although such economic value may constitute a fortuitous "windfall" to the patient * * *, the fortuitous nature of the economic value does not justify the creation of a novel exception from conversion liability which sanctions the intentional misappropriation of that value from the patient.

* * *

It is certainly arguable that, as a matter of policy or morality, it would be wiser to prohibit any private individual or entity from profiting from the fortuitous value that adheres in a part of a human body, and instead to require all valuable excised body parts to be deposited in a public repository which would make such materials freely available to all scientists for the betterment of society as a whole * * *. But the majority's rejection of plaintiff's conversion cause of action does not mean that body parts may not be bought or sold for research or commercial purposes or that no private individual or entity may benefit economically from the fortuitous value of plaintiff's diseased cells. Far from elevating these biological materials above the marketplace, the majority's holding simply bars *plaintiff*, the source of the cells, from obtaining the benefit of the cells' value, but permits *defendants*, who allegedly obtained the cells from plaintiff by improper means, to retain and exploit the full economic value of their ill-gotten gains free of their ordinary common law liability for conversion.

* * *

MOSK, J., dissenting.

* * *

[T]he majority conclude that the patent somehow cut off all Moore's rights—past, present, and future—to share in the proceeds of defendants' commercial exploitation of the cell line derived from his own body tissue. The majority cite no authority for this unfair result, and I cannot believe it is compelled by the general law of patents: a patent is not a license to defraud. * * *

* * * [I]t does not necessarily follow that, as the majority claim, application of the law of conversion to this area "will hinder research by restricting access to the necessary raw materials," i.e., to cells, cell cultures, and cell lines.

* * *

To begin with, if the relevant exchange of scientific materials was ever "free and efficient," it is much less so today. Since biological products of genetic engineering became patentable in 1980 [under Diamond v. Chakrabarty], human cell lines have been amenable to patent protection and, * * * "[t]he rush to patent for exclusive use has been rampant." * * *

* * *

"Record keeping would not be overly burdensome because researchers generally keep accurate records of tissue sources for other reasons: to trace anomalies to the medical history of the patient, to maintain title for other researchers and * * * to insure reproducibility of the experiment."

* * *

In any event, in my view whatever merit the majority's single policy consideration may have is outweighed by two contrary considerations, i.e., policies that are promoted by recognizing that every individual has a legally protectible property interest in his own body and its products. First, our society acknowledges a profound ethical imperative to respect the human body as the physical and temporal expression of the unique human persona. One manifestation of that respect is our prohibition against direct abuse of the body by torture or other forms of cruel or unusual punishment. Another is our prohibition against indirect abuse of the body by its economic exploitation for the sole benefit of another person. The most abhorrent form of such exploitation, of course, was the institution of slavery. Lesser forms, such as indentured servitude or even debtor's prison, have also disappeared. Yet their specter haunts the laboratories and boardrooms of today's biotechnological research-industrial complex. It arises wherever scientists or industrialists claim, as defendants claim here, the right to appropriate and exploit a patient's tissue for their sole economic benefit—the right, in other words, to freely mine or harvest valuable physical properties of the patient's body.

* * *

The majority's final reason for refusing to recognize a conversion cause of action [here] is that "there is no pressing need" to do so because the complaint also states another a cause of action [for] "breach of a fiduciary duty to disclose facts material to the patient's consent or, alternatively, . . . the performance of medical procedures without first having obtained the patient's informed consent".

* * *

The remedy is largely illusory * * *. Few if any judges or juries are likely to believe that disclosure of such a possibility of research or development would dissuade a reasonably prudent person from consenting to the treatment. For example, * * * no trier of fact is likely to believe that if defendants had disclosed their plans for using Moore's cells, no reasonably prudent person in Moore's position—i.e., a leukemia patient suffering from a grossly enlarged spleen—would have consented to the routine operation that saved or at least prolonged his life.

* * *

The second reason why the nondisclosure cause of action is inadequate for the task that the majority assign to it is that it fails to solve half the problem before us: it gives the patient only the right to *refuse* consent, i.e., the right to prohibit the commercialization of his tissue; it does not give him the right to *grant* consent to that commercialization on the condition that he share in its proceeds.

* * *

In sum, the nondisclosure cause of action (1) is unlikely to be successful in most cases, (2) fails to protect patients' rights to share in the proceeds of the commercial exploitation of their tissue, and (3) may allow the true exploiters to escape liability. It is thus not an adequate substitute, in my view, for the conversion cause of action.

GREENBERG V. MIAMI CHILDREN'S HOSPITAL RESEARCH INSTITUTE, INC.

264 F.Supp.2d 1064 (S.D. Fla. 2003).

MORENO, J.

[The parents of children afflicted with Canavan disease and non-profit organizations that supported Defendants' efforts to identify the Canavan disease gene brought this diversity action against physician-researcher, Dr. Reuben Matalon; Miami Children's Hospital (MCH); and the hospital's research affiliate, Miami Children's Hospital Research Institute. Canavan disease is an incurable, progressive, neurological genetic disease. Affected children usually develop symptoms in infancy and typically do not live beyond 10 years. The condition mostly affects children of Ashkenazi Jewish and Saudi Arabian descent.

The plaintiffs alleged that, in 1987, before the gene for Canavan disease had been discovered, Daniel Greenberg approached Dr. Matalon, to request his involvement in identifying the genetic variants responsible for Canavan disease so that carrier and prenatal tests for the fatal condition could be developed. Greenberg and the Chicago Chapter of the National Tay-Sachs and Allied Disease Association, Inc. persuaded other Canavan families to provide blood, urine, and autopsy samples, financial support, and help in identifying Canavan families internationally.]

* * *

The individual Plaintiffs allege that they provided Matalon with these samples and confidential information "with the understanding and expectations that such samples and information would be used for the specific purpose of researching Canavan disease and identifying mutations in the Canavan disease which could lead to carrier detection within their families and benefit the population at large." Plaintiffs further allege that it was their "understanding that any carrier and prenatal testing developed in connection with the research for which they were providing essential support would be provided on an affordable and accessible basis, and that Matalon's research would remain in the public domain to promote the discovery of more effective prevention techniques and treatments and, eventually, to effectuate a cure for Canavan disease." This understanding stemmed from their "experience in community testing for Tay-Sachs disease, another deadly genetic disease that occurs most frequently in families of Ashkenazi Jewish descent."

Using Plaintiffs' blood and tissue samples, familial pedigree information, contacts, and financial support, Matalon and his research team successfully isolated the gene responsible for Canavan disease. * * * [U]nbeknownst to Plaintiffs, a patent application was submitted for the genetic sequence that Defendants had identified. This application was granted in October 1997. * * * Through patenting, Defendants acquired the ability to restrict any activity related to the Canavan disease gene, including without limitation: carrier and prenatal testing, gene therapy and other treatments for Canavan disease and research involving the gene and its mutations.

Plaintiffs allege that they did not learn of [the patent] until November 1998, when MCH revealed their intention to limit Canavan disease testing through a campaign of restrictive licensing of the Patent.

* * *

Based on these facts, Plaintiffs filed a six-count complaint on October 30, 2000, against Defendants asserting * * *: (1) lack of informed consent; (2) breach of fiduciary duty; (3) unjust enrichment; (4) fraudulent concealment; (5) conversion; and (6) misappropriation of trade secrets. Plaintiffs generally seek a permanent injunction restraining Defendants from enforcing their patent rights, damages in the form of all royalties Defendants have received on the Patent as well as all financial contributions Plaintiffs made to benefit Defendants' research. Plaintiffs allege that Defendants have earned significant royalties from Canavan disease testing in excess of $75,000 through enforcement of their gene patent, and that Dr. Matalon has personally profited by receiving a recent substantial federal grant to undertake further research on the gene patent.

* * *

A.   LACK OF INFORMED CONSENT

[Plaintiffs claim Defendants breached the duty of informed consent when they 1) failed to disclose the intent to patent and enforce for their own economic benefit the Canavan disease gene and 2) misrepresented the research purpose described on the consent forms. Plaintiffs allege they would not have made the contributions if they had known Defendants would "commercialize" the results of their contributions.]

* * *

The question of informed consent in the context of medical research, however, is a relatively novel one in Florida. Medical consent law does not apply to medical researchers. Florida Statute § 760.40 does require, however, that a person's informed consent must be obtained when any genetic analysis is undertaken on his or her tissue.

* * *

Since the law regarding a duty of informed consent for research subjects is unsettled and fact-specific and further, Defendants conceded at oral argument that a duty does attach at some point in the relationship, the Court finds that in certain circumstances a medical researcher does have a duty of informed consent. Nevertheless, without clear guidance from Florida jurisprudence, the Court must consider whether this duty of informed consent in medical research can be extended to disclosure of a researcher's economic interests.

* * *

Defendants assert that extending a possible informed consent duty to disclosing economic interests has no support in established law, and more ominously, this requirement would have pernicious effects over medical research, as it would give each donor complete control over how medical research is used and who benefits from that research. The Court agrees and declines to extend the duty of informed consent to cover a researcher's economic interests in this case.

* * *

In declining to extend the duty of informed consent to cover economic interests, the Court takes note of the practical implications of retroactively imposing a duty of this nature. First, imposing a duty of the character that Plaintiffs seek would be unworkable and would chill medical research as it would mandate that researchers constantly evaluate whether a discloseable event has occurred. Second, this extra duty would give rise to a type of dead-hand control that research subjects could hold because they would be able to dictate how medical research progresses. Finally, the Plaintiffs are more accurately portrayed as donors rather than objects of human experimentation, and thus the voluntary nature of their submissions warrants different treatment. Accordingly, the Court finds that Plaintiffs have failed to state a claim upon which relief may be granted, and this count is DISMISSED.

B.   BREACH OF FIDUCIARY DUTY

The individual Plaintiffs allege in Count II of the Complaint that all the Defendants were in a fiduciary relationship with them, and as such, they should have disclosed all material information relating to the Canavan disease research they were conducting, including any economic interests of the Defendants relating to that research.

* * *

Defendants assert that the Complaint does not allege any facts that show that the trust was recognized and accepted. Plaintiffs allege, however, that Defendants accepted the trust by undertaking research that they represented as being for the benefit of the Plaintiffs. * * * Taking all the facts alleged as true, the Court finds that Plaintiffs have not sufficiently alleged the second element of acceptance of trust by Defendants and therefore have failed to state a claim. There is no automatic fiduciary relationship that attaches when a researcher accepts medical donations and the acceptance of trust, the second constitutive element of finding a fiduciary duty, cannot be assumed once a donation is given. Accordingly, this claim is DISMISSED.

C.   UNJUST ENRICHMENT

In Count III of the Complaint, Plaintiffs allege that MCH is being unjustly enriched by collecting license fees under the Patent. * * * The Court finds that Plaintiffs have sufficiently alleged the elements of a claim for unjust enrichment to survive Defendants' motion to dismiss.

* * *

[T]he facts paint a picture of a continuing research collaboration that involved Plaintiffs also investing time and significant resources in the race to isolate the Canavan gene. Therefore, given the facts as alleged, the Court finds that Plaintiffs have sufficiently pled the requisite elements of an unjust enrichment claim and the motion to dismiss for failure to state a claim is DENIED as to this count.

D.   FRAUDULENT CONCEALMENT

Count IV of the Complaint alleges that MCH fraudulently concealed from the Plaintiffs that (1) the Hospital would economically benefit from Canavan research; (2) it would patent the Canavan gene mutation; and (3) it would license the testing under the Patent.

* * *

[T]here was no duty of disclosure to the Plaintiffs. Allegations of fraudulent concealment by silence must be accompanied by allegations of a special relationship that gives rise to a duty to speak. * * * [T]he facts asserted as fraudulently concealed were accessible to the Plaintiffs. A patent becomes public knowledge when issued and Plaintiffs could have undertaken due diligence to uncover the facts surrounding the patent application. Plaintiffs' allegations that they were prevented from making reasonable inquiries because they had no reason to believe that patenting would occur is unavailing because if they were so concerned about a possible intent to patent then a simple phone inquiry to the Defendants would have uncovered this fact.

* * *

Plaintiffs contend that, but for the fraudulent non-disclosure, they would have acted differently. Nevertheless, fraud must be specially pled, and the Complaint does not adequately allege a claim based on a special relationship or of injury nor does it allege more specifics about efforts at concealment or about any representations made by Matalon as to what he would do with the test results. Therefore, the Court finds that the Complaint lacks the specificity required by Fed.R.Civ.P. 9(b). Accordingly, the fraudulent concealment claim is DISMISSED.

E.   CONVERSION

The Plaintiffs allege in Count V of their Complaint that they had a property interest in their body tissue and genetic information, and that they owned the Canavan registry in Illinois which contained contact information, pedigree information and family information for Canavan families worldwide. They claim that MCH and Matalon converted the names on the register and the genetic information by utilizing them for the hospitals' "exclusive economic benefit." The Court disagrees and declines to find a property interest for the body tissue and genetic information voluntarily given to Defendants. These were donations to research without any contemporaneous expectations of return of the body tissue and genetic samples, and thus conversion does not lie as a cause of action.

In Florida, the tort of "conversion is an unauthorized act which deprives another of his property permanently or for an indefinite time." Using property given for one purpose for another purpose constitutes conversion.

First, Plaintiffs have no cognizable property interest in body tissue and genetic matter donated for research under a theory of conversion. This case is similar to Moore v. Regents of the University of California, where the Court declined to extend liability under a theory of conversion to misuse of a person's excised biological materials * * * because the donor had no property interest [in excised bodily material used in research] after the donation was made. The [Moore] Court also recognized that the patented result of research is "both factually and legally distinct" from excised material used in the research.

Second, limits to the property rights that attach to body tissue have been recognized in Florida state courts * * * Similarly, the property right in blood and tissue samples also evaporates once the sample is voluntarily given to a third party.

Plaintiffs rely on Pioneer Hi-Bred v. Holden Foundation, 1987 WL 341211 (S.D.Iowa, Oct.30, 1987), aff'd, 35 F.3d 1226 (8th Cir.1994), for their assertion that genetic information itself can constitute property for the purposes of the tort of conversion. In that case, the Court held that a corn seed's property interest in the genetic message contained in a corn seed variety is property protected by the laws of conversion. Plaintiffs argue that giving permission for one purpose (gene discovery) does not mean they agreed to other uses (gene patenting and commercialization). Yet, the Pioneer court recognized that, "where information is gathered and arranged at some cost and sold as a commodity on the market, it is properly protected as property." This seemingly provides more support for property rights inherent in Defendants' research rather than the donations of Plaintiffs' DNA. * * *

Plaintiffs have not cited any case that interprets the statute [Fla. Stat. § 760.40, which provides that the results of DNA analysis "are the exclusive property of the person tested"] as applying to an analogous factual situation, and this Court's investigation did not find any relevant case either. Moreover, even assuming, arguendo, that the statute does create a property right in genetic material donated for medical research purposes, it is unclear whether this confers a property right for conversion, a common law cause of action.

Finally, although the Complaint sets out that Plaintiff Greenberg owned the Canavan Registry, the facts alleged do not sufficiently allege the elements of a prima facie case of conversion, as the Plaintiffs have not alleged how the Defendants' use of the Registry in their research was an expressly unauthorized act. The Complaint only alleges that the Defendants "utilized the information and contacts for their exclusive economic benefit." There is no further allegation of the circumstances or conditions that were attached to the Defendants' use of the Canavan Registry. Nor are there any allegations about any of the Plaintiffs' entitlement to possess the Registry.

The Court finds that Florida statutory and common law do not provide a remedy for Plaintiffs' donations of body tissue and blood samples under a theory of conversion liability. Indeed, the Complaint does not allege that the Defendants used the genetic material for any purpose but medical research. Plaintiffs claim that the fruits of the research, namely the patented material, was commercialized. This is an important distinction and another step in the chain of attenuation that renders conversion liability inapplicable to the facts as alleged. If adopted, the expansive theory championed by Plaintiffs would cripple medical research as it would bestow a continuing right for donors to possess the results of any research conducted by the hospital. At the core, these were donations to research without any contemporaneous expectations of return. Consequently, the Plaintiffs have failed to state a claim upon which relief may be granted on this issue. Accordingly, this claim is DISMISSED.

F.   MISAPPROPRIATION OF TRADE SECRETS

The Canavan Registry was not misappropriated by MCH because there is no allegation that MCH knew or should have known that the Canavan Registry was a confidential trade secret guarded by Plaintiffs, and furthermore, that Matalon had acquired through improper means. Plaintiffs cannot donate information that they prepared for fighting a disease and then retroactively claim that it was a protected secret. * * * This claim is therefore DISMISSED.

AMERICAN MEDICAL ASSOCIATION, COUNCIL ON ETHICAL AND JUDICIAL AFFAIRS, CODE OF MEDICAL ETHICS: CURRENT OPINIONS WITH ANNOTATIONS, 2012–2013 ED.

(2013).

2.08 Commercial Use of Human Tissue

The rapid growth of the biotechnology industry has resulted in the commercial availability of numerous therapeutic and other products developed from human tissue. Physicians contemplating the commercial use of human tissue should abide by the following guidelines:

(1) Informed consent must be obtained from patients for the use of organs or tissues in clinical research.

(2) Potential commercial applications must be disclosed to the patient before a profit is realized on products developed from biological materials.

(3) Human tissue and its products may not be used for commercial purposes without the informed consent of the patient who provided the original cellular material.

(4) Profits from the commercial use of human tissue and its products may be shared with patients, in accordance with lawful contractual agreements.

(5) The diagnostic and therapeutic alternatives offered to patients by their physicians should conform to standards of good

medical practice and should not be influenced in any way by the commercial potential of the patient's tissue.

Issued June 1994 based on the report Who Should Profit from the Economic Value of Human Tissue? An Ethical Analysis, adopted June 1990.

NOTES AND QUESTIONS

1.   Like the *Moore* and *Greenberg* courts, the Eighth Circuit held that prostate cancer patients who voluntarily provided biological samples as research participants for genetics research at Washington University had no ownership or proprietary interests in the samples. Since the early 1980s, Dr. William Catalona, a prostate cancer surgeon, had asked his patients if they were willing to let him use the tissue removed during their surgery, blood, and other tissue for research. Over the years he amassed over 30,000 tissue samples and an enviable set of research results. Thanks to Dr. Catalona's research, men now routinely use a simple blood test to screen for prostate cancer. When Dr. Catalona decided to leave his job at Washington University to take a new position at Northwestern University, he intended to take the tissue samples with him to continue his research. He sought permission from the research subjects to move the samples and over 6,000 people asked that their samples be transferred to Northwestern University.

Washington University sought to prevent the transfers by asking a federal court to declare that the university was the legal owner of the samples. The patients were eventually added as necessary parties to the matter; they argued that they owned their samples and could thus transfer them. Washington University argued that the patients had no ownership rights to tissue that had been donated for research purposes. The patients and Dr. Catalona disputed that depiction, claiming that the tissue samples had not been donated or gifted to the university, but were instead provided to Dr. Catalona for a particular use—research on prostate cancer. The patients also claimed that, under the research informed consent forms, they had retained rights to control what happened to their tissue samples, including the right to withdraw samples from research and in some cases to have samples destroyed, and as such there could not have been a gift of their tissue samples to the university. In April 2006, the district court ruled that the informed consent form under which the patients retained rights was "inconsequential" and held that the samples were the property of Washington University. The court stated that the patients released their samples to Washington University as *inter vivos* gifts, finding all the elements of a gift were present on the facts: (1) present donative intent, (2) delivery of the gift, and (3) acceptance of the gift. Washington University v. Catalona et al., 437 F.Supp.2d 985 (E.D. Mo.2006).

The Court of Appeals for the Eighth Circuit affirmed the judgment of the district court. In addressing whether the patients' limited rights to withdraw their tissue from research prevented them from making an *inter vivos* gift, the appellate court noted that under Missouri law, an individual can give a charitable donation as a valid gift, even if the donation is subject to a condition of revocation. In this case, the condition of revocation would be the patients' rights to withdraw from research. Thus, according to the court, the patients made valid *inter vivos* gifts to Washington University under Missouri law.

Additionally, the appellate court clarified what it meant if the patients withdrew from research. The district court had indicated that federal regulations permitted Washington University to use a patient's tissue for research if it removed all donor-identifying information, even if the patient expressed a desire to withdraw from the research process. In contrast, the Eighth Circuit stated that patients have the right to withdraw from research by (1) prohibiting future research of any kind on their samples, (2) refusing to donate more samples, and (3) refusing to answer additional questions. Washington University v. Catalona, 490 F.3d 667, 673–676 (8th Cir. 2007), cert. denied, 552 U.S. 1166 (2008).

The district court had ruled that Washington University, not the patients, had a property interest in the biological samples. Does the Eighth Circuit ruling also deny patients a property interest in their biological samples because it views the donations of the samples as a " 'voluntary transfer of property by the owner to another.' " What is the effect of the Eighth Circuit's holding that patients can prohibit further research of any kind on their samples? Does it mean that patients retain some property interest in their tissue?

2.   On what legal grounds does the patient have a right to be informed of a physician's research interests and commercial interests? Why does Justice Mosk believe that the nondisclosure causes of action are inadequate?

3.   Is it likely that granting property interests in the biological samples of Moore, the families in *Greenberg*, or the patients in *Catalona* have hampered research? If so, how?

4.   Should the courts formally recognize a property interest in excised tissue or genes? If so, how extensive should this interest be? Should individuals retain control of their samples even after donating them to research? Should relatives of donors be able to control the use of the donor's sample after the donor's death?

Radhika Rao has noted the law's inconsistency surrounding ownership of body parts. Blood is treated as "a full-fledged commodity" when courts treat the sale of blood as taxable income. On the other hand, the status of organs and other body parts is less clear. Rao notes they cannot be bought or sold for transplant under the National Organ Transplant Act, which makes it unlawful "to knowingly acquire, receive or otherwise transfer any human organ for valuable consideration for use in human transplantation," although she suggests it may be permissible to donate them for transplant or perhaps even to sell them for other purposes. She argues the Uniform Anatomical Gift Act treats bodies and body parts of the deceased as property by giving the "owners" the right to donate their bodies or body parts after death for transplant, therapy, or research. These rights pass to close relatives, who may donate a loved one's body after death if there is no evidence the decedent would decide otherwise.

Cadavers, however, cannot be sold, although they can be donated. The common law treats them as "quasi property." Close relatives retain certain rights, such as "the right to possess the body for purposes of burial, the right to control the body's use in certain ways, the right to exclude others, and the right to direct the body's ultimate disposal." Rao describes the quasi-property right in cadavers as a "legal fiction created to enable relatives to recover for the tort of mental distress." In redressing "emotional harm rather than pecuniary injury," she describes it as falling under the" umbrella of privacy."

Rao suggests courts have treated one's interest in reproductive material like sperm and embryos at times like property and at others like privacy. In a dispute over the disposal of a decedent's sperm, which he had wanted to bequeath to his girlfriend, the California Court of Appeals initially treated the sperm as property and therefore part of the estate and subject to the probate court's jurisdiction. Hecht v. Superior Court (Kane), 20 Cal. Rptr. 2d 275 (Cal. Dist. Ct. App. 1993). The court later rejected the notion that the sperm was property or an asset of the estate. Instead it viewed the decedent's decisions concerning the use of his sperm as central to his procreative interests, Hecht v. Superior Court (Kane), 59 Cal. Rptr. 2d 222 (Cal. Dist. App. Ct. 1996), which Rao views as a constitutional privacy interest. Similarly, frozen embryos have been treated as property in cases where disputes over their disposition was resolved based on the idea that a couple's cryopreservation agreement with a fertility clinic regarding the couple's frozen embryo created a bailment relationship. Other cases, however, suggest the right of progenitors to make decisions about the disposition of their embryos, which implicates constitutional privacy interests in reproduction. Radhika Rao, Property, Privacy, and the Human Body, 80 B.U. L. Rev. 359, 371–88, 414–17 (2000). Is it possible to describe a unifying theory for the law's varied treatment of different kinds of body parts?

5.   Although property rights were initially understood to entitle one to absolute control over the subject of ownership, the more contemporary view is that property interests range from limited to absolute. They include among other things, interests in exclusive possession or use of the object, control over how it is used or kept from use (transferability), alienability, and devisability. While individuals possess the DNA and cells in their bodies, can they restrict others from accessing them by controlling the disposal of body parts? Can only the individuals in whose cells the DNA resides modify, destroy or alienate the genetic information therein? Are individuals immune from expropriation of the information in their DNA? Can only the person whose cells contain the DNA give away that information through donations of the cells or by passing on the DNA through reproduction? Can individuals control their genetic information during their lifetime or after? Can individuals bequeath or devise their genetic information? See Catherine M. Valerio Barrad, Genetic Information and Property Theory, 87 Nw.U. L. Rev. 1037 (1993).

6. As of 2019, five states have enacted laws identifying genetic information as the property of the person from whom it came or to whom it pertains: Alaska Stat. Ann. § 18.13.010 (2) ("exclusive property"); Colo. Rev. Stat. Ann. 10–3–1104.7(1) ("unique property"); Fla. Stat. Ann. § 760.40(2)(a) ("exclusive property"); Ga. Code Ann. § 33–54–1(1) ("unique property"); 22:1023(E) ("property of the insured or enrollee").

Alaska is unique in also identifying "a DNA sample" as "the exclusive property of the person sampled or analyzed." Alaska Stat. Ann. § 18.13.010 (2). Are the legal, ethical, and social implications of defining genetic *information* as property different from those of defining *DNA samples* as property? Why might so few states have created property rights in genetic information and even fewer in DNA samples?

7. The statutes that create property rights in genetic information and/or genetic samples do so in the context of protecting genetic privacy. What are some rationales for using the language of property to protect privacy interests? Sonia Suter suggests various rationales that might motivate such legislation:

1) "The use of property language in talking about genetic information is compelling because we use the possessive to refer to that which is deeply meaningful" like our bodies and our loved ones.

2) "Property has always been a powerful tool to protect important interests because it is familiar and effective. . . . [I]t has always suggested a power to restrict others."

3) "Property's long legal tradition not only suggests power and protection but also offers the illusion of simplicity. . . . To many, property appears to offer simpler and clearer protections than the newer or more contested concept of privacy."

4) "One of the most common reasons for creating property rights in personal information is the control property seems to provide. . . . Control is central to informational privacy, and 'property' works as a proxy for such control."

5) "Property rights in personal or genetic information are also attractive to many because the term suggests . . . the ability to buy and sell the object as a commodity. . . . Even the Restatement of Property states that '[P]roperty interests are, in general, alienable.' "

Sonia M. Suter, Disentangling Privacy from Property, 72 Geo. Wash. L. Rev. 737, 750–757 (2004). Which of these reasons most strongly supports creating property rights in genetic information or samples? Are there additional reasons to use property rights to protect our interests in our genetic information or DNA?

8. In *Moore*, Justice Broussard makes a compelling argument for property rights with respect to genetic information or tissue samples: markets

already exist for personal information and body parts. If others can own and profit from them, why can't the source of the genetic information or DNA?

Justice Broussard suggests an alternative to patenting: making cell lines and genes available to all scientists through a public repository. Would this more communitarian alternative address the profit imbalance by preventing patients and scientists from having a property right in cells or genes? Does this approach present any challenges?

9.   Suter argues in favor of privacy protections over property protections on the grounds that the latter threatens to commodify something integral to the self and introduces and potentially infects the relationships of trust in which genetic information is disclosed. Suter, *supra*. Would allowing a person to have a property right in his or her genes "commodify" individuals? If selling genes is permitted, what about other parts of people like organs? What about selling people as a whole—i.e., slavery? It is important to note that just because something is legally considered to be property does not preclude limiting its sale or use. What restrictions, if any, are appropriate for genes?

10.   Various scholars have argued that we have property rights of sorts in our genetic information. For example, Jorge Contreras argues that a de facto property regime has been created through informed consent requirements, which give individuals the right to exclude, the right to destroy, dead hand control, divisibility, and alienability. In fact, he critiques "propertizing consent" in research as giving "individuals excessive and inappropriate control over genetic data" and stymying "socially valuable biomedical research." Jorge Contreras, Genetic Property, 105 Geo. L.J. 1, 7 (2016).

Jessica Roberts argues that individuals have "three limited property entitlements that make up the personal genetic ownership bundle" with respect to genetic information. She identifies a right to exclude through informed consent; genetic access rights, through the HIPAA rule and other regulations; and the right to commercialize, given that some companies offer individuals commercial interests and researchers must tell participants whether their research will be used for commercial purposes. Jessica Roberts, Progressive Genetic Ownership, 93 Notre Dame L. Rev. 1105, 1129–33 (2018).

In a different vein, Natalie Ram argues that the law of property, specifically tenancy by the entirety, offers a useful framework to recognize that genetic information is "shared immutably and nonvolitionally" between biological relatives. She reasons that this property concept is preferable to privacy because it is less individualistic and considers the shared interests in genetic information among family members in the context of forensic familial searching (see Chapter 20, Part V), genetic research, and personal genetic testing. Natalie Ram, DNA by the Entirety, 115 Columbia L. Rev. 873, 877 (2015).

Are these theories of property rights persuasive? Are they preferable to privacy or other theories of law to protect the interests at stake? Roberts identifies the conflicting views regarding genetic ownership rights. Some view these rights as creating "positive incentives" for researchers, biotech companies, and individuals to engage in research. Others worry they create an anticommons problem, where "ownership leads to underuse"; a collective action problem, where individuals opt out leading potentially to selection bias; and perverse incentives, where rights like patents discourage the sharing necessary for innovation. Roberts, *supra* at 1133–45.

11.   Recently, a few courts have allowed conversion claims with respect to genetic information. For example, the Federal District Court of Alaska, in Cole v. Gene by Gene, Ltd., No. 1:14–cv–00004, 2017 WL 2838256 (D. Ala. June 30, 2017), seemed willing to recognize a conversion cause of action with respect to the unauthorized use of someone's genetic information. In that case, Michael Cole had taken a DNA ancestry test and signed up for optional participation in projects run by third-party volunteers. A few months later, after receiving excessive amounts of junk mail, he searched for his email address on the internet. Not only did he find it on a website, he also discovered that his DNA results were publicly available. Cole sued Gene by Gene for violating the Alaska Genetic Privacy Act, which states that DNA samples and the results of DNA analysis "are the exclusive property of the person sampled or analyzed," and which allows for a private right of action for violations of the act. In allowing the claim to proceed, the district court observed that the "statutory entitlements bear a close relationship to the common law torts of conversion of property and invasion of privacy, which have each historically provided a basis for a lawsuit in American courts." *Id.* at *3–4.

Similarly, a Florida trial court allowed plaintiffs, Mr. and Mrs. Perlmutter, to bring a claim for conversion against Harold Peerenboom for allegedly "collecting, analyzing, and testing the genetic material to obtain the Perlmutters' confidential genetic information" and for exercising "dominion and authority" in a way that "deprived the Perlmutters of their rights of ownership, possession, control and privacy." The Perlmutters claimed that, after a dispute over the management of a tennis court on a property where Peerenboom lived, Peerenboom hired a forensic testing company to test their DNA on a discarded water bottle. Finding that the Perlmutters "plainly retain important intangible rights to their genetic information," the court found it appropriate to extend "conversion's definition of property to one's intangible rights in his or her genetic information." Am. Countercl. at 24, Peerenboom v. Perlmutter, No. 2013–CA–015257 (Fla. Cir. Ct. Apr. 7, 2017).

The *Perlmutter* court reconciled its decision with *Greenberg* and *Moore* by reasoning that those cases dealt with genetic material, whereas *Perlmutter* dealt with genetic information. Moreover, in *Greenberg*, the plaintiffs donated their samples, whereas Peerenboom allegedly collected the plaintiffs' DNA without consent. Order Den. Pl.'s Mot. to Dismiss Def.'s Countercl., Peerenboom v. Perlmutter, No. 2013–CA–015257, at 10–12 (Fla. Cir. Ct. Jan. 23, 2017). Is this distinction persuasive? Does the fact that both states have legislation recognizing property rights in genetic information play a role in the courts' willingness to contemplate conversion claims?

12.   Although much attention has been paid to the John Moore case, he is not the first person whose cell lines were made commercially available. In 1951, a 31-year-old African-American woman, Henrietta Lacks, was dying of cervical cancer. Dr. George Otto Gey, a cell biologist at Johns Hopkins University at the time, used her cancerous tissue to create the first immortalized human cell line, the HeLa cell line, which could grow continuously in vitro. The HeLa cells have been used by generations of scientists for research. In an interview, her husband said, "As far as them selling my wife's cells without my knowledge and making a profit—I don't like it at all. They are exploiting us both." Harriet A. Washington, Henrietta Lacks—An Unsung Hero, Emerge, Oct. 1994, at 29; Rebecca Skloot, The Immortal Life of Henrietta Lacks (2010).

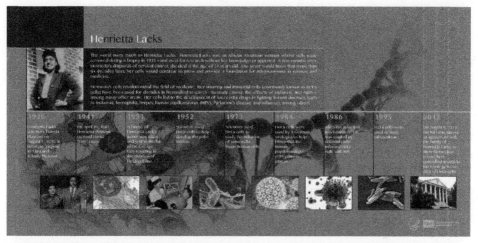

This timeline includes events from 1920 (when Lacks was born) to 2013 (when NIH announced an agreement with the Lacks family to allow biomedical researchers controlled access to the whole genome data of HeLa cells).
Credit: Darryl Leja, National Human Genome Research Institute, www.genome.gov.

13.   Patients' tissue samples are now a commercial resource for hospitals. Duke University Medical Center entered into a commercial agreement with Ardais, granting the start-up genomics company access to Duke's patients' tissue. Harvard Beth Israel Deaconess Medical Center entered into a similar arrangement. Should patients whose tissue is part of these deals be informed of the arrangements? Should they receive compensation? The Revised Common rule requires the researchers to include a statement, as part of the informed consent process, "that the subject's biospecimens (even if identifiers are removed) may be used for commercial profit and whether the subject will or will not share in this commercial profit." 45 C.F.R. § 46.116(c)(7).

14.   In *Moore*, Justice Mosk suggested that patients or research subjects who were the source of genes or cell lines could be listed as co-inventors on the patent. A decade later, in 2000, the patient group PXE International followed that approach. The patients suffered from pseudoxanthoma elasticum (PXE), a genetic disorder that causes connective tissue in the skin, eyes, and arteries

to calcify. Because PXE had been under-researched, PXE International set up a tissue bank of families afflicted with the disease. To gain access to the tissue bank, researchers had to sign a contract saying that they would share with PXE International the ownership and profits from research using those samples. When University of Hawaii pathobiologist Charles Boyd found the PXE gene in 2000, he filed a patent application listing Sharon Terry, the founder of PXE International and the mother of two children with the disorder, as a co-inventor on the patent. PXE International will split royalties gained from the patent equally with the university, and will have control over licensing arrangements for the gene patent. Matt Fleisher, Seeking Rights to Crucial Genes, Nat'l L.J., June 25, 2001, at C 1.

If you were representing a patient group, what provisions might you want to put into an agreement with researchers?

15. When arrangements to be a co-inventor or co-owner of a patent are not made in advance, the people whose DNA was used to find a particular gene may not be able to assert a claim to be recognized on the patent. Eric Fuchs realized he had been repeatedly exposed to HIV infection without becoming symptomatic. He suggested to researchers that they search his blood for the unique factor that appeared to make him immune. When researchers at the Aaron Diamond AIDS Research Center found it, they patented it. Fuchs believes that his role in the research should be recognized via co-ownership of the patent. Is he correct that his role should be recognized? Why or why not? What about other people who serve as controls in such studies? Should their role be recognized?

PART V

NON-MEDICAL USES OF GENETICS

■ ■ ■

Part II described the various uses of genetic testing in medical care and clinical research. Genetic analysis is also helpful in many non-medical contexts, far more than can be covered in this textbook. Part V will focus on three specific areas where non-clinical applications of genetics are important in the law: forensics, criminal litigation, and civil litigation. Because our genetic profiles are unique (unless we have an identical twin), genetic testing can be used for identification purposes. As Chapters 18–21 discuss in detail below, DNA analysis has become a vital part of forensic analysis, helping to identify suspects based on crime scene samples or to identify the remains of victims in accidents, crimes, or battles in war. Chapter 18 describes the science of forensic DNA analysis, the admissibility issues of forensic DNA evidence, and the legal issues that arise from various methods of collecting DNA samples for forensic purposes. Chapter 19 explores the constitutional issues surrounding the expanding forensic DNA databases, while Chapter 20 examines the uses and regulations of these databases, including an emerging technique called familial searching. Finally, Chapter 21 discusses post-conviction DNA testing.

Sometimes genetics, particularly behavioral genetics, enters the criminal justice system at the behest of defendants who wish to claim that their genetic profile should exculpate them from conviction or mitigate their punishment. Chapter 22 provides some background on behavioral genetics, particularly in criminal litigation, to examine the legal and scientific limitations of using genetics in this context.

The last chapter of Part V, Chapter 23 explores the use of genetics in civil litigation. It discusses the science, law, and policy of tort recovery for toxicogenomic and epigenetic based harms. It also considers the introduction of genetic information in occupational and environmental regulation, and the admissibility and weight given to general and individual-specific genetic information.

Before turning to these three non-clinical uses of genetics, we take a moment to describe a few other contexts in which genetic analysis is used outside of the medical setting. Because close relatives share more genetic material with one another than with unrelated individuals, genetic testing can help identify biological kin. DNA-based paternity testing became a booming industry in the 1990s. It can resolve uncertainty about paternity for various purposes, including legal determinations of paternity, proving adultery in divorce, inheritance disputes, and family mix-ups. Sometimes, the results have devastating consequences, however, when they demonstrate presumed biological fathers are not, in fact, genetic fathers.

More recently, the search for familial connections through DNA has become a popular pastime with the growth of direct-to-consumer (DTC) DNA ancestry testing. DTC genetic testing companies, as noted in Section III of Chapter 5, can provide information about certain health risks or fun facts—such as whether your genes make you more likely to sneeze in bright light, prefer cilantro, have a longer second toe than big toe, prefer sweet or salty snacks, or produce a particular odor in your urine after eating asparagus (all things we likely already know about ourselves without genetic testing). Through companies like AncestryDNA and 23andMe, individuals can also learn about their ethnic identity and locate relatives. By the start of 2019, over 26 million people had taken a genetic ancestry test from such companies, a number that surpassed sales of all previous years. With an estimated worth of $359 million in 2017, the booming DNA testing market is projected to be worth $928 million by 2023. We take a moment to describe genetic ancestry testing here because, as discussed in Chapter 20 below, law enforcement has begun using the genealogical databases of these companies to try to solve cold cases, raising numerous ethical and legal questions.

Ancestry testing involves analysis of single nucleotide polymorphisms (SNPs). Using algorithms, the companies compare an individual's SNP patterns with a reference database of SNPs from populations in Asia, Africa, Europe, and the Americas to estimate the probabilities that the individual has ancestors from various parts of the world. The companies' proprietary reference databases, however, disproportionately represent regions for people of European heritage. As a result, the reports are less informative for some ethnic groups than others. For example, genetic diversity within the African population is greater than that between African and European populations. Consequently, larger reference panels are necessary to offer meaningful ancestry reports for people of African ancestry. Companies are therefore working to enhance their references databases for minority groups. Until they do, ancestry reports can offer more fine-grained distinctions between, for example, Irish and Anglo-Saxon ancestry than between groups within Africa. At this point, ancestry testing is most accurate with respect to identifying continental origins.

Ancestry testing has other limitations. First, the reference groups are based on self-reporting of ethnicity. Second, humans' constant migration and mixing with nearby groups throughout history makes it difficult to distinguish populations from one another. Moreover, because the reference databases use DNA from modern populations, ancestry reports can only offer educated guesses about where someone's ancestors lived long ago. The results provide much better information about where individuals with similar DNA to us exist today than where our DNA came from in the distant past. Third, marketing for ancestry testing falsely suggests that DNA ancestry will reveal our heritage. Knowing how much DNA we share with people in certain parts of the world, of course, tells us nothing about our ancestor's culture. Fourth, there is a danger that genetic tests may be viewed as the ultimate arbiter of race, when race is actually a contested concept and in many ways is culturally constructed. At its worst, ancestry testing promotes a focus on racial differences. Some groups that seek to divide by race, for example, use DNA ancestry results to highlight genetic differences (and to flaunt their allegedly exclusive European ancestry), obscuring the fact that we are 99.99% identical to one another.

The controversy that arose when presidential candidate, Elizabeth Warren, used ancestry testing to disprove President Trump's claim that she does not have Native American heritage highlights some of the problems with ancestry testing. Although the results determined with "high confidence" that she was between 1/64th and 1/1024th Native American, the fact that the database for Native Americans is sparse seriously limits the reliability of the results. Second, critics argued that DNA has virtually nothing to do with Native American identity. The Cherokee Nation Secretary of State issued a statement that Warren's use of a DNA test to "lay claim to any connection to the Cherokee Nation" dishonored "legitimate tribal governments and their citizens, whose ancestors are well-documented and whose heritage is proven."

What ancestry testing can do more reliably is identify familial relatives like third, fourth, or even ninth or more distant cousins. Often people want to discover far-removed relatives. Sometimes, however, such discoveries can be painful and confusing. They may reveal the lack of genetic connection to one's presumed biological family by uncovering unknown adoptions, conception through gamete donation, or infidelity. They can also expose unexpected genetic connections. In recent years, ancestry testing has revealed the identity of gamete donors whose anonymity had been promised by fertility clinics. In notorious examples, fertility physicians who claimed to use sperm from anonymous donors to inseminate patients, were found to have used their own sperm to father multitudes of children. Sometimes the genetic discoveries are more amusing than distressing. An author in the Wall Street Journal described how she and her husband discovered through 23andMe that they are third cousins. She noted, however, that for Ashkenazi Jews like them, this was not so surprising; the genetic variation in that ethnic group is far less than in other groups. A study in 2014, for example, found that all Ashkenazi Jews are at least 30th cousins having descended from a founding population of 350 people in the Middle East. As we shall see in Chapter 20, recently law enforcement has taken advantage of the ability to find relatives through ancestry testing to try to identify perpetrators of serious crimes like rape and murder, raising numerous legal and ethical questions.

CHAPTER 18

FORENSICS: DNA EVIDENCE IN CRIMINAL CASES

■ ■ ■

Since 1985, law enforcement officials have increasingly used DNA testing in solving crimes. Chapters 18–21 will explore the various ethical and legal issues that arise in this context. Chapter 18 describes the techniques that have been used to help identify perpetrators by assessing the similarity of their DNA to that of semen, blood, or other tissue from the crime scene. Since these comparisons provide a statistical probability that a given individual was present at the crime scene, courts face questions about whether an evolving series of DNA tests are admissible and what weight to give a DNA match. Law enforcement officials face questions about the circumstances under which they can compel suspects—or even the relatives of suspects—to provide blood, saliva, or other tissue for DNA testing.

In 1989, states began passing laws to require the collection of DNA samples from convicted violent offenders before their release from prison so their DNA could be compared to DNA collected from crime scenes. Law enforcement officials heralded the possibility of solving crimes with "the flick of a computer switch." All 50 states have passed laws to mandate the collection of DNA from offenders. As Chapter 19 will explore, however, the collection of DNA in forensic banks raises constitutional, policy, and practical issues. Does the collection of DNA from convicted offenders violate the Fourth Amendment of the U.S. Constitution? Should DNA be banked, as it is in many states, from people convicted of lesser offenses, such as non-violent crimes, misdemeanors, juvenile offenses, or even from arrestees? Should DNA from all citizens be put in a DNA bank for law enforcement purposes?

The use of forensic DNA identification techniques goes beyond the criminal justice system, however. A military DNA bank has been established for future use to identify the remains of any soldiers killed in battle. Recently, the Trump Administration is using DNA testing to reunite families, identify fraudulent families, and, perhaps in the future, to store DNA test results of undocumented immigrants in the custody of Customs and Border Protection. In the future, DNA testing might be used to identify individuals as members of particular ethnic groups in order to provide social benefits.

Chapter 20 will describe the various uses of government (and genealogical) databases for forensic purposes. It discusses regulations of these databases, the interests various individuals have in the information therein, and whether the regulations sufficiently protect against potential abuses of those databases. It also explores a new technique called familial searching, which allows law enforcement to draw on familial connections to try to identify perpetrators of crimes. Finally, Chapter 21 discusses the use of post-conviction DNA testing, which has led to the exoneration of hundreds of defendants.

I. THE SCIENCE OF FORENSIC TESTING

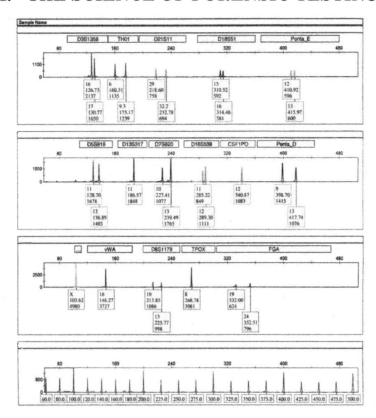

Forensic DNA Profile.

THE NATIONAL COMMISSION ON THE FUTURE OF DNA
EVIDENCE, THE FUTURE OF FORENSIC DNA TESTING:
PREDICTIONS OF THE RESEARCH AND
DEVELOPMENT WORKING GROUP

13–20, 46–61 (U.S. Department of Justice, Washington, D.C., Nov. 2000).

The first genetic markers that were useful for human identification were the ABO blood groups discovered in the same year (1900) that Mendel's rules of inheritance were rediscovered. * * * [Scientists discovered] that human blood cells fell into four antigenic groups * * * designated A, B, AB, and O. It was quickly realized that the blood groups were inherited * * *. * * *

Different human populations were found to differ in the frequencies of the four types. * * * Over the years, several more independently inherited red blood cell systems were discovered. * * * Along with this battery of serological tests some laboratories included a few serum proteins and enzymes. Although it was quite probable that two blood samples from different persons would agree for one blood group or enzyme, it was less and less probable that two unrelated persons would agree for all loci as more tests were added.

The frequencies of a combination of such markers were typically one in a few hundred or less, although in some instances, when samples contained rare types, the probability of matching of samples could be much smaller. By the mid-1970s, analysis of evidence samples and calculations of random matches could be calculated. A combination of blood groups and serum proteins were sometimes used for identification in criminal investigations. Much more often, such probabilities were used in paternity testing and accepted as evidence of parentage, where civil criterion "preponderance of evidence," rather than the criminal criterion "beyond reasonable doubt," prevailed.

* * *

The nature of forensic identification changed abruptly in 1985. That year Alec Jeffreys and colleagues in England first demonstrated the use of DNA in a criminal investigation. He made use of DNA regions in which short segments are repeated a number of times [VNTRs—variable number of tandem repeats]. This number of repeats varies greatly from person to person. Jeffreys used such variable-length segments of DNA, first to exonerate one suspect in two rape homicides of young girls and later to show that another man had a DNA profile matching that of the sperm in the evidence samples from both girls. Soon after, some commercial laboratories made use of this "fingerprinting" procedure, and in 1988 the FBI implemented the techniques, after improving their robustness and sensitivity and collecting extensive data on the frequency of different repeat lengths in different populations.

* * *

After a first flush of immediate acceptance by the courts, the molecular methodology and the results of evidence analysis were challenged as unreliable. Although the majority of courts admitted the DNA evidence, a few highly publicized cases were overturned by higher courts, citing failure of sufficient DNA testing to meet the *Frye* or other standards for admissibility of scientific evidence as the reason.

* * *

During the decade 1985–1995, a revolutionary technical innovation became more and more widely used in molecular biology, so that by now it is almost universal. This is the polymerase chain reaction (PCR), a technique for amplifying a tiny quantity of DNA into almost any desired amount. It uses essentially the same principle as that by which DNA is normally copied in the cell, except that instead of a whole chromosome being copied only a short chosen segment of the DNA in a chromosome is amplified. This has made it possible to process the very tiny amounts of DNA often left behind as evidence of a crime and has greatly increased the sensitivity of the forensic systems available to the criminal justice system. Thanks to PCR, minute amounts of DNA extracted from hairs, postage stamps, cigarette butts, coffee cups, and similar evidence sources can often be successfully analyzed.

What's That?: The diagram below shows how PCR amplifies segments of DNA. A double-stranded DNA segment (A) is first denatured, i.e., separated into two single strands. Then a primer (B), DNA nucleotide bases, and a special enzyme are added (C) for the creation of a second strand where the primer binds to the single strands (D). The denaturing and synthesis of new double-stranded DNA segments is repeated (E) resulting in time twice as many double-stranded segments of DNA (F). Each iteration doubles the DNA segments (G-J) Typically, the process is repeated 20–40 times.

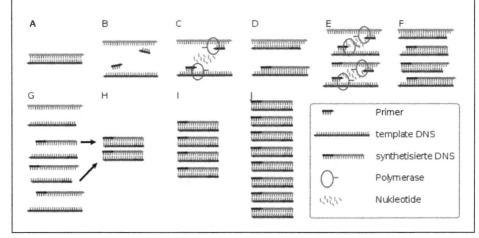

* * *

STRs (short tandem repeats) are similar to VNTRs in that they are based on repeated sequences dispersed throughout the chromosomes. While methods of interpretation for STRs and VNTRs are similar, STRs have smaller repeat units (usually 3 to 5 base pairs) and fewer of them (usually 7 to 15 alleles per locus). The small size makes them amenable to PCR amplification so that much smaller quantities of DNA are needed for analysis.

* * *

The FBI has selected 13 STR loci to serve as a standard battery of core loci, and increasingly laboratories are developing the capability to process these loci. [In 2017, seven STR loci were added for a total of 20 loci.] As laboratories throughout the Nation employ the same loci, comparisons and cooperation between laboratories are facilitated * * *. The FBI and others are actively involved in getting frequency data from a number of populations of different population groups and subgroups. These populations are being continuously subdivided. * * * With the 13 core loci the most common profile has an estimated frequency less than 1 in 10 billion. Of the 10 STR loci that the British system now uses, 8 are included in the 13 core loci, so international comparisons are feasible.

* * *

Techniques for using mitochondrial DNA (mtDNA) have been available for some years, but application to problems of forensic identification began in 1990. Several laboratories now have the necessary equipment and techniques to use this system. Mitochondria are intracellular particles (organelles) outside the nucleus in the cytoplasm of the cell. They contain their own small DNA genomes; circular molecules of 16,569 base pairs and the variants are identified by sequence determination. Each cell contains hundreds to thousands of mitochondria. For this reason, a single hair shaft, old bones, or charred remains, which are generally unsuitable for chromosomal DNA, sometimes provide enough intact material for mtDNA analysis. Mitochondria are transmitted by the egg but not by the sperm, so mtDNA is uniquely suited for tracing ancestry through the female line. It was used recently to identify some of the bodies of the Russian royal family, the Romanovs. Limitations of mtDNA include its relatively low discriminatory power and the dependence for that power on the creation of large databases of mtDNA sequences.

NOTES AND QUESTIONS

1.   The STR technique, like other DNA forensic techniques, has been promoted based on the idea that the section of DNA analyzed is "junk DNA" from the non-coding regions of the genome and thus provides only identifying information and not information about the individual's health. However, the DNA in these regions turns out to have many important functions and can

sometimes be used to predict some health risks. The STR loci can also identify genetic profiles from biobanks.

Even if all the STR loci chosen for analysis are in non-coding regions, their analyses could provide health information. An STR variation could identify disease susceptibility when (1) the STR variation occurs in a regulatory region, e.g., promoter or intron splice site, and thereby alters gene activity; or (2) the STR variation occurs in an intron or outside a gene and is positioned close enough (typically within 200,000 base pairs) to a functional mutation that it is almost always inherited with the mutation. See Jennifer M. Kwon & Alison M. Goate, Genes and Mutations, 24 Alcohol Research & Health 167 (2000); William E. Evans & Mary V. Relling, Pharmacogenetics: Translating Functional Genomics into Rational Therapeutics, 286 Sci. 487 (1999).

2.   What privacy concerns are raised when forensic DNA testing also provides potential health information? Should care be taken to choose STR sites that are not likely to be in gene regulatory regions or near known disease mutations? Should laws be adopted to prevent third parties from gaining access to information and samples in forensic DNA banks? Should relatives of offenders have a right to prevent a criminal's DNA from being stored on the grounds that the DNA potentially reveals health information about them?

EMERGING TECHNOLOGIES: YSTR, LOW COPY NUMBERS, SNPS, AND MASSIVE PARALLEL SEQUENCING

Standard STR DNA tests sometimes produce inconclusive results when the sample size is small or when there is a mixture of DNA, such as that of the rape victim and the rapist. New technologies are being developed to circumvent those problems. But, as each new technology is applied by forensic laboratories, the question of admissibility needs to be reconsidered.

As an alternative to the STR DNA test when there is an admixture of DNA, a method known as YSTR was developed, which is specific to male DNA only. YSTR tests for short tandem repeats only on the Y chromosome. YSTR was held to be admissible under the *Frye* standard in Arizona v. Sanders, CR-2000 2900 (Dec. 16, 2003) and in Shabazz v. State, 592 SE2d 876 (Ga. Ct. App. 2004).

The low copy number (LCN) DNA test was designed to deal with the problem of having just a small amount of DNA. However, because it multiplies the DNA in the sample by using more PCR cycles than traditional forensic DNA typing, there is more possibility of contamination. For example, the DNA of someone in the lab might be introduced into the sample. Courts have disagreed about the reliability and admissibility of LCN DNA tests. In People v. Megnath, a New York trial court found that LCN DNA testing was both "generally accepted as reliable in the forensic scientific community" and also was "*not a novel* scientific procedure within the scope of the *Frye* doctrine." 898 N.Y.S.2d 408, 415 (Sup.Ct. 2010). In U.S. v. McCluskey, the court did not allow the government to introduce LCN DNA testing. It found the government had not met the burden of proof to show the technique was "reliable and admissible under Daubert and Rule 702." 954 F.Supp.2d 1224, 1288 (D.N.M. 2013).

Another emerging forensic technology is based on SNPs. A single nucleotide polymorphism (SNP) represents a single base difference in the more than three billion bases of DNA in the human genome. SNPs are considered the most common form of genetic variation with each person carrying his or her own distinctive set of SNPs. SNP analysis purportedly can generate accurate matches using much shorter segments of DNA than other approaches. Although no public forensic DNA laboratory in the U.S. routinely analyzes forensic evidence for SNPs, the technique has been used for identification of human remains, as in the World Trade Center bombing. SNPs are not likely to replace STRs for most forensic applications, but SNPs may help solve special problems in forensic genetics. For example, SNPs might help identify male DNA by measuring polymorphisms on the Y chromosome (found only in men) from degraded samples. This approach is expected to be particularly useful in constructing the male profile in samples that contain mixtures of DNA from both a man and a woman.

A relatively recent development in DNA typing, massive parallel sequencing (MPS), is making waves in DNA forensics analysis. MPS or "next-generation" sequencing originally hit the commercial markets in 2005. Whereas early DNA sequencing technology required high-quality and large samples of DNA and only allowed analysis of one sequence at a time, massive parallel sequencing improves sequencing time, reduces the amount of DNA samples needed for analysis, and allows for simultaneous analysis of several samples at the same time across millions of DNA fragments. MPS can support both STR and SNP analysis.

While faster and cheaper than early sequencing technology (with the cost of sequencing dropping from the millions to the thousands), MPS has limitations. It relies on a reference library of DNA from a population. If there is not a large population for a reference, it is not as efficient as it could be. In 2018, scientists at the National Institute of Standards and Technology (NIST) developed a statistical foundation for calculating match statistics when using MPS. This development could potentially make MPS more useful in solving crimes by making more efficient use of smaller DNA samples. Questions concerning the admissibility of testimony based on MPS, however, are beginning to emerge. A validation study by Illumina, a company that develops integrated systems for the analysis of genetic variation, indicated that experts can draw accurate inferences from MPS results. It is still too early to determine how the court system will respond to this quickly developing technology.

NOTES AND QUESTIONS

1. Identical twins have long presented a problem in forensic DNA testing, as traditional testing cannot distinguish between their DNA. When a female student was raped and assaulted in Grand Rapids, Michigan, the police obtained a DNA match to Jerome Cooper. However, Cooper had an identical twin brother Tyrone. Both men had records for sexual assault and both denied involvement. Police were unable to convict either since they could not prove through DNA testing which brother was responsible. Alison Gee, Twin DNA Test: Why Identical Criminals May No Longer Be Safe, BBC World Service, BBC.com, January 14, 2014, www.bbc.com/news/magazine-25371014.

By undertaking analyses of large portions of two twins' genomes—or even their whole genomes—scientists can determine which twin's DNA was left at the crime scene. Jacqueline Weber-Lehmann et al., Finding the Needle in the Haystack: Differentiating "Identical" Twins in Paternity Testing and Forensics by Ultra-Deep Next Generation Sequencing, 9 Forensic Sci. Int'l: Genetics 42 (2014). In Boston, police found that Dwayne McNair's DNA matched samples collected from two rapes in 2004. Because McNair had an identical twin, prosecutors had his DNA sequenced for $130,000. The prosecutor provided statistical analysis showing it was "two billion times more likely that the rapist's DNA belonged to Dwayne McNair than to his brother." Although the judge found the technique was based on valid scientific principles, because the study had not been replicated by other labs, she refused to admit the evidence. She noted jurors "would not have the luxury of many days of rumination, as this gatekeeper has needed, to untie this Gordian knot" of complex scientific principles. As a result of this ruling, prosecutors in the Cooper case in Grand Rapids Michigan, who had been considering using sequencing, decided not to. Ultimately, McNair was found guilty in January 2018 based on the STR analysis and testimony by the other rapist that Dwayne was the second rapist in the crimes. Carl Zimmer, One Twin Committed the Crime—But Which One? A New DNA Test Can Finger the Culprit, N.Y. Times, Mar. 1, 2019, https://www.nytimes.com/2019/03/01/science/twins-dna-crime-paternity.html.

2. Traditional DNA testing generally takes weeks or even months to return a sample. However, Rapid DNA machines, introduced in the United States in 2011, can produce a DNA profile in a fraction of that time. IntegenX markets a product called RapidHIT 200 that can "generate a DNA profile, check it against a database, and report on whether it found a match" in just 90 minutes. Police have already used this technology in Arizona, Florida, South Carolina, and California. The Rapid DNA Act of 2017 authorizes criminal justice agencies to upload profiles created through rapid DNA analysis to the FBI's Combined DNA Index System (CODIS). The FBI is currently developing the program, although it will not allow submission of Rapid DNA generated

> **What's That?:** The DNA Identification Act of 1994 gave the FBI authority to establish the national Combined DNA Index System (CODIS). CODIS blends forensic science and computer technology, enabling federal, state, and local forensic labs to compare DNA profiles electronically. This allows them to link serial violent crimes to each other and to known offenders.

profiles from unknown crime scenes to be added to the CODIS database. Tom Jackman, FBI Plans 'Rapid DNA' Network for Quick Database Checks on Arrestees, Wash. Post, Dec. 13, 2018, https://www.washingtonpost.com/crime-law/2018/12/13/fbi-plans-rapid-dna-network-quick-database-checks-arrestees/?noredirect=on.

As rapid DNA testing becomes less expensive and more widely available, how should it be regulated? Are critics right to be concerned that no agency is controlling its rollout and that anyone can buy Rapid DNA machines? Will it encourage law enforcement to collect and store a larger number of DNA profiles? See Jackman, *supra*.

II. THE LEGAL STANDARDS FOR ADMISSIBILITY

NATIONAL RESEARCH COUNCIL (NRC), THE EVALUATION OF FORENSIC DNA EVIDENCE
171–173 (1996).

GENERAL ACCEPTANCE AND SOUND METHODOLOGY

The technology used to examine VNTRs, STRs, or other loci must satisfy the standard required of scientific evidence. In the United States, two major standards exist for deciding whether scientific findings will be admitted into evidence: the "general-acceptance" test and the "sound-methodology" standard. In addition, some jurisdictions have adopted special statutes that provide for the admissibility of genetic testing in general or of DNA analyses in particular in criminal or civil cases. If a timely objection is raised, the judge must determine whether the applicable standard has been met.

The general-acceptance standard was first articulated in an influential 1923 federal case, Frye v. United States, 293 F. 1013 (D.C.Cir. 1923). In jurisdictions that follow *Frye*, the proponent of the scientific evidence must establish that the underlying theory and methodology are generally accepted within the relevant portions of the scientific community.

* * *

The sound-methodology standard is derived from phrases in the Federal Rules of Evidence. In Daubert v. Merrell Dow Pharmaceuticals [509 U.S. 579 (1993)], the Supreme Court held that these rules implicitly jettison general acceptance as an absolute prerequisite to the admissibility of scientific evidence. Instead of the *Frye* test, the Court prescribed a broader framework for deciding whether proposed testimony has sufficient scientific validity and reliability to be admitted as relevant "scientific knowledge" that would "assist the trier of fact." In that framework, the lack of general acceptance weighs against admissibility but is not invariably fatal. The Court discussed other factors that might be considered. Its nonexhaustive list includes the extent to which the theory and technology have been tested, the existence of a body of peer-reviewed studies, and the known error rates of the procedure.

III. ASSESSING THE RELIABILITY OF DNA EVIDENCE

The Florida Supreme Court in Brim v. State, 695 So.2d 268, 271 (Fla. 1997) pointed out that "The fact that a match is found in the first step of the DNA testing process may be 'meaningless' without qualitative or quantitative estimates demonstrating the significance of the match." The DNA analysis assesses whether the accused's sample is similar to that from a crime scene. But a statistical analysis must be done to calculate the likelihood that such a match could occur by chance. The most common method of calculating these statistics is the multiplication or product rule. The product rule requires an expert to determine the frequency of certain genetic markers and then multiply those frequencies together.

Under the product rule, the probability of the joint occurrence of mutually independent events is equal to the product of the individual probabilities that each of the events will occur. If a person is rolling a die, there is a 1 in 6 chance that she will roll the number two. The chance that she will roll the number two twice in a row is $1/6 \times 1/6$—a 1 in 36 chance. But if the chance of a man having a beard is 1 in 6 and the chance of a man having a mustache is 1 in 6, these probabilities cannot be multiplied together to produce an estimate of 1 in 36, because the factors are not independent. (Many men with beards also have mustaches). So if a victim describes her assailant as a man with a beard and mustache and police arrest a man matching that description, it cannot be said that the probability that they have the wrong man is 1 in 36; the probability of a random match is higher.

Individual frequencies must be trustworthy for this rule to produce accurate results, but sometimes they are not because of the limited size of DNA databases. These limited databases, established for calculating population frequencies for broad racial categories, may not be representative of isolated subpopulations where intermarriage and inbreeding occur. The product rule also presents potential problems because it is based on an assumption that the genetic markers used for matching are independent (that is, not close enough to each other on chromosomes so that they are likely to be inherited together), but this is not always the case. See Paul C. Giannelli & Edward J. Imwinkelried, Scientific Evidence § 18 (3d ed. 1999). For instance, the admission of DNA evidence can be misleading in cases where the potential suspects are related and share common genetic markers.

An additional issue is misinterpretation of DNA, which has grown more complex with recent technologies. Whereas DNA profiling in the 1980s required samples the size of a quarter, today it is possible to analyze samples as small as "touch DNA," traces of DNA left from a smeared thumbprint or speck of spit. With single-source DNA samples, the DNA profile of the sample is compared with the suspect's DNA profile, and if there is a match the analyst testifies as to how rare the profile is based on the frequency of the markers in a given population. In comparing the alleles at now twenty locations, the odds are lower than one in 1 billion that unrelated people will share the same pattern.

> With mixtures, the math gets a lot more complicated: The number of alleles in a sample doubles in the case of two contributors, and triples in the case of three. . . . The analyst must determine how many contributors are involved, and which alleles belong to whom. If the sample is very small or degraded—the two often go hand in hand—alleles might drop out in some locations or appear to exist where they do not. Suddenly, we are dealing not so much with an objective science as an interpretive art.

Matthew Shaer, The False Promise of DNA Testing, Atlantic, June 2016, https://www.theatlantic.com/magazine/archive/2016/06/a-reasonable-doubt/480747/.

A 2010 study gave mixture DNA samples from an adjudicated sexual assault to 17 lab technicians and asked them to determine whether it included the defendant's DNA. Two experts had previously concluded the defendant could not be excluded as a contributor, and therefore his DNA was a possible match. Unaware of those findings, only one of the technicians found the defendant could not be excluded, twelve concluded the DNA was exclusionary, and four said it was inconclusive. As the authors of the study stated, "[i]t seems . . . that at least in complex situations (such as with DNA mixtures) DNA does require and rely on human examiners making a variety of subjective judgements that are susceptible to bias." Itiel E. Dror & Greg Hampikian, Subjectivity and Bias in Forensic DNA Mixture Interpretation, 51 Sci. & Just. 204 (2011). Incentives to interpret forensic evidence as inculpatory is just one such bias. A study found that in North Carolina, law-enforcement agencies that operated crime labs received $600 compensation for DNA analysis that resulted in convictions. Roger Koppl & Meghan Sacks, Incentives for False Convictions, 32 Crim. Just. Ethics 126 (2012).

NOTES AND QUESTIONS

1.   Because of the difficulties analyzing complex DNA mixtures, especially with small samples that are of poor quality and degraded, algorithms have been developed to establish the evidentiary weight of the samples. These "probabilistic genotyping" algorithms are "designed to weigh

the probability that the sample is either missing information or contains incorrect or misleading information, not truly from the DNA source, and the likelihood of the two hypotheticals given this uncertainty." Essentially, they determine likelihood ratios by comparing the probabilities of two hypotheses: 1) the likelihood that the suspect is the source of some of the DNA and 2) the likelihood that the suspect is not the source. The results are presented in the conditional: " 'given this piece of evidence, it is x times more likely that the suspect is the source of the DNA than it is likely that an unknown unrelated person is the source.' " In seeming to answer whether the defendant is the source of the DNA, these calculations can be misleading. Because ratios do not objectively determine how likely either hypothesis is, juries can easily misunderstand the results as expressing the probability of the defendant's guilt. Are there concerns that, because the likelihood ratios are generated by "first presuming guilt (inclusion), they undermine the presumption of innocence . . . and water down the burden of proof beyond a reasonable doubt in a criminal trial"? Bess Stiffelman, No Longer the Gold Standard: Probabilistic Genotyping Is Changing the Nature of DNA Evidence in Criminal Trials, 24 Berkeley J. Crim. L. 110 (2019).

In People v. Collins, 15 N.Y.S.3d 564 (N.Y. Sup. Ct. 2015), the court ruled that a software program for DNA analysis (as well as low copy number analysis) was not admissible under *Frye* because it was "not generally accepted in the DNA scientific community." Sometimes these algorithms raise additional concerns if they remain a "black box." See Jessica Goldthwaite et al., Mixing It Up: Legal Challenges to Probabilistic Genotyping Programs for DNA Mixture Analysis, Champion, May 2018, at 12. In Commonwealth v. Knight, 2017 WL 5951725 (Pa. Super. Ct. 2017), however, the Pennsylvania Superior Court affirmed the trial court's refusal to compel a company whose software was used for DNA to release its source code.

2.   Some form of forensic DNA testing is admissible in every state. As new DNA technologies are introduced, such as low copy number, massive parallel sequencing, Rapid DNA testing, or algorithms, courts must undertake *Frye* or *Daubert* analyses to determine whether the results from these techniques are admissible.

3.   Courts have grappled with the difficulties of determining the probability of a random match when the accused individual is a member of a minority ethnic group and that group is not adequately represented in the genetic database to which the sample from the crime scene is being compared. In United States v. Chischilly, 30 F.3d 1144 (9th Cir. 1994), a Navajo man accused of murder argued that the FBI's database of Native American DNA was too small and contained too few Navajos to determine accurately the odds of a random match between the suspect's DNA and crime scene DNA. The defendant also raised questions about "substructuring"—the fact that there is less genetic variability among ethnically homogeneous, non-randomly mating populations and consequently "the probability of a random match between two of its members is greater than the likelihood of such a match between two members of the population at large." The Ninth Circuit acknowledged that the

defendant had raised legitimate concerns that may warrant review by the FBI and revision of its procedures. But the court held that these concerns went to the weight of the evidence, and not its admissibility.

Other challenges to the weight of DNA evidence have focused on the probability of matches between the genetic profile of DNA evidence found at a crime scene and the genetic profiles stored in DNA databases, such as CODIS. The FBI estimates that a match between a crime scene sample and DNA in CODIS has the odds of occurring only one in 113 billion times. But a technician working in the Arizona Department of Public Safety Crime Laboratory, Kathryn Troyer, found 122 men in the Arizona database that matched at 9 loci, 20 at 10 loci, one match at 11 loci, and one match at 12 loci. Other laboratory workers claimed to have seen similar matches in their own crime labs. Jason Felch & Maura Dolan, The Verdict is Out on DNA Profiles, L.A. Times, July 20, 2008, articles.latimes.com/2008/jul/20/local/me-dna20.

4.   Scientists have developed a few ways to create artificial DNA evidence containing anyone's DNA they choose. The processes are simple—in fact, according to the author of a study in Forensic Science International, "anyone with the proper equipment and basic understanding of molecular biology" can do it. One technique involves collecting a small sample of a person's DNA from a drinking cup or hair follicle. Next, using "whole genome amplification," scientists can make multiple copies of the person's DNA. The amplified DNA can then be inserted into a fake saliva or blood sample stripped of endogenous DNA. Another technique does not even require a physical sample of DNA. Using a DNA profile from the CODIS-allele library, the researchers generated a completely new DNA sample with molecular cloning. Does this technology raise new issues about the admissibility and reliability of DNA evidence? Kristen Bolden, DNA Fabrication, A Wake Up Call: The Need to Reevaluate the Admissibility and Reliability of DNA Evidence, 27 Ga. St. U. L. Rev. 409 (2011). Considering that "DNA is a lot easier to plant at a crime scene than fingerprints," do law enforcement officials and the public place too much faith in DNA evidence? Andrew Pollack, DNA Evidence Can Be Fabricated, Scientists Show, N.Y. Times, Aug. 18, 2009, at D3.

5.   Hundreds of thousands of DNA analyses are conducted annually in the United States at more than 400 publicly funded forensic laboratories and a growing number of privately funded labs. In 2005, Congress authorized the National Academy of Sciences (NAS) to conduct a study on forensics science, including DNA analysis, in the Science, State, Justice, Commerce, and Related Agencies Appropriations Act of 2006. The NAS report states that "DNA typing is now universally recognized as the standard against which many other forensic individualization techniques are judged." Although its probabilities for false positives are quantifiable and often miniscule, the report cautions that even a very small, but nonzero, probability of false positives can affect the odds that a suspect is the source of a matching DNA profile. When errors occur, they usually involve ambiguities, inappropriate processing or contamination of samples by the laboratory, or limited test information because of small amounts of DNA. National Research Council of the National Academies,

Descriptions of Some Forensic Science Disciplines, Strengthening Forensic Science in the United States: A Path Forward, 129–131 (2009), books.nap.edu/catalog.php?record_id=12589.

One scholar points out the difference between DNA forensics and DNA medical diagnostics. The latter

> can be conducted under optimal laboratory conditions: the samples are fresh, clean, and from a single individual. If uncertainty arises in the results, new samples can be taken and the test can be redone, which makes for a high standard of accuracy in the procedure. By contrast, DNA forensics compels the biologist to work with whatever samples happen to be found at the scene of a crime. Samples may have been exposed to numerous environmental insults: they may be degraded; they may be mixtures of samples from different individuals, as happens in a multiple rape. The forensic biologist often has only a microgram or less of sample DNA, enough to do perhaps only one test. If the test has ambiguous results, it often cannot be repeated because the sample will have been used up.

Eric E. Lander, DNA Fingerprinting: Science Law, and the Ultimate Identifier in the Code of Codes: Scientific and Social Issues in the Human Genome Project, 195–196 (Daniel J. Kevles & Leroy Hood eds. 1993). Lander points out that clinical laboratory errors in all areas occur between roughly 1 percent and 5 percent of the time. He suggests "that it makes no sense to report DNA fingerprinting results as accurate to one part in a hundred million, if the rate of laboratory errors is on the order of even 1 percent." Lander, *supra* at 208. Do Lander's points and the reports of poor laboratory procedures undermine the probative value of DNA testing?

6. A 2009 NAS report indicated that the field of forensic science generally needs reform to address "poor documentation, serious analytical and interpretative errors, the absence of quality assurance programs, inadequately trained personnel, erroneous reporting, the use of inaccurate and misleading statistics, and even 'drylabbing' (the falsification of laboratory results)." National Research Council of the National Academies, Introduction, Strengthening Forensic Science in the United States: A Path Forward, 188, 193 (2009), books.nap.edu/catalog.php?record_id=12589.

In spite of various reports about the problems with forensic science and the fact that some forensic methods have not been validated, in April 2017, the Department of Justice (DOJ) terminated the National Commission on Forensic Science, which had been charged with "advising the federal government on improving the parlous state of forensic science." The DOJ proposed opening a new office for forensic science in place of the commission and named a prosecutor to lead it. Is it problematic to have the DOJ "be involved in evaluating the use of forensic science"? Why or why not? See Suzanne Bell et al., A Call for More Science in Forensic Science, 115 PNAS 4541, 4543 (2018).

7.   In late 2012, Lukis Anderson was arrested and charged with first degree murder in the commission of a burglary. Law enforcement had previously discovered that Anderson's DNA was under the victim's fingernails. After a month of waiting in jail for further criminal proceedings, Anderson's defense attorney discovered that Anderson had been in a hospital, detoxing the night of the homicide. The airtight alibi resulted in Anderson's release from jail. How could Anderson's DNA have gotten underneath the victim's fingernails when they had never even met each other? It seems that the phenomenon of DNA transfer occurred. The paramedics who picked up and took Anderson to the hospital on the night of the murder also responded to the victim's residence three hours later. The prosecutors, defense attorney, and police all agreed that when the paramedics checked the victim's vitals, they transferred some of Anderson's DNA to the scene of the crime. Katie Worth, Framed for Murder by His Own DNA, Wired, Apr. 19, 2018, https://www.wired.com/story/dna-transfer-framed-murder/.

DNA transfer (or "touch" DNA) is not uncommon. People can pick up traces of other people's DNA from other people simply from touching objects, like pens or doorknobs, without touching each other. Roland A. H. van Oorschot, DNA Fingerprints from Fingerprints, 387 Sci. 797 (June 19, 1997). A recent study found that 91% of public items like escalator rails, shopping basket handles, and coins contain human DNA from as many as a half a dozen people. More striking, approximately one in five of us has someone else's DNA under our fingernails. Margreet van den Berge et al., Prevalence of Cell Material: DNA and RNA Profiling of Public and Private Objects, 21 Forensics Sci. Int'l Genetics 81 (2016). DNA and sperm can even be transferred from one person to another during laundering of clothes. Sarah Noel et al., DNA Transfer During Laundering May Yield Complete DNA Profiles, 23 Forensics Sci. Int'l Genetics 240 (2016). Various factors affect whether DNA transfer occurs—the quantity of DNA, the intensity of contact, and the time that passes between contact, and how prone a person is to shed DNA.

Not surprisingly, studies have found DNA on three-quarters of crime scene tools and even in the cleanest parts of the laboratory. See Ane E. Fonnelop, Contamination During Criminal Investigation: Detecting Police Contamination and Secondary DNA Transfer from Evidence Bags, 23 Forensics Sci. Int'l Genetics 121 (2016); Duncan Taylor et al., Observations of DNA Transfer with an Operational Forensic Biology Laboratory, 23 Forensics Sci. Int'l Genetics 33 (2016).

> **Food for Thought:** The fact that DNA analysis can identify people on the basis of just a few cells heightens the problems of DNA transfer. The European Network of Forensic Science Institutes suggests that forensic scientists shift from reporting not only the source of DNA (whose DNA is it?), to also reporting on how the DNA got there. Europe has been slow to adopt this change, and the United States has not adopted this change. Should such a shift be made? What concerns might explain the reluctance to move in that direction?

8.   In Williams v. Illinois, 567 U.S. 50 (2012), Sandy Williams challenged his conviction for rape, arguing that the prosecution's use of an expert witness violated the Confrontation Clause. The expert had testified that a DNA profile

produced by an outside laboratory, Cellmark, matched the profile the state police lab created from William's blood sample. She also testified that Cellmark was an accredited laboratory; that it provided the police with a DNA profile; and that, according to records, the police lab sent the vaginal swabs from the victim to Cellmark and later received them back. The expert did not make any statements that were offered to identify the biological sample Cellmark used to create the DNA profile, explain how Cellmark handled and analyzed the sample, or vouch for the accuracy of the DNA profile Cellmark created.

In a 5–4 decision, the Supreme Court found that the expert's testimony did not violate the Confrontation Clause because that provision has no application to out-of-court statements that are not offered to prove the truth of the matter asserted. The Court also concluded that even if the Cellmark report had been entered into evidence there would have been no Confrontation Clause exception. It reasoned that Cellmark's DNA profile was not "inherently inculpatory," in fact DNA profiles tend "to exculpate all but one of the more than 7 billion people in the world today. . . . If DNA profiles could not be introduced without calling the technicians who participated in the preparation of the profile, economic pressures would encourage prosecutors to forgo DNA testing and rely instead on older [and less reliable] forms of evidence, such as eye witness identification . . . "

The dissent argued that the Confrontation Clause is a method for ensuring that forensic evidence is reliable. Cross-examination of the analyst is especially likely to reveal whether vials have been switched, samples contaminated, tests incompetently run, or results inaccurately recorded. The dissent lamented the departure of two Supreme Court precedents that required a prosecutor wishing to admit the results of forensic testing to produce the technician responsible for the analysis. Is the majority or dissent more persuasive?

9.   When prosecutors have not yet identified a suspect, but have the suspect's DNA profile, they have sometimes obtained DNA arrest warrants and indictments that contain the profile. These are used to toll the statute of limitations until the offender is identified. A New York appellate court held that the use of a DNA profile in a criminal indictment did not violate a defendant's Sixth Amendment or state constitutional right to notice of the charges brought against him. The court reasoned that the charges read against the defendant at his arraignment provided him with sufficient notice. Therefore, the use of a DNA profile in the indicting document did not deprive the defendant of any constitutional rights. The court also noted that the use of DNA profiles for this purpose was increasingly popular due to the ability of DNA to accurately identify an individual and was therefore appropriate for use in an indicting document. People v. Martinez, 855 N.Y.S.2d 522 (N.Y. App. Div. 2008). See also Wisconsin v. Dabney, 663 N.W.2d 366 (Wis. Ct. App. 2003).

IV.   OBTAINING DNA SAMPLES FOR A MATCH

EDWARD IMWINKELRIED & D. H. KAYE, DNA TYPING: EMERGING OR NEGLECTED ISSUES

76 Wash. L. Rev. 413, 416–445 (2001).

* * *

Traditionally, DNA has been employed to link a suspect to a crime. Finding that a suspect's DNA matches the DNA left at a crime scene, for example, tends to incriminate the suspect. Inversely, when the DNA does not match, the suspect usually can be excluded as the source of the crime-scene DNA. If trace evidence is to be used in these ways, the police must secure samples of DNA from individuals who might have committed the crime under investigation. Officials can secure such samples in many ways. They can seek a court order to compel an individual to submit to sampling; they can turn to a preexisting collection of DNA samples; they can take a sample with the consent of the individual; or they can try to locate a sample that the suspect has abandoned.

As a matter of constitutional law, the principal constraint on such government action is the Search and Seizure Clause of the Fourth Amendment to the U.S. Constitution, which states:

> The right of the people to be secure in their persons, houses, papers, and effects, against unreasonable searches and seizures, shall not be violated, and no Warrants shall issue, but upon probable cause, supported by Oath or affirmation, and particularly describing the place to be searched, and the persons or things to be seized.

* * *

Because Schmerber [v. California, 384 U.S. 757 (1966)] established that the Fourth Amendment applies to removing material from a suspect's body, as a general rule, police must persuade a judge or magistrate that there is probable cause to believe that the desired DNA sample will produce evidence linking the suspect to the crime. With judicial authorization, police can use necessary force to extract the biological material. Furthermore, once the authorities legally have acquired a suspect's profile, they are permitted to compare it to profiles from unrelated, unsolved crime-scene stains. The current state of the law appears to allow evidence legitimately acquired for one purpose to be used for another purpose, at least if the additional use entails no further search or seizure of the person.

* * *

It also is likely that an order compelling a person to give a sample could be issued on something less than probable cause. [The Supreme Court's dictum in Davis v. Mississippi, 394 U.S. 721, 727 (1969) suggested as much. Overturning a conviction for rape based on fingerprint evidence because the defendant was detained without a warrant and without probable cause, the Court hinted that an arrest made solely for the purpose of obtaining fingerprints could be allowed without probable cause.] Although Justice Brennan, writing for the majority of the Court, emphasized that "detentions for the sole purpose of obtaining fingerprints are * * * subject to the constraints of the Fourth Amendment," he added that:

> It is arguable, however, that, because of the unique nature of the fingerprinting process, such detentions might, under narrowly defined circumstances, be found to comply with the Fourth Amendment even though there is no probable cause in the traditional sense * * *. Detention for fingerprinting may constitute a much less serious intrusion upon personal security than other types of police searches and detentions. Fingerprinting involves none of the probing into an individual's private life and thoughts that marks an interrogation or search. Nor can fingerprint detention be employed repeatedly to harass an individual, since the police need only one set of each person's prints. Furthermore, fingerprinting is an inherently more reliable and effective crime solving tool than eyewitness identifications or confessions * * *. Finally, because there is no danger of destruction of fingerprints, the limited detention need not come unexpectedly or at an inconvenient time.

The Court opened the door to the possibility that "the requirements of the Fourth Amendment could be met by narrowly circumscribed procedures for obtaining, during the course of a criminal investigation, the fingerprints of individuals for whom there is no probable cause to arrest." The Court virtually invited states to devise procedures to obtain evidence of identifying characteristics on the basis of something less than probable cause.

Many states seized on this invitation by adopting statutes or court rules permitting the police to obtain evidence of identifying physical characteristics after a showing of founded or reasonable suspicion. For instance, Arizona authorizes magistrates to issue "an order authorizing * * * temporary detention, for the purpose of obtaining evidence of identifying physical characteristics" on a showing of "reasonable cause for belief that a felony has been committed" and proof that the "physical characteristics * * * may contribute to the identification of the individual who committed such offense." As in this instance, the language of many of these statutes and court rules is broad enough to apply to DNA samples.

One might argue that these statutes or rules are too broad—that unlike the fingerprints in *Davis*, blood, urine, or hair samples should be treated differently because they have the potential to reveal information that is more significant than the pattern of whorls and ridges in a fingerprint. Some support for this distinction can be found in Skinner v. Railway Labor Executives' Ass'n [489 U.S. 602 (1989)], which involved drug testing of railway employees. The Court observed that "chemical analysis of urine, like that of blood, can reveal a host of private medical facts about an employee, including whether he or she is epileptic, pregnant, or diabetic." The same concern with "private medical facts" arises with any samples that can be subjected to DNA analysis. To this extent, it would be facile to say that DNA typing, like the fingerprinting in *Davis*, "involves none of the probing into an individual's private life and thoughts that marks an interrogation or search." Certain parts of one's genome—those that are related to otherwise nonobvious disease states or behavioral characteristics—are as much, if not more, a part of "an individual's private life" as are the hormones or other chemicals found in one's urine.

However, all the other factors listed in the *Davis* dictum apply to DNA sampling. Detention to obtain the sample cannot "be employed repeatedly to harass an individual, since the police need only one set of each person's [DNA types]." DNA analysis "is an inherently more reliable and effective crime-solving tool than eyewitness identifications or confessions." And, "the limited detention need not come unexpectedly or at an inconvenient time." Moreover, in describing these features of fingerprinting, the *Davis* Court recognized the possibility that the police might abuse even fingerprinting to harass or inconvenience a suspect. The suggestion of relaxing the probable cause requirement presupposes the police will conform to the court order and the judiciary will issue orders that avoid these problems. This premise applies as well to the informational privacy concern voiced in *Skinner*. Just as there is no need to detain an individual repeatedly or to detain a person in the middle of the night, there is no reason for the police to probe parts of the genome that conceivably could be used to indicate disease states, susceptibilities, or the like. Because the judicial order can limit the search to loci that are of strictly biometric interest, the analogy to *Davis* is apt. Detention for DNA typing, as much as detention for fingerprinting, "may constitute a much less serious intrusion upon personal security than other types of police searches and detentions." If a person can be compelled to submit to fingerprinting on reasonable suspicion rather than probable cause, he or she can be required to submit to DNA sampling on the same showing.

* * *

The police [have] also * * * obtain[ed] a suspect's DNA sample surreptitiously, without detaining the person. Saliva deposited on a coffee cup at a restaurant, for example, can be collected and analyzed. Police unsuccessfully chasing a wounded felon might find sufficient blood has dripped onto the sidewalk for DNA profiling to be conducted. It could be argued that such activity is not a search (and hence requires neither probable cause nor a warrant) because the individual, having abandoned the material in a public place, retains no reasonable expectation of privacy in it. The Supreme Court used this reasoning in California v. Greenwood [486 U.S. 35 (1988)] in holding that the Fourth Amendment does not prohibit "the warrantless search and seizure of garbage left for collection outside the curtilage of a home." The Court commented:

> It is common knowledge that plastic garbage bags left on or at the side of a public street are readily accessible to animals, children, scavengers, snoops, and other members of the public * * *. Moreover, respondents placed their refuse at the curb for the express purpose of conveying it to a third party, the trash collector, who might himself have sorted through respondents' trash or permitted others, such as the police, to do so.

However, depositing DNA in the ordinary course of life when drinking, sneezing, or shedding hair, dandruff, or other cells differs from placing private papers in a container on the street to be collected as garbage. Depositing paper in the trash is generally a volitional act. Someone intent on preserving the secrecy of the papers can shred the papers or dispose of them in other ways that would defeat normal police surveillance. Leaving a trail of DNA, however, is not a conscious activity. The deposition of DNA in public places cannot be avoided unless one is a hermit or is fanatical in using extraordinary containment measures. In this setting, the inference of intent to abandon is markedly weaker.

If the police collection of inadvertently deposited DNA cannot be justified solely on an abandonment theory, under Katz [v. United States, 389 U.S. 347 (1967), a case about the application of the Fourth Amendment to electronic eavesdropping on public phone booth calls], the question becomes whether society does or should recognize as reasonable the expectation that government agents will not follow one about to obtain and analyze DNA that almost inevitably is left in public places. A case can be constructed that such an expectation exists. The public is extremely concerned with preserving genetic privacy.

NOTES AND QUESTIONS

1.   The Supreme Court has never examined the constitutionality of surreptitious searches of DNA, although lower courts have found such actions constitutional. In State v. Athan, 158 P.3d 27 (Wash. 2007), police collected DNA from the saliva of a return envelope the defendant sent to the police in response to their fictitious letter, purportedly from a law firm, inviting him to join a class action lawsuit. The court observed that the Fourth Amendment allows police to "surreptitiously follow a suspect to collect DNA, fingerprints, footprints, or other possibly incriminating evidence." As a result, it concluded that the police's ruse to obtain the defendant's DNA for DNA fingerprinting

was not a search under the Fourth Amendment. Similarly, in Raynor v. State, 99 A.3d 753 (Md. Ct. App. 2014), the court found that DNA collected from a defendant's sweat on the armchair in which he had been interrogated did not constitute a search or seizure. The court saw no distinction between dusting the chair for fingerprints and collecting DNA from the chair for DNA fingerprinting because the defendant had no reasonable expectation of privacy "in the identifying characteristics of his DNA."

2.   As noted in the Imwinkelried & Kaye excerpt, under California v. Greenwood, items abandoned in public lack Fourth Amendment protection against unreasonable search and seizure by law enforcement agents. Is DNA abandoned in the same way that garbage is left out on the street? And does it matter where it is abandoned? The law surrounding this issue is currently in flux. A New York court accepted that DNA on a piece of gum a suspect gave to police officers was abandoned. The suspect gave the gum to the officers while participating in a staged Pepsi taste-test that the police department had designed to acquire DNA evidence from the suspect. People v. LaGuerre, 815 N.Y.S.2d 211, 213 (N.Y. App. Div. 2006). In contrast, the North Carolina Court of Appeals prevented DNA from being used as evidence in a criminal trial because it had been collected from a cigarette butt found on the defendant's patio. The court concluded that a reasonable expectation of privacy still attached to the cigarette butt and its DNA because it was seized on a private piece of property rather than in a public place. State v. Reed, 641 S.E.2d 320, 322–323 (N.C. Ct. App. 2007). But in State v. Borders, 762 S.E.2d 490 (N.C. Ct. App. 2014), the same court found another criminal defendant had no reasonable expectation of privacy in a cigarette butt he relinquished to police officers in the curtilage of his home following his arrest. See Laura A. Matejik, DNA Sampling: Privacy and Police Investigation in a Suspect Society, 61 Ark. L. Rev. 53 (2008) for a discussion of this issue.

3.   The Fourth Amendment protects individuals who have a reasonable expectation of privacy. Should the reasonable expectation of privacy be affected by the fact that DNA analysis has become more accessible through direct-to-consumer testing (see Chapter 5) and increasingly possible through DIY DNA analysis kits, like the Bento lab? See Bento Lab, 34 Nature Biotech. 455, May 2016. Should the mere fact that technology makes certain invasions of privacy easier to accomplish override an individual's beliefs and social expectations that such information should be private? Just because people can learn about their ancestry or propensity to develop certain diseases through DTC genetic testing does not mean they expect that information to be publicly available.

In Kyllo v. United States, 533 U.S. 27 (2001), police used novel thermal imaging technology to scan an individual's home to obtain evidence that he probably was using high-intensity lamps that aided the indoor growth of marijuana. The Ninth Circuit did not deem the scanning a search in violation of the Fourth Amendment. It held that the defendant had no expectation of privacy because he had not attempted to conceal the heat emanating from his home. Plus, the imagery did not expose intimate details of his life. The Supreme Court reversed, holding "Where, as here, the Government uses a device that is not in general public use, to explore details of the home that would previously have been unknowable without physical intrusion, the surveillance is a 'search' and is presumptively unreasonable without a warrant."

The Maryland court of appeals in Raynor v. State, 99 A.3d 753 (Md. Ct. App. 2014), rejected the idea that *Kyllo* stands "for the broad proposition that 'using "sense-enhancing technology" to acquire information about an individual is, ipso facto, a search.' " Instead, it understood *Kyllo* as treating the thermal scanner as a search because it was "a substitute for a physical trespass into the home," whereas DNA fingerprinting, whether or not " 'in general public use,' " was not "a substitute for a 'trespass' on or into Petitioner's body."

In 2018, the Supreme Court held that collecting cell-tower data from a wireless carrier constituted a search and seizure under the Fourth Amendment. Timothy Carpenter was convicted of robbery based in part on cell-site data, which allowed the FBI to produce maps placing Carpenter's phone near four robberies. The Court found that government access to such information contravened a reasonable person's expectation that law enforcement would not secretly monitor their movements for an extended period of time. It observed that "[m]apping a cell phone's location over the course of 127 days provides an all-encompassing record of the holder's whereabouts." Moreover, "the retrospective quality of the data . . . gives police access to a category of information otherwise unknowable." The Court noted that before the digital age, collection of such information was expensive and difficult, whereas now it is "remarkably easy, cheap, and efficient."

The Court declined to apply the third-party doctrine, even though it noted that continuously revealing one's location to one's wireless carrier "implicates the third-party principles." While acknowledging that the doctrine "stems from the notion that an individual has a reduced expectation of privacy in information knowingly shared with another," the Court reasoned that the Fourth Amendment does not " 'fall[] out of the picture entirely.' " It found that cell-phone tower data—which provides a "detailed chronical of a person's physical presence compiled every day, every moment, over several years"— implicated "privacy concerns far beyond" that of information to which the third-party doctrine had applied, like phone company's telephone call logs and bank's records of account activity. The Court also concluded that cell-site "information is not truly 'shared.' " First, cell phones are indispensable. Second, the carrier receives cell-phone location information "without any affirmative act on the part of the user beyond powering up." Therefore, the Court held that the search "invaded Carpenter's reasonable expectation of privacy in the whole of his physical movements."

Four dissenting opinions were issued. Justice Kennedy, joined by Justices Alito and Thomas, criticized the majority for transforming the third-party doctrine "into an unprincipled and unworkable doctrine" by applying a balancing test that allows "weighty" privacy interests to " 'overcome' the third-party disclosure." Not only did the Court fail to explain what makes cell-site records distinct from other business records, its "multifactor analysis—considering intimacy, comprehensiveness, expense, retrospectivity, and voluntariness—puts the law on a new and unstable foundation."

Justice Thomas argued that "the Government did not search Carpenter's property" because the cell-site records belonged to the cell phone carriers. "To come within the text of the Fourth Amendment, Carpenter must prove that the cell-site records are his. . . ." He also faulted the majority for relying on Katz v. United States, 389 U.S. 347 (1967), which shifted "the focus of the Fourth Amendment from property to privacy." Instead, the Court should have reconsidered the "failed experiment" of *Katz.*

Justice Alito, joined by Justice Thomas, dissented, in part, to criticize the Court for allowing "a defendant to object to the search of a third party's property." The cell-site records, he reasoned, "belong to Carpenter's cell service providers, not to Carpenter," who did not create, possess, or have "meaningful control over" them. As a result, he found "no plausible ground for maintaining that the information at issue here represents Carpenter's 'papers' or 'effects.' "

Finally, Justice Gorsuch faulted the majority for keeping the third-party doctrine "on life support," rather than concluding its rationale is wrong. Because we rely on the Internet for so much, he noted, nothing is really safe from police review under the doctrine. "Even our most private documents . . . now reside on third party servers." Would, he queried, the doctrine allow the government to "demand a copy of all your e-mails from Google or Microsoft without implicating your Fourth Amendment rights?" Could it take "your DNA from 23andMe without a warrant or probable cause?" The doctrine, he reasoned, is inconsistent with the fact that "people often do reasonably expect that information they entrust to third parties, especially information subject to confidentiality agreements, will be kept private."

Gorsuch also criticized the majority for supplementing the doctrine "with a new and multilayered inquiry." Lower courts must first find a reasonable expectation of privacy. Then, they must determine whether to apply the third-party doctrine by "asking whether the fact of disclosure to a third party outweighs privacy interests in the 'category of information' so disclosed." They should also consider "the need to avoid 'arbitrary power' and the importance of 'plac[ing] obstacles in the way of a too permeating police surveillance.' " Yet, he lamented, the Court offers little guidance. All it tells us, is "that historical cell-site location information (for seven days, anyway) escapes" the application of the doctrine, "while a lifetime of bank or phone records does not." Lower courts must "stay tuned" with respect to "any other kind of information."

Justice Gorsuch advocated, instead, a "traditional approach" where you have a Fourth Amendment interest in things that are "yours." He found it "entirely possible a person's cell-site data could qualify as his papers or effects under existing law" because "customers have substantial legal interests in this information, including at least some right to include, exclude, and control its use. Those interests might even rise to the level of a property right." Because Carpenter "did not invoke the law of property or any analogies to the common law," Gorsuch concluded that Carpenter "forfeited perhaps his most promising line of argument." Carpenter v. United States, 138 S. Ct. 2206 (2018).

What do the majority and dissenting opinions suggest about our Fourth Amendment interests in our genetic information now that it is easier than ever to analyze DNA? What do they suggest about our interests in such information if we use consumer services like 23andMe or Ancestry.com for genetic analysis?

4.   DNA dragnet operations have been used to obtain blood samples. Following a rape by a black man in Ann Arbor, Michigan, the police stopped more than seven hundred African-American men and took DNA samples from 160 of them. One of the men, Blair Shelton, lost his job after the police quizzed his manager about him. When they asked him for a sample, he insisted he was innocent. After they threatened to seek a search warrant if he refused, however, he complied. Although his DNA did not match the crime scene sample, the police continued to intimidate him, repeatedly stopping him and requiring him to show a receipt to prove his blood had already been tested. An officer even "held him at gunpoint until he could 'prove' his genetic innocence. The receipt in effect became his 'passport' to avoid further questioning." In 1997, after the rapist was found, Shelton won a lawsuit to have the police return his blood sample. "Now, says Shelton, he keeps the two tubes in his refrigerator to 'remind me how angry this whole thing makes me.'" Lori Andrews & Dorothy Nelkin, Body Bazaar: The Market for Human Tissue in the Biotechnology Age 102–103 (2001).

Was Blair Shelton's provision of a blood sample sufficiently coerced so as not to be considered "voluntary"? Under what circumstances should the police be able to request blood samples from individuals to match to a crime scene?

5.   States are free to find their state constitutions provide greater privacy protection than the U.S. Constitution. In State v. Goss, 834 A.2d 316 (N.H. 2003), for example, the Supreme Court of New Hampshire interpreted the New Hampshire Constitution as providing greater protection than the Federal Constitution with respect to warrantless searches of garbage. It observed that "[c]lues to people's most private traits and affairs can be found in their garbage. Almost every human activity ultimately manifests itself in waste products and any individual may understandably wish to maintain the confidentiality of his refuse."

6.   Under what circumstances may law enforcement officials obtain genetic information (or even DNA samples) from physicians when their patients are suspected of committing a crime? The U.S. Department of Health and Human Services has promulgated health privacy regulations pursuant to the Health Insurance Portability and Accountability Act of 1996 (HIPAA). Under the HIPAA privacy regulations, a health care provider or institution may disclose otherwise-protected health care information to law enforcement officials pursuant to a court order. Even if there is no court order, law enforcement officials may obtain certain protected health information (such as the type of injury, ABO blood type, and a description of distinguishing physical characteristics) for purposes of "identifying or locating a suspect, fugitive,

material witness or missing person." However, without a court order, the police may *not* obtain "information related to the individual's DNA or DNA analysis, dental records, or typing, samples or analysis of body fluids or tissue." Note that the covered entity is not required to disclose the information without court order. See 45 C.F.R. § 164.512(f).

7.   After Christa Worthington was murdered on Cape Cod, DNA samples from suspects were collected, but it took over a year for the state crime lab to analyze the results and identify her killer. Pam Belluck, Slow DNA Trail Leads to Suspect in Cape Cod Case, N.Y. Times, Apr. 16, 2005, at A1. Other women were outraged that her alleged killer had been allowed to remain free, perhaps to kill again during that time period. But such delays are common. In fact, a poll of U.S. law enforcement officials found a reluctance to collect DNA evidence, especially in cases involving non-violent offenses, because of a belief that due to cost, backlogs, and storage problems, the evidence will never be sent to the lab and therefore never result in an arrest. See Nicholas P. Lovrich et al., National Forensic DNA Study Report, Dec. 12, 2003, www.ncjrs.gov/pdffiles1/nij/grants/203970.pdf.

8.   Since 2004, the Department of Justice has awarded close to $1 billion in grants to states and local jurisdictions through the DNA Capacity Enhancement and Backlog Reduction (CEBR) grant program to increase lab capacity and reduce labs' backlog of DNA evidence. Unfortunately, although these grants allow labs to process more requests, backlogs of crime scene evidence in labs continue to increase. From 2011 to 2017, the number of backlogged requests for crime scene DNA analysis at state and local government labs had increased by 85 percent (from about 91,000 to about 169,000). A GAO report "identified several factors that are reported to have contributed to an increased demand for DNA analysis of crime scene evidence beyond labs' capacities": 1) scientific advancements, that allow for analysis of ever smaller amounts of biological material, including "touch" DNA (DNA transferred by touching an object); 2) decreased turnaround times; 3) increased awareness among law enforcement of the potential value of DNA analysis in solving crimes; and 4) increased legislation requiring sexual assault kit analysis. U.S. Gov't Accountability Office, GAO–19–216 DNA Evidence: DOJ Should Improve Performance Measurement and Properly Design Controls for Nationwide Grant Program 1, 17, 21–22 (2019).

9.   Given the backlog in the processing of DNA evidence, should law enforcement agencies reopen cold cases that, because of older technologies, were not solvable in the past but might be solvable now? Should statutes of limitations be extended so that perpetrators of a crime can be brought to justice at some point in the future? Does "the growing capacity of today's forensics to reach farther and farther into the past seem[ ] likely to undermine the law's time-ingrained notions, embodied in statutes of limitations, about how long people should be liable to criminal prosecutions"? Scott Turow, Still Guilty After All These Years, N.Y. Times, Apr. 8, 2007, at C11.

CHAPTER 19

CONSTITUTIONALITY OF FORENSIC DNA DATABASES

■ ■ ■

JONES V. MURRAY
962 F.2d 302 (4th Cir. 1992).

NIEMEYER, J.

Section 19.2–310.2 of the Virginia Code, effective July 1, 1990, requires convicted felons to submit blood samples for DNA analysis "to determine identification characteristics specific to the person" and provides for the creation of a data bank of the information for future law enforcement purposes. Six inmates have challenged the statute's constitutionality, contending that it authorizes the involuntary extraction of blood in violation of the Fourth Amendment prohibition against unreasonable searches and seizures.

* * *

II.

The principal argument advanced by the inmates is grounded on the contention that Virginia's blood testing program violates the inmates' Fourth Amendment rights against unreasonable searches and seizures by authorizing the search of their bodies in the absence of any individualized suspicion. They argue that the general purpose of enforcing the law by improving methods of identification is not sufficient to justify testing an entire class of people merely because the recidivism rate is higher for them. They note that several classifications of persons, for example, those affected by mental disease or environmental factors, who have never before been convicted of a crime, might statistically be equally likely to commit future crimes. They contend that the district court's ruling sustaining the Virginia program is "the first instance . . . that a pure law enforcement search has ever been sustained in the absence of any individualized suspicion."

The Commonwealth of Virginia observes that if individualized suspicion must exist before any felon can be required to submit to a blood test, any meaningful DNA identification bank will be impossible. The very idea of establishing a data bank refutes the possibility of establishing individualized suspicion because the collection of the blood samples is designed to solve future cases for which no present suspicion can exist. It argues that the special needs of the government warrant application of the balancing test identified in Skinner v. Railway Labor Executives' Ass'n, 489 U.S. 602 [(1989)] and National Treasury Employees Union v. Von Raab, 489 U.S. 656 [(1989)]. When considering the minimal level of intrusion, the Commonwealth argues, demonstrably higher rates of recidivism among felons and the improved methods of identification provided by DNA analysis justify the search. They refer to studies, including one which concluded:

> Of the 108,580 persons released from prisons in 11 states in 1983, * * * an estimated 62.5% were arrested for a felony or serious misdemeanor within 3 years. . . . Before their release from prison, the prisoners had been arrested and charged with an average of more than 12 offenses each; nearly two-thirds had been arrested at least once in the past for a violent offense; and two-thirds had previously been in jail or prison. . . . An estimated 22.7% of all prisoners were rearrested for a violent offense within 3 years of their release.

* * *

It appears to be established, at least with respect to free persons, that the bodily intrusion resulting from taking a blood sample constitutes a search within the scope of the Fourth Amendment. And in the view of the inmates, all governmental searches conducted in the context of criminal law enforcement require individualized suspicion to satisfy the Fourth Amendment's requirement of reasonableness.

We have not been made aware of any case, however, establishing a per se Fourth Amendment requirement of probable cause, or even a lesser degree of individualized suspicion, when government officials conduct a limited search for the purpose of ascertaining and recording the identity of a person who is lawfully confined to prison. This is not surprising when we consider that probable cause had already supplied the basis for bringing the person within the criminal justice system. With the person's loss of liberty upon arrest comes the loss of at least some, if not all, rights to personal privacy otherwise protected by the Fourth Amendment. Thus, persons lawfully arrested on probable cause and detained lose a right of privacy from routine searches of the cavities of their bodies and their jail cells as do convicted felons. Even probationers lose the protection of the Fourth Amendment with respect to their right to privacy against searches of their homes pursuant to an established program to ensure rehabilitation and security.

Similarly, when a suspect is arrested upon probable cause, his identification becomes a matter of legitimate state interest and he can hardly claim privacy in it. * * * As with fingerprinting, therefore, we find that the Fourth Amendment does not require an additional finding of individualized suspicion before blood can be taken from incarcerated felons for the purpose of identifying them.[2]

In the absence of a requirement for individualized suspicion, assuming that the Fourth Amendment continues to apply to lawfully confined prisoners, we must nevertheless determine the reasonableness of any search. We recognize that the search effected by the taking of blood samples may be considered a greater intrusion than fingerprinting. Yet blood tests are commonplace, and the intrusion occasioned by them is "not significant." The procedure "involves virtually no risk, trauma, or pain." In *Skinner*, the Supreme Court upheld a program which required mandatory blood testing of an entire class of railway employees, albeit not for law enforcement purposes. In a similar vein, mandatory blood testing of all prisoners to detect the presence of the Human Immunodeficiency Virus, which causes Acquired Immune Deficiency Syndrome (AIDS), has been justified by the governmental interests in controlling AIDS in prison. These decisions instruct that blood testing can be reasonable under the Fourth Amendment, even with respect to free persons, where the slight intrusion is outweighed by the governmental interest advanced by the intrusion.

Against the minor intrusion, therefore, we weigh the government's interest in preserving a permanent identification record of convicted felons for resolving past and future crimes. It is a well-recognized aspect of criminal conduct that the perpetrator will take unusual steps to conceal not only his conduct, but also his identity. Disguises used while committing a crime may be supplemented or replaced by changed names, and even changed physical features. Traditional methods of identification by photographs, historical records, and fingerprints often prove inadequate. The DNA, however, is claimed to be unique to each individual and cannot, within current scientific knowledge, be altered. The individuality of the DNA provides a dramatic new tool for the law enforcement effort to match suspects and criminal conduct. Even a suspect with altered physical features cannot escape the match that his DNA might make with a sample contained in a DNA bank, or left at the scene of a crime within samples of blood, skin, semen or hair follicles. The governmental justification for this form of identification, therefore, relies on no argument different in kind from that traditionally advanced for taking fingerprints and photographs, but with additional force because of the potentially greater precision of DNA sampling and matching methods.

---

[2]   Because we consider the cases which involve the Fourth Amendment rights of prison inmates to comprise a separate category of cases to which the usual per se requirement of probable cause does not apply, there is no cause to address whether the so-called "special needs" exception, relied on by the district court, applies in this case. We do, however, find support for our holding in the fact that the Supreme Court has not categorically required individualized suspicion in the case of every search which advances a law enforcement objective. * * *

Thus, in the case of convicted felons who are in custody of the Commonwealth, we find that the minor intrusion caused by the taking of a blood sample is outweighed by Virginia's interest, as stated in the statute, in determining inmates' "identification characteristics specific to the person" for improved law enforcement.

The inmates argue that the usefulness of DNA as an identification technique is largely limited to violent crimes, based upon the unlikelihood of recovering from the scene of a nonviolent crime a DNA sample from the perpetrator that is sufficient for comparison with the suspect's DNA. According to statistics presented by the inmates, there is only a remote possibility that a nonviolent offender will commit a future violent crime which will produce sufficient DNA for an identification match. These statistics indicate that 97% of the cases in which DNA evidence was used to link a defendant with a crime involved murder or rape, and further, less than 1% of all nonviolent offenders are later arrested on murder or rape charges. They contend therefore that the DNA program cannot be justified with respect to the testing of nonviolent felons.

These numbers persuasively demonstrate, given the DNA technology that is currently available, that Virginia's interest in DNA testing is significantly more compelling with regard to those felons convicted of violent crimes than those not. However, we note that the fact that fingerprints are not found at a particular crime scene does not negate the Commonwealth's interest in fingerprinting the criminal suspect when caught. There may be uses for DNA technology other than merely verifying a suspect's presence at the scene of a crime. As we have noted, a DNA print might be used to identify a criminal suspect who has attempted to alter or conceal his or her identity. Moreover, if DNA technology becomes more common (and particularly if it is established as a reliable and judicially accepted identification tool), then it is likely that law enforcement officials will become more aware of the technology and thus more likely to make use of the DNA clues that are left as a result of crimes other than murder or rape. The effectiveness of the Commonwealth's plan, in terms of percentage, need not be high where the objective is significant and the privacy intrusion limited.

* * * While greater utility for use of DNA data can be supposed when the future crime is one of violence and those crimes can statistically be related more directly to inmates now incarcerated for crimes of violence, the utility of more exact identification in all cases still justifies the minor intrusion. We therefore agree with the district court's conclusion that § 19.2–310.2 does not violate the Fourth Amendment as applied by the Fourteenth Amendment to the Commonwealth of Virginia.

* * *

MURNAGHAN, J., concurring in part and dissenting in part:

To the extent that the majority opinion upholds the Virginia DNA testing procedure as applied to violent felons, and holds that the statute qualifies as an *ex post facto* law with respect to its effect on the mandatory release of prisoners convicted prior to its effective date, I concur in the decision. But I must respectfully dissent from the majority's determination of the constitutionality of the statute as applied to prisoners convicted of non-violent crimes. Prisoners do not lose an expectation of privacy with regard to blood testing, and the Commonwealth's articulated interest in the testing of non-violent felons does not counter-balance the privacy violation involved in the procedure.

I.

* * *

Prisoners most assuredly do give up specific aspects of their reasonable expectation of privacy because of practical concerns relating to living conditions, and because of the necessities involved in ensuring prison security. However, in the present case, appellants have not forfeited their expectation of privacy with respect to blood testing, and no practical penal concern justifies the departure involved in the DNA procedure. Accordingly, the Commonwealth's DNA testing procedure should be reviewed under the standard applied to a search of any individual when such a search is not based on individualized suspicion: the privacy interest of the prisoner in remaining free of bodily invasion should be balanced against the state interest in carrying out the search.

* * *

A prisoner certainly cannot stake a claim to the kind of sanctity of dominion to a cell that a non-incarcerated individual can to a home. Moreover, the Supreme Court has indicated that there are situations in which even a private citizen's expectation of privacy diminishes, or disappears altogether. It is apparent, however, that the search involved in the present case, blood testing, violates a privacy interest that even a prisoner, living in close quarters under constant security surveillance, reasonably can expect to enjoy.

No precedential justification exists for the majority's holding that convicted felons, violent or non-violent, solely because of past criminal activity, lose the expectation that their bodily fluids will be free of unjustified search. As the Supreme Court stated in Skinner v. Railway Labor Association, 489 U.S. 602 (1989), "it is obvious that this physical invasion [a blood test] penetrating beneath the skin, infringes an expectation of privacy that society is prepared to recognize as reasonable." Although *Skinner* involved the testing of free citizens, its determination that an individual has a reasonable expectation of privacy within one's own body applies equally to prisoners, unless the prisoner's privacy right is incompatible with the objectives of incarceration.

* * *

II.

The DNA testing of felons convicted of non-violent crimes is not justified, given the limited and non-compelling state interest in including them in the testing procedure. The only state interest offered by the Commonwealth for including non-violent felons is administrative ease. I cannot conclude that the government interest in administrative ease suffices to outweigh a prisoner's expectation of privacy in not having blood withdrawn from his body when that prisoner is not significantly more likely to commit a violent crime in the future than a member of the general population.

* * *

The record supports appellants' contention that there is an extremely tenuous link connecting persons convicted of non-violent felonies to the commission of future violent crime. It, therefore, contains nothing to substantiate a theory that DNA testing of non-violent felons would assist in solution of future crimes. United States Justice Department statistics provided in the record show that only 0.4% of non-violent felons are later arrested on rape charges, and only 0.8% are later arrested on murder charges. One might assume non-violent drug offenders would be more likely to commit violent crime subsequent to release than other non-violent felons; yet, only 0.4% of them are later arrested for rape, and 0.3% for murder.

The record does not provide similar percentage statistics for the general population. It can be readily inferred that the testing of all citizens, regardless of criminal record, would create a DNA data bank with a similar statistical likelihood of solving future crime as is provided by the testing of non-violent felons. Additionally, the testing of other discrete populations, e.g., racial minorities or residents of underprivileged areas, might produce significantly better statistics than 0.4%.

Lacking a significant statistical likelihood to justify the inclusion of non-violent felons, the Commonwealth is forced to justify the inclusion of these individuals based on its amorphous concern for administrative efficiency * * *. Therefore, the majority opinion * * * leads me to a deep, disturbing, and overriding concern that, without a proper and compelling justification, the Commonwealth may be successful in taking significant strides towards the establishment of a future police state, in which broad and vague concerns for administrative efficiency will serve to support substantial intrusions into the privacy of citizens.

* * *

MARYLAND V. KING

569 U.S. 435 (2013).

JUSTICE KENNEDY delivered the opinion of the Court.

In 2003 a man concealing his face and armed with a gun broke into a woman's home in Salisbury, Maryland. He raped her. The police were unable to identify or apprehend the assailant based on any detailed description or other evidence they then had, but they did obtain from the victim a sample of the perpetrator's DNA.

In 2009 Alonzo King was arrested in Wicomico County, Maryland, and charged with first- and second-degree assault for menacing a group of people with a shotgun. As part of a routine booking procedure for serious offenses, his DNA sample was taken by applying a cotton swab or filter paper—known as a buccal swab—to the inside of his cheeks. The DNA was found to match the DNA taken from the Salisbury rape victim. King was tried and convicted for the rape. * * * [T]here seems to be no doubt that it was the DNA from the cheek sample taken at the time he was booked in 2009 that led to his first having been linked to the rape and charged with its commission.

* * *

In a divided opinion, the Maryland Court of Appeals struck down the portions of the Act authorizing collection of DNA from felony arrestees as unconstitutional [and overturned King's conviction]. The majority concluded that a DNA swab was an unreasonable search in violation of the Fourth Amendment because King's "expectation of privacy is greater than the State's purported interest in using King's DNA to identify him." * * *

Both federal and state courts have reached differing conclusions as to whether the Fourth Amendment prohibits the collection and analysis of a DNA sample from persons arrested, but not yet convicted, on felony charges. This Court granted certiorari, 568 U.S. [1006] (2012), to address the question [and now reverses the judgment of the Maryland court]. * * *

Although the DNA swab procedure used here presents a question the Court has not yet addressed, the framework for deciding the issue is well established. The Fourth Amendment, binding on the States by the Fourteenth Amendment, provides that "[t]he right of the people to be secure in their persons, houses, papers, and effects, against unreasonable searches and seizures, shall not be violated." It can be agreed that using a buccal swab on the inner tissues of a person's cheek in order to obtain DNA samples is a search. [Citing cases that find intrusions of human bodies to be searches].

A buccal swab is a far more gentle process than a venipuncture to draw blood. It involves but a light touch on the inside of the cheek; and although it can be deemed a search within the body of the arrestee, it requires no "surgical intrusions beneath the skin." *Winston,* 470 U.S., at 760. The fact than an intrusion is negligible is of central relevance to determining reasonableness, although it is still a search as the law defines that term.

To say that the Fourth Amendment applies here is the beginning point, not the end of the analysis. * * * "As the text of the Fourth Amendment indicates, the ultimate measure of the constitutionality of a governmental search is 'reasonableness.'" In giving content to the inquiry whether an intrusion is reasonable, the Court has preferred "some quantum of individualized suspicion . . . [as] a prerequisite to a constitutional search or seizure. But the Fourth Amendment imposes no irreducible requirement of such suspicion."

In some circumstances, such as "[w]hen faced with special law enforcement needs, diminished expectations of privacy, minimal intrusions, or the like, the Court has found that certain general, or individual, circumstances may render a warrantless search or seizure reasonable." * * * The need for a warrant is perhaps least when the search involves no discretion that could properly be limited by the "interpo[lation of] a neutral magistrate between the citizen and the law enforcement officer." Treasury Employees v. Von Raab, 489 U.S. 656 (1989).

The legitimate government interest served by the Maryland DNA Collection Act is one that is well established: the need for law enforcement officers in a safe and accurate way to process and identify the persons and possessions they must take into custody. It is beyond dispute that "probable cause provides legal justification for arresting a person suspected of crime, and for a brief period of detention to take the administrative steps incident to arrest. . . . The validity of the search of a person incident to a lawful arrest has been regarded as settled from its first enunciation, and has remained virtually unchallenged." Even in that context, the Court has been clear that individual suspicion is not necessary, because "[t]he constitutionality of a search incident to an arrest does not depend on whether there is any indication that the person arrested possesses weapons or evidence. The fact of a lawful arrest, standing alone, authorizes a search."

Perhaps the most direct historical analogue to the DNA technology used to identify respondent is the familiar practice of fingerprinting arrestees. From the advent of this technique, courts had no trouble determining that fingerprinting was a natural part of "the administrative steps incident to arrest."

DNA identification is an advanced technique superior to fingerprinting in many ways, so much so that to insist on fingerprints as the norm would make little sense to either the forensic expert or a layperson. * * * A suspect who has changed his facial features to evade photographic identification or even one who has undertaken the more arduous task of altering his fingerprints cannot escape the revealing power of his DNA.

In sum, there can be little reason to question "the legitimate interest of the government in knowing for an absolute certainty the identity of the person arrested, in knowing whether he is wanted elsewhere, and in ensuring his identification in the event he flees prosecution."

In light of the context of a valid arrest supported by probable cause respondent's expectations of privacy were not offended by the minor intrusion of a brief swab of his cheeks. By contrast, that same context of arrest gives rise to significant state interests in identifying respondent not only so that the proper name can be attached to his charges but also so that the criminal justice system can make informed decisions concerning pretrial custody. Upon these considerations the Court concludes that DNA identification of arrestees is a reasonable search that can be considered part of a routine booking procedure. When officers make an arrest supported by probable cause to hold for a serious offense and they bring the suspect to the station to be detained in custody, taking and analyzing a cheek swab of the arrestee's DNA is, like fingerprinting and photographing, a legitimate police booking procedure that is reasonable under the Fourth Amendment.

The judgment of the Court of Appeals of Maryland is reversed.

JUSTICE SCALIA, with whom JUSTICE GINSBURG, JUSTICE SOTOMAYOR, and JUSTICE KAGAN join, dissenting.

The Fourth Amendment forbids searching a person for evidence of a crime when there is no basis for believing the person is guilty of the crime or is in possession of incriminating evidence. That prohibition is categorical and without exception; it lies at the very heart of the Fourth Amendment. Whenever this Court has allowed a suspicionless search, it has insisted upon a justifying motive apart from the investigation of crime.

It is obvious that no such noninvestigative motive exists in this case. The Court's assertion that DNA is being taken, not to solve crimes, but to *identify* those in the State's custody, taxes the credulity of the credulous. And the Court's comparison of Maryland's DNA searches to other techniques, such as fingerprinting, can seem apt only to those who know no more than today's opinion has chosen to tell them about how those DNA searches actually work.

* * *

Although there is a "closely guarded category of constitutionally permissible suspicionless searches," that has never included searches designed to serve "the normal need for law enforcement." * * * Even the common name for suspicionless searches—"special needs" searches—itself reflects that they must be justified, *always,* by concerns "other than crime detection." ** *

So while the Court is correct to note that there are instances in which we have permitted searches without individualized suspicion, "[i]n none of these cases . . . did we indicate approval of a [search] whose primary purpose was to detect evidence of ordinary criminal wrongdoing." That limitation is crucial. It is only when a governmental purpose aside from crime-solving is at stake that we engage in the free-form "reasonableness" inquiry that the Court indulges at length today. To put it another way, both the legitimacy of the Court's method and the correctness of its outcome hinge entirely on the truth of a single proposition: that the primary purpose of these DNA searches is something other than simply discovering evidence of criminal wrongdoing. That proposition is wrong.

It is on the fingerprinting of arrestees * * * that the Court relies most heavily. The Court does not actually say whether it believes that taking a person's fingerprints is a Fourth Amendment search, and our cases provide no ready answer to that question. Even assuming so, however, law enforcement's post-arrest use of fingerprints could not be more different from its post-arrest use of DNA. Fingerprints of arrestees are taken primarily to identify them (though that process sometimes solves crimes); the DNA of arrestees is taken to solve crimes (and nothing else). Contrast CODIS, the FBI's nationwide DNA database, with IAFIS, the FBI's Integrated Automated Fingerprint Identification System.

Fingerprints	DNA Samples
The "average response time for an electronic criminal fingerprint submission is about 27 minutes." IAFIS.	DNA analysis can take months—far too long to be useful for identifying someone.
IAFIS includes detailed identification information, including "criminal histories; mug shots; scars and tattoo photos; physical characteristics like height, weight, and hair and eye color."	CODIS contains "[n]o names or other personal identifiers of the offenders, arrestees, or detainees." See CODIS and NDIS Fact Sheet.
"Latent prints" recovered from crime scenes are not systematically compared against the database of known fingerprints, since that requires further forensic work.	The entire point of the DNA database is to check crime scene evidence against the profiles of arrestees and convicts as they come in.

* * *

Today, it can fairly be said that fingerprints really are used to identify people—so well, in fact, that there would be no need for the expense of a separate, wholly redundant DNA confirmation of the same information. What DNA adds—what makes it a valuable weapon in the law-enforcement arsenal—is the ability to solve unsolved crimes, by matching old crime-scene evidence against the profiles of people whose identities are already known. That is what was going on when King's DNA was taken, and we should not disguise the fact. Solving unsolved crimes is a noble objective, but it occupies a lower place in the American pantheon of noble objectives than the protection of our people from suspicionless law-enforcement searches. The Fourth Amendment must prevail.

* * *

The most regrettable aspect of the suspicionless search that occurred here is that it proved to be quite unnecessary. All parties concede that it would have been entirely permissible, as far as the Fourth Amendment is concerned, for Maryland to take a sample of King's DNA as a consequence of his conviction for second-degree assault. So the ironic result of the Court's error is this: The only arrestees to whom the outcome here will ever make a difference are those who *have been acquitted* of the crime of arrest (so that their DNA could not have been taken upon conviction). In other words, this Act manages to burden uniquely the sole group for whom the Fourth Amendment's protections ought to be most jealously guarded: people who are innocent of the State's accusations.

Today's judgment will, to be sure, have the beneficial effect of solving more crimes; then again, so would the taking of DNA samples from anyone who flies on an airplane (surely the Transportation Security Administration needs to know the "identity" of the flying public), applies for a driver's license, or attends a public school. Perhaps the construction of such a genetic panopticon is wise. But I doubt that the proud men who wrote the charter of our liberties would have been so eager to open their mouths for royal inspection.

I therefore dissent, and hope that today's incursion upon the Fourth Amendment, like an earlier one, will some day be repudiated.

* * *

NOTES AND QUESTIONS

1.   In State v. Medina, 102 A.3d 661 (Vt. 2014), the Vermont Supreme Court addressed the constitutionality of a 2011 Amendment to Vermont's DNA database statute, which authorized warrantless, suspicionless DNA collection and analysis from anyone arraigned for a felony after a determination of probable cause. Lower Vermont courts had ruled that the amendment violated Article 11 of the Vermont Constitution, the Fourth Amendment of the U.S. Constitution, or both. Because those decisions were made prior to the decision in Maryland v. King, the Vermont Supreme Court focused only on the

constitutionality of the Vermont statute under Article 11 of the Vermont Constitution, which protects against unlawful searches and seizures.

Distinguishing the Maryland and Vermont statutes, the Vermont Court observed that the former law is triggered by arrest, whereas the latter is triggered by a finding of probable cause at arraignment for a felony, which normally occurs after the defendant is brought to court. In *King*, the rationale for upholding the Maryland law was based in part on the right of police officers to search suspects incident to an arrest and to accurately identify the person arrested and charged with a crime. The identification of arrested persons, however, is not even included in the stated purposes for the Vermont DNA-collection law.

The Vermont Court further noted that "the current system of photographs and [routine] fingerprints fully responds to the need for identification of" arrestees. Moreover, because DNA sampling involves two searches—the taking of a DNA sample and the analysis of the sample—the Court refused to "equate a procedure that takes an image of the skin of a finger with the capture of intimate bodily fluids." Although ordinary fingerprinting is constitutional under the Vermont Constitution, the Court observed that the "real functionality" of DNA fingerprinting is "to solve open criminal cases or ones that may occur in the future." It was also unpersuaded by the *King* decision that there is "any limit on what information may be gathered about an arrestee and the effect of that information gathering on the decision whether to arrest." Because the "weight of the privacy interest of arraignees prior to conviction" defeats the "marginal weight of the State's interest in DNA collection at the point of arraignment," the Court found the amendment unconstitutional under Article 11 of the Vermont Constitution.

In contrast, the California Supreme Court, "employing the same mode of analysis that the high court applied in *King*," ruled that California's collection and analysis of DNA samples taken at booking from adult felony arrestees did not violate the California Constitution's protection against unreasonable search and seizures. People v. Buza, 4 Cal. 5th 658, 684 (Cal. 2018).

2.   Who has the better argument as to the differences or similarities between ordinary and DNA fingerprints, the *King* majority or the Vermont Supreme Court?

Like the Vermont Court, Mark Rothstein and Sandra Carnahan find "fundamental differences between DNA and fingerprints," given that a DNA sample contains information that could reveal "one's genetic predisposition to disease, physical and mental characteristics, and a host of other private facts not evident to the public." The fact that DNA samples are retained indefinitely by law enforcement "on the chance that technological advancements might require re-testing of the samples," heightens the risk of misuse or abuse of the samples and privacy violations. "Moreover, many state statutes allow access to the samples for undefined law enforcement purposes and humanitarian identification purposes, or authorize the use of samples for assisting medical research or to support identification research and protocol development."

Noting that "the Supreme Court has recognized that a laboratory analysis of blood and other bodily fluids constitutes a 'second search' subject to the Fourth Amendment's reasonableness requirement," they conclude that "any reasonableness determination ought to include an analysis of the use that law enforcement authorities intend to make of the DNA sample." Mark A. Rothstein & Sandra Carnahan, Legal and Policy Issues in Expanding the Scope of Law Enforcement DNA Data Banks 67 Brooklyn L. Rev. 127 (2001).

3.   One court rejected a convicted felon's assertions that the DNA Analysis Backlog Elimination Act of 2000 (DNA Act), mandating the collection and analysis of biological samples to create a DNA profile to enter into CODIS, violated his rights under the First Amendment and the Religious Freedom Restoration Act (RFRA). It found the DNA Act did not burden the free exercise of the felon's alleged religious belief that " 'DNA sampling, collection and storage' 'defile[s] God's temple' " because, even if the Act incidentally affects religiously motivated action, it is a religion-neutral, generally applicable law. It also held that the Act did not violate RFRA. First, the mandatory collection, analysis and storage of DNA information was not a substantial burden on religious exercise because it did not require the felon "to modify his religious behavior in any way." Second, even if it did, the DNA Act is in furtherance of a compelling government interest to solve past and future crimes in order to protect the public and ensure conviction of the guilty and exoneration of the innocent. And it is the least restrictive means of furthering that interest. In addition, to finding that the Act did not violate the First Amendment and RFRA, the court found it did not violate the Fifth Amendment or Fourth Amendment. Kaemmerling v. Lapping 553 F.3d 669 (D.C. Cir. 2008).

4.   Originally, state and federal databases were limited to DNA samples from sexual offenders and a few other violent felons, such as murderers. However, as of 2013, 48 states collect DNA for all felony convictions and 42 states now collect DNA for some misdemeanor convictions. Two states collect DNA only for some felony and misdemeanor convictions. Additionally, 31 states collect DNA from convicted juveniles. National Conference of State Legislatures, Convicted Offender DNA Collection and Analysis Laws, (2013), www.ncsl.org/Documents/cj/ConvictedOffendersDNALaws.pdf.

As of 2019, 33 states collect DNA samples from arrestees for certain offenses. Federal Bureau of Investigation, CODIS-NDIS Statistics, https://www.fbi.gov/services/laboratory/biometric-analysis/codis/ndis-statistics.

Some argue that DNA data banks should be limited to DNA obtained from individuals convicted of violent sex offenses and other violent felonies. What are the pros and cons of that view? And what are the pros and cons of allowing DNA collection on arrestees? Supporters of arrestee DNA collection claim that the policy will help law enforcement solve crimes more quickly and efficiently. Opponents claim that the increase in DNA samples to be collected and processed at the federal level each year would significantly increase the current workload and cost to the country. Is the *King* majority or dissent more persuasive with respect to whether DNA testing of arrestees is appropriate?

5.　The expansion of DNA testing led to a significant increase in uploads of convicted offender and arrestee sample DNA profiles into CODIS from 2003 through 2010. (This is in addition to the backlogs of crime scene samples discussed in Chapter 18, notes 7–8, page 411.) Not surprisingly, laboratory backlogs for DNA testing of samples of convicted offenders and arrestees grew. Between 2005 and 2010, however, the National Institute of Justice provided more than $58 million to reduce those backlogs. "According to officials from NIJ, the FBI, and the American Society of Crime Lab Directors, this funding helped build labs' capacities such that convicted offender and arrestee backlogs are no longer an issue of concern." U.S. Gov't Accountability Office, GAO–19–216 DNA Evidence: DOJ Should Improve Performance Measurement and Properly Design Controls for Nationwide Grant Program 70–71 (2019).

6.　Because minorities are disproportionately arrested, prosecuted, and convicted, DNA databases disproportionately include profiles from those groups, which are not reflective of their representation in society. According to Hank Greely, 12% of the United States population is African American, while 40% of the genetic profiles in the federal database belong to African-American individuals. Solomon Moore, F.B.I. and States Vastly Expanding Databases of DNA, N.Y. Times, Apr. 19, 2009, at 1. Would the creation of universal databases, where samples are collected from everyone, potentially even at birth through newborn screening, solve this problem? See David H. Kaye & Michael E. Smith, DNA Databases for Law Enforcement: The Coverage Question and the Case for a Population-Wide Database, in DNA and the Criminal Justice System 247, 269–71 (David Lazer ed., 2004).

Would universal databases raise civil liberty concerns for everyone, however, rather than just some groups? And would they make it more difficult to prevent other more dangerous uses of the information by the government? See Mark A. Rothstein & Meghan K. Talbott, The Expanding Use of DNA in Law Enforcement: What Role for Privacy?, 34 J. L. Med. & Ethics 153–164 (2006). Or would universal databases improve our privacy by ending the need for more intrusive investigative techniques, particularly if privacy safeguards, like destruction of samples after profiles are generated and restrictions on the use of samples, are put in place? Kirsten Dedrickson, Universal DNA Databases: A Way to *Improve* Privacy, 4 J.L. & Biosci. 637 (2018).

> **Food for Thought:** Would universal databases solve more crimes? Or would they offer limited benefits because most offenders, as recidivists, already have their DNA in a database, and expanded databases could overburden labs and slow down DNA analysis?

7.　The issue of the constitutionality of DNA databases also arose with respect to the Department of Defense's DNA Registry program, which collects and stores DNA samples from active and reserve personnel to help identify soldiers' remains. Members of the United States Marine Corps who had refused to provide biological samples for the DNA repository were charged with violating orders. They brought suit claiming that the program violated their Fourth Amendment interests.

In Mayfield v. Dalton, 901 F. Supp. 300 (D. Haw.1995), vacated as moot, 109 F.3d 1423 (9th Cir. 1997), the federal district court concluded that, although the compulsory taking of biological samples is a seizure, it was not unreasonable. It found the collection of cheek swabs and blood samples to identify soldiers' remains "a far less intrusive infringement of Plaintiffs' Fourth Amendment privacy rights" than blood, urine, or breath tests to be used as evidence in criminal prosecutions or disciplinary actions. Although the military "has a significant interest" in being able to identify the remains of its members, the court observed that family members "derive the greatest benefit, and solace, from the speedy and definite identification of the remains of their loved ones." Moreover, the court found no evidence that the military has used or has any plans to use the "samples for some less innocuous purpose, such as the diagnosis of hereditary diseases or disorders and the use or dissemination of such diagnoses to potential employers, insurers and others with a possible interest in such information." In short, it found that the military's compelling interest in being able to identify its service members and ensure the "peace of mind of their next of kin" outweighed the minimal intrusion on the service members of taking blood samples and oral swabs for the military's DNA registry.

Should the Department of Defense be allowed to use the DNA in its bank for any purpose other than identification of soldiers' remains? Under what circumstances, if any, should law enforcement officials be able to gain access to the DOD DNA bank to see if a soldier's DNA profile matches the DNA profile from a crime scene? Section 1565a of the 2003 National Defense Authorization Act allows DNA samples to be made available pursuant to a valid court order "for the purposes of an investigation or prosecution of a felony or any sexual offense, for which no other source of DNA information is reasonably available." 10 U.S.C.A. § 1565a.

Under what circumstances, if any, should genetic researchers be able to gain access to samples in the DOD DNA bank? If identification is the only permissible use of the DOD DNA bank, should members of the military be able to direct that the DNA be held privately by the soldier's relatives, rather than in the government DNA bank?

8.   DNA analysis has also been used in the immigration context. In 2018, a Federal District Court ordered the reunification of immigrant children under the age of five with their parents after the families were separated at the border. To comply with the court order, the U.S. Department of Health and Human Services announced it would conduct DNA tests to verify relationships before reuniting families. Since then, Immigration and Customs Enforcement (ICE) has begun using Rapid DNA testing along the border to identify fraudulent familial relationships. The government argues that the testing is voluntary. Is that persuasive when the DHS and ICE state that refusing to submit to testing could be a "factor in ICE's assessment of the validity of the claimed parent-child relationship"? See Privacy Impact Assessment for the Rapid DNA Operational Use, https://www.dhs.gov/sites/default/files/publications/privacy-pia-ice-rapiddna-june2019_1.pdf. In addition to privacy

and consent concerns, critics worry about the accuracy of the Rapid DNA testing used (see Chapter 18).

In the fall of 2019, it was reported by officials of the Department of Homeland Security (DHS) that the Department of Justice (DOJ) is developing a federal regulation to give immigration officers authority to collect DNA samples from undocumented immigrants in the custody of Customs and Border Protection (CBP). Although the DNA Fingerprint Act of 2005 allows federal agencies to collect DNA from people in their custody, previous DOJ regulations exempted agencies under DHS, like CBP and ICE. In 2010, DHS narrowed the exemption to those who were not detained on criminal charges or who were awaiting deportation proceedings. Under the new proposal, the exemption would disappear altogether. The plan is to add the DNA test results to CODIS, the national DNA database. As one DHS official stated under condition of anonymity, "There is a criminal aspect to this population."

Does this plan raise Fourth Amendment or other concerns in collecting DNA without a warrant? The government argues it has authority to conduct DNA testing under 8 U.S.C. § 1357(b), which allows ICE to "take and consider evidence concerning the privilege of any person to enter, reenter, pass through, or reside in the United States." Given that this statute has generally applied to "evidence" like inspecting entry documents as opposed to invasive DNA testing, is the government's position persuasive?

CHAPTER 20

USES OF FORENSIC DNA DATABASES

■ ■ ■

I. REGULATION OF DNA DATABASES

SETH AXELRAD, USE OF FORENSIC DNA DATABASE INFORMATION FOR MEDICAL OR GENETIC RESEARCH

Am. Soc'y L., Med. & Ethics (2005).

The state legislatures in all 50 states established DNA databases in order to aid and enhance law enforcement. Alabama's statute declares, "[T]he creation and establishment of a statewide DNA database is the most reasonable and certain method or means to rapidly identify repeat or habitually dangerous criminals." Ala. Code § 36–18–20(g). The state statutes also recognize, however, that the criminals' DNA information can be used for other purposes, including for medical and genetic research.

Eight states—Indiana, Rhode Island, South Dakota, Texas, Utah, Vermont, Washington, and Wyoming—expressly prohibit the use of the DNA database to obtain information on human physical traits, predisposition to disease, or medical or genetic disorders. Alabama, on the other hand, explicitly authorizes the use of DNA information for medical research, and is the only state to do so. Ala. Code §§ 36–18–20 and 36–18–31.

Michigan authorizes use of anonymous database information for an "academic" or "research" purpose, although it is unclear from the statutory language whether the state legislature meant to include medical or genetic research as an authorized use of database information. Mich. Comp. Laws Ann. § 28.176. The remaining 40 state statutes are either silent on this issue * * *, or they neither expressly authorize nor prohibit such research * * *.

Thus, with regard to most state DNA database statutes, the issue of the use of database information for medical or genetic research is not directly addressed. An indirect answer to the question of research uses may be gleaned from those statutes which provide a list of "authorized uses." For example, Alaska limits use of the DNA database "only for (1) providing DNA or other blood grouping tests for identification analysis; (2) criminal investigations, prosecutions, and identification analysis; (3) statistical blind analysis; (4) improving the operation of the system; or (5) exoneration of the innocent." Alaska Stat. § 41.41.035(f). This exclusive list does not include medical or genetic research and, presumably, such research uses would violate the statute. Therefore, by examining the "authorized uses" provisions of the statutes, one may get a clearer picture of how most US states regulate research use of database information. Furthermore, where the authorized uses apparently exclude research use, the states also may deter the dissemination of DNA information to researchers by criminalizing the disclosure of database information to unauthorized persons. Thirty states currently criminalize such disclosures.

STEPHEN MERCER & JESSICA GABEL, SHADOW DWELLERS: THE UNDERREGULATED WORLD OF STATE AND LOCAL DNA DATABASES

69 N.Y.U. Ann. Surv. Am. L. 639, 653–56 (2014).

* * *

[T]he FBI is limited in what profiles it can include in the national databank. NDIS [the national DNA index system] can only include profiles authorized by statute. Further, Congress expressly prohibited the FBI from including in NDIS any DNA samples that are voluntarily submitted for elimination purposes. The FBI implemented additional quality standards that restrict the inclusion of profiles of known persons and from crime scenes. The FBI does not allow state or local CODIS laboratories to upload enhanced DNA profiles created from very low-level amounts of human cells. The concern is that part of the profile may be an artifact created during the testing process that enhanced testing techniques have amplified to seemingly detectable levels. The imperative for reliable matches between DNA profiles in the national databank also means that the FBI limits state and local laboratories to uploading only profiles that are reasonably probative of the identity of a putative perpetrator. Partial profiles and mixtures of DNA from crime scenes are also prohibited in the national databank unless the expected number of contributors to the mixture is fewer than the number of matches expected by chance from a search of the relentlessly expanding databank.

C. State Regulation

States are responsible for developing their own regulations governing state and local DNA databases. A minority of states regulate the categories of DNA profiles that can be stored and searched at the state or local levels. For example, Alaska permits only certain categories of DNA samples that cannot be uploaded to NDIS to be retained in the state database. * * *

By contrast, Michigan allows a suspect's DNA to be taken, but limits that "any other DNA identification profile obtained by the department shall not be permanently retained by the department but shall be retained only as long as it is needed for a criminal investigation or criminal prosecution." Vermont permits DNA profiles to be stored only at the state level and prohibits the entry into the state database of DNA "voluntarily submitted or obtained by the execution of a nontestimonial identification order . . . ." Other states that subject local DNA databases to statutory requirements include Connecticut, Missouri, and Washington. Yet other states appear to prohibit the use of local DNA databases altogether.

The vast majority of states, however, do not curb or regulate the categories of DNA samples from known persons that may be stored in the state or local databases. These states allow the warehousing of far more DNA profiles and information than is allowed at the national level or by other states. In the absence of affirmative statutory authorization for these local databases to contain DNA profiles that cannot be entered into the national databank, state law limiting the collection of DNA to qualifying offenders may implicitly prohibit the entry of such profiles. Underregulated DNA databases may also violate state privacy law. Further, the passage of state statutes to regulate the mandatory collection of DNA from convicted offenders and arrestees is a legislative recognition of the potential for misuse of DNA databases. Nevertheless, state and local governments are empowered, subject to constitutional limitations, to authorize official police agencies to investigate and prevent crime to further the health, general welfare, and safety of the community, which may include the use of underregulated state or local DNA databases.

* * *

II.   *Sleeper Cells: The Development of Local DNA Databases*

In spite of the threat to individual privacy, law enforcement officials trumpet the value of local DNA databases as an effective crime-solving tool. Local DNA databases "operate under their own rules," and as a result, they can catalogue a far greater number of DNA samples than their state and federal counterparts. Laws regulating local DNA databases exist in a very small number of states. Even among the limited laws regulating local DNA databases, there is "little consensus about what DNA retention policies are appropriate at the local level." Without strict rules governing local DNA databases, local law enforcement agencies are able to exercise great discretion in the collection and use of DNA samples. According to experts, with technological advances allowing for "rapid DNA testing," local DNA databases will continue to expand.

* * *

* * * Commentators have noted the opportunity for police to create "offline" DNA databases that are not connected to CODIS to target the "usual suspects" who are defined by demographics like race, class, and geographic location. However, police are expanding state and local DNA databases that are connected to CODIS in ways that were probably never legislatively intended. Police have discovered the backdoor to CODIS: federal law limits the DNA profiles that can be stored in the national databank, but these limits do not extend to state and local DNA databases.

* * * While many states have * * * adopted requisite standards for their own statewide DNA databases, some local police departments have established their own databases with little or no regulation. In recent years, "a growing number of law enforcement agencies collect DNA for their own 'offline' databases." Out of either frustration with the inefficiencies of state DNA laboratories or a desire to utilize DNA samples ineligible for collection under state or federal law, many local law enforcement agencies view local DNA databases "as valuable investigative tools." Rather than limiting collection of DNA samples to convicted offenders and arrestees, many local law enforcement agencies also collect samples from "volunteers, victims, and suspects." Innocent crime victims may "not necessarily realize their DNA will be saved for future searches." Such collections are "profoundly disturbing" because DNA voluntarily given to the police to clear a name can be retained and used in the investigation of future crimes.

* * * While some local labs are proactive in their use of local databases, there are many that limit their own profiles to those that are permissible at the national level. Those labs that are proactive in this regard—that is, those that include more legally obtained samples in the local database than may ultimately be submitted to the national databank—claim they are providing a more valuable service to their communities because they are likely to provide more investigative leads through CODIS.

For example, during the course of the typical investigation, police will frequently collect many investigative reference samples. Even if some of these samples are not eligible for entry into the national databank, some localities are allowed to keep the DNA profiles in their own local databases. In addition, securing samples from otherwise ineligible defendants through plea bargains provides additional opportunities to solve crimes through CODIS. Because criminals often commit crimes repeatedly in the same geographic area, local law enforcement is able to make the case for these local databases. Little concern is expressed over the potential for gerrymandering the contours of a geographic area to follow lines of race or class, the pooling of data between laboratories, the enhanced "CODIS-plus" profiles that include information necessary to identify a male's paternal line, or the cynicism of bartering for a young male's DNA that will permanently put him—and effectively his family—in a database with uncertain opportunities to expunge his genetic information.

The scope of the problem is magnified when the casework of a local DNA laboratory intersects—as it often does—with DNA dragnets to identify the source of DNA collected at a crime scene. When there is no hit of the unknown suspect profile to any offender profile in the national DNA databank, police may utilize a DNA dragnet—requesting DNA swabs from a target population that may largely be defined by economic class, race, or sex—to expand the collection of DNA to a selected group of individuals who are "associated" with the crime. * * * Usually, individual targets in the group are excluded as suspects through DNA testing. * * * And while these voluntarily submitted samples cannot be uploaded to the national DNA databank, police maintain that they may upload the profiles into local and state DNA databases that participate in CODIS to search for evidence connecting the person to other crimes beyond the purview of the dragnet.

A major concern is that the profiles of the individuals excluded as the source of any crime scene evidence may be permanently retained in the local and state databases because these casework profiles are treated as evidence.

* * *

The underregulation of state and local DNA databases also means that low-quality DNA profiles developed from crime scene samples that cannot be uploaded to the national DNA databank are placed in state and local databases. The risk of misidentification increases when degraded, partial, or irrelevant crime scene profiles are stored in databases. DNA analysis of low amounts of DNA, called "low-copy number DNA," often fails to detect a complete profile and can add erroneous information. In addition, state and local DNA databases are now being expanded to include other poor-quality DNA samples like "touch" DNA, driven by the increasing sensitivity of DNA analysis and an insatiable demand for DNA testing in a wide array of cases from property and drug crimes to quality-of-life offenses.

NOTES AND QUESTIONS

1.   Consider each of the following policies that have been recommended with respect to DNA in DNA Databanks.

a)   *DNA to be analyzed*—Only non-coding regions of DNA should be used for analysis, thereby ensuring that the only possible use of the DNA analysis is identification.

b)   *Statistical and reporting issues*—All statistical methodologies used for determining a match between a crime scene or other sample and a DNA profile in the data bank should adhere to the latest scientific principles.

c)   *Destruction of samples*—Law enforcement officials, including the FBI, favor retaining samples indefinitely for quality assurance and to re-type the samples in the event of changing technology. Twenty-nine state laws either authorize or require that agencies retain samples after analysis; only one state (Wisconsin) requires the destruction of samples, and no samples have actually been destroyed. [As of 2016, 16 states have no provisions regarding the expungement or retention of DNA samples.] The retention of samples, however, even under conditions of stringent security, raises concerns among the public that the samples could be re-analyzed for purposes other than identification. Therefore, samples should be destroyed immediately after analysis.

d) *Access to data bank*—Access to the data banks should be limited to law enforcement personnel, and data banks should not be used for any purpose other than identification, including research.

Mark A. Rothstein & Sandra Carnahan, Legal and Policy Issues in Expanding the Scope of Law Enforcement DNA Data Banks 67 Brooklyn L. Rev. 127 (2001). What are the pros and cons of each recommendation? What are the pros and cons of retaining the printout of the DNA forensic tests instead of the samples themselves?

Should a convicted felon have a say about whether medical studies are undertaken on his or her DNA? Why or why not?

2. Mercer and Gabel propose various rules regarding destruction of samples and records. They believe convicted felons should "receive the least amount of privacy protection" and therefore should not have the option of having their samples and records expunged. In contrast, samples from victims, suspects, and individuals who voluntarily submit samples for elimination purposes should be expunged once "the criminal investigatory interest ends or the duration of the investigation reaches a defined point." In addition, arrested individuals should qualify for automatic expungement if the qualifying charge does not result in a conviction. Is it appropriate to draw such lines? Are these proposed regulations sufficient to address the problems they describe with respect to unregulated local databases?

3. In 2008, the European Court of Human Rights found that the United Kingdom's policy of retaining DNA profiles, cellular tissues, and fingerprints from people charged with a crime but later acquitted violated Article 8 of the European Convention on Human Rights. Article 8 states, in relevant parts, "1. Everyone has the right to respect for his private and family life . . . . 2. There shall be no interference by a public authority with the exercise of this right except such as in accordance with the law and is necessary in a democratic society . . . for the prevention of disorder or crime . . . ." The Court found that:

In addition to the highly personal nature of cellular samples, the Court notes that they contain much sensitive information about an individual, including information about his or her health. Moreover, samples contain a unique genetic code of great relevance to both the individual and his relatives. In this respect the Court concurs with [the lower court's decision that "there could be little, if anything more private to the individual than the knowledge of his genetic make-up."]

Given the nature and amount of personal information contained in cellular samples, their retention *per se* must be regarded as interfering with the right to respect for private lives of the individuals concerned.

* * *

The Court observes * * * that the [DNA] profiles contain substantial amounts of unique personal data. * * * In the Court's view, the DNA profiles' capacity to provide a means of identifying genetic relationships between individuals is in itself sufficient to conclude that their retention interferes with the right to the private life of the individuals concerned. The frequency of familial searches, the safeguards attached thereto and the likelihood of detriment in a particular case are immaterial in this respect. * * *

The Court also found that "[t]he possibility the DNA profiles create for inferences to be drawn as to ethnic origin makes their retention all the more sensitive and susceptible of affecting the right to private life." Additionally, in weighing the public interest of increasing the chances of capturing future offenders, the court concluded that:

> the blanket and indiscriminate nature of the powers of retention of the fingerprints, cellular samples and DNA profiles of persons suspected but not convicted of offences * * * fails to strike a fair balance between the competing public and private interests and that the respondent State has overstepped any acceptable margin of appreciation in this regard. Accordingly, the retention at issue constitutes a disproportionate interference with the applicants' right to respect for private life and cannot be regarded as necessary in a democratic society.

S. and Marper v. The United Kingdom, Nos. 30562/04 and 30566/04, 4 December 2008. In response, the UK enacted the Protection of Freedoms Act 2012, which requires the destruction of fingerprints and DNA profiles of individuals arrested or charged, who have not been convicted of an offense. When the destruction occurs depends on the case. Those arrested but not convicted of a minor offense will have their DNA destroyed at the end of the investigation. In contrast, those arrested, but not convicted of a qualifying offense, like a serious sexual offense, could have their DNA retained for up to five years. The first three years depend on the consent of the Biometrics Commissioner and the last two years require an application to the courts.

4.   Should crime scene DNA be analyzed—and forensic DNA bank samples be analyzed—for "DNA phenotyping," the process of attempting to ascertain someone's physical characteristics from DNA? A few companies are offering DNA phenotyping for a fee. Parabon NanoLabs, for example, does DNA analysis to predict "skin color, eye color, hair color, freckles, ancestry, and face shape." Some traits, like eye color, are influenced by relatively few genetic variants and are easier to predict than more "polygenetic traits." Caitlin Curtis

& James Hereward, How Accurately Can Scientists Reconstruct A Persons' Face from DNA?, Smithsonian.com, May 4, 2018, https://www.smithsonian mag.com/innovation/how-accurately-can-scientists-reconstruct-persons-face-from-dna-180968951/.

In 2004, a DNA test called "DNA Witness" help law enforcement solve a series of rapes and murders in Louisiana. Relying on witness testimony, the police had been searching for a white male. The test, however, predicted the perpetrator was a light-skinned black man, which redirected the search and led to the capture and conviction of Derrick Todd Lee. Duana Fullwiley, Can DNA "Witness" Race?: Forensic Use of an Imperfect Ancestry Testing Technology, 21 Genewatch 12 (2008). The first forensic image based on a DNA sample was created in 2011 on the fourth anniversary of a still-unsolved double homicide in South Carolina. Clive Cookson, DNA: The Next Frontier in Forensics, Jan. 30, 2015, https://www.ft.com/content/012b2b9c-a742-11e4-8a71-00144feab7de.

In China, scientists are using DNA phenotyping to create images of faces, which experts fear may be used to "justify and intensify racial profiling and other state discrimination against Uighurs" as well as general mass surveillance to track dissidents, protestors, and criminals. Sui-Lee Wee & Paul Mozur, China Uses DNA to Map Faces, with Help from the West, N.Y. Times, Dec. 3, 2019, https://www.nytimes.com/2019/12/03/business/china-dna-uighurs-xinjiang.html?searchResultPosition=1.

5.   A 2011 study found that DNA analysis of only about 30–35 single nucleotide polymorphisms (SNPs) "can provide significant information on the pigmentation and ancestry of an individual." Katherine Butler et al., Molecular "Eyewitness": Forensic Prediction of Phenotype and Ancestry, 3 Forensic Sci. Int'l: Genetics Supp. Series e498–e499 (2011). This study relied on volunteers' self-reports regarding their ancestry and phenotype and used spectrophotometry to measure skin pigmentation. How should the problems of quantifying race and ancestry affect the use of these techniques in investigations? What precautions should be taken to address potential problems of standardization and accuracy?

6.   Arguments for using race, ancestry, or phenotype information in the forensic context include its ability to lead to swifter and more efficient investigations. Race is already used ubiquitously in suspect descriptions. Testing can serve to confirm or contradict eyewitness accounts, which are often unreliable. Using a DNA-based description of a phenotype could help alleviate racial bias in the investigation by providing potentially more objective information to guide police searches. Proponents of this technique also argue that we do not have a constitutional privacy interest in DNA abandoned at a crime scene. Further, they note that the type of information used to identify someone is not highly sensitive because it generally constitutes observable traits—eye, hair, and skin color. They argue we can mitigate any privacy risks further by limiting testing and reporting to visible characteristics.

Nevertheless, serious issues arise regarding the use of DNA to predict race. Because race does not correlate to a gene or allele, DNA testing that purports to predict race necessarily incorporates assumptions, inferences, and cultural biases. It also reinforces the idea that race is a biological reality. Even if testing proves sufficiently accurate, it could be used to justify law enforcement's use of extreme and "intrusive search methods, such as DNA dragnets" when testing reveals a suspect who is a racial minority. Further, using genetics to bolster definitions of race inaccurately and inappropriately increases our cultural linkage of crime and race, regardless of the race of suspects. It may even increase racist attitudes. A study of public health messages showed that racist attitudes increased where these messages mentioned a person's race, either white or black, in the messages, even if the content was not negative. Pilar Ossorio, About Face: Forensic Genetic Testing for Race and Visible Traits, 34 J.L. Med. & Ethics 277 (2006).

Given its potential to perpetuate racial bias, should DNA phenotyping be used? Would the issue be resolved by reporting results of DNA analysis both to law enforcement and the public in terms of a specific, narrow phenotype rather than race?

The use of DNA phenotyping raises other concerns. It may be more accurate for certain phenotypes or ethnicities than others. For example, genetic variants linked to hair color are more reliable for some colors (black or red) than others (blonde or brown), and Caucasian ancestry is more accurate than African ancestry. See Curtis & Hereward, *supra*; Samuel D. Hodge, Current Controversies in the Use of DNA in Forensic Investigations, 48 U. Balt. L. Rev. 39 (2018). Finally, SNPs could potentially be used to predict a perpetrator's susceptibility to certain diseases, which raises serious privacy issues.

7.   Although DNA phenotyping is not referenced in the federal legislation regulating DNA identification records, the Federal Bureau of Investigation "has interpreted federal law to permit determining sex and drawing inferences pertaining to ancestry and family kinship for the purposes of investigation." Of the few state laws that address DNA phenotyping, three (Rhode Island, Indiana, and Wyoming) ban it. Louisiana seems to allow the practice in describing a "DNA record" as " 'identification information stored in' " a database for purposes of " 'generating investigative leads' " including "characteristics . . . of value in establishing the identity of individuals.' " A few states (Texas, Vermont, and Michigan) impliedly allow it, although Vermont and Michigan prohibit the use of DNA to identify medical or genetic disorders. Hodge, *supra* at 64. How should states address DNA phenotyping, if at all?

II. DNA FAMILIAL SEARCHES

SONIA M. SUTER, ALL IN THE FAMILY: PRIVACY AND DNA FAMILIAL SEARCHING

23 Harv. J.L. & Tech. 309, 311, 318–20 (2010).

* * *

Familial searching builds on one of the most basic facts of genetics: DNA is shared among family members. As a result, a forensic DNA profile "not only reveal[s] extensive genetic information about the individual whose 'genetic fingerprint' is on file, but also about his or her close relatives." Familial searching uses this principle to infer that someone whose DNA is a close, but not perfect, match to a crime scene sample might be related to the offender. England has pursued such leads to powerful effect in some well-celebrated cases, including the "shoe rapist" case. It has also been used successfully in a few states in America. [T]he federal government (via the FBI) and some states have begun * * * to identify criminals through familial searches.

* * *

The technique that is most commonly understood to be familial searching * * * [uses] DNA databases to locate possible relatives who might be perpetrators of the crime. This expansion has far-reaching implications because it effectively includes individuals based on genetic association, rather than suspicion or even conviction of crimes.

The technique * * * applies modern computer technology to the principle that * * * we share more of our genetic material with biological relatives than with others. In a typical DNA search, only a * * * perfect match * * * at all thirteen [now 20] loci between an individual's DNA and that of a crime scene sample indicates that the individual was the source of the crime scene sample. A "partial match" or "near miss"—for example, sixteen out of twenty-six alleles (two at each locus)—suggests that a close biological relative of the individual whose DNA partially matches the crime scene sample might have been the source. Of course, a close match might also occur randomly because "unrelated people can have some of the same genetic markers." * * * How strong or weak the lead is likely to be * * * can be estimated. The closer the match, or the lower the frequency of the matched alleles in the general population, the more likely that the samples come from a biological relative, although we do not know which one.

**ERIN MURPHY, LAW AND POLICY OVERSIGHT OF FAMILIAL
SEARCHES IN RECREATIONAL GENEALOGY DATABASES**
292 Forensic Sci. Int'l e5, e5–e8 (2018).

In April of 2018, police announced that they had used a recreational genealogy site to identify a man suspected of committing a series of rapes and murders attributed to the "Golden State Killer." * * * [I]t appears that investigators used several publicly available databases (including YSearch and GEDMatch) to find potential DNA matches to a profile developed from biological evidence left at one of the crime scenes. After finding a match to an apparent distant relative, an investigator built up the family tree of that person all the way back to their great-great-great-grandparents in the 1800s. Following a branch of that tree down a line that settled on the west coast, the investigator then found at least two possible suspects, but DNA taken from them did not match. A third lead identified a former police officer named Joseph DeAngelo as a suspect. Police conducted surveillance of DeAngelo and obtained two DNA samples without his knowledge, and when the second clearly matched, DeAngelo was arrested. Since then, over 100 crime scene samples have been uploaded to GEDMatch alone, and law enforcement have used the same methods to make arrests in similarly serious cold cases, and in at least one active investigation.

Searches in recreational genealogical databases are in many respects an outgrowth of familial searches within government DNA databases * * *. The debates over such searches in law enforcement DNA databases have aired * * * arguments regarding their efficacy, legality, and fairness, which apply equally as strongly to searches in recreational databases. * * * But there are also added concerns raised by recreational database searches, which differ both in kind and magnitude. Specifically, searches in recreational databases affect a far greater number of innocent persons, and are conducted with no oversight or governance of any kind. By contrast, familial searches in government databases, while intrusive, rely on scientific methods that carry less of a threat to privacy, affect fewer people in sheer numbers, and are more likely to be governed by laws or policies that impose some safeguards for genetic privacy. * * *

1.   STRs v SNPs

* * * Familial searches in government databases rely on a DNA method known as STRs, rather than the SNPs used in genealogical research. This is significant for two reasons. First, STRs arguably reveal little to nothing about a person's medical or clinical history. * * * In contrast, SNPs—and particularly the SNPs used for genealogy and recreational databases—are chosen precisely for their informational richness. * * * 23andMe, for instance, offers information about disease carrier status, predictive wellness, and cosmetic conditions, relying on

hundreds of thousands of SNPs rather than the 13–20 STRs in the typical forensic profile. * * *

The informational rich quality of SNPs also allows them to locate far more distant relatives than STRs. A familial search in a CODIS database * * * can at best identify a potential sibling, parent, or child of the target. * * * [T]he number of persons affected by such a search and the nature of the ensuing investigation is therefore limited. A familial search in a genealogical database, however, produces leads much farther out—to "relatives" unlikely to know of each other's relatedness, much less consider each other relatives in the colloquial sense. As a result, the sheer number of persons who must be investigated, and the amount of information law enforcement must amass on those persons in order to winnow down candidates, far exceeds that of a typical familial search. * * * The Golden State Killer investigator told reporters he mapped "thousands" of relatives, creating 25 distinct lines on the family tree.

* * * An STR search invites investigation into a handful of a genetic match's immediate male family members. A SNP search invites law enforcement to probe both more deeply and more broadly into a family's history. The SNP search thus raises the specter of both greater intrusiveness and more false positives. Indeed, after such a search, one would expect that the police would know far more about an individual's biological family than does any individual member of that family. * * *

2. *Differences in regulatory oversight*

Second, genealogy searches * * * are also less were regulated. Most officials authorizing familial searches of government databases * * * erected a series of regulatory constraints intended to further quality control, privacy, and oversight interests. * * *

* * *

These restraints * * * represent an effort to balance the right of individuals to genetic privacy, and to be free from government intrusion in the absence of suspicion, against the desire to apprehend law breakers.

* * *

But a search in a genealogical database carries no such restrictions or constraints. Law enforcement may conduct searches hoping to find victims, witnesses, or bystanders to a crime—not just the putative perpetrator. A search in a genealogical database could use an incomplete profile from a crime scene, allowing an even broader "fishing expedition." And law enforcement officers searching genealogical databases and building out family trees face no restrictions on the kind of follow-up investigations they conduct. They are not required to use public sources, and can pursue even the dodgiest or most intimate leads, such as learning through birth records that a person had a child, then through adoption records that the child was placed elsewhere—without regard to whether the child or the current spouse of the woman knows. And this knowledge of intimate familial structure is available to the officials who come into daily contact with the investigated persons, as there is no mandatory separation between the investigator and the investigation.

In addition, a genealogical detective can take endless amounts of surreptitious samples: whereas a policy like California's limits such sampling to those taken to directly identify the perpetrator[;] * * * a recreational database search bears no such limits. In the Golden State Killer case, police took two DNA samples from persons they believed to be suspects but were in fact innocent. But no regulation would prohibit police from sneak sampling persons in the "family tree" even though they are not suspects, simply because such samples might help expedite the investigation by eliminating potential suspect "branches." Samples could likewise be taken from victims, victims' family members or loved ones, or purported witnesses to a crime—all without those persons knowing that they had been targeted by police. * * *

It does not take special insight to see that law enforcement is likely to turn to genealogical databases not just to find matches in cold cases that fail to return any hits in the forensic databases, but also in situations where federal or state laws expressly forbid such searches for quality control or privacy reasons. * * * [This] end-run around the regulatory structures of forensic DNA should be alarming to any person concerned about unbridled police power. * * * [Moreover,] it seems odd that the immediate sibling of a convicted offender has greater protection against genetic surveillance— because familial searches in offender databases are governed by both the CODIS database rules and the state's familial search policy—than a distant biological relation of a person interested in recreational genomics. * * *

3. Lack of transparency and accountability

The lack of oversight at the front-end of genealogical DNA database searches is coupled with an equally alarming lack of transparency and accountability at the back-end. Not only may law enforcement set its own terms for when and how to conduct such searches, but also they can refuse to disclose those terms—or their success and failure rates—to the public. Indeed, in the press conference announcing the DeAngelo's arrest, * * * the police [did not] admit that the suspect was identified through a genealogical database * * *. Even after the use of the GEDMatch database came to light, police guarded detailed information about the search process. * * * We still do not know whether [the] profiles [of the two persons whose DNA was sampled] have been preserved in a government database; whether there were any other persons surreptitiously sampled, or what law enforcement learned from constructing a family tree so elaborate that * * * there were "thousands" of innocent people to rule out as suspects. We do not even know the identity of the distant relative who made the initial link * * *.

Of course, law enforcement DNA databases suffer from the same lack of transparency * * *. * * * As a result, investigators have broad latitude to conduct such searches and compile genetic information on innocent people who otherwise would never have come under law enforcement suspicion, and who are not required by law to submit their DNA to a known offender databases.

* * *

* * * Without greater transparency about the number and nature of recreational genetic searches, it is impossible for the public to reach an informed decision about their permissible scope.

4.   A de facto universal DNA database

In the absence of legal or political intervention, * * * [e]ssentially, everyone will be a police database now. For instance, the study of 600,000 profiles in a recreational genealogy database concluded that "long range familial searches [could] return a match to virtually anyone with genetic databases that cover even a small fraction of the target population." Given that almost 2% of the profiles from the white population of the United States is already contained in recreational genealogy databases, "in the near future, virtually any European-descent US person could be implicated by this technique."

One interesting consequence of the broad reach of a genealogical search is that the racial composition of genealogical DNA sites—which heavily skew white—may end up balancing and complementing that of government databases, which disproportionately contain profiles from persons of color. It is thus oddly possible to imagine a scenario in which communities of color have *greater* protection from intrusive genetic searches simply because *government* database searches use STRs and impose regulatory restrictions, while genealogical searches do not. But the pessimistic view is that the prevalence of genealogical DNA database searches will instead * * * prompt the loosening of existing regulations rather than the enhancement of the regulatory architecture for genealogical searches.

* * * If such searches are to be done, there is much to recommend an approach that would ensure the continued genetic privacy of any innocent families who were once targets of suspicion. But, then, perhaps even that does not matter: * * * the fact that a fifth cousin once removed uploaded their DNA to an online site means that the government still has one's profile, anyway.

NOTES AND QUESTIONS

1. When crime labs compare DNA profiles from crime scene samples with DNA profiles in government databases, they can use high-stringency searches that require a match at all 20 loci, or lower-stringency searches that detect partial (or close) matches. Although not designed to find familial matches, lower-stringency searches can fortuitously identify potential family relationships by detecting partial matches. Some labs use algorithms specifically designed to detect family relationships, which is deliberate familial DNA searching.

Only some jurisdictions have formal law or policies concerning deliberate familial DNA searching (FDS) or partial matching (PM) in government databases. Maryland and DC prohibit FDS by statute and Indiana, by policy. Alaska and Georgia prohibit PM, but are silent as to FDS. California policy allows both FDS and PM, whereas the policies of Arkansas, Colorado, Texas, and Virginia allow FDS, and those of New York, Texas, Washington, and West Virginia allow PM. FBI policy prohibits searches of the national database intended to find familial matches, but it allows such searches in state and local CODIS databases. Sara Debus-Sherrill & Michael Field, Understanding Familial DNA Searching: Policies, Procedures, and Potential Impact 3–4, 10–12 (June 2017), https://www.ncjrs.gov/pdffiles1/nij/grants/251043.pdf.

A survey of over 100 crime labs suggests these practices are fairly widespread. Twelve labs in 11 states reported doing familial DNA searches, forty labs in 24 states (and Puerto Rico) reported disclosing or proceeding with partial matches; and seven labs did both. Three quarters of labs that do not conduct familial searches had discussed using that technology in the past, and nearly half (42%) were considering using it in in the future. Sara Debus-Sherrill & Michael Field, Familial DNA Searching: An Emerging Forensic Investigative Tool, 59 Sci. & Justice 20 (2019). Should more labs be using this technology? Why or why not?

2. Various concerns have been raised with respect to familial searches of *government databases*. One is the possibility that they could reveal biological connections (or lack of connections) within the family because of adoption, the use of assisted reproductive technologies, adultery, or incest. If shrouded in secrecy, these revelations not only threaten the privacy interests of family members, but also "the integrity of the family as a whole." Another concern is that it places relatives of offenders or arrestees under a cloud of suspicion simply because of genetic relatedness to the offender or arrestee. The worry is compounded by the potential long-term retention of samples relatives provide upon request by the police, given that many state laboratories have undocumented databases of samples collected voluntarily. (See Mercer & Gabel, *supra*). Additionally, given the disproportionate rate of arrests, prosecutions, and convictions of minority population members, their DNA profiles are disproportionately represented within government databases. Finally, familial searches may have detrimental effects on investigations by tempting investigators to avoid " 'traditional lines of investigation' " that may

be more fruitful. As a result, the use of these databases to conduct familial searches magnifies the odds of identifying suspects in minority communities. See Suter, *supra*.

California has been at the forefront of developing policies for familial searches, which some states have copied. It requires that 1) they be conducted to solve only the most serious cases; 2) an oversight committee decides when a familial match is strong enough to disclose to local investigators; 3) any incidental findings, such as non-paternity are distanced from local law enforcement; and 4) leads are winnowed through public or police resources to minimize intrusions on individuals who are ultimately ruled out as potential leads or suspects. Murphy, *supra*. Do these measures sufficiently address the privacy and justice issues that arise with familial searches in *government databases*? If not, why not? Even if these policies do not fully address those concerns, are such familial searches justified by their investigative efficiencies?

3. As Murphy notes in the excerpt above, few regulations constrain the use of familial searches in *genealogical databases*. Decisions about how they are used currently depend on individual companies. In 2019, FamilyTreeDNA was the first consumer genealogy DNA-testing company to grant the FBI access to its nearly 2 million genetic profiles. That decision doubled the genetic data to which the FBI already had access through the open-source database of GEDmatch (used in the Golden State Killer case). Access is not "unfettered," however. FamilyTreeDNA will only test samples and upload profiles to its database for the FBI on a case-by-case basis. Kristen Brown, Major DNA Testing Company Sharing Genetic Data with the FBI, Bloomberg, Feb. 1, 2019, https://www.bloomberg.com/news/articles/2019-02-01/major-dna-testing-company-is-sharing-genetic-data-with-the-fbi.

FamilyTreeDNA decided to cooperate with the FBI, reasoning that the FBI would have probable cause to access the database given that studies show that ancestry DNA databases can currently identify 60% of Americans of European ancestry. (See *infra* note 10, p. 447). The company limits law enforcement searches to identifying deceased remains or rapists and murderers. Its default setting in the United States and the rest of the world

FYI: The General Data Protection Regulation (GDPR) (EU) 2016/679 was adopted by the European Union in 2016 and became enforceable in 2018. It provides strong data protection and privacy for citizens of the European Union. FamilyTreeDNA required its European customers to explicitly opt-in to share their information with law enforcement to comply with the GDPR's requirement that consent be freely given, unambiguous, and not be presumed by inactivity.

except Europe is to opt in, with an option to opt-out. In Europe, the default is to opt out, with the option to opt in. Seth Augenstein, Exclusive: The FBI Had Already Accessed FamilyTreeDNA's Database Before Cooperation, Forensic Mag., Mar. 19, 2019.

Other companies are more reluctant to share information with law enforcement. 23andMe, for example, states on its website that it "uses all practical legal and administrative resources to resist requests from law enforcement." https://www.23and

me.com/law-enforcement-guide/. In addition, its transparency report as of July 2019, indicates it received six data requests since 2015 and zero instances in which the data were produced without "prior, explicit consent by the individual(s) specified in the request." https://www.23andme.com/transparency-report/. Even GEDMatch changed its privacy terms of service to a default opt out for use in police searches. This limits law enforcement access to only profiles of users who explicitly opt-in. Because it is open-source, however, police could potentially use the site "pretending to be normal customers." Peter Aldhouse, This Genealogy Database Helped Solve Dozens of Crimes, BuzzFeed.News, May 19, 2019, https://www.buzzfeednews.com/article/peteraldhous/this-genealogy-database-helped-solve-dozens-of-crimes-but.

It turns out, it may not matter what a company's disclosure policies are. In 2019, a Florida detective was trying to solve the case of a serial rapist. Frustrated by GEDmatch's new privacy protections, he sought a search warrant to override its privacy settings. A judge in the Ninth Judicial Circuit Court of Florida granted the request, giving him access to the profiles of all 1.2 million users, including those who did not consent to police access. Experts call this warrant, the first of its kind, a "game-changer." They believe it will encourage other law enforcement agencies to seek similar search warrants of even larger, closed databases, like 23andMe and Ancestry.com, which have, respectively, 10 million and 15 million users. Kashmir Hill & Heather Murphy, Your DNA Profile is Private? A Florida Judge Just Said Otherwise, N.Y. Times, Nov. 5, 2019, https://www.nytimes.com/2019/11/05/business/dna-database-search-warrant.html.

4.   The Department of Justice (DOJ) issued an interim policy for forensic genetic genealogy DNA analysis and searching (FGGS), which became effective Nov. 1, 2019. The policy only applies to federally funded or federal criminal investigations or research. It "is designed to balance the [DOJ's] relentless commitment to solving violent crimes and protecting public safety against equally important public interests—such as preserving the privacy and civil liberties of all citizens." To achieve those goals it imposes various restrictions. First, it limits FGGS to unsolved violent crimes, unidentified human remains from suspected homicide victims, and authorized cases that threaten "public safety or national security."

Second, investigative agencies may not "arrest a suspect based solely on a genetic association generated by" FGGS. Instead, "[t]raditional genealogy research and other investigative work is required to determine the true nature of any genetic association," and STR forensic analysis is required to confirm a potential match.

Third, if samples from third parties who may be related to the putative perpetrator are necessary, investigative agencies must seek their "informed consent" to collect reference samples that will be used for FGGS, unless "case-specific circumstances provide reasonable grounds to believe that this request would compromise the integrity of the investigation."

Fourth, genealogy profiles may only be used for "law enforcement identification purposes." Because government laboratories do not perform SNP analysis, they must use outside vendors laboratories to create forensic genetic genealogy (FGG) profiles. Investigators must therefore take "all reasonable and necessary steps and precautions to ensure that same limited use by others who have authorized access to those samples and profiles." More specifically, biological samples and genealogy profiles "[s]hall not be used by agencies, vendor laboratories, [genealogy] services, or others to determine the sample donor's genetic predisposition for diseases or any other medical condition or psychological trait."

Finally, all FGG profiles and associated data must be removed from the genealogical services and provided to the investigative agency if a suspect has been arrested and charged with a criminal offense. United States Department of Justice Interim Policy: Forensic Genetic Genealogical DNA Analysis and Searching, https://www.justice.gov/olp/page/file/1204386/download.

The final DOJ policy will be issued in 2020. Are these regulations sufficient? Is it problematic that the government outsources the creation of FGGS analysis to companies like Parabon, which profit from forensic analysis? Would other issues arise if the government were to begin doing SNP analysis for genetic genealogy purposes?

5.   A survey of 1,500 people found that 91% support the use of genealogy databases to solve violent crimes like rape and murder, although only 46% support its use in nonviolent crimes. Christi J. Guerrini et al., Should Police Have Access to Genetic Genealogy Databases? Capturing the Golden State Killer and Other Criminals Using a Controversial New Forensic Technique, 16 PLOS Biology 1 (2018). A week after FamilyTree announced the option to opt-out of law enforcement access to its database, only 0.7% opted out. Of the 10% European customers who were automatically removed, 1000 opted back in to support law enforcement. Are these data relevant in regulating law enforcement searches of consumer DNA databases and if so, how?

6.   Are there privacy concerns with respect to distant relatives in genealogy databases who are useful links in finding serial killers or rapist? If so what is the nature of these concerns? What are their legal implications?

7.   Three DTC consumer companies—Ancestry, 23andMe, and Helix—formed the Coalition for Genetic Data Protection, whose website states that it seeks "reasonable and uniform privacy regulation that will ensure the responsible and ethical handling of every person's genetic data." https://geneticdataprotection.com/. Skeptics argue that this is simply a lobbying effort to "make sure there are no carve-outs in a federal privacy law for genetic information" so that these companies face no more stringent regulations than companies like Facebook or Google. David Lazarus, High Stakes in Genetic Privacy Battle, L.A. Times, July 2, 2019, 2019 WLNR 20177565. Should the scope of law enforcement access to these databases be set by the government or by "best practices" defined by the industry? If the former, how should the

government restrict when and how law enforcement can access these databases?

8.   In response to the issues Murphy raises with respect to familial searches in *genealogical databases*, she proposes a few solutions: 1) ban such searches entirely, 2) impose the same constraints on law enforcement that exist with respect to familial searches in government databases, 3) restrict leads from genealogical searches to third-degree relatives to minimize the size of the family tree probed, 4) only allow surreptitious sampling when the target is a suspected perpetrator, 5) require destruction of all samples and profiles created in the search that do not match crime scene evidence, 6) require disclosure of law enforcement activity, "including the number of persons investigated or sampled but found to be innocent."

Natalie Ram et al. argue that the Stored Communications Act, which protects digital information maintained on the internet, offers a model for how the law might limit the use of genealogy databases. The Act allows courts to order the disclosure of electronic records if the government " 'offers specific and articulable facts showing that there are reasonable grounds to believe' that the records sought 'are relevant and material to an ongoing criminal investigation.' " Natalie Ram et al., Genealogy Databases and the Future of Criminal Investigations, 360 Nature 1078 (2018) (quoting 18 U.S.C. § 2703(d)). Do these various recommendations address the problems associated with these suspicionless searches? Why or why not? Should any of these recommendations apply to familial searches in *government databases*?

> **Connect the Dots:** Recall *Carpenter v. United States*, which held that warrantless police use of cell-tower data from a wireless carrier violated the Fourth Amendment. See Chapter 18, note 3, page 408. Does *Carpenter's* reasoning apply to police use of DNA genealogy databases for criminal investigations? Are the expectations of privacy regarding DNA data in consumer genetic databases and cell-site data similar? The Court did not apply the third-party doctrine in *Carpenter* because the cellphone user's only "affirmative act" in providing cell-tower data is "powering up" the phone. 138 S. Ct. at 2220. Should the third-party doctrine apply to DNA information in consumer genetic databases based on the reasoning of the majority or dissenting opinions?

9.   Given that genetic information is shared between biological relatives, Natalie Ram proposes using the property concept, tenancy by the entirety, as a framework to address familial searches (and other uses of genetic information). See Chapter 17, note 10, p. 379. Because tenancy by the entirety does not allow one spouse to encumber shared property without her partner's consent, Ram argues by analogy that "courts should constrain the government to using genetic information it has lawfully obtained only to search for matches implicating the matching offender—but not to search for matches implicating a matching offender's close genetic relatives." Natalie Ram, DNA by the Entirety, 115 Columbia L. Rev. 873, 919–29 (2015).

10. A recent study found that roughly 60% of searches for individuals of Northern European ancestry in consumer genealogical databases will find a third-cousin or closer match. Because this ethnic group is so well represented

in these databases, the odds of finding a match are 30% more likely than for individuals with sub-Saharan African ancestry. As Murphy notes, the racial representation in genealogical databases is the mirror opposite of those of government databases, which disproportionately include minority profiles. The study's authors predict that once databases include 2% of a target population, 99% of that group would have at least a third-cousin match, and 65% would have at least one second-cousin match. Yaniv Erlich et al., Identity Inference of Genomic Data Using Long-Range Familial Searches, 362 Sci. 690 (2018).

Interestingly, although fewer minority families will be investigated through genetic genealogy searches, this forensic tool leads to a different kind of racial inequity than that of familial searches in government databases. When constructing family trees, genetic genealogists rely on public records to determine the relationships between people who share DNA and where they fall on the branches of the family tree. This helps rule out relatives as potential subjects of investigation. However, because there is less public information about minority populations, it is harder to fill in their family trees and exclude biological relatives as suspects. As a result, the minority families that are investigated may be subject to more false positives and more intrusive law enforcement probing as compared with families of Northern European descent. Hearings on Familial DNA and Criminal Investigations Before the House Judiciary Subcommittee, Maryland House of Delegates, Nov. 7, 2019 (statement of Dr. Timothy D. O'Connor),

11. For interesting podcasts about the use of genealogical databases to investigate cold cases, listen to A New Way to Solve Murder, Part 1: The Genetic Detectives, The Daily, Jun. 6, 2019, https://www.nytimes.com/2019/06/06/podcasts/the-daily/dna-genealogy-crime.html; A New Way to Solve Murder, Part 2: The Future of Genetic Privacy, The Daily, Jun. 7, 2019, https://www.nytimes.com/2019/06/07/podcasts/the-daily/genealogy-dna-crime-privacy.html?module=inline; Podcast: The Golden State Killer and Genetic Privacy, Constitution Daily, June 21, 2018, https://constitutioncenter.org/blog/podcast-the-golden-state-killer-and-genetic-privacy.

CHAPTER 21

POST-CONVICTION DNA TESTING

■ ■ ■

SETH AXELRAD & JULIANA RUSSO, SURVEY OF POST-CONVICTION DNA TESTING STATUTES

Am. Soc'y L., Med. & Ethics (2005).

Thirty-eight [now all fifty] states and the federal government have passed statutes specifically providing for post-conviction DNA testing of biological evidence relating to a crime for which an offender has been convicted * * *.

* * *

- Who May Apply for Post-Conviction DNA Testing?

* * *

With respect to the severity of the offense, more than half of the state statutes limit eligible convicts to felons or a subset of felons. [Alabama] represent[s] the extreme case[ ], limiting applicability to capital offenders. Less than half of the states, and the federal government, include those who have been convicted for any crime. The second criterion, [requiring that the individual be in] state custody, provides a means of restricting the potential postconviction remedy to those who need it to escape or reduce their imprisonment.

* * *

- What Evidence Can Be Tested? / What Criteria Must the Evidence Meet?

All of the state statutes place some restriction on the evidence that can be subjected to the requested DNA testing. The restrictions may be minimal, as in the case of Washington (requiring only that the evidence still exists); more common, however, are requirements that the evidence was secured in relation to the crime, was maintained or stored in a manner to ensure that the evidence has not degraded or been tampered with, and/or either was not previously tested, or was previously tested, but there exists good reason for retesting.

- Is the Prosecutor Involved in the Process?

The American criminal justice system is an adversarial system; accordingly, all of the post-conviction statutes except for * * * Oregon [and Washington] explicitly provide for prosecutorial involvement. At the minimum is the requirement of notice to the prosecution of the motion for post-conviction DNA testing * * *. A typical statute will require notice to the prosecution and afford the prosecution an opportunity to respond to the motion.

* * *

- What Are the Review Criteria for the Petition?

This section lists the criteria that the decision-maker (usually the judge) will use in reviewing the defendant's motion for post-conviction DNA testing. Thus, this section identifies the barriers that the defendant must overcome in order to persuade a court to grant his or her post-conviction motion. In general, the courts require a showing that: the identity of the perpetrator (or accomplice) was an issue at trial; the evidence to be tested is relevant to the identity of the perpetrator; the evidentiary criteria have been met; and/or exculpatory DNA results, had they been introduced at trial, likely would have resulted in a different outcome at trial.

* * *

- Who Pays for the Costs of Testing?

This section identifies the allocation of the costs of DNA testing, if present in the statutory provision. The federal Justice for All Act of 2004 exemplifies a typical provision. The statute allocates the costs of testing to the applicant, except in cases where the applicant is indigent.

* * *

- What are the Consequences if the Results Do Not Favor the Petitioner?

* * * Some statutes, like Maryland, simply deny the petition for post-conviction relief upon unfavorable test results. Others penalize the petitioner in some manner, e.g., by requiring inclusion of the petitioner's DNA profile into the DNA database. The federal statute's punitive consequences arise as a result of its requirement that the petition for post-conviction DNA test contain an assertion of actual innocence under penalty of perjury; thus, upon the receipt of unfavorable test results, the petitioner can be held in contempt, or potentially prosecuted for making false assertions.

- What are the Consequences if the Results Do Favor the Petitioner?

In the event that the test results exclude the petitioner as the source of DNA evidence, the state and federal statutes specify the subsequent procedural steps a petitioner may take to challenge his conviction. The federal statute requires the petitioner to file a motion for a new trial, which the court shall grant upon a showing of compelling evidence that the new trial would result in an acquittal. The state statutes either similarly require a motion for a new trial, or provide the court more procedural flexibility upon reception of the favorable test results. North Carolina, for example, allows the court to enter any order "that serves the interests of justice," which may include an order setting a new trial or an order vacating and setting aside the petitioner's conviction.

* * *

- Will Compensation Be Awarded if the Petitioner is Exonerated?

Missouri, Montana, and the Federal Government have statutes providing for restitution for wrongfully imprisoned persons exonerated through DNA testing. The Montana statute provides educational aid to exonerated petitioners, whereas the Missouri and Federal statutes provide direct financial restitution. [There are also other state laws, such as Mass. Gen. Laws Ann. Ch. 444 § 1, that provide compensation for certain exonerated individuals regardless of the nature of the evidence used to convict them.]

NOTES AND QUESTIONS

1.   Since the first DNA exoneration in 1989, DNA testing has led to the exoneration of 367 persons who were wrongfully convicted, with the average time served being 14 years. All 50 states and the District of Columbia now have laws that allow inmates to apply for postconviction DNA testing. States differ on the types of convictions for which testing is allowed: 21 states allow testing for any crime; Iowa allows testing for all felonies and some misdemeanors; 16 states allow testing for any felony; and 10 states limit testing to enumerated felonies. Alabama allows testing only for capital offenses, the District of Columbia for any crime of violence, and Maine allows testing for crimes with a minimum of a one-year sentence. National Conference of State Legislatures, Post-Conviction DNA Testing, 50 State Survey, (2013), www.ncsl.org/Documents/cj/PostConvictionDNATesting.pdf. Should there be limitations on the types of convictions for which a person may seek postconviction DNA testing?

2.   The federal government, the District of Columbia, and 30 states have compensation statutes, which automatically award compensation to qualifying exonerees in accordance with the law. The requirements for compensation vary in requirements and award amount. While New Hampshire caps compensation at $20,000 total, Texas entitles exonerees to $80,000 per year of wrongful incarceration, an annuity of $80,000 per year until death, and other social benefits. Some statutes restrict who qualifies for compensation or attach conditions to compensation. For example, states like Wisconsin will not compensate individuals who "contributed" to their wrongful conviction through false confessions or pleading guilty. Other states, like Florida, will not

compensate those with a prior criminal record. Some states, like Missouri, require exonerees to waive their right to sue for additional compensation in order to receive the statute award. Nearly three-quarters of DNA exonerees have been awarded some type of compensation. Innocence Project: DNA Exonerations, 1989–2014: Review of the Data and Findings from the First 25 Years, 79 Albany L. Rev. 717, 771–73 (2015–16).

3.   Should courts require a person to raise an identity defense at trial in order to preserve a right to postconviction DNA testing? Should postconviction testing be available to those who have confessed or pled guilty? See Justin Brooks & Alexander Simpson, Blood Sugar Sex Magik: A Review of Postconviction DNA Testing Statutes and Legislative Recommendations, 59 Drake L. Rev. 799, 818 (2010–2011).

4.   Exonerations have provided insight into the potential problems in the criminal justice system. An Innocence Project study of exonerations from 1989–2014 revealed that "nearly all of the wrongful convictions . . . (91%) contain a sexual assault element to the crime (64% sexual assault; 27% sexual assault and homicide). Fewer than 10% represent homicides without a sexual assault or other violent crimes (e.g., home invasions or carjackings)." Innocence Project: DNA Exonerations, 1989–2014, *supra* at 725 (2015–16). Wrongful convictions are usually the result of multiple failures: 69% involved eyewitness misidentification, 44% involved misapplication of forensic science, and 28% involved false confessions. Innocence Project: DNA Exonerations in the United States, https://www.innocenceproject.org/dna-exonerations-in-the-united-states/.

5.   William Osborne was identified as the perpetrator of a sexual assault and attempted murder after his accomplice implicated him and police discovered an axe handle similar to the one used at the crime scene in Osborne's residence. The state performed DQ Alpha testing on sperm found in a condom left at the crime scene. An inexact form of DNA testing, DQ Alpha testing can clear some wrongly accused individuals, but generally cannot narrow the perpetrator down to less than 5% of the population. The semen found on the condom had a genotype matching that of Osborne, who was ultimately convicted of kidnapping, assault, and sexual assault.

Osborne sued state officials in federal court, claiming that the Due Process Clause and other constitutional provisions gave him a constitutional right to access the State's DNA evidence for more discriminating short-tandem-repeat (STR) testing. The District Court granted summary judgment for Osborne, and the Court of Appeals affirmed. In a 5–4 decision, the U.S. Supreme Court held that Osborne had no substantive due process right of access to DNA evidence. Noting its reluctance to "expand the concept of substantive due process," it reasoned that "[e]stablishing a freestanding right to access DNA evidence for testing would force [the Court] to act as policymakers," and it would undercut the legislature's ongoing response to "the challenges DNA technology poses."

The dissent found that Osborne established a due process right to test the State's evidence. Supporting this view was the fact that 46 states and the federal government had passed statutes providing access to evidence for DNA testing, and three additional states provided similar access through court-made rules. It also noted recent trends in legal ethics recognizing prosecutors' obligations to disclose all forms of exculpatory evidence that come into their possession following conviction. According to the dissent, a "decision to recognize a limited federal right of postconviction access to DNA evidence would not prevent the States from creating procedures by which litigants request and obtain such access; it would merely ensure that States do so in a manner that is nonarbitrary." District Attorney's Office for the Third Judicial District v. Osborne, 557 U.S. 52 (2009).

> **Make the Connection:** Is a right to postconviction DNA testing analogous to the prosecutor's duty to disclose exculpatory evidence when it is not clear that the results of the DNA test will exculpate the individual?

6.   Should there be a duty to store evidentiary items that might have DNA on them? With the advent of DNA technologies, forensic officials who had been pack rats were able to convict people of decades-old crimes by applying new techniques to stored evidence from the original crime scene evidence. Such evidence has also been retested through efforts like the Innocence Project, letting many innocent men go free. In fact, in 2009, volunteer lawyers in Virginia were trained on how to contact the 881 Virginia felons whose old cases included evidence ripe for potentially-exculpatory genetic testing.

With such technological miracles at hand, forensic specialists became reluctant to throw anything away. Beds, cars, clothes—who knew what new technologies would be developed in the future to allow the crime scene investigators to coax clues out of evidence?

The storage situation worsened in Colorado in 2008 when, after an innocent murder suspect was freed after nine years' imprisonment, a broad law was adopted requiring storage of every piece of evidence that might contain DNA. It required storage for the life of the defendant of "all reasonable and relevant evidence that may contain DNA." A recent amendment, Colorado Statutes Section 18–1–1104, made clear that an entire large item, such as a car, need not be stored if the DNA can be lifted off the item. The new law does not require retention "if DNA evidence is of such a size, bulk, or physical character as to render retention impracticable." What policies should be developed for the storage of evidence?

CHAPTER 22

MENTAL AND BEHAVIORAL GENETICS
IN CRIMINAL LAW

■ ■ ■

Genetics can play a role in criminal law to identify people, as the previous section on forensic uses of genetics discussed. But it can also be relevant in criminal law with respect to issues of culpability, sentencing, and even commitment proceedings. In particular, the field of behavioral genetics has relevance in this context. Although the applications of this field have clinical and other implications, this chapter focuses on the use of developments in the science of behavioral genetics to assess culpability and potential mitigation for sentencing after a conviction.

TROY DUSTER, BEHAVIORAL GENETICS AND
EXPLANATIONS OF THE LINK BETWEEN CRIME, VIOLENCE,
AND RACE IN WRESTLING WITH BEHAVIORAL GENETICS:
SCIENCE, ETHICS, AND PUBLIC CONVERSATION
154–156 (Erik Parens, Audrey R. Chapman & Nancy Press eds. 2006).

* * * Behavioral genetics has long been interested in "the genetics of criminality." At the same time the prospect of discerning a relationship between genes and violent behavior has been very contentious.

Critics have raised a variety of issues. One concern is whether violent behavior is a well-defined classification amenable to scientific analysis. Crime, by definition an act or the commission of activity that is forbidden, is socially constructed; that is, the very categorization of an act as criminal depends on social standards of behavior, the identity of the actor, and the environment in which it takes place. Criminal behavior can be a one-time phenomenon (impulsive homicide after discovery of adultery), or it can be a profession (the cat burglar—the professional thief, or the "hit-man" specialist for organized crime). * * * Crime can be an occasional diversion from one's ordinary life * * * or it can be a compulsive-neurotic habituation (sexual abuse of the young by adults); alternatively, crime can be a rational, calculated decision (stealing a loaf of bread to feed one's family), or a routine occupational imperative, as was the case with the price-fixing scandal among the largest electrical companies in the United States. Crime can be a bureaucratic response to turf invasion, such as with organized crime during Prohibition, or a violation of existing social stratifying practices, such as the crime of teaching a slave to read—or assisting a slave to run away.

In short, what is criminal is as variable, and as variably explained, as any wide range of human behaviors that are legal. To place in the same taxonomic system the theft of bread, exposing oneself in public, cat burglary, and euthanasia, as a single, examinable phenotype is to engage in a breathtaking mystification of the classification of crime. * * * Today, we place in the same criminal category someone who leaves lethal nerve gas on a subway station (anonymous killings) and someone who shoots in the back a doctor working in an abortion clinic. Fifty years from now, if some researcher went through the police records to show whether adoptees had a similar "inclination to commit crime" as did those in then biological families, someone might point out the quite reasonable objection that the system of classification was constructed in such a way as to make any claims about a genetic basis for these crimes highly problematic. The search for a genetic explanation for such a demonstrably variegated "phenotype" (criminal) requires a theoretical warrant that has never been delivered. * * * [G]iven this demonstrably high empirical variability * * * in what constitutes a crime * * * across social time and space, how is it possible to search for a genotype? The answer, and the conclusion provide strong reasons for deep concern.

* * * The very classification of criminals or criminal behavior as a biological category may also affect the way people understand a particular kind of behavior. The sheer knowledge of such categories can have a looping effect. That is, it may affect people's attitudes and behavior in a way that feeds back on the classification scheme itself.

MARK A. ROTHSTEIN, APPLICATIONS OF BEHAVIOURAL GENETICS: OUTPACING THE SCIENCE?

6 Nature Reviews Genetics 793, 795–796 (2005).

* * *

Criminal Law. Genetic explanations of anti-social behaviour represent an important area of research and one of the earliest applications of behavioural genetics. Behavioural genetics could potentially be used in several ways—from the earliest stages of a criminal investigation through to almost every aspect of the criminal justice system.

DNA forensic * * * profiling can be used for several purposes—to identify the gender of and make predictions about the race or ethnicity, health status, age, or physical characteristics of the sample source. Behavioural genetic forensic profiling might be increasingly used in law enforcement to predict the perpetrator's behavioural traits and psychiatric conditions, such as learning disabilities and personality traits.

Once a suspect is arrested and charged with a crime, behavioural genetic information could be presented at a bail hearing. Prosecutors might urge that bail should not be granted or should be set at a high amount because of the defendant's genetic predisposition to impulsivity (for example, risk of flight) or aggression (for example, risk of committing further crimes).

At trial, evidence of behavioural genetic variations within the normal range is unlikely to establish an independent basis for acquittal. More extreme deviations might be part of the scientific evidence used to support an insanity defence. Behavioural genetic evidence might also be used to claim that the defendant lacked the mental capacity to form the intent necessary to commit the crime. For example, on this basis a defendant charged with premeditated murder might be convicted of a lesser offence, such as manslaughter.

In many states in the United States it is common for convicted defendants to introduce evidence that relatives across many generations have engaged in violent criminal activities, that the defendant has inexplicably engaged in antisocial activities from a young age, or that the individual has been diagnosed with a neurogenetic disorder. This is then used to assert that defendants who commit crimes caused at least in part by a genetic predisposition or compulsion are not as morally culpable and do not deserve the harshest sentences. It is difficult to determine whether such arguments have had an effect on the sentences imposed, but the willingness of some courts to consider such evidence leaves open the possibility that behavioural genetics could be afforded greater weight in the future.

Behavioural genetic information could also be introduced in parole hearings. Ironically, the positions of the government and the inmate with respect to the behavioural genetic evidence are likely to be the opposite of their arguments at the trial. At a parole hearing, the government might attempt to use genetic predisposition as a basis for denying parole; the inmate might use the absence of genetic predisposition as a basis for release under the theory that he or she is less likely to commit another crime in the future.

Finally, many states in the United States have enacted 'sexual predator laws', which permit the indefinite confinement of individuals who have been convicted of multiple sex crimes against children and who are considered likely to commit further crimes if released. In theory, behavioural genetic evidence might be used to predict the likelihood of the individual committing future sex crimes.

LORI B. ANDREWS, PREDICTING AND PUNISHING ANTISOCIAL ACTS: HOW THE CRIMINAL JUSTICE SYSTEM MIGHT USE BEHAVIORAL GENETICS, IN BEHAVIORAL GENETICS: THE CLASH OF CULTURE AND BIOLOGY

120–122 (Ronald A. Carson & Mark A. Rothstein eds. 1999).

Criminal law is viewed as a "choosing system" in that people are seen as having a choice about whether to engage in criminal behavior. People are seen as culpable when they *choose* to violate the law. This involves both a voluntary wrongful act *(actus rea)* and the mental state to know that the act was wrongful *(mens rea)*. In situations in which the individual was not acting under free will, however, the law provides a variety of mechanisms to avoid traditional criminal penalties.

Evidence of one's genotype might be used to exculpate an individual or to mitigate punishment. A person may claim that his genes provoked involuntary actions that caused the inappropriate act (such as involuntarily physically harming someone during a seizure). Or he may argue that his genotype influenced his mental processes so as to prevent him from realizing his act was wrongful and controlling himself. Or he might argue that it is unjust to punish him because his actions are compelled by an illness rather than a "chosen" behavior.

With respect to the voluntary act requirement for criminal conviction, genetic defenses would be unlikely to be accepted if there was evidence that the individual could have ascertained his or her genetic status and done something about it. For example, a driver who unexpectedly blacks out and causes a fatal accident would not be criminally liable; however, a driver who knows he is prone to blackouts could be found guilty of manslaughter if he has a fatal traffic accident during a blackout. This is in keeping with the traditional legal approach, which holds that "the powerful influences exercised by one's hereditary make-up by his developmental and environmental background are not ignored, but the law takes the position 'that most men, in most of the relations of life, can act purposefully and can inhibit antisocial, illegal tendencies.'"

There is more potential to prove that a particular genotype influenced a defendant's mental status. If a person's genetic status causes him or her to be insane, the individual can be found not guilty by reason of insanity. There are a variety of legal tests for insanity, * * * [including] a strict rule requiring proof that the defendant did not know the nature or the quality of the act he was committing, or if he did know it, that he did not know he was doing wrong. * * * [A] more liberal approach * * * require[s] the defendant to prove that he lacked substantial capacity to appreciate the criminality of his or her conduct or to control that conduct to the requirements of law.

* * * [U]nder federal law, individuals can be found not guilty by reason of insanity only if they are unable to appreciate the nature and quality or wrongfulness of their acts. Merely not being able to conform their conduct is not enough.

* * * [T]he majority of states amended their criminal laws to create a verdict of guilty but mentally ill to avoid (except in rare instances) acquitting someone who had committed an antisocial act. This newer "guilty but mentally ill" verdict recognizes culpability but allows mitigation of the sentence in terms of its length or the type of facility in which the offender is institutionalized.

In traditional criminal law, several justifications are put forth for punishing people who have committed antisocial acts. People are institutionalized to deter them from committing future antisocial acts, to rehabilitate them, to deter others from committing antisocial acts, to incapacitate them, and to exact retribution (an institutionalized vengeance). If a genetic deterministic view is taken, the first two justifications may be eliminated on the ground that there would be nothing that could be done to change the individual. However, institutionalizing the offender might serve other purposes by deterring others from committing crimes (or from attempting to "game" the system by purporting to have a genetic defense), by preventing the offender (through incarceration) from having the opportunity to commit another crime, and by satisfying society's need for revenge.

Lawyer Maureen Coffey advocates that, "In light of increasing knowledge and understanding, traditional yet outdated notions of freedom and responsibility should be modified to square with a scientific view of human conduct." She argues that people with genetic susceptibilities for antisocial behavior are "innately different from the 'normal' person," but that their lessened free will should not make such individuals immune from punishment. Rather, punishment should be based, not on a subjective, moral culpability justification, but on "the legitimate objectives of social control and public welfare." Even though she acknowledges that "punishing an individual for crimes for which he is not responsible in the traditional sense seems to be morally offensive," she feels it can be outweighed by the greater social good.

Coffey's argument will probably be attractive to policymakers, who seem to have given up on a rehabilitative model of prison in favor of a punitive one. Thus, even in instances in which it is proven that the defendant acted in conformity with a genetic predisposition, people who argue that their genes caused them to commit an antisocial act may ultimately be incarcerated to prevent them from committing other acts, to deter others, or to satisfy society's need for vengeance.

STEPHEN J. MORSE, GENETICS AND CRIMINAL RESPONSIBILITY

15 Trends Cognitive Sci. 378, 379 (2011).

* * *

TRANSLATING GENETIC RESEARCH FOR ASSESSING CRIMINAL RESPONSIBILITY

Genetics concerns mechanistic causation. Genes do not have mental states and do not commit crimes; people do. To make a useful internal contribution to criminal responsibility, the genetic data must be 'translated' into the law's folk psychological responsibility criteria. It must be shown how, precisely, the genetic data are relevant to whether a defendant acted, whether he or she possessed a particular mens rea, and whether the mental states relevant to defenses were present.

It is not sufficient to indicate that genetics played a causal role in explaining the criminal behavior * * *. Causation and predictability are not excusing conditions in law and causation is not the equivalent of legal compulsion (most action is not the causal result of dire threats or uncontrollable desires). If they were, no one would be responsible because we inhabit a causal universe, but we nonetheless hold people responsible. A genetic predisposition to criminal conduct does not per se mitigate or excuse. Causation is relevant only if it tends to show the presence of a genuine excusing condition, but it is the latter that does the legal work. Believing that causation per se mitigates or excuses responsibility is the most pernicious confusion bedeviling the attempt to relate scientific findings to criminal responsibility. I have termed it the 'fundamental psycholegal error'. In the few legal cases in which genetic information has been used to mitigate responsibility, this error has been common.

We are reasonably confident that having a genetically induced MAO-A deficiency in interaction with childhood abuse causally increases the risk of criminal and antisocial behavior more than ninefold. Nonetheless, there is no reason to believe that offenders exposed to that interaction did not act or form the required mental states. If exposure to that interaction somehow diminished their rationality or produced some type of uncontrollable internal desire, then mitigation or excuse might be warranted. Such a diminished rationality or control problem would have to be demonstrated independently by evidence other than causation data.

MILLARD V. MARYLAND

261 A.2d 227 (Md. Ct. Spec. App. 1970).

MURPHY, J.

Charged with the offense of robbery with a deadly weapon, appellant filed a written plea that he was insane at the time of the commission of the crime under Maryland Code, Article 59, Section 9(a), which provides:

"A defendant is not responsible for criminal conduct and shall be found insane at the time of the commission of the alleged crime if, at the time of such conduct as a result of mental disease or defect, he lacks substantial capacity either to appreciate the criminality of his conduct or to conform his conduct to the requirements of law. As used in this section, the terms 'mental disease or defect' do not include an abnormality manifested only by repeated criminal or otherwise antisocial conduct."

The basis for appellant's insanity plea, as later unfolded at the trial, was that he had an extra Y chromosome in the brain and other cells of his body which constituted, within the meaning of Section 9(a), a mental defect resulting in his lacking substantial capacity either to appreciate the criminality of his conduct or to conform his conduct to the requirements of law.

* * * [A]ppellant adduced evidence through the testimony of a Lieutenant at the Prince George's County jail showing that while in confinement appellant was agitated, nervous, upset, and became so violent on occasions that he had to be handcuffed and shackled in leg irons; that appellant cut himself five or six times on his arm between the elbow and the wrist, resulting in severe bleeding, although no arteries were severed; that these cuts "ran the gamut from scratches to very severe cuts requiring quite a number of sutures"; and that as a result of his condition, appellant was sent to three different hospitals for treatment and evaluation.

[The appellant's only medical witness was Dr. Cecil Jacobson, an Assistant Professor in the Department of Obstetrics and Gynecology and Chief of the Reproduction Genetics Unit of the George Washington University School of Medicine. He testified that he earned a medical degree and licensure to practice medicine, had published 42 articles, and conducted extensive research in the field of genetics. Although he received formal training and clinical experience in psychiatry as a medical student and intern, he was not a psychiatrist and had no more competence in the field of psychiatry than a "conventional physician."] * * *

Dr. Jacobson testified that on December 16, 1968, appellant was examined and his body cells found to contain an extra Y chromosome (XYY); that the presence of this extra chromosome constituted a "basic defect in the genetic complement of the cell" affecting not only the way the cells grow in the body, but also the physical growth of the body itself; that the presence of the extra Y chromosome caused "marked physical and mental problems" affecting the manner in which persons possessing the extra Y chromosome "will react to certain stimulus; certain physiological problems; certain behavioral characteristics." Dr. Jacobson then told of approximately 40 published reports indicating that persons possessed of an extra Y chromosome tended to be very tall, with limbs disproportionate to their body; that such persons had marked antisocial, aggressive and schizoid reactions and were in continual conflict with the law.

* * * [Article 59,] Section 9(a) was * * * read to Dr. Jacobson, and he was then asked whether appellant was insane. Dr. Jacobson * * * [stated] that "if the definition of insanity has a mental defect, the answer is yes, he has a mental defect based upon his abnormal [chromosome] test." Asked whether the "defect" was such as to cause appellant to lack "substantial capacity either to appreciate the criminality of his conduct or to conform his conduct to the requirements of law," Dr. Jacobson answered:

> "I cannot say that because I have not examined him as a psychiatrist. I have no competence in that area."

Appellant's counsel then told the court that he intended to show through "case histories" that individuals having the extra Y chromosome have extremely aggressive personalities, "to the extent that most of them end up in jail for one reason or another because of their aggressive reactions." Dr. Jacobson was then asked to examine appellant's arms to determine whether the cuts thereon were "suicidal or merely attention cuts." Dr. Jacobson did so briefly and stated that based on his experience as a medical doctor, he believed the cuts constituted an actual attempt at suicide; that based on this fact, and his brief questioning of appellant during a five-minute court recess, he felt appellant's "reactions" were not normal; that appellant had a fear of "forceful activity with an attempt at extension of this regression and a lack of adequately controlling this;" that although he was "greatly restricted" by not knowing the "developmental history" of appellant, he believed, based upon the testimony of the jail lieutenant concerning appellant's conduct while in confinement, including the suicide attempts, coupled with appellant's genetic defect, that "this does not fall within the realm of sanity, as I understand it." Dr. Jacobson then testified that the extra Y chromosome in appellant's genetic make-up affected his behavioral patterns, as reported in other cases of persons similarly possessed of the extra Y chromosome. He conceded that persons having the extra Y chromosome may differ among themselves depending upon "what other physical effects are found in the body of the XYY," environment also being a factor accounting for differences between XYY individuals.

Under further questioning by the trial judge, the prosecutor, and defense counsel, Dr. Jacobson stated that appellant's genetic defect—which he characterized as a mental defect—influenced "his competence or ability to recognize the area of his crime;" that appellant had a "propensity" toward crime because of his genetic abnormality; that based upon the medical literature, the appellants' conduct and behavioral patterns, and his genetic defect, he was insane and not even competent to stand trial. The doctor defined insanity in terms of the "ability to comprehend reality" or the "inability to judge one's action as far as consequence." Dr. Jacobson next testified that he had "insufficient evidence" upon which to base a conclusion whether appellant appreciated the consequences of his action, but that because he had attempted to commit suicide, such an act constituted "an inability to comprehend the consequences of his act, the act of suicide, being death;" and that appellant's actions were "not consistent with sanity."

* * *

[Ruling that Dr. Jacobson's testimony did not, with reasonable medical certainty, overcome the presumption that appellant was sane, the trial judge declined to submit the issue of appellant's sanity to the jury. The jury] found appellant guilty of robbery with a deadly weapon and he was sentenced to eighteen years under the jurisdiction of the Department of Correction.

We see no merit in appellant's contention on appeal that the trial judge erred in ruling that there had not been presented evidence of insanity under Article 59, Section 9(a) sufficient to overcome the presumption of sanity. Dr. Jacobson's testimony, if believed, clearly established that appellant possessed an extra Y chromosome (XYY) and that he was therefore genetically abnormal. It also tended to show in a general way that appellant's possession of the extra Y chromosome caused him to be antisocial, aggressive, in continual conflict with the law, and to have a "propensity" toward the commission of crime. But, * * * the test of responsibility for criminal conduct under Section 9(a) is predicated upon "mental disease or defect," the existence of which is "first and foremost a medical problem;" and that an opinion as to the ultimate fact whether an accused is insane under Section 9(a) should be reached "by a medical diagnosis," based on "reasonable medical certainty." The mere fact then that appellant had a genetic abnormality which Dr. Jacobson characterized as "a mental defect" would not, of itself, suffice to show that, under Section 9(a), he lacked, because of such defect, "substantial capacity either to appreciate the criminality of his conduct or to conform his conduct to the requirements of law." And to simply state that persons having the extra Y chromosome are prone to aggressiveness, are antisocial, and continually run afoul of the criminal laws, is hardly sufficient to rebut the presumption of sanity and show the requisite lack of "substantial capacity" under Section 9(a). Moreover, we think it entirely plain from the record that in testifying that appellant had a "mental defect," Dr. Jacobson did so only in a most general sense, without full appreciation for the meaning of the term as used in Section 9(a), and particularly without an understanding that such term expressly excludes "an abnormality manifested only by repeated criminal or otherwise antisocial conduct." But even if it were accepted that appellant had a "mental defect" within the contemplation of Section 9(a), Dr. Jacobson, by his own testimony, indicated an inability to meaningfully relate the effect of such defect to the "substantial capacity" requirements of the subsection. Not only did Dr. Jacobson candidly admit that he had "no competence" in the field of psychiatry, but he demonstrated that fact by showing that he had not theretofore familiarized himself with the substance of Section 9(a); indeed, his conception of the test of criminal responsibility in Maryland was shallow at best, at least until the test was read to him during his testimony. While Dr. Jacobson did ultimately testify in conclusory fashion that he thought appellant insane and even incompetent to stand trial, his testimony in this connection was obviously predicated on a definition of "insanity" different than that prescribed under Section 9(a)—a definition so general as to encompass as insane a person who would attempt suicide.

* * *

* * * [T]o constitute proof of insanity sufficient to raise a doubt in the minds of reasonable men, competent medical evidence must be adduced to the positive effect that the accused, as a result of mental disease or defect, lacked substantial capacity either to appreciate the criminality of his conduct or to conform his conduct to the requirements of law; and evidence of some undefined mental disorder or instability is insufficient proof to overcome the presumption of sanity. On the record before us, we think Dr. Jacobson's opinion as to appellant's sanity under Section 9(a) was not competent in that it was not based on reasonable medical certainty, and that the trial judge, had he so concluded, would not have been in error.

> **FYI:** The defense's expert witness, Dr. Cecil Jacobson, was actually a fertility doctor. In 1992, he was convicted of 52 felony counts for perjury and fraud for using his sperm for artificial insemination procedures instead of the promised sperm of patients' husbands or anonymous donors. Up to 75 children were born as a result. He was sentenced to five years in prison, required to pay a $75,000 fine and $39,205 in restitution, and his license was revoked. Parents of the children he allegedly fathered brought several suits against him for fraud, battery, negligence, outrage, negligent infliction of emotional distress, medical malpractice, and child support.

NOTES AND QUESTIONS

1. In 1965, a chromosomal study of 197 mentally subnormal males with dangerous, violent, or criminal tendencies in an institution in Scotland found that seven of the men had a karyotype of XYY. This was a surprisingly high percentage of 3.5%. In addition, the average height of the seven men was 6 feet, 1 inch, whereas the average height for the rest of the men was 5 feet, 7

inches. It was not long before an XYY genetic defense was asserted in several criminal cases, based on the assumption that men with an extra Y chromosome were genetically programmed to commit violent acts for which they should not be responsible. The courts generally rejected the defense. See, e.g., People v. Tanner, 91 Cal.Rptr. 656 (Cal. Ct. App. 1970); People v. Yukl, 372 N.Y.S.2d 313 (N.Y.Sup.1975); State v. Roberts, 544 P.2d 754 (Wash.App.1976). Subsequent research indicated that men with an XYY karyotype tend to have lower intellectual functioning or even to be mildly intellectually impaired. Cognitive impairment, irrespective of genetic makeup, correlates with being institutionalized for crime.

2.   Based on the Andrews excerpt above, what would a criminal defendant have to prove to make out a genetic defense to a crime? How, if at all, would it differ from an insanity defense?

3.   Glenda Sue Caldwell was tried for the murder of her son and the aggravated assault of her daughter. She was found guilty but mentally ill and sentenced to life imprisonment. Her defense at trial was that she was insane, brought on by the fear of contracting Huntington disease and the stress of her separation from her husband. The psychiatrist who testified for the defense said that she was under stress and exhibited a borderline personality disorder, but she was not psychotic. Caldwell v. State, 354 S.E.2d 124 (Ga. 1987). After spending nine years in prison, Caldwell was granted a new trial and subsequently acquitted. By the time of the retrial, her Huntington disease symptoms had become more pronounced, which may have convinced the judge that she was not responsible for the shootings. Woman Wins Acquittal in Murder Case by Claiming Huntington's Disease, AP News Archive, Sept. 28, 1994. What effect, if any, should her later development of symptoms of Huntington disease have on her guilt or innocence? As predictive testing improves for various late-onset neurological disorders and dementias, what principles should the courts apply in determining the admissibility and effects of this evidence?

4.   In State v. Waldroup, the defense expert was allowed to testify that Bradley Waldroup had a variant of the monoamine oxidase A (MAO-A) gene, which, in combination with his history of child abuse, "constituted a risk factor or a vulnerability" for violence. The expert testified that some studies found a 400 percent increased chance of being convicted of a violent offense if one has the high-risk gene and suffered from child abuse. The expert also noted that other studies did not find that correlation. A jury convicted Waldroup of voluntary manslaughter instead of murder for killing his wife's friend. According to some of the jurors, the genetic evidence was a major, if not the only factor, in finding that Waldroup's actions were not premeditated. Barbara B. Hagerty, Can Your Genes Make You Murder?, Morning Edition, Nat'l Pub. Radio, July 1, 2010, https://www.npr.org/templates/story/story.php?storyId= 128043329.

One concern with the use of population-based data like that used in the Waldroup case is the "ecological fallacy." Because the data describe a heterogeneous population, "population-level associations do not apply to all individuals within the populations." For example, the combination of the high-risk variant of the MAO-A gene and child abuse in a defendant does not demonstrate definitively whether or not the crime was related to genetics. J. Bradley Segal, Inherited Proclivity: When Should Neurogenetics Mitigate Moral Culpability for Purposes of Sentencing?, 3 J.L. & Biosci. 227, 233–34 (2016).

5.   Defendants have also argued that their "genetic makeup" should be a mitigating factor in sentencing. In Mobley v. State, 455 S.E.2d 61 (Ga.), cert. denied, 516 U.S. 942 (1995), Stephen Mobley was convicted of murdering a Domino's Pizza store manager. Based on his family history of violence, the defense requested expert and financial assistance to conduct genetic analysis to determine whether Mobley had a genetic mutation associated with MAO-A deficiency. The trial court denied the request based on insufficient scientific evidence of a correlation between MAO-A deficiency and aggression. The Georgia Supreme Court affirmed. Mobley subsequently filed a habeas corpus petition in which he alleged ineffective assistance of counsel for attempting to present such an unorthodox mitigation defense, using genetic evidence. The Georgia Supreme Court held that Mobley's counsel had made a "reasonable strategic decision." Turpin v. Mobley, 502 S.E.2d 458 (Ga. 1998), and the Eleventh Circuit agreed, Mobley v. Head, 267 F.3d 1312 (11th Cir. 2001), cert. denied, 536 U.S. 968 (2002).

In United States v. Duran, No. 2011200440, 2014 CCA LEXIS 38 (N.M. Ct. Crim. App. Jan. 31, 2014), Alex Duran appealed his conviction for attempted murder, maiming, and assault. In contrast to Mobley, he claimed ineffective assistance of counsel because his defense counsel *failed* to pursue behavioral genetic testing, which he believed might have shown he was "genetically predisposed to violence" and mitigated his sentence. In rejecting the appeal, the court noted that "the practical value" of behavioral genetics may not be possible for at least a decade.

Is introducing genetic evidence at the sentencing stage likely to help or hurt the defendant? Although genetic propensity may explain the predisposition of the plaintiff (ostensibly militating toward a less harsh sentence), the determinist view of genes argued by the defendant may cause the court to think that a maximum sentence is necessary to keep the defendant off the streets as long as possible. As one court noted, while evidence of a defendant's mental condition and inability to control his "explosive behavior" could have some "mitigating effect," it could also be "a two-edged sword" by indicating his propensity for future violence. Gilson v. Sirmonts, 520 F.3d 1196, 1248 (10th Cir. 2008).

6.   In Roper v. Simmons, 543 U.S. 551 (2005), the Supreme Court held it unconstitutional to execute individuals who were under 18 years old when they committed their crime. The decision was based largely on "evolving national and international standards of decency" and the consensus that children lack the emotional and mental maturity necessary for the most culpable criminal

intent. Amicus briefs submitted on behalf of the defendant emphasized, among other things, that teenagers have "an underdeveloped sense of responsibility." Studies using modern neuroscience imaging techniques were offered to show that the brain does not mature until the age of 20–25 and therefore teenagers do not have fully developed frontal lobes capable of impulse control.

Based on this line of reasoning, how should courts rule in a future case where the defendant argues it is cruel and unusual punishment to execute an adult who does not suffer from mental retardation, but whose impulse control has been compromised by a genetic mutation? Could such a claim be made with respect to attention deficit/hyperactivity disorder, whose primary causes are thought to be genetic and biological and which has been deemed the "paradigmatic disorder of self-control." See Robert Eme, The Neuroscience of ADHD, the Paradigmatic Disorder of Self Control, 3 J.L. & Biosci. 350 (2016).

7.   In Robinson v. California, 370 U.S. 660 (1962) (narcotic addiction) and Powell v. Texas, 392 U.S. 514 (1968) (alcohol addiction), the Supreme Court held that individuals may be convicted for unlawful acts, but it is unconstitutional to punish someone for having the status of an addict. If an individual were found to have a genetic mutation linked to a predisposition to violence, would incarcerating the individual before he or she committed a crime be cruel and unusual punishment? Again, would it matter the degree of correlation between the mutation and the likelihood of committing the violent act? Would Robinson and Powell prohibit compelled treatment of an individual to prevent acts of violence, or to prevent additional acts of violence for an individual who already has been convicted?

8.   Richard M. Ewanisyzk was an attorney who abused alcohol and misappropriated client funds. His disbarment was affirmed by the courts. In re Ewaniszyk, 788 P.2d 690 (Cal.1990). John David Baker, another attorney who abused alcohol and misappropriated client funds was only suspended. The state bar and courts considered it a mitigating factor that Baker conceded he "had a genetic predisposition to addiction." Baker v. State Bar of California, 781 P.2d 1344 (Cal.1989). To what degree, if any, should the genetic basis of the addictive behavior (assuming it could be established) affect the appropriate discipline in these cases or sentencing in criminal cases?

9.   Issues concerning the use of predictive medical information could arise at all stages of the criminal justice system, from bail to parole. As to bail, in United States v. Salerno, 481 U.S. 739 (1987), the Supreme Court upheld the use of predictions of future criminal conduct as a factor in deciding whether to grant bail and the proper amount. As to parole, parole boards use a wide range of considerations and are given broad discretion, subject to considerations of due process. See Greenholtz v. Inmates of Nebraska Penal & Correctional Complex, 442 U.S. 1 (1979).

In general, a more lax evidentiary standard is used in bail, sentencing, and parole matters than is applied at trial. What standard should be applied to the introduction of proffered behavioral genetic evidence?

10. Might genetic evidence one day be relevant to civil commitment decisions? Many states have laws like the Kansas Sexually Violent Predator Act, Kan. Stat. Ann. § 59–29a01 et seq (1994), the interpretation of which was at issue in Kansas v. Crane, 534 U.S. 407 (2002). The statute "requires a finding of dangerousness either to one's self or to others" and "links that finding to the existence of a 'mental abnormality' or 'personality disorder' that makes it difficult, if not impossible, for the person to control his dangerous behavior." Could someone who has demonstrated a genetic basis for inability to control dangerous behavior be civilly committed under this statute?

In *Crane*, the Supreme Court vacated and remanded the Kansas Supreme Court's judgment that Michael Crane, a previously convicted sexual offender with exhibitionism and antisocial personality disorder, should not be civilly committed. It found that the Kansas court erred in thinking that an earlier decision, Kansas v. Hendricks, 521 U.S. 346 (1997), required the State to prove that "a dangerous individual is *completely* unable to control his behavior." Nevertheless, the Court did require "proof of serious difficulty in controlling behavior." It did not offer a "narrow or technical meaning" of the phrase "lack of control," reasoning that "precise bright-line rules" were not especially effective at safeguarding "liberty in the area of mental illness" for two reasons: States have "considerable leeway" in defining what mental abnormalities or personality disorders make someone eligible for commitment, and distinctions in the "ever-advancing" field of psychiatry "do not seek precisely to mirror those of the law."

After remand of Mr. Crane's case, doctors determined that he was no longer a threat, and he was released in January 2002. On October 14, 2003, he was found guilty of forcible rape, kidnapping, third-degree assault, and three counts of forcible sodomy. He was sentenced to life in prison.

11. The Supreme Court in *Crane* recognized the difficulty of demonstrating "with mathematical precision" someone's "inability to control behavior." How might that language affect a court's determination regarding civil commitment when evidence is introduced of a genetic predisposition to impulsive and violent behavior? Would it matter the degree of correlation between the mutation and the likelihood of committing the violent act?

12. For a further discussion, see J. Bradley Segal, Inherited Proclivity: When Should Neurogenetics Mitigate Moral Culpability for Purposes of Sentencing?, 3 J.L. & Biosci. 227 (2016); Paul S. Appelbaum, The Double Helix Takes the Witness Stand: Behavioral and Neuropsychiatric Genetics in Court, 82 Neuron 946 (2014); Paula Kim, Psychopathy, Genes and the Criminal Justice System, 15 Colum. Sci. & Tech. L. Rev. 375 (2014); Diane E. Hoffmann & Karen H. Rothenberg, Judging Genes: Implications of the Second Generation of Genetic Tests in the Courtroom, 66 Md. L. Rev. 858 (2007); Nita A. Farahany & James E. Coleman, Jr., Genetics and Responsibility: To Know the Criminal from the Crime, 69 L. & Contemp. Probs. 115 (2006); Karen H. Rothenberg & Alice Wang, The Scarlet Gene: Behavioral Genetics, Criminal Law, and Racial and Ethnic Stigma, 69 L. & Contemp. Probs. 343 (2006).

CHAPTER 23

ENVIRONMENTAL AND OCCUPATIONAL REGULATION AND PERSONAL INJURY CASES

■ ■ ■

I. INTRODUCTION

Prior chapters have explored the relationship between genetic and environmental factors in human health and development in the context of clinical genetics (Chapters 6–8), pharmacogenomics (Chapter 14), and behavioral genetics (Chapter 22). Another interaction between genetics and the environment with important legal applications involves laws that protect the air, water, earth, wildlife, and food supply from pollutants. Similar issues are raised by laws that attempt to ensure that workers have safe and healthful workplaces. The overarching question is the degree to which human genetic variation should be considered in setting exposure limits and in prescribing other measures to prevent harm. One concern is that an overemphasis on genetic factors will shift the blame from polluters to the "faulty genes" of certain individuals. The regulatory consequences of adopting such an approach could include changing the focus from lowering exposures merely to warning at-risk individuals or, in the workplace setting, excluding them from employment. At the same time, it may simply not be technologically or economically feasible to lower all exposures to levels where the most vulnerable individuals can be exposed without any adverse health effects. It is difficult to decide what ethical and legal principles should be applied in these circumstances, especially when the scientific evidence is incomplete or inconclusive.

Regulatory agencies have begun considering genetic studies, and to a lesser extent epigenetic studies, in assessing the human health risks from environmental and occupational exposures. This chapter will consider the legal significance of developments in toxicogenomics and related avenues of scientific inquiry. In addition to discussing the applicable statutes, the chapter will also consider the admissibility and significance of genetic information proffered by either plaintiffs or defendants in personal injury litigation to prove or disprove exposure, causation, and damages. These legal actions could be based on negligence, strict liability, products liability, or other theories.

469

II. REGULATION

A. ENVIRONMENTAL

NATIONAL RESEARCH COUNCIL, APPLICATIONS OF TOXICOGENOMIC TECHNOLOGIES TO PREDICTIVE TOXICOLOGY AND RISK ASSESSMENT
186–189 (2007).

Toxicogenomic data have numerous potential applications in environmental, pharmaceutical, and occupational health regulation. Regulatory agencies such as the Environmental Protection Agency (EPA) and the [Food and Drug Administration (FDA)] have already produced guidance documents on the incorporation of genomic information into their regulatory programs. Some examples of potential regulatory applications of toxicogenomics and their implications are discussed below.

DEFINING NEW ADVERSE EFFECTS

Many regulatory requirements are based on a finding of "adverse effect." For example, national ambient air-quality standards set under the Clean Air Act are set at a level that protects against adverse effects in susceptible populations. Some subclinical effects (for example, changes in erythrocyte protoporphyrin concentration in blood) have been found to be adverse effects under this statutory provision and have required more stringent standards to prevent such effects from occurring in exposed populations. Furthermore, many EPA regulations for noncarcinogenic substances are based on the reference concentrations (RfC) or reference dose (RfD). Some gene expression or other changes measured with toxicogenomic technologies may constitute new adverse effects under these programs and thus lower RfDs and RfCs, resulting in more stringent regulations. Manufacturers of pesticides and toxic chemicals are required to notify the EPA of new scientific findings about adverse effects associated with their products. In pharmaceutical regulation, the detection of a biomarker that suggests an adverse effect may likewise trigger additional regulatory scrutiny or restrictions.

Therefore, a critical issue in the regulatory application of toxicogenomics will be determining whether and when a change constitutes an adverse effect. Many changes in gene expression, protein levels, and metabolite profiles will be adaptive responses to a stimulus that are not representative or predictive of a toxic response. Other toxicogenomic changes may be strongly indicative of a toxic response. Therefore, it will be important to distinguish true biomarkers of toxicity from reversible or adaptive responses and to do so in a way that is transparent, predictable, and consistent for the affected entities. At least initially, phenotypic anchoring of toxicogenomics changes to well-established toxicologic end points will likely be necessary to identify toxicologically significant markers.

REGULATORY DECISIONS BASED ON SCREENING ASSAYS

The availability of relatively inexpensive and quick toxicogenomics assays that can be used for hazard characterization of otherwise untested materials offers a number of potential regulatory opportunities. Full toxicologic characterization of the approximately 80,000 chemicals in commerce using a battery of traditional toxicology tests (for example, chronic rodent bioassay) is not economically or technologically feasible in the foreseeable future. Screening with a toxicogenomic assay, such as gene expression analysis that classifies agents based on transcript profiles, might be useful to quickly screen chemicals for prioritizing substances for further investigation and possible regulation. Another possibility is to require the manufacturer of a new chemical substance, or an existing substance that will be used in a new application, to include the results of a standardized toxicogenomics assay as part of a premanufacturing notice required under Section 5 of the Toxic Substances Control Act.

PROTECTION OF GENETICALLY SUSCEPTIBLE INDIVIDUALS

Many regulatory programs specifically require protection of susceptible individuals. For example, the Clean Air Act requires that national ambient air-quality standards be set at a level that protects the most susceptible subgroups within the population. Under this program, the EPA focuses its standard-setting activities on susceptible subgroups such as children with asthma. Recent studies indicate a significant genetic role in susceptibility to air pollution, which may lead to air-quality standards being based on the risks to genetically susceptible individuals. Regulations under other environmental statutes, such as pesticide regulations under the Food Quality Protection Act and drinking water standards under the Safe Drinking Water Act, may likewise focus on genetically susceptible individuals in the future, as might occupational exposure standards promulgated by the Occupational Safety and Health Administration. Likewise, pharmaceutical approvals may require considering and protecting individuals with genetic susceptibilities to a particular drug.

The identification of genetic susceptibilities to chemicals, consumer products, pharmaceuticals, and other materials raises a number of regulatory issues. One issue is the question of the feasibility of protecting genetically susceptible individuals. On the one hand, protecting the most susceptible individual in society may be extremely costly, and perhaps even infeasible without major, formidable changes in our industrial society. On the other hand, the concept of government regulators leaving the health of some individuals unprotected, who through no fault of their own are born with a susceptibility to a particular product or chemical, also seems politically and ethically infeasible. As more information on individual genetic susceptibility becomes available, regulators and society generally will confront difficult challenges in deciding whether and how to protect the most genetically vulnerable citizens in our midst.

Gary E. Marchant, Toxicogenomics and Environmental Regulation, in Genomics and Environmental Regulation: Science, Ethics, and Law

11–14 (Richard R. Sharp, Gary E. Marchant & Jamie A. Grodsky eds. 2008).

Major uncertainties and data gaps limit the utility and credibility of risk assessment for informing regulatory decisions. These uncertainties include extrapolating results from animals to humans and from high-dose to more typical low-dose human exposures, understanding the mechanism of action of a toxicant and its implications for risk assessment, determining the shape of the dose-response curve, and estimating the exposure levels for actual human populations. Gene expression data have the potential to help address many of these unknowns.

Toxicogenomic data can improve risk assessment in several ways. First, gene expression data, by providing a characteristic "fingerprint" of different toxicological mechanisms, can be used to characterize the mechanism or mode of action of a toxicant. Regulatory agencies such as the U.S. Environmental Protection Agency (EPA) have recently focused on mode of action as a key factor in risk assessment, because this information is critical for addressing the issues raised above and for deciding whether an agent is likely to exhibit a threshold below which there is no significant toxicity. As noted in EPA's 2002 Interim Policy on Genomics, toxicogenomics will "likely provide a better understanding of the mechanism or mode of action of a stressor and thus assist in predictive toxicology, in the screening of stressors, and in the design of monitoring activities and exposure studies."

Second, gene expression will be useful in extrapolating results obtained in animal and epidemiology studies that typically involve higher dose levels than those more relevant for the general human population. Until now, low-dose effects have generally been refractory to empirical analysis, and risk assessors have had to rely on models to extrapolate results from high to low dose levels. A finding that gene expression changes characteristic of the carcinogenic response of a particular agent at high doses are also observed in low-dose groups, even though those low-dose animals may not develop tumors, may indicate that low-dose exposures present a carcinogenic risk in large populations. Alternatively, the absence of any characteristic gene expression response in low-dose animals may suggest that the carcinogenetic response occurs only at high doses.

Third, gene expression patterns may help to assess the relevance of animal studies for humans. Most toxicology data comes from animal studies, which are often but not always relevant to humans. By providing a quick and inexpensive test of whether a chemical is causing a similar response in rodents and humans, gene expression assays can help prevent false positives for chemicals that cause toxicity in rodents but not in humans and false negatives for chemicals that cause toxicity in humans but not rodents.

Fourth, gene expression data may also be beneficial for exposure assessment. Many types of environmental exposures lack adequate exposure data, which severely limits the ability to accurately determine the relationship between dose and response that underlies risk-assessment estimates. By characterizing gene expression patterns in exposed persons, microarrays have the potential to provide more precise quantitative estimates of exposure to specific toxic substances in contemporaneous and prospective human studies.

Fifth, gene expression profiling may be particularly useful for evaluating the toxicity of chemical mixtures, which is difficult to do with traditional chemical-by-chemical toxicological methods. DNA microarrays permit the simultaneous monitoring of all gene expression changes within a cell in a single experiment, thus they are "particularly suitable to evaluate any kind of combinational effect resulting from combined exposure to toxicants."

These potential applications of gene expression data may help reduce many of the most important uncertainties in risk assessment, although by no means eliminating such uncertainties altogether. The effect may be to give risk regulation greater credibility and certainty, which will allow environmental regulation to more directly target the most serious risks to human health and the environment.

HIGH-THROUGHPUT TOXICITY SCREENING OF CHEMICALS

The majority of chemicals in commercial use in the United States have not been comprehensively tested for human toxicity and carcinogenicity potential. EPA and the chemical industry have begun to address this data gap for chemical risk assessment with the high-production volume (HPV) chemical testing initiative. However, given that there are now some 80,000 chemicals in commerce, it is not feasible to conduct full toxicological testing for all or even most of these chemicals using existing methods. As the then-director of the National Institute of Environmental Health Sciences testified to Congress in 2002, many commercial products require additional testing, but "we can never satisfy this testing requirement using traditional technologies."

Gene expression assays have the potential to provide rapid, inexpensive, and high-throughput screening of chemicals for a wide range of genotoxic and nongenotoxic responses. Microarrays can be used to interrogate the gene expression of cells either in tissue culture or in living laboratory animals that have been treated with putative toxic agents. The resulting gene expression profiles can be used to classify those chemicals in specific toxicological categories to characterize likely risks. In addition to their relatively low cost and rapid results, microarrays offer possible advantages as a screening assay. Microassays can monitor changes in the expression of all genes within a cell, potentially permitting simultaneous evaluation of all toxicological endpoints in a single assay, something that is not possible with traditional toxicological technologies. In addition, microassays allow a more sensitive assay of potential toxicity, because they test for the initial molecular events in a toxic response. This is more sensitive than other assay methods that tend to monitor clinical effects that do not occur until much later in the disease process.

Initially, gene expression assays will need to be conducted in association with traditional toxicity testing until a sufficiently robust and validated data set has been accumulated to reliably correlate specific gene expression profiles with particular toxicological mechanisms and endpoints. Used in conjunction with traditional toxicology tests, gene expression data have the potential to improve the sensitivity and interoperability of the standard tests. After an adequate relational database has been established, gene expression assays might replace some or all of the current toxicological screening and testing assays or at least select the specific assays indicated by the observed gene expression pattern.

NOTES AND QUESTIONS

1.   Toxicogenomics is defined as the application of genomic technologies to study the adverse effects of environmental and pharmaceutical chemicals on human health and the environment. National Research Council, Applications of Toxicogenomic Technologies to Predictive Toxicology and Risk Assessment 12 (2007).

2.   There are thousands of commonly used industrial and consumer chemicals that could have toxicogenomic-mediated adverse effects on human health. A possible strategy to protect individuals is to issue warnings, perhaps because of regulatory requirements or the desire to limit tort liability. Imagine the shelves of the neighborhood grocery or hardware store, with numerous products containing genotype-specific warnings about exposures and harms. How helpful do you think this information would be? Might there be harms from such warnings?

3.   One likely effect of toxicogenomics is to increase the amount of individual genomic information. What risks to privacy are raised by this additional information? How, if at all, would you protect against the adverse uses and effects?

MARK A. ROTHSTEIN, YU CAI & GARY E. MARCHANT, ETHICAL IMPLICATIONS OF EPIGENETICS RESEARCH

10 Nature Revs. Genetics 224 (2009).

* * *

First we consider environmental justice. Epigenetic effects have been associated with exposure to various toxic chemicals, airborne pollutants, pesticides and other harmful substances. Many of these exposures are linked with poverty, discriminatory land use, and substandard living and working conditions. At the same time, many individuals with these harmful exposures are considered medically vulnerable because of pre-existing health conditions that are frequently complicated by poor clinical management. Both the exposure to environmental hazards and the social, nutritional, medical and psychological stresses of low-income communities can separately and, perhaps even more importantly, cumulatively cause epigenetic changes that place exposed populations at increased risk. Epigenetics therefore provides a new window for understanding and possibly addressing the co-morbidities associated with disparate environmental exposures.

The second issue regards the intergenerational effects and equity of epigenetics research. A key implication of epigenetics research is that many environmental and hazardous exposures will affect not only the exposed individuals, but possibly their progeny and subsequent generations. This insight will create new challenges for environmental and health regulation, as well as for intergenerational equity. Intergenerational equity refers to the obligations of each generation to serve as a custodian or steward of the planet and its inhabitants for future generations. Thus, it could be asserted that each generation has an obligation to its descendants not to damage the genomes and epigenomes of future generations, such as through exposure to environmental hazards. It remains to be seen whether or how the possible transgenerational damage caused by environmentally induced epigenetic changes will affect environmental regulatory policies.

* * *

Some of the ethical concerns discussed above are similar to those already raised by genetics, but the role of environmental exposures in producing epigenetic effects adds new concerns. The use of epigenetics in environmental risk assessment will probably be among the first applications of the new research. Once epigenetic testing of individuals becomes available, concerns are likely to arise about possible privacy violations and epigenetic discrimination. The prospect of such non-genetic discrimination casts doubt on the wisdom and efficacy of current genetic-specific laws, and it suggests that broader laws are needed to prohibit adverse treatment on the basis of health status or biological markers.

Epigenetic research raises other profound issues, including individual and societal responsibilities to prevent hazardous exposures, monitor health status and provide treatment. Epigenetics also serves to highlight the effects of inequality in living and working conditions and adds a multigenerational dimension to environmentally caused adverse health effects.

NOTES AND QUESTIONS

1.   Epigenetics, which is discussed briefly in Chapter 4, literally means "above the genes." It refers to modifications of the genome that do not involve a change in the DNA sequence. The recent understanding of epigenetic processes stands in contrast to the traditional assumption that genetic variation was exclusively the result of changes in DNA sequence. Epigenetic changes or "marks" result from a wide range of environmental exposures, including diet, toxic substances, and environmental stressors. Epigenetic changes tend to occur at much higher rates than mutations in DNA sequences from similar exposures. Susceptibility is not only a function of dose, but also of the stage of development when exposure takes place, such as prenatal and neonatal exposure. Whereas genetic mutations tend to be irreversible, epigenetic changes can be reversed. How, if at all, should these factors influence legal regulation of substances causing epigenetic changes?

2.   A distinctive feature of epigenetics, especially changes resulting from the process of methylation, is that the effects may persist in future generations despite the lack of DNA sequence modification. Thus, parental exposures (e.g., to diesel exhaust fumes) may be expressed not only in the exposed generation in the form of respiratory disease, but in future generations as well. The issue of intergenerational equity raised in the article excerpt has been applied in the context of various environmental hazards, such as nuclear waste disposal, climate change, and extinction of species of plants and animals. Do you think the present generation is the steward of the genomes and epigenomes of future generations? If so, how can such an abstract concern be implemented in laws? See Mark A. Rothstein, Heather L. Harrell, & Gary E. Marchant, Transgenerational Epigenetics and Environmental Justice, 3(3) Envtl. Epigenetics 1–11 (2017).

3.   There are many unresolved scientific questions surrounding epigenetics that will have significant effects on social policy. For example: How many substances and environmental conditions cause epigenetic effects, at what exposure levels, and at what time during human development? Are there predispositions that make certain individuals more susceptible to epigenetic changes? When will tests be commonly available to measure epigenetic effects? When will therapies be available to reverse epigenetic effects? Is it possible to regulate in the absence of answers to these questions?

4.   For further discussion, see Mark A. Rothstein, Yu Cai & Gary E. Marchant, The Ghost in Our Genes: Legal and Ethical Implications of Epigenetics, 19 Health Matrix 1 (2009).

B. OCCUPATIONAL

MARK A. ROTHSTEIN, OCCUPATIONAL HEALTH AND DISCRIMINATION ISSUES RAISED BY TOXICOGENOMICS IN THE WORKPLACE IN GENOMICS AND ENVIRONMENTAL REGULATION: SCIENCE, ETHICS, AND LAW

184–188 (Richard R. Sharp, Gary E. Marchant & Jamie A. Grodsky eds. 2008).

The Occupational Safety and Health Act of 1970 is the primary federal law regulating worker safety and health. The OSH Act covers employment in every state and territory—an estimated six million workplaces and ninety million employees. Unlike many labor and unemployment laws, there is no minimum number of employees or dollar volume of business needed for coverage. The OSH Act applies to all employers engaged in a business affecting interstate commerce—an easy standard to satisfy.

Among other requirements, each covered employer must comply with two provisions of the statute. First, section 5(a)(1) requires each covered employer to keep its workplace free from recognized hazards that are causing or likely to cause death or serious physical harm to its employees. Second, section 5(a)(2) requires each covered employer to comply with occupational safety and health standards promulgated by the Occupational Safety and Health Administration (OSHA) of the U.S. Department of Labor. The failure to comply with these requirements may result in the assessment of a range of civil penalties depending on the nature and gravity of the violation as well as on other factors.

STANDARD SETTING

Section 6 of the statute provides for the promulgation of standards in three ways. First, under section 6(a) the secretary of labor was authorized from 1971 to 1973 to adopt as OSHA standards, without rulemaking procedures, two types of existing standards—national consensus standards (developed by private organizations) and established federal standards (promulgated under other federal laws). This provision was designed to ensure the existence of OSHA standards soon after the effective date of the OSH Act in 1971, by adopting standards with which industry already was familiar. Second, under section 6(b), the secretary may modify, revoke, or issue new standards by complying with detailed rule-making procedures. This is the most important standards promulgation provision for new health standards. Third, under section 6(c), the secretary may issue emergency temporary standards in extraordinary circumstances, which may remain in effect for up to six months. Because standards promulgated under this provision have been difficult to sustain on judicial review, it has been rarely used.

Occupational safety and health standards generally have not been developed with an explicit concern for individual variability in response to toxic substances. Although such standards are designed to provide the maximum protection possible, OSHA has recognized that it may not be possible to protect workers with heightened sensitivity. For example, the preamble to the coke oven emissions standard provides: "Because of the variability of individual response to carcinogens and other factors, the concept of a 'threshold level' may have little applicability on the basis of existing knowledge. Some individuals may be more susceptible than others. Thus, while a 'threshold' exposure level, below which exposure does not cause cancer, may conceivably exist for an individual, susceptible individuals in the working population may have cancer induced by doses so low as to be effectively zero." New toxicogenomic studies will identify an increasing number of substances for which a particular genotype confers greater risk of illness based on occupational exposures. OSHA will need to decide if, or to what extent, individual variability should be incorporated into the agency's standards promulgation strategy.

As an initial matter, it is necessary to consider OSHA's statutory authority to promulgate health standards and the judicial construction of the exercise of that authority. Section 6(b)(5) of the OSH Act, which deals with the promulgation of standards for toxic substances and harmful physical agents, provides in part: "The Secretary of Labor shall set the standard which most adequately assures, to the extent feasible. . . . that no employee will suffer material impairment of health." This seemingly absolute language might be read as requiring OSHA to set standards at a level where even the most sensitive employee could work without ill effects. However, in *Industrial Union Department, AFL-CIO v. American Petroleum Institute* (1980)—also known as the *Benzene* decision—the Supreme Court rejected the notion that the OSH Act requires regulation at the level of zero risk.

The *Benzene* decision involved an industry challenge to OSHA rulemaking that lowered the permissible exposure limit for benzene from 10 parts per million to 1 part per million. In striking down the benzene standard, the Fifth Circuit held that, based on section 3(5) of the OSH Act, the secretary was required to prove that the benefits of the standard bear a reasonable relationship to the costs. The Supreme Court affirmed, but on different grounds. According to the plurality opinion, the secretary must initially demonstrate the need for a new standard by establishing that exposure at current levels poses a "significant risk" of harm. Because the secretary failed to make this finding, the benzene standard was struck down. The Court also cautioned that the duty imposed on employers by the statute was not absolute. "The statute was not designed to require employers to provide absolutely risk-free workplaces whenever it is technologically feasible to do so . . . [but] was intended to require the elimination, as far as feasible, of significant risks of harm."

Although the Supreme Court never explicitly stated whether the OSH Act requires employers to set exposure levels that would protect the most sensitive workers, *Benzene* implicitly holds that it does not. OSHA standards for toxic substances could be set to avoid requiring absolute levels of protection in two main ways: they could be limited to control measures that are economically and technologically feasible, or they could establish permissible exposure levels that would not protect the most sensitive workers. Although these appear to be distinct concepts, as a scientific and practical matter, they are closely related. Figure 11.1 plots a hypothetical linear dose-response curve.

As the dose increases (along the horizontal axis), the percentage of affected workers increases (along the vertical axis), and as the percentage of workers increases, even less sensitive individuals will exhibit the biological response. The lowest feasible level for reducing exposure is indicated by f. The intersection of f with the dose-response line, point 0, results in setting the susceptibility cutoff at s. Consequently, a standard lowering exposures only to the *Benzene* requirement of feasibility will necessarily result in a lack of protection for some of the most susceptible workers.

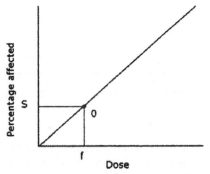

Figure 11.1. The intersection of feasibility
and susceptibility in dose-response analysis

NOTES AND QUESTIONS

1.   The *Benzene* case implicitly acknowledges it is impossible to protect the most sensitive workers from adverse health effects caused by occupational exposures. If Congress or the Supreme Court were to make this principle more explicit, what would it say? What would be the likely public reaction?

2.   The *Benzene* case fills 118 pages of the U.S. Reports—an indication of the complexity of the issues and the divisions within the Court. Toxicogenomics is likely to make the scientific issues even more complicated. Is judicial review of regulatory action now beyond the technical competence of the judiciary? Are there alternatives?

3. In American Textile Mfrs. Institute, Inc. v. Donovan, 452 U.S. 490 (1981), the Supreme Court rejected the industry argument that the Occupational Safety and Health Act (OSHA) requires the use of cost-benefit analysis. Relying on the plain meaning of the word "feasible" in § 6(b)(5) as "capable of being done," the Court held that imposing a cost-benefit requirement would be inconsistent with the mandate of Congress.

MARK A. ROTHSTEIN, GENETICS AND THE WORK FORCE OF THE NEXT HUNDRED YEARS

2000 Colum. Bus. L. Rev. 371, 393–95 (2000).

Autonomy and paternalism conflict in the area of genetic predisposition to occupational disease. Should workers be screened for polymorphic markers of varied sensitivity to toxic chemicals and other hazards in some workplaces? One view is that workers should not be screened; instead, the employer should be required to make the workplace safe and healthful for all workers. The problem is that reducing exposures to levels where even the most sensitive individual can work safely is neither technologically nor economically feasible because of the wide variability among individuals and because the difficulty and cost of reducing exposure levels increases exponentially as exposures are reduced to very low levels. The opposite view is that employers should be free to use genetic screening as a way of protecting the health of employees and their own financial interests. This approach, however, shifts the economic burden of working with dangerous substances from the employer to the worker, removes an important incentive to clean up workplaces for the benefit of even "low-risk" workers, and runs counter to the notion of autonomy embraced in *Johnson Controls* as well as the ADA.

[In International Union, UAW v. Johnson Controls, Inc., 499 U.S. 187 (1991), the Supreme Court held that the employer's rule prohibiting assignment of any fertile women to work with exposure to lead (which may cause in utero birth defects to the fetus of a pregnant woman employee) was sex discrimination because women have the right to decide which risks to their reproductive health are acceptable.]

A middle position is that a worker who is currently capable of performing the job should have the option of learning whether he or she is at increased risk of occupational disease based on genetic factors. This information should not be available to the employer, but should be used by the employee in deciding whether to accept or continue in the position. A threshold issue is whether a scientific test has sufficient analytical and clinical utility to be used as a screening device for individuals, as opposed to a research tool for population studies. Another issue is what criteria should be used in evaluating whether there is scientific justification for the individual to avoid a job with a certain exposure. Finally, other logistical questions include how individuals get referred for genetic testing, who pays for the testing, and who has access to test results.

In my view, where employers know or should know that research has identified genetic markers of increased risk based on exposure to substances in their workplace, they have a duty to inform applicants and employees. The applicants and employees then should have the option of undergoing genetic testing at the employer's expense, administered by a physician of the applicant's or employee's choosing, with the results available only to the individual. If the test is positive, the physician or a genetic counselor should discuss the risks of employment with the individual. The choice of whether to accept or continue in the job would rest with the individual. Only where employment of an individual would create a direct, immediate, and severe risk of harm to self, others, or property would the employer be justified in performing its own testing and excluding the individual from employment. These situations are likely to be rare.

NOTES AND QUESTIONS

1.   Section 202(b)(5) of GINA, provides that it is not unlawful for an employer to offer employees voluntary genetic monitoring to determine whether prior occupational exposures have caused genetic changes. GINA does not permit employers to offer new employees and those initially being assigned to work where there are certain exposures voluntary genetic screening to assess whether they are at increased risk from occupational exposures. Would you favor extending the exception to pre-exposure genetic screening?

2.   One of the first applications of toxicogenomic testing in the workplace involves occupational exposure to beryllium, a lightweight metal widely used in aircraft components, nuclear weapons, and a variety of industrial products. Exposure to beryllium can result in chronic beryllium disease (CBD), a serious respiratory condition. Individuals with a particular genetic marker, HLA-DPB1-Glu69, have been shown to be at an increased risk of CBD. At least two employers have used voluntary genetic screening for new workers, who could elect to undergo testing at no cost by an independent laboratory, with individual results not reported to the employer. Such efforts at genetic screening have raised a variety of scientific, ethical, and legal issues, many of them stemming from the low positive predictive value of the test. For a further discussion, see Ken Silver & Richard R. Sharp, Ethical Considerations in Testing Workers for the -Glu69 Marker of Genetic Susceptibility to Chronic Beryllium Disease, 48 J. Occup. & Envtl. Med. 434 (2006).

GENETIC TESTING FOR SUSCEPTIBILITY
TO CARPAL TUNNEL SYNDROME

Burlington Northern Santa Fe Railroad (BNSF) is the nation's second largest railroad company. The railroad operates 33,500 route miles of track covering 28 states and two Canadian provinces. In March 2000, BNSF began a pilot program that included genetic testing for employees who claimed work-related carpal tunnel disease. Rail industry safety rules and negotiated union contracts allow BNSF to require employees to undergo medical examinations to evaluate work-related injury claims. Since the initiation of the new policy, approximately 125 of its 40,000 active employees filed claims for carpal tunnel-related injuries. Of those 125, genetic testing was performed on 23 employees. None of the employees was told that the blood sample they were giving was being sent to a research laboratory for genetic analysis.

BNSF's practice of requiring genetic tests came to the attention of the Equal Employment Opportunity Commission (EEOC) when Janice Avary, a registered nurse and wife of a BNSF employee, began looking into the reason why BNSF was requiring her husband to submit seven vials of blood after he filed a claim for a carpal tunnel injury. Avary was concerned that her husband was asked to furnish such a large amount of blood and that he was not instructed to fast to ensure accurate results, as is typical when blood tests are taken. Two days before the scheduled exam, Avary called the company to ask for an explanation and to get a list of the lab tests that her husband would undergo. When the company's medical liaison mentioned possible genetic tests, Avary became alarmed. She called the railroad's headquarters to inform them that they could not subject her husband to a genetic test without his permission (under Iowa state law). According to Avary, BNSF told her that if her husband refused the exam, he could face an investigation for insubordination.

As a result of this experience, Gary Avary filed a complaint with the EEOC. Soon after, five more workers told the EEOC that they had given blood during the medical exams but were unaware of its ultimate use. While the union and the EEOC were investigating the claims against BNSF, Gary Avary received a disciplinary letter from BNSF as a result of his failure to comply with the examination. In response to this letter and to BNSF's practice of requiring genetic testing, on February 9, 2001, EEOC filed its first court action challenging genetic testing. EEOC v. Burlington Northern Santa Fe R.R. Co., No. C01–4013 (N.D. Iowa, filed Feb. 9, 2001). In its petition, the EEOC asked for a preliminary injunction against BNSF requiring the company to end genetic testing of employees who have filed claims for work-related injuries based on carpal tunnel syndrome. The EEOC alleged that the employees were unaware that they were submitting to a genetic test and further, that they were not asked to consent to such a test. The EEOC asked the court to order the railroad to end its nationwide policy of requiring employees who have submitted claims of work-related carpal tunnel syndrome to provide blood samples which are then used for a genetic DNA test for a chromosome 17 deletion associated with hereditary pressure palsy neuropathy, a rare condition which may predict some forms of carpal tunnel syndrome. For a discussion of the scientific basis of the genetic testing, see Paul A. Schulte & Geoffrey Lomax, Assessment of the Scientific Basis for Genetic Testing of Railroad Workers with Carpal Tunnel Syndrome, 45 J. Occup. & Envt'l Med. 592 (2003).

The EEOC also sought to halt any disciplinary action or termination of an employee who has refused to submit a blood sample. The EEOC claimed that the genetic testing violated the Americans with Disabilities Act (ADA) because it is not job-related or consistent with business necessity. Section 102 (d)(4) of the ADA provides that any medical examinations or inquiries of current employees must be either voluntary or job-related and consistent with business necessity, meaning that they measure the ability to perform the job safely and efficiently. EEOC's position was that the unproven test was not job-related. On February 12, 2001, BNSF announced that it would suspend its practice of requiring genetic testing, and a settlement agreement was approved by the court on April 18, 2001.

The *Burlington Northern* case generated a substantial amount of publicity. It was widely reported as the first action brought by the EEOC alleging genetic discrimination. Part of the publicity may be attributable to the fact that the case arose within days of the joint publication in *Nature* and *Science* of the completed draft sequence of the human genome. Thus, it provided the counterpoint for the scientific marvel—the possibility that genetics could result in discrimination. Yet, it is arguable that the case has little to do with genetics. What ADA and common law legal theories could be asserted by the EEOC and individual plaintiffs? How strong a case is this? What is the central ethical issue surrounding this incident?

Burlington Northern and Norman Bloodsaw v. Lawrence Berkeley Lab., 135 F.3d 1260 (9th Cir. 1998) (holding nonconsensual sickle cell testing violated Title VII) were the two genetic discrimination cases relied on by Congress to demonstrate the need to enact GINA. See Jessica L. Roberts, Preempting Discrimination: Lessons from the Genetic Information Nondiscrimination Act, 63 Vand. L. Rev. 439 (2010).

III. LITIGATION

Several constitutional, statutory, regulatory, and common law causes of action already have been discussed in this book, including medical malpractice, intellectual property, discrimination, criminal law, and forensics. In this section, we consider three additional uses of genetic information in litigation. First is the use of genetic information to prove or disprove that the plaintiff suffered an injury. Second is the use of genetic information to prove or disprove that the plaintiff's injury was caused by a harmful exposure rather than the plaintiff's genetic predisposition. These are mostly toxic tort cases. The third type of case considered in this section is any personal injury lawsuit in which genetic information is used to predict the life expectancy or future health of the plaintiff and therefore may be relevant to the issue of the plaintiff's damages.

A. INJURY

BRYSON V. PILLSBURY CO.
573 N.W.2d 718 (Minn.Ct.App.1998).

KALITOWSKI, J.

Appellant Nora Bryson challenges the district court's grant of summary judgment in favor of respondents Pillsbury Company, et al., arguing the district court erred because: (1) Bryson submitted evidence that raised a genuine issue of material fact as to whether she suffered a present injury; and (2) Bryson presented sufficient evidence to establish her claim for damages based on her alleged increased risk of developing cancer.

FACTS

Appellant Nora Bryson boarded her horse at the farm of an individual who, like Bryson, was an employee of respondent Pillsbury's subsidiary, Green Giant (company). On July 23, 1990, Bryson discovered that her horse had fallen into a pit filled with water from a storm. The pit, which was 20 feet by 20 feet with a 17-foot depth, had allegedly been used by the company to dispose of waste. Bryson entered the pit in an attempt to rescue the horse and, while in the pit, observed what she believed to be Captan-treated seeds floating in the water. Captan is a chemical treatment for seed that protects it from insects in the soil until germination.

Bryson and others succeeded in getting the horse out of the water. Later that day, Bryson broke out in a rash that covered her body. She presented evidence that she has subsequently developed additional rashes. Bryson, through her expert from the University of Minnesota, presented evidence that she suffered extensive chromosome breakage as a result of exposure to Captan and that, because of the chromosome breakage, she has an increased risk of developing cancer. The company made a motion for summary judgment arguing: (1) Bryson assumed the risk of harm by not leaving the pit when she saw the Captan-treated seeds; and (2) Bryson's alleged damages were too speculative. The district court denied the company's summary judgment motion on assumption of risk, but granted summary judgment in favor of the company stating that Bryson suffered no present injury and concluding that her claimed damages for future harm were too speculative as a matter of law.

ISSUES

1.   Did Bryson present sufficient evidence to support her claim of a present injury?

2.   Did Bryson present sufficient evidence to support her claim for damages based on her alleged increased risk of developing cancer?

ANALYSIS

* * *

Bryson contends the district court erred in granting summary judgment, claiming she presented sufficient evidence to raise a genuine fact issue as to whether her chromosome damage constituted a present injury. The company asserts that because Bryson's claimed chromosome damage is asymptomatic, it does not constitute a legally compensable present injury. In a memorandum supporting its order for summary judgment, the district court, without reference to Bryson's allegations regarding present damages, stated: "In this matter there are no present injuries * * *." We conclude the district court erred by granting summary judgment where there is a genuine issue of disputed material fact regarding whether there was a present injury.

In Werlein v. United States, 746 F.Supp. 887, 901 (D.Minn.1990), vacated in part on other grounds, 793 F.Supp. 898 (D.Minn.1992), the United States District Court addressed a case in which the plaintiffs claimed that exposure to contaminated air and drinking water resulted in chromosome damage. The defendants argued that the plaintiffs did not suffer a present injury. In denying the defendants' summary judgment motion, the court in Werlein stated that it could not

> rule as a matter of law that plaintiffs' alleged injuries are not "real" simply because they are subcellular. The effect of volatile organic compounds on the human body is a subtle, complex matter. It is for the trier of fact, aided by expert testimony, to determine whether plaintiffs have suffered present harm.

The asymptomatic, subcellular damages claimed in Werlein are similar to the injury claimed by Bryson. Here Bryson's expert witness presented evidence that Bryson's exposure to Captan resulted in chromosome breakage, and that such breakage is a "real and present physical and biologic injury." This testimony was disputed by the company, whose expert testified that

> an elevated number of chromosome aberrations are not considered an "injury" per se because they do not in and of themselves result in any physical impairment.

Following the reasoning of Werlein, we conclude the trier of fact should resolve this fact dispute.

Further, like the plaintiffs in Werlein, Bryson claims emotional distress damages and medical monitoring expenses because of her alleged chromosome damage. The court in Werlein determined that the existence and extent of these alleged damages also presented fact questions for the jury. Again, following *Werlein*, we conclude that because there are genuine fact issues concerning the existence of Bryson's present injuries and damages, summary judgment on this claim is inappropriate.

Bryson next argues that because she has offered expert evidence that she has a present injury, she need only present evidence that is "fair comment" on the medical implications of chromosome breakage to establish future damages resulting from her increased risk of cancer. Alternatively, Bryson argues that she has presented sufficient evidence to a reasonable medical certainty that entitles her to compensation for future damages as a result of her increased risk of cancer. The district court concluded that because Bryson can neither prove that her increased risk of future harm is more likely than not to occur, nor quantify her increased risk of developing cancer, her claimed damages for increased risk of future harm are too speculative as a matter of law. We agree.

A plaintiff must prove every element of a claim by a preponderance of the evidence. For Bryson to establish her claim for future damages, she must show: (1) that the future harm is more likely than not to occur; and (2) that her future damages are not too speculative. Bryson failed to present evidence on both issues.

We disagree with Bryson's contention that she need only present evidence that is "fair comment" on the medical implications of chromosome breakage. The term "fair comment" has been used to characterize expert medical testimony for purposes of determining the admissibility of evidence, not to provide the standard for proving future injury. Here, Bryson's expert admitted that Bryson's increased risk of cancer could not be measured or quantified. Thus, the evidence presented by Bryson does not, as a matter of law, permit a factfinder to determine that Bryson is more likely than not to develop cancer.

Further, this court [has] affirmed the principle that plaintiffs may not recover damages that are too speculative. The determination of whether damages are too speculative or remote "should usually be left to the judgment of the trial court." Because Bryson has presented no evidence to quantify her risk of developing cancer, we conclude the district court properly granted summary judgment in favor of the company on Bryson's claim for future damages.

DECISION

The district court properly granted summary judgment in favor of the company on Bryson's claim for damages based on an alleged increased risk of future harm because: (1) Bryson has not presented evidence that it is more likely than not that she will develop cancer; and (2) Bryson's claimed damages for the increased risk of cancer are too speculative as a matter of law. We conclude, however, Bryson has presented sufficient evidence to establish a genuine issue of material fact concerning the existence of a present injury and damages as a result of the alleged injury. We, therefore, reverse and remand this claim for further proceedings.

Affirmed in part, reversed in part, and remanded; motion to strike denied.

SHORT, J. (concurring in part, dissenting in part).

I concur insofar as the majority concludes the trial court properly granted summary judgment in favor of Pillsbury Company on Bryson's "risk of cancer" claim. I respectfully dissent on the narrow remand concerning Bryson's "chromosome breakage" claim because there is no evidence supporting an award of damages for present physical injury. Mere allegations of emotional distress and possible medical monitoring expenses are insufficient to create a fact issue on whether Bryson now suffers from a present physical injury.

Even if an asymptomatic chromosome condition constitutes evidence of a present physical injury, Bryson also failed to offer any evidence that her alleged damages are capable of proof to a reasonable certainty. Under these circumstances, Bryson has no compensable injury and Pillsbury Company is entitled to judgment as a matter of law. I would affirm the trial court's grant of summary judgment.

NOTES AND QUESTIONS

1.   How can biomarkers of a genetic, unexpressed or preclinical "injury" help to prove causation and to establish a compensable harm?

> The power of biomarkers to validate latent risk claims is demonstrated by the following hypothetical. A young woman is exposed to vinyl chloride emitted by a nearby factory. A blood test reveals the presence of DNA adducts in her lymphocytes that are consistent with a significant recent exposure to vinyl chloride. Two years later, the woman has a son with a mutation that inactivates ("knocks out") one of his two copies of the *p53* tumor suppressor gene. The mutation has the "genetic fingerprint" that is characteristic of vinyl chloride. Genetic testing of the mother reveals that most of her cells contain no such mutation, although a few of her cells have similar mutations. Moreover, other sequence variations in the mother's *p53* genes confirm that the son's defective copy of the gene came from the mother, thus indicating that the mutation must have arisen in the mother's germ cells. With only one functioning copy of the *p53* gene, the son is at a permanent, significantly increased risk of cancer. A mutation to the remaining functional copy of the *p53* gene, arising either spontaneously or from some other exposure later in life, would almost certainly result in cancer. By providing objective and specific evidence of an increased risk and the probable cause of

such risk, the genetic biomarker strengthens the case for such a plaintiff to recover damages for his permanent and irreversible risk.

Gary E. Marchant, Genetic Susceptibility and Biomarkers in Toxic Injury Litigation, 41 Jurimetrics 67, 87 (2000). See also Jamie A. Grodsky, Genomics and Toxic Torts: Dismantling the Risk-Injury Divide, 59 Stan. L. Rev. 1671 (2007); Gary E. Marchant, Genetic Data in Toxic Tort Litigation, 45 The Brief no. 2 (2016), https://www.americanbar.org/groups/tort_trial_insurance_practice/publications/the_brief/2016_17/winter/genetic_data_in_toxic_tort_litigation/.

2.   Is subclinical damage compensable, either by itself or because it signifies increased risk? In general, the courts have not been receptive to such claims based on products liability, see In re Rezulin Products Liability Litigation, 361 F. Supp.2d 268 (S.D.N.Y. 2005), or emotional distress, see Parker v. Wellman, 230 Fed. Appx. 878 (11th Cir. 2007). A physical injury or disabling sign or symptom is required.

3.   The measure of the damages for increased risk of future harms will, undoubtedly, be smaller than the damages for any harms that actually occur. Why not simply wait to see whether the injury manifests itself and then sue? What effect would statutes of limitation have in calculating whether to sue immediately after the injury or wait until the damage appears clinically? See Christopher H. Schroeder, Corrective Justice and Liability for Increasing Risks, 37 UCLA L. Rev. 439 (1990).

4.   Two other issues are also relevant: (1) the availability of damages for the psychological harm of worrying whether certain illnesses will become manifest, see James F. D'Entremont, Fear Factor: The Future of Cancerphobia and Fear of Future Disease Claims in the Toxicogenomic Age, 52 Loy. L. Rev. 807 (2006); and (2) the damages associated with increased medical monitoring to detect the early symptoms of disease at a time when treatment will be most effective, see James M. Garner et al., Medical Monitoring: The Evolution of a Cause of Action, 30 Envt'l L. Rep. 10,024 (2000).

B. CAUSATION

WINTZ V. NORTHROP CORP.
110 F.3d 508 (7th Cir. 1997).

COFFEY, J.

Plaintiffs-appellants Van Wintz and Jill Wintz, both individually and on behalf of their daughter Jessica (the "Wintzes"), appeal the district court's order granting the jointly-filed motion for summary judgment of defendants-appellees Northrop Corporation ("Northrop") and Eastman Kodak Company ("Kodak"). The Wintzes sought damages for injuries allegedly suffered by Jessica as a result of her *in utero* exposure to the chemical bromide, allegedly contained in photographic developing material manufactured by Kodak and used by Jill Wintz in the course of her employment with Northrop. The questions presented are whether the district court erred in excluding the proffered testimony of a toxicologist hired by the Wintzes, and whether, absent that testimony, the Wintzes failed to establish a genuine issue of fact as to whether exposure to bromide caused injury to Jessica. We affirm.

I.   BACKGROUND

Prior to and during her pregnancy with Jessica, Jill Wintz was employed by Northrop as an Industrial Engineer Associate in Northrop's Defense Systems Division. Her employment with Northrop began in May 1979, and continued through March 1982. From March 1980 through October 1980, while she was pregnant, Jill's duties involved the mixing of certain chemicals manufactured by Kodak to develop photographic film used in the manufacturing process of the "black box" for jet fighter aircraft. One of these chemicals, Kodalith Developer B, contained bromide. The chemicals came in powdered form in paper-type bags, and Jill poured them from the bag into a container for mixing with water. During this process, the powder from the bags would create a dust in the air, and Jill alleges that she inhaled this dust while mixing the chemicals. According to Jill's affidavit, she was "never given or advised to use any type of protective breathing mask or other protective equipment during mixing or use of the chemical powders." Jill Wintz worked in this capacity for Northrop from March 1980 until she took a maternity leave of absence on October 31, 1980, approximately five weeks before giving birth to Jessica, and she mixed the chemicals on a daily basis during this period.

Jessica was born at Lutheran General Hospital in Park Ridge, Illinois on December 6, 1980, and shortly thereafter she began displaying a number of atypical symptoms for newborns. Most noticeably, according to the deposition of Dr. Henry Mangurten, a neonatologist who treated Jessica at that time, she displayed hypotonia (low muscle tone), poor sucking reflexes, and weak or infrequent cry, as well as abnormal facial features. When she was but four days old, the baby was placed in a neonatal intensive care unit and came under Dr. Mangurten's care. In an effort to determine the cause of these abnormal behavioral symptoms, Dr. Mangurten ordered a variety of tests but they came back inconclusive, at which time the specialist saw fit to interview and gain additional background information from Jill Wintz. Upon learning that Jill worked in an environment in which bromide was present, Dr. Mangurten, based on his previous experience in which he had treated a baby with elevated bromide levels and who had displayed symptoms similar to Jessica's, ordered a bromide test on the baby. A urine sample was obtained when she was 11 days old and prior to learning the results of this test, Jessica's condition showed signs of improvement and she was released from the neonatal intensive care unit when she was but 13 days old. Shortly thereafter, the test revealed elevated levels of bromide in Jessica's system.

The doctor, at this time, ordered another urine sample taken when Jessica was 20 days old and this test again revealed the presence of bromide in her system but at a decreased level. This time, Dr. Mangurten also ordered a bromide test on her mother, Jill, which also revealed elevated bromide levels in her system as well.

Dr. Mangurten stated that Jessica's condition had improved somewhat, though not entirely, at the time she was released from the neonatal intensive care unit. According to Dr. Mangurten, Jessica's condition was tracked for roughly four years after she left Lutheran General pursuant to a follow-up program the hospital maintains for infants who have spent time in the neonatal intensive care unit. In an affidavit, Dr. Barbara Burton, Director for the Center of Medical and Reproductive Genetics at Michael Reese Hospital in Chicago, who reviewed Jessica's complete medical records, stated that Jessica has continued to display abnormal symptoms through the present, including strabismus (deviation of the eye), myopia, frequent upper respiratory infections, enamel defects in her teeth, and delayed development in mental and physical milestones. Dr. Burton, who is an expert in genetics and genetic disorders, opined in her affidavit that Jessica's symptoms are all "classical" symptoms of a person afflicted with a genetic disorder known as Prader-Willi Syndrome ("PWS").[1]

In the course of her follow-up care after being discharged, it was learned (and is not disputed by the Wintzes) that Jessica was in fact born with PWS. PWS is caused by a deletion of genetic material from the father's chromosomes. It is a purely genetic disorder which occurs prior to conception, and it cannot be caused by environmental exposure. As the Wintzes have acknowledged, all of the abnormal symptoms Jessica has experienced throughout her life are very similar, if not identical, to those experienced by children with PWS. During his deposition, Dr. Mangurten agreed with the statement that Jessica's developmental problems have "almost certainly" been caused by PWS.

In addition to Dr. Mangurten, the Wintzes listed Gilbert Elenbogen ("Elenbogen"), a toxicologist, as an expert witness. The Wintzes asserted that Elenbogen would testify that exposure to bromide caused Jessica's abnormalities. Elenbogen opined in an affidavit that Jill Wintz's exposure to bromide while mixing the photographic chemicals caused Jessica to be exposed to bromide, and that this exposure, as stated in Elenbogen's affidavit, "caused the child's symptoms at birth and her permanent developmental damage and problems." Elenbogen did acknowledge that Jessica had PWS, and that her symptoms which he attributed to her

---

[1]   Prader-Willi Syndrome is defined as "a congenital disorder characterized by rounded face, almond-shaped eyes, strabismus, low forehead, hypogonadism, hypotomia, insatiable appetite, early hypotonia, failure to thrive, and mental retardation." *Dorland's Illustrated Medical Dictionary* 1638 (28th ed. 1994).

prenatal exposure to bromide were identical to those caused by PWS. No other expert testified for the Wintzes on the issue of causation.

Kodak and Northrop filed a combined motion for summary judgment after deposing Elenbogen and Mangurten. They argued that Elenbogen's testimony was inadmissible under rule 702 of the Federal Rules of Evidence as interpreted by the Supreme Court in Daubert v. Merrell Dow Pharmaceuticals, 509 U.S. 579 (1993). They argued that the toxicologist Elenbogen was not a licensed physician and surgeon and lacked sufficient experience with bromide or with PWS, and was thus not qualified to render an opinion as an expert as to the cause of Jessica's injuries. Northrop and Kodak further argued that, because Elenbogen's opinion that bromide caused Jessica's injuries was inadmissible due to his lack of qualifications, and because Dr. Mangurten agreed in his deposition testimony that PWS was the cause of Jessica's developmental problems, the Wintzes failed to establish a genuine issue of material fact as to whether bromide exposure was a proximate cause of any of Jessica's abnormalities. In a memorandum opinion dated December 21, 1995, the district judge agreed with Kodak and Northrop. The district court entered a summary judgment order in favor of Kodak and Northrop on December 21, and the Wintzes appealed.

* * *

In the present case, Dr. Mangurten's deposition established in clear and unequivocal language that, in his opinion, PWS caused Jessica's long-term developmental problems. It also established that he could not offer an opinion with any reasonable degree of medical certainty that Jessica's short-term problems at birth were caused by bromide, notwithstanding the observation that her symptoms decreased at the same time the bromide levels decreased. Whatever support the Wintzes hope to find in [Champion v. Knasiak, 323 N.E.2d 62 (Ill.App.Ct. 1974)], we do not agree that it can be read to suggest that they did not have the obligation to come forward with affirmative evidence to support their causation argument. Thus, the trial court did not err in concluding that Dr. Mangurten's testimony was insufficient to create a genuine issue of fact as to whether bromide caused any of Jessica's long-term or short-term symptoms.

The district court's decision excluding the proffered testimony of the Wintzes' toxicologist was not manifestly erroneous, and the evidence, when considered in its totality, fell short of raising a genuine issue of material fact as to the cause of Jessica's short-term or long-term symptoms. WE AFFIRM the grant of summary judgment in favor of Kodak and Northrop.

NOTES AND QUESTIONS

1. As indicated in *Bryson* and *Wintz,* genetic information may be helpful to the plaintiff or the defendant.

2.   The issue of causation has been one of the great conundrums of tort law. Toxic injuries and toxicogenomics add a layer of complexity to the issue of causation in fact. For example, scientists may demonstrate convincingly that if 1,000 people are exposed to substance A at B levels for C amount of time per day, over D number of years there will be E cases of cancer, which greatly exceeds the F number of cases for a similar group of unexposed people. Are these facts enough to establish that any particular individual's exposure to substance A caused his or her cancer? If not, what additional evidence is necessary? Genetic biomarkers may help to prove that the exposure actually caused a particular individual's cancer. If the science has not developed appropriate measures for the substance and disease at issue, what level of statistically increased risk should be required to prove causation in fact for legal purposes? See Daniel A. Farber, Toxic Causation, 71 Minn. L. Rev. 1219 (1987); Steve C. Gold, The More We Know, the Less Intelligent We Are?—How Genetic Information Should and Should not, Change Toxic Tort Causation Doctrine, 34 Harv. Envt'l L. Rev. 369 (2010); Sander Greenland & James M. Robins, Epidemiology, Justice, and the Probability of Causation, 40 Jurimetrics J. 321 (2000).

A Closer Look: Benzene causes leukemia, but not all people exposed to benzene get leukemia, and only a small percentage of leukemia cases are caused by benzene exposure. Because it is very difficult to prove that exposure to benzene (e.g., by living next to a chemical plant), caused a plaintiff's leukemia, some courts hold that if exposure to a toxic substance at levels present in the case doubles the risk of disease, then this "general causation" permits recovery. If genetic biomarkers can prove that a plaintiff's leukemia was caused by benzene exposure (e.g., because of a unique mutation pattern), then this establishes "specific causation." The absence of a unique mutation also might be used by a defendant to prove that benzene exposure was not the cause of a plaintiff's leukemia. Are there any concerns about using such genetic information?

C. DAMAGES

MARK A. ROTHSTEIN, PREVENTING THE DISCOVERY OF PLAINTIFF GENETIC PROFILES BY DEFENDANTS SEEKING TO LIMIT DAMAGES IN PERSONAL INJURY LITIGATION
71 Ind. L.J. 877, 878–880 (1996).

Imagine the following situation: Dr. Jane Smith is a thirty-five year-old neurosurgeon who entered private practice three years ago upon completion of her training. She has an annual income of $200,000. One day, while crossing the street from the doctors' parking lot to the hospital, she is run over by a Zippy Express delivery truck, whose unlicensed, intoxicated driver was speeding to a delivery and failed to stop for a red light. As a result of the accident, Dr. Smith has become quadriplegic and will be unable to perform surgery again.

In a negligence action against Zippy Express, a key component of Dr. Smith's economic damages is her lost income. Assuming she would have been able to work for thirty more years, with an income of $200,000 per year, this would amount to six million in current dollars, exclusive of projected earnings increases, merely for lost income.

Suppose, however, that Dr. Smith is in the unaffected, presymptomatic stage of Huntington's disease, amyotrophic lateral sclerosis, or some other late-onset genetic disorder. Further suppose that experts will testify that, in all likelihood, irrespective of the accident, she would not have been able to practice medicine beyond age forty-five and that her life expectancy is fifty years. Applying traditional damages principles, this information would reduce her recovery for economic injury by at least four million dollars.

Zippy Express and its insurers therefore would have a great economic incentive to discover information about Dr. Smith's genetic profile and to introduce this information at trial. Should the defendants be able to discover this information by obtaining access to Dr. Smith's medical records? Should they be able to obtain a court order directing Dr. Smith to submit to genetic testing? Should it matter whether genetic testing previously had been performed on Dr. Smith or whether there was something in her family or medical history to suspect a genetic disorder? Should it matter whether Dr. Smith was suspected of having a genetic risk of a monogenic disorder, such as Huntington's disease, or a multifactorial disorder, such as cancer? What effect, if any, should be given to the penetrance, variable expressivity, and treatability of the disorder? Should it matter if Dr. Smith objects to genetic testing?

* * *

NOTES AND QUESTIONS

1. Should the same rules apply to discovery of genetic information for proof of harm and causation as are applied to estimations of life expectancy?

2. If you think that limits should be placed on the compelled disclosure of genetic information to defendants for proof of damages, should the limitation be judge-made through application of procedural rules or pursuant to legislative enactment?

3. For a further discussion of these issues, see Diane E. Hoffmann & Karen H. Rothenberg, Judging Genes: Implications of the Second Generation of Genetic Tests in the Courtroom, 66 Md. L. Rev. 858 (2007); Anthony S. Niedwiecki, Science Fact or Science Fiction? The Implications of Court-Ordered Genetic Testing Under Rule 35, 34 U.S.F.L. Rev. 295 (2000).

PART VI

PRIVACY AND CONFIDENTIALITY

■ ■ ■

For experts and lay people alike, privacy is the defining issue in determining whether advances in genetics can be integrated into medical practice and other aspects of daily life without unacceptable social consequences. Virtually everyone is in favor of genetic privacy in the abstract, but agreement among individuals and interest groups on this issue rarely extends beyond the abstract.

On closer examination, it is extraordinarily difficult to: (1) reach consensus on the definition of privacy and the related concepts of confidentiality, security, and anonymity; (2) distinguish genetic privacy from more general notions of medical privacy; (3) differentiate among the tangible and intangible benefits and harms associated with the presence or absence of privacy, including the complex concept of genetic discrimination; (4) balance the interests in genetic privacy and confidentiality against other valid social interests, such as research, clinical care, public health, law enforcement, and cost; and (5) devise thoughtful, practical, and effective legislative and regulatory measures to protect genetic privacy.

This chapter challenges you to think critically about genetic privacy and confidentiality. There are few cases in the chapter because cases based on alleged invasions of privacy tend to be context-specific and therefore they are included in, for example, succeeding chapters on insurance and employment. Nevertheless, the readings and statutory materials are crucial because they explore the conceptual foundations on which all genetic privacy and confidentiality law, ethics, and policy are based.

ELLEN WRIGHT CLAYTON ET AL., THE LAW OF GENETIC PRIVACY: APPLICATIONS, IMPLICATIONS, AND LIMITATIONS
J.L. & Biosciences 1, 2–3 (2019), doi:10.1093/jlb/lsz007.

People often view genetic information about themselves as private. Each person's genome, or full complement of DNA, is unique, but the specific variants within an individual's genome may be widely shared with biological relatives or even across the entire human population. This mixed character of the genome—as a uniquely individual assemblage of widely shared common elements—imbues it with a dual private and public significance that confounds any discussion of policy addressing genetic privacy.

On one hand, DNA has been conceptualized as a unique identifier and a person's book of life, which provides insights into many aspects of the person's future, although perhaps not as much as many people might think. This conceptualization leads many people to want to control who has access to genetic information about them and drives calls for strong privacy protection or even personal genetic data ownership. On the other hand, genetic data are not limited to one individual, with information about one person revealing information about the person's close and distant biological relatives. Only by studying genetic information from many people can the significance of the individual's variants be discerned. The importance of understanding the causes of health and disease has led some to argue that people have some obligation to share data about themselves for low-risk research. This public nature and value of the genome makes it difficult to decide what level of control individuals should have and how to provide appropriate privacy protections.

At the same time, the very concept of 'privacy' has evolved in recent decades and a new model of privacy has gained ground. The traditional view of privacy as secrecy or concealment—as a 'right to be let alone'—has grown increasingly strained in the Information Age. The Internet and ubiquitous communication technologies facilitate broad sharing of information, including highly personal information, often without the individual's knowledge or consent. A new theorization of privacy has emerged, in which concealing one's secrets 'is less relevant than being in control of the distribution and use by others' of the data people generate in the course of seeking healthcare, conducting consumer transactions, and going about their lives. 'The leading paradigm on the Internet and in the "real," ' or off-line world, conceives of privacy as a personal right to control the use of one's data', including enjoying access and using it by oneself.

NOTES AND QUESTIONS

1. Privacy is not the same as confidentiality. Confidentiality means that information disclosed in the course of a confidential relationship (e.g., physician-patient) will not be redisclosed outside of the relationship without the consent of the individual who supplied the information. It has been a core value of the medical profession ever since the time of the Hippocratic Oath, which provides, in pertinent part: "And whatsoever I shall see or hear in the course of my profession, as well as outside my profession in my intercourse with men, if it be what should not be published abroad, I will never divulge, holding such things to be holy secrets." The principle of confidentiality is also widely endorsed by the modern ethical codes of the medical profession. See Mark A. Rothstein, Privacy and Confidentiality, in Medical Ethics: Analysis of the Issues Raised by the Codes, Opinions and Statements (Baruch A. Brody et al. eds. 2001).

2.   The confidentiality of genetic information was addressed by the Institute of Medicine's Committee on Assessing Genetic Risks:

> Confidentiality as a principle implies that some body of information is sensitive, and hence, access to it must be controlled and limited to parties authorized to have such access. The information provided within the relationship is given in confidence, with the expectation that it will not be disclosed to others or will be disclosed to others only within limits. The state or condition of nondisclosure or limited disclosure may be protected by moral, social, or legal principles and rules, which can be expressed in terms of rights or obligations.

Committee on Assessing Genetic Risks, Institute of Medicine, Assessing Genetic Risks: Implications for Health and Social Policy 205 (Lori B. Andrews et al. eds. 1994). See also Eugene Pergament, A Clinical Geneticist Perspective of the Patient-Physician Relationship in Genetic Secrets: Protecting Privacy and Confidentiality in the Genetic Era 92 (Mark A. Rothstein ed. 1997); Madison Powers, Genetic Information, Ethics, Privacy and Confidentiality: Overview, in 1 Encyclopedia of Ethical, Legal, and Policy Issues in Biotechnology 405 (Thomas H. Murray & Maxwell J. Mehlman eds. 2000).

3.   Another important concept is security, which refers to the administrative, physical, and technical standards used to ensure that access to electronic personal health information is restricted to those with authorization. The HIPAA Security Rule appears at 45 C.F.R. Part 160, 164 subparts A and C. Among its many provisions are those dealing with access controls, user authentication, transmission security, and breach notification.

CHAPTER 24

GENETIC PRIVACY AND CONFIDENTIALITY

■ ■ ■

I. HEALTHCARE

AMY L. MCGUIRE ET AL., CONFIDENTIALITY, PRIVACY, AND SECURITY OF GENETIC AND GENOMIC TEST INFORMATION IN ELECTRONIC HEALTH RECORDS: POINTS TO CONSIDER

10 Genetics in Med. 495, 495, 499 (2009).

The clinical use of genetic/genomic information is becoming an increasingly important aspect of modern health care delivery. At the same time, the increasing role of health information technology platforms in organizing health information has led to the need to review the confidentiality, privacy, and security of electronic information. Electronic health records (EHRs) provide a useful way to manage complex medical information; as such, EHRs will become established in the future as the means to manage the large and complex datasets that accompany genetic/genomic tests and interpretations. The inclusion of genetic/genomic information in EHRs should inform the determination of disease risk, appropriate drug dosing to avoid adverse events, and the selection of effective treatment. However, electronic health information is portable and mobile; the ease with which information can be disseminated through EHRs raises concern about the potential for unauthorized access to and use of this information. A major policy question, then, is whether special protections should be created for genetic/genomic information that is stored in the EHR.

* * *

The inclusion of genetic/genomic information in the EHR will greatly impact personalized health care by informing disease risk determination, appropriate drug dosing, and the selection of effective treatment or preventive action. To realize the full potential of personalized medicine, however, policies must be implemented to protect the confidentiality, privacy, and security of genetic/genomic test information appropriately with regard to access and use. Genetic/genomic information features a series of attributes that must be carefully considered in the aggregate with regard to policy development. Genetic/genomic data should be afforded the same provisions as other sensitive health information with regard to potential restricted access in the EHR. Protection against potential discrimination based on genetic/genomic information must be ensured, and proper disclosures must also be made for the use of such data for research purposes. Attention to the issues raised by these discussions will help policy developers and health care professionals ensure that confidentiality, privacy, and security are appropriately maintained for genetic/genomic information contained in the EHR.

NOTES AND QUESTIONS

1.   The American Recovery and Reinvestment Act of 2009, Pub. L. 111–5, 123 Stat. 115 (2009), includes the Health Information Technology for Economic and Clinical Health Act (HITECH Act), which commits the nation to shifting from paper to electronic health records (EHRs) in an attempt to make the practice of medicine safer, more effective, and more efficient. The HITECH Act provided substantial grants to develop new technologies and assist in their adoption and implementation. By 2015, aided by $35 billion in federal financial incentives, 78% of physicians and 96% of hospitals had an EHR system certified by HHS.

2.   There are three essential attributes of EHRs and the networks designed to connect them. First, they are interoperable, meaning that they may be accessed and used from remote locations and utilize a standard system for transmitting and receiving information. Second, they are comprehensive, meaning that they compile information from all of an individual's health care encounters with various physicians, hospitals, pharmacies, laboratories, etc. Third, they are longitudinal, meaning that they contain an individual's records over an extended period of time. These three attributes enhance coordination of care, help avoid duplication of services, prevent errors, improve effectiveness of care, and facilitate outcomes and other research. They also challenge privacy, confidentiality, and security by providing easier access to a wider range of health information—sometimes when health care providers or third-party users have no need to know the information. See generally Sharona Hoffman & Andy Podgurski, In Sickness, Health, and Cyberspace: Protecting the Security of Electronic Private Health Information, 48 B.C.L. Rev. 331 (2007): Mark A. Rothstein & Stacey A. Tovino, Privacy Risks of Interoperable Electronic Health Records: Segmentation of Sensitive Information Will Help, 47 J.L. Med. & Ethics 771–777 (2019); Nicolas P. Terry & Leslie P. Francis, Ensuring the Privacy and Confidentiality of Electronic Health Records, 2007 U. Ill. L. Rev. 681 (2007).

II. COMPELLED DISCLOSURES

MARK A. ROTHSTEIN & MEGHAN K. TALBOTT, COMPELLED DISCLOSURES OF HEALTH RECORDS: UPDATED ESTIMATES
45 J.L. Med. & Ethics 149, 153–154 (2017).

* * *

In both the popular media and scholarly literature, breaches of health privacy, confidentiality, and security are often associated with unlawful or unethical actions that result in disclosures of health information to individuals or entities with no right to access them. Although it is important to address wrongful access, disclosure, and use of health information, the focus on wrongful acts frequently overlooks the significant threat to health privacy posed by lawful disclosure of health information to individuals and entities with the economic or other leverage to require individuals to sign authorizations for the disclosure of their health information. We have termed this common practice "compelled disclosures" or "compelled authorizations." It includes instances in which individuals are required to sign an authorization as well as the times in which individuals are required to obtain their own health records and submit them directly.

* * *

Annual Compelled Authorizations in the United States

Type of Authorization	Estimate
Employment entrance examinations	12,320,000
Individual health insurance applications	0
Individual life insurance applications	5,021,000
Individual long-term care insurance applications	65,000
Individual disability insurance applications	303,000
Disability insurance claims (individual and group)	2,160,000
Automobile insurance claims	1,480,000
Social Security Disability Insurance applications	1,930,000
Workers' compensation claims	743,000
Veterans' disability claims	800,000
Personal injury lawsuits	185,000
Total	25,007,000

* * *

We will be the first to concede that "guesstimate" may be a more appropriate description of our calculations than "estimate." In some cases, we were forced to rely on old or incomplete data and had to assume what percentage of health assessments would include the compelled disclosure of health records. Nevertheless, we believe that focusing on possible flaws in our methodology or errors in our estimates would miss the entire point of this research. The simple, indisputable fact is that each year there are millions of lawful, compelled disclosures of health records associated with important activities of individuals with private and public sector entities that have the economic and legal leverage to require disclosure of health information.

The entities we studied have a legitimate need to obtain individual health information, but compelled disclosures often include more than the required information. In many cases, a compelled authorization is for an individual's complete health records, which frequently include sensitive information unrelated to the reason for the disclosure. In other cases, even if the request is for limited health information, health care providers simply disclose the complete record because it is easier, faster, and cheaper than reviewing lengthy files and selecting the information that appears to be relevant. Furthermore, most EHR systems lack the technical capacity to limit disclosures. Although unnecessarily broad disclosure of sensitive health information is one of the greatest sources of health privacy lapses, adopting measures to alleviate the problem has not been a priority for individuals, health care providers, EHR vendors, or policy makers.

* * *

Finally, it bears mentioning that the harms from inadequately protecting health privacy go well beyond embarrassment or even discrimination. When people fear that their medical secrets will not be protected from repeated, harmful disclosures for an unlimited period of time they may be less likely to seek timely care for stigmatizing conditions, such as substance abuse, mental illness, and sexually transmitted infections. The result is to put the individuals' own health at risk as well as to endanger the health of the public.

CHAPTER 25

LEGAL PROTECTIONS FOR MEDICAL AND GENETIC PRIVACY

■ ■ ■

I. CONSTITUTIONAL LAW

NASA v. NELSON
562 U.S. 134 (2011).

JUSTICE ALITO delivered the opinion of the Court.

In two cases decided more than 30 years ago, this Court referred broadly to a constitutional privacy "interest in avoiding disclosure of personal matters." Whalen v. Roe, 429 U.S. 589, 599–600 (1977); Nixon v. Administrator of General Services, 433 U.S. 425, 457 (1977). Respondents in this case, federal contract employees at a Government laboratory, claim that two parts of a standard employment background investigation violate their rights under *Whalen* and *Nixon*. Respondents challenge a section of a form questionnaire that asks employees about treatment or counseling for recent illegal-drug use. They also object to certain open-ended questions on a form sent to employees' designated references.

We assume, without deciding, that the Constitution protects a privacy right of the sort mentioned in *Whalen* and *Nixon*. We hold, however, that the challenged portions of the Government's background check do not violate this right in the present case. The Government's interests as employer and proprietor in managing its internal operations, combined with the protections against public dissemination provided by the Privacy Act of 1974, 5 U.S.C. § 552a, satisfy any "interest in avoiding disclosure" that may "arguably ha[ve] its roots in the Constitution."

The National Aeronautics and Space Administration (NASA) is an independent federal agency charged with planning and conducting the Government's "space activities." NASA's workforce numbers in the tens of thousands of employees. While many of these workers are federal civil servants, a substantial majority are employed directly by Government contractors. Contract employees play an important role in NASA's mission, and their duties are functionally equivalent to those performed by civil servants.

One NASA facility, the Jet Propulsion Laboratory (JPL) in Pasadena, California, is staffed exclusively by contract employees. NASA owns JPL, but the California Institute of Technology (Cal Tech) operates the facility under a Government contract. JPL is the lead NASA center for deep-space robotics and communications.

* * *

Twenty-eight JPL employees are respondents here. Many of them have worked at the lab for decades, and none has ever been the subject of a Government background investigation. At the time when respondents were hired, background checks were standard only for federal civil servants.* * *

The Government has recently taken steps to eliminate this two-track approach to background investigations. In 2004, a recommendation by the 9/11 Commission prompted the President to order new, uniform identification standards for "[f]ederal employees," including "contractor employees." The Department of Commerce implemented this directive by mandating that contract employees with long-term access to federal facilities complete a standard background check, typically the National Agency Check with Inquiries (NACI).

* * *

As noted, respondents contend that portions of [the background check form] violate their "right to informational privacy." This Court considered a similar claim in *Whalen,* which concerned New York's practice of collecting "the names and addresses of all persons" prescribed dangerous drugs with both "legitimate and illegitimate uses." In discussing that claim, the Court said that "[t]he cases sometimes characterized as protecting 'privacy'" actually involved "at least two different kinds of interests": one, an "interest in avoiding disclosure of personal matters"; the other, an interest in "making certain kinds of important decisions" free from government interference. The patients who brought suit in *Whalen* argued that New York's statute "threaten[ed] to impair" both their "nondisclosure" interests and their interests in making healthcare decisions independently. The Court, however, upheld the statute as a "reasonable exercise of New York's broad police powers."

Whalen acknowledged that the disclosure of "private information" to the State was an "unpleasant invasion of privacy," but the Court pointed out that the New York statute contained "security provisions" that protected against "public disclosure" of patients' information, this sort of "statutory or regulatory duty to avoid unwarranted disclosures" of "accumulated private data" was sufficient, in the Court's view, to protect a privacy interest that "arguably ha[d] its roots in the Constitution." The

Court thus concluded that the statute did not violate "any right or liberty protected by the Fourteenth Amendment."

* * *

As was our approach in *Whalen,* we will assume for present purposes that the Government's challenged inquiries implicate a privacy interest of constitutional significance. We hold, however, that, whatever the scope of this interest, it does not prevent the Government from asking reasonable questions of the sort included * * * in an employment background investigation that is subject to the Privacy Act's safeguards against public disclosure.

With these interests in view, we conclude that the challenged portions of both [forms] consist of reasonable, employment-related inquiries that further the Government's interests in managing its internal operations. As to SF-85, the only part of the form challenged here is its request for information about "any treatment or counseling received" for illegal-drug use within the previous year. The "treatment or counseling" question, however, must be considered in context. It is a follow-up to SF-85's inquiry into whether the employee has "used, possessed, supplied, or manufactured illegal drugs" during the past year. The Government has good reason to ask employees about their recent illegal-drug use. Like any employer, the Government is entitled to have its projects staffed by reliable, law-abiding persons who will " 'efficiently and effectively' " discharge their duties. Questions about illegal-drug use are a useful way of figuring out which persons have these characteristics.

In context, the follow-up question on "treatment or counseling" for recent illegal-drug use is also a reasonable, employment-related inquiry. The Government, recognizing that illegal-drug use is both a criminal and a medical issue, seeks to separate out those illegal-drug users who are taking steps to address and overcome their problems. The Government thus uses responses to the "treatment or counseling" question as a mitigating factor in determining whether to grant contract employees long-term access to federal facilities.

This is a reasonable, and indeed a humane, approach, and respondents do not dispute the legitimacy of the Government's decision to use drug treatment as a mitigating factor in its contractor credentialing decisions. Respondents' argument is that, if drug treatment is only used to mitigate, then the Government should change the mandatory phrasing of SF-85—"Include [in your answer] any treatment or counseling received"—so as to make a response optional. As it stands, the mandatory "treatment or counseling" question is unconstitutional, in respondents' view, because it is "more intrusive than necessary to satisfy the government's objective."

We reject the argument that the Government, when it requests job-related personal information in an employment background check, has a constitutional burden to demonstrate that its questions are "necessary" or the least restrictive means of furthering its interests. So exacting a standard runs directly contrary to *Whalen*. The patients in *Whalen*, much like respondents here, argued that New York's statute was unconstitutional because the State could not "demonstrate the necessity" of its program. The Court quickly rejected that argument, concluding that New York's collection of patients' prescription information could "not be held unconstitutional simply because" a court viewed it as "unnecessary, in whole or in part."

That analysis applies with even greater force where the Government acts, not as a regulator, but as the manager of its internal affairs. SF-85's "treatment or counseling" question reasonably seeks to identify a subset of acknowledged drug users who are attempting to overcome their problems. The Government's considered position is that phrasing the question in more permissive terms would result in a lower response rate, and the question's effectiveness in identifying illegal-drug users who are suitable for employment would be "materially reduced." That is a reasonable position, falling within the " 'wide latitude' " granted the Government in its dealings with employees.

* * *

Not only are SF-85 and Form 42 reasonable in light of the Government interests at stake, they are also subject to substantial protections against disclosure to the public. Both *Whalen* and *Nixon* recognized that government "accumulation" of "personal information" for "public purposes" may pose a threat to privacy. But both decisions also stated that a "statutory or regulatory duty to avoid unwarranted disclosures" generally allays these privacy concerns. The Court in *Whalen*, relying on New York's "security provisions" prohibiting public disclosure, turned aside a challenge to the collection of patients' prescription information. In *Nixon*, the Court rejected what it regarded as an even "weaker" claim by the former President because the Presidential Recordings and Materials Preservation Act "[n]ot only . . . mandate[d] regulations" against "undue dissemination," but also required immediate return of any "purely private" materials flagged by the Government's archivists.

Respondents in this case, like the patients in *Whalen* and former President Nixon, attack only the Government's *collection* of information on SF-85 and Form 42. And here, no less than in *Whalen* and *Nixon*, the information collected is shielded by statute from "unwarranted disclosur[e]." The Privacy Act, which covers all information collected during the background-check process, allows the Government to maintain records "about an individual" only to the extent the records are "relevant and necessary to accomplish" a purpose authorized by law. The Act requires written consent before the Government may disclose records pertaining to any individual. And the Act imposes criminal liability for willful violations of its nondisclosure obligations. These requirements, as we have noted, give "forceful recognition" to a Government employee's interest in maintaining the "confidentiality of sensitive information . . . in his personnel files." Like the protections against disclosure in Whalen and Nixon, they "evidence a proper concern" for individual privacy.

* * *

In light of the protection provided by the Privacy Act's nondisclosure requirement, and because the challenged portions of the forms consist of reasonable inquiries in an employment background check, we conclude that the Government's inquiries do not violate a constitutional right to informational privacy.

* * *

For these reasons, the judgment of the Court of Appeals is reversed, and the case is remanded for further proceedings consistent with this opinion.

It is so ordered.

JUSTICE KAGAN took no part in the consideration or decision of this case.

JUSTICE SCALIA, with whom JUSTICE THOMAS joins, concurring in the judgment.

I agree with the Court, of course, that background checks of employees of government contractors do not offend the Constitution. But rather than reach this conclusion on the basis of the never-explained assumption that the Constitution requires courts to "balance" the Government's interests in data collection against its contractor employees' interest in privacy, I reach it on simpler grounds. Like many other desirable things not included in the Constitution, "informational privacy" seems like a good idea—wherefore the People have enacted laws at the federal level and in the states restricting the government's collection and use of information. But it is up to the People to enact those laws, to shape them, and, when they think it appropriate, to repeal them. A federal constitutional right to "informational privacy" does not exist.

* * *

NOTES AND QUESTIONS

1.   Based on *Whalen*, the Court assumed, without deciding, that there was a constitutional right to informational privacy, but still found that the government action was reasonable. Two justices would hold there was no such

constitutional right. Do you think there is much likelihood of success for plaintiffs to allege a constitutional privacy violation? See Mark A. Rothstein, Constitutional Right to Informational Health Privacy in Critical Condition, 39 J.L. Med. & Ethics 280 (2011).

2.   In Matson v. Bd. of Educ., 631 F.3d 57 (2d Cir. 2011), the Second Circuit, relying on circuit precedent, held that there was a limited constitutional right to informational health privacy. It held that the privacy protection afforded medical information will vary with the medical condition. To be protected, the medical condition must be stigmatizing and lead to "discrimination and intolerance." Applying this test, the court held that disclosure of the plaintiff's fibromyalgia was not a constitutional violation. How would the disclosure of genetic information fare under this test? Would it matter what the genetic information revealed?

3.   Even claims involving stigmatizing conditions have not fared well in the courts. For example, in Doe v. Southeastern Pennsylvania Transp. Auth. (SEPTA), 72 F.3d 1133 (3d Cir.1995), cert. denied, 519 U.S. 808 (1996), the plaintiff was an employee who was the manager of his company's employee assistance program. Before he had a prescription filled under the company's drug plan, he asked his supervisor, the head of the medical department, whether the company was able to identify what prescriptions individual employees had filled. When he was assured that the company did not get such information, the employee had his prescription for AZT, an antiviral drug used to treat AIDS, refilled under the company plan. When the pharmacy chain submitted its mandatory utilization report, which included a list of the names of all employees and the medications they were taking, the employer's medical department, including this particular employee's supervisors, learned that he was HIV-positive, a fact that they then indiscriminately shared. In an action for invasion of privacy, the jury awarded the plaintiff $125,000, but the Third Circuit reversed. The court held that the employer's "important interests" in the prescription information outweighed the "minimal intrusion" into the plaintiff's privacy. For a discussion of possible tort actions for invasion of genetic privacy, see June Mary Z. Makdisi, Genetic Privacy: New Intrusion a New Tort?, 34 Creighton L. Rev. 965 (2001).

4.   In what settings and in what ways do you think constitutional privacy issues could be raised with regard to genetics?

II. LEGISLATION

A. STATE LEGISLATION

NEW MEXICO GENETIC INFORMATION PRIVACY ACT
(ENACTED 1998).

N.M. Stat. Ann.

§§ 24–21–2 Definitions.

As used in the Genetic Information Privacy Act [24–21–1 to 24–21–7 NMSA 1978]:

§§ 24–21–3 Genetic analysis prohibited without informed consent; exceptions.

A. Except as provided in Subsection C of this section, no person shall obtain genetic information or samples for genetic analysis from a person without first obtaining informed and written consent from the person or the person's authorized representative.

B. Except as provided in Subsection C of this section, genetic analysis of a person or collection, retention, transmission or use of genetic information without the informed and written consent of the person or the person's authorized representative is prohibited.

C. A person's DNA, genetic information or the results of genetic analysis may be obtained, retained, transmitted or used without the person's written and informed consent pursuant to federal or state law or regulations only:

(1) to identify a person in the course of a criminal investigation by a law enforcement agency;

(2) if the person has been convicted of a felony, for purposes of maintaining a DNA database for law enforcement purposes;

(3) to identify deceased persons;

(4) to establish parental identity;

(5) to screen newborns;

(6) if the DNA, genetic information or results of genetic analysis are not identified with the person or person's family members;

(7) by a court for determination of damage awards pursuant to the Genetic Information Privacy Act [24–21–1 to 24–21–7 NMSA 1978];

(8) by medical repositories or registries;

(9) for the purpose of medical or scientific research and education, including retention of gene products, genetic information or genetic analysis if the identity of the person or person's family members is not disclosed; or

(10) for the purpose of emergency medical treatment consistent with applicable law.

D.   Actions of an insurer and third parties dealing with an insurer in the ordinary course of conducting and administering the business of life, disability income or long-term care insurance are exempt from the provisions of this section if the use of genetic analysis or genetic information for underwriting purposes is based on sound actuarial principles or related to actual or reasonably anticipated experience. However, before or at the time of collecting genetic information for use in conducting and administering the business of life, disability income or long-term care insurance, the insurer shall notify in writing an applicant for insurance or the insured that the information may be used, transmitted or retained solely for the purpose of conducting and administering the business of life, disability income or long-term care insurance, the insurer shall notify in writing an applicant for insurance or the insured that the information may be used, transmitted or retained solely for the purpose of conducting and administering the business of life, disability income or long-term care insurance.

E.   Nothing in Paragraph (5), (6), (8), (9) or (10) of Subsection C of Section 3 [24–21–3 NMSA 1978] of the Genetic Information Privacy Act authorizes obtaining, retaining, transmitting or using a person's DNA, genetic information or the results of genetic analysis if the person, his authorized representative or guardian, or the parent or guardian of a minor child, objects on the basis of religious tenets or practices.

* * *

§§ 24–21–5   Rights of retention.

A.   Unless otherwise authorized by Subsection C of Section 3 [24–21–3 NMSA 1978] of the Genetic Information Privacy Act, no person shall retain a person's genetic information, gene products or samples for genetic analysis without first obtaining informed and written consent from the person or the person's authorized representative. This subsection does not affect the status of original medical records of patients, and the rules of confidentiality and accessibility applicable to the records continue in force.

B.   A person's genetic information or samples for genetic analysis shall be destroyed promptly upon the specific request by that person or that person's authorized representative unless:

(1)   retention is necessary for the purposes of a criminal or death investigation or a criminal or juvenile proceeding;

(2) retention is authorized by order of a court of competent jurisdiction;

(3) retention is authorized under a research protocol approved by an institution review board pursuant to federal law or a medical registry or repository authorized by state or federal law; or

(4) the genetic information or samples for genetic analysis have been obtained pursuant to Subsection C of Section 3 of the Genetic Information Privacy Act.

C. Actions of an insurer and third parties dealing with an insurer in the ordinary course of conducting and administering the business of life, disability income or long-term care insurance are exempt from the provisions of this section. However, before or at the time of collecting genetic information for use in conducting and administering the business of life, disability income or long-term care insurance, the insurer shall notify in writing an applicant for insurance or the insured that the information may be used, transmitted or retained solely for the purpose of conducting and administering the business of life, disability income or long-term care insurance.

D. Nothing in Paragraph (3) or (4) of Subsection B of Section 5 [24–21–5 NMSA 1978] of the Genetic Information Privacy Act authorizes retention of a person's authorized representative or guardian, or the parent or guardian of a minor child, objects on the basis of religious tenets or practices.

NOTES AND QUESTIONS

1. As of 2019, most states had enacted genetic privacy laws similar to the New Mexico law in at least some respects, although they may be limited to certain entities, such as employers or insurers. These laws typically contain one or more of the following provisions: (1) personal access to genetic information is required; (2) informed consent is required to perform a genetic test or obtain, retain, or disclose genetic information; (3) genetic information or DNA samples are defined as personal property; and (4) penalties for violations are provided. State genetic privacy laws are collected and updated by the LawSeq project at the University of Minnesota, http://lawseq.umn.edu.

2. What are the benefits of enacting a law such as New Mexico's? Are there costs?

B. FEDERAL LEGISLATION

HEALTH INSURANCE PORTABILITY AND ACCOUNTABILITY ACT (HIPAA)

The Health Insurance Portability and Accountability Act (HIPAA), 42 U.S.C. §§ 300gg–300gg–2, enacted in 1996, contains a provision that required Congress to enact privacy legislation by August 21, 1999. If Congress failed to enact legislation by the deadline, the law directed the Secretary of Health and Human Services to promulgate regulations for the privacy of medical information. Following unsuccessful attempts to pass federal legislation, proposed regulations were issued in November 1999. After considering over 52,000 comments, the final regulations were issued on December 2000, and had a compliance date of April 2003. The regulations appear at 45 C.F.R. Parts 160 and 164. The key substantive provisions of HIPAA related to genetics and group health insurance are discussed in Chapter 26. The following excerpt describes in very basic terms the complicated and detailed HIPAA Privacy Rule.

OFFICE FOR CIVIL RIGHTS, DEPARTMENT OF HEALTH AND HUMAN SERVICES, SUMMARY OF THE HIPAA PRIVACY RULE

https://www.hhs.gov/hipaa/for-professionals/privacy/laws-regulations/index.html.

Who is Covered by the Privacy Rule

The Privacy Rule, as well as all the Administrative Simplification rules, apply to health plans, health care clearinghouses, and to any health care provider who transmits health information in electronic form in connection with transactions for which the Secretary of HHS has adopted standards under HIPAA (the "covered entities").

Health Plans. Individual and group plans that provide or pay the cost of medical care are covered entities. Health plans include health, dental, vision, and prescription drug insurers, health maintenance organizations ("HMOs"), Medicare, Medicaid, Medicare+Choice and Medicare supplement insurers, and long-term care insurers (excluding nursing home fixed-indemnity policies). Health plans also include employer-sponsored group health plans, government and church-sponsored health plans, and multi-employer health plans. There are exceptions—a group health plan with less than 50 participants that is administered solely by the employer that established and maintains the plan is not a covered entity.

* * *

Health Care Providers. Every health care provider, regardless of size, who electronically transmits health information in connection with certain transactions, is a covered entity. These transactions include claims, benefit eligibility inquiries, referral authorization requests, or other transactions for which HHS has established standards under the HIPAA Transactions Rule.

* * *

Health Care Clearinghouses. *Health care clearinghouses* are entities that process nonstandard information they receive from another entity into a standard (i.e., standard format or data content), or vice versa. In most instances, health care clearinghouses will receive individually identifiable health information only when they are providing these processing services to a health plan or health care provider as a business associate.

* * *

Business Associates

Business Associate Defined. In general, a business associate is a person or organization, other than a member of a covered entity's workforce, that performs certain functions or activities on behalf of, or provides certain services to, a covered entity that involve the use or disclosure of individually identifiable health information. Business associate functions or activities on behalf of a covered entity include claims processing, data analysis, utilization review, and billing. Business associate services to a covered entity are limited to legal, actuarial, accounting, consulting, data aggregation, management, administrative, accreditation, or financial services. However, persons or organizations are not considered business associates if their functions or services do not involve the use or disclosure of protected health information, and where any access to protected health information by such persons would be incidental, if at all. A covered entity can be the business associate of another covered entity.

* * *

What Information is Protected

Protected Health Information. The Privacy Rule protects all "individually identifiable health information" held or transmitted by a covered entity or its business associate, in any form or media, whether electronic, paper, or oral. The Privacy Rule calls this information "protected health information (PHI)."

* * *

General Principle for Uses and Disclosures

Basic Principle. A major purpose of the Privacy Rule is to define and limit the circumstances in which an individual's protected heath information may be used or disclosed by covered entities. A covered entity may not use or disclose protected health information, except either: (1) as the Privacy Rule permits or requires; or (2) as the individual who is the subject of the information (or the individual's personal representative) authorizes in writing.

Required Disclosures. A covered entity must disclose protected health information in only two situations: (a) to individuals (or their personal representatives) specifically when they request access to, or an accounting of disclosures of, their protected health information; and (b) to HHS when it is undertaking a compliance investigation or review or enforcement action.

Permitted Uses and Disclosures

Permitted Uses and Disclosures. A covered entity is permitted, but not required, to use and disclose protected health information, without an individual's authorization, for the following purposes or situations: (1) To the Individual (unless required for access or accounting of disclosures); (2) Treatment, Payment, and Health Care Operations; (3) Opportunity to Agree or Object; (4) Incident to an otherwise permitted use and disclosure; (5) Public Interest and Benefit Activities; and (6) Limited Data Set for the purposes of research, public health or health care operations. Covered entities may rely on professional ethics and best judgments in deciding which of these permissive uses and disclosures to make.

* * *

Authorized Uses and Disclosures

Authorization. A covered entity must obtain the individual's written authorization for any use or disclosure of protected health information that is not for treatment, payment or health care operations or otherwise permitted or required by the Privacy Rule. A covered entity may not condition treatment, payment, enrollment, or benefits eligibility on an individual granting an authorization, except in limited circumstances.

An authorization must be written in specific terms. It may allow use and disclosure of protected health information by the covered entity seeking the authorization, or by a third party. Examples of disclosures that would require an individual's authorization include disclosures to a life insurer for coverage purposes, disclosures to an employer of the results of a pre-employment physical or lab test, or disclosures to a pharmaceutical firm for their own marketing purposes.

All authorizations must be in plain language, and contain specific information regarding the information to be disclosed or used, the person(s) disclosing and receiving the information, expiration, right to revoke in writing, and other data.

Psychotherapy Notes. A covered entity must obtain an individual's authorization to use or disclose psychotherapy notes with the following exceptions:

* * *

Limiting Uses and Disclosures to the Minimum Necessary

Minimum Necessary. A central aspect of the Privacy Rule is the principle of "minimum necessary" use and disclosure. A covered entity must make reasonable efforts to use, disclose, and request only the minimum amount of protected health information needed to accomplish the intended purpose of the use, disclosure, or request. A covered entity must develop and implement policies and procedures to reasonably limit uses and disclosures to the minimum necessary. When the minimum necessary standard applies to a use or disclosure, a covered entity may not use, disclose, or request the entire medical record for a particular purpose, unless it can specifically justify the whole record as the amount reasonably needed for the purpose.

The minimum necessary requirement is not imposed in any of the following circumstances: (a) disclosure to or a request by a health care provider for treatment; (b) disclosure to an individual who is the subject of the information, or the individual's personal representative; (c) use or disclosure made pursuant to an authorization; (d) disclosure to HHS for complaint investigation, compliance review or enforcement; (e) use or disclosure that is required by law; or (f) use or disclosure required for compliance with the HIPAA Transactions Rule or other HIPAA Administrative Simplification Rules.

* * *

State Law

Preemption. In general, State laws that are contrary to the Privacy Rule are preempted by the federal requirements, which means that the federal requirements will apply. "Contrary" means that it would be impossible for a covered entity to comply with both the State and federal requirements, or that the provision of State law is an obstacle to accomplishing the full purposes and objectives of the Administrative Simplification provisions of HIPAA. The Privacy Rule provides exceptions to the general rule of federal preemption for contrary State laws that (1) relate to the privacy of individually identifiable health information and provide greater privacy protections or privacy rights with respect to such information, (2) provide for the reporting of disease or injury, child abuse, birth, or death, or for public health surveillance, investigation, or intervention, or (3) require certain health plan reporting, such as for management or financial audits.

* * *

Enforcement and Penalties for Noncompliance

Compliance. The Standards for Privacy of Individually Identifiable Health Information (Privacy Rule) establishes a set of national standards for the use and disclosure of an individual's health information—called protected health information—by covered entities, as well as standards for providing individuals with privacy rights to understand and control how their health information is used. The Department of Health and Human Services, Office for Civil Rights (OCR) is responsible for administering and enforcing these standards and may conduct complaint investigations and compliance reviews.

* * *

Civil Money Penalties. OCR may impose a penalty on a covered entity for a failure to comply with a requirement of the Privacy Rule. Penalties will vary significantly depending on factors such as the date of the violation, whether the covered entity knew or should have known of the failure to comply, or whether the covered entity's failure to comply was due to willful neglect. Penalties may not exceed a calendar year cap for multiple violations of the same requirement.

* * *

Criminal Penalties. A person who knowingly obtains or discloses individually identifiable health information in violation of the Privacy Rule may face a criminal penalty of up to $50,000 and up to one-year imprisonment. The criminal penalties increase to $100,000 and up to five years imprisonment if the wrongful conduct involves false pretenses, and to $250,000 and up to 10 years imprisonment if the wrongful conduct involves the intent to sell, transfer, or use identifiable health information for commercial advantage, personal gain or malicious harm. The Department of Justice is responsible for criminal prosecutions under the Privacy Rule.

III. COMMON LAW

MARK A. ROTHSTEIN, GENETIC STALKING AND VOYEURISM: A NEW CHALLENGE TO PRIVACY
57 Kan. L. Rev. 539, 546–548 (2009).

* * *

In 1890, two young law partners from Boston, Samuel D. Warren and Louis D. Brandeis, published a seminal article on the right to privacy at common law. According to most historians, the impetus for the article was Warren's great concern about the allegedly intrusive social reporting of the Boston press, but it is not clear what, if any, specific stories aroused his ire.

Brandeis collaborated with Warren to write their seminal and legendary law review article, *The Right to Privacy*. Although it was inspired by perceived abuses by the press, Warren and Brandeis argued more broadly in favor of a comprehensive common law right of individuals to be free of unwanted and unreasonable intrusions of their "inviolate personality."

Warren and Brandeis expanded on Judge Thomas M. Cooley's notion of privacy as the right "to be let alone." They proposed a general legal principle of protecting "the privacy of private life" and urged creating a cause of action to redress "the more flagrant breaches of decency and propriety . . ." They concluded their article by observing the irony between the different standards used by the law in dealing with public and private interferences with peaceful habitation: "The common law has always recognized a man's house as his castle, impregnable, often, even to its own officers engaged in the execution of its commands. Shall the courts thus close the front entrance to constituted authority, and open wide the back door to idle or prurient curiosity?"

Louis D. Brandeis

Despite its well-deserved acclaim in the academic literature, the Warren and Brandeis article did not immediately translate into a concrete common law doctrine that could be invoked to redress private wrongs. Beginning in the 1930s, courts in several states began to recognize a right of privacy, but the contours of the right were not well defined. The task of developing a cohesive doctrine fell to William L. Prosser who, in a famous law review article in 1960, proposed that the common law right to privacy was actionable in tort in four discrete situations: (1) intrusion upon the plaintiff's seclusion or solitude, or into his private affairs; (2) public disclosure of embarrassing private facts about the plaintiff; (3) publicity which places the plaintiff in a false light in the public eye; and (4) appropriation, for the defendant's advantage, of the plaintiff's name or likeness.

Some scholars have argued that, in carving out limited categories of protected interests, Prosser engaged in reductionism and oversimplification of the human dignity embodied in the right to privacy. Nevertheless, the *Restatement (Second) of Torts* adopted Prosser's classifications, and the limited, categorical approach to common law torts for invasion of privacy steadily gained widespread acceptance in the United States.

NOTES AND QUESTIONS

1.   Of the four common law torts for invasion of privacy, public disclosure of private facts is the one most likely to be alleged in the context of genetics. According to the *Restatement (Second) of Torts* § 652D, there are four essential elements to the tort: (1) disclosure to the public or a large number of persons; (2) of a fact that is private in nature; (3) which would be highly offensive to a reasonable person; and (4) is not of a legitimate concern to the public. This theory has been used when other types of health information were unreasonably disclosed without consent. See, e.g., Urbaniak v. Newton, 277 Cal.Rptr. 354 (Cal. Civ. App. 1991) (disclosure of HIV status); Levias v. United Airlines, 500 N.E.2d 370 (Ohio App. 1985) (disclosure of reproductive health).

2.   Are common law invasion of privacy actions appropriate to redress invasion of genetic privacy? If not, why not, and what would be better?

IV.   DATA PRIVACY LEGISLATION

MARK A. ROTHSTEIN & STACEY A. TOVINO, CALIFORNIA TAKES THE LEAD ON DATA PRIVACY
49 Hastings Center Report No. 5, at 4–5 (2019).

* * *

Signaling a new direction in state data privacy and consumer protection law, the California Consumer Privacy Act (CCPA) establishes important rights and protections for California residents with regard to the collection, use, disclosure, and sale of their personal information. The CCPA is the brainchild of Alastair Mactaggart, a wealthy Californian who spent millions of dollars gathering signatures to place an initiative on the state's November 2018 ballot and subsequently negotiated a deal with lawmakers to enact a scaled-back version of his desired legislation. The CCPA was signed into law by Governor Jerry Brown in mid-summer 2018 and most of the CCPA will become operational on January 1, 2020. The California Attorney General has enforcement authority beginning six months after publication of final regulations implementing the CCPA or July 1, 2020, whichever is sooner. Because the CCPA is certain to spur similar legislation in other states and to affect national and international businesses that collect data from California's 40 million residents, understanding the CCPA is important for all data-driven industries, including the health care industry.

* * *

The rights set forth in the CCPA apply to personal information, defined as information that identifies, relates to, describes, is capable of being associated with, or could reasonably be linked, directly or indirectly, with a particular consumer or household. The CCPA includes an illustrative list of items that fall within this definition, including names, physical addresses, email addresses, Internet Protocol addresses, geolocation data, social security numbers, telephone numbers, driver's license numbers, account numbers, biometric identifiers, physical descriptions, medical information, insurance information, financial information, employment information, purchase histories, and browser histories, as well as inferences that can be drawn from the preceding items regarding consumer preferences, psychological trends, predispositions, behavior, attitudes, intelligence, abilities, and aptitudes.

The CCPA gives California residents several important privacy rights with respect to their personal information. These rights include: (1) the right to be informed of the categories of personal information being collected and the purposes for which such information shall be used, (2) the right not to have additional personal information collected without further notice, (3) the right to request deletion of personal information, (4) the right to know whether personal information is being sold or disclosed and to whom, (5) the right to opt out of the sale of personal information, (6) the right to access personal information, and (7) the right to equal services and prices regardless of whether they exercise privacy rights under the CCPA. The first, fourth, sixth, and seventh rights are similar to rights that patients and insureds have under the HIPAA Privacy Rule. The first, second, third, fourth, and sixth rights are similar to rights that data subjects have under the EU General Data Protection Regulation (GDPR).

* * *

Because of the timing of its enactment and its codification of "fair information practices," the CCPA has been referred to as "GDPR light." The actual GDPR contains several rights of data subjects that go beyond any current laws in the United States. These include the right of data subjects to have their data erased, the so-called right to be forgotten; the right of data subjects to receive their personal data in a commonly used format and have it transmitted to another data controller, the so-called right to data portability; and the right not to be subject to an adverse decision based solely on the application of artificial intelligence. Some of these rights could be adopted by amending the CCPA or by new legislation in other jurisdictions.

The CCPA has inspired the introduction of consumer privacy legislation in several states, including Connecticut, Hawaii, Maryland, Massachusetts, Rhode Island, and Texas. Some of the state bills would go beyond the CCPA, such as by authorizing private lawsuits by individuals for all violations of the privacy law, not just data breaches. Because the CCPA and some of the other state consumer privacy bills exempt information subject to the HIPAA Privacy Rule, the results may be paradoxical. Thus, the enactment of more stringent, state consumer privacy laws could mean that information about individuals' Amazon book orders and other common consumer transactions would be protected more vigorously than their health information.

NOTES AND QUESTIONS

1.   Beyond the healthcare area, genetic information has been used for identification, establishing relationships, predicting future health, and other purposes. Thus, there are numerous applications of genetic information, including the following: (1) criminal justice (e.g., identification, criminal capacity); (2) education (e.g., admissions, educational placement); (3) employment (e.g., sensitivity to occupational exposures); (4) family law (e.g., adoption, child custody, and parentage); (5) government benefits (e.g., etiology of a health condition); (6) immigration (e.g., relatedness of individuals); (7) insurance (e.g., life expectancy, source of disability); (8) personal injury litigation (e.g., causation in toxic tort cases); and (9) real property (e.g., future earning capacity for mortgages, risk for dementia in retirement facilities). Which uses do you think raise the most serious threats to privacy? See Ellen Wright Clayton et al., The Law of Genetic Privacy: Applications, Implications, and Limitations, J.L. & Biosciences 1, 21–26 (2019), doi:10.1093/jlb/lsz007.

Food for Thought: In the U.S., any concerns about genetic privacy have been addressed through genetic-specific legislation at the state or federal level. By contrast, the General Data Protection Regulation GDPR represents a comprehensive effort by the E.U. to establish "data protection" through a single piece of legislation. Why do you think the U.S. prefers genetic-specific approaches? Are such approaches better at protecting genetic privacy? See Mark A. Rothstein, Genetic Exceptionalism and Legislative Pragmatism, 35 Hastings Ctr. Rep. No. 4, at 27–33 (2005).

PART VII

INSURANCE

■ ■ ■

Insurance is a system for pooling resources against contingent risks. In the United States, the insurance market is a private, largely for-profit enterprise, and there are thousands of companies selling insurance. Many of the insurance products, such as homeowners insurance, auto insurance, fire and flood insurance, property and casualty insurance, and professional liability insurance attempt to protect against the harms caused by natural occurrences or human errors. Other product lines, including medical expense insurance (health insurance), life insurance, disability insurance, and long-term care insurance, attempt to cover expenses and provide replacement income in the event of unpredictable illness or death.

Risk classification lies at the heart of insurance. To use life insurance as an example, it is impossible to predict how long any particular individual will live. But, it is possible to predict how long the average member of a clearly defined group will live. Thus, if we know the individual's age, current health status, occupation, lifestyle (e.g. smoking, drinking), and other relevant factors, it is possible to predict the average life expectancy of a group of individuals with the same relevant characteristics. Underwriting is the process of assigning individuals to actuarially relevant groups for purposes of predicting risk and thus deciding the appropriate terms and rates for insurance coverage.

Predictive genetic assessments of individuals have a curious relationship with insurance. If insurance is based on coverage against unknown risks, to the extent that any individual's future illness or death becomes predictable, then insurance would be either (1) unnecessary (where there is little chance of serious illness or death within a given period of time) or (2) unavailable or unaffordable (where there is a virtual certainty of serious illness or death in a given period of time).

Genetic prognostications involving asymptomatic individuals have not yet reached the point where it is possible to make accurate estimates of future illness and death. This is true for monogenic disorders with high penetrance rates, and predictions are even more venturesome for complex disorders and disorders with lower rates of penetrance. Nevertheless, because risk classification is concerned with group experience rather than individual experience, it is clear that genetic information may well be relevant in risk classification.

The interests of consumers and insurers may be summarized in the following way. First, consumers are concerned that genetic information may be used inaccurately, such as during the early 1970s when some unaffected carriers of sickle cell trait were denied access to insurance despite a lack of scientific evidence of increased risk of morbidity or mortality. Second, they are concerned about the invasion of their privacy in insurance companies requiring that they undergo genetic tests they would prefer not to take or companies obtaining, retaining, and disclosing their genetic information. Third, consumers assert that even actuarially accurate insurance decisions may result in great unfairness in denying them access to essential services such as health care and long-term care.

On the other hand, insurers are extremely worried about adverse selection. This is the tendency of those who need insurance the most to purchase it and in the greatest amounts. Insurers argue that as more genetic tests are run in the clinical setting and by direct-to-consumer companies, greater numbers of individuals learn of their genetic risks. Those who learn that they are at greater risk of illness are more likely to seek insurance. Insurers assert that unless they have access to the same information as the individuals, then it is impossible to assign policy holders to the appropriate risk pool for purposes of underwriting. The result is that low-risk individuals will be subsidizing the policies of high-risk individuals who have knowledge of their genetic risks, resulting in unfairness among policy holders as well as threatening the economic viability of the insurance companies.

Because of conflicts between the consumer and insurer positions, the use of genetic information in insurance is one of the most contentious social issues arising from the genetics revolution. Among the many questions raised are the following: First, when is the science sufficiently developed that it is appropriate to use genetic information in risk classification? Second, even if actuarially justified, are there social reasons why genetic information should not be used? Answering this question demands an inquiry into the social function of the particular insurance product; the harms associated with obtaining, storing, and using the information; and the existence of alternatives to a genetic-based risk classification scheme. Third, how should the insurance industry be regulated to accomplish social policy?

In this part we will consider the use of genetic information in four main contexts: health, life, disability, and long-term care insurance. Although this area has been a fertile ground for scholarship and legislative activity at all levels, there have been few cases thus far. As you consider these materials, try to determine the underlying social policies at issue and whether each proposal or enactment operates to further those policies.

CHAPTER 26

HEALTH INSURANCE

■ ■ ■

I. BACKGROUND

The American system for payment of health care is incredibly complicated. It is public and private, commercial and noncommercial, federal and state, group and individual, premium-based and tax-supported. Efforts to make the system more effective, efficient, and equitable invariably succeed in making the system more complex.

According to the U.S. Census Bureau, in 2018, employer-based health insurance covered 55.1% of the population for some or all of the calendar year, followed by Medicaid (10.8%), Medicare (17.8%), direct-purchase coverage (14.1%), and military coverage (3.6%). Note that multiple coverage in a single year accounts for the sum total greater than 100%. A total of 27.5 million people (8.5%) did not have health insurance at any point during the year. U.S. Census Bureau, Health Insurance Coverage in the United States: 2018 (Nov. 2019).

Government-sponsored health coverage is not medically underwritten. If an individual satisfies the statutory criteria (e.g., age or permanent disability for Medicare; income limits for Medicaid), then the individual's health status is irrelevant. Non-government health coverage principally has been employer-sponsored group health plans and individual health insurance. Both of these private markets used to be relatively unregulated, but over the last 40 years a series of enactments have attempted to make health coverage more widely available and in accord with public notions of fairness.

Several federal laws dealing with private health coverage have had significant effects on genetic-based distinctions and genetic information in health coverage. The following are some of the key laws and some of their relevant provisions.

- The Employee Retirement Income Security Act of 1974 (ERISA), 29 U.S.C. §§ 1001–1046, regulates employer-sponsored pension and welfare plans—the latter includes health coverage. ERISA does not require employers to provide any benefits, but if they do the beneficiaries are given federal protections to enforce employer promises.

- The Health Insurance Portability and Accountability Act of 1996 (HIPAA), Pub. L. No. 104–191, 110 Stat. 1936, limits the ability of employer-sponsored group health plans (both commercially insured and self-insured) to apply preexisting condition exclusions to individuals moving from one job to another and prohibits the charging of differential premiums to individuals within a group plan.

- The Genetic Information Nondiscrimination Act of 2008 (GINA), 42 U.S.C. § 2000ff, prohibits health insurers in both the individual and group markets from discriminating on the basis of "genetic information," but the law does not protect adverse treatment based on an individual's health condition that has already manifested.

- The Affordable Care Act of 2010 (ACA), Pub. L. No. 111–148, 124 Stat. 119, prohibits medical underwriting in the individual health insurance market, and it attempts to guard against adverse selection by requiring large employers (those with 50 or more employees) to provide coverage for "essential health benefits." The ACA also establishes health marketplaces for individuals to purchase coverage, and it provides government subsidies for those with a limited income.

Traditionally, states have been responsible for regulating all forms of insurance sold in the state. Thus, it is not surprising that state genetic nondiscrimination in health insurance laws actually predate federal involvement. As of 2019, every state except Mississippi has enacted legislation prohibiting one or more aspects of genetic-based discrimination. With the increasingly significant role of federal legislation, however, state measures have become less important.

II. STATE LAWS

State genetic nondiscrimination laws were first enacted in the early 1970s to combat irrational sickle cell trait discrimination that arose from the federal government's poorly conceived and implemented sickle cell screening programs. Florida, Louisiana, and North Carolina enacted the first laws prohibiting discrimination in employment and health insurance. In 1981, New Jersey enacted a broader law that prohibited discrimination based on an individual's "atypical hereditary cellular or blood type," defined to include sickle cell trait, hemoglobin C trait, thalassemia trait, Tay-Sachs trait, or cystic fibrosis trait. Oregon, New York, Wisconsin, and other states followed suit. In the 1990s, with the Human Genome Project serving as the impetus, numerous other states enacted laws prohibiting genetic discrimination in health insurance. Because ERISA preempts state regulation of employer-sponsored group health plans, these state laws applied only to individual health insurance and some small, non-employer group plans. For an updated list of the state laws, see http://www.genome.gov/27552194.

KAN. STAT. ANN. § 40–2259
(ENACTED 1997, amended 2010).

40–2259. Genetic screening or testing; prohibiting the use of; exceptions. (a) As used in this section, "genetic screening or testing" means a laboratory test of a person's genes or chromosomes for abnormalities, defects or deficiencies, including carrier status, that are linked to physical or mental disorders or impairments, or that indicate a susceptibility to illness, disease or other disorders, whether physical or mental, which test is a direct test for abnormalities, defects or deficiencies, and not an indirect manifestation of genetic disorders.

(b) An insurance company, health maintenance organization, nonprofit medical and hospital, dental, optometric or pharmacy corporation, or a group subject to K.S.A. 12–2616 et seq., and amendments thereto, offering group policies providing hospital, medical or surgical expense benefits, shall not:

(1) Require or request directly or indirectly any individual or a member of the individual's family to obtain a genetic test;

(2) require or request directly or indirectly any individual to reveal whether the individual or a member of the individual's family has obtained a genetic test or the results of the test, if obtained by the individual or a member of the individual's family;

(3) condition the provision of insurance coverage or health care benefits on whether an individual or a member of the individual's family has obtained a genetic test or the results of the test, if obtained by the individual or a member of the individual's family; or

(4) consider in the determination of rates or any other aspect of insurance coverage or health care benefits provided to an individual whether an individual or a member of the individual's family has obtained a genetic test or the results of the test, if obtained by the individual or a member of the individual's family;

(5) require any individual, as a condition of enrollment or continued enrollment, to pay a premium or contribution which is greater than such premium or contribution for a similarly situated individual on the basis of whether the individual or a member of the individual's family has obtained a genetic test or the results of such test; or

(6)   adjust premium or contribution amounts on the basis of whether the individual or a member of the individual's family has obtained a genetic test or the result of such test.

(c)   Subsection (b) does not apply to an insurer writing life insurance, disability income insurance or long-term care insurance coverage.

(d)   An insurer writing life insurance, disability income insurance or long-term care insurance coverage that obtains information under paragraphs (1) or (2) of subsection (b), shall not:

(1)   Use the information contrary to paragraphs (3) or (4) of subsection (b) in writing a type of insurance coverage other than life for the individual or a member of the individual's family; or

(2)   provide for rates or any other aspect of coverage that is not reasonably related to the risk involved.

NOTES AND QUESTIONS

1.   The Kansas statute is typical of the state genetic nondiscrimination laws, although each one differs to some degree. Would the Kansas law prohibit discrimination in health insurance based on an individual's family history of genetic disease? Should insurers be prohibited from considering such information? Does the Kansas law prohibit an individual from voluntarily submitting favorable genetic information to an insurer to get a lower rate?

2.   The exclusion in the Kansas law of life, disability, and long-term care insurance is typical of most of the state laws. These other forms of insurance are discussed later in this chapter.

III.   FEDERAL LAWS

HEALTH INSURANCE PORTABILITY AND ACCOUNTABILITY ACT
42 U.S.C. §§ 300gg—300gg-2.

(ALSO CODIFIED IN PART AT 26 U.S.C. § 9801, AND IN FULL AT 29 U.S.C. §§ 1181–1191c.)

PART A—GROUP MARKET REFORMS

Subpart 1—Portability, Access, and Renewability Requirements

§ 300gg.   Increased portability through limitation on preexisting condition exclusions

(a) Limitation on preexisting condition exclusion period; crediting for periods of previous coverage

Subject to subsection (d) of this section, a group health plan, and a health insurance issuer offering group health insurance coverage, may, with respect to a participant or beneficiary, impose a preexisting condition exclusion only if—

(1)　such exclusion relates to a condition (whether physical or mental), regardless of the cause of the condition, for which medical advice, diagnosis, care, or treatment was recommended or received within the 6-month period ending on the enrollment date;

(2)　such exclusion extends for a period of not more than 12 months (or 18 months in the case of a late enrollee) after the enrollment date; and

(3)　the period of any such preexisting condition exclusion is reduced by the aggregate of the periods of creditable coverage (if any, as defined in subsection (c)(1) of this section) applicable to the participant or beneficiary as of the enrollment date.

(b)　Definitions

For purposes of this part—

(1)　Preexisting condition exclusion

(A)　In general

The term "preexisting condition exclusion" means, with respect to coverage, a limitation or exclusion of benefits relating to a condition based on the fact that the condition was present before the date of enrollment for such coverage, whether or not any medical advice, diagnosis, care, or treatment was recommended or received before such date.

(B)　Treatment of genetic information

Genetic information shall not be treated as a condition described in subsection (a)(1) of this section in the absence of a diagnosis of the condition related-to such information.

* * *

§ 300gg–1.

(a)　In eligibility to enroll

(1)　In general

Subject to paragraph (2), a group health plan, and a health insurance issuer offering group health insurance coverage in connection with a group health plan, may not establish rules for eligibility (including continued eligibility) of any individual to enroll under the terms of the plan based on any of the following health status-related factors in relation to the individual or a dependent of the individual:

(A)　Health status.

(B) Medical condition (including both physical and mental illnesses).

(C) Claims experience.

(D) Receipt of health care.

(E) Medical history.

(F) Genetic information.

(G) Evidence of insurability (including conditions arising out of acts of domestic violence).

(H) Disability.

(2) No application to benefits or exclusions

To the extent consistent with section 701, paragraph (1) shall not be construed—

(A) to require a group health plan, or group health insurance coverage, to provide particular benefits other than those provided under the terms of such plan or coverage, or

(B) to prevent such a plan or coverage from establishing limitations or restrictions on the amount, level, extent, or nature of the benefits or coverage for similarly situated individuals enrolled in the plan or coverage.

(3) Construction

For purposes of paragraph (1), rules for eligibility to enroll under a plan include rules defining any applicable waiting periods for such enrollment.

NOTES

1.   HIPAA was enacted in 1996, and the language applicable to genetic information was included late in the legislative process. HIPAA applies to employer-sponsored group health plans, the main avenue by which individuals obtain health care coverage in the private sector. According to HIPAA, genetic information may not be considered to be a preexisting condition and may not be used as a basis for denying coverage or setting rates.

2.   HIPAA does not require that any employer offer health benefits, it does not set a defined minimum benefits package, it does not limit the amount of money that employers charge employees to participate in the plan, and it does not prohibit an employer from dropping coverage altogether. HIPAA also does not apply to individual health insurance policies or non-employer group plans. The more comprehensive legislation was enacted later.

GENETIC INFORMATION NONDISCRIMINATION ACT (GINA)
P.L. 110–233 (2008).

* * *

SEC. 2. FINDINGS.

Congress makes the following findings:

* * *

(5) Federal law addressing genetic discrimination in health insurance and employment is incomplete in both the scope and depth of its protections. Moreover, while many States have enacted some type of genetic non-discrimination law, these laws vary widely with respect to their approach, application, and level of protection. Congress has collected substantial evidence that the American public and the medical community find the existing patchwork of State and Federal laws to be confusing and inadequate to protect them from discrimination. Therefore, Federal legislation establishing a national and uniform basic standard is necessary to fully protect the public from discrimination and allay their concerns about the potential for discrimination, thereby allowing individuals to take advantage of genetic testing, technologies, research, and new therapies.

TITLE I—GENETIC NONDISCRIMINATION IN HEALTH INSURANCE

SEC. 101. AMENDMENTS TO EMPLOYEE RETIREMENT INCOME SECURITY ACT OF 1974.

(a) NO DISCRIMINATION IN GROUP PREMIUMS BASED ON GENETIC INFORMATION.—Section 702(b) of the Employee Retirement Income Security Act of 1974 (29 U.S.C. 1182(b)) is amended—

* * *

(3) NO GROUP-BASED DISCRIMINATION ON BASIS OF GENETIC INFORMATION.—

(A) IN GENERAL.—For purposes of this section, a group health plan, and a health insurance issuer offering group health insurance coverage in connection with a group health plan, may not adjust premium or contribution amounts for the group covered under such plan on the basis of genetic information.

* * *

SEC. 102. AMENDMENTS TO THE PUBLIC HEALTH SERVICE ACT.

* * *

(b) AMENDMENT RELATING TO THE INDIVIDUAL MARKET.—

(1) IN GENERAL.—The first subpart 3 of part B of title XXVII of the Public Health Service Act (42 U.S.C. 300gg–51 et seq.) (relating to other requirements) is amended—

SEC. 2753. PROHIBITION OF HEALTH DISCRIMINATION ON THE BASIS OF GENETIC INFORMATION.

(a) PROHIBITION ON GENETIC INFORMATION AS A CONDITION OF ELIGIBILITY.—

(1) IN GENERAL.—A health insurance issuer offering health insurance coverage in the individual market may not establish rules for the eligibility (including continued eligibility) of any individual to enroll in individual health insurance coverage based on genetic information.

(2) RULE OF CONSTRUCTION.—Nothing in paragraph (1) or in paragraphs (1) and (2) of subsection (e) shall be construed to preclude a health insurance issuer from establishing rules for eligibility for an individual to enroll in individual health insurance coverage based on the manifestation of a disease or disorder in that individual, or in a family member of such individual where such family member is covered under the policy that covers such individual.

(b) PROHIBITION ON GENETIC INFORMATION IN SETTING PREMIUM RATES.—

(1) IN GENERAL.—A health insurance issuer offering health insurance coverage in the individual market shall not adjust premium or contribution amounts for an individual on the basis of genetic information concerning the individual or a family member of the individual.

(2) RULE OF CONSTRUCTION.—Nothing in paragraph (1) or in paragraphs (1) and (2) of subsection (e) shall be construed to preclude a health insurance issuer from adjusting premium or contribution amounts for an individual on the basis of a manifestation of a disease or disorder in that individual, or in a family member of such individual where such family member is covered under the policy that covers such individual. In such case, the manifestation of a disease or disorder in one individual cannot also be used as genetic information about other individuals covered under the policy issued to such individual and to further increase premiums or contribution amounts.

(c) PROHIBITION ON GENETIC INFORMATION AS PREEXISTING CONDITION.—

(1) IN GENERAL.—A health insurance issuer offering health insurance coverage in the individual market may not, on the basis of genetic information, impose any preexisting condition exclusion (as defined in section 2701(b)(1)(A)) with respect to such coverage.

(2) RULE OF CONSTRUCTION.—Nothing in paragraph (1) or in paragraphs (1) and (2) of subsection (e) shall be construed to preclude a health insurance issuer from imposing any preexisting condition exclusion for an individual with respect to health insurance coverage on the basis of a manifestation of a disease or disorder in that individual.

(d) GENETIC TESTING.—

(1) LIMITATION ON REQUESTING OR REQUIRING GENETIC TESTING.—A health insurance issuer offering health insurance coverage in the individual market shall not request or require an individual or a family member of such individual to undergo a genetic test.

(2) RULE OF CONSTRUCTION.—Paragraph (1) shall not be construed to limit the authority of a health care professional who is providing health care services to an individual to request that such individual undergo a genetic test.

MARK A. ROTHSTEIN, GINA AT TEN AND THE FUTURE OF GENETIC NONDISCRIMINATION LAW

48 Hastings Center Report No. 3, at 5–6 (2018).

* * *

Even within the two areas of its current applicability, health insurance and employment, GINA has major gaps in coverage. Title I of GINA prohibits discrimination in health insurance on the basis of genetic information. Section 101(d)(6)(A) of GINA defines genetic information with respect to any individual as "(i) such individual's genetic tests; (ii) the genetic tests of family members of such individual [section 101(d)(5) (B) defines "family member" to include up to fourth-degree relatives]; and (iii) the manifestation of a disease or disorder in family members of such individual." GINA does not prohibit discrimination based on an individual's own health history because such a provision would prohibit health insurers from using health status in underwriting. The Affordable Care Act, enacted in 2010, prohibits discrimination based on health status, making Title I of GINA largely irrelevant. If Congress repealed the ACA or significantly amended it with regard to health insurance underwriting, then GINA would once again have a role in prohibiting a subset of health-based discrimination attributable to genetic information.

Another gap in coverage stems from GINA's narrow conception and definition of "genetic." Section 101(d)(7)(A) defines a "genetic test" as "an analysis of human DNA, RNA, chromosomes, proteins or metabolites that detects genotypes, mutations, or chromosomal changes." The definition does not appear to cover epigenetic marks, microbiome data, or various other emerging biological measures. As a matter of science, GINA has been frozen in time for at least ten years, and it may be increasingly difficult to prove discrimination resulting from information developed by emerging technologies.

AFFORDABLE CARE ACT OF 2010

On March 30, 2010, President Barack Obama signed the Health Care and Education Reconciliation Act, P.L. 111–152, also known as the Reconciliation Act, making changes to the Patient Protection and Affordable Care Act, P.L. 111–148, also known as the Affordable Care Act, or ACA, which passed one week earlier. The Acts collectively make numerous changes to existing laws and add a variety of new programs in an effort to expand access to health care, improve quality, prohibit discriminatory practices by insurers, and reduce costs. The legislation was designed to augment rather than supplant employer-based group health plans, and in several ways the new laws attempt to promote and support the role of employers in health care finance.

President Obama signing into law the Affordable Care Act, March 23, 2010.
Photo credit: Pete Souza.

The health reform law is a notoriously long and complicated piece of legislation. The following discussion focuses on a selection of key issues.

EMPLOYER RESPONSIBILITIES

Large Employer Penalty. Under the ACA, employers are not required to provide health insurance coverage; however, beginning in 2014, certain large employers (those with 50 or more employees) that do not offer health insurance to their employees will be penalized. The ACA provides that "applicable large employers" that do not offer minimum essential health coverage under an eligible employer-sponsored plan, and that have at least one full-time employee who enrolls in a plan on the state health exchange using a federal premium tax credit or costsharing reduction, will be liable for a penalty. This penalty is also known as the "play-or-pay" mandate and the "free rider penalty." ACA § 1513 imposes a penalty in the amount of $2,000 on large employers that do not offer minimum essential health coverage each year (or $166.67 for each month the employer does not provide a plan), multiplied by the number of full-time employees. The first 30 employees do not count towards the penalty. The penalties for employers with 100 or more employees were postponed until January 1, 2015, and for employers with 50–99 employees they were postponed until January 1, 2016.

An "applicable large employer" is defined as an employer with at least 50 full-time employees on business days during the preceding calendar year. A "full-time employee" is defined as an employee who works an average of at least 30 hours per week. "Essential health benefits" includes the following non-comprehensive list of features:

(A) Ambulatory patient services;

(B) Emergency services;

(C) Hospitalization;

(D) Maternity and newborn care;

(E) Mental health and substance use disorder services, including behavioral health treatment;

(F) Prescription drugs;

(G) Rehabilitative and habilitative services and devices;

(H) Laboratory services;

(I) Preventive and wellness services and chronic disease management;

and

(J) Pediatric services, including oral and vision care.

Furthermore, large employers that offer coverage described above but whose coverage is not "affordable" or whose coverage does not provide a certain value must pay an additional penalty. To be "affordable" the premium of the employer-sponsored plan must cost less than 9.5% of the employee's household income. The plan must also provide a minimum value of at least 60% of the coverage (i.e., the employer's share must constitute 60% of the employee's covered medical expenses). If the large employer does not meet either of these minimum requirements of coverage, the employer will be liable for a penalty in the amount of $3,000 per year for each full-time employee (or $250 each month that the employer offers coverage below these levels). ACA § 1513(c)(2) provides a limitation on this penalty, which cannot exceed $2,000 per full-time employee per year (or $166.67 for each month), and the first 30 employees will not count towards the penalty.

Exempt from these penalties are large employers with seasonal workers and large employers that have over 50 full-time employees for only 120 days or less out of the calendar year, and the employees in excess of the 50 employees during that 120-day period are seasonal workers. A "seasonal worker" is defined as a "worker who performs labor or services on a seasonal basis as defined by the Secretary of Labor," and retail workers employed exclusively during holiday seasons.

Automatic Enrollment. The ACA amended the Fair Labor Standards Act (FLSA) to impose another duty on larger employers. Larger employers that have more than 200 full-time employees and offer group health plans are required to enroll automatically new full-time employees in a health benefits plan. They are also required to continue the enrollment of current employees. These employers must provide adequate notice to their employees of the automatic enrollment program, along with an opportunity for the employee to opt out of the program. Employees must affirmatively opt out of the program if they do not want coverage under their employer. The relevant provision is silent regarding the effective date of this mandate, but most experts have interpreted the provision to be effective in 2014.

Lifetime and Annual Limits. As of 2014, lifetime and annual limits are prohibited.

Rescissions. Rescissions of coverage for enrollees once they are covered are prohibited, except in cases of fraud or intentional misrepresentation of material fact (e.g., where employer has misstated its claims experience to obtain a group health policy). This provision took effect in 2010.

Coverage of Dependents. Individual and group health plans that provide coverage to dependents must continue to make coverage available to adult dependents up to age 26, regardless of marriage status (effective 2010).

Coverage of Individuals with Preexisting Conditions. Exclusions are prohibited for children up to age 18 with preexisting conditions (effective 2010). The prohibition with respect to preexisting conditions was extended to adults beginning in 2014.

Appeals Process. An internal and external appeals process must be established for appeals of coverage determinations and claims. The plan must allow an enrollee to review his or her file, present evidence and testimony, and receive continued coverage pending the outcome of the appeals process. Notice of the available internal and external processes must be given to enrollees (effective 2010). The internal process and external process both must meet requirements under certain state and/or federal law, and both processes must be updated with any new standards published by the Secretary of HHS.

Nondiscrimination. The ACA has a number of provisions designed to prohibit discrimination, shaping rules ranging from enrollment eligibility to marketing. Insurers are prohibited from having eligibility rules for enrollment based on health status, medical condition (including physical or mental illnesses) or medical history, claims experience, receipt of health care, genetic information, disability, evidence of insurability, or any factor determined appropriate by HHS (effective 2014). In addition, there is a prohibition on eligibility rules based on wages, or rules that otherwise have the effect of discriminating in favor of higher wage employees (effective six months after enactment). Insurers are also prohibited from utilizing discriminatory premium rates. Premium rates may only vary based only on the following factors: family composition, age, tobacco use, and geographic area. No rating variation is allowed based on health, race, or gender (effective 2014). Insurers may not employ marketing practices that have the effect of discouraging enrollment by individuals with significant health needs.

STATE HEALTH EXCHANGES

By January 1, 2014, states were required to establish an "American Health Benefit Exchange" or state health exchange, where individuals who do not have coverage under their employer can purchase qualified health plans. States are also required to establish a Small Business Health Options Program, or "SHOP Exchange," to assist small employers in enrolling their employees in qualified health plans. The state may establish only one exchange to serve both individuals and small employers; moreover, states may establish subsidiary exchanges for different geographical regions, and more than one state can coordinate to establish an interstate health exchange with the approval of the Secretary of HHS. The exchange will facilitate the purchase of health coverage by providing a website where individuals and small employers can compare different plans, which are assigned ratings by the exchange. The state health exchange must be a government agency or nonprofit entity established by the state. Only qualified health plans may be offered in the exchange.

As of 2019, only 12 states and the District of Columbia have health exchanges. Individuals in other states use the federal health exchange.

NONDISCRIMINATION BASED ON GENETIC INFORMATION

The ACA contains only one provision on genetics in the entire act, but it is very important. Section 2705 of the ACA (42 U.S.C. § 300gg–4) provides: "A group health plan or health insurance issuer offering group or individual health insurance may not establish rules for new or continued eligibility based on several health status-related factors, including genetic information."

NOTES AND QUESTIONS

1. How does this provision differ from the relevant provisions under HIPAA and GINA?

2. Does the ACA strike the right balance between risk and responsibility? See Tom Baker, Health Insurance, Risk, and Responsibility after the Patient Protection and Affordable Care Act, 159 U. Pa. L. Rev. 1577 (2011); Jessica L. Roberts, Healthism: A Critique of the Antidiscrimination Approach to Health Insurance and Health-Care Reform, 2012 Ill. L. Rev. 1159.

3. If the ACA were repealed or significantly weakened, what do you think would happen to the genetic nondiscrimination provision or the protections for individuals with genetic conditions?

CHAPTER 27

LIFE INSURANCE

∎ ∎ ∎

MARK A. ROTHSTEIN, TIME TO END THE USE OF GENETIC
TEST RESULTS IN LIFE INSURANCE UNDERWRITING
46 J.L. Med. & Ethics 794, 795–797 (2018).

* * *

**Insurer access to genetic test results is unnecessary to avoid
adverse selection**

* * *

Relatively few genetic-related disorders have demonstrable
importance for medical underwriting in life insurance because they must
have the following six characteristics. First, they must be adult-onset. A
person having a disorder with childhood onset, such as type 1 diabetes, will
be symptomatic by the time of a typical application for life insurance.
Second, they must have a high penetrance, which means a significant
likelihood that a gene variant will be expressed. Third, they must have a
high absolute risk, meaning there is a substantial risk that an individual
with a risk-conferring genotype will get the disorder. Fourth, they must
have a high relative risk, meaning that individuals with the risk-conferring
genotype are significantly more likely to express the particular condition
than other individuals. Fifth, there must be a high mortality rate for the
condition and a lack of effective treatment, especially if the disease is not
detected early. Sixth, there must be a lack of family history of the disorder,
because if there were a family history then genetic test results would be
less valuable. The lack of family history for a life insurance applicant with
a positive genetic test is most likely to occur when a young adult applies
for life insurance before the applicant's parent, the carrier of the autosomal
dominant allele, has begun to exhibit symptoms or the affected parent has
died of other causes before reaching the age when the genetic-related
condition would manifest. Some conditions meeting these six criteria are
early-onset Alzheimer's disease; some neurodegenerative diseases, such as
amyotrophic lateral sclerosis and Huntington disease; some hereditary
cancers, such as some breast and colon cancers; and some syndromic
conditions, including Li-Fraumeni syndrome and Lynch syndrome.

* * *

Maintaining the privacy of genetic test results will save lives

The most powerful argument in favor of ending the use of genetic test results in life insurance underwriting is that doing so will save lives. A wealth of survey data indicate that many at-risk individuals are reluctant to undergo genetic testing or genome sequencing for two main reasons. First, some individuals do not think they can handle the psychological strain associated with a result indicating a high risk of serious illness. Second, other individuals decline testing in clinical and research settings because they fear the potential economic consequences of the results in terms of genetic discrimination in employment and various types of insurance. Genetic counselors confirm these survey results with numerous personal accounts. The economic fears are rational, even though there have been few reported incidents of genetic discrimination. GINA only prohibits discrimination based on genetic information in health insurance and employment. The few state laws to address life insurance add little protection. One of the most restrictive state laws, in Vermont, prohibits genetic testing as a condition of applying for any type of insurance as well as using the results of genetic tests of family members. Life insurance companies may still exclude from coverage or charge higher rates to individuals at genetically increased risks based on the results of genetic tests performed in the clinical setting and documented in an applicant's health record. Therefore, it seems that even in Vermont many individuals would be reluctant to undergo genetic testing.

For some at-risk individuals the failure to undergo genetic testing and to embark on heightened surveillance and appropriate prophylactic or therapeutic intervention can be catastrophic. This is especially the case for certain gene-mediated cancers, including hereditary nonpolyposis colon cancer, familial adenomatous polyposis colon cancer, and hereditary diffuse gastric cancer. Early detection and timely intervention can markedly improve these individuals' long-term survival.

* * *

VERMONT. STAT. ANN. TIT. 18, CH. 217
(ENACTED 1997).

§ 9331. Definitions

For purposes of this chapter:

* * *

(2) "DNA" means deoxyribonucleic acid and "RNA" means ribonucleic acid.

* * *

(6) "Genetic information" means the results of "genetic testing" contained in any report, interpretation, evaluation, or other record thereof.

(7)(A)　"Genetic testing" means a test, examination or analysis that is diagnostic or predictive of a particular heritable disease or disorder and is of:

(i)　a human chromosome or gene;

(ii)　human DNA or RNA; or

(iii)　a human genetically encoded protein.

(B) The test for human genetically encoded protein referred to in subdivision (A)(iii) of this subdivision shall be generally accepted in the scientific and medical communities as being specifically determinative for the presence or absence of a mutation, alteration, or deletion of a gene or chromosome.

(C) For the purposes of sections 9332 and 9333 of this title, as they apply to insurers, section 9334 of this title, and section 4727 of Title 8, and notwithstanding any language in this section to the contrary, "genetic testing" does not include:

(i)　a test, examination or analysis which reports on an individual's current condition unless such a test, examination or analysis is designed or intended to be specifically determinative for the presence or absence of a mutation, alteration, or deletion of a gene or chromosome; or

(ii)　a test, examination or analysis of a human chromosome or gene, of human DNA or RNA, or of a human genetically encoded protein that is diagnostic or predictive of a particular heritable disease or disorder, if, in accordance with generally accepted standards in the medical community, the potential presence or absence of a mutation, alteration or deletion of a gene or chromosome has already manifested itself by causing a disease, disorder or medical condition or by symptoms highly predictive of the disease, disorder or medical condition.

(8) "Insurance" means a policy of insurance regulated under Title 8, offered or issued in this state, including health, life, disability and long-term care insurance policies, hospital and medical service corporation service contracts, and health maintenance organization benefit plans.

* * *

§ 9334.　Genetic testing as a condition of insurance coverage

(a)　No policy of insurance offered for delivery or issued in this state shall be underwritten or conditioned on the basis of:

(1)　any requirement or agreement of the individual to undergo genetic testing; or

(2) the results of genetic testing of a member of the individual's family.

(b) A violation of this section shall be considered an unfair method of competition or unfair or deceptive act or practice in the business of insurance in violation of section 4724 of Title 8.

(c) In addition to other remedies available under the law, a person who violates this section shall be subject to the enforcement provisions available under Title 8.

§ 9335. Remedies

(a) Any person who intentionally violates section 9333 or subsection 9334(a) of this chapter shall be imprisoned not more than one year or fined not more than $10,000.00, or both.

(b) Any person aggrieved by a violation of this chapter may bring an action for civil damages, including punitive damages, equitable relief, including restraint of prohibited acts, restitution of wages or other benefits and reinstatement, costs, and reasonable attorney's fees and other appropriate relief.

NOTES AND QUESTIONS

1. Although most states have enacted legislation addressing genetic discrimination in health insurance, only a handful of states have enacted legislation dealing with other forms of insurance. In California, a life or disability insurance carrier may not refuse to sell or renew a policy "solely by reason of the fact that the person to be insured carries a gene which may, under some circumstances, be associated with disability in that person's offspring, but which causes no adverse effects on the carrier." Cal. Ins. Code § 10143(a). Is this provision helpful? Note that another provision prohibits differentiation "because of a physical or mental impairment, except where the refusal, limitation or rate differential is based on sound actuarial principles or is related to actual and reasonably anticipated experience." Cal. Ins. Code § 10144.

> **Food for Thought:** The use of genetic information in life insurance has been considered in numerous countries around the world. Many countries already have acted to limit the use of genetic test results in life insurance. In the U.S., life insurance is a matter of state law, and some states have enacted laws purporting to regulate the use of genetic information in life insurance, although they are weak, and none limit the ability of life insurers to use the results of genetic tests previously run in the clinical setting. Suppose you have been invited by your state legislature to testify on a new bill. What are your most persuasive and politically appealing arguments in favor of limiting the use of genetic information or genetic test results in life insurance? What are the most persuasive and politically appealing arguments against such legislation? What is the difference between regulating "information" versus "test results"?

2. Enacting a law prohibiting genetic discrimination in life insurance raises several difficult policy issues, including the following: (1) whether an insurer may require or use the results of genetic tests of family members; (2)

whether genetically at-risk individuals may voluntarily submit favorable genetic test results; (3) whether insurers may use genetic test results for life insurance policies above a certain amount and, if so, what amount; (4) whether insurers may charge higher rates to individuals at a genetically increased risk and, if so, how much; (5) whether genetic test results may be used for certain approved genetic tests and, if so, how the approval process would work; (6) whether legislation would be necessary if there were an industry-wide policy of not using genetic test results; and (7) whether antitrust laws would prevent the adoption of such an industry-wide policy. How would you address these issues? See Mark A. Rothstein, Time to End the Use of Genetic Test Results in Life Insurance Underwriting, 46 J.L., Med. & Ethics 794, 799 (2018).

3.   Legislation prohibiting the use of genetic test results by life insurers has been enacted in numerous countries, including Argentina, Belgium, Bulgaria, Denmark, Estonia, France, Germany, Iceland, Ireland, Israel, Lithuania, Luxembourg, the Netherlands, Portugal, Sweden, and Switzerland. In other countries, such as Canada and the UK, life insurers have agreed to moratoria on the use of genetic test results, often for policies below a certain threshold.

CHABNER V. UNITED OF OMAHA LIFE INSURANCE CO.
225 F.3d 1042 (9th Cir. 2000).

HUG, J.

* * *

Howard Chabner suffers from a progressive condition called facioscapulohumeral muscular dystrophy (FSH MD), a rare form of muscular dystrophy. The condition has confined Chabner to a wheelchair since 1991 and has caused "marked wasting" of his extremities. Chabner takes medication to help control the condition, and his doctor administers annual electrocardiograms to detect any cardiomyopathy that may arise.

On May 3, 1993, Chabner, who was 35 years old at the time, applied to United for whole life insurance. United forwarded Chabner's application to an underwriter who had experience in underwriting insurance policies for applicants with muscular dystrophy, but not with FSH MD. United possessed no internally developed actuarial data for people with FSH MD, and so its underwriter turned to external sources to estimate Chabner's mortality risk. The underwriter, who was not a doctor, arranged to have Chabner examined by a paramedic, reviewed Chabner's medical records, and consulted two underwriting source materials: the Cologne Life Reinsurance Company's "Life Underwriting Manual" ("Cologne manual"); and "Medical Selection of Life Risks" by R.D.C. Brackenridge and W. John Elder ("Brackenridge manual"). After reviewing these materials, the underwriter authorized a policy with a "Table 6" rating, which corresponded to a mortality rate of 150 percent above standard.

United offered Chabner a $100,000 whole life policy at a cost of $1,076 per year. Of the $1,076 annual premium, $305.44 was applied to the cost of insurance, and the remainder was invested in the policy's cash accumulation and surrender values. By contrast, even though the annual premium for a standard whole life policy (without an increased mortality rating) would have been the same $1,076, only $155.44 of that annual premium would have been applied to the cost of insurance, which would result in an additional $150 being invested in the policy's cash accumulation and surrender values each year.

Chabner accepted the policy, but inquired about the reason for his nonstandard premium. United's Vice President and Senior Medical Director of Underwriting sent Chabner a letter attempting to explain the nonstandard rating. In the letter, United acknowledged that FSH MD "has only a small effect on mortality" and stated that it reduced life expectancy by four years for a non-smoking man of his age. Unsatisfied, Chabner wrote United on two more occasions to inquire why his premium was 96.5% greater than standard if his condition had only a small effect on mortality. United did not respond, and Chabner filed this action.

Chabner filed his original complaint in California Superior Court on January 3, 1995, alleging violations of California's Insurance Code, its Business and Professions Code, its Unruh Civil Rights Act, and common law fraud. After United removed the case to federal court based on diversity jurisdiction, Chabner amended his complaint to add a claim under the ADA. Chabner sought class certification and moved for summary judgment on all but his fraud claim. The district court denied class certification, but granted Chabner's motion for summary judgment. The district court held that the ADA applies to insurance underwriting, that California law provides Chabner with a private cause of action for the alleged violation of the state insurance code, and that United's actions in this case violated the ADA, the California Insurance Code and the Business and Professions Code, and the Unruh Civil Rights Act.

* * *

I.   THE ADA

Chabner alleges that the nonstandard premium that United charged him for his insurance policy violated the ADA. Recently, however, we held that although Title III of the ADA requires an insurance office to be physically accessible to the disabled, it does not address the terms of the policies the insurance companies sell. See Weyer v. Twentieth Century Fox Film Corp., 198 F.3d 1104, 1115 (9th Cir.2000). We therefore hold that United did not violate the ADA by offering Chabner a nonstandard policy.

Title III of the ADA provides: "No individual shall be discriminated against on the basis of disability in the full and equal enjoyment of the goods, services, facilities, privileges, advantages, or accommodations of any place of public accommodation by any person who owns, leases (or leases to), or operates a place of public accommodation." 42 U.S.C. § 12181(a). The ADA also includes a "safe harbor" provision, which says that "[the ADA] shall not be construed to prohibit or restrict ... an insurer ... from underwriting risks, classifying risks, or administering such risks that are based on or not inconsistent with State law. . . ." 42 U.S.C. § 12201(c).

Weyer, which was handed down after the district court's order was issued, concerned the question of whether an insurance company that administers an employer-provided disability plan was a "place of public accommodation" under Title III of the Americans with Disabilities Act. We found that the term "place of public accommodation" required a connection between the good or service complained of and an actual physical place. As we explained: "[c]ertainly, an insurance office is a place where the public generally has access. But this case is not about such matters as ramps and elevators so that disabled people can get to the office. The dispute in this case, over terms of a contract that the insurer markets through an employer, is not what Congress addressed in the public accommodations provisions." In adopting this approach, we followed the Third and Sixth Circuits, each of which agreed that an insurance company that administered an employer-provided disability plan was not a "place of public accommodation" under the ADA because the employees received their benefits through employment, and not through a public accommodation. See Parker v. Metropolitan Life Ins. Co., 121 F.3d 1006, 1010–12 (6th Cir.1997) (en banc); Ford v. Schering-Plough Corp., 145 F.3d 601, 612–13 (3d Cir.1998). Taking these cases at face value, we are led to conclude that a similar distinction between "access" and "content" applies to this case. Here, we reiterate our observation, set forth in *Weyer*, that "an insurance office must be physically accessible to the disabled but need not provide insurance that treats the disabled equally with the non-disabled." Therefore, we do not uphold the district court's decision based upon the ADA.

II. CALIFORNIA LAW

A. Business and Professions Code section 17200 and Insurance Code section 10144

In his complaint Chabner alleged violations of California Insurance Code section 10144, and California Business and Professions Code section 17200. Insurance Code Section 10144 provides, in relevant part: "No insurer issuing [life insurance] shall refuse to insure, or refuse to continue to insure ... or charge a different rate for the same coverage solely because of a physical or mental impairment, except where the refusal ... or rate differential is based on sound actuarial principles or is related to actual and reasonably anticipated experience. . . ." Cal. Ins. Code § 10144. This statutory provision would have prohibited United from charging Chabner a nonstandard premium due to his FSH MD, unless the premium was based on sound actuarial principles or was related to actual and reasonably anticipated experience. However, it is unclear whether this insurance code section provides Chabner with a private cause of action. The parties did not address this issue in their briefs, and therefore we do not address it.

Chabner, however, also claimed violations of California Business and Professions Code section 17200. Section 17200 is part of the Unfair Competition Law, Cal. Bus. & Prof. Code §§ 17200–18209, and provides, in relevant part, that "unfair competition shall mean and include any unlawful, unfair or fraudulent business act or practice." Cal. Bus. & Prof. Code § 17200. Private causes of action for violations of Business and Professions Code section 17200 are authorized by Business and Professions Code section 17204. The district court held that Insurance Code section 10144 may be used to define the contours of a private cause of action under Business and Professions Code section 17200. We agree.

* * *

As applied to this case, the district court was correct in holding that Chabner could maintain a cause of action under section 17200 for United's alleged violation of section 10144. Setting the premium for a life insurance policy can quite "properly be called a business practice." Also, United's alleged misconduct (charging Chabner a discriminatory premium that is neither actuarially sound nor based on reasonably anticipated experience) would run afoul of section 10144, if proven. Accordingly, the prerequisites for "borrowing" a violation of section 10144 and treating it as a violation of section 17200 exist in this case.

* * *

B. The Unruh Civil Rights Act

Chabner also claims that United's actions violated California's Unruh Civil Rights Act. The Unruh Civil Rights Act provides, in relevant part, that "[a]ll persons within the jurisdiction of this state are free and equal, and no matter what their . . . disability are entitled to the full and equal accommodations, advantages, facilities, privileges, or services in all business establishments of every kind whatsoever." Cal. Civ. Code § 51. The Act also provides that a violation of the ADA is also a violation of the Unruh Act. Cal. Civ. Code § 51. The district court held that because United had violated the ADA, it also violated the Unruh Act. In light of our decision in Weyer v. Twentieth Century Fox Film Corp., 198 F.3d 1104 (9th Cir.2000), as discussed above, the district court's decision cannot be upheld on this basis.

We may, however, "affirm the district court on a ground not selected by the district judge so long as the record fairly supports such an alternative disposition." Chabner, and the State of California as amicus curiae, argue that United's actions violated the Unruh Act, regardless of whether they also violated the ADA. We agree that Chabner's allegations support an Unruh Civil Rights Act claim independently of the alleged ADA violation.

The Unruh Civil Rights Act works to ensure that all persons receive the full accommodations of any business within California, regardless of the person's disabilities. Cal. Civ. Code § 51. The insurance business is subject to the Unruh Civil Rights Act. Cal. Ins. Code § 1861.03 (a). Unruh prevents more than discrimination in access to a business or its services; it also prevents discrimination in the form of pricing differentials. However, disparities in treatment and pricing that are reasonable do not violate the Unruh Act. The critical question, therefore, is whether the nonstandard premium United charged Chabner was "reasonable."

To determine whether the nonstandard premium was reasonable, we are again informed by Insurance Code section 10144. Section 10144 prevents an insurer from charging "a different rate for the same coverage solely because of a physical or mental impairment," unless the "rate differential is based on sound actuarial principles or is related to actual and reasonably anticipated experience." Cal. Ins. Code § 10144. If Chabner's nonstandard premium was based on "sound actuarial principles" or "actual and reasonably anticipated experience," then it would certainly be reasonable for purposes of the Unruh Act because it would have been specifically allowed by statute. By contrast, if the premium was not based on one of the section 10144 prongs, then there would be no reasonable justification for it, and in that case we may consider the nonstandard premium to be arbitrary and a violation of the Unruh Act. Therefore, we hold that if United violated Insurance Code section 10144, it also violated the Unruh Act, but if section 10144 authorized United's actions, then Chabner's Unruh Act claim necessarily fails as well.

* * *

D. *Summary Judgment*

* * *

The parties argue at length about the proper definitions of "sound actuarial principles" or "actual and reasonably anticipated experience." For example, they dispute whether an insurance company must base its rating decisions on "hard data" that is specific to each person, or whether it may take into account more generalized estimates of mortality when it lacks specific data. We need not resolve the debate about exactly what can justify a mortality decision as actuarially sound or related to actual and reasonably anticipated experience, for in this case there is no question that United's mortality rating was arbitrarily high.

The mortality rating United assigned to Chabner was not actuarially sound. United assigned Chabner a "Table 6" rating, which corresponds with a 150% mortality rating. The 150% mortality rating, in turn, reflects an estimate that Chabner's life expectancy is nine to eleven years less than that of a standard male non-smoker. United points to the Brackenridge manual, which recommended a mortality rating of 75%—150%, and the Cologne manual, which recommended a mortality rating of 300%, to argue that the 150% mortality rating was justified. However, United's own admissions subvert its reliance on these manuals. In his letter to Chabner, Dr. Robert Quinn, the Vice President and Senior Medical Director of Underwriting at United, admitted that FSH MD "has only a small effect on mortality." Moreover, Dr. Quinn estimated Chabner's life expectancy to be only four years less than standard. Even assuming that the estimate of a four year decrease in life expectancy is correct, it does not justify a rating that estimates a nine to eleven year decrease. Accordingly, by United's own admission, the 150% mortality rating (i.e., the estimate of a nine to eleven year decrease in life expectancy) was not actuarially sound.

Nor does the second prong of section 10144, which allows rate differentials if they are based on actual and reasonably anticipated experience, provide refuge for the 150% mortality rating. United's underwriter handling Chabner's application had experience with muscular dystrophy, but not with Chabner's rare fascioscapulohumeral muscular dystrophy. She thus had no "actual experience" with underwriting applicants with FSH MD. Moreover, she was not a doctor, she did not have a doctor examine Chabner, and she did not have a doctor review Chabner's medical records. Thus, the underwriter's basis for "reasonably anticipated experience" in evaluating an applicant with FSH MD was virtually nonexistent, especially considering that Dr. Quinn, who was a medical doctor and who was familiar with FSH MD, subsequently admitted that FSH MD has little effect on mortality. Therefore, viewing the evidence in the light most favorable to United, we hold that no reasonable jury could find that the 150% mortality rating was either based on sound actuarial principles or related to actual and reasonably anticipated experience. Section 10144 did not justify the discriminatory premium, and summary judgment on Chabner's Business and Professions Code section 17200 claim, and on his Unruh Civil Rights Act claim, was therefore proper.

* * *

CONCLUSION

For the foregoing reasons, the district court's grant of summary judgment for Appellee Chabner, and its judgment ordering Appellant United to modify the insurance policy, are AFFIRMED.

NOTES AND QUESTIONS

1.   The Ninth Circuit's holding that Title III of the ADA does not permit individuals to challenge the substantive provisions of insurance contracts is in accord with the weight of authority. See, e.g., Pallozzi v. Allstate Life Insurance Co., 198 F.3d 28 (2d Cir.1999). See generally Maxwell J. Mehlman et al., When Do Health Care Decisions Discriminate Against Persons with Disabilities?, 22 J. Health Pol., Pol'y & L. 1385 (1997).

2.   State unfair trade practice laws or other regulation of insurance practices exist in every state, although the remedies and the interpretation of the statutory provisions differ widely. Who should have the burden of proof with regard to underwriting decision making? What degree of deference, if any, should be given to the insurance company?

3.   The most commonly raised issue regarding genetics and life insurance is that actuarial fairness does not necessarily equate with moral fairness when allocating essential goods. *Chabner* raises a second concern, that the medical underwriting will not be based on sound actuarial principles. Which of the two issues is the more vexing problem? Why?

CHAPTER 28

DISABILITY INSURANCE

■ ■ ■

Disability insurance policies pay a percentage of the wages of the insured individual (often about 70% to reflect after-tax income) in the event of short-term or long-term disability. Disability is tied to the ability to work in one's chosen profession and, not surprisingly, most disability policies are issued through employer-sponsored groups. Risk selection and pricing is done on a group basis, and the percentage of income replacement offered and premiums charged are influenced by the nature of the employment and the claims experience of the employer. Some employment-based group policies offer individuals a "buy up" option whereby they can purchase additional coverage. These supplements may be individually underwritten or they may be offered on a group-rate basis, where the pricing structure takes into account the likelihood for adverse selection.

Individual policies represent about 12 percent of all policies sold. Because of the cost, these policies are mostly bought by self-employed individuals and professionals such as lawyers and physicians. As with other individual policies (e.g. life, health), there is individual underwriting.

There are three main government disability insurance programs. Workers' compensation provides income replacement for workers who are injured or become ill from workplace exposures. Except for a few categories of workers, such as federal employees, employee eligibility, benefit levels, and administration are determined by the states. Social Security Disability Insurance (SSDI) provides disability payments to workers (and survivors of disabled workers) who qualify for Social Security but who become permanently and totally disabled before reaching retirement age. Supplemental Security Income (SSI) provides disability payments linked to financial need.

Disability insurance policies are regulated at the state level, but the policies adopted by the states on issues such as the use of predictive genetic information in underwriting may have an effect on both state and federal disability insurance programs.

As of 2019, about one-third of the states have enacted legislation regulating the use of genetic information by disability insurers. Most of these state statutes, however, only have limited applicability. The most common provisions prohibit discrimination that is not actuarially justified or require separate consent for an insurer to conduct genetic testing or use genetic information. State genetic nondiscrimination laws are collected by the LawSeq project at the University of Minnesota, http://lawseq.umn.edu.

SUSAN M. WOLF & JEFFREY P. KAHN, GENETIC TESTING AND THE FUTURE OF DISABILITY INSURANCE: ETHICS, LAW, AND POLICY

35 J.L. Med. & Ethics (Supp. 2) 6, 11, 13 (2007).

Genetics may play a larger role in private disability insurance than private health insurance or life insurance. State and federal statutes place some limits on health insurers' use of such information, and very few limits on disability insurers. Further, in the realm of private individual life insurance, individual underwriting is less stringent than in disability insurance, as life insurers cover a single event—death. Because an individual may be disabled early in life precluding decades of income, disability insurers are exposed for longer periods of time than life insurers and for potentially much larger amounts of money. This exposure creates an incentive for disability insurers to use predictive medical information including genetic information, since genetics may help predict whether a disability precluding work will manifest at all, when, how, and for what duration.

To underwrite individual disability insurance, the insurer must carefully review the medical history of the applicant. On the basis of that information, the insurer may issue the coverage as applied for, charge additional premiums for the coverage, exclude specific conditions from coverage, change the benefit or elimination periods, or refuse to issue the coverage. As noted above, disability insurers providing individual policies generally rely less than group insurers on pre-existing conditions exclusions. The insurer is thus motivated to perform careful health research on an applicant. The insurer is also motivated by the requirement in most states that the policy include an incontestability clause. The incontestability clause provides that after two years, the insurer cannot deny benefits or cancel a policy if it discovers error in the information supplied by the applicant, so long as the insured did not intentionally defraud the insurer. Once this period has expired, the insurer thus loses the option to deny or cancel a contract due to pre-existing conditions that it failed to uncover. Incontestability clauses add to the insurer's incentives to discover as much as possible about an applicant's medical history— including genetic susceptibility to future disability—at the time of application, or at least within two years of it.

* * *

Given the importance of disability insurance, ideally legislators and regulators would impose the same restrictions on disability insurers as they do on health insurers. Norman Daniels analyzes the implications of setting up a disability insurance social safety net by eliminating medical underwriting (including consideration of genetics) while requiring that everyone have a minimum amount of disability insurance. Daniels does not go so far as to advocate this, but he recognizes it as an option to preserve equality of opportunity in the face of disability disrupting employment and income. For many individuals, this goal might be met through group insurance and public disability programs. When an individual can obtain the minimum amount of disability insurance needed through these other mechanisms, then individuals with a higher level of income can buy additional private individual insurance for additional income protection. Yet there will be some individuals without access to group insurance and unable to qualify for public programs who need access to a minimum safety net of individual disability insurance.

NOTES AND QUESTIONS

1. As with health insurance, public and private interests clearly intersect in the area of disability insurance. Disability income replacement is an important part of the Social Security system (SSDI), and private disability insurance provides supplemental protection for many workers. How might Social Security be affected by changes in the way that private disability insurance is regulated with regard to the use of genetic information?

2. Based on the legislative treatment of health insurance versus life insurance, at the moment, U.S. public policy seems to regard health insurance more as an entitlement or right to which all individuals have a claim, whereas life insurance is considered more of a commercial transaction to which actuarial principles should apply. Assuming this analysis is correct, how should disability insurance be regarded, and how might this consideration affect public policy for disability insurance?

CHAPTER 29

LONG-TERM CARE INSURANCE

■ ■ ■

MARK A. ROTHSTEIN, PREDICTIVE GENETIC TESTING FOR
ALZHEIMER'S DISEASE IN LONG-TERM CARE INSURANCE
35 Ga. L. Rev. 707, 716–731 (2001).

* * *

Long-term care insurance is expensive; paying for the costs of long-term care out-of-pocket can be a catastrophic financial experience for individuals and their families. As long-term care for the elderly increases in expense and a larger portion of the population closes in on their twilight years, the number of insurance policies should be expected to grow. Nevertheless, private insurance is likely to have only a limited role in financing long-term care unless at least the following three things occur: First, long-term care insurance must become a more widely available employee benefit offered through "cafeteria plans" by employers and purchased by employees with pre-tax dollars. Second, because younger, working employees are unlikely to purchase a benefit that they probably will not need, if at all, until after they retire and are no longer paying the premiums needed to keep the policy in force, some "paid up" forms of long-term care insurance will be necessary.

* * *

On average, Alzheimer's disease patients live eight to ten years after they are diagnosed. Consequently, each additional patient with Alzheimer's disease represents a significant increase in the likely expenditures for long-term care. Insurance companies can easily identify symptomatic individuals, but identifying those asymptomatic individuals who are likely to get Alzheimer's disease is much more difficult. Any tests used today by insurers would be poor predictors of future cognitive impairment in asymptomatic and younger applicants. If new tests, including genetic tests, were developed that were better predictors of future dementia (or if they were believed to be better predictors), long-term care insurance companies would have a considerable economic interest in using them. If predictive testing were available, then insurers could learn of the individual's risk status, which may cause adverse selection. Testing by insurers would thus be merely "defensive" in nature.

* * *

In trying to discern the appropriate public policy for the use of predictive genetic information in long-term care insurance, it is valuable to contrast the public policy for health insurance with that for life insurance. For health insurance, restrictions on access due to genetic-based predictions of future health status are unacceptable. There are not clear indications of the specific reasons for this public policy. It may well be a combination of at least the following reasons: (1) the importance of private health insurance to well-being in a nation that does not provide for universal access to health care; (2) the lack of alternatives to health insurance as a way of spreading risk and, in the era of managed care, obtaining health services at negotiated rates; (3) the speculative nature of many types of predictive genetic information; (4) the asserted moral blamelessness of individuals with genetic predisposition to illness; and (5) successful lobbying by groups with an interest in genetic-specific health protections—genetic disease advocacy groups, public health officials, and pharmaceutical and biotechnology companies concerned that individuals will not take their genetic tests if they fear discrimination.

For life insurance, at least in the United States, restrictions on access or cost based on predictions of future health status currently are generally acceptable. The reasons for this policy are likely to include at least the following: (1) life insurance serves a valuable role in promoting peace of mind and in providing financial security for one's heirs, but it is not a necessity for the person who is insured; (2) there are various investment alternatives to some forms of life insurance; (3) medical underwriting based on predictions of mortality risk are commonly performed for various health and lifestyle measures, including smoking and drinking habits, diet, occupation, recreational activities, and various presymptomatic health measures ranging from weight to cholesterol levels; (4) unlike health insurance, where the benefits are largely defined, life insurance can be purchased in extremely large amounts, thereby increasing the incentives for adverse selection; and (5) life insurance has not yet been the subject of intense lobbying activity.

If the preceding arguments generally capture the current public sentiments with regard to health and life insurance, to determine the appropriate policy for long-term care insurance one must merely resolve the following question: As a policy matter, is long-term care insurance more like health insurance or life insurance? Arguing in favor of long-term care insurance being closer to health insurance is the fact that long-term care is a type of health care which is merely provided in a different setting, and even though there are different pricing levels among long-term care facilities, commercial policies are generally sold with certain defined benefits. Arguing in favor of long-term care insurance being closer to life insurance is the fact that there are alternatives to long-term care policies and the premium structure is based on mortality risk, much the way that life insurance (and disability insurance) is.

* * *

As with the use of genetic information in numerous other contexts, the issue of using genetic information in long-term care insurance cannot be resolved in isolation. If public policy prohibits long-term care insurers from requiring genetic testing or using the results of a genetic test, what about using predictive genetic information based on family history? If the use of *any* predictive genetic information should be prohibited, what about non-genetic health information predictive of dementia, such as a history of head trauma, smoking, or drinking? What about other non-health factors predictive of dementia, such as socio-economic status? What about underwriting based on medical and nonmedical factors predictive of other disabling conditions?

Ultimately, the question becomes who should have access to long-term care, or, at least, who should have access to long-term care insurance? The most logical, and defensible line of demarcation for risk classification may not be genetic versus nongenetic factors. It may be whether the applicant is asymptomatic or symptomatic, with only age as an underwriting factor for individuals who are asymptomatic and all actuarially relevant criteria permitted in underwriting symptomatic individuals.

CATHLEEN D. ZICK ET AL., GENETIC TESTING FOR ALZHEIMER'S DISEASE AND ITS IMPACT ON INSURANCE PURCHASING BEHAVIOR
24 Health Affairs 483, 484–488 (2005).

STUDY DATA AND METHODS

Study design.

The Risk Evaluation and Education for Alzheimer's Disease (REVEAL) Study is a recently completed randomized controlled trial (RCT) evaluating the impact of a genetic education and counseling program for adult children of Alzheimer's patients. As the largest study of its kind, it provides a rare opportunity to gain initial insights into the relationship between genetic testing for Alzheimer's disease and insurance purchasing behavior.

Participants in the REVEAL Study were either self-referred or systematically ascertained through their family's membership in existing Alzheimer's research registries in Boston, Cleveland, or New York City. Recruitment began in August 2000, and the last of the follow-up respondents surveys was completed in October 2003. A total of 162 participants were randomized into the clinical trial. All study participants were at higher-than-average risk for developing Alzheimer's because they have at least one parent affected by the disease.

In the control arm of the REVEAL Study, participants were informed of their risk of developing Alzheimer's based on sex and family history alone, with lifetime risk estimates ranging from 18 to 29 percent. Meanwhile, intervention-group participants learned their APOE genotype and were informed of their risk on the basis of sex, family history, and genotype, with lifetime risk estimates ranging from 13 to 57 percent.

Of the 162 people in the study, 148 were included in the analyses that follow. The remaining fourteen were excluded because they had missing data on one or more of the covariates. Among the 148 subjects, 46 were in the arm of the study where there was no APOE disclosure, 54 learned that they were a4 negative, and the remaining 48 learned that they were a4 positive (that is, had one or two a4 alleles).

Participants' characteristics.

Participants' sociodemographic information illustrates that the REVEAL sample, like all research volunteer samples, is not a representative sample of the population. People in this study were more likely to be white, female, and well educated than members of the general population. Participants were also typically older than the general population, since participants had to be an adult child of a diagnosed Alzheimer's patient. Before intervention, it was ascertained that 97 percent of the sample had health insurance, 78 percent had life insurance, and 19.8 had long-term care insurance. These high rates of insurance coverage likely reflect the age, education, and ethnic composition of the sample.

* * *

Adverse selection.

First, there was little evidence of adverse selection in the health, life, and disability insurance markets despite the fact that the sample consisted of highly motivated people (that is, all had a family history of Alzheimer's disease and were highly educated) who were participating in a closed research trial where confidentiality of genetic information was guaranteed. This finding might be expected, however, given the ages of the participants, the relatively short period of follow-up (one year), people's typical insurance buying patterns, and the unique attributes of various insurance products.

Long-term care insurance.

Second, the one insurance domain where we found suggestive evidence of adverse selection is long-term care. Almost 17 percent of those who tested positive subsequently changed their long-term care insurance coverage in the year after APOE disclosure, compared with approximately 2 percent of those who tested negative and 4 percent of those who did not receive APOE disclosure. The overall percentage with long-term care insurance rose from 19.8 percent at baseline to 27 percent just one year later. Roughly three quarters of this increase is attributable to study participants' having learned that they had tested positive for the a4 allele. Controlling for other insurance-related covariates, we found that participants who tested positive were 5.76 times more likely to change their long-term care insurance coverage during the subsequent year than were those who did not receive APOE disclosure (although this finding is not reinforced by the sensitivity analyses).

Potential for adverse selection.

Policymakers who are attempting to balance consumers' concerns regarding potential genetic discrimination against insurers' concerns that the withholding of genetic test results would make insurance markets unprofitable should proceed with caution. Our findings imply that the potential for adverse selection may vary considerably by insurance market, thus making it difficult to design a public policy that works well in all instances.

It may be that the natural history of Alzheimer's disease combines with APOE testing and the characteristics of the mostly private long-term care insurance market to create the "perfect storm" with regard to adverse selection. That is, (1) Alzheimer's is a condition that has a high probability of requiring formal, long-term care services; (2) APOE testing gives significant, albeit incomplete, predictive information for the at-risk population; and (3) long-term care insurance is generally a private insurance market where an information asymmetry can have serious consequences. Taken in combination, these conditions create a situation where adverse selection may occur and where its consequences for insurers and consumers may be significant. This premise is consistent with the fact that we observe a positive relationship between testing positive and changing one's long-term care insurance coverage even in our relatively small sample.

NOTES AND QUESTIONS

1.   Taken together, what do the Rothstein and Zick articles indicate about the nature and consequences of genetic information for long-term care insurance? According to another study, healthy people with an increased risk of illness based on predictive genetic tests were more likely to purchase long-term care insurance. Donald H. Taylor, Jr. et al., Genetic Testing for Alzheimer's and Long-Term Care Insurance, 29 Health Affairs 102 (2010).

2.   Long-term care insurance is declining. In 2004, there were 362,000 policies sold in the United States, but by 2015, there were only 104,000 policies

sold. What effect, if any, do you think that declining sales will have on insurers' interest in using genetic information?

3. Genetic information may have an effect on a variety of other insurance products. Medical malpractice (for negligence in diagnosis or treatment) and products liability (for pharmacogenomic medications) quickly come to mind. But there are other less obvious implications as well. For example, would it be permissible for an auto insurance company to test applicants to determine whether they were genetically predisposed to be risk takers?

PART VIII

EMPLOYMENT DISCRIMINATION

∎ ∎ ∎

CHAPTER 30

INTRODUCTION

■ ■ ■

Along with genetic discrimination in insurance, the topic of Chapters 26–29, genetic discrimination in employment is a topic of enormous concern to individuals and policy makers. Employment is not only a source of income, but also the source of health insurance for the majority of Americans. Therefore, it is extremely important to resolve whether employers may get access to individuals' genetic information and, if so, what they may lawfully do with it. At the same time, it is necessary to consider the employers' interests in efficiency, employee health, and the health and safety of the public.

Employers have a keen interest in the health of their employees. A healthy work force is more stable, more productive, safer, and less costly in various ways than one composed of workers who are ill or likely to become ill in the future. Accordingly, medical screening of workers, the use of medical criteria in selecting and maintaining a work force, makes sense from a business standpoint and, if appropriately performed, from a health and policy standpoint as well. Medical screening of workers is not new; the only recent changes have been in the specific financial incentives for having healthier employees and the science used to make such determinations.

Medical screening became common in the United States at the beginning of the twentieth century. With industrialization, and the emergence of large manufacturing and other centralized employment facilities, employers attempted to ensure that their employees were free of tuberculosis and other communicable diseases. They also wanted to determine whether applicants and employees had the necessary vision, hearing, strength, stamina, dexterity, and other physical (and later mental) attributes necessary to perform the job safely and efficiently. Thus, "factory surgeons" were hired to screen out individuals who were deemed to be unacceptable. The nascent state of occupational medicine and the vulnerability of employer-paid physicians to making decisions for non-medical reasons, such as screening out union sympathizers for "medical reasons," sometimes compromised the integrity of the medical screening process during the first half of the twentieth century.

After World War II, there were new incentives to use more extensive medical screening. Besides workers' compensation and unemployment compensation liability for injuries and illnesses and employee turnover, employers began assuming a portion of employee (and later dependent) health insurance costs and, for some employers, disability insurance. In 1970, the Occupational Safety and Health Act subjected employers to civil penalties for safety and health violations, including those associated with occupational diseases or employee-caused accidents. The prospect of substantial tort liability for physical injuries and property damage sustained by the public resulting from employee-based mishaps further encouraged employers to select employees carefully based on medical criteria.

While pressures to increase medical screening were growing, civil rights legislation was enacted to limit employer prerogatives in employee selection. Title VII of the Civil Rights Act of 1964, as amended, and the Age Discrimination in Employment Act of 1967 (ADEA) prohibited discrimination based on race, color, religion, sex, pregnancy, national origin, or age. These laws had the effect of prohibiting employers from using stereotypical assumptions of individuals' abilities, thereby requiring an individualized determination of physical ability. In 1990, Congress enacted the Americans with Disabilities Act (ADA), which differed from Title VII and the ADEA in at least two important ways. First, Congress realized that it had to go beyond merely prohibiting discrimination based on disability; it was also necessary to address the previously unregulated process of selecting employees based on medical criteria. Thus, the ADA limits the timing and permissible scope of medical inquiries so that individuals with disabilities will not be excluded from consideration because of their disabilities before they have a chance to demonstrate their abilities. Second, the ADA requires that employers provide "reasonable accommodation" to enable individuals with disabilities to perform their jobs.

In 2008, Congress enacted the Genetic Information Nondiscrimination Act (GINA), Title II of which prohibits discrimination in employment on the basis of genetic information. Following the general framework of state laws enacted in the 1990s, GINA's main purpose is to reassure individuals that they can undergo genetic testing or genetic consultations without adverse consequences to their employment.

This chapter considers the broader context of genetic information and discrimination in the workplace. It explores what it means to "discriminate," whether genetic-specific or more general laws would be more effective in preventing discrimination, and the specifics of GINA and other legislation applicable to genetics in employment.

I.   WHAT IS GENETIC DISCRIMINATION?

MARK A. ROTHSTEIN & MARY R. ANDERLIK, WHAT IS GENETIC DISCRIMINATION AND WHEN AND HOW CAN IT BE PREVENTED?
3 Genetics in Med. 354, 354–355 (2001).

The two most common uses of the term discrimination differ dramatically in the degree of disapproval they connote. On the one hand, the term discrimination may be used to indicate a type of distinction that invariably is or should be socially unacceptable. We refer to this as the civil rights definition. For example, the Council for Responsible Genetics position paper on genetic discrimination does not define the term discrimination, but the negative connotation is clear from its use. Discrimination is linked to evaluating people based on "questionable stereotypes" rather than their individual merits and abilities, invading people's privacy, the morally and publicly unacceptable stratification of the community into "haves" and "have-nots," and the punishment of people for characteristics over which they have no control in violation of cherished beliefs in justice and equality. The proper response to discrimination is legal prohibition.

On the other hand, the term discrimination may be used as an all-purpose descriptor for the practice of making distinctions. Further, some individuals and entities link social unacceptability with irrationality, that is, they believe that only irrational distinctions should be socially unacceptable. We refer to this as the actuarial definition. For example, in the insurance industry, the term discrimination is considered neutral and simply refers to classification for purposes of underwriting. On the industry view, discrimination only becomes problematic where there is no sound actuarial basis for the manner in which risks are classified, or individuals with equivalent risks are treated differently. Often, in the business context, "irrational" means that the distinction cannot be defended in economic terms or, in the case of insurance, by reference to sound actuarial principles.

For both definitions, the term genetic discrimination also conveys that adverse treatment is based solely on the genotype of asymptomatic individuals. Differential treatment on the basis of phenotype is frequently rational and accepted as a social necessity, such as where an employer bases a hiring decision on a job-related need for visual acuity. Cases of adverse treatment based on the phenotypic expression of a genetic characteristic fit well within the analytical framework of laws dealing with disability-based or health status-based discrimination generally. The most important of these laws is the Americans with Disabilities Act. To the contrary, cases of adverse treatment of phenotypically "normal" individuals fit poorly within the disability discrimination framework. A large majority of the public considers discrimination against these individuals as unfair because current opportunities are being denied to seemingly unaffected individuals merely because a genetic test or assessment indicates an increased risk of future incapacity.

We define discrimination as drawing a distinction among individuals or groups plus an element of either irrationality or social unacceptability or both. Our definition draws upon elements of both the civil rights and actuarial definitions. When discrimination is defined in this way, the term clearly has a negative connotation, but it does not necessarily equate with a legal proscription of the classification. The appropriate legal and policy response to social unacceptability—a widely shared sense within a polity that some activity or state of affairs is "wrong"—will depend on the circumstances. In addition to or in lieu of legal prohibitions backed by criminal, civil, or administrative penalties are withdrawals of public funding, public condemnation, professional standards, and direct citizen action against the offending parties, for example, in the form of an economic boycott. Our definition recognizes that some forms of irrational discrimination are accepted, or at least tolerated, by society and some forms of discrimination are socially unacceptable despite the fact that they are rational.

Table 1 illustrates the application of our definition of discrimination by indicating how a sample of selection criteria for employment would be arrayed along dimensions of social acceptability and rationality. Note that standards for judging social acceptability will vary according to the context. While employers are generally not prohibited from basing hiring decisions on Zodiac signs, even though this is clearly irrational, an insurer would have to offer some actuarial basis for the distinction in order to meet the requirements of state insurance laws. One justification for differences in the law of employment and insurance is that, in our society, there is no history of systematic mistreatment of Virgos relative to Capricorns in employment, and the costs of policing idiosyncratic factors in isolated hiring decisions would be very high. On the other hand, risk classification in insurance involves assigning individuals to risk pools and hence insurance practices have the potential to create systematic mistreatment. Insurance underwriting policies also are more amenable to regulation than hiring decisions.

Table 1. Categories of Discrimination in Employment

	Rational	Irrational
Acceptable	• Choosing based on relative skill or other job-related criteria • Choosing based on medical assessment of ability to perform the job	• Choosing based on Zodiac sign • Choosing based on a coin toss
Unacceptable	• Excluding persons with cancer based on concerns about health care costs • Excluding pregnant women because they may shortly go on maternity leave	• Excluding based on religion (in a secular enterprise) • Excluding based on national origin

NOTES AND QUESTIONS

1. "Genetic discrimination" has long been an essential and accepted component of employee selection practices. For example, genes are a factor in height, vision, cognitive ability, and numerous other attributes of interest to employers. Thus, in a sense, it is "genetic discrimination" for a professional basketball team to select players based on their height. It is also "genetic discrimination" for an employer to refuse to hire an individual whose intellectual deficits preclude understanding key assignments or whose expressed genetic disorder precludes him or her from working. These forms of discrimination are generally considered legally and ethically permissible. Thus, "genetic discrimination" of a legally and ethically problematic nature, and as the term is commonly used, really means discrimination based on an unexpressed genotype. It is discrimination against presymptomatic or at-risk individuals.

2. Based on this definition, where would you place genetic discrimination on the preceding table? Can you make an argument for including genetic discrimination in any of the other "boxes"?

3. What is the nature of the harm suffered by a victim of genetic discrimination? How does it compare with the harm suffered by the victims of other forms of discrimination in employment?

II. EMPLOYER ACCESS TO
GENETIC INFORMATION

Employers have a considerable interest in the current and future health of their employees. The nature of the business and the work force will determine the specific interests, but in general, a healthy work force will be more productive; have less absenteeism and turnover; have fewer workers' compensation, disability insurance, and unemployment compensation claims; have fewer Family and Medical Leave Act requests for personal leave; require fewer accommodations under the Americans with Disabilities Act; and cause fewer OSHA violations.

The most important economic reason to have a healthy work force is to control health insurance costs. In the United States, about 55% of individuals have health care coverage through their employer. The cost of health care coverage is the largest single non-salary compensation expense and, despite a moderating of increases in the 1990s attributable to managed care, the costs have begun increasing at a faster rate. In any given year, 5% of claimants represent 50% of expenditures, and therefore if the high-cost users could be excluded, dramatic savings (or cost-shifting to other, largely public payers) would be realized.

Employers attempting to limit their health insurance costs by selecting employees based on their health status may run afoul of the Americans with Disabilities Act as well as the Health Insurance Portability and Accountability Act of 1996 (HIPAA), the Affordable Care Act, and the Genetic Information Nondiscrimination Act. As a result, it might seem that employers have no lawful interest in the likely future health of individual employees and their dependents. Nevertheless, claims experience may be used in pricing the policy for an employer's group coverage and self-insured employers (mostly large employers) will have the solvency of their plan affected by the claims filed.

NOTE ON EMPLOYER ACCESS TO EMPLOYEE
HEALTH INFORMATION

Employers lawfully obtain medical information about employees in numerous ways. The following are 10 of the most common ways.

1.   Application forms. Under the Americans with Disabilities Act (ADA), it is unlawful for an employer to make any medical inquiries of an applicant for employment until after there has been a conditional offer of employment. Therefore, it would be unlawful for an employer to require that the individual provide medical information on an application form. It is lawful, however, for an application form to ask an individual about previous jobs held and the reason why the individual left each prior job. The answer to one of these questions might be: "took time off work for cancer treatment."

2. Interviews. It is unlawful for an employer to ask about health matters at the interview before a conditional offer of employment. But nothing would prevent an employer from asking, for example, why the individual is interested in working for a particular employer. The answer to such a question could be: "Your health benefits are excellent, and there is a good chance I will need a liver transplant in a few years."

3. References. References sometimes disclose information about individuals that the individual would prefer not to have divulged to a potential employer. For example, a reference, trying to be helpful might say: "He has not let the fact that he tested positive for the Huntington disease mutation affect his positive outlook on life."

4. Post-offer medical exams. Under the ADA, after a conditional offer of employment, the employer can require that the individual submit to a preplacement medical examination. These examinations may be unlimited in scope, regardless of the nature of the job or the individual's health history.

5. Releases of medical records. Under the ADA, after a conditional offer of employment, an employer may require that an individual sign a blanket release authorizing disclosure to the employer of all of the individual's medical records. Under GINA, it is unlawful for an employer to request, require, or purchase genetic information about an employee or family member of an employee, but genetic information is generally interspersed with non-genetic information in medical records. Because there is no easy or low-cost method of separating this information in paper or electronic health records, the custodians of health records often send the entire files in response to a more limited request.

6. FMLA requests. Under the Family and Medical Leave Act (FMLA), an employer of 50 or more employees is required to provide up to 12 weeks of unpaid leave for, among other things, the worker's own serious health condition that prevents him or her from working. The employer may require medical certification of the employee's need for leave, notwithstanding the ADA, which otherwise prohibits employers from requiring current employees to undergo non-job-related medical examinations. GINA, which prohibits employers from requesting genetic information from their employees, contains an exception for information related to an FMLA certification.

7. Periodic medical exams. Employers often require that employees periodically undergo medical examinations. For jobs with certain workplace exposures, periodic examinations are required under the Occupational Safety and Health Act. Under the ADA, medical examinations of current employees must be job-related or voluntary.

8. Workers' compensation claims. Employees sustaining work-related injuries and illnesses are eligible for workers' compensation. By submitting a claim, however, the employee places his or her medical condition at issue. The employer is therefore entitled to an independent medical examination of the claimant as well as access to the employee's medical records.

9.   Health insurance claims. Employers often have widespread access to claims information submitted under an employer-sponsored health benefits plan. With a self-insured, self-administered plan, the physicians' bills and fee explanations are sent directly to the employer for payment. Even when a third-party administrator is used, employers often have access to the information. Employers also gain access to the health claims of the employee's dependents.

10.   Voluntary disclosure. One of the most frequently used forms of disclosure of health information in the workplace occurs when employees voluntarily disclose their illnesses to co-workers and supervisors.

CHAPTER 31

GENETIC DISCRIMINATION UNDER THE AMERICANS WITH DISABILITIES ACT (ADA)

■ ■ ■

I. COVERAGE

The Americans with Disabilities Act of 1990 (ADA), 42 U.S.C. §§ 12101–12213, was the first comprehensive federal law to prohibit discrimination in employment against the estimated 43 million Americans with physical or mental disabilities. The ADA's five titles deal with employment (Title I), public services (Title II), public accommodations operated by private entities (Title III), telecommunications (Title IV), and miscellaneous issues (Title V). The ADA draws heavily upon Title VII of the Civil Rights Act of 1964, 42 U.S.C. § 2000e, and the Rehabilitation Act of 1973, 29 U.S.C. §§ 701–796i.

The ADA applies to employers with 15 or more employees. It also applies to state and local government employers and the United States Congress. Federal employees are not covered by the ADA, but they are covered by comparable provisions of section 501 of the Rehabilitation Act.

Section 102(a) of the ADA contains the general prohibition on employment discrimination. "No covered entity shall discriminate against a qualified individual with a disability because of the disability of such individual in regard to job application procedures, the hiring, advancement, or discharge of employees, employee compensation, job training, and other terms, conditions, and privileges of employment." There can be no liability if the employer did not know that the individual had a disability at the time it took the adverse action and therefore direct or circumstantial proof of employer motive is often determinative.

Besides the ADA, nearly every state has its own civil rights law prohibiting discrimination in employment on the basis of disability or handicap. Section 501(b) of the ADA provides that the ADA does not preempt any state or local law "that provides greater or equal protection for the rights of individuals with disabilities than are afforded by this [Act]." There are three main ways in which state laws are important to complement the protections of the ADA. First, the state law may apply to a wider class of employers. Twenty-five states and the District of Columbia have laws that apply to employers with fewer than 15 employees. Second, the state law may apply to a wider range of impairments than the ADA, such as individuals who are obese, who have substance abuse problems, or whose disabilities are not severe enough to meet the ADA definition. Third, the state law may more closely regulate certain medical or hiring procedures in employment. For example, in California and Minnesota preplacement medical examinations must be limited to assessing job-related health conditions. Medical examinations are discussed in Section II of this Chapter.

The ADA Amendments Act of 2008, P.L. 110–325, 110th Cong., 2d Sess. (2008), was signed into law on September 25, 2008. It was enacted to overturn Supreme Court decisions narrowly interpreting the definition of an individual with a disability. The essence of the new amendments is captured by the following rule of construction: "The definition of a disability in this Act shall be construed in favor of broad coverage of individuals under this Act, to the maximum extent permitted by the terms of this Act." ADA Amendments Act § 3(4). Among the Supreme Court decisions overturned were Sutton v. United Air Lines, Inc., 527 U.S. 471 (1999), and its companion cases. In *Sutton*, twin sisters with correctable vision problems were denied an opportunity to become airline pilots because their uncorrected vision did not meet the airline's medical standards. In the ADA action, however, the airline argued that they were not covered by the ADA because in their "mitigated" state they did not have a substantially limiting impairment. The Supreme Court, rejecting the EEOC's interpretation that impairments should be considered in their unmitigated state, held that the lower court was required to consider the effect of eyeglasses on their condition. The Court relied on the congressional finding that the ADA provided coverage to 43 million Americans with disabilities to conclude that the ADA was only intended to apply to individuals with substantially limiting impairments. Although Congress overturned *Sutton*, the ADA Amendments Act did not address the issue of genetic discrimination or discrimination based on the risk of future impairment. Perhaps Congress did not believe this was necessary in light of GINA (discussed below), which was signed into law four months earlier on May 21, 2008.

II. MEDICAL EXAMINATIONS

AMERICANS WITH DISABILITIES ACT
42 U.S.C. §§ 12101–12213.

SECTION 102. (§ 12112) DISCRIMINATION

(a) GENERAL RULE.—No covered entity shall discriminate against a qualified individual with a disability because of the disability of such individual in regard to job application procedures, the hiring, advancement, or discharge of employees, employee compensation, job training, and other terms, conditions, and privileges of employment.

* * *

(d) MEDICAL EXAMINATIONS AND INQUIRIES.—

(1) IN GENERAL.—The prohibition against discrimination as referred to in subsection (a) shall include medical examinations and inquiries.

(2) PREEMPLOYMENT—

(A) PROHIBITED EXAMINATION OR INQUIRY.—Except as provided in paragraph (3), a covered entity shall not conduct a medical examination or make inquiries of a job applicant as to whether such applicant is an individual with a disability or as to the nature or severity of such disability.

(B) ACCEPTABLE INQUIRY.—A covered entity may make preemployment inquiries into the ability of an applicant to perform job-related functions.

(3) EMPLOYMENT ENTRANCE EXAMINATION.—A covered entity may require a medical examination after an offer of employment has been made to a job applicant and prior to the commencement of the employment duties of such applicant, and may condition an offer of employment on the results of such examination, if—

(A) all entering employees are subjected to such an examination regardless of disability;

(B) information obtained regarding the medical condition or history of the applicant is collected and maintained on separate forms and in separate medical files and is treated as a confidential medical record, except that—

(i) supervisors and managers may be informed regarding necessary restrictions on the work or duties of the employee and necessary accommodations;

(ii) first aid and safety personnel may be informed, when appropriate, if the disability might require emergency treatment; and

(iii) government officials investigating compliance with this Act shall be provided relevant information on request; and

(C) the results of such examination are used only in accordance with this title.

(4) EXAMINATION AND INQUIRY.—

(A) PROHIBITED EXAMINATIONS AND INQUIRIES.—A covered entity shall not require a medical examination and shall not make inquiries of an employee as to whether such employee is an individual with a disability or as to the nature or severity of the disability, unless such examination or inquiry is shown to be job-related and consistent with business necessity.

(B) ACCEPTABLE EXAMINATIONS AND INQUIRIES.—A covered entity may conduct voluntary medical examinations, including voluntary medical histories, which are part of an employee health program available to employees at that work site. A covered entity may make inquiries into the ability of an employee to perform job-related functions.

(C) REQUIREMENT.—Information obtained under subparagraph (B) regarding the medical condition or history of any employee are subject to the requirements of subparagraphs (B) and (C) of paragraph (3).

NOTES AND QUESTIONS

1. Section 102(d) of the ADA has three different sets of rules for employee medical examinations and inquiries, depending on the stage of employment at which the examination or inquiry is conducted. Can you summarize the three different sets of rules? Are these privacy protection rules or antidiscrimination rules?

2. For a discussion of the legislative history of this section, see Chai Feldblum, Medical Examinations and Inquiries Under the Americans with Disabilities Act: A View From the Inside, 64 Temp. L. Rev. 521 (1991); Sharona Hoffman, Preplacement Examinations and Job-Relatedness: How to Enhance Privacy and Diminish Discrimination in the Workplace, 49 U. Kan. L. Rev. 517 (2001). For a discussion of the ADA and genetics, see Mark A. Rothstein, Genetic Discrimination in Employment and the Americans with Disabilities Act, 29 Hous. L. Rev. 23 (1992).

3. In Shell v. Burlington Northern Santa Fe Railway Co. (BNSF), 941 F.3d 331 (7th Cir. 2019), BNSF withdrew a conditional offer of employment following a medical examination indicating that Mr. Shell was 5'10" tall and weighed 331 pounds. The withdrawal was based on BNSF's view that individuals with this level of obesity are at a substantially increased risk of developing conditions such as sleep apnea, diabetes, and heart disease that can result in sudden incapacitation. The Eighth Circuit held that in refusing to hire Mr. Shell because of a fear that he was at a higher risk of future impairment, BNSF did not regard him as having a disability under the ADA. The court expressly declined to give any weight to section 902.8 of EEOC's Compliance Manual, which provides that if an employer refused to hire an individual because of an increased risk of colon cancer the individual would be

covered under the regarded as part of the definition of disability. This provision was specifically written to cover genetic discrimination.

OTHER LAWS APPLICABLE TO GENETIC DISCRIMINATION IN EMPLOYMENT

Title VII of the Civil Rights Act of 1964 prohibits discrimination in employment on the basis of race, color, religion, sex, and national origin. 42 U.S.C. § 2000e–2(a)(1). Because genetic disorders often appear in higher frequencies in distinct population groups, discrimination against individuals with certain disorders or traits (e.g., sickle cell) might be alleged as disparate impact discrimination under Title VII. This was the theory used in Norman-Bloodsaw v. Lawrence Berkeley Laboratory, 135 F.3d 1260 (9th Cir. 1998). Without their knowledge or consent, blood and urine samples of certain employees obtained during their preplacement medical examinations were tested for pregnancy, syphilis, and sickle cell trait. Seven current and former employees sued under the U.S. and California Constitutions, Title VII, and the ADA. The Ninth Circuit, in reversing the district court's dismissal of all claims, held that the facts raised a valid constitutional claim. "One can think of few subject areas more personal and more likely to implicate privacy interests than that of one's health and genetic make-up." 135 F.3d at 1269. The court also held that a cognizable Title VII claim for sex discrimination was alleged by the pregnancy testing and a race discrimination claim because the sickle cell testing was limited to black employees. The dismissal of the ADA claims was affirmed, however, because, under the ADA, preplacement medical examinations can be of unlimited scope and need not be job-related.

The Employee Retirement Income Security Act (ERISA) makes it unlawful to discriminate against a participant or beneficiary "for the purpose of interfering with the attainment of any right to which such participant may become entitled under the plan * * *." 29 U.S.C. § 1140. However, ERISA applies only to current employees and therefore is inapplicable to a refusal to hire based on perceived future health insurance costs. The ADA and state genetic nondiscrimination laws would be the best recourse for discrimination before hiring.

CHAPTER 32

GENETIC NONDISCRIMINATION LAWS

■ ■ ■

I. STATE LAWS

State laws prohibiting genetic discrimination in employment date back to the 1970s. At that time, widespread and ill-advised carrier testing for sickle cell trait caused confusion, resulting in discrimination against unaffected carriers. Florida, Louisiana, and North Carolina enacted laws prohibiting discrimination based on sickle cell trait. The first comprehensive genetic nondiscrimination law was enacted in Wisconsin in 1991. In the years since then, over half the states have enacted laws prohibiting genetic discrimination in employment, and new measures are introduced in more states every year.

The laws fall into two general categories. First, the laws in all but two of the states to enact genetic nondiscrimination legislation prohibit employers from requiring genetic testing as a condition of employment and prohibit discrimination based on genetic information. The definition of genetic information includes family health history in some states; in others it is limited to the results of a DNA-based genetic test. The laws do not prohibit employers from requiring that individuals sign a blanket release of their medical records after there has been a conditional offer of employment. The second category of laws, represented by only California and Minnesota, adopt a more generic approach, and prohibit employers from obtaining any non-job-related medical information at any time. Presumably, this also prohibits employers from requiring broad releases of medical information, which could include genetic information and family health history information from which genetic risks may be inferred.

II. FEDERAL LAWS

OVERVIEW OF THE GENETIC INFORMATION NONDISCRIMINATION ACT OF 2008 (GINA)

The Genetic Information Nondiscrimination Act of 2008 (GINA), was signed into law by President Bush on May 21, 2008, after a 13-year struggle in Congress. Previously, in 2000, President Clinton issued Executive Order 13145, which prohibited genetic discrimination in federal government employment. The executive order was designed to pave the way for legislation covering the private sector, but GINA was considered unnecessary or intrusive by some members of Congress until various objections were resolved.

Title II of GINA prohibits discrimination in employment. Specifically, it prohibits employers from requesting, requiring, or purchasing genetic information about employees or applicants. Genetic information is defined as information about the individual's genetic tests, the genetic tests of family members, or the manifestation of a disease or disorder in a family member. It does not apply to manifested diseases or disorders of the individual. Thus, as with Title I, applicable to health insurance (discussed in Chapter 15), Title II of GINA applies only to individuals who are asymptomatic.

Employers are prohibited from engaging in various unlawful employment practices, including refusing to hire, discharging, or discriminating in terms or conditions of employment, based on genetic information. There are several exceptions to the ban on acquiring genetic information, including inadvertent acquisition (e.g., disclosures by the employee), employer requests for health information in accordance with the Family and Medical Leave Act (FMLA), and optional genetic monitoring for the effects of occupational exposures.

For private sector employers, GINA has the same coverage and remedies as Title VII, except that disparate impact claims may not be brought. Title II took effect on November 21, 2009, 18 months after GINA was signed into law. The Equal Employment Opportunity Commission (EEOC) has responsibility for issuing regulations and enforcement of GINA.

GENETIC INFORMATION NONDISCRIMINATION ACT OF 2008 (GINA)

P.L. 110–233, 122 Stat 881 (2008).

* * *

TITLE II—PROHIBITING EMPLOYMENT DISCRIMINATION ON THE BASIS OF GENETIC INFORMATION

§ 201.   DEFINITIONS

* * *

(4) GENETIC INFORMATION—

(A) IN GENERAL—The term 'genetic information' means, with respect to any individual, information about—

(i)   such individual's genetic tests,

(ii) the genetic tests of family members of such individual, and

(iii) the manifestation of a disease or disorder in family members of such individual.

(B) INCLUSION OF GENETIC SERVICES AND PARTICIPATION IN GENETIC RESEARCH—Such term includes, with respect to any individual, any request for, or receipt of, genetic services, or participation in clinical research which includes genetic services, by such individual or any family member of such individual.

(C) EXCLUSIONS—The term 'genetic information' shall not include information about the sex or age of any individual.

(5) GENETIC MONITORING—The term 'genetic monitoring' means the periodic examination of employees to evaluate acquired modifications to their genetic material, such as chromosomal damage or evidence of increased occurrence of mutations, that may have developed in the course of employment due to exposure to toxic substances in the workplace, in order to identify, evaluate, and respond to the effects of or control adverse environmental exposures in the workplace.

(6) GENETIC SERVICES—The term 'genetic services' means—

(A) a genetic test;

(B) genetic counseling (including obtaining, interpreting, or assessing genetic information); or

(C) genetic education.

(7) GENETIC TEST—

(A) IN GENERAL—The term 'genetic test' means an analysis of human DNA, RNA, chromosomes, proteins, or metabolites, that detects genotypes, mutations, or chromosomal changes.

(B) EXCEPTIONS—The term 'genetic test' does not mean an analysis of proteins or metabolites that does not detect genotypes, mutations, or chromosomal changes.

§ 202.   EMPLOYER PRACTICES.

(a) Discrimination Based on Genetic Information—It shall be an unlawful employment practice for an employer—

(1) to fail or refuse to hire, or to discharge, any employee, or otherwise to discriminate against any employee with respect to the compensation, terms, conditions, or privileges of employment

of the employee, because of genetic information with respect to the employee; or

(2) to limit, segregate, or classify the employees of the employer in any way that would deprive or tend to deprive any employee of employment opportunities or otherwise adversely affect the status of the employee as an employee, because of genetic information with respect to the employee.

(b) Acquisition of Genetic Information—It shall be an unlawful employment practice for an employer to request, require, or purchase genetic information with respect to an employee or a family member of the employee except—

(1) where an employer inadvertently requests or requires family medical history of the employee or family member of the employee;

(2) where—

(A) health or genetic services are offered by the employer, including such services offered as part of a wellness program;

(B) the employee provides prior, knowing, voluntary, and written authorization;

(C) only the employee (or family member if the family member is receiving genetic services) and the licensed health care professional or board certified genetic counselor involved in providing such services receive individually identifiable information concerning the results of such services; and

(D) any individually identifiable genetic information provided under subparagraph (C) in connection with the services provided under subparagraph (A) is only available for purposes of such services and shall not be disclosed to the employer except in aggregate terms that do not disclose the identity of specific employees;

(3) where an employer requests or requires family medical history from the employee to comply with the certification provisions of section 103 of the Family and Medical Leave Act of 1993 (29 U.S.C. 2613) or such requirements under State family and medical leave laws;

(4) where an employer purchases documents that are commercially and publicly available (including newspapers, magazines, periodicals, and books, but not including medical databases or court records) that include family medical history;

(5) where the information involved is to be used for genetic monitoring of the biological effects of toxic substances in the workplace, but only if—

(A) the employer provides written notice of the genetic monitoring to the employee;

(B)(i)   the employee provides prior, knowing, voluntary, and written authorization; or

(ii) the genetic monitoring is required by Federal or State law;

(C) the employee is informed of individual monitoring results;

(D) the monitoring is in compliance with—

(i) any Federal genetic monitoring regulations, including any such regulations that may be promulgated by the Secretary of Labor pursuant to the Occupational Safety and Health Act of 1970 (29 U.S.C. 651 et seq.), the Federal Mine Safety and Health Act of 1977 (30 U.S.C. 801 et seq.), or the Atomic Energy Act of 1954 (42 U.S.C. 2011 et seq.); or

(ii) State genetic monitoring regulations, in the case of a State that is implementing genetic monitoring regulations under the authority of the Occupational Safety and Health Act of 1970 (29 U.S.C. 651 et seq.); and

(E) the employer, excluding any licensed health care professional or board certified genetic counselor that is involved in the genetic monitoring program, receives the results of the monitoring only in aggregate terms that do not disclose the identity of specific employees; or

(6) where the employer conducts DNA analysis for law enforcement purposes as a forensic laboratory or for purposes of human remains identification, and requests or requires genetic information of such employer's employees, but only to the extent that such genetic information is used for analysis of DNA identification markers for quality control to detect sample contamination.

(c) Preservation of Protections-In the case of information to which any of paragraphs (1) through (6) of subsection (b) applies, such information may not be used in violation of paragraph (1) or (2) of subsection (a) or treated or disclosed in a manner that violates section 206.

* * *

§ 206.   CONFIDENTIALITY OF GENETIC INFORMATION.

(a) Treatment of Information as Part of Confidential Medical Record—If an employer, employment agency, labor organization, or joint labor-management committee possesses genetic information about an employee or member, such information shall be maintained on separate forms and in separate medical files and be treated as a confidential medical record of the employee or member. An employer, employment agency, labor organization, or joint labor-management committee shall be considered to be in compliance with the maintenance of information requirements of this subsection with respect to genetic information subject to this subsection that is maintained with and treated as a confidential medical record under section 102(d)(3)(B) of the Americans With Disabilities Act (42 U.S.C. 12112(d)(3)(B)).

(b) Limitation on Disclosure—An employer, employment agency, labor organization, or joint labor-management committee shall not disclose genetic information concerning an employee or member except—

    (1)   to the employee or member of a labor organization (or family member if the family member is receiving the genetic services) at the written request of the employee or member of such organization;

    (2)   to an occupational or other health researcher if the research is conducted in compliance with the regulations and protections provided for under part 46 of title 45, Code of Federal Regulations;

    (3)   in response to an order of a court, except that—

        (A)   the employer, employment agency, labor organization, or joint labor-management committee may disclose only the genetic information expressly authorized by such order; and

        (B)   if the court order was secured without the knowledge of the employee or member to whom the information refers, the employer, employment agency, labor organization, or joint labor-management committee shall inform the employee or member of the court order and any genetic information that was disclosed pursuant to such order;

    (4)   to government officials who are investigating compliance with this title if the information is relevant to the investigation;

    (5)   to the extent that such disclosure is made in connection with the employee's compliance with the certification provisions of section 103 of the Family and Medical Leave Act of 1993 (29

U.S.C. 2613) or such requirements under State family and medical leave laws; or

(6) to a Federal, State, or local public health agency only with regard to information that is described in section 201(4)(A)(iii) and that concerns a contagious disease that presents an imminent hazard of death or life-threatening illness, and that the employee whose family member or family members is or are the subject of a disclosure under this paragraph is notified of such disclosure.

(c) Relationship to HIPAA Regulations—With respect to the regulations promulgated by the Secretary of Health and Human Services under part C of title XI of the Social Security Act (42 U.S.C. 1320d et seq.) and section 264 of the Health Insurance Portability and Accountability Act of 1996 (42 U.S.C. 1320d–2 note), this title does not prohibit a covered entity under such regulations from any use or disclosure of health information that is authorized for the covered entity under such regulations. The previous sentence does not affect the authority of such Secretary to modify such regulations.

§ 207. REMEDIES AND ENFORCEMENT.

(a) Employees Covered by Title VII of the Civil Rights Act of 1964—

(1) IN GENERAL—The powers, procedures, and remedies provided in sections 705, 706, 707, 709, 710, and 711 of the Civil Rights Act of 1964 (42 U.S.C. 2000e–4 et seq.) to the Commission, the Attorney General, or any person, alleging a violation of title VII of that Act (42 U.S.C. 2000e et seq.) shall be the powers, procedures, and remedies this title provides to the Commission, the Attorney General, or any person, respectively, alleging an unlawful employment practice in violation of this title against an employee described in section 201(2)(A)(i), except as provided in paragraphs (2) and (3).

(2) COSTS AND FEES—The powers, remedies, and procedures provided in subsections (b) and (c) of section 722 of the Revised Statutes of the United States (42 U.S.C. 1988), shall be powers, remedies, and procedures this title provides to the Commission, the Attorney General, or any person, alleging such a practice.

(3) DAMAGES—The powers, remedies, and procedures provided in section 1977A of the Revised Statutes of the United States (42 U.S.C. 1981a), including the limitations contained in subsection (b)(3) of such section 1977A, shall be powers, remedies, and procedures this title provides to the Commission, the Attorney General, or any person, alleging such a practice (not an employment practice specifically excluded from coverage under section 1977A(a)(1) of the Revised Statutes of the United States).

* * *

(f) Prohibition Against Retaliation—No person shall discriminate against any individual because such individual has opposed any act or practice made unlawful by this title or because such individual made a charge, testified, assisted, or participated in any manner in an investigation, proceeding, or hearing under this title. The remedies and procedures otherwise provided for under this section shall be available to aggrieved individuals with respect to violations of this subsection.

* * *

JESSICA L. ROBERTS, PREEMPTING DISCRIMINATION: LESSONS FROM THE GENETIC INFORMATION NONDISCRIMINATION ACT
63 Vand. L. Rev. 439, 440–41 (2010).

Historically, antidiscrimination law has been Janus-like, one face reflecting upon a legacy of discrimination with the other gazing forward to stop discrimination in the future. The four major employment discrimination statutes prior to GINA—Title VII of the Civil Rights Act, the Age Discrimination in Employment Act, the Rehabilitation Act, and the Americans with Disabilities Act—were all retrospective: each looked to discrimination in the past to justify protection in the present and the future.

Conversely, GINA has little upon which to reflect. GINA prohibits health insurers and employers from making decisions based on genetic information. While some examples do exist, both GINA's advocates and adversaries agreed that scant evidence indicated a significant history of genetic-information discrimination. Thus, whereas the preceding laws were retrospective, GINA is *preemptive*. It anticipates a form of discrimination that may pose a future threat. GINA's opponents cited the lack of existing genetic-information discrimination as evidence that the law was premature or unnecessary. Its proponents, however, presented GINA as a unique opportunity to stop discrimination before it starts. It is this preemptive nature, basing protection on future-rather than past or even present-discrimination, that truly makes GINA novel.

Novelty aside, preemptive antidiscrimination legislation has its benefits and its drawbacks. By passing GINA before genetic information discrimination could take hold, Congress may have effectively bypassed a new variety of discriminatory treatment. GINA's ability to preempt discrimination is perhaps its greatest strength. Yet the statute's preemptive qualities carry with them potentially serious hurdles regarding GINA's enforcement and effectiveness.

NOTES AND QUESTIONS

1. Professor Roberts goes on to note that two main arguments in favor of the legislation were made by proponents of GINA: (1) that fear of discrimination has impeded the ability of researchers to recruit potential research subjects; and (2) the use of genetic information for discrimination is unjust, especially because it involves immutable characteristics over which the individual has no control. The congressional findings section of GINA (section 2(5)), concludes with the reasons for GINA's enactment: "Therefore Federal legislation establishing a national and uniform standard is necessary to fully protect the public from discrimination and allay their concerns about the potential for discrimination, thereby allowing individuals to take advantage of genetic testing, technologies, research, and new therapies."

2. Is "preemptive" legislation necessary or a good idea? What do you think the major impetus was for enacting GINA?

3. On the role of immutability, see Sharona Hoffman, The Importance of Immutability in Employment Discrimination Law, 52 Wm. & Mary L. Rev. 1483 (2010–2011).

4. The implementing regulations promulgated by the EEOC appear at 29 C.F.R. Part 1635.

MARK A. ROTHSTEIN, GINA, THE ADA, AND GENETIC DISCRIMINATION IN EMPLOYMENT
36 J.L. Med. & Ethics 837, 838–839 (2008).

* * *

GINA

Both the health insurance and employment provisions of GINA expressly limit their protections to asymptomatic individuals who have been subjected to adverse treatment based on genetic information. GINA defines "genetic information" as information about an individual's genetic tests, the genetic tests of family members, and the manifestation of a disease or disorder in family members. Of critical importance, GINA provides that it is not unlawful to use, acquire, or disclose medical information "about a manifested disease, disorder, or pathological condition of an employee . . . , including a manifested disease, disorder, or pathological condition that has or may have a genetic basis."

Unfortunately, GINA does not define "a manifested disease, disorder, or pathological condition." GINA instead defines a "genetic test" as "an analysis of human DNA, RNA, chromosomes, proteins, or metabolites, that detects genotypes, mutations, or chromosomal changes." The definition does not include "(1) an analysis of proteins or metabolites that does not detect genotypes, mutations, or chromosomal changes; or (2) an analysis of proteins or metabolites that is directly related to a manifested disease, disorder, or pathological condition that could reasonably be detected by a health care professional with appropriate training and expertise in the field of medicine involved." These definitions do not provide much guidance as to the types of tests considered genetic, let alone when a disease, disorder, or pathological condition is "manifested."

READING THE ADA AND GINA TOGETHER

As illustrated in Figure 1, the coverage of the ADA and GINA are mirror images at the extremes. In the context of genetic discrimination in employment, asymptomatic individuals are unlikely to be covered by the ADA, but they are expressly covered by GINA. Conversely, severely affected individuals are covered by the ADA, but they are expressly not covered by GINA. The greatest uncertainty is in the middle. Under the ADA, an individual with a mild, temporary, or presymptomatic condition does not come within the statutory definition of an individual with a disability. Similarly, under GINA, an individual with a genetically based, biologically determinable difference beyond genotypic variation but short of phenotypic variation is unlikely to be protected.

FIGURE 1 COVERAGE OF GINA AND THE ADA			
	ASYMPTOMATIC	BIOMARKERS, ENDOPHENOTYPES, MILD SYMPTOMS	MANIFESTATION OF DISEASE
GINA	Yes	?	No
ADA	No	No	Yes

The problems in interpreting GINA stem from the fact that the law is based on a scientifically dubious dichotomy between genetic and non-genetic information, tests, and disorders. It has been generally acknowledged by scientists for decades that virtually all human disease has both genetic and environmental components. New developments in proteomics, transcriptomics, metabonomics, epigenetics, and other fields have blurred the line between asymptomatic and symptomatic. The various biological processes by which a gene becomes expressed are still being elucidated. Increasingly sensitive biomarkers and sophisticated analyses of endophenotypes add further complexity to disease mechanisms. Regardless of the policy issues implicated by different definitions under GINA, the distinctions drawn in the statute are scientifically untenable today and are likely to be increasingly problematic.

CONCLUSION

The employment discrimination provisions of GINA take effect November 21, 2009, and the EEOC is charged with issuing regulations implementing GINA by May 21, 2009 [29 CFR §§ 1635.1–1635.12]. One of the most important tasks for the EEOC is to devise practical, understandable, and scientifically compelling rules for determining what degree of biological response or symptoms constitutes manifestation of a disease, thereby precluding an individual from coverage by GINA. Under any conceivable definition of "manifestation," however, an individual will be too affected to be covered under GINA long before having a substantial limitation of a major life activity necessary to be covered under the ADA.

NOTES AND QUESTIONS

1.   On the issue of "manifestation," the EEOC's GINA regulations provide:

> (g) *Manifestation or manifested* means, with respect to a disease, disorder, or pathological condition, that an individual has been or could reasonably be diagnosed with the disease, disorder, or pathological condition by a health care professional with appropriate training and expertise in the field of medicine involved. For purposes of this part, a disease, disorder, or pathological condition is not manifested if the diagnosis is based principally on genetic information.

29 C.F.R. § 1635(g).

2.   Does this definition resolve the "gap" between the ADA and GINA? Can the gap be eliminated through regulation? See Anya E.R. Prince & Benjamin E. Berkman, When Does an Illness Begin: Genetic Discrimination and Disease Manifestation, 40 J.L. Med. & Ethics 655 (2012). Will the need for protection against genetic discrimination lessen over time? See Robert C. Green, Denise Bautenbach & Amy L. McGuire, GINA, Genetic Discrimination, and Genomic Medicine, 372 New Eng. J. Med. 397 (2015).

LOWE V. ATLAS LOGISTICS GROUP RETAIL SERVICES (ATLANTA), LLC
102 F.Supp. 3d 1360 (N.D. Ga. 2015).

AMY TOTENBERG, DISTRICT JUDGE.

Atlas Logistics Group Retail Services (Atlanta), LLC ("Atlas") operates warehouses for the storage of products sold at a variety of grocery stores. So one could imagine Atlas's frustration when a mystery employee began habitually defecating in one of its warehouses. To solve the mystery of the devious defecator, Atlas requested some of its employees, including Jack Lowe and Dennis Reynolds, to submit to a cheek swab. The cheek cell samples were then sent to a lab where a technician compared the cheek cell DNA to DNA from the offending fecal matter. Lowe and Dennis were not a match. With the culprit apparently still on the loose, Lowe and Dennis filed suit under the Genetic Information Nondiscrimination Act ("GINA"), 42

U.S.C. § 2000ff et seq., which generally prohibits employers from requesting genetic information from its employees.

The matter is before the Court on the parties' Cross-Motions for Summary Judgment. The legal question before the Court is whether the information requested and obtained by Atlas was "genetic information" covered by GINA. For the reasons that follow, the Court concludes that it is. Thus, the Court **GRANTS** Plaintiffs' Motion for Partial Summary Judgment and **DENIES** Defendant's Motion for Summary Judgment.

* * *

II. FACTUAL BACKGROUND

Atlas provides long-haul transportation and storage services for the grocery industry. As part of its services, Atlas maintains warehouse facilities to store grocery items which are then distributed to grocery retailers. Beginning in 2012, an unknown number of Atlas employees began defecating in Atlas's Bouldercrest Warehouse. The defecations occurred numerous times and necessitated the destruction of grocery products on at least one occasion.

Atlas attempted to remedy the defecation issue by asking its Loss Prevention Manager, Don Hill, to conduct an investigation. Mr. Hill began his investigation by comparing employee work schedules to the timing and location of the defecation episodes in order to create a list of employees who may have been responsible. Plaintiffs Jack Lowe and Dennis Reynolds were two of the employees Mr. Hill identified.

Once Mr. Hill created the list of potential suspects, he hired Speckin Forensic Labratories ("Speckin Labs") to assist in the investigation. Hill retained Speckin Labs to perform a comparison of buccal swab samples to the fecal matter collected in the Warehouse. Atlas requested that the results of the comparison be transmitted to Atlas.

In order to perform the comparison, Speckin Labs suggested using Short Tandem Repeat analysis ("STR analysis"). STR analysis compares samples by analyzing "genetic spacers" at various sites. "Genetic spacers" are the space between an individual's genes and vary drastically from person to person. STR analysis can be used to compare DNA from one sample to another for identification purposes. STR analysis cannot, however, determine an individual's propensity for disease or disorder.

Speckin Labs sent Dr. Julie Howenstine to the Warehouse in October 2012 to collect buccal swab samples from Lowe and Reynolds. Lowe and Reynolds provided samples to Dr. Howenstine, who then sent the samples to GenQuest DNA Analysis Laboratory ("GenQuest") via an intermediary, Semen and Sperm Detection, Inc. Dr. Howenstine requested that GenQuest use the PowerPlex 21 System ("PowerPlex 21") to perform the STR analysis of Lowe's and Reynolds's buccal swab samples. The

PowerPlex 21 measures the length of spaces between two genes at twenty chromosome spaces to compare various DNA samples. The PowerPlex 21 produces an electropherogram, which graphs the PowerPlex 21's analysis of DNA samples.

After performing the PowerPlex 21 analysis on Lowe's and Reynolds's DNA samples, GenQuest sent Dr. Howenstine the electropherogram with the PowerPlex 21 analysis' findings. Using the data provided in the electropherogram, Dr. Howenstine compared the DNA samples of Lowe and Reynolds to the DNA of the fecal matter and determined that neither Lowe nor Reynolds were the culprits. Dr. Howenstine documented this mismatch in a letter to Mr. Hill on October 22, 2012.

On March 27, 2013, Lowe and Reynolds filed charges of discrimination with the Equal Employment Opportunity Commission ("EEOC"). The Plaintiffs alleged that Atlas violated the Genetic Information Nondiscrimination Act, 42 U.S.C. § 2000ff et seq. ("GINA") because Atlas illegally requested and required them to provide their genetic information and illegally disclosed their genetic information. The EEOC dismissed Lowe's and Reynolds's charges against Atlas on April 24, 2013.

* * *

III. ANALYSIS

According to Plaintiffs Jack Lowe and Dennis Reynolds, the undisputed facts show that Atlas requested information about Speckin Labs's comparison of Lowe's and Reynolds's DNA to the fecal sample. These facts, Plaintiffs argue, demonstrate that Atlas violated 42 U.S.C. § 2000ff–1(b), which makes it "an unlawful employment practice for an employer to request, require, or purchase genetic information with respect to an employee." Plaintiffs therefore move for Partial Summary Judgment as to Atlas's liability under this section of GINA.

Atlas responds and argues in its Motion for Summary Judgment that the information the company requested concerning Lowe's and Reynolds's DNA analysis does not constitute "genetic information" as defined in GINA. According to Defendant's interpretation of GINA, "genetic information" refers only to information related to an individual's propensity for disease. For this reason, Defendant moves for summary judgment as to all of Plaintiffs' claims. The issue before the Court, therefore, is whether the term "genetic information" as used in GINA encompasses the information Atlas requested in this case.

"As with any question of statutory interpretation, [the Court] begin[s] by examining the text of the statute to determine whether its meaning is clear." The Court's analysis stops at a review of the text of GINA "if the statutory language is unambiguous and the statutory scheme is coherent and consistent." If the statutory language may be reasonably interpreted in more than one way, however, the statutory language is deemed ambiguous and additional tools of statutory interpretation should be used. Only "in rare and exceptional circumstances" may a court "decline to follow the plain meaning of a statute because overwhelming extrinsic evidence demonstrates a legislative intent contrary to the text's plain meaning."

As discussed below, the Court determines that the unambiguous language of GINA covers Atlas's requests for Lowe's and Reynolds's genetic information and thus compels judgment in favor of Lowe and Reynolds. This case is not one of the rare instances where overwhelming extrinsic evidence demonstrates a legislative intent contrary to the text's plain meaning. For these reasons, the Court grants Plaintiffs' Motion for Partial Summary Judgment and denies Defendant's Motion for Summary Judgment.

A. The Unambiguous Statutory Language of GINA

The Court begins its analysis with the language of GINA. GINA makes it "an unlawful employment practice for an employer to request, require, or purchase genetic information with respect to an employee." 42 U.S.C. § 2000ff–1(b). Section 2000ff–1(b) lists six exceptions to this general prohibition, but Atlas admits that none of the statutory exceptions apply here. The parties also agree that Atlas is an "employer" and Lowe and Reynolds are "employees" as defined by GINA. The parties' disagreement centers on a single phrase in Section 2000ff–1(b): "genetic information."

GINA defines genetic information as "with respect to any individual, information about (i) such individual's genetic tests, (ii) the genetic tests of family members of such individual, and (iii) the manifestation of a disease or disorder in family members of such individual." 42 U.S.C. § 2000ff(4). Parts (ii) and (iii) do not apply to Lowe and Reynolds's claims, as the PowerPlex 21 analysis was not performed on DNA of their family members. Therefore, the DNA analysis would only qualify as "genetic information" under GINA if the analysis qualifies as a "genetic test."

"Genetic test" is also defined in GINA. The statute defines "genetic test" as "an analysis of human DNA, RNA, chromosomes, proteins, or metabolites, that detects genotypes, mutations, or chromosomal changes." 42 U.S.C. § 2000ff(7). The extent of GINA's guidance ends with its definition of "genetic test:" none of the words included in 42 U.S.C. § 2000ff(7) are further defined in GINA.

If all the Court considers is the language of GINA, the undisputed evidence in the record establishes that the DNA analysis at issue here clearly falls within the definition of "genetic test." The parties agree that Dr. Howenstine conducted an "analysis" of Lowe's and Reynolds's DNA. And the undisputed evidence in the record shows that this analysis at a minimum detects genotypes and mutations. Because the parties agree that Atlas requested a comparison of Lowe's and Reynolds's DNA to the fecal

DNA found in the warehouse, Atlas's request and course of action appear to constitute a violation of 42 U.S.C. § 2000ff–1(b)'s prohibition against requesting genetic information from employees.

Defendant argues that this straightforward but broad interpretation of GINA is erroneous. Defendant urges the Court to interpret the "genetic test" language of GINA to exclude analyses of DNA, RNA, chromosomes, proteins, or metabolites if such analyses do not reveal an individual's propensity for disease. This proposed definition of "genetic tests"—a definition which limits genetic tests to those related to one's propensity for disease—renders other language in GINA superfluous, and should thus be rejected.

Section 2000ff–1(b) makes it unlawful to request, require, or purchase genetic information, except in six contexts. Section 1(b)(6), in turn, expressly allows employers to request, require, or purchase some genetic information which has nothing to do with the propensity for disease. 42 U.S.C. § 2000ff–1(b)(6). Specifically, an employer is not liable under GINA where it conducts a "DNA analysis . . . for purposes of human remains identification, and requests or requires genetic information of such employer's employees, but only to the extent that such genetic information is used for analysis of DNA identification markers for quality control to detect sample contamination." 42 U.S.C. § 2000ff–1(b)(6). This exception would be unnecessary if Atlas's construction of GINA were correct, because under Atlas's construction, the term "genetic information" already excludes DNA analyses for purposes of human remains identification—a type of analysis unrelated to testing for disease propensity. Thus, the exception in § 2000ff–1(b)(6) weighs against Atlas's interpretation.

* * *

B. Evidence of Legislative Intent

Despite the plain, unambiguous language of GINA providing a broad definition of "genetic information," which covers the information Atlas requested in this case, Atlas urges the Court to adopt its narrow definition. It is true that "in rare and exceptional circumstances [a court] may decline to follow the plain meaning of a statute because overwhelming extrinsic evidence demonstrates a legislative intent contrary to the text's plain meaning."

Atlas first relies on the Congressional Findings, included in GINA, to urge the Court to adopt its definition of "genetic information," but the Congressional Findings lend Atlas only limited support. The Congressional Findings do indeed express a concern that advances in genetic testing, which "can allow individuals to take steps to reduce the likelihood that they will contract a particular disorder," also "give rise to the potential misuse of genetic information to discriminate in health insurance and employment." And as Atlas highlights, the Findings include historical examples of discrimination on the basis of genetic testing that reveals the existence of or propensity for disease, such as state-sanctioned sterilization of individuals with genetic defects and state-sanctioned sickle cell anemia testing. But Atlas ignores the Findings' more general pronouncement of GINA's purpose: to "establish[ ] a national and uniform basic standard" of unacceptable use of genetic information in health insurance and employment, in order "to fully protect the public from discrimination and allay their concerns about the potential for discrimination, thereby allowing individuals to take advantage of genetic testing, technologies, research, and new therapies." It is not unreasonable for Congress to achieve this "national and uniform basic standard" of full protection by broadly prohibiting employers from requesting, requiring, or purchasing genetic information of their employees, except under limited circumstances. On the contrary, GINA's statutory regime, which errs on the side of prohibiting employer-mandated or requested genetic testing, seems fully consistent with these Congressional Findings.

* * *

IV. CONCLUSION

For the reasons discussed above, the Court finds Atlas liable under 42 U.S.C. § 2000ff and **GRANTS** Plaintiffs Jack Lowe and Dennis Reynolds Partial Motion for Summary Judgment as to liability. The Court **DENIES** Defendant Atlas Logistics Group Retail Services (Atlanta), LLC Motion for Summary Judgment.

* * *

NOTES AND QUESTIONS

1.   There has been very little litigation under GINA. A study of the law's first ten years indicated that there were only 48 cases of "plausible" claims of discrimination based on genetic information. See Bradley A. Areheart & Jessica L. Roberts, GINA, Big Data, and the Future of Employee Privacy, 128 Yale L.J. 710, 730–731 (2019). This contrasts with tens of thousands of cases in the same time period alleging discrimination based on race or sex. Why are there so few cases under GINA? Is it a lack of genetic discrimination or a lack of knowledge of GINA by potential plaintiffs? Does GINA have value notwithstanding the low number of cases? If so, what is it?

2.   In AARP v. EEOC, 292 F. Supp. 3d 238 (D.D.C. 2017), the plaintiffs challenged EEOC's regulations pertaining to wellness programs under the ADA and GINA. The regulations provided that employer-sponsored wellness programs may collect health information (otherwise unlawful under the ADA and GINA) so long as participation is "voluntary." Employers may offer an incentive of up to 30% of self-only health coverage if employees divulge information about a spouse's manifestation of a disease or disorder, which

qualifies as "genetic information" under GINA. The plaintiffs argued that that the 30% incentive is inconsistent with the ordinary meaning of voluntary because it is too high to give employees a meaningful choice about whether to participate. The court agreed. It also noted that the 30% level was likely to disproportionately affect people with disabilities who, on average, have lower incomes than those without disabilities. See generally Kathy L. Hudson & Karen Pollitz, Undermining Genetic Privacy? Employee Wellness Programs and the Law, 377 New Eng. J. Med. 1 (2017).

MARK A. ROTHSTEIN, GINA AT TEN AND THE FUTURE OF GENETIC NONDISCRIMINATION LAW
48 Hastings Center Report No. 3, at 5–6 (2018).

* * *

In the coming years, the nature of predictive genetic information is likely to change in both clinical and nonclinical applications. Precision medicine promises to utilize genomic data in combination with diverse "big data" sources, such as data from exposures, mobile devices and health apps, wearable devices, consumer transactions, geolocation logs, and numerous other publicly and privately available data sources. Computer algorithms will then calculate health risks or other end points. This process raises interesting and weighty privacy issues, including whether individuals ought to have a right not to have their diverse data aggregated and used without their consent. Genetic information will have an important part in the policy formulation, but measures to address these emerging issues extend well beyond current approaches to genetic discrimination.

Ever since the 1960s, antidiscrimination laws generally have adopted a civil rights model, under which all individuals are considered essentially the same. Therefore, with only a few exceptions, Title VII of the Civil Rights Act of 1964 and the Age Discrimination in Employment Act provide that employers must ignore race, color, religion, sex, national origin, and age in all employment decisions, even when distinctions may be relevant in some way. For example, where workplace exposures below limits set by the Occupational Safety and Health Administration contain teratogenic risks to female reproductive health, employers may not exclude female employees, but they need not take other action beyond allowing women to decide whether to accept such risks.

By contrast, the ADA requires that employers and other covered entities provide reasonable accommodation to enable individuals to access employment and other essential aspects of daily life. For example, accommodations may help overcome physical barriers (as adding ramps does) or sensory barriers (by providing sign language interpreters or accessible websites, for instance). Using the Title VII model of ignoring genetic differences may be inconsistent with advancing the interests of individuals who have genetic-based sensitivities to certain environments or who need other reasonable accommodations, some of which may even be unfathomable today.

Considering genotype along with other biological factors is a hallmark of future precision medicine, and thus there may be a growing tension between modern medicine and current civil rights laws. In my view, it is possible to be cognizant of and responsive to genetic diversity and still actively pursue the goals of nondiscrimination, equal opportunity, privacy, autonomy, and human dignity. Nevertheless, implementing a new vision of genomic diversity will require new conceptions of and new approaches to antidiscrimination laws.

Today, at GINA's tenth anniversary, Title I of the act, dealing with health insurance, is largely irrelevant, and Title II, dealing with employment, is rarely invoked. GINA undoubtedly has important symbolic value in proclaiming the social unacceptability of certain uses of genetic information, but it is not clear what policies ought to or can be adopted next. As we look to the future, we should reexamine the assumptions on which GINA is based. Other areas of potential genetic discrimination also should be studied for possible legislation. Finally, policy-makers should contemplate a new civil rights paradigm to encourage the beneficial uses of genetic information without giving rise to stigmatization or discrimination. There will be much to consider in the next ten years and beyond.

> **Food for Thought:** In 2033, GINA will be 25 years old. What changes do you think will be needed to account for likely changes in technology or access to genomic information? What changes do you think Congress will make in the coming years? Do you think genetic discrimination in employment will be greater, lesser, or similar to today?

INDEX

References are to Pages
